Family Maps
of
Kemper County, Mississippi
Deluxe Edition

With Homesteads, Roads, Waterways, Towns, Cemeteries, Railroads, and More

Family Maps
of
Kemper County, Mississippi
Deluxe Edition

With Homesteads, Roads, Waterways, Towns, Cemeteries, Railroads, and More

by Gregory A. Boyd, J.D.

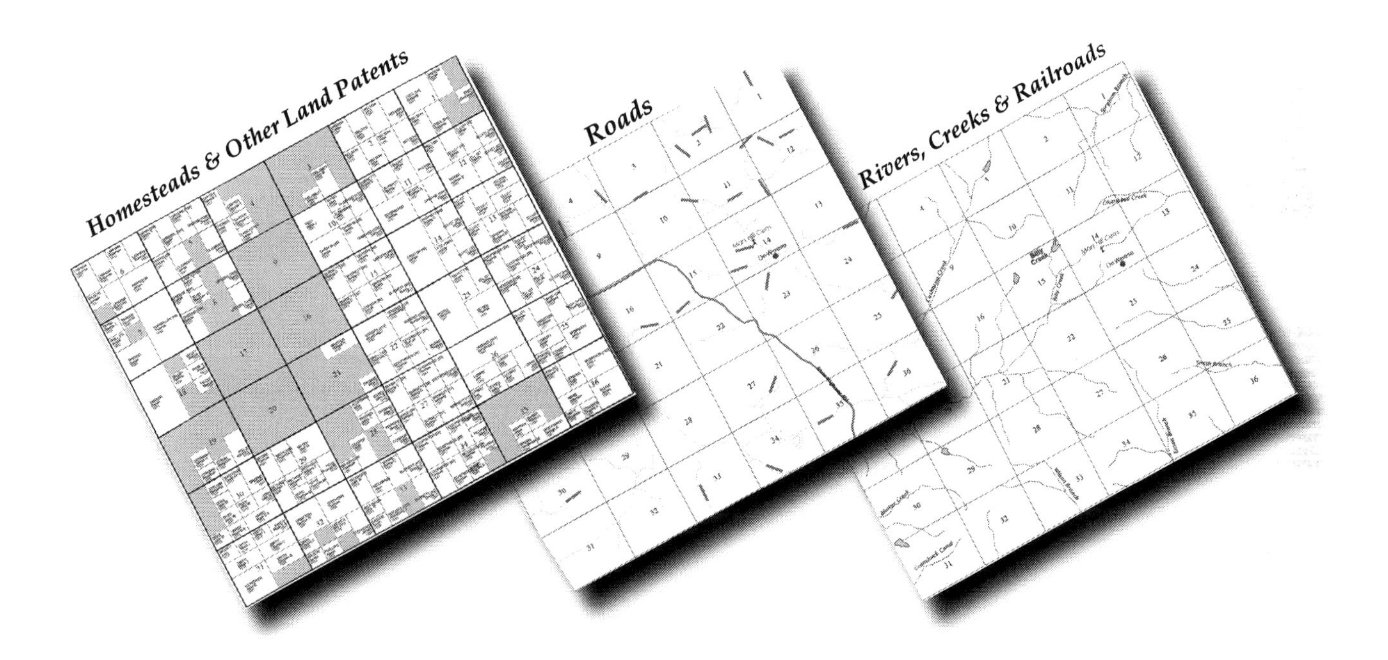

Featuring 3 Maps Per Township...

Arphax Publishing Co.
www.arphax.com

Family Maps of Kemper County, Mississippi, Deluxe Edition: With Homesteads, Roads, Waterways, Towns, Cemeteries, Railroads, and More.
by Gregory A. Boyd, J.D.

ISBN 1-4203-1137-9

Printed in the United States of America

Published by Arphax Publishing Co., 2210 Research Park Blvd., Norman, Oklahoma, USA 73069
www.arphax.com

First Edition

—LEGAL—

This book is dedicated to my wonderful family:

Vicki, Jordan, & Amy Boyd

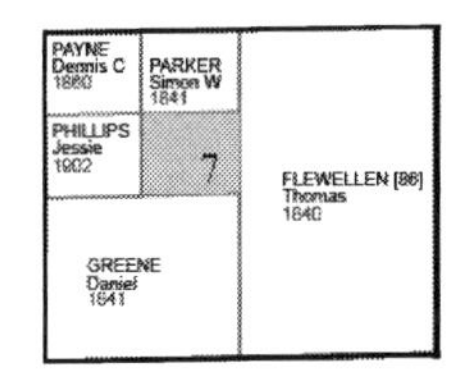

Contents

- Part I -

The Big Picture

- Part II -

Township Map Groups

(each Map Group contains a Patent Index, Patent Map, Road Map, & Historical Map)

Appendices

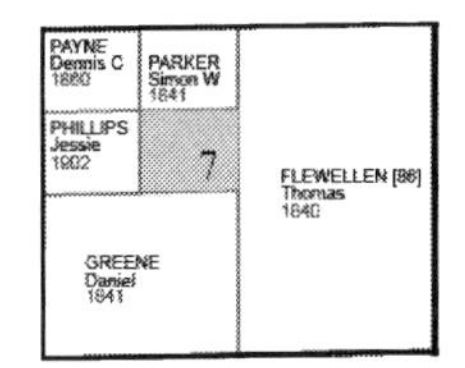

Preface

The quest for the discovery of my ancestors' origins, migrations, beliefs, and life-ways has brought me rewards that I could never have imagined. The *Family Maps* series of books is my first effort to share with historical and genealogical researchers, some of the tools that I have developed to achieve my research goals. I firmly believe that this effort will allow many people to reap the same sorts of treasures that I have.

Our Federal government's General Land Office of the Bureau of Land Management (the "GLO") has given genealogists and historians an incredible gift by virtue of its enormous database housed on its web-site at glorecords.blm.gov. Here, you can search for and find millions of parcels of land purchased by our ancestors in about thirty states.

This GLO web-site is one of the best FREE on-line tools available to family researchers. But, it is not for the faint of heart, nor is it for those unwilling or unable to to sift through and analyze the thousands of records that exist for most counties.

My immediate goal with this series is to spare you the hundreds of hours of work that it would take you to map the Land Patents for this county. Every Kemper County homestead or land patent that I have gleaned from public GLO databases is mapped here. Consequently, I can usually show you in an instant, where your ancestor's land is located, as well as the names of nearby land-owners.

Originally, that was my primary goal. But after speaking to other genealogists, it became clear that there was much more that they wanted. Taking their advice set me back almost a full year, but I think you will agree it was worth the wait. Because now, you can learn so much more.

Now, this book answers these sorts of questions:

- Are there any variant spellings for surnames that I have missed in searching GLO records?
- Where is my family's traditional home-place?
- What cemeteries are near Grandma's house?
- My Granddad used to swim in such-and-such-Creek—where is that?
- How close is this little community to that one?
- Are there any other people with the same surname who bought land in the county?
- How about cousins and in-laws—did they buy land in the area?

And these are just for starters!

The rules for using the *Family Maps* books are simple, but the strategies for success are many. Some techniques are apparent on first use, but many are gained with time and experience. Please take the time to notice the roads, cemeteries, creek-names, family names, and unique first-names throughout the whole county. You cannot imagine what YOU might be the first to discover.

I hope to learn that many of you have answered age-old research questions within these pages or that you have discovered relationships previously not even considered. When these sorts of things happen to you, will you please let me hear about it? I would like nothing better. My contact information can always be found at www.arphax.com.

One more thing: please read the "How To Use This Book" chapter; it starts on the next page. This will give you the very best chance to find the treasures that lie within these pages.

My family and I wish you the very best of luck, both in life, and in your research. Greg Boyd

How to Use This Book - A Graphical Summary

Part I

"The Big Picture"

Map A ▸ *Counties in the State*
Map B ▸ *Surrounding Counties*
Map C ▸ *Congressional Townships (Map Groups) in the County*
Map D ▸ *Cities & Towns in the County*
Map E ▸ *Cemeteries in the County*
Surnames in the County ▸ *Number of Land-Parcels for Each Surname*
Surname/Township Index ▸ Directs you to Township Map Groups in Part II

The Surname/Township Index can direct you to any number of **Township Map Groups**

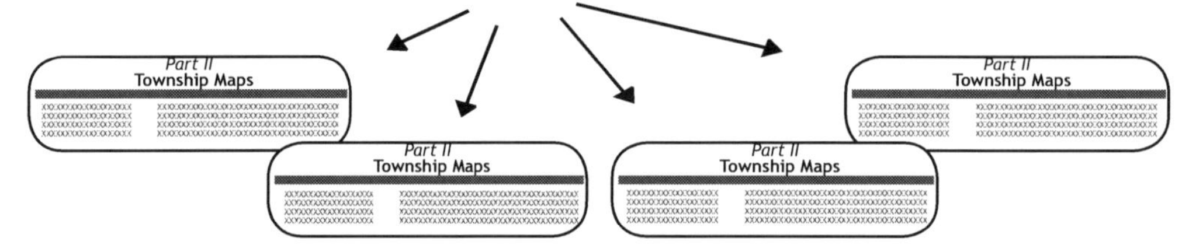

Part II

Township Map Groups

(1 for each Township in the County)

Each Township Map Group contains all four of of the following tools . . .

Land Patent Index ▸ *Every-name Index of Patents Mapped in this Township*
Land Patent Map ▸ *Map of Patents as listed in above Index*
Road Map ▸ *Map of Roads, City-centers, and Cemeteries in the Township*
Historical Map ▸ *Map of Railroads, Lakes, Rivers, Creeks, City-Centers, and Cemeteries*

Appendices

Appendix A ▸ *Congressional Authority enabling Patents within our Maps*
Appendix B ▸ *Section-Parts / Aliquot Parts (a comprehensive list)*
Appendix C ▸ *Multi-patentee Groups (Individuals within Buying Groups)*

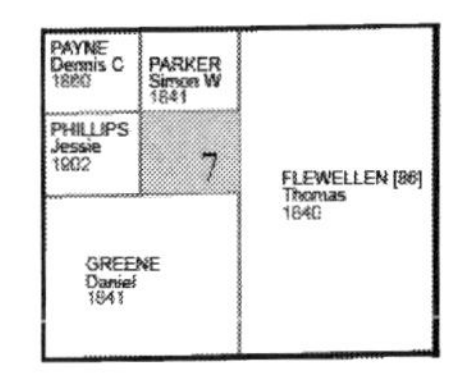

How to Use This Book

The two "Parts" of this *Family Maps* volume seek to answer two different types of questions. Part I deals with broad questions like: what counties surround Kemper County, are there any ASHCRAFTs in Kemper County, and if so, in which Townships or Maps can I find them? Ultimately, though, Part I should point you to a particular Township Map Group in Part II.

Part II concerns itself with details like: where exactly is this family's land, who else bought land in the area, and what roads and streams run through the land, or are located nearby. The Chart on the opposite page, and the remainder of this chapter attempt to convey to you the particulars of these two "parts", as well as how best to use them to achieve your research goals.

Part I
"The Big Picture"

Within Part I, you will find five "Big Picture" maps and two county-wide surname tools.

These include:

- Map A - Where Kemper County lies within the state
- Map B - Counties that surround Kemper County
- Map C - Congressional Townships of Kemper County (+ Map Group Numbers)
- Map D - Cities & Towns of Kemper County (with Index)
- Map E - Cemeteries of Kemper County (with Index)
- Surnames in Kemper County Patents (with Parcel-counts for each surname)
- Surname/Township Index (with Parcel-counts for each surname by Township)

The five "Big-Picture" Maps are fairly self-explanatory, yet should not be overlooked. This is particularly true of Maps "C", "D", and "E", all of which show Kemper County and its Congressional Townships (and their assigned Map Group Numbers).

Let me briefly explain this concept of Map Group Numbers. These are a device completely of our own invention. They were created to help you quickly locate maps without having to remember the full legal name of the various Congressional Townships. It is simply easier to remember "Map Group 1" than a legal name like: "Township 9-North Range 6-West, 5th Principal Meridian." But the fact is that the TRUE legal name for these Townships IS terribly important. These are the designations that others will be familiar with and you will need to accurately record them in your notes. This is why both Map Group numbers AND legal descriptions of Townships are almost always displayed together.

Map "C" will be your first intoduction to "Map Group Numbers", and that is all it contains: legal Township descriptions and their assigned Map Group Numbers. Once you get further into your research, and more immersed in the details, you will likely want to refer back to Map "C" from time to time, in order to regain your bearings on just where in the county you are researching.

Remember, township boundaries are a completely artificial device, created to standardize land descriptions. But do not let them become a boundary in your mind when choosing which townships to research. Your relative's in-laws, children, cousins, siblings, and mamas and papas, might just as easily have lived in the township next to the one your grandfather lived in—rather than in the one where he actually lived. So Map "C" can be your guide to which other Townships/ Map Groups you likewise ought to analyze.

Of course, the same holds true for County lines; this is the purpose behind Map "B". It shows you surrounding counties that you may want to consider for further reserarch.

Map "D", the Cities and Towns map, is the first map with an index. Map "E" is the second (Cemeteries). Both, Maps "D" and "E" give you broad views of City (or Cemetery) locations in the County. But they go much further by pointing you toward pertinent Township Map Groups so you can locate the patents, roads, and waterways located near a particular city or cemetery.

Once you are familiar with these *Family Maps* volumes and the county you are researching, the "Surnames In Kemper County" chapter (or its sister chapter in other volumes) is where you'll likely start your future research sessions. Here, you can quickly scan its few pages and see if anyone in the county possesses the surnames you are researching. The "Surnames in Kemper County" list shows only two things: surnames and the number of parcels of land we have located for that surname in Kemper County. But whether or not you immediately locate the surnames you are researching, please do not go any further without taking a few moments to scan ALL the surnames in these very few pages.

You cannot imagine how many lost ancestors are waiting to be found by someone willing to take just a little longer to scan the "Surnames In Kemper County" list. Misspellings and typographical errors abound in most any index of this sort. Don't miss out on finding your Kinard that was written Rynard or Cox that was written Lox. If it looks funny or wrong, it very often is. And one of those little errors may well be your relative.

Now, armed with a surname and the knowledge that it has one or more entries in this book, you are ready for the "Surname/Township Index." Unlike the "Surnames In Kemper County", which has only one line per Surname, the "Surname/Township Index" contains one line-item for each Township Map Group in which each surname is found. In other words, each line represents a different Township Map Group that you will need to review.

Specifically, each line of the Surname/Township Index contains the following four columns of information:

1. Surname
2. Township Map Group Number (these Map Groups are found in Part II)
3. Parcels of Land (number of them with the given Surname within the Township)
4. Meridian/Township/Range (the legal description for this Township Map Group)

The key column here is that of the Township Map Group Number. While you should definitely record the Meridian, Township, and Range, you can do that later. Right now, you need to dig a little deeper. That Map Group Number tells you where in Part II that you need to start digging.

But before you leave the "Surname/Township Index", do the same thing that you did with the "Surnames in Kemper County" list: take a moment to scan the pages of the Index and see if there are similarly spelled or misspelled surnames that deserve your attention. Here again, is an easy opportunity to discover grossly misspelled family names with very little effort. Now you are ready to turn to . . .

Part II
"Township Map Groups"

You will normally arrive here in Part II after being directed to do so by one or more "Map Group Numbers" in the Surname/Township Index of Part I.

Each Map Group represents a set of four tools dedicated to a single Congressional Township that is either wholly or partially within the county. If you are trying to learn all that you can about a particular family or their land, then these tools should usually be viewed in the order they are presented.

These four tools include:

1. a Land Patent Index
2. a Land Patent Map
3. a Road Map, and
4. an Historical Map

As I mentioned earlier, each grouping of this sort is assigned a Map Group Number. So, let's now move on to a discussion of the four tools that make up one of these Township Map Groups.

Land Patent Index

Each Township Map Group's Index begins with a title, something along these lines:

MAP GROUP 1: Index to Land Patents

Township 16-North Range 5-West (2nd PM)

The Index contains seven (7) columns. They are:

1. ID (a unique ID number for this Individual and a corresponding Parcel of land in this Township)
2. Individual in Patent (name)
3. Sec. (Section), and
4. Sec. Part (Section Part, or Aliquot Part)
5. Date Issued (Patent)
6. Other Counties (often means multiple counties were mentioned in GLO records, or the section lies within multiple counties).
7. For More Info . . . (points to other places within this index or elsewhere in the book where you can find more information)

While most of the seven columns are self-explanatory, I will take a few moments to explain the "Sec. Part." and "For More Info" columns.

The "Sec. Part" column refers to what surveryors and other land professionals refer to as an Aliquot Part. The origins and use of such a term mean little to a non-surveyor, and I have chosen to simply call these sub-sections of land what they are: a "Section Part". No matter what we call them, what we are referring to are things like a quarter-section or half-section or quarter-quarter-section. See Appendix "B" for most of the "Section Parts" you will come across (and many you will not) and what size land-parcel they represent.

The "For More Info" column of the Index may seem like a small appendage to each line, but please recognize quickly that this is not so. And to understand the various items you might find here, you need to become familiar with the Legend that appears at the top of each Land Patent Index.

Here is a sample of the Legend . . .

LEGEND

"For More Info . . . " column

A = Authority (Legislative Act, See Appendix "A")
B = Block or Lot (location in Section unknown)
C = Cancelled Patent
F = Fractional Section
G = Group (Multi-Patentee Patent, see Appendix "C")
V = Overlaps another Parcel
R = Re-Issued (Parcel patented more than once)

Most parcels of land will have only one or two of these items in their "For More Info" columns, but when that is not the case, there is often some valuable information to be gained from further investigation. Below, I will explain what each of these items means to you you as a researcher.

A = Authority
(Legislative Act, See Appendix "A")

All Federal Land Patents were issued because some branch of our government (usually the U.S. Congress) passed a law making such a transfer of title possible. And therefore every patent within these pages will have an "A" item next to it in the index. The number after the "A" indicates which item in Appendix "A" holds the citation to the particular law which authorized the transfer of land to the public. As it stands, most of the Public Land data compiled and released by our government, and which serves as the basis for the patents mapped here, concerns itself with "Cash Sale" homesteads. So in some Counties, the law which authorized cash sales will be the primary, if not the only, entry in the Appendix.

B = Block or Lot (location in Section unknown)

A "B" designation in the Index is a tip-off that the EXACT location of the patent within the map is not apparent from the legal description. This Patent will nonetheless be noted within the proper

Section along with any other Lots purchased in the Section. Given the scope of this project (many states and many Counties are being mapped), trying to locate all relevant plats for Lots (if they even exist) and accurately mapping them would have taken one person several lifetimes. But since our primary goal from the onset has been to establish relationships between neighbors and families, very little is lost to this goal since we can still observe who all lived in which Section.

C = Cancelled Patent

A Cancelled Patent is just that: cancelled. Whether the original Patentee forfeited his or her patent due to fraud, a technicality, non-payment, or whatever, the fact remains that it is significant to know who received patents for what parcels and when. A cancellation may be evidence that the Patentee never physically re-located to the land, but does not in itself prove that point. Further evidence would be required to prove that. *See also*, Re-issued Patents, *below*.

F = Fractional Section

A Fractional Section is one that contains less than 640 acres, almost always because of a body of water. The exact size and shape of land-parcels contained in such sections may not be ascertainable, but we map them nonetheless. Just keep in mind that we are not mapping an actual parcel to scale in such instances. Another point to consider is that we have located some fractional sections that are not so designated by the Bureau of Land Management in their data. This means that not all fractional sections have been so identified in our indexes.

G = Group

(Multi-Patentee Patent, see Appendix "C")

A "G" designation means that the Patent was issued to a GROUP of people (Multi-patentees). The "G" will always be followed by a number. Some such groups were quite large and it was impractical if not impossible to display each individual in our maps without unduly affecting readability. EACH person in the group is named in the Index, but they won't all be found on the Map. You will find the name of the first person in such a Group on the map with the Group number next to it, enclosed in [square brackets].

To find all the members of the Group you can either scan the Index for all people with the same Group Number or you can simply refer to Appendix "C" where all members of the Group are listed next to their number.

O = Overlaps another Parcel

An Overlap is one where PART of a parcel of land gets issued on more than one patent. For genealogical purposes, both transfers of title are important and both Patentees are mapped. If the ENTIRE parcel of land is re-issued, that is what we call it, a Re-Issued Patent (*see below*). The number after the "O" indicates the ID for the overlapping Patent(s) contained within the same Index. Like Re-Issued and Cancelled Patents, Overlaps may cause a map-reader to be confused at first, but for genealogical purposes, all of these parties' relationships to the underlying land is important, and therefore, we map them.

R = Re-Issued (Parcel patented more than once)

The label, "Re-issued Patent" describes Patents which were issued more than once for land with the EXACT SAME LEGAL DESCRIPTION. Whether the original patent was cancelled or not, there were a good many parcels which were patented more than once. The number after the "R" indicates the ID for the other Patent contained within the same Index that was for the same land. A quick glance at the map itself within the relevant Section will be the quickest way to find the other Patentee to whom the Parcel was transferred. They should both be mapped in the same general area.

I have gone to some length describing all sorts of anomalies either in the underlying data or in their representation on the maps and indexes in this book. Most of this will bore the most ardent reseracher, but I do this with all due respect to those researchers who will inevitably (and rightfully) ask: *"Why isn't so-and-so's name on the exact spot that the index says it should be?"*

In most cases it will be due to the existence of a Multi-Patentee Patent, a Re-issued Patent, a Cancelled Patent, or Overlapping Parcels named in separate Patents. I don't pretend that this discussion will answer every question along these lines, but I hope it will at least convince you of the complexity of the subject.

Not to despair, this book's companion web-site will offer a way to further explain "odd-ball" or errant data. Each book (County) will have its own web-page or pages to discuss such situations. You can go to www.arphax.com to find the relevant web-page for Kemper County.

Land Patent Map

On the first two-page spread following each Township's Index to Land Patents, you'll find the corresponding Land Patent Map. And here lies the real heart of our work. For the first time anywhere, researchers will be able to observe and analyze, on a grand scale, most of the original land-owners for an area AND see them mapped in proximity to each one another.

We encourage you to make vigorous use of the accompanying Index described above, but then later, to abandon it, and just stare at these maps for a while. This is a great way to catch misspellings or to find collateral kin you'd not known were in the area.

Each Land Patent Map represents one Congressional Township containing approximately 36-square miles. Each of these square miles is labeled by an accompanying Section Number (1 through 36, in most cases). Keep in mind, that this book concerns itself solely with Kemper County's patents. Townships which creep into one or more other counties will not be shown in their entirety in any one book. You will need to consult other books, as they become available, in order to view other countys' patents, cities, cemeteries, etc.

But getting back to Kemper County: each Land Patent Map contains a Statistical Chart that looks like the following:

Township Statistics

Parcels Mapped	:	173
Number of Patents	:	163
Number of Individuals	:	152
Patentees Identified	:	151
Number of Surnames	:	137
Multi-Patentee Parcels	:	4
Oldest Patent Date	:	11/27/1820
Most Recent Patent	:	9/28/1917
Block/Lot Parcels	:	0
Parcels Re-Issued	:	3
Parcels that Overlap	:	8
Cities and Towns	:	6
Cemeteries	:	6

This information may be of more use to a social statistician or historian than a genealogist, but I think all three will find it interesting.

Most of the statistics are self-explanatory, and what is not, was described in the above discussion of the Index's Legend, but I do want to mention a few of them that may affect your understanding of the Land Patent Maps.

First of all, Patents often contain more than one Parcel of land, so it is common for there to be more Parcels than Patents. Also, the Number of Individuals will more often than not, not match the number of Patentees. A Patentee is literally the person or PERSONS named in a patent. So, a Patent may have a multi-person Patentee or a single-person patentee. Nonetheless, we account for all these individuals in our indexes.

On the lower-righthand side of the Patent Map is a Legend which describes various features in the map, including Section Boundaries, Patent (land) Boundaries, Lots (numbered), and Multi-Patentee Group Numbers. You'll also find a "Helpful Hints" Box that will assist you.

One important note: though the vast majority of Patents mapped in this series will prove to be reasonably accurate representations of their actual locations, we cannot claim this for patents lying along state and county lines, or waterways, or that have been platted (lots).

Shifting boundaries and sparse legal descriptions in the GLO data make this a reality that we have nonetheless tried to overcome by estimating these patents' locations the best that we can.

Road Map

On the two-page spread following each Patent Map you will find a Road Map covering the exact same area (the same Congressional Township).

For me, fully exploring the past means that every once in a while I must leave the library and travel to the actual locations where my ancestors once walked and worked the land. Our Township Road Maps are a great place to begin such a quest.

Keep in mind that the scaling and proportion of these maps was chosen in order to squeeze hundreds of people-names, road-names, and place-names into tinier spaces than you would traditionally see. These are not professional road-maps, and like any secondary genealogical source, should be looked upon as an entry-way to original sources—in this case, original patents and applications, professionally produced maps and surveys, etc.

Both our Road Maps and Historical Maps contain cemeteries and city-centers, along with a listing of these on the left-hand side of the map. I should note that I am showing you city center-points, rather than city-limit boundaries, because in many instances, this will represent a place where settlement began. This may be a good time to mention that many cemeteries are located on private property, Always check with a local historical or genealogical society to see if a particular cemetery is publicly accessible (if it is not obviously so). As a final point, look for your surnames among the road-names. You will often be surprised by what you find.

Historical Map

The third and final map in each Map Group is our attempt to display what each Township might have looked like before the advent of modern roads. In frontier times, people were usually more determined to settle near rivers and creeks than they were near roads, which were often few and far between. As was the case with the Road Map, we've included the same cemeteries and city-centers. We've also included railroads, many of which came along before most roads.

While some may claim "Historical Map" to be a bit of a misnomer for this tool, we settled for this label simply because it was almost as accurate as saying "Railroads, Lakes, Rivers, Cities, and Cemeteries," and it is much easier to remember.

In Closing . . .

By way of example, here is *A Really Good Way to Use a Township Map Group*. First, find the person you are researching in the Township's Index to Land Patents, which will direct you to the proper Section and parcel on the Patent Map. But before leaving the Index, scan all the patents within it, looking for other names of interest. Now, turn to the Patent Map and locate your parcels of land. Pay special attention to the names of patent-holders who own land surrounding your person of interest. Next, turn the page and look at the same Section(s) on the Road Map. Note which roads are closest to your parcels and also the names of nearby towns and cemeteries. Using other resources, you may be able to learn of kin who have been buried here, plus, you may choose to visit these cemeteries the next time you are in the area.

Finally, turn to the Historical Map. Look once more at the same Sections where you found your research subject's land. Note the nearby streams, creeks, and other geographical features. You may be surprised to find family names were used to name them, or you may see a name you haven't heard mentioned in years and years—and a new research possibility is born.

Many more techniques for using these *Family Maps* volumes will no doubt be discovered. If from time to time, you will navigate to Kemper County's web-page at www.arphax.com (use the "Research" link), you can learn new tricks as they become known (or you can share ones you have employed). But for now, you are ready to get started. So, go, and good luck.

– Part I –

The Big Picture

Map A - Where Kemper County, Mississippi Lies Within the State

Legend

State Boundary

County Boundaries

Kemper County, Mississippi

Helpful Hints

1 We start with Map "A" which simply shows us where within the State this county lies.

2 Map "B" zooms in further to help us more easily identify surrounding Counties.

3 Map "C" zooms in even further to reveal the Congressional Townships that either lie within or intersect Kemper County.

Map B - Kemper County, Mississippi and Surrounding Counties

Pickens
Noxubee
Winston
Greene
Mississippi
Kemper
Neshoba
Alabama
Lauderdale
Newton
Sumter

Legend

State Boundaries (when applicable)
County Boundary

Helpful Hints

1 Many Patent-holders and their families settled across county lines. It is always a good idea to check nearby counties for your families.

2 Refer to Map "A" to see a broader view of where this County lies within the State, and Map "C" to see which Congressional Townships lie within Kemper County.

Map C - Congressional Townships of Kemper County, Mississippi

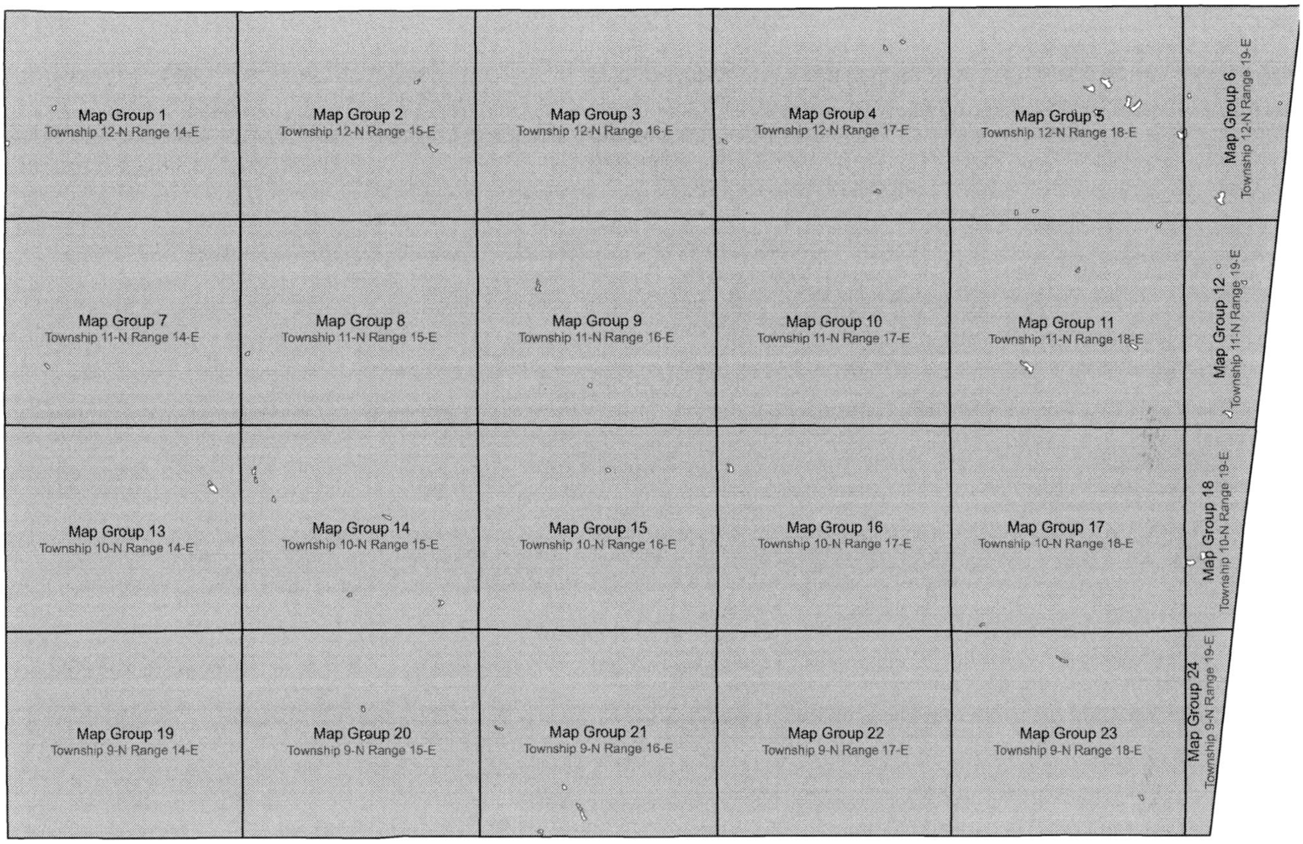

Map Group 1
Township 12-N Range 14-E
Map Group 2
Township 12-N Range 15-E
Map Group 3
Township 12-N Range 16-E
Map Group 4
Township 12-N Range 17-E
Map Group 5
Township 12-N Range 18-E
Map Group 6
Township 12-N Range 19-E

Map Group 7
Township 11-N Range 14-E
Map Group 8
Township 11-N Range 15-E
Map Group 9
Township 11-N Range 16-E
Map Group 10
Township 11-N Range 17-E
Map Group 11
Township 11-N Range 18-E
Map Group 12
Township 11-N Range 19-E

Map Group 13
Township 10-N Range 14-E
Map Group 14
Township 10-N Range 15-E
Map Group 15
Township 10-N Range 16-E
Map Group 16
Township 10-N Range 17-E
Map Group 17
Township 10-N Range 18-E
Map Group 18
Township 10-N Range 19-E

Map Group 19
Township 9-N Range 14-E
Map Group 20
Township 9-N Range 15-E
Map Group 21
Township 9-N Range 16-E
Map Group 22
Township 9-N Range 17-E
Map Group 23
Township 9-N Range 18-E
Map Group 24
Township 9-N Range 19-E

Legend

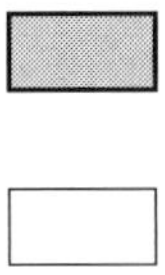

Kemper County, Mississippi

Congressional Townships

Helpful Hints

1. Many Patent-holders and their families settled across county lines. It is always a good idea to check nearby counties for your families (See Map "B").
2. Refer to Map "A" to see a broader view of where this county lies within the State, and Map "B" for a view of the counties surrounding Kemper County.

Map D Index: Cities & Towns of Kemper County, Mississippi

The following represents the Cities and Towns of Kemper County, along with the corresponding Map Group in which each is found. Cities and Towns are displayed in both the Road and Historical maps in the Group.

City/Town	Map Group No.
Akron	16
Antioch (historical)	10
Ayanabi (historical)	14
Beckville (historical)	17
Binnsville	6
Blackwater	21
Bloomfield	8
Bluff Springs	7
Bogue Toocolo Chitto (historical)	9
Carters	10
Center Ridge (historical)	16
Chomontakali (historical)	20
Cleveland	7
Cow Creek (historical)	7
Coy	1
Cullum	21
Cuthi Uckehaca (historical)	16
Damascus	19
Darnall (historical)	13
De Kalb	9
East Abeika (historical)	9
East Coongetto (historical)	14
East Yazo Skatane (historical)	15
Electric Mills	11
Enondale	23
Giles	12
Haanka Ullah (historical)	14
Hatchette (historical)	11
Herbert (historical)	13
Holihtasha (historical)	9
Kemper Springs	22
Kipling	15
Klondike	20
Liberty	20
Lynville	1
Millington	5
Moscow	14
Mount Nebo	15
Narkeeta (historical)	23
Oak Grove	16
Oktibbeha (historical)	20
Old Narkeetah (historical)	17
Old Scooba (historical)	11
Old Wahalak (historical)	5
Peden (historical)	8
Porterville	17
Preston	1
Prince Chapel	1
Prismatic	20
Red Bud (historical)	7
Rio	19
Rocky Mount (historical)	16
Sciples Mill	2
Scooba	11
Spinks (historical)	13
Sucarnoochee	17
Tamola	23
Texas (historical)	19
Townsend	10
Wahalak	4

Map D - Cities & Towns of Kemper County, Mississippi

Prince Chapel
Coy
Map Group 1
Township 12-N Range 14-E
Preston
Lynville
Map Group 2
Township 12-N Range 15-E
Scipies Mill
Map Group 3
Township 12-N Range 16-E
Map Group 4
Township 12-N Range 17-E
Wahalak
Old Wahalak (historical)
Millington
Map Group 5
Township 12-N Range 18-E
Binnsville
Map Group 6
Township 12-N
Range 19-E

Cow Creek (historical)
Map Group 7
Township 11-N Range 14-E
Bluff Springs
Red Bud (historical)
Cleveland
Peden (historical)
Bloomfield
Map Group 8
Township 11-N Range 15-E
Bogue Toocolo Chitto (historical)
East Abeika (historical)
Map Group 9
Township 11-N Range 16-E
Holihtasha (historical)
De Kalb
Antioch (historical)
Map Group 10
Township 11-N Range 17-E
Carters
Townsend
Scooba
Old Scooba (historical)
Hatchettie (historical)
Map Group 11
Township 11-N Range 18-E
Electric Mills
Giles
Map Group 12
Township 11-N
Range 19-E

Map Group 13
Township 10-N Range 14-E
Spinks (historical)
Darnall (historical)
Herbert (historical)
Map Group 14
Township 10-N Range 15-E
Moscow
East Coongetto (historical)
Ayanabi (historical)
Haanka Ullah (historical)
Map Group 15
Township 10-N Range 16-E
Mount Nebo
East Yazo Skatane (historical)
Kipling
Akron
Map Group 16
Township 10-N Range 17-E
Rocky Mount (historical)
Cuthi Uckehaca (historical)
Oak Grove
Center Ridge (historical)
Sucarnoochee
Map Group 17
Township 10-N Range 18-E
Old Narkeetah (historical)
Porterville
Beckville (historical)
Map Group 18
Township 10-N Range 19-E

Damascus
Map Group 19
Township 9-N Range 14-E
Rio
Texas (historical)
Liberty
Map Group 20
Township 9-N Range 15-E
Klondike
Chomontakali (historical)
Prismatic
Oktibbeha (historical)
Cullum
Blackwater
Map Group 21
Township 9-N Range 16-E
Map Group 22
Township 9-N Range 17-E
Kemper Springs
Narkeeta (historical)
Enondale
Map Group 23
Township 9-N Range 18-E
Tamola
Map Group 24
Township 9-N Range 19-E

Legend

Kemper County, Mississippi

Congressional Townships

Helpful Hints

1 Cities and towns are marked only at their center-points as published by the USGS and/or NationalAtlas.gov. This often enables us to more closely approximate where these might have existed when first settled.

2 To see more specifically where these Cities & Towns are located within the county, refer to both the Road and Historical maps in the Map-Group referred to above. See also, the Map "D" Index on the opposite page.

Map E Index: Cemeteries of Kemper County, Mississippi

The following represents many of the Cemeteries of Kemper County, along with the corresponding Township Map Group in which each is found. Cemeteries are displayed in both the Road and Historical maps in the Map Groups referred to below.

Cemetery	Map Group No.
Antioch Cem.	4
Bethany Springs Cem.	16
Binnsville Cem.	6
Blackwater Cem.	21
Blue Chapel Cem.	11
Bluff Springs Cem.	7
Briggs Chapel Cem.	24
Cedar Lawn Memorial Cem.	11
Center Ridge Cem.	16
Chamberlin Cem.	2
Chapel Hill Cem.	16
Cherry Cem.	10
Chisholm Cem.	19
Cole Cem.	13
Damascus Cem.	19
DeKalb Cem.	9
Dry Creek Cem.	1
Enondale Cem.	23
Felton Cem.	4
Giles Cem.	12
Hampton Cem.	15
Hensons Cem.	7
Hopewell Cem.	13
Jerusalem Cem.	9
Klondike Cem.	20
Liberty Cem.	13
Linwood Cem.	19
Macedonia Cem.	16
McDonald Cem.	13
McRae Cem.	8
Mount Hebron Cem.	23
Mount Olive Cem.	20
Mount Pleasant Cem.	20
New Hope Cem.	14
New Hope Cem.	14
Old Scooba Cem.	11
Old Wahalak Cem.	5
Pawticfaw Cem.	15
Pinecrest Cem.	9
Pleasant Springs Cem.	1
Pleasant Springs Church Cem.	1
Robbins Cem.	17
Rush Cem.	15
Salem Cem.	2
Shepard Grove Cem.	1
Shepherd Cem.	7
Shiloh Cem.	14
Smith Cem.	8
Smyrna Cem.	8
Spring Hill Cem.	3
Talbert Cem.	13
Tubb Cem.	2
Twin Cemeteries	4
Union Cem.	16
Union Cem.	20
Van Devender Cem.	3
Wahalak Cem.	4
West Kemper Cem.	14
Zion Cem.	19

Map E - Cemeteries of Kemper County, Mississippi

Dry Creek
Tubb
Van Devender
Old Wahalak
Map Group 1
Township 12-N Range 14-E
Shepard Grove
Pleasant Springs Church
Pleasant Springs
Map Group 2
Township 12-N Range 15-E
Salem
Chamberlin
Map Group 3
Township 12-N Range 16-E
Spring Hill
Wahalak
Twin Cemeteries
Map Group 4
Township 12-N Range 17-E
Felton
Antioch
Map Group 5
Township 12-N Range 18-E
Binnsville
Map Group 6
Township 12-N
Range 19-E

Map Group 7
Township 11-N Range 14-E
Hensons
Bluff Springs
Shepherd
Map Group 8
Township 11-N Range 15-E
Smyrna
McRae
Smith
Jerusalem
Map Group 9
Township 11-N Range 16-E
DeKalb
Pinecrest
Map Group 10
Township 11-N Range 17-E
Cherry
Blue Chapel
Cedar Lawn Memorial
Old Scooba
Map Group 11
Township 11-N Range 18-E
Giles
Map Group 12
Township 11-N Range 19-E

Cole
McDonald
Liberty
Hopewell
Map Group 13
Township 10-N Range 14-E
Talbert
New Hope
West Kemper
New Hope
Shiloh
Map Group 14
Township 10-N Range 15-E
Hampton
Map Group 15
Township 10-N Range 16-E
Pawticfaw
Rush
Macedonia
Bethany Springs
Map Group 16
Township 10-N Range 17-E
Chapel Hill
Union
Center Ridge
Map Group 17
Township 10-N Range 18-E
Robbins
Map Group 18
Township 10-N Range 19-E

Damascus
Linwood
Chisholm
Zion
Map Group 19
Township 9-N Range 14-E
Mount Pleasant
Mount Olive
Klondike
Map Group 20
Township 9-N Range 15-E
Union
Map Group 21
Township 9-N Range 16-E
Blackwater
Map Group 22
Township 9-N Range 17-E
Enondale
Map Group 23
Township 9-N Range 18-E
Mount Hebron
Map Group 24
Township 9-N
Range 19-E
Briggs Chapel

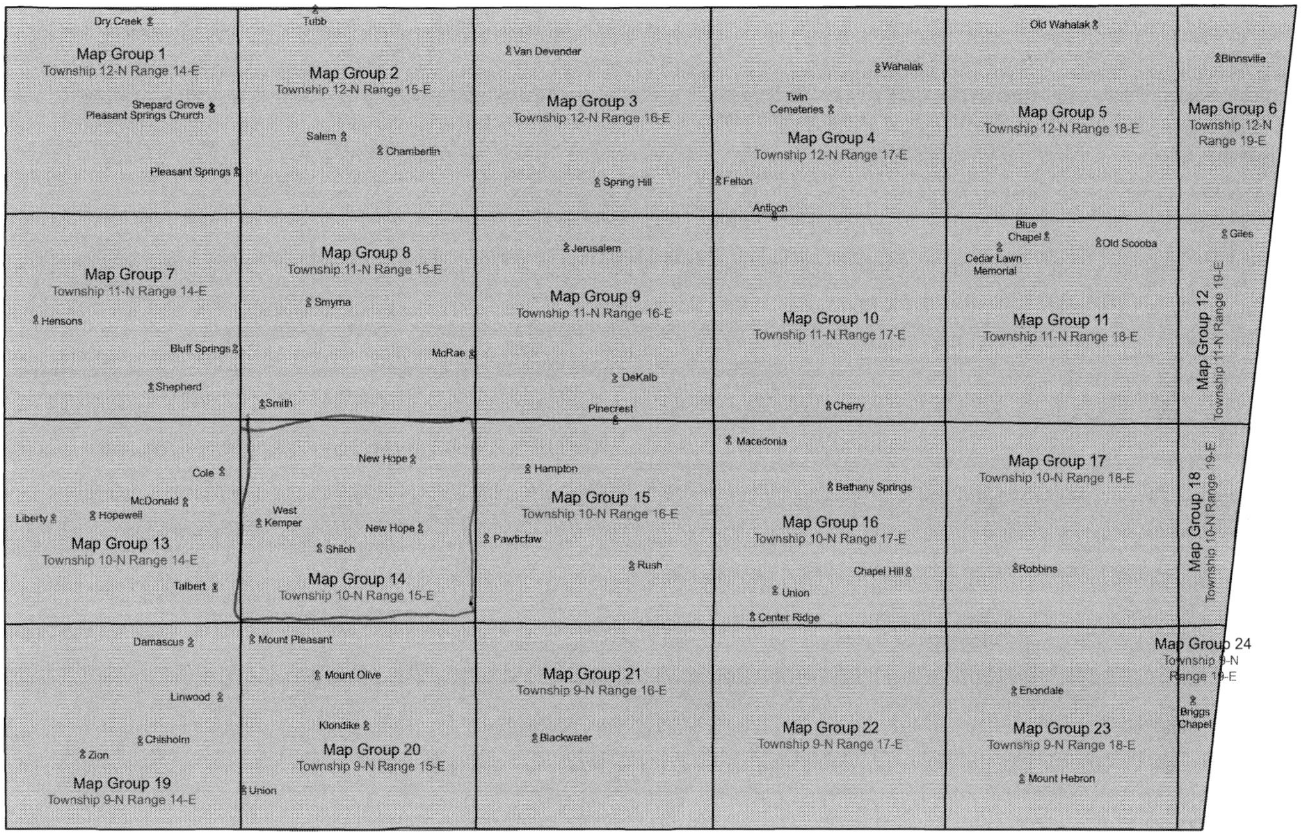

Legend

Kemper County, Mississippi

Congressional Townships

Helpful Hints

1 Cemeteries are marked at locations as published by the USGS and/or NationalAtlas.gov.

2 To see more specifically where these Cemeteries are located, refer to the Road & Historical maps in the Map-Group referred to above. See also, the Map "E" Index on the opposite page to make sure you don't miss any of the Cemeteries located within this Congressional township.

Surnames in Kemper County, Mississippi Patents

The following list represents the surnames that we have located in Kemper County, Mississippi Patents and the number of parcels that we have mapped for each one. Here is a quick way to determine the existence (or not) of Patents to be found in the subsequent indexes and maps of this volume.

Surname	# of Land Parcels
ABBERCROMBIE	1
ABBOTT	2
ABELS	1
ABERCROMBIE	10
ABERCROMBRIE	3
ABERNATHY	19
ADAIR	5
ADAMS	24
ADCOCK	18
ADCOX	1
AH	1
ALDERMAN	1
ALEXANDER	2
ALLEN	12
ALLIS	1
ALLWOOD	2
ANDERSON	36
ANDREWS	3
ARCHER	1
ARCHIBALD	1
ARTHUR	1
ASKIN	2
AULD	7
AUTRY	1
AVERY	8
AYLETT	1
AYRES	1
BACON	2
BAIRD	1
BALDWIN	3
BALLARD	1
BANKS	8
BANNON	1
BAREFIELD	5
BAREFOOT	1
BARFIELD	2
BARFOOT	3
BARNES	6
BARNETT	22
BARTLETT	10
BARTON	2
BASKIN	3
BATES	3
BAUGHMAN	1
BECK	2
BEESON	9
BELANCY	1
BELCHER	1
BELEW	3
BELL	4
BENNET	1
BENNETT	5
BENTON	2
BERRYMAN	1
BESTER	7
BETHANY	10
BETSILL	1
BEVIL	19
BEVILL	28
BIGGS	1
BILLINGSLEY	1
BINNS	1
BIRD	1
BIRDSONG	2
BISHOP	2
BLACKWELL	2
BLAKELY	2
BLANTON	3
BLUE	1
BOBBITT	3
BOBO	4
BOHANNON	3
BONNER	1
BORDEN	16
BOSTIAN	6
BOSTICK	6
BOUGHTON	1
BOUNDS	11
BOWEN	3
BOYD	16
BOYKIN	1
BOYLS	5
BOZEMAN	1
BRACKENRIDGE	1
BRANNING	12
BRANTLEY	4
BREAZEALE	1
BRECKENRIDGE	1
BREWTON	2
BRICKELL	2
BRIGGS	2
BRISTER	2
BRITTAIN	5
BROADWAY	2
BRODANAX	1
BROOKE	3
BROOKS	2
BROOM	1
BROWN	29
BROWNLEE	2
BUCHANAN	2
BUCHANNAN	1
BUCHANNON	2
BURFOOT	1
BURFORD	2
BURNETT	34
BURRAGE	8
BURROUGHS	1
BURTON	11
BUTCHEE	1
BUTLER	5
BUTTERWORTH	3
BYRD	1
BYRN	16
CADE	1
CALHOUN	6
CALLAHAN	3
CALLAWAY	1
CALVART	5
CALVERT	10
CAMPBELL	14
CAMRON	1
CANNON	25
CAPERS	1
CARLISLE	6
CARMICHAEL	4
CAROTHERS	1
CARRAWAY	2
CARRIEL	1
CARTER	23
CATES	13
CAVANAH	2
CHAMBERS	1
CHANCELOR	2
CHANEY	5
CHARLTON	5
CHEATHAM	1
CHERRY	10
CHILDS	1
CHIPMAN	2
CHISOLM	3
CLARK	21
CLAY	9
CLEARMAN	1
CLEMENT	11
COATES	3
COBB	1
COCHRAN	1
COCKRELL	1
COLBERT	4
COLE	34
COLEMAN	21
COLGLAZER	6
COLLUM	4
CONELLY	2
CONN	2
CONNER	1
COOK	9
COOKE	1
COOLEDGE	3
COOLIDGE	3
COOPER	3
COOPWOOD	70
CORLEY	1
CORNATHORN	1
COTTON	1
COWAN	2
COWSAR	2
COWSER	1
COX	2
CRAIN	1
CRANFORD	1
CRAWFORD	9
CRAWLEY	1
CREEKMORE	1
CREER	1
CRENSHAW	1
CROCKER	1
CROKER	1
CROOK	2
CROSBY	1
CROWTHER	7
CUBBA	1
CULBERTSON	1
CULLUM	4
CULPEPPER	3
CUNNINGHAM	3
CURRIE	2
DADE	1
DAFFAN	1
DANIEL	8
DARNAL	2
DARNALL	16
DAVIDSON	2
DAVIES	7
DAVIS	23
DAWE	1
DAWKINS	3
DAWS	3
DEAN	1
DEES	7
DEESE	2
DEGGES	1
DEJARNAT	2
DELK	5
DENNIS	2
DENTON	2
DEW	1
DEWEESE	2
DICKENS	1
DICKINS	10
DICKSON	1
DILLON	1
DOBBS	1
DODSON	1
DOLBEAR	4
DONALD	4
DONALDS	2
DOOLY	1
DORR	1
DOZIER	5
DREWRY	1
DUNCAN	10
DUNGER	1
DUNKIN	1
DUNLAP	2
DUNN	4
DYER	10
EAKES	1
EAKIN	2
EAKS	1
EARL	1
EARLE	26
EARNEST	1
EASON	3
EASTHAM	3
ECHOLS	2
ECKFORD	4
EDGE	2
EDMONDS	1
EDMONDSON	1
EDWARDS	18
EGGERTON	1
EKES	3
ELLINGTON	1
ELLIOT	28
ELLIOTT	16
ELLIS	5

Surname	# of Land Parcels
EMMONS	2
ESKRIDGE	2
ESTELL	2
ESTES	1
ETHRIDGE	4
EUBANKS	1
EVANS	12
EVERETT	13
EVERITT	1
FAIN	2
FALKNER	4
FARMER	1
FARRAR	4
FAUCETT	2
FELTON	7
FELTS	10
FELTZ	1
FERGUSON	2
FEW	1
FINLEY	1
FLANAGIN	3
FLEMMING	19
FLETCHER	1
FLEWVELLAN	1
FLOORE	2
FLORD	1
FLOURNOY	2
FLOYD	6
FOOTE	3
FORESTER	2
FORRESTER	1
FOSTER	1
FOWCETT	4
FOWLER	9
FOX	7
FRANKLIN	3
FREELAND	2
FULLER	1
FULTON	18
FUTRELL	1
GAINES	6
GALES	1
GALLASPY	1
GAMBLE	2
GARRARD	7
GARRETT	1
GARRISON	1
GASTON	4
GAY	5
GENTRY	1
GEORGE	2
GERMANY	5
GERRARD	1
GEWIN	4
GIBBS	1
GIBSON	2
GIFFORD	22
GILBERT	1
GILCHRIST	32
GILES	10
GILL	3
GILLESPIE	3
GILLIS	3
GIVAN	3
GLOVER	6
GOODE	9
GOODGER	2
GOODWIN	1
GORDON	2
GOYNE	1
GOYNES	2
GRACE	3
GRADY	5
GRAHAM	4
GRANT	11
GRANTHAM	4
GRAY	7
GREEN	20
GREENE	144
GREENLEE	2
GREENLEES	1
GREGORY	3
GRIFFIN	22
GRIFFITH	5
GRIGGS	4
GRIGSBY	12
GRISOM	3
GROCE	1
GRUBBS	1
GUINN	2
GULLY	15
GUNN	1
GUNTER	1
HAGEWOOD	1
HAGGARD	4
HAGOOD	2
HAILLY	1
HAIR	2
HALE	3
HALL	24
HALLFORD	3
HAMBRICK	1
HAMLETT	1
HAMMACK	1
HAMMOCK	3
HAMPTON	2
HAMRICK	1
HANLEY	1
HANNA	3
HARBOUR	6
HARDEMAN	1
HARDIMAN	1
HARDIN	1
HARDY	3
HARGROVE	1
HARMON	2
HARPER	33
HARREL	2
HARRELL	7
HARRINGTON	3
HARRIS	16
HARRISON	2
HARVEY	1
HASKINS	3
HATCH	4
HAWES	2
HAWS	1
HAYNES	2
HEARON	1
HENDERSON	15
HENDON	1
HENDRICK	4
HENDRICKS	1
HENSON	14
HERNDON	1
HERRINGTON	8
HICKMAN	1
HICKS	1
HIGGINBOTHAM	2
HILL	1
HILLHOUSE	2
HITCHCOCK	1
HITT	3
HODGE	2
HODGES	33
HOLCROFT	1
HOLDER	1
HOLDERNESS	24
HOLLAND	1
HOLMES	2
HOLT	6
HOLTON	2
HOMES	1
HOPSON	7
HORN	1
HOTAH	1
HOUSTON	16
HUBBARD	108
HUDNALL	1
HUDNELL	2
HUDSON	4
HUGHES	10
HULL	8
HUMPHRIES	2
HUNDLEY	12
HUNNEYCUTT	1
HUNNICUTT	3
HUNT	2
HUNTER	1
HUNTINGTON	3
HUSBANDS	1
HUSE	3
HUSTON	3
HUTCHINS	7
HUTTON	7
IKARD	1
IVY	1
JACK	3
JACKSON	27
JACOWAY	4
JAGGANS	1
JAGGERS	1
JAMES	1
JAMISON	3
JARVIS	6
JEMISON	28
JENKINS	24
JENNINGS	1
JINCKS	3
JINKINS	1
JOHNSON	52
JOHNSTON	4
JOINER	5
JONAS	1
JONES	42
JORDAN	3
JORDEN	2
JOYNER	6
JUDSON	15
JUMPER	1
KEAHEY	1
KEAKY	1
KEELAND	2
KEENAN	2
KELLEY	2
KEMPER	1
KENNON	6
KEY	3
KILLIN	1
KING	10
KNAPP	1
KNIGHT	1
KNIGHTEN	2
KOONCE	1
KYLE	1
LA HO LO	1
LA MA	1
LACY	15
LAKE	12
LAMPLEY	12
LAMPLY	3
LAND	3
LANDRUM	4
LANG	16
LANHAM	1
LANHAN	1
LANKAM	1
LARK	1
LATHAM	12
LAUDERDALE	1
LEACH	1
LEE	4
LENTON	1
LEVENS	2
LEVINE	1
LEWIS	163
LILES	1
LINCECUM	3
LIPSCOMB	2
LITTLE	5
LLOYD	10
LOCKLIN	1
LOFTIN	4
LONG	3
LOVE	11
LOVELADY	4
LOVEN	1
LOWE	1
LOYD	1
LUKE	3
LYLE	3
MA	2
MABRY	2
MADDEN	1
MADERSON	1
MADISON	6
MAHON	2
MAJORS	2
MALLORY	3
MALONE	13
MARR	1
MARS	3
MARSHALL	17
MARTIN	5
MASSEY	3
MATHENY	4
MATHEWS	5
MATTHEWS	7
MAURY	6
MAY	2
MAYBRY	2
MAYFIELD	1
MAYNOR	2
MAYO	5
MCAFEE	3
MCALISTER	1
MCALLISTER	1
MCALLUM	3
MCARTHUR	10
MCBRAYER	4

Surname	# of Land Parcels
MCBRYDE	3
MCCALEBB	1
MCCALL	3
MCCASKILL	4
MCCLAIN	1
MCCLELAND	1
MCCLURG	1
MCCONNELL	6
MCCOWN	19
MCCOY	5
MCCRANIE	2
MCCRAY	2
MCCRIMON	3
MCCRORY	9
MCDADE	9
MCDANIEL	1
MCDONALD	18
MCDOWELL	1
MCFARLAND	4
MCGEE	88
MCGEHEE	3
MCGOWEN	2
MCINTOSH	14
MCINTUSH	1
MCINTYRE	4
MCKAY	1
MCKEE	1
MCKELLAR	11
MCKELVAIN	1
MCKELVIN	3
MCKINNEY	4
MCKLEVAIN	1
MCLAMORE	1
MCLAUGHLIN	4
MCLAURIN	8
MCLAWREN	1
MCLEAN	3
MCLELAND	2
MCLELLAND	1
MCLENDON	2
MCLEROY	1
MCMAHON	6
MCMILLAN	1
MCMILLON	1
MCMURRY	2
MCNEAL	3
MCNEES	1
MCNEIL	2
MCNEILL	10
MCPHERSON	1
MCQUEEN	2
MCRAE	6
MCRIGHT	2
MCSIVEEN	3
MCSWEAN	1
MCWHORTER	3
MCWOOTAN	2
MEEKS	4
MEYATTE	1
MIDDLEBROOKS	3
MIETT	1
MILLARD	2
MILLING	1
MILLS	126
MINNIECE	1
MISSISSIPPI	12
MITCHEL	2
MITCHELL	3
MITCHUM	2
MONK	1
MONTAGUE	1
MOODY	11
MOONEY	2
MOORE	36
MORGAN	4
MORRAH	2
MORRIS	3
MORRISON	2
MORROW	5
MORSE	1
MOSBY	1
MOSELEY	17
MOSELY	4
MOSLEY	11
MULDROW	1
MULHOLLAND	1
MULLINS	2
MURPHEY	6
MURPHY	5
MURRAY	1
MURRY	3
NAIL	1
NASH	16
NAVE	2
NAYLOR	3
NEADHAM	1
NEAL	5
NEEDHAM	1
NEEL	1
NEOTLCAH	1
NESTER	3
NETHERRY	1
NETTLES	4
NEW	1
NEWBERRY	2
NEWCOMB	2
NEWELL	3
NEWTON	1
NICHOLAS	6
NICHOLSON	44
NOATEMAH	2
NOLES	1
NORDEN	1
NORRIS	1
NORRISS	4
NUNN	1
OBANNON	1
ODEN	20
ODOM	10
OLIVE	5
ONEAL	1
ONEIL	1
ONEILL	2
OREILLY	7
ORNE	22
OVERSTREET	11
OWEN	7
OWENS	1
PACE	4
PADEN	11
PAGE	12
PALMER	9
PARKER	18
PARRISH	1
PATRICK	1
PATTON	1
PAYNE	1
PEARCE	1
PEARL	7
PEARSON	1
PEDEN	74
PEEL	3
PEGG	2
PENNINGTON	2
PERKINS	7
PERMENTER	1
PERRY	4
PERSON	6
PERSONS	1
PETTIS	1
PETTUS	6
PFISTER	1
PHARMER	2
PHILLIPS	2
PICKETT	2
PIERCE	5
POLLARD	1
POLLOCK	8
POOL	6
POOLE	4
POPE	3
PORTER	2
POSEY	1
POWE	9
POWELL	2
PRESTON	2
PREUIT	5
PREWIT	4
PREWITT	1
PRICE	1
PRIDDY	2
PRUIT	6
PRUITT	10
PUCKETT	2
PULLER	2
QUARLES	3
RAINER	1
RAINEY	2
RAWLS	1
REA	3
REED	2
REID	2
RENCHER	1
REY	1
REYNOLDS	5
RHODES	3
RICHARDSON	3
RICHEY	14
RIDDLE	2
RIDGWAY	2
RIGBY	6
RIGDON	2
RILEY	6
ROACH	1
ROBBINS	6
ROBERTS	6
ROBERTSON	2
ROBINSON	3
ROCHEL	1
RODES	3
RODGERS	1
ROEBUCK	1
ROGERS	19
RORY	1
ROSAMOND	3
ROSS	16
ROUNDTREE	2
ROWE	19
RUPERT	42
RUSH	7
RUSHING	1
RUSSELL	2
RUTHERFORD	1
RUTHVEN	2
SADERFIELD	2
SADLER	3
SALTER	1
SANDERS	16
SANDERSON	3
SANDFORD	1
SANFORD	2
SAUNDERS	1
SAYRE	11
SCITZS	4
SCONYERS	1
SCOTT	59
SCUDDAY	6
SCUDDY	4
SEAL	1
SEALE	8
SECREST	1
SELBY	3
SELLERS	4
SESSIONS	2
SESSUMS	1
SHANDS	1
SHANNON	1
SHARP	10
SHAW	1
SHEPARD	3
SHEPHERD	1
SHIKLE	2
SHIP	1
SHIPP	2
SHIRLEY	2
SHUMATE	9
SIGGARS	1
SILLIMAN	6
SIMMONS	5
SIMMS	1
SIMPSON	1
SIMS	1
SINCLAIR	2
SITZS	1
SKINNER	4
SLATON	3
SLAUGHTER	2
SMALL	1
SMITH	39
SMYTH	4
SNEAD	7
SNEED	1
SNOWDEN	1
SORSBY	12
SPEAR	4
SPEARS	1
SPEED	1
SPEIR	1
SPENCE	1
SPENCER	6
SPIER	1
SPINKS	21
STANTON	1
STARLING	1
STEDE	1
STEEL	4
STEELE	29
STENNIS	28
STEPHENS	6
STEPHENSON	1

Surname	# of Land Parcels
STEVENSON	3
STEWARD	1
STEWART	27
STOCKTON	2
STOKES	11
STONE	2
STOVALL	11
STOWALL	1
STRAHAN	1
STRAIT	3
STRAITZ	2
STRANGE	1
STUART	3
SUGGS	1
SULLINS	1
SWARENGIN	2
SWEARINGEN	4
SWIFT	3
TABER	1
TAH	1
TAPPAN	107
TART	1
TARTT	11
TATE	1
TAYLOR	5
TEER	4
TERRY	27
TEW	2
THOMAS	15
THOMPSON	6
THORN	1
THORNELL	2
THURMOND	3
TINDALL	1
TINSLEY	7
TISDALE	4
TOAL	1
TODD	2
TOLES	2
TOWNSEND	2
TREWHITT	1
TRIPLETT	3
TRUSSELL	1
TUBB	1
TUBBEE	2
TUBBS	1
TUBBY	1
TUCKER	5
TURNER	5
TURNEY	1
TUTT	8
ULMER	3
ULMORE	1
UPCHURCH	1
VAN HAWES	1
VANCE	9
VANDEAVENDER	1
VANDERVANDER	1
VANDEVANDER	6
VANDEVENDER	2
VAUGHAN	2
WADE	2
WAIR	2
WALKER	11
WALL	9
WALTER	1
WALTHALL	15
WALTON	1
WARD	6
WARE	3
WARREN	35
WARRIN	1
WASHINGTON	2
WATKINS	3
WATSON	15
WATT	1
WATTERS	10
WATTS	1
WEBB	1
WEIR	12
WELLS	3
WELSH	13
WEST	4
WESTMORELAND	2
WHITE	43
WHITEHEAD	2
WHITFIELD	8
WHITLEY	3
WHITSETT	23
WHITTLE	5
WIER	1
WIGGIN	1
WIGGINS	5
WILKINS	1
WILKINSON	2
WILKS	1
WILLIAMS	51
WILLIAMSON	9
WILLSON	1
WILSON	16
WIMBERLY	1
WINDHAM	8
WINN	5
WINSTON	35
WITHERS	1
WITTLERS	2
WOLFE	1
WOODS	1
WOODSON	1
WOOTAN	3
YAGER	1
YATES	6
YERBY	2
YOUNG	36

Surname/Township Index

This Index allows you to determine which *Township Map Group(s)* contain individuals with the following surnames. Each *Map Group* has a corresponding full-name index of all individuals who obtained patents for land within its Congressional township's borders. After each index you will find the Patent Map to which it refers, and just thereafter, you can view the township's Road Map and Historical Map, with the latter map displaying streams, railroads, and more.

So, once you find your Surname here, proceed to the Index at the beginning of the **Map Group** indicated below.

Surname	Map Group	Parcels of Land	Meridian/Township/Range
ABBERCROMBIE	**14**	1	Choctaw 10-N 15-E
ABBOTT	**14**	2	Choctaw 10-N 15-E
ABELS	**1**	1	Choctaw 12-N 14-E
ABERCROMBIE	**14**	6	Choctaw 10-N 15-E
" "	**11**	3	Choctaw 11-N 18-E
" "	**7**	1	Choctaw 11-N 14-E
ABERCROMBRIE	**14**	3	Choctaw 10-N 15-E
ABERNATHY	**19**	8	Choctaw 9-N 14-E
" "	**13**	4	Choctaw 10-N 14-E
" "	**2**	4	Choctaw 12-N 15-E
" "	**1**	3	Choctaw 12-N 14-E
ADAIR	**20**	5	Choctaw 9-N 15-E
ADAMS	**14**	5	Choctaw 10-N 15-E
" "	**4**	5	Choctaw 12-N 17-E
" "	**15**	4	Choctaw 10-N 16-E
" "	**5**	4	Choctaw 12-N 18-E
" "	**10**	3	Choctaw 11-N 17-E
" "	**8**	2	Choctaw 11-N 15-E
" "	**11**	1	Choctaw 11-N 18-E
ADCOCK	**3**	9	Choctaw 12-N 16-E
" "	**10**	6	Choctaw 11-N 17-E
" "	**2**	2	Choctaw 12-N 15-E
" "	**4**	1	Choctaw 12-N 17-E
ADCOX	**10**	1	Choctaw 11-N 17-E
AH	**22**	1	Choctaw 9-N 17-E
ALDERMAN	**13**	1	Choctaw 10-N 14-E
ALEXANDER	**14**	2	Choctaw 10-N 15-E
ALLEN	**13**	4	Choctaw 10-N 14-E
" "	**24**	4	Choctaw 9-N 19-E
" "	**2**	2	Choctaw 12-N 15-E
" "	**9**	1	Choctaw 11-N 16-E
" "	**5**	1	Choctaw 12-N 18-E
ALLIS	**9**	1	Choctaw 11-N 16-E
ALLWOOD	**14**	1	Choctaw 10-N 15-E
" "	**20**	1	Choctaw 9-N 15-E
ANDERSON	**13**	11	Choctaw 10-N 14-E
" "	**5**	8	Choctaw 12-N 18-E
" "	**18**	5	Choctaw 10-N 19-E
" "	**14**	3	Choctaw 10-N 15-E
" "	**8**	3	Choctaw 11-N 15-E
" "	**7**	2	Choctaw 11-N 14-E
" "	**1**	2	Choctaw 12-N 14-E
" "	**17**	1	Choctaw 10-N 18-E
" "	**4**	1	Choctaw 12-N 17-E

Surname	Map Group	Parcels of Land	Meridian/Township/Range
ANDREWS	22	2	Choctaw 9-N 17-E
" "	17	1	Choctaw 10-N 18-E
ARCHER	22	1	Choctaw 9-N 17-E
ARCHIBALD	11	1	Choctaw 11-N 18-E
ARTHUR	9	1	Choctaw 11-N 16-E
ASKIN	22	2	Choctaw 9-N 17-E
AULD	21	7	Choctaw 9-N 16-E
AUTRY	15	1	Choctaw 10-N 16-E
AVERY	10	2	Choctaw 11-N 17-E
" "	11	2	Choctaw 11-N 18-E
" "	16	1	Choctaw 10-N 17-E
" "	17	1	Choctaw 10-N 18-E
" "	9	1	Choctaw 11-N 16-E
" "	23	1	Choctaw 9-N 18-E
AYLETT	10	1	Choctaw 11-N 17-E
AYRES	20	1	Choctaw 9-N 15-E
BACON	9	2	Choctaw 11-N 16-E
BAIRD	19	1	Choctaw 9-N 14-E
BALDWIN	18	2	Choctaw 10-N 19-E
" "	14	1	Choctaw 10-N 15-E
BALLARD	9	1	Choctaw 11-N 16-E
BANKS	15	4	Choctaw 10-N 16-E
" "	14	3	Choctaw 10-N 15-E
" "	20	1	Choctaw 9-N 15-E
BANNON	23	1	Choctaw 9-N 18-E
BAREFIELD	8	5	Choctaw 11-N 15-E
BAREFOOT	21	1	Choctaw 9-N 16-E
BARFIELD	8	1	Choctaw 11-N 15-E
" "	22	1	Choctaw 9-N 17-E
BARFOOT	21	2	Choctaw 9-N 16-E
" "	7	1	Choctaw 11-N 14-E
BARNES	4	4	Choctaw 12-N 17-E
" "	9	1	Choctaw 11-N 16-E
" "	2	1	Choctaw 12-N 15-E
BARNETT	12	17	Choctaw 11-N 19-E
" "	18	4	Choctaw 10-N 19-E
" "	11	1	Choctaw 11-N 18-E
BARTLETT	8	4	Choctaw 11-N 15-E
" "	2	4	Choctaw 12-N 15-E
" "	17	1	Choctaw 10-N 18-E
" "	7	1	Choctaw 11-N 14-E
BARTON	18	2	Choctaw 10-N 19-E
BASKIN	10	2	Choctaw 11-N 17-E
" "	4	1	Choctaw 12-N 17-E
BATES	12	2	Choctaw 11-N 19-E
" "	13	1	Choctaw 10-N 14-E
BAUGHMAN	8	1	Choctaw 11-N 15-E
BECK	3	2	Choctaw 12-N 16-E
BEESON	15	7	Choctaw 10-N 16-E
" "	20	2	Choctaw 9-N 15-E
BELANCY	9	1	Choctaw 11-N 16-E
BELCHER	19	1	Choctaw 9-N 14-E
BELEW	7	3	Choctaw 11-N 14-E
BELL	15	2	Choctaw 10-N 16-E
" "	9	1	Choctaw 11-N 16-E
" "	21	1	Choctaw 9-N 16-E
BENNET	15	1	Choctaw 10-N 16-E
BENNETT	12	2	Choctaw 11-N 19-E
" "	11	1	Choctaw 11-N 18-E
" "	3	1	Choctaw 12-N 16-E

Surname	Map Group	Parcels of Land	Meridian/Township/Range
BENNETT (Cont'd)	**5**	1	Choctaw 12-N 18-E
BENTON	**12**	2	Choctaw 11-N 19-E
BERRYMAN	**21**	1	Choctaw 9-N 16-E
BESTER	**11**	7	Choctaw 11-N 18-E
BETHANY	**3**	10	Choctaw 12-N 16-E
BETSILL	**16**	1	Choctaw 10-N 17-E
BEVIL	**13**	17	Choctaw 10-N 14-E
" "	**19**	2	Choctaw 9-N 14-E
BEVILL	**17**	18	Choctaw 10-N 18-E
" "	**13**	3	Choctaw 10-N 14-E
" "	**19**	3	Choctaw 9-N 14-E
" "	**20**	2	Choctaw 9-N 15-E
" "	**21**	1	Choctaw 9-N 16-E
" "	**23**	1	Choctaw 9-N 18-E
BIGGS	**17**	1	Choctaw 10-N 18-E
BILLINGSLEY	**1**	1	Choctaw 12-N 14-E
BINNS	**9**	1	Choctaw 11-N 16-E
BIRD	**1**	1	Choctaw 12-N 14-E
BIRDSONG	**17**	2	Choctaw 10-N 18-E
BISHOP	**8**	2	Choctaw 11-N 15-E
BLACKWELL	**7**	1	Choctaw 11-N 14-E
" "	**8**	1	Choctaw 11-N 15-E
BLAKELY	**10**	2	Choctaw 11-N 17-E
BLANTON	**12**	3	Choctaw 11-N 19-E
BLUE	**3**	1	Choctaw 12-N 16-E
BOBBITT	**22**	3	Choctaw 9-N 17-E
BOBO	**13**	4	Choctaw 10-N 14-E
BOHANNON	**9**	3	Choctaw 11-N 16-E
BONNER	**13**	1	Choctaw 10-N 14-E
BORDEN	**12**	16	Choctaw 11-N 19-E
BOSTIAN	**21**	6	Choctaw 9-N 16-E
BOSTICK	**7**	5	Choctaw 11-N 14-E
" "	**1**	1	Choctaw 12-N 14-E
BOUGHTON	**5**	1	Choctaw 12-N 18-E
BOUNDS	**14**	8	Choctaw 10-N 15-E
" "	**13**	3	Choctaw 10-N 14-E
BOWEN	**19**	3	Choctaw 9-N 14-E
BOYD	**10**	4	Choctaw 11-N 17-E
" "	**23**	4	Choctaw 9-N 18-E
" "	**1**	3	Choctaw 12-N 14-E
" "	**16**	2	Choctaw 10-N 17-E
" "	**24**	2	Choctaw 9-N 19-E
" "	**19**	1	Choctaw 9-N 14-E
BOYKIN	**3**	1	Choctaw 12-N 16-E
BOYLS	**19**	5	Choctaw 9-N 14-E
BOZEMAN	**13**	1	Choctaw 10-N 14-E
BRACKENRIDGE	**1**	1	Choctaw 12-N 14-E
BRANNING	**7**	12	Choctaw 11-N 14-E
BRANTLEY	**23**	4	Choctaw 9-N 18-E
BREAZEALE	**15**	1	Choctaw 10-N 16-E
BRECKENRIDGE	**1**	1	Choctaw 12-N 14-E
BREWTON	**19**	2	Choctaw 9-N 14-E
BRICKELL	**13**	2	Choctaw 10-N 14-E
BRIGGS	**23**	2	Choctaw 9-N 18-E
BRISTER	**10**	2	Choctaw 11-N 17-E
BRITTAIN	**8**	3	Choctaw 11-N 15-E
" "	**9**	2	Choctaw 11-N 16-E
BROADWAY	**2**	1	Choctaw 12-N 15-E
" "	**21**	1	Choctaw 9-N 16-E
BRODANAX	**23**	1	Choctaw 9-N 18-E

Surname	Map Group	Parcels of Land	Meridian/Township/Range
BROOKE	**20**	3	Choctaw 9-N 15-E
BROOKS	**9**	2	Choctaw 11-N 16-E
BROOM	**5**	1	Choctaw 12-N 18-E
BROWN	**21**	8	Choctaw 9-N 16-E
" "	**10**	7	Choctaw 11-N 17-E
" "	**24**	5	Choctaw 9-N 19-E
" "	**9**	4	Choctaw 11-N 16-E
" "	**14**	1	Choctaw 10-N 15-E
" "	**15**	1	Choctaw 10-N 16-E
" "	**7**	1	Choctaw 11-N 14-E
" "	**1**	1	Choctaw 12-N 14-E
" "	**6**	1	Choctaw 12-N 19-E
BROWNLEE	**16**	1	Choctaw 10-N 17-E
" "	**5**	1	Choctaw 12-N 18-E
BUCHANAN	**3**	1	Choctaw 12-N 16-E
" "	**24**	1	Choctaw 9-N 19-E
BUCHANNAN	**2**	1	Choctaw 12-N 15-E
BUCHANNON	**2**	2	Choctaw 12-N 15-E
BURFOOT	**5**	1	Choctaw 12-N 18-E
BURFORD	**5**	2	Choctaw 12-N 18-E
BURNETT	**3**	7	Choctaw 12-N 16-E
" "	**13**	6	Choctaw 10-N 14-E
" "	**19**	4	Choctaw 9-N 14-E
" "	**22**	4	Choctaw 9-N 17-E
" "	**14**	3	Choctaw 10-N 15-E
" "	**16**	3	Choctaw 10-N 17-E
" "	**17**	3	Choctaw 10-N 18-E
" "	**1**	2	Choctaw 12-N 14-E
" "	**2**	1	Choctaw 12-N 15-E
" "	**21**	1	Choctaw 9-N 16-E
BURRAGE	**1**	7	Choctaw 12-N 14-E
" "	**14**	1	Choctaw 10-N 15-E
BURROUGHS	**18**	1	Choctaw 10-N 19-E
BURTON	**10**	5	Choctaw 11-N 17-E
" "	**23**	4	Choctaw 9-N 18-E
" "	**8**	2	Choctaw 11-N 15-E
BUTCHEE	**22**	1	Choctaw 9-N 17-E
BUTLER	**24**	4	Choctaw 9-N 19-E
" "	**5**	1	Choctaw 12-N 18-E
BUTTERWORTH	**3**	3	Choctaw 12-N 16-E
BYRD	**2**	1	Choctaw 12-N 15-E
BYRN	**23**	12	Choctaw 9-N 18-E
" "	**2**	4	Choctaw 12-N 15-E
CADE	**4**	1	Choctaw 12-N 17-E
CALHOUN	**2**	2	Choctaw 12-N 15-E
" "	**22**	2	Choctaw 9-N 17-E
" "	**3**	1	Choctaw 12-N 16-E
" "	**23**	1	Choctaw 9-N 18-E
CALLAHAN	**11**	3	Choctaw 11-N 18-E
CALLAWAY	**20**	1	Choctaw 9-N 15-E
CALVART	**4**	4	Choctaw 12-N 17-E
" "	**10**	1	Choctaw 11-N 17-E
CALVERT	**19**	7	Choctaw 9-N 14-E
" "	**17**	1	Choctaw 10-N 18-E
" "	**4**	1	Choctaw 12-N 17-E
" "	**23**	1	Choctaw 9-N 18-E
CAMPBELL	**8**	9	Choctaw 11-N 15-E
" "	**13**	1	Choctaw 10-N 14-E
" "	**15**	1	Choctaw 10-N 16-E
" "	**5**	1	Choctaw 12-N 18-E

Surname	Map Group	Parcels of Land	Meridian/Township/Range
CAMPBELL (Cont'd)	**20**	1	Choctaw 9-N 15-E
" "	**23**	1	Choctaw 9-N 18-E
CAMRON	**11**	1	Choctaw 11-N 18-E
CANNON	**11**	20	Choctaw 11-N 18-E
" "	**12**	5	Choctaw 11-N 19-E
CAPERS	**23**	1	Choctaw 9-N 18-E
CARLISLE	**16**	5	Choctaw 10-N 17-E
" "	**2**	1	Choctaw 12-N 15-E
CARMICHAEL	**22**	3	Choctaw 9-N 17-E
" "	**13**	1	Choctaw 10-N 14-E
CAROTHERS	**5**	1	Choctaw 12-N 18-E
CARRAWAY	**22**	2	Choctaw 9-N 17-E
CARRIEL	**14**	1	Choctaw 10-N 15-E
CARTER	**11**	12	Choctaw 11-N 18-E
" "	**13**	3	Choctaw 10-N 14-E
" "	**22**	3	Choctaw 9-N 17-E
" "	**18**	2	Choctaw 10-N 19-E
" "	**23**	2	Choctaw 9-N 18-E
" "	**5**	1	Choctaw 12-N 18-E
CATES	**5**	7	Choctaw 12-N 18-E
" "	**6**	3	Choctaw 12-N 19-E
" "	**2**	2	Choctaw 12-N 15-E
" "	**3**	1	Choctaw 12-N 16-E
CAVANAH	**8**	2	Choctaw 11-N 15-E
CHAMBERS	**1**	1	Choctaw 12-N 14-E
CHANCELOR	**3**	2	Choctaw 12-N 16-E
CHANEY	**17**	2	Choctaw 10-N 18-E
" "	**3**	2	Choctaw 12-N 16-E
" "	**8**	1	Choctaw 11-N 15-E
CHARLTON	**6**	5	Choctaw 12-N 19-E
CHEATHAM	**1**	1	Choctaw 12-N 14-E
CHERRY	**10**	6	Choctaw 11-N 17-E
" "	**16**	3	Choctaw 10-N 17-E
" "	**17**	1	Choctaw 10-N 18-E
CHILDS	**21**	1	Choctaw 9-N 16-E
CHIPMAN	**13**	2	Choctaw 10-N 14-E
CHISOLM	**11**	2	Choctaw 11-N 18-E
" "	**19**	1	Choctaw 9-N 14-E
CLARK	**13**	5	Choctaw 10-N 14-E
" "	**15**	5	Choctaw 10-N 16-E
" "	**7**	5	Choctaw 11-N 14-E
" "	**8**	2	Choctaw 11-N 15-E
" "	**2**	1	Choctaw 12-N 15-E
" "	**19**	1	Choctaw 9-N 14-E
" "	**22**	1	Choctaw 9-N 17-E
" "	**23**	1	Choctaw 9-N 18-E
CLAY	**24**	4	Choctaw 9-N 19-E
" "	**19**	3	Choctaw 9-N 14-E
" "	**23**	2	Choctaw 9-N 18-E
CLEARMAN	**3**	1	Choctaw 12-N 16-E
CLEMENT	**14**	6	Choctaw 10-N 15-E
" "	**2**	3	Choctaw 12-N 15-E
" "	**16**	1	Choctaw 10-N 17-E
" "	**8**	1	Choctaw 11-N 15-E
COATES	**14**	1	Choctaw 10-N 15-E
" "	**10**	1	Choctaw 11-N 17-E
" "	**21**	1	Choctaw 9-N 16-E
COBB	**10**	1	Choctaw 11-N 17-E
COCHRAN	**20**	1	Choctaw 9-N 15-E
COCKRELL	**9**	1	Choctaw 11-N 16-E

Surname	Map Group	Parcels of Land	Meridian/Township/Range
COLBERT	**2**	4	Choctaw 12-N 15-E
COLE	**1**	10	Choctaw 12-N 14-E
" "	**20**	9	Choctaw 9-N 15-E
" "	**15**	5	Choctaw 10-N 16-E
" "	**14**	4	Choctaw 10-N 15-E
" "	**13**	3	Choctaw 10-N 14-E
" "	**9**	2	Choctaw 11-N 16-E
" "	**8**	1	Choctaw 11-N 15-E
COLEMAN	**3**	9	Choctaw 12-N 16-E
" "	**4**	6	Choctaw 12-N 17-E
" "	**5**	4	Choctaw 12-N 18-E
" "	**8**	1	Choctaw 11-N 15-E
" "	**1**	1	Choctaw 12-N 14-E
COLGLAZER	**21**	3	Choctaw 9-N 16-E
" "	**3**	2	Choctaw 12-N 16-E
" "	**2**	1	Choctaw 12-N 15-E
COLLUM	**19**	4	Choctaw 9-N 14-E
CONELLY	**14**	2	Choctaw 10-N 15-E
CONN	**14**	1	Choctaw 10-N 15-E
" "	**3**	1	Choctaw 12-N 16-E
CONNER	**9**	1	Choctaw 11-N 16-E
COOK	**10**	4	Choctaw 11-N 17-E
" "	**2**	3	Choctaw 12-N 15-E
" "	**8**	1	Choctaw 11-N 15-E
" "	**1**	1	Choctaw 12-N 14-E
COOKE	**2**	1	Choctaw 12-N 15-E
COOLEDGE	**2**	3	Choctaw 12-N 15-E
COOLIDGE	**2**	3	Choctaw 12-N 15-E
COOPER	**9**	2	Choctaw 11-N 16-E
" "	**22**	1	Choctaw 9-N 17-E
COOPWOOD	**3**	20	Choctaw 12-N 16-E
" "	**20**	17	Choctaw 9-N 15-E
" "	**2**	13	Choctaw 12-N 15-E
" "	**21**	11	Choctaw 9-N 16-E
" "	**16**	4	Choctaw 10-N 17-E
" "	**15**	3	Choctaw 10-N 16-E
" "	**1**	2	Choctaw 12-N 14-E
CORLEY	**9**	1	Choctaw 11-N 16-E
CORNATHORN	**3**	1	Choctaw 12-N 16-E
COTTON	**1**	1	Choctaw 12-N 14-E
COWAN	**16**	2	Choctaw 10-N 17-E
COWSAR	**8**	2	Choctaw 11-N 15-E
COWSER	**8**	1	Choctaw 11-N 15-E
COX	**9**	2	Choctaw 11-N 16-E
CRAIN	**2**	1	Choctaw 12-N 15-E
CRANFORD	**3**	1	Choctaw 12-N 16-E
CRAWFORD	**20**	4	Choctaw 9-N 15-E
" "	**15**	2	Choctaw 10-N 16-E
" "	**3**	2	Choctaw 12-N 16-E
" "	**11**	1	Choctaw 11-N 18-E
CRAWLEY	**23**	1	Choctaw 9-N 18-E
CREEKMORE	**9**	1	Choctaw 11-N 16-E
CREER	**22**	1	Choctaw 9-N 17-E
CRENSHAW	**13**	1	Choctaw 10-N 14-E
CROCKER	**11**	1	Choctaw 11-N 18-E
CROKER	**11**	1	Choctaw 11-N 18-E
CROOK	**3**	2	Choctaw 12-N 16-E
CROSBY	**22**	1	Choctaw 9-N 17-E
CROWTHER	**19**	7	Choctaw 9-N 14-E
CUBBA	**22**	1	Choctaw 9-N 17-E

Surname	Map Group	Parcels of Land	Meridian/Township/Range		
CULBERTSON	**13**	1	Choctaw	10-N	14-E
CULLUM	**16**	4	Choctaw	10-N	17-E
CULPEPPER	**11**	3	Choctaw	11-N	18-E
CUNNINGHAM	**16**	2	Choctaw	10-N	17-E
" "	**23**	1	Choctaw	9-N	18-E
CURRIE	**22**	2	Choctaw	9-N	17-E
DADE	**2**	1	Choctaw	12-N	15-E
DAFFAN	**1**	1	Choctaw	12-N	14-E
DANIEL	**11**	6	Choctaw	11-N	18-E
" "	**5**	2	Choctaw	12-N	18-E
DARNAL	**11**	2	Choctaw	11-N	18-E
DARNALL	**13**	5	Choctaw	10-N	14-E
" "	**18**	5	Choctaw	10-N	19-E
" "	**11**	5	Choctaw	11-N	18-E
" "	**17**	1	Choctaw	10-N	18-E
DAVIDSON	**16**	2	Choctaw	10-N	17-E
DAVIES	**13**	5	Choctaw	10-N	14-E
" "	**1**	2	Choctaw	12-N	14-E
DAVIS	**7**	7	Choctaw	11-N	14-E
" "	**18**	4	Choctaw	10-N	19-E
" "	**20**	4	Choctaw	9-N	15-E
" "	**13**	2	Choctaw	10-N	14-E
" "	**2**	2	Choctaw	12-N	15-E
" "	**14**	1	Choctaw	10-N	15-E
" "	**15**	1	Choctaw	10-N	16-E
" "	**19**	1	Choctaw	9-N	14-E
" "	**22**	1	Choctaw	9-N	17-E
DAWE	**7**	1	Choctaw	11-N	14-E
DAWKINS	**14**	2	Choctaw	10-N	15-E
" "	**15**	1	Choctaw	10-N	16-E
DAWS	**13**	2	Choctaw	10-N	14-E
" "	**7**	1	Choctaw	11-N	14-E
DEAN	**16**	1	Choctaw	10-N	17-E
DEES	**7**	7	Choctaw	11-N	14-E
DEESE	**7**	2	Choctaw	11-N	14-E
DEGGES	**15**	1	Choctaw	10-N	16-E
DEJARNAT	**20**	2	Choctaw	9-N	15-E
DELK	**23**	4	Choctaw	9-N	18-E
" "	**17**	1	Choctaw	10-N	18-E
DENNIS	**20**	1	Choctaw	9-N	15-E
" "	**24**	1	Choctaw	9-N	19-E
DENTON	**17**	1	Choctaw	10-N	18-E
" "	**3**	1	Choctaw	12-N	16-E
DEW	**5**	1	Choctaw	12-N	18-E
DEWEESE	**9**	1	Choctaw	11-N	16-E
" "	**3**	1	Choctaw	12-N	16-E
DICKENS	**3**	1	Choctaw	12-N	16-E
DICKINS	**2**	4	Choctaw	12-N	15-E
" "	**3**	3	Choctaw	12-N	16-E
" "	**20**	2	Choctaw	9-N	15-E
" "	**1**	1	Choctaw	12-N	14-E
DICKSON	**4**	1	Choctaw	12-N	17-E
DILLON	**10**	1	Choctaw	11-N	17-E
DOBBS	**5**	1	Choctaw	12-N	18-E
DODSON	**2**	1	Choctaw	12-N	15-E
DOLBEAR	**13**	4	Choctaw	10-N	14-E
DONALD	**8**	2	Choctaw	11-N	15-E
" "	**1**	2	Choctaw	12-N	14-E
DONALDS	**7**	2	Choctaw	11-N	14-E
DOOLY	**3**	1	Choctaw	12-N	16-E

Surname	Map Group	Parcels of Land	Meridian/Township/Range
DORR	23	1	Choctaw 9-N 18-E
DOZIER	10	3	Choctaw 11-N 17-E
" "	11	2	Choctaw 11-N 18-E
DREWRY	2	1	Choctaw 12-N 15-E
DUNCAN	19	4	Choctaw 9-N 14-E
" "	1	2	Choctaw 12-N 14-E
" "	6	2	Choctaw 12-N 19-E
" "	4	1	Choctaw 12-N 17-E
" "	21	1	Choctaw 9-N 16-E
DUNGER	22	1	Choctaw 9-N 17-E
DUNKIN	19	1	Choctaw 9-N 14-E
DUNLAP	9	1	Choctaw 11-N 16-E
" "	3	1	Choctaw 12-N 16-E
DUNN	1	3	Choctaw 12-N 14-E
" "	7	1	Choctaw 11-N 14-E
DYER	13	5	Choctaw 10-N 14-E
" "	1	2	Choctaw 12-N 14-E
" "	21	2	Choctaw 9-N 16-E
" "	3	1	Choctaw 12-N 16-E
EAKES	13	1	Choctaw 10-N 14-E
EAKIN	16	1	Choctaw 10-N 17-E
" "	10	1	Choctaw 11-N 17-E
EAKS	13	1	Choctaw 10-N 14-E
EARL	11	1	Choctaw 11-N 18-E
EARLE	11	13	Choctaw 11-N 18-E
" "	5	13	Choctaw 12-N 18-E
EARNEST	8	1	Choctaw 11-N 15-E
EASON	17	2	Choctaw 10-N 18-E
" "	13	1	Choctaw 10-N 14-E
EASTHAM	22	2	Choctaw 9-N 17-E
" "	21	1	Choctaw 9-N 16-E
ECHOLS	7	2	Choctaw 11-N 14-E
ECKFORD	14	2	Choctaw 10-N 15-E
" "	2	2	Choctaw 12-N 15-E
EDGE	9	2	Choctaw 11-N 16-E
EDMONDS	4	1	Choctaw 12-N 17-E
EDMONDSON	16	1	Choctaw 10-N 17-E
EDWARDS	22	6	Choctaw 9-N 17-E
" "	3	4	Choctaw 12-N 16-E
" "	7	2	Choctaw 11-N 14-E
" "	2	2	Choctaw 12-N 15-E
" "	23	2	Choctaw 9-N 18-E
" "	8	1	Choctaw 11-N 15-E
" "	21	1	Choctaw 9-N 16-E
EGGERTON	2	1	Choctaw 12-N 15-E
EKES	13	3	Choctaw 10-N 14-E
ELLINGTON	12	1	Choctaw 11-N 19-E
ELLIOT	13	8	Choctaw 10-N 14-E
" "	2	7	Choctaw 12-N 15-E
" "	10	6	Choctaw 11-N 17-E
" "	19	4	Choctaw 9-N 14-E
" "	14	3	Choctaw 10-N 15-E
ELLIOTT	10	10	Choctaw 11-N 17-E
" "	2	2	Choctaw 12-N 15-E
" "	3	2	Choctaw 12-N 16-E
" "	4	2	Choctaw 12-N 17-E
ELLIS	8	5	Choctaw 11-N 15-E
EMMONS	1	2	Choctaw 12-N 14-E
ESKRIDGE	15	1	Choctaw 10-N 16-E
" "	16	1	Choctaw 10-N 17-E

Surname	Map Group	Parcels of Land	Meridian/Township/Range
ESTELL	**2**	1	Choctaw 12-N 15-E
" "	**20**	1	Choctaw 9-N 15-E
ESTES	**21**	1	Choctaw 9-N 16-E
ETHRIDGE	**19**	3	Choctaw 9-N 14-E
" "	**5**	1	Choctaw 12-N 18-E
EUBANKS	**19**	1	Choctaw 9-N 14-E
EVANS	**16**	8	Choctaw 10-N 17-E
" "	**9**	2	Choctaw 11-N 16-E
" "	**1**	1	Choctaw 12-N 14-E
" "	**19**	1	Choctaw 9-N 14-E
EVERETT	**23**	4	Choctaw 9-N 18-E
" "	**10**	3	Choctaw 11-N 17-E
" "	**14**	2	Choctaw 10-N 15-E
" "	**9**	2	Choctaw 11-N 16-E
" "	**16**	1	Choctaw 10-N 17-E
" "	**5**	1	Choctaw 12-N 18-E
EVERITT	**18**	1	Choctaw 10-N 19-E
FAIN	**2**	2	Choctaw 12-N 15-E
FALKNER	**8**	4	Choctaw 11-N 15-E
FARMER	**22**	1	Choctaw 9-N 17-E
FARRAR	**24**	4	Choctaw 9-N 19-E
FAUCETT	**13**	2	Choctaw 10-N 14-E
FELTON	**3**	3	Choctaw 12-N 16-E
" "	**17**	2	Choctaw 10-N 18-E
" "	**9**	2	Choctaw 11-N 16-E
FELTS	**11**	8	Choctaw 11-N 18-E
" "	**5**	2	Choctaw 12-N 18-E
FELTZ	**11**	1	Choctaw 11-N 18-E
FERGUSON	**3**	2	Choctaw 12-N 16-E
FEW	**15**	1	Choctaw 10-N 16-E
FINLEY	**21**	1	Choctaw 9-N 16-E
FLANAGIN	**20**	3	Choctaw 9-N 15-E
FLEMMING	**6**	12	Choctaw 12-N 19-E
" "	**4**	7	Choctaw 12-N 17-E
FLETCHER	**5**	1	Choctaw 12-N 18-E
FLEWVELLAN	**21**	1	Choctaw 9-N 16-E
FLOORE	**2**	2	Choctaw 12-N 15-E
FLORD	**2**	1	Choctaw 12-N 15-E
FLOURNOY	**9**	2	Choctaw 11-N 16-E
FLOYD	**14**	6	Choctaw 10-N 15-E
FOOTE	**16**	3	Choctaw 10-N 17-E
FORESTER	**9**	2	Choctaw 11-N 16-E
FORRESTER	**9**	1	Choctaw 11-N 16-E
FOSTER	**19**	1	Choctaw 9-N 14-E
FOWCETT	**10**	4	Choctaw 11-N 17-E
FOWLER	**3**	4	Choctaw 12-N 16-E
" "	**13**	2	Choctaw 10-N 14-E
" "	**20**	1	Choctaw 9-N 15-E
" "	**22**	1	Choctaw 9-N 17-E
" "	**23**	1	Choctaw 9-N 18-E
FOX	**7**	3	Choctaw 11-N 14-E
" "	**11**	2	Choctaw 11-N 18-E
" "	**8**	1	Choctaw 11-N 15-E
" "	**9**	1	Choctaw 11-N 16-E
FRANKLIN	**13**	1	Choctaw 10-N 14-E
" "	**7**	1	Choctaw 11-N 14-E
" "	**20**	1	Choctaw 9-N 15-E
FREELAND	**24**	2	Choctaw 9-N 19-E
FULLER	**8**	1	Choctaw 11-N 15-E
FULTON	**1**	15	Choctaw 12-N 14-E

Surname	Map Group	Parcels of Land	Meridian/Township/Range
FULTON (Cont'd)	**7**	2	Choctaw 11-N 14-E
" "	**8**	1	Choctaw 11-N 15-E
FUTRELL	**21**	1	Choctaw 9-N 16-E
GAINES	**5**	6	Choctaw 12-N 18-E
GALES	**1**	1	Choctaw 12-N 14-E
GALLASPY	**20**	1	Choctaw 9-N 15-E
GAMBLE	**20**	2	Choctaw 9-N 15-E
GARRARD	**1**	7	Choctaw 12-N 14-E
GARRETT	**21**	1	Choctaw 9-N 16-E
GARRISON	**18**	1	Choctaw 10-N 19-E
GASTON	**1**	4	Choctaw 12-N 14-E
GAY	**2**	2	Choctaw 12-N 15-E
" "	**24**	2	Choctaw 9-N 19-E
" "	**10**	1	Choctaw 11-N 17-E
GENTRY	**16**	1	Choctaw 10-N 17-E
GEORGE	**15**	2	Choctaw 10-N 16-E
GERMANY	**7**	4	Choctaw 11-N 14-E
" "	**9**	1	Choctaw 11-N 16-E
GERRARD	**1**	1	Choctaw 12-N 14-E
GEWIN	**15**	4	Choctaw 10-N 16-E
GIBBS	**23**	1	Choctaw 9-N 18-E
GIBSON	**8**	2	Choctaw 11-N 15-E
GIFFORD	**3**	19	Choctaw 12-N 16-E
" "	**1**	3	Choctaw 12-N 14-E
GILBERT	**17**	1	Choctaw 10-N 18-E
GILCHRIST	**3**	21	Choctaw 12-N 16-E
" "	**13**	7	Choctaw 10-N 14-E
" "	**1**	3	Choctaw 12-N 14-E
" "	**4**	1	Choctaw 12-N 17-E
GILES	**12**	7	Choctaw 11-N 19-E
" "	**6**	3	Choctaw 12-N 19-E
GILL	**9**	3	Choctaw 11-N 16-E
GILLESPIE	**21**	3	Choctaw 9-N 16-E
GILLIS	**7**	3	Choctaw 11-N 14-E
GIVAN	**22**	3	Choctaw 9-N 17-E
GLOVER	**5**	6	Choctaw 12-N 18-E
GOODE	**5**	9	Choctaw 12-N 18-E
GOODGER	**14**	2	Choctaw 10-N 15-E
GOODWIN	**4**	1	Choctaw 12-N 17-E
GORDON	**21**	1	Choctaw 9-N 16-E
" "	**22**	1	Choctaw 9-N 17-E
GOYNE	**8**	1	Choctaw 11-N 15-E
GOYNES	**15**	1	Choctaw 10-N 16-E
" "	**10**	1	Choctaw 11-N 17-E
GRACE	**18**	2	Choctaw 10-N 19-E
" "	**15**	1	Choctaw 10-N 16-E
GRADY	**9**	3	Choctaw 11-N 16-E
" "	**15**	1	Choctaw 10-N 16-E
" "	**3**	1	Choctaw 12-N 16-E
GRAHAM	**14**	1	Choctaw 10-N 15-E
" "	**16**	1	Choctaw 10-N 17-E
" "	**2**	1	Choctaw 12-N 15-E
" "	**4**	1	Choctaw 12-N 17-E
GRANT	**2**	5	Choctaw 12-N 15-E
" "	**21**	4	Choctaw 9-N 16-E
" "	**22**	2	Choctaw 9-N 17-E
GRANTHAM	**17**	2	Choctaw 10-N 18-E
" "	**23**	2	Choctaw 9-N 18-E
GRAY	**16**	5	Choctaw 10-N 17-E
" "	**15**	1	Choctaw 10-N 16-E

Surname	Map Group	Parcels of Land	Meridian/Township/Range
GRAY (Cont'd)	**4**	1	Choctaw 12-N 17-E
GREEN	**5**	15	Choctaw 12-N 18-E
" "	**11**	2	Choctaw 11-N 18-E
" "	**19**	1	Choctaw 9-N 14-E
" "	**20**	1	Choctaw 9-N 15-E
" "	**21**	1	Choctaw 9-N 16-E
GREENE	**6**	36	Choctaw 12-N 19-E
" "	**13**	28	Choctaw 10-N 14-E
" "	**5**	25	Choctaw 12-N 18-E
" "	**12**	16	Choctaw 11-N 19-E
" "	**14**	9	Choctaw 10-N 15-E
" "	**16**	8	Choctaw 10-N 17-E
" "	**20**	7	Choctaw 9-N 15-E
" "	**19**	5	Choctaw 9-N 14-E
" "	**24**	4	Choctaw 9-N 19-E
" "	**15**	2	Choctaw 10-N 16-E
" "	**17**	1	Choctaw 10-N 18-E
" "	**21**	1	Choctaw 9-N 16-E
" "	**22**	1	Choctaw 9-N 17-E
" "	**23**	1	Choctaw 9-N 18-E
GREENLEE	**24**	2	Choctaw 9-N 19-E
GREENLEES	**11**	1	Choctaw 11-N 18-E
GREGORY	**15**	3	Choctaw 10-N 16-E
GRIFFIN	**23**	9	Choctaw 9-N 18-E
" "	**24**	4	Choctaw 9-N 19-E
" "	**13**	3	Choctaw 10-N 14-E
" "	**14**	2	Choctaw 10-N 15-E
" "	**22**	2	Choctaw 9-N 17-E
" "	**3**	1	Choctaw 12-N 16-E
" "	**5**	1	Choctaw 12-N 18-E
GRIFFITH	**9**	3	Choctaw 11-N 16-E
" "	**8**	2	Choctaw 11-N 15-E
GRIGGS	**5**	4	Choctaw 12-N 18-E
GRIGSBY	**16**	4	Choctaw 10-N 17-E
" "	**6**	2	Choctaw 12-N 19-E
" "	**19**	2	Choctaw 9-N 14-E
" "	**22**	2	Choctaw 9-N 17-E
" "	**3**	1	Choctaw 12-N 16-E
" "	**4**	1	Choctaw 12-N 17-E
GRISOM	**23**	2	Choctaw 9-N 18-E
" "	**19**	1	Choctaw 9-N 14-E
GROCE	**13**	1	Choctaw 10-N 14-E
GRUBBS	**7**	1	Choctaw 11-N 14-E
GUINN	**2**	2	Choctaw 12-N 15-E
GULLY	**8**	5	Choctaw 11-N 15-E
" "	**3**	5	Choctaw 12-N 16-E
" "	**14**	2	Choctaw 10-N 15-E
" "	**13**	1	Choctaw 10-N 14-E
" "	**7**	1	Choctaw 11-N 14-E
" "	**9**	1	Choctaw 11-N 16-E
GUNN	**23**	1	Choctaw 9-N 18-E
GUNTER	**15**	1	Choctaw 10-N 16-E
HAGEWOOD	**23**	1	Choctaw 9-N 18-E
HAGGARD	**13**	2	Choctaw 10-N 14-E
" "	**14**	1	Choctaw 10-N 15-E
" "	**2**	1	Choctaw 12-N 15-E
HAGOOD	**21**	1	Choctaw 9-N 16-E
" "	**23**	1	Choctaw 9-N 18-E
HAILLY	**2**	1	Choctaw 12-N 15-E
HAIR	**4**	2	Choctaw 12-N 17-E

Surname	Map Group	Parcels of Land	Meridian/Township/Range
HALE	**20**	3	Choctaw 9-N 15-E
HALL	**15**	11	Choctaw 10-N 16-E
" "	**19**	3	Choctaw 9-N 14-E
" "	**24**	3	Choctaw 9-N 19-E
" "	**17**	2	Choctaw 10-N 18-E
" "	**4**	2	Choctaw 12-N 17-E
" "	**10**	1	Choctaw 11-N 17-E
" "	**3**	1	Choctaw 12-N 16-E
" "	**21**	1	Choctaw 9-N 16-E
HALLFORD	**3**	2	Choctaw 12-N 16-E
" "	**9**	1	Choctaw 11-N 16-E
HAMBRICK	**21**	1	Choctaw 9-N 16-E
HAMLETT	**23**	1	Choctaw 9-N 18-E
HAMMACK	**3**	1	Choctaw 12-N 16-E
HAMMOCK	**3**	3	Choctaw 12-N 16-E
HAMPTON	**15**	2	Choctaw 10-N 16-E
HAMRICK	**21**	1	Choctaw 9-N 16-E
HANLEY	**13**	1	Choctaw 10-N 14-E
HANNA	**7**	2	Choctaw 11-N 14-E
" "	**22**	1	Choctaw 9-N 17-E
HARBOUR	**14**	4	Choctaw 10-N 15-E
" "	**20**	2	Choctaw 9-N 15-E
HARDEMAN	**2**	1	Choctaw 12-N 15-E
HARDIMAN	**2**	1	Choctaw 12-N 15-E
HARDIN	**4**	1	Choctaw 12-N 17-E
HARDY	**13**	2	Choctaw 10-N 14-E
" "	**1**	1	Choctaw 12-N 14-E
HARGROVE	**8**	1	Choctaw 11-N 15-E
HARMON	**7**	2	Choctaw 11-N 14-E
HARPER	**20**	7	Choctaw 9-N 15-E
" "	**12**	5	Choctaw 11-N 19-E
" "	**13**	4	Choctaw 10-N 14-E
" "	**14**	4	Choctaw 10-N 15-E
" "	**16**	4	Choctaw 10-N 17-E
" "	**19**	4	Choctaw 9-N 14-E
" "	**23**	4	Choctaw 9-N 18-E
" "	**18**	1	Choctaw 10-N 19-E
HARREL	**14**	2	Choctaw 10-N 15-E
HARRELL	**15**	6	Choctaw 10-N 16-E
" "	**16**	1	Choctaw 10-N 17-E
HARRINGTON	**23**	3	Choctaw 9-N 18-E
HARRIS	**22**	3	Choctaw 9-N 17-E
" "	**15**	2	Choctaw 10-N 16-E
" "	**2**	2	Choctaw 12-N 15-E
" "	**3**	2	Choctaw 12-N 16-E
" "	**6**	2	Choctaw 12-N 19-E
" "	**19**	2	Choctaw 9-N 14-E
" "	**16**	1	Choctaw 10-N 17-E
" "	**4**	1	Choctaw 12-N 17-E
" "	**5**	1	Choctaw 12-N 18-E
HARRISON	**7**	1	Choctaw 11-N 14-E
" "	**12**	1	Choctaw 11-N 19-E
HARVEY	**23**	1	Choctaw 9-N 18-E
HASKINS	**3**	3	Choctaw 12-N 16-E
HATCH	**21**	4	Choctaw 9-N 16-E
HAWES	**16**	2	Choctaw 10-N 17-E
HAWS	**22**	1	Choctaw 9-N 17-E
HAYNES	**2**	2	Choctaw 12-N 15-E
HEARON	**23**	1	Choctaw 9-N 18-E
HENDERSON	**8**	5	Choctaw 11-N 15-E

Surname	Map Group	Parcels of Land	Meridian/Township/Range
HENDERSON (Cont'd)	**7**	4	Choctaw 11-N 14-E
" "	**1**	3	Choctaw 12-N 14-E
" "	**6**	1	Choctaw 12-N 19-E
" "	**19**	1	Choctaw 9-N 14-E
" "	**21**	1	Choctaw 9-N 16-E
HENDON	**13**	1	Choctaw 10-N 14-E
HENDRICK	**7**	3	Choctaw 11-N 14-E
" "	**19**	1	Choctaw 9-N 14-E
HENDRICKS	**17**	1	Choctaw 10-N 18-E
HENSON	**7**	14	Choctaw 11-N 14-E
HERNDON	**14**	1	Choctaw 10-N 15-E
HERRINGTON	**21**	6	Choctaw 9-N 16-E
" "	**22**	2	Choctaw 9-N 17-E
HICKMAN	**1**	1	Choctaw 12-N 14-E
HICKS	**13**	1	Choctaw 10-N 14-E
HIGGINBOTHAM	**15**	2	Choctaw 10-N 16-E
HILL	**1**	1	Choctaw 12-N 14-E
HILLHOUSE	**14**	1	Choctaw 10-N 15-E
" "	**5**	1	Choctaw 12-N 18-E
HITCHCOCK	**8**	1	Choctaw 11-N 15-E
HITT	**17**	3	Choctaw 10-N 18-E
HODGE	**21**	2	Choctaw 9-N 16-E
HODGES	**1**	10	Choctaw 12-N 14-E
" "	**20**	9	Choctaw 9-N 15-E
" "	**14**	6	Choctaw 10-N 15-E
" "	**13**	5	Choctaw 10-N 14-E
" "	**24**	3	Choctaw 9-N 19-E
HOLCROFT	**18**	1	Choctaw 10-N 19-E
HOLDER	**17**	1	Choctaw 10-N 18-E
HOLDERNESS	**14**	10	Choctaw 10-N 15-E
" "	**1**	5	Choctaw 12-N 14-E
" "	**2**	5	Choctaw 12-N 15-E
" "	**3**	3	Choctaw 12-N 16-E
" "	**21**	1	Choctaw 9-N 16-E
HOLLAND	**3**	1	Choctaw 12-N 16-E
HOLMES	**15**	1	Choctaw 10-N 16-E
" "	**5**	1	Choctaw 12-N 18-E
HOLT	**7**	6	Choctaw 11-N 14-E
HOLTON	**8**	2	Choctaw 11-N 15-E
HOMES	**5**	1	Choctaw 12-N 18-E
HOPSON	**9**	5	Choctaw 11-N 16-E
" "	**23**	2	Choctaw 9-N 18-E
HORN	**9**	1	Choctaw 11-N 16-E
HOTAH	**22**	1	Choctaw 9-N 17-E
HOUSTON	**23**	12	Choctaw 9-N 18-E
" "	**14**	2	Choctaw 10-N 15-E
" "	**7**	1	Choctaw 11-N 14-E
" "	**8**	1	Choctaw 11-N 15-E
HUBBARD	**13**	16	Choctaw 10-N 14-E
" "	**10**	16	Choctaw 11-N 17-E
" "	**4**	11	Choctaw 12-N 17-E
" "	**6**	10	Choctaw 12-N 19-E
" "	**16**	8	Choctaw 10-N 17-E
" "	**11**	8	Choctaw 11-N 18-E
" "	**12**	7	Choctaw 11-N 19-E
" "	**19**	7	Choctaw 9-N 14-E
" "	**5**	4	Choctaw 12-N 18-E
" "	**20**	4	Choctaw 9-N 15-E
" "	**22**	4	Choctaw 9-N 17-E
" "	**24**	4	Choctaw 9-N 19-E

Surname	Map Group	Parcels of Land	Meridian/Township/Range
HUBBARD (Cont'd)	**14**	3	Choctaw 10-N 15-E
" "	**21**	3	Choctaw 9-N 16-E
" "	**23**	3	Choctaw 9-N 18-E
HUDNALL	**21**	1	Choctaw 9-N 16-E
HUDNELL	**21**	2	Choctaw 9-N 16-E
HUDSON	**16**	2	Choctaw 10-N 17-E
" "	**15**	1	Choctaw 10-N 16-E
" "	**23**	1	Choctaw 9-N 18-E
HUGHES	**7**	4	Choctaw 11-N 14-E
" "	**1**	2	Choctaw 12-N 14-E
" "	**22**	2	Choctaw 9-N 17-E
" "	**9**	1	Choctaw 11-N 16-E
" "	**2**	1	Choctaw 12-N 15-E
HULL	**8**	5	Choctaw 11-N 15-E
" "	**14**	1	Choctaw 10-N 15-E
" "	**15**	1	Choctaw 10-N 16-E
" "	**9**	1	Choctaw 11-N 16-E
HUMPHRIES	**13**	2	Choctaw 10-N 14-E
HUNDLEY	**2**	12	Choctaw 12-N 15-E
HUNNEYCUTT	**9**	1	Choctaw 11-N 16-E
HUNNICUTT	**15**	1	Choctaw 10-N 16-E
" "	**16**	1	Choctaw 10-N 17-E
" "	**10**	1	Choctaw 11-N 17-E
HUNT	**2**	2	Choctaw 12-N 15-E
HUNTER	**23**	1	Choctaw 9-N 18-E
HUNTINGTON	**16**	3	Choctaw 10-N 17-E
HUSBANDS	**16**	1	Choctaw 10-N 17-E
HUSE	**22**	3	Choctaw 9-N 17-E
HUSTON	**19**	3	Choctaw 9-N 14-E
HUTCHINS	**13**	7	Choctaw 10-N 14-E
HUTTON	**7**	5	Choctaw 11-N 14-E
" "	**1**	2	Choctaw 12-N 14-E
IKARD	**9**	1	Choctaw 11-N 16-E
IVY	**9**	1	Choctaw 11-N 16-E
JACK	**9**	2	Choctaw 11-N 16-E
" "	**10**	1	Choctaw 11-N 17-E
JACKSON	**11**	9	Choctaw 11-N 18-E
" "	**1**	7	Choctaw 12-N 14-E
" "	**2**	7	Choctaw 12-N 15-E
" "	**14**	2	Choctaw 10-N 15-E
" "	**13**	1	Choctaw 10-N 14-E
" "	**19**	1	Choctaw 9-N 14-E
JACOWAY	**7**	3	Choctaw 11-N 14-E
" "	**8**	1	Choctaw 11-N 15-E
JAGGANS	**14**	1	Choctaw 10-N 15-E
JAGGERS	**14**	1	Choctaw 10-N 15-E
JAMES	**10**	1	Choctaw 11-N 17-E
JAMISON	**7**	3	Choctaw 11-N 14-E
JARVIS	**1**	3	Choctaw 12-N 14-E
" "	**2**	3	Choctaw 12-N 15-E
JEMISON	**21**	6	Choctaw 9-N 16-E
" "	**13**	5	Choctaw 10-N 14-E
" "	**14**	4	Choctaw 10-N 15-E
" "	**15**	4	Choctaw 10-N 16-E
" "	**16**	3	Choctaw 10-N 17-E
" "	**19**	3	Choctaw 9-N 14-E
" "	**22**	2	Choctaw 9-N 17-E
" "	**23**	1	Choctaw 9-N 18-E
JENKINS	**4**	11	Choctaw 12-N 17-E
" "	**3**	4	Choctaw 12-N 16-E

Surname	Map Group	Parcels of Land	Meridian/Township/Range
JENKINS (Cont'd)	**5**	4	Choctaw 12-N 18-E
" "	**13**	2	Choctaw 10-N 14-E
" "	**19**	2	Choctaw 9-N 14-E
" "	**18**	1	Choctaw 10-N 19-E
JENNINGS	**14**	1	Choctaw 10-N 15-E
JINCKS	**5**	2	Choctaw 12-N 18-E
" "	**11**	1	Choctaw 11-N 18-E
JINKINS	**7**	1	Choctaw 11-N 14-E
JOHNSON	**15**	19	Choctaw 10-N 16-E
" "	**9**	5	Choctaw 11-N 16-E
" "	**23**	5	Choctaw 9-N 18-E
" "	**11**	4	Choctaw 11-N 18-E
" "	**3**	4	Choctaw 12-N 16-E
" "	**5**	4	Choctaw 12-N 18-E
" "	**14**	2	Choctaw 10-N 15-E
" "	**10**	2	Choctaw 11-N 17-E
" "	**2**	2	Choctaw 12-N 15-E
" "	**13**	1	Choctaw 10-N 14-E
" "	**7**	1	Choctaw 11-N 14-E
" "	**1**	1	Choctaw 12-N 14-E
" "	**4**	1	Choctaw 12-N 17-E
" "	**19**	1	Choctaw 9-N 14-E
JOHNSTON	**14**	2	Choctaw 10-N 15-E
" "	**15**	1	Choctaw 10-N 16-E
" "	**22**	1	Choctaw 9-N 17-E
JOINER	**19**	3	Choctaw 9-N 14-E
" "	**14**	2	Choctaw 10-N 15-E
JONAS	**17**	1	Choctaw 10-N 18-E
JONES	**11**	9	Choctaw 11-N 18-E
" "	**16**	7	Choctaw 10-N 17-E
" "	**23**	7	Choctaw 9-N 18-E
" "	**20**	6	Choctaw 9-N 15-E
" "	**14**	4	Choctaw 10-N 15-E
" "	**9**	3	Choctaw 11-N 16-E
" "	**22**	3	Choctaw 9-N 17-E
" "	**1**	2	Choctaw 12-N 14-E
" "	**5**	1	Choctaw 12-N 18-E
JORDAN	**8**	2	Choctaw 11-N 15-E
" "	**14**	1	Choctaw 10-N 15-E
JORDEN	**1**	1	Choctaw 12-N 14-E
" "	**2**	1	Choctaw 12-N 15-E
JOYNER	**19**	4	Choctaw 9-N 14-E
" "	**17**	1	Choctaw 10-N 18-E
" "	**12**	1	Choctaw 11-N 19-E
JUDSON	**6**	8	Choctaw 12-N 19-E
" "	**4**	7	Choctaw 12-N 17-E
JUMPER	**19**	1	Choctaw 9-N 14-E
KEAHEY	**2**	1	Choctaw 12-N 15-E
KEAKY	**2**	1	Choctaw 12-N 15-E
KEELAND	**14**	2	Choctaw 10-N 15-E
KEENAN	**2**	2	Choctaw 12-N 15-E
KELLEY	**7**	1	Choctaw 11-N 14-E
" "	**3**	1	Choctaw 12-N 16-E
KEMPER	**9**	1	Choctaw 11-N 16-E
KENNON	**10**	4	Choctaw 11-N 17-E
" "	**15**	2	Choctaw 10-N 16-E
KEY	**10**	2	Choctaw 11-N 17-E
" "	**15**	1	Choctaw 10-N 16-E
KILLIN	**3**	1	Choctaw 12-N 16-E
KING	**19**	7	Choctaw 9-N 14-E

Surname	Map Group	Parcels of Land	Meridian/Township/Range
KING (Cont'd)	**23**	2	Choctaw 9-N 18-E
" "	**5**	1	Choctaw 12-N 18-E
KNAPP	**4**	1	Choctaw 12-N 17-E
KNIGHT	**17**	1	Choctaw 10-N 18-E
KNIGHTEN	**17**	2	Choctaw 10-N 18-E
KOONCE	**12**	1	Choctaw 11-N 19-E
KYLE	**5**	1	Choctaw 12-N 18-E
LA HO LO	**22**	1	Choctaw 9-N 17-E
LA MA	**22**	1	Choctaw 9-N 17-E
LACY	**12**	11	Choctaw 11-N 19-E
" "	**9**	2	Choctaw 11-N 16-E
" "	**3**	2	Choctaw 12-N 16-E
LAKE	**11**	5	Choctaw 11-N 18-E
" "	**5**	5	Choctaw 12-N 18-E
" "	**22**	2	Choctaw 9-N 17-E
LAMPLEY	**8**	5	Choctaw 11-N 15-E
" "	**3**	5	Choctaw 12-N 16-E
" "	**2**	2	Choctaw 12-N 15-E
LAMPLY	**8**	2	Choctaw 11-N 15-E
" "	**2**	1	Choctaw 12-N 15-E
LAND	**8**	3	Choctaw 11-N 15-E
LANDRUM	**1**	4	Choctaw 12-N 14-E
LANG	**9**	12	Choctaw 11-N 16-E
" "	**10**	2	Choctaw 11-N 17-E
" "	**2**	1	Choctaw 12-N 15-E
" "	**21**	1	Choctaw 9-N 16-E
LANHAM	**8**	1	Choctaw 11-N 15-E
LANHAN	**13**	1	Choctaw 10-N 14-E
LANKAM	**9**	1	Choctaw 11-N 16-E
LARK	**22**	1	Choctaw 9-N 17-E
LATHAM	**20**	7	Choctaw 9-N 15-E
" "	**19**	3	Choctaw 9-N 14-E
" "	**13**	2	Choctaw 10-N 14-E
LAUDERDALE	**14**	1	Choctaw 10-N 15-E
LEACH	**16**	1	Choctaw 10-N 17-E
LEE	**18**	2	Choctaw 10-N 19-E
" "	**19**	2	Choctaw 9-N 14-E
LENTON	**3**	1	Choctaw 12-N 16-E
LEVENS	**6**	2	Choctaw 12-N 19-E
LEVINE	**23**	1	Choctaw 9-N 18-E
LEWIS	**4**	33	Choctaw 12-N 17-E
" "	**10**	30	Choctaw 11-N 17-E
" "	**13**	17	Choctaw 10-N 14-E
" "	**6**	16	Choctaw 12-N 19-E
" "	**16**	12	Choctaw 10-N 17-E
" "	**11**	9	Choctaw 11-N 18-E
" "	**19**	8	Choctaw 9-N 14-E
" "	**12**	7	Choctaw 11-N 19-E
" "	**24**	5	Choctaw 9-N 19-E
" "	**14**	4	Choctaw 10-N 15-E
" "	**5**	4	Choctaw 12-N 18-E
" "	**20**	4	Choctaw 9-N 15-E
" "	**22**	4	Choctaw 9-N 17-E
" "	**23**	4	Choctaw 9-N 18-E
" "	**21**	3	Choctaw 9-N 16-E
" "	**17**	1	Choctaw 10-N 18-E
" "	**7**	1	Choctaw 11-N 14-E
" "	**3**	1	Choctaw 12-N 16-E
LILES	**4**	1	Choctaw 12-N 17-E
LINCECUM	**21**	3	Choctaw 9-N 16-E

Surname	Map Group	Parcels of Land	Meridian/Township/Range		
LIPSCOMB	11	2	Choctaw	11-N	18-E
LITTLE	7	2	Choctaw	11-N	14-E
" "	14	1	Choctaw	10-N	15-E
" "	16	1	Choctaw	10-N	17-E
" "	2	1	Choctaw	12-N	15-E
LLOYD	20	8	Choctaw	9-N	15-E
" "	5	1	Choctaw	12-N	18-E
" "	19	1	Choctaw	9-N	14-E
LOCKLIN	22	1	Choctaw	9-N	17-E
LOFTIN	4	4	Choctaw	12-N	17-E
LONG	16	1	Choctaw	10-N	17-E
" "	9	1	Choctaw	11-N	16-E
" "	22	1	Choctaw	9-N	17-E
LOVE	8	5	Choctaw	11-N	15-E
" "	14	3	Choctaw	10-N	15-E
" "	3	3	Choctaw	12-N	16-E
LOVELADY	8	3	Choctaw	11-N	15-E
" "	13	1	Choctaw	10-N	14-E
LOVEN	13	1	Choctaw	10-N	14-E
LOWE	8	1	Choctaw	11-N	15-E
LOYD	20	1	Choctaw	9-N	15-E
LUKE	1	3	Choctaw	12-N	14-E
LYLE	13	1	Choctaw	10-N	14-E
" "	14	1	Choctaw	10-N	15-E
" "	5	1	Choctaw	12-N	18-E
MA	22	2	Choctaw	9-N	17-E
MABRY	2	2	Choctaw	12-N	15-E
MADDEN	5	1	Choctaw	12-N	18-E
MADERSON	10	1	Choctaw	11-N	17-E
MADISON	11	2	Choctaw	11-N	18-E
" "	3	2	Choctaw	12-N	16-E
" "	8	1	Choctaw	11-N	15-E
" "	9	1	Choctaw	11-N	16-E
MAHON	1	2	Choctaw	12-N	14-E
MAJORS	20	2	Choctaw	9-N	15-E
MALLORY	22	3	Choctaw	9-N	17-E
MALONE	5	9	Choctaw	12-N	18-E
" "	3	3	Choctaw	12-N	16-E
" "	18	1	Choctaw	10-N	19-E
MARR	15	1	Choctaw	10-N	16-E
MARS	15	1	Choctaw	10-N	16-E
" "	10	1	Choctaw	11-N	17-E
" "	3	1	Choctaw	12-N	16-E
MARSHALL	2	12	Choctaw	12-N	15-E
" "	3	3	Choctaw	12-N	16-E
" "	15	1	Choctaw	10-N	16-E
" "	21	1	Choctaw	9-N	16-E
MARTIN	24	4	Choctaw	9-N	19-E
" "	21	1	Choctaw	9-N	16-E
MASSEY	8	1	Choctaw	11-N	15-E
" "	4	1	Choctaw	12-N	17-E
" "	5	1	Choctaw	12-N	18-E
MATHENY	16	2	Choctaw	10-N	17-E
" "	8	2	Choctaw	11-N	15-E
MATHEWS	3	3	Choctaw	12-N	16-E
" "	15	1	Choctaw	10-N	16-E
" "	17	1	Choctaw	10-N	18-E
MATTHEWS	20	4	Choctaw	9-N	15-E
" "	16	2	Choctaw	10-N	17-E
" "	21	1	Choctaw	9-N	16-E

Surname	Map Group	Parcels of Land	Meridian/Township/Range
MAURY	**3**	6	Choctaw 12-N 16-E
MAY	**20**	2	Choctaw 9-N 15-E
MAYBRY	**2**	2	Choctaw 12-N 15-E
MAYFIELD	**13**	1	Choctaw 10-N 14-E
MAYNOR	**15**	1	Choctaw 10-N 16-E
" "	**21**	1	Choctaw 9-N 16-E
MAYO	**1**	5	Choctaw 12-N 14-E
MCAFEE	**2**	3	Choctaw 12-N 15-E
MCALISTER	**4**	1	Choctaw 12-N 17-E
MCALLISTER	**4**	1	Choctaw 12-N 17-E
MCALLUM	**8**	2	Choctaw 11-N 15-E
" "	**13**	1	Choctaw 10-N 14-E
MCARTHUR	**2**	9	Choctaw 12-N 15-E
" "	**3**	1	Choctaw 12-N 16-E
MCBRAYER	**1**	3	Choctaw 12-N 14-E
" "	**2**	1	Choctaw 12-N 15-E
MCBRYDE	**8**	3	Choctaw 11-N 15-E
MCCALEBB	**5**	1	Choctaw 12-N 18-E
MCCALL	**21**	3	Choctaw 9-N 16-E
MCCASKILL	**6**	4	Choctaw 12-N 19-E
MCCLAIN	**9**	1	Choctaw 11-N 16-E
MCCLELAND	**21**	1	Choctaw 9-N 16-E
MCCLURG	**5**	1	Choctaw 12-N 18-E
MCCONNELL	**21**	3	Choctaw 9-N 16-E
" "	**23**	3	Choctaw 9-N 18-E
MCCOWN	**23**	6	Choctaw 9-N 18-E
" "	**24**	4	Choctaw 9-N 19-E
" "	**22**	3	Choctaw 9-N 17-E
" "	**17**	2	Choctaw 10-N 18-E
" "	**20**	2	Choctaw 9-N 15-E
" "	**21**	2	Choctaw 9-N 16-E
MCCOY	**21**	2	Choctaw 9-N 16-E
" "	**16**	1	Choctaw 10-N 17-E
" "	**20**	1	Choctaw 9-N 15-E
" "	**22**	1	Choctaw 9-N 17-E
MCCRANIE	**14**	1	Choctaw 10-N 15-E
" "	**22**	1	Choctaw 9-N 17-E
MCCRAY	**3**	2	Choctaw 12-N 16-E
MCCRIMON	**2**	3	Choctaw 12-N 15-E
MCCRORY	**9**	5	Choctaw 11-N 16-E
" "	**3**	4	Choctaw 12-N 16-E
MCDADE	**16**	4	Choctaw 10-N 17-E
" "	**10**	3	Choctaw 11-N 17-E
" "	**17**	2	Choctaw 10-N 18-E
MCDANIEL	**18**	1	Choctaw 10-N 19-E
MCDONALD	**1**	5	Choctaw 12-N 14-E
" "	**7**	4	Choctaw 11-N 14-E
" "	**19**	3	Choctaw 9-N 14-E
" "	**13**	2	Choctaw 10-N 14-E
" "	**14**	1	Choctaw 10-N 15-E
" "	**15**	1	Choctaw 10-N 16-E
" "	**16**	1	Choctaw 10-N 17-E
" "	**3**	1	Choctaw 12-N 16-E
MCDOWELL	**24**	1	Choctaw 9-N 19-E
MCFARLAND	**8**	3	Choctaw 11-N 15-E
" "	**13**	1	Choctaw 10-N 14-E
MCGEE	**11**	40	Choctaw 11-N 18-E
" "	**5**	20	Choctaw 12-N 18-E
" "	**6**	18	Choctaw 12-N 19-E
" "	**20**	5	Choctaw 9-N 15-E

Surname	Map Group	Parcels of Land	Meridian/Township/Range
MCGEE (Cont'd)	**14**	2	Choctaw 10-N 15-E
" "	**12**	2	Choctaw 11-N 19-E
" "	**21**	1	Choctaw 9-N 16-E
MCGEHEE	**19**	3	Choctaw 9-N 14-E
MCGOWEN	**13**	2	Choctaw 10-N 14-E
MCINTOSH	**6**	14	Choctaw 12-N 19-E
MCINTUSH	**19**	1	Choctaw 9-N 14-E
MCINTYRE	**3**	3	Choctaw 12-N 16-E
" "	**13**	1	Choctaw 10-N 14-E
MCKAY	**15**	1	Choctaw 10-N 16-E
MCKEE	**19**	1	Choctaw 9-N 14-E
MCKELLAR	**14**	4	Choctaw 10-N 15-E
" "	**7**	3	Choctaw 11-N 14-E
" "	**9**	2	Choctaw 11-N 16-E
" "	**13**	1	Choctaw 10-N 14-E
" "	**8**	1	Choctaw 11-N 15-E
MCKELVAIN	**22**	1	Choctaw 9-N 17-E
MCKELVIN	**9**	1	Choctaw 11-N 16-E
" "	**3**	1	Choctaw 12-N 16-E
" "	**21**	1	Choctaw 9-N 16-E
MCKINNEY	**13**	4	Choctaw 10-N 14-E
MCKLEVAIN	**21**	1	Choctaw 9-N 16-E
MCLAMORE	**23**	1	Choctaw 9-N 18-E
MCLAUGHLIN	**5**	4	Choctaw 12-N 18-E
MCLAURIN	**8**	4	Choctaw 11-N 15-E
" "	**14**	2	Choctaw 10-N 15-E
" "	**7**	1	Choctaw 11-N 14-E
" "	**3**	1	Choctaw 12-N 16-E
MCLAWREN	**10**	1	Choctaw 11-N 17-E
MCLEAN	**9**	3	Choctaw 11-N 16-E
MCLELAND	**20**	2	Choctaw 9-N 15-E
MCLELLAND	**21**	1	Choctaw 9-N 16-E
MCLENDON	**16**	1	Choctaw 10-N 17-E
" "	**22**	1	Choctaw 9-N 17-E
MCLEROY	**9**	1	Choctaw 11-N 16-E
MCMAHON	**13**	5	Choctaw 10-N 14-E
" "	**10**	1	Choctaw 11-N 17-E
MCMILLAN	**16**	1	Choctaw 10-N 17-E
MCMILLON	**21**	1	Choctaw 9-N 16-E
MCMURRY	**24**	2	Choctaw 9-N 19-E
MCNEAL	**14**	3	Choctaw 10-N 15-E
MCNEES	**3**	1	Choctaw 12-N 16-E
MCNEIL	**8**	2	Choctaw 11-N 15-E
MCNEILL	**22**	7	Choctaw 9-N 17-E
" "	**11**	2	Choctaw 11-N 18-E
" "	**8**	1	Choctaw 11-N 15-E
MCPHERSON	**22**	1	Choctaw 9-N 17-E
MCQUEEN	**24**	2	Choctaw 9-N 19-E
MCRAE	**8**	3	Choctaw 11-N 15-E
" "	**9**	3	Choctaw 11-N 16-E
MCRIGHT	**13**	2	Choctaw 10-N 14-E
MCSIVEEN	**2**	3	Choctaw 12-N 15-E
MCSWEAN	**3**	1	Choctaw 12-N 16-E
MCWHORTER	**21**	3	Choctaw 9-N 16-E
MCWOOTAN	**21**	2	Choctaw 9-N 16-E
MEEKS	**15**	4	Choctaw 10-N 16-E
MEYATTE	**14**	1	Choctaw 10-N 15-E
MIDDLEBROOKS	**15**	3	Choctaw 10-N 16-E
MIETT	**13**	1	Choctaw 10-N 14-E
MILLARD	**23**	2	Choctaw 9-N 18-E

Surname	Map Group	Parcels of Land	Meridian/Township/Range
MILLING	**1**	1	Choctaw 12-N 14-E
MILLS	**7**	24	Choctaw 11-N 14-E
" "	**8**	15	Choctaw 11-N 15-E
" "	**9**	15	Choctaw 11-N 16-E
" "	**1**	13	Choctaw 12-N 14-E
" "	**14**	11	Choctaw 10-N 15-E
" "	**13**	10	Choctaw 10-N 14-E
" "	**19**	10	Choctaw 9-N 14-E
" "	**15**	8	Choctaw 10-N 16-E
" "	**20**	6	Choctaw 9-N 15-E
" "	**2**	5	Choctaw 12-N 15-E
" "	**23**	4	Choctaw 9-N 18-E
" "	**16**	2	Choctaw 10-N 17-E
" "	**21**	2	Choctaw 9-N 16-E
" "	**22**	1	Choctaw 9-N 17-E
MINNIECE	**4**	1	Choctaw 12-N 17-E
MISSISSIPPI	**2**	3	Choctaw 12-N 15-E
" "	**15**	2	Choctaw 10-N 16-E
" "	**11**	2	Choctaw 11-N 18-E
" "	**3**	2	Choctaw 12-N 16-E
" "	**18**	1	Choctaw 10-N 19-E
" "	**4**	1	Choctaw 12-N 17-E
" "	**19**	1	Choctaw 9-N 14-E
MITCHEL	**16**	2	Choctaw 10-N 17-E
MITCHELL	**10**	2	Choctaw 11-N 17-E
" "	**16**	1	Choctaw 10-N 17-E
MITCHUM	**13**	2	Choctaw 10-N 14-E
MONK	**17**	1	Choctaw 10-N 18-E
MONTAGUE	**14**	1	Choctaw 10-N 15-E
MOODY	**2**	7	Choctaw 12-N 15-E
" "	**3**	2	Choctaw 12-N 16-E
" "	**13**	1	Choctaw 10-N 14-E
" "	**21**	1	Choctaw 9-N 16-E
MOONEY	**8**	2	Choctaw 11-N 15-E
MOORE	**2**	8	Choctaw 12-N 15-E
" "	**1**	5	Choctaw 12-N 14-E
" "	**22**	5	Choctaw 9-N 17-E
" "	**7**	4	Choctaw 11-N 14-E
" "	**13**	3	Choctaw 10-N 14-E
" "	**16**	2	Choctaw 10-N 17-E
" "	**9**	2	Choctaw 11-N 16-E
" "	**19**	2	Choctaw 9-N 14-E
" "	**8**	1	Choctaw 11-N 15-E
" "	**10**	1	Choctaw 11-N 17-E
" "	**3**	1	Choctaw 12-N 16-E
" "	**20**	1	Choctaw 9-N 15-E
" "	**23**	1	Choctaw 9-N 18-E
MORGAN	**17**	4	Choctaw 10-N 18-E
MORRAH	**9**	2	Choctaw 11-N 16-E
MORRIS	**9**	2	Choctaw 11-N 16-E
" "	**10**	1	Choctaw 11-N 17-E
MORRISON	**22**	2	Choctaw 9-N 17-E
MORROW	**15**	5	Choctaw 10-N 16-E
MORSE	**3**	1	Choctaw 12-N 16-E
MOSBY	**22**	1	Choctaw 9-N 17-E
MOSELEY	**6**	12	Choctaw 12-N 19-E
" "	**21**	4	Choctaw 9-N 16-E
" "	**1**	1	Choctaw 12-N 14-E
MOSELY	**6**	4	Choctaw 12-N 19-E
MOSLEY	**6**	6	Choctaw 12-N 19-E

Surname	Map Group	Parcels of Land	Meridian/Township/Range
MOSLEY (Cont'd)	**21**	3	Choctaw 9-N 16-E
" "	**19**	1	Choctaw 9-N 14-E
" "	**20**	1	Choctaw 9-N 15-E
MULDROW	**15**	1	Choctaw 10-N 16-E
MULHOLLAND	**19**	1	Choctaw 9-N 14-E
MULLINS	**24**	2	Choctaw 9-N 19-E
MURPHEY	**22**	5	Choctaw 9-N 17-E
" "	**21**	1	Choctaw 9-N 16-E
MURPHY	**17**	5	Choctaw 10-N 18-E
MURRAY	**4**	1	Choctaw 12-N 17-E
MURRY	**3**	3	Choctaw 12-N 16-E
NAIL	**2**	1	Choctaw 12-N 15-E
NASH	**16**	7	Choctaw 10-N 17-E
" "	**3**	3	Choctaw 12-N 16-E
" "	**13**	2	Choctaw 10-N 14-E
" "	**15**	2	Choctaw 10-N 16-E
" "	**19**	1	Choctaw 9-N 14-E
" "	**20**	1	Choctaw 9-N 15-E
NAVE	**9**	1	Choctaw 11-N 16-E
" "	**10**	1	Choctaw 11-N 17-E
NAYLOR	**22**	2	Choctaw 9-N 17-E
" "	**16**	1	Choctaw 10-N 17-E
NEADHAM	**1**	1	Choctaw 12-N 14-E
NEAL	**2**	3	Choctaw 12-N 15-E
" "	**1**	1	Choctaw 12-N 14-E
" "	**3**	1	Choctaw 12-N 16-E
NEEDHAM	**1**	1	Choctaw 12-N 14-E
NEEL	**9**	1	Choctaw 11-N 16-E
NEOTLCAH	**22**	1	Choctaw 9-N 17-E
NESTER	**3**	2	Choctaw 12-N 16-E
" "	**9**	1	Choctaw 11-N 16-E
NETHERRY	**17**	1	Choctaw 10-N 18-E
NETTLES	**21**	3	Choctaw 9-N 16-E
" "	**9**	1	Choctaw 11-N 16-E
NEW	**18**	1	Choctaw 10-N 19-E
NEWBERRY	**23**	2	Choctaw 9-N 18-E
NEWCOMB	**21**	2	Choctaw 9-N 16-E
NEWELL	**3**	2	Choctaw 12-N 16-E
" "	**16**	1	Choctaw 10-N 17-E
NEWTON	**16**	1	Choctaw 10-N 17-E
NICHOLAS	**3**	6	Choctaw 12-N 16-E
NICHOLSON	**12**	14	Choctaw 11-N 19-E
" "	**4**	12	Choctaw 12-N 17-E
" "	**3**	8	Choctaw 12-N 16-E
" "	**11**	4	Choctaw 11-N 18-E
" "	**5**	2	Choctaw 12-N 18-E
" "	**15**	1	Choctaw 10-N 16-E
" "	**8**	1	Choctaw 11-N 15-E
" "	**10**	1	Choctaw 11-N 17-E
" "	**2**	1	Choctaw 12-N 15-E
NOATEMAH	**22**	2	Choctaw 9-N 17-E
NOLES	**10**	1	Choctaw 11-N 17-E
NORDEN	**15**	1	Choctaw 10-N 16-E
NORRIS	**7**	1	Choctaw 11-N 14-E
NORRISS	**11**	4	Choctaw 11-N 18-E
NUNN	**2**	1	Choctaw 12-N 15-E
OBANNON	**23**	1	Choctaw 9-N 18-E
ODEN	**9**	7	Choctaw 11-N 16-E
" "	**16**	6	Choctaw 10-N 17-E
" "	**19**	5	Choctaw 9-N 14-E

Surname	Map Group	Parcels of Land	Meridian/Township/Range
ODEN (Cont'd)	**18**	2	Choctaw 10-N 19-E
ODOM	**22**	4	Choctaw 9-N 17-E
" "	**21**	3	Choctaw 9-N 16-E
" "	**17**	2	Choctaw 10-N 18-E
" "	**16**	1	Choctaw 10-N 17-E
OLIVE	**11**	3	Choctaw 11-N 18-E
" "	**9**	2	Choctaw 11-N 16-E
ONEAL	**22**	1	Choctaw 9-N 17-E
ONEIL	**13**	1	Choctaw 10-N 14-E
ONEILL	**13**	2	Choctaw 10-N 14-E
OREILLY	**21**	3	Choctaw 9-N 16-E
" "	**2**	2	Choctaw 12-N 15-E
" "	**3**	2	Choctaw 12-N 16-E
ORNE	**3**	19	Choctaw 12-N 16-E
" "	**1**	3	Choctaw 12-N 14-E
OVERSTREET	**9**	4	Choctaw 11-N 16-E
" "	**14**	3	Choctaw 10-N 15-E
" "	**8**	2	Choctaw 11-N 15-E
" "	**3**	2	Choctaw 12-N 16-E
OWEN	**6**	4	Choctaw 12-N 19-E
" "	**19**	2	Choctaw 9-N 14-E
" "	**20**	1	Choctaw 9-N 15-E
OWENS	**15**	1	Choctaw 10-N 16-E
PACE	**2**	3	Choctaw 12-N 15-E
" "	**8**	1	Choctaw 11-N 15-E
PADEN	**8**	11	Choctaw 11-N 15-E
PAGE	**22**	10	Choctaw 9-N 17-E
" "	**16**	1	Choctaw 10-N 17-E
" "	**18**	1	Choctaw 10-N 19-E
PALMER	**2**	7	Choctaw 12-N 15-E
" "	**7**	2	Choctaw 11-N 14-E
PARKER	**10**	3	Choctaw 11-N 17-E
" "	**2**	3	Choctaw 12-N 15-E
" "	**16**	2	Choctaw 10-N 17-E
" "	**18**	2	Choctaw 10-N 19-E
" "	**3**	2	Choctaw 12-N 16-E
" "	**21**	2	Choctaw 9-N 16-E
" "	**22**	2	Choctaw 9-N 17-E
" "	**15**	1	Choctaw 10-N 16-E
" "	**1**	1	Choctaw 12-N 14-E
PARRISH	**17**	1	Choctaw 10-N 18-E
PATRICK	**22**	1	Choctaw 9-N 17-E
PATTON	**17**	1	Choctaw 10-N 18-E
PAYNE	**22**	1	Choctaw 9-N 17-E
PEARCE	**5**	1	Choctaw 12-N 18-E
PEARL	**2**	4	Choctaw 12-N 15-E
" "	**4**	2	Choctaw 12-N 17-E
" "	**22**	1	Choctaw 9-N 17-E
PEARSON	**8**	1	Choctaw 11-N 15-E
PEDEN	**8**	47	Choctaw 11-N 15-E
" "	**7**	20	Choctaw 11-N 14-E
" "	**2**	3	Choctaw 12-N 15-E
" "	**13**	2	Choctaw 10-N 14-E
" "	**14**	2	Choctaw 10-N 15-E
PEEL	**17**	3	Choctaw 10-N 18-E
PEGG	**22**	2	Choctaw 9-N 17-E
PENNINGTON	**16**	2	Choctaw 10-N 17-E
PERKINS	**14**	3	Choctaw 10-N 15-E
" "	**13**	1	Choctaw 10-N 14-E
" "	**7**	1	Choctaw 11-N 14-E

Surname	Map Group	Parcels of Land	Meridian/Township/Range
PERKINS (Cont'd)	**8**	1	Choctaw 11-N 15-E
" "	**20**	1	Choctaw 9-N 15-E
PERMENTER	**3**	1	Choctaw 12-N 16-E
PERRY	**11**	4	Choctaw 11-N 18-E
PERSON	**3**	4	Choctaw 12-N 16-E
" "	**4**	2	Choctaw 12-N 17-E
PERSONS	**1**	1	Choctaw 12-N 14-E
PETTIS	**5**	1	Choctaw 12-N 18-E
PETTUS	**5**	6	Choctaw 12-N 18-E
PFISTER	**2**	1	Choctaw 12-N 15-E
PHARMER	**2**	1	Choctaw 12-N 15-E
" "	**22**	1	Choctaw 9-N 17-E
PHILLIPS	**7**	1	Choctaw 11-N 14-E
" "	**8**	1	Choctaw 11-N 15-E
PICKETT	**11**	1	Choctaw 11-N 18-E
" "	**2**	1	Choctaw 12-N 15-E
PIERCE	**8**	3	Choctaw 11-N 15-E
" "	**9**	1	Choctaw 11-N 16-E
" "	**5**	1	Choctaw 12-N 18-E
POLLARD	**3**	1	Choctaw 12-N 16-E
POLLOCK	**14**	4	Choctaw 10-N 15-E
" "	**20**	3	Choctaw 9-N 15-E
" "	**15**	1	Choctaw 10-N 16-E
POOL	**10**	2	Choctaw 11-N 17-E
" "	**19**	2	Choctaw 9-N 14-E
" "	**15**	1	Choctaw 10-N 16-E
" "	**5**	1	Choctaw 12-N 18-E
POOLE	**19**	4	Choctaw 9-N 14-E
POPE	**5**	2	Choctaw 12-N 18-E
" "	**16**	1	Choctaw 10-N 17-E
PORTER	**8**	1	Choctaw 11-N 15-E
" "	**23**	1	Choctaw 9-N 18-E
POSEY	**20**	1	Choctaw 9-N 15-E
POWE	**6**	8	Choctaw 12-N 19-E
" "	**5**	1	Choctaw 12-N 18-E
POWELL	**11**	1	Choctaw 11-N 18-E
" "	**20**	1	Choctaw 9-N 15-E
PRESTON	**9**	2	Choctaw 11-N 16-E
PREUIT	**19**	5	Choctaw 9-N 14-E
PREWIT	**19**	4	Choctaw 9-N 14-E
PREWITT	**14**	1	Choctaw 10-N 15-E
PRICE	**21**	1	Choctaw 9-N 16-E
PRIDDY	**22**	2	Choctaw 9-N 17-E
PRUIT	**19**	5	Choctaw 9-N 14-E
" "	**5**	1	Choctaw 12-N 18-E
PRUITT	**19**	10	Choctaw 9-N 14-E
PUCKETT	**11**	2	Choctaw 11-N 18-E
PULLER	**10**	2	Choctaw 11-N 17-E
QUARLES	**6**	2	Choctaw 12-N 19-E
" "	**5**	1	Choctaw 12-N 18-E
RAINER	**18**	1	Choctaw 10-N 19-E
RAINEY	**1**	1	Choctaw 12-N 14-E
" "	**22**	1	Choctaw 9-N 17-E
RAWLS	**1**	1	Choctaw 12-N 14-E
REA	**3**	3	Choctaw 12-N 16-E
REED	**1**	2	Choctaw 12-N 14-E
REID	**21**	2	Choctaw 9-N 16-E
RENCHER	**11**	1	Choctaw 11-N 18-E
REY	**9**	1	Choctaw 11-N 16-E
REYNOLDS	**16**	5	Choctaw 10-N 17-E

Surname	Map Group	Parcels of Land	Meridian/Township/Range
RHODES	**22**	3	Choctaw 9-N 17-E
RICHARDSON	**2**	2	Choctaw 12-N 15-E
" "	**1**	1	Choctaw 12-N 14-E
RICHEY	**3**	7	Choctaw 12-N 16-E
" "	**20**	3	Choctaw 9-N 15-E
" "	**15**	2	Choctaw 10-N 16-E
" "	**9**	1	Choctaw 11-N 16-E
" "	**21**	1	Choctaw 9-N 16-E
RIDDLE	**1**	1	Choctaw 12-N 14-E
" "	**2**	1	Choctaw 12-N 15-E
RIDGWAY	**11**	1	Choctaw 11-N 18-E
" "	**6**	1	Choctaw 12-N 19-E
RIGBY	**21**	3	Choctaw 9-N 16-E
" "	**16**	2	Choctaw 10-N 17-E
" "	**15**	1	Choctaw 10-N 16-E
RIGDON	**17**	2	Choctaw 10-N 18-E
RILEY	**8**	4	Choctaw 11-N 15-E
" "	**5**	2	Choctaw 12-N 18-E
ROACH	**15**	1	Choctaw 10-N 16-E
ROBBINS	**7**	5	Choctaw 11-N 14-E
" "	**17**	1	Choctaw 10-N 18-E
ROBERTS	**4**	2	Choctaw 12-N 17-E
" "	**15**	1	Choctaw 10-N 16-E
" "	**8**	1	Choctaw 11-N 15-E
" "	**22**	1	Choctaw 9-N 17-E
" "	**23**	1	Choctaw 9-N 18-E
ROBERTSON	**16**	1	Choctaw 10-N 17-E
" "	**20**	1	Choctaw 9-N 15-E
ROBINSON	**11**	1	Choctaw 11-N 18-E
" "	**2**	1	Choctaw 12-N 15-E
" "	**19**	1	Choctaw 9-N 14-E
ROCHEL	**21**	1	Choctaw 9-N 16-E
RODES	**18**	2	Choctaw 10-N 19-E
" "	**14**	1	Choctaw 10-N 15-E
RODGERS	**6**	1	Choctaw 12-N 19-E
ROEBUCK	**1**	1	Choctaw 12-N 14-E
ROGERS	**5**	8	Choctaw 12-N 18-E
" "	**6**	6	Choctaw 12-N 19-E
" "	**7**	2	Choctaw 11-N 14-E
" "	**15**	1	Choctaw 10-N 16-E
" "	**17**	1	Choctaw 10-N 18-E
" "	**12**	1	Choctaw 11-N 19-E
RORY	**4**	1	Choctaw 12-N 17-E
ROSAMOND	**1**	3	Choctaw 12-N 14-E
ROSS	**15**	8	Choctaw 10-N 16-E
" "	**6**	3	Choctaw 12-N 19-E
" "	**21**	2	Choctaw 9-N 16-E
" "	**16**	1	Choctaw 10-N 17-E
" "	**8**	1	Choctaw 11-N 15-E
" "	**20**	1	Choctaw 9-N 15-E
ROUNDTREE	**1**	1	Choctaw 12-N 14-E
" "	**5**	1	Choctaw 12-N 18-E
ROWE	**10**	10	Choctaw 11-N 17-E
" "	**4**	8	Choctaw 12-N 17-E
" "	**5**	1	Choctaw 12-N 18-E
RUPERT	**5**	24	Choctaw 12-N 18-E
" "	**13**	6	Choctaw 10-N 14-E
" "	**4**	6	Choctaw 12-N 17-E
" "	**19**	2	Choctaw 9-N 14-E
" "	**1**	1	Choctaw 12-N 14-E

Surname	Map Group	Parcels of Land	Meridian/Township/Range
RUPERT (Cont'd)	**3**	1	Choctaw 12-N 16-E
" "	**20**	1	Choctaw 9-N 15-E
" "	**21**	1	Choctaw 9-N 16-E
RUSH	**15**	5	Choctaw 10-N 16-E
" "	**22**	2	Choctaw 9-N 17-E
RUSHING	**19**	1	Choctaw 9-N 14-E
RUSSELL	**15**	1	Choctaw 10-N 16-E
" "	**22**	1	Choctaw 9-N 17-E
RUTHERFORD	**8**	1	Choctaw 11-N 15-E
RUTHVEN	**7**	2	Choctaw 11-N 14-E
SADERFIELD	**7**	2	Choctaw 11-N 14-E
SADLER	**15**	2	Choctaw 10-N 16-E
" "	**8**	1	Choctaw 11-N 15-E
SALTER	**19**	1	Choctaw 9-N 14-E
SANDERS	**5**	7	Choctaw 12-N 18-E
" "	**16**	2	Choctaw 10-N 17-E
" "	**17**	2	Choctaw 10-N 18-E
" "	**4**	2	Choctaw 12-N 17-E
" "	**18**	1	Choctaw 10-N 19-E
" "	**9**	1	Choctaw 11-N 16-E
" "	**22**	1	Choctaw 9-N 17-E
SANDERSON	**21**	2	Choctaw 9-N 16-E
" "	**20**	1	Choctaw 9-N 15-E
SANDFORD	**11**	1	Choctaw 11-N 18-E
SANFORD	**1**	1	Choctaw 12-N 14-E
" "	**2**	1	Choctaw 12-N 15-E
SAUNDERS	**16**	1	Choctaw 10-N 17-E
SAYRE	**11**	11	Choctaw 11-N 18-E
SCITZS	**21**	4	Choctaw 9-N 16-E
SCONYERS	**9**	1	Choctaw 11-N 16-E
SCOTT	**10**	26	Choctaw 11-N 17-E
" "	**13**	9	Choctaw 10-N 14-E
" "	**16**	5	Choctaw 10-N 17-E
" "	**4**	4	Choctaw 12-N 17-E
" "	**5**	4	Choctaw 12-N 18-E
" "	**9**	3	Choctaw 11-N 16-E
" "	**11**	3	Choctaw 11-N 18-E
" "	**23**	3	Choctaw 9-N 18-E
" "	**8**	1	Choctaw 11-N 15-E
" "	**6**	1	Choctaw 12-N 19-E
SCUDDAY	**4**	5	Choctaw 12-N 17-E
" "	**5**	1	Choctaw 12-N 18-E
SCUDDY	**5**	4	Choctaw 12-N 18-E
SEAL	**23**	1	Choctaw 9-N 18-E
SEALE	**23**	6	Choctaw 9-N 18-E
" "	**1**	2	Choctaw 12-N 14-E
SECREST	**19**	1	Choctaw 9-N 14-E
SELBY	**23**	3	Choctaw 9-N 18-E
SELLERS	**3**	4	Choctaw 12-N 16-E
SESSIONS	**5**	2	Choctaw 12-N 18-E
SESSUMS	**14**	1	Choctaw 10-N 15-E
SHANDS	**1**	1	Choctaw 12-N 14-E
SHANNON	**9**	1	Choctaw 11-N 16-E
SHARP	**22**	6	Choctaw 9-N 17-E
" "	**17**	2	Choctaw 10-N 18-E
" "	**15**	1	Choctaw 10-N 16-E
" "	**21**	1	Choctaw 9-N 16-E
SHAW	**5**	1	Choctaw 12-N 18-E
SHEPARD	**8**	2	Choctaw 11-N 15-E
" "	**1**	1	Choctaw 12-N 14-E

Surname	Map Group	Parcels of Land	Meridian/Township/Range
SHEPHERD	**2**	1	Choctaw 12-N 15-E
SHIKLE	**9**	1	Choctaw 11-N 16-E
" "	**3**	1	Choctaw 12-N 16-E
SHIP	**13**	1	Choctaw 10-N 14-E
SHIPP	**13**	2	Choctaw 10-N 14-E
SHIRLEY	**2**	2	Choctaw 12-N 15-E
SHUMATE	**21**	5	Choctaw 9-N 16-E
" "	**15**	2	Choctaw 10-N 16-E
" "	**16**	2	Choctaw 10-N 17-E
SIGGARS	**23**	1	Choctaw 9-N 18-E
SILLIMAN	**23**	6	Choctaw 9-N 18-E
SIMMONS	**23**	4	Choctaw 9-N 18-E
" "	**22**	1	Choctaw 9-N 17-E
SIMMS	**8**	1	Choctaw 11-N 15-E
SIMPSON	**9**	1	Choctaw 11-N 16-E
SIMS	**15**	1	Choctaw 10-N 16-E
SINCLAIR	**15**	1	Choctaw 10-N 16-E
" "	**16**	1	Choctaw 10-N 17-E
SITZS	**21**	1	Choctaw 9-N 16-E
SKINNER	**14**	2	Choctaw 10-N 15-E
" "	**20**	1	Choctaw 9-N 15-E
" "	**22**	1	Choctaw 9-N 17-E
SLATON	**17**	2	Choctaw 10-N 18-E
" "	**19**	1	Choctaw 9-N 14-E
SLAUGHTER	**1**	2	Choctaw 12-N 14-E
SMALL	**2**	1	Choctaw 12-N 15-E
SMITH	**14**	10	Choctaw 10-N 15-E
" "	**13**	7	Choctaw 10-N 14-E
" "	**8**	7	Choctaw 11-N 15-E
" "	**10**	7	Choctaw 11-N 17-E
" "	**9**	2	Choctaw 11-N 16-E
" "	**1**	2	Choctaw 12-N 14-E
" "	**19**	2	Choctaw 9-N 14-E
" "	**7**	1	Choctaw 11-N 14-E
" "	**22**	1	Choctaw 9-N 17-E
SMYTH	**7**	3	Choctaw 11-N 14-E
" "	**5**	1	Choctaw 12-N 18-E
SNEAD	**15**	4	Choctaw 10-N 16-E
" "	**14**	3	Choctaw 10-N 15-E
SNEED	**13**	1	Choctaw 10-N 14-E
SNOWDEN	**20**	1	Choctaw 9-N 15-E
SORSBY	**20**	5	Choctaw 9-N 15-E
" "	**14**	4	Choctaw 10-N 15-E
" "	**21**	3	Choctaw 9-N 16-E
SPEAR	**9**	3	Choctaw 11-N 16-E
" "	**8**	1	Choctaw 11-N 15-E
SPEARS	**1**	1	Choctaw 12-N 14-E
SPEED	**16**	1	Choctaw 10-N 17-E
SPEIR	**7**	1	Choctaw 11-N 14-E
SPENCE	**8**	1	Choctaw 11-N 15-E
SPENCER	**5**	6	Choctaw 12-N 18-E
SPIER	**7**	1	Choctaw 11-N 14-E
SPINKS	**20**	19	Choctaw 9-N 15-E
" "	**5**	1	Choctaw 12-N 18-E
" "	**19**	1	Choctaw 9-N 14-E
STANTON	**23**	1	Choctaw 9-N 18-E
STARLING	**15**	1	Choctaw 10-N 16-E
STEDE	**4**	1	Choctaw 12-N 17-E
STEEL	**14**	2	Choctaw 10-N 15-E
" "	**2**	1	Choctaw 12-N 15-E

Surname	Map Group	Parcels of Land	Meridian/Township/Range
STEEL (Cont'd)	**4**	1	Choctaw 12-N 17-E
STEELE	**5**	12	Choctaw 12-N 18-E
" "	**14**	9	Choctaw 10-N 15-E
" "	**4**	4	Choctaw 12-N 17-E
" "	**10**	2	Choctaw 11-N 17-E
" "	**11**	2	Choctaw 11-N 18-E
STENNIS	**8**	19	Choctaw 11-N 15-E
" "	**7**	7	Choctaw 11-N 14-E
" "	**3**	2	Choctaw 12-N 16-E
STEPHENS	**10**	5	Choctaw 11-N 17-E
" "	**21**	1	Choctaw 9-N 16-E
STEPHENSON	**20**	1	Choctaw 9-N 15-E
STEVENSON	**8**	2	Choctaw 11-N 15-E
" "	**20**	1	Choctaw 9-N 15-E
STEWARD	**9**	1	Choctaw 11-N 16-E
STEWART	**3**	9	Choctaw 12-N 16-E
" "	**2**	4	Choctaw 12-N 15-E
" "	**20**	3	Choctaw 9-N 15-E
" "	**23**	3	Choctaw 9-N 18-E
" "	**15**	2	Choctaw 10-N 16-E
" "	**7**	2	Choctaw 11-N 14-E
" "	**10**	1	Choctaw 11-N 17-E
" "	**1**	1	Choctaw 12-N 14-E
" "	**21**	1	Choctaw 9-N 16-E
" "	**22**	1	Choctaw 9-N 17-E
STOCKTON	**13**	2	Choctaw 10-N 14-E
STOKES	**1**	7	Choctaw 12-N 14-E
" "	**2**	4	Choctaw 12-N 15-E
STONE	**9**	2	Choctaw 11-N 16-E
STOVALL	**7**	6	Choctaw 11-N 14-E
" "	**14**	2	Choctaw 10-N 15-E
" "	**9**	1	Choctaw 11-N 16-E
" "	**11**	1	Choctaw 11-N 18-E
" "	**5**	1	Choctaw 12-N 18-E
STOWALL	**7**	1	Choctaw 11-N 14-E
STRAHAN	**17**	1	Choctaw 10-N 18-E
STRAIT	**22**	3	Choctaw 9-N 17-E
STRAITZ	**24**	2	Choctaw 9-N 19-E
STRANGE	**20**	1	Choctaw 9-N 15-E
STUART	**15**	2	Choctaw 10-N 16-E
" "	**9**	1	Choctaw 11-N 16-E
SUGGS	**1**	1	Choctaw 12-N 14-E
SULLINS	**3**	1	Choctaw 12-N 16-E
SWARENGIN	**14**	2	Choctaw 10-N 15-E
SWEARINGEN	**14**	4	Choctaw 10-N 15-E
SWIFT	**22**	3	Choctaw 9-N 17-E
TABER	**3**	1	Choctaw 12-N 16-E
TAH	**22**	1	Choctaw 9-N 17-E
TAPPAN	**13**	16	Choctaw 10-N 14-E
" "	**10**	16	Choctaw 11-N 17-E
" "	**4**	11	Choctaw 12-N 17-E
" "	**6**	10	Choctaw 12-N 19-E
" "	**16**	8	Choctaw 10-N 17-E
" "	**11**	8	Choctaw 11-N 18-E
" "	**12**	7	Choctaw 11-N 19-E
" "	**19**	7	Choctaw 9-N 14-E
" "	**5**	4	Choctaw 12-N 18-E
" "	**20**	4	Choctaw 9-N 15-E
" "	**22**	4	Choctaw 9-N 17-E
" "	**24**	4	Choctaw 9-N 19-E

Surname	Map Group	Parcels of Land	Meridian/Township/Range
TAPPAN (Cont'd)	**14**	3	Choctaw 10-N 15-E
" "	**21**	3	Choctaw 9-N 16-E
" "	**23**	2	Choctaw 9-N 18-E
TART	**11**	1	Choctaw 11-N 18-E
TARTT	**11**	7	Choctaw 11-N 18-E
" "	**22**	3	Choctaw 9-N 17-E
" "	**20**	1	Choctaw 9-N 15-E
TATE	**3**	1	Choctaw 12-N 16-E
TAYLOR	**19**	3	Choctaw 9-N 14-E
" "	**10**	1	Choctaw 11-N 17-E
" "	**4**	1	Choctaw 12-N 17-E
TEER	**1**	3	Choctaw 12-N 14-E
" "	**3**	1	Choctaw 12-N 16-E
TERRY	**7**	12	Choctaw 11-N 14-E
" "	**8**	10	Choctaw 11-N 15-E
" "	**14**	4	Choctaw 10-N 15-E
" "	**13**	1	Choctaw 10-N 14-E
TEW	**17**	2	Choctaw 10-N 18-E
THOMAS	**2**	4	Choctaw 12-N 15-E
" "	**4**	3	Choctaw 12-N 17-E
" "	**5**	3	Choctaw 12-N 18-E
" "	**10**	2	Choctaw 11-N 17-E
" "	**15**	1	Choctaw 10-N 16-E
" "	**1**	1	Choctaw 12-N 14-E
" "	**22**	1	Choctaw 9-N 17-E
THOMPSON	**19**	2	Choctaw 9-N 14-E
" "	**13**	1	Choctaw 10-N 14-E
" "	**7**	1	Choctaw 11-N 14-E
" "	**9**	1	Choctaw 11-N 16-E
" "	**22**	1	Choctaw 9-N 17-E
THORN	**10**	1	Choctaw 11-N 17-E
THORNELL	**13**	2	Choctaw 10-N 14-E
THURMOND	**5**	3	Choctaw 12-N 18-E
TINDALL	**15**	1	Choctaw 10-N 16-E
TINSLEY	**19**	7	Choctaw 9-N 14-E
TISDALE	**8**	3	Choctaw 11-N 15-E
" "	**14**	1	Choctaw 10-N 15-E
TOAL	**2**	1	Choctaw 12-N 15-E
TODD	**14**	1	Choctaw 10-N 15-E
" "	**7**	1	Choctaw 11-N 14-E
TOLES	**19**	2	Choctaw 9-N 14-E
TOWNSEND	**16**	2	Choctaw 10-N 17-E
TREWHITT	**20**	1	Choctaw 9-N 15-E
TRIPLETT	**1**	2	Choctaw 12-N 14-E
" "	**3**	1	Choctaw 12-N 16-E
TRUSSELL	**20**	1	Choctaw 9-N 15-E
TUBB	**9**	1	Choctaw 11-N 16-E
TUBBEE	**22**	1	Choctaw 9-N 17-E
" "	**23**	1	Choctaw 9-N 18-E
TUBBS	**15**	1	Choctaw 10-N 16-E
TUBBY	**1**	1	Choctaw 12-N 14-E
TUCKER	**19**	3	Choctaw 9-N 14-E
" "	**9**	1	Choctaw 11-N 16-E
" "	**1**	1	Choctaw 12-N 14-E
TURNER	**18**	4	Choctaw 10-N 19-E
" "	**15**	1	Choctaw 10-N 16-E
TURNEY	**3**	1	Choctaw 12-N 16-E
TUTT	**19**	7	Choctaw 9-N 14-E
" "	**10**	1	Choctaw 11-N 17-E
ULMER	**12**	2	Choctaw 11-N 19-E

Surname	Map Group	Parcels of Land	Meridian/Township/Range
ULMER (Cont'd)	**11**	1	Choctaw 11-N 18-E
ULMORE	**12**	1	Choctaw 11-N 19-E
UPCHURCH	**23**	1	Choctaw 9-N 18-E
VAN HAWES	**16**	1	Choctaw 10-N 17-E
VANCE	**19**	9	Choctaw 9-N 14-E
VANDEAVENDER	**2**	1	Choctaw 12-N 15-E
VANDERVANDER	**2**	1	Choctaw 12-N 15-E
VANDEVANDER	**2**	6	Choctaw 12-N 15-E
VANDEVENDER	**1**	1	Choctaw 12-N 14-E
" "	**2**	1	Choctaw 12-N 15-E
VAUGHAN	**15**	1	Choctaw 10-N 16-E
" "	**4**	1	Choctaw 12-N 17-E
WADE	**5**	2	Choctaw 12-N 18-E
WAIR	**10**	2	Choctaw 11-N 17-E
WALKER	**3**	4	Choctaw 12-N 16-E
" "	**1**	3	Choctaw 12-N 14-E
" "	**23**	2	Choctaw 9-N 18-E
" "	**14**	1	Choctaw 10-N 15-E
" "	**2**	1	Choctaw 12-N 15-E
WALL	**9**	4	Choctaw 11-N 16-E
" "	**3**	3	Choctaw 12-N 16-E
" "	**23**	2	Choctaw 9-N 18-E
WALTER	**16**	1	Choctaw 10-N 17-E
WALTHALL	**20**	8	Choctaw 9-N 15-E
" "	**14**	7	Choctaw 10-N 15-E
WALTON	**11**	1	Choctaw 11-N 18-E
WARD	**13**	2	Choctaw 10-N 14-E
" "	**10**	2	Choctaw 11-N 17-E
" "	**21**	2	Choctaw 9-N 16-E
WARE	**16**	2	Choctaw 10-N 17-E
" "	**1**	1	Choctaw 12-N 14-E
WARREN	**15**	24	Choctaw 10-N 16-E
" "	**21**	3	Choctaw 9-N 16-E
" "	**23**	3	Choctaw 9-N 18-E
" "	**13**	2	Choctaw 10-N 14-E
" "	**9**	2	Choctaw 11-N 16-E
" "	**14**	1	Choctaw 10-N 15-E
WARRIN	**14**	1	Choctaw 10-N 15-E
WASHINGTON	**1**	1	Choctaw 12-N 14-E
" "	**3**	1	Choctaw 12-N 16-E
WATKINS	**14**	1	Choctaw 10-N 15-E
" "	**2**	1	Choctaw 12-N 15-E
" "	**3**	1	Choctaw 12-N 16-E
WATSON	**10**	7	Choctaw 11-N 17-E
" "	**8**	4	Choctaw 11-N 15-E
" "	**2**	3	Choctaw 12-N 15-E
" "	**11**	1	Choctaw 11-N 18-E
WATT	**17**	1	Choctaw 10-N 18-E
WATTERS	**16**	4	Choctaw 10-N 17-E
" "	**20**	3	Choctaw 9-N 15-E
" "	**22**	2	Choctaw 9-N 17-E
" "	**2**	1	Choctaw 12-N 15-E
WATTS	**21**	1	Choctaw 9-N 16-E
WEBB	**22**	1	Choctaw 9-N 17-E
WEIR	**6**	4	Choctaw 12-N 19-E
" "	**4**	2	Choctaw 12-N 17-E
" "	**19**	2	Choctaw 9-N 14-E
" "	**22**	2	Choctaw 9-N 17-E
" "	**5**	1	Choctaw 12-N 18-E
" "	**20**	1	Choctaw 9-N 15-E

Surname	Map Group	Parcels of Land	Meridian/Township/Range
WELLS	**19**	1	Choctaw 9-N 14-E
" "	**20**	1	Choctaw 9-N 15-E
" "	**22**	1	Choctaw 9-N 17-E
WELSH	**5**	10	Choctaw 12-N 18-E
" "	**15**	2	Choctaw 10-N 16-E
" "	**16**	1	Choctaw 10-N 17-E
WEST	**3**	2	Choctaw 12-N 16-E
" "	**9**	1	Choctaw 11-N 16-E
" "	**11**	1	Choctaw 11-N 18-E
WESTMORELAND	**13**	2	Choctaw 10-N 14-E
WHITE	**20**	6	Choctaw 9-N 15-E
" "	**21**	6	Choctaw 9-N 16-E
" "	**13**	5	Choctaw 10-N 14-E
" "	**14**	5	Choctaw 10-N 15-E
" "	**12**	5	Choctaw 11-N 19-E
" "	**1**	5	Choctaw 12-N 14-E
" "	**5**	3	Choctaw 12-N 18-E
" "	**15**	2	Choctaw 10-N 16-E
" "	**8**	2	Choctaw 11-N 15-E
" "	**22**	2	Choctaw 9-N 17-E
" "	**2**	1	Choctaw 12-N 15-E
" "	**4**	1	Choctaw 12-N 17-E
WHITEHEAD	**2**	1	Choctaw 12-N 15-E
" "	**22**	1	Choctaw 9-N 17-E
WHITFIELD	**14**	4	Choctaw 10-N 15-E
" "	**11**	2	Choctaw 11-N 18-E
" "	**2**	1	Choctaw 12-N 15-E
" "	**21**	1	Choctaw 9-N 16-E
WHITLEY	**4**	2	Choctaw 12-N 17-E
" "	**10**	1	Choctaw 11-N 17-E
WHITSETT	**11**	6	Choctaw 11-N 18-E
" "	**12**	4	Choctaw 11-N 19-E
" "	**21**	3	Choctaw 9-N 16-E
" "	**6**	2	Choctaw 12-N 19-E
" "	**13**	1	Choctaw 10-N 14-E
" "	**14**	1	Choctaw 10-N 15-E
" "	**16**	1	Choctaw 10-N 17-E
" "	**17**	1	Choctaw 10-N 18-E
" "	**19**	1	Choctaw 9-N 14-E
" "	**22**	1	Choctaw 9-N 17-E
" "	**23**	1	Choctaw 9-N 18-E
" "	**24**	1	Choctaw 9-N 19-E
WHITTLE	**9**	4	Choctaw 11-N 16-E
" "	**10**	1	Choctaw 11-N 17-E
WIER	**10**	1	Choctaw 11-N 17-E
WIGGIN	**13**	1	Choctaw 10-N 14-E
WIGGINS	**24**	4	Choctaw 9-N 19-E
" "	**11**	1	Choctaw 11-N 18-E
WILKINS	**1**	1	Choctaw 12-N 14-E
WILKINSON	**9**	2	Choctaw 11-N 16-E
WILKS	**3**	1	Choctaw 12-N 16-E
WILLIAMS	**4**	32	Choctaw 12-N 17-E
" "	**18**	5	Choctaw 10-N 19-E
" "	**17**	4	Choctaw 10-N 18-E
" "	**16**	2	Choctaw 10-N 17-E
" "	**9**	2	Choctaw 11-N 16-E
" "	**1**	2	Choctaw 12-N 14-E
" "	**14**	1	Choctaw 10-N 15-E
" "	**12**	1	Choctaw 11-N 19-E
" "	**2**	1	Choctaw 12-N 15-E

Surname	Map Group	Parcels of Land	Meridian/Township/Range
WILLIAMS (Cont'd)	**19**	1	Choctaw 9-N 14-E
WILLIAMSON	**9**	4	Choctaw 11-N 16-E
" "	**8**	3	Choctaw 11-N 15-E
" "	**22**	2	Choctaw 9-N 17-E
WILLSON	**1**	1	Choctaw 12-N 14-E
WILSON	**1**	5	Choctaw 12-N 14-E
" "	**7**	4	Choctaw 11-N 14-E
" "	**14**	2	Choctaw 10-N 15-E
" "	**5**	2	Choctaw 12-N 18-E
" "	**8**	1	Choctaw 11-N 15-E
" "	**2**	1	Choctaw 12-N 15-E
" "	**3**	1	Choctaw 12-N 16-E
WIMBERLY	**11**	1	Choctaw 11-N 18-E
WINDHAM	**19**	8	Choctaw 9-N 14-E
WINN	**22**	5	Choctaw 9-N 17-E
WINSTON	**20**	8	Choctaw 9-N 15-E
" "	**5**	7	Choctaw 12-N 18-E
" "	**13**	6	Choctaw 10-N 14-E
" "	**14**	6	Choctaw 10-N 15-E
" "	**11**	5	Choctaw 11-N 18-E
" "	**6**	3	Choctaw 12-N 19-E
WITHERS	**5**	1	Choctaw 12-N 18-E
WITTLERS	**21**	2	Choctaw 9-N 16-E
WOLFE	**20**	1	Choctaw 9-N 15-E
WOODS	**8**	1	Choctaw 11-N 15-E
WOODSON	**9**	1	Choctaw 11-N 16-E
WOOTAN	**21**	3	Choctaw 9-N 16-E
YAGER	**1**	1	Choctaw 12-N 14-E
YATES	**9**	3	Choctaw 11-N 16-E
" "	**19**	2	Choctaw 9-N 14-E
" "	**1**	1	Choctaw 12-N 14-E
YERBY	**18**	2	Choctaw 10-N 19-E
YOUNG	**16**	15	Choctaw 10-N 17-E
" "	**7**	7	Choctaw 11-N 14-E
" "	**3**	4	Choctaw 12-N 16-E
" "	**1**	3	Choctaw 12-N 14-E
" "	**19**	3	Choctaw 9-N 14-E
" "	**22**	2	Choctaw 9-N 17-E
" "	**20**	1	Choctaw 9-N 15-E
" "	**23**	1	Choctaw 9-N 18-E

– Part II –

Township Map Groups

Map Group 1: Index to Land Patents

Township 12-North Range 14-East (Choctaw)

After you locate an individual in this Index, take note of the Section and Section Part then proceed to the Land Patent map on the pages immediately following. You should have no difficulty locating the corresponding parcel of land.

The "For More Info" Column will lead you to more information about the underlying Patents. See the *Legend* at right, and the "How to Use this Book" chapter, for more information.

LEGEND

"For More Info . . . " column

A = Authority (Legislative Act, See Appendix "A")
B = Block or Lot (location in Section unknown)
C = Cancelled Patent
F = Fractional Section
G = Group (Multi-Patentee Patent, see Appendix "C")
V = Overlaps another Parcel
R = Re-Issued (Parcel patented more than once)

(A & G items require you to look in the Appendixes referred to above. All other Letter-designations followed by a number require you to locate line-items in this index that possess the ID number found after the letter).

ID	Individual in Patent	Sec.	Sec. Part	Date Issued	Other Counties	For More Info . . .
120	ABELS, Mary	2	W½NW	1844-05-04		A1 G2
104	ABERNATHY, John T	15	E½SW	1841-02-27		A1 G5
103	" "	32	E½SE	1841-02-27		A1 G9
102	" "	32	W½SE	1841-02-27		A1 G13
47	ANDERSON, Frank	29	NESE	1878-06-24		A2
48	" "	29	W½SE	1878-06-24		A2
54	BILLINGSLEY, George W	6	NWNE	1859-10-01		A1
41	BIRD, Ebenezer P	21	SWSE	1859-10-01		A1
167	BOSTICK, Tandy C K	7	SWNW	1909-03-11		A2
19	BOYD, Archibald	7	NWNW	1850-12-05		A1
18	" "	7	NENW	1859-10-01		A1
131	BOYD, Robert	6	SWNW	1859-10-01		A1
156	BRACKENRIDGE, Samuel J	11	SESW	1860-05-01		A1
157	BRECKENRIDGE, Samuel J	11	NESW	1850-12-05		A1
164	BROWN, Stephen	8	NWNE	1892-09-02		A2
23	BURNETT, Boling C	5	E½NW	1841-02-27		A1 G62
24	" "	5	W½NW	1841-02-27		A1 G62
16	BURRAGE, Ann	6	NESE	1906-06-04		A2
80	BURRAGE, James W	18	SENE	1854-03-15		A1
81	" "	18	SENW	1854-03-15		A1
82	" "	7	SENE	1861-07-01		A1
83	" "	8	NWSW	1861-07-01		A1
90	BURRAGE, John H	10	W½NW	1848-09-01		A1
91	" "	9	E½NE	1848-09-01		A1
191	CHAMBERS, William E	4	NWNE	1892-03-23		A2
104	CHEATHAM, Thomas M	15	E½SW	1841-02-27		A1 G5
139	COLE, Roscow	15	E½NW	1841-02-27		A1 G94
140	" "	15	W½NW	1841-02-27		A1 G94
141	" "	15	W½SW	1841-02-27		A1 G94
143	" "	34	E½NE	1841-02-27		A1 G94
144	" "	34	E½SE	1841-02-27		A1 G94
145	" "	34	W½NE	1841-02-27		A1 G94
146	" "	34	W½SE	1841-02-27		A1 G94
147	" "	9	E½SW	1841-02-27		A1 G94
148	" "	9	W½SW	1841-02-27		A1 G94
142	" "	21	W½	1846-08-10		A1 G94
117	COLEMAN, Louisa	9	SENW	1892-04-29		A2
190	COOK, William	12	NESW	1848-09-01		A1
168	COOPWOOD, Thomas	29	E½SW	1841-02-27		A1 G119
169	" "	29	W½SW	1841-02-27		A1 G119
163	COTTON, Si	8	SWSE	1901-12-30		A2
52	DAFFAN, George H	3	W½SW	1848-09-01		A1
87	DAVIES, John	29	E½NW	1841-02-27		A1 G122
88	" "	29	W½NW	1841-02-27		A1 G122
132	DICKINS, Robert	14	E½SE	1841-02-27		A1 G124
34	DONALD, David	8	E½NW	1846-09-01		A1

ID	Individual in Patent	Sec.	Sec. Part	Date Issued	Other Counties	For More Info . . .
35	DONALD, David (Cont'd)	8	SWNW	1848-09-01		A1
25	DUNCAN, Charles B	34	NWSW	1850-12-05		A1
127	DUNCAN, Patience A	34	E½SW	1856-04-01		A1
209	DUNN, Zack M	21	N½NE	1895-08-08		A2
210	" "	21	SWNE	1895-08-08		A2
211	" "	22	NWNW	1895-08-08		A2
87	DYER, Otis	29	E½NW	1841-02-27		A1 G122
88	" "	29	W½NW	1841-02-27		A1 G122
30	EMMONS, Daniel	9	NWNE	1849-12-01		A1
29	" "	10	SESW	1852-05-22		A1
130	EVANS, Richard	25	W½SE	1846-09-01		A1
51	FULTON, George	35	SWSE	1859-10-01		A1
50	" "	35	SESW	1860-05-01		A1
55	FULTON, George W	26	S½SW	1896-12-14		A2
56	" "	27	SESE	1896-12-14		A2
57	" "	35	NWNW	1896-12-14		A2
62	FULTON, Green	27	S½SW	1895-06-27		A2
63	" "	34	N½NW	1895-06-27		A2
155	FULTON, Samuel	26	NW	1846-12-01		A1
152	FULTON, Samuel D	26	E½SE	1846-09-01		A1
150	" "	25	NESE	1859-10-01		A1
151	" "	25	SWNW	1859-10-01		A1
153	" "	27	SWNE	1859-10-01		A1
154	" "	36	NWNW	1859-10-01		A1
192	FULTON, William	11	E½NW	1847-04-01		A1
193	" "	11	W½NE	1847-04-01		A1
174	GALES, Tom	29	SWNE	1915-04-05		A2
96	GARRARD, John L	21	NESE	1875-07-01		A2
97	" "	21	SENE	1875-07-01		A2
98	" "	22	NWSW	1875-07-01		A2
99	" "	22	SWNW	1875-07-01		A2
119	GARRARD, Marrion M	27	SWSE	1905-05-09		A2
197	GARRARD, William H	35	N½NE	1901-11-08		A2
198	" "	35	NENW	1901-11-08		A2
112	GASTON, Leroy B	13	W½SE	1847-04-01		A1
196	GASTON, William	13	S½NW	1848-09-01		A1
195	" "	13	NWSW	1859-10-01		A1
194	" "	13	NENW	1860-05-01		A1
162	GERRARD, Sarah J	14	SW	1882-05-20		A2
6	GIFFORD, Alden	17	E½NE	1841-02-27		A1 G164
7	" "	31	E½SW	1841-02-27		A1 G164
8	" "	31	W½SW	1841-02-27		A1 G164
6	GILCHRIST, Malcolm	17	E½NE	1841-02-27		A1 G164
7	" "	31	E½SW	1841-02-27		A1 G164
8	" "	31	W½SW	1841-02-27		A1 G164
26	HARDY, Charles	30	E½	1841-02-27		A1 G217
9	HENDERSON, Allen J	35	SENW	1861-01-01		A1
134	HENDERSON, Robert W	23	NENW	1875-11-20		A2
158	HENDERSON, Samuel L	10	SWSE	1884-12-30		A2
121	HICKMAN, Mary	18	W½NW	1847-04-01		A1
92	HILL, John	2	W½NE	1845-06-03		A1
139	HODGES, Armstrong J	15	E½NW	1841-02-27		A1 G94
140	" "	15	W½NW	1841-02-27		A1 G94
141	" "	15	W½SW	1841-02-27		A1 G94
143	" "	34	E½NE	1841-02-27		A1 G94
144	" "	34	E½SE	1841-02-27		A1 G94
145	" "	34	W½NE	1841-02-27		A1 G94
146	" "	34	W½SE	1841-02-27		A1 G94
147	" "	9	E½SW	1841-02-27		A1 G94
148	" "	9	W½SW	1841-02-27		A1 G94
142	" "	21	W½	1846-08-10		A1 G94
123	HOLDERNESS, Mckinney	14	E½NE	1841-02-27		A1
132	" "	14	E½SE	1841-02-27		A1 G124
124	" "	14	W½NE	1841-02-27		A1
125	" "	17	W½NW	1841-02-27		A1 G229 V149
103	" "	32	E½SE	1841-02-27		A1 G9
40	HUGHES, E R	6	S½SW	1860-05-01		A1
46	HUGHES, Ellison R	7	W½SW	1861-07-01		A1
108	HUTTON, Joseph A	22	N½SE	1893-12-21		A2
109	" "	22	SESE	1893-12-21		A2
28	JACKSON, Christopher C	9	W½SE	1875-11-20		A2
64	JACKSON, Harris	2	E½NW	1844-05-04		A1 G243
120	" "	2	W½NW	1844-05-04		A1 G2

ID	Individual in Patent	Sec.	Sec. Part	Date Issued	Other Counties	For More Info . . .
94	JACKSON, John	13	SESE	1859-10-01		A1
95	" "	24	NENE	1859-10-01		A1
118	JACKSON, Mack	8	E½SE	1881-09-17		A2
170	JACKSON, Thomas	13	NESW	1860-05-01		A1
58	JARVIS, George W	3	NENW	1892-03-17		A2
59	" "	3	W½NE	1892-03-17		A2
86	JARVIS, John B	1	SW	1891-05-20		A2
27	JOHNSON, Charles M	14	W½SE	1841-02-27		A1
113	JONES, Leroy H	5	N½SE	1895-02-21		A2
114	" "	5	N½SW	1895-02-21		A2
199	JORDEN, William	17	E½SW	1848-09-01		A1
89	LANDRUM, John F	24	W½SW	1892-07-25		A2
159	LANDRUM, Samuel R	23	N½SE	1890-08-16		A2
160	" "	23	NESW	1890-08-16		A2
161	" "	23	SWNE	1890-08-16		A2
12	LUKE, Allen V	20	E½NE	1901-12-04		A2
13	" "	20	SWNE	1901-12-04		A2
36	LUKE, David F	22	NENW	1899-07-15		A2
23	MAHON, Archimedes	5	E½NW	1841-02-27		A1 G62
24	" "	5	W½NW	1841-02-27		A1 G62
14	MAYO, Alonzo C	6	NENE	1906-06-16		A2
42	MAYO, Elias L	21	SESE	1850-12-05		A1
43	" "	27	NWNW	1850-12-05		A1
44	" "	27	SWNW	1859-10-01		A1
165	MAYO, Stephen D	22	SWSE	1850-12-05		A1
37	MCBRAYER, David	10	NENW	1854-03-15		A1
38	" "	3	E½SW	1854-03-15		A1
39	" "	3	SENW	1854-03-15		A1
10	MCDONALD, Allen	12	SESW	1859-10-01		A1
11	" "	13	NWNW	1859-10-01		A1
32	MCDONALD, Daniel	5	E½NE	1841-02-27		A1 G283
33	" "	5	W½NE	1841-02-27		A1 G283
31	" "	2	SENE	1850-12-05		A1
101	MILLING, John	12	NE	1846-09-01		A1
178	MILLS, Willard C	27	E½NE	1859-10-01		A1
179	" "	27	NWNE	1859-10-01		A1
183	" "	36	NESE	1859-10-01		A1
184	" "	36	NWSE	1859-10-01		A1
185	" "	36	NWSW	1859-10-01		A1
186	" "	36	S½NE	1859-10-01		A1
188	" "	36	SWNW	1859-10-01		A1
177	" "	20	SESE	1860-05-01		A1
180	" "	29	SENE	1860-05-01		A1
181	" "	33	NENE	1860-05-01		A1
182	" "	33	SESW	1860-05-01		A1
187	" "	36	SENW	1860-05-01		A1
189	" "	9	NENW	1860-05-01		A1
66	MOORE, Henry	24	E½SW	1848-09-01		A1
67	" "	24	NWNE	1848-09-01		A1
68	" "	24	NWSE	1848-09-01		A1
69	" "	24	S½NE	1859-10-01		A1
70	" "	24	SWSE	1859-10-01		A1
122	MOSELEY, Mathew	3	E½NE	1847-04-01		A1
204	NEADHAM, William	24	NW	1848-09-01		A1
171	NEAL, Thomas	1	NW	1879-05-06		A2
205	NEEDHAM, William	13	SESW	1850-12-05		A1
6	ORNE, Edward	17	E½NE	1841-02-27		A1 G164
7	" "	31	E½SW	1841-02-27		A1 G164
8	" "	31	W½SW	1841-02-27		A1 G164
72	PARKER, Ira V	6	NWSW	1860-05-01		A1
26	PERSONS, Nicholas W	30	E½	1841-02-27		A1 G217
206	RAINEY, William	2	E½SE	1860-05-01		A1
85	RAWLS, Jesse A	7	NESW	1850-12-05		A1
78	REED, James	19	W½SE	1897-06-02		A1
176	REED, Will	32	SWNE	1879-05-06		A2
202	RICHARDSON, William M	25	E½NE	1889-11-23		A2
110	RIDDLE, Joseph N	4	SWNE	1848-09-01		A1
107	ROEBUCK, John W	2	NENE	1892-06-15		A2
1	ROSAMOND, Addison	11	E½NE	1848-09-01		A1
3	" "	12	W½NW	1848-09-01		A1
2	" "	11	NWSE	1850-12-05		A1
45	ROUNDTREE, Elias	21	NWSE	1886-04-10		A2
125	RUPERT, James C	17	W½NW	1841-02-27		A1 G229 V149

ID	Individual in Patent	Sec.	Sec. Part	Date Issued	Other Counties	For More Info . . .
75	SANFORD, James A	36	S½SE	1895-02-21		A2
73	SEALE, Isham T	5	SESW	1861-07-01		A1
74	" "	8	NWNW	1861-07-01		A1
71	SHANDS, Hilliard J	10	NWSE	1848-09-01		A1
65	SHEPARD, Henry H	34	SENW	1859-10-01		A1
207	SLAUGHTER, William	4	SE	1846-09-01		A1
208	SLAUGHTER, Wyatt	6	SWSE	1860-10-01		A1
53	SMITH, George	6	SESE	1901-03-23		A2
79	SMITH, James	2	E½SW	1841-02-27		A1
203	SPEARS, William N	12	E½NW	1848-09-01		A1
128	STEWART, Reuben	32	NWNE	1884-12-30		A2
4	STOKES, Albert P	7	NENE	1895-05-11		A2
5	" "	7	W½NE	1895-05-11		A2
15	STOKES, Andy W	6	E½NW	1905-12-13		A2
100	STOKES, John M	25	SESE	1904-08-10		A2
129	STOKES, Richard B	35	SWNW	1860-05-01		A1
200	STOKES, William L	22	NESW	1879-05-06		A2
201	" "	22	W½NE	1879-05-06		A2
116	SUGGS, Lewis S	11	SWNW	1860-05-01		A1
76	TEER, James M	26	SWNE	1906-06-16		A2
115	TEER, Leroy	27	NWSW	1896-12-14		A2
175	TEER, Wiley	27	NESW	1859-10-01		A1
105	THOMAS, John	4	NW	1847-04-01		A1
22	TRIPLETT, Berlin	4	SENE	1895-10-09		A2
126	TRIPLETT, Nimrod	4	NENE	1859-10-01		A1
149	TUBBY, Sam	17	SWNW	1906-06-16		A2 V125
106	TUCKER, John	2	W½SW	1842-06-06		A1 G329
166	VANDEVENDER, Sterritt A	24	E½SE	1893-12-21		A2
77	WALKER, James M	2	W½SE	1841-02-01		A1
102	WALKER, Lawrence W	32	W½SE	1841-02-27		A1 G13
111	" "	32	E½SW	1846-08-10		A1
64	WARE, John	2	E½NW	1844-05-04		A1 G243
17	WASHINGTON, Ann	5	SWSW	1896-12-14		A2
32	WHITE, Isham	5	E½NE	1841-02-27		A1 G283
33	" "	5	W½NE	1841-02-27		A1 G283
135	WHITE, Robert W	11	E½SE	1848-09-01		A1
136	" "	12	W½SW	1848-09-01		A1
137	" "	13	NESE	1848-09-01		A1
133	WILKINS, Robert S	35	SESE	1905-12-30		A2
172	WILLIAMS, Thomas	17	E½SE	1841-02-27		A1
173	" "	17	W½SE	1841-02-27		A1
20	WILLSON, Asa K	34	SWSW	1848-09-01		A1
106	WILSON, George	2	W½SW	1842-06-06		A1 G329
84	WILSON, James	12	SE	1846-09-01		A1
168	WILSON, Joseph	29	E½SW	1841-02-27		A1 G119
169	" "	29	W½SW	1841-02-27		A1 G119
138	WILSON, Robert	13	NE	1846-09-01		A1
21	YAGER, Bartholomew	6	NWSE	1859-10-01		A1
93	YATES, John J	22	SENW	1860-05-01		A1
60	YOUNG, George	35	N½SE	1897-10-05		A2 G340
61	" "	35	S½NE	1897-10-05		A2 G340
49	YOUNG, George Frank	35	SWSW	1908-10-26		A2
60	YOUNG, Martha J	35	N½SE	1897-10-05		A2 G340
61	" "	35	S½NE	1897-10-05		A2 G340

Patent Map

T12-N R14-E
Choctaw Meridian

Map Group 1

Township Statistics

Parcels Mapped	:	211
Number of Patents	:	175
Number of Individuals	:	142
Patentees Identified	:	133
Number of Surnames	:	100
Multi-Patentee Parcels	:	32
Oldest Patent Date	:	2/1/1841
Most Recent Patent	:	4/5/1915
Block/Lot Parcels	:	0
Parcels Re - Issued	:	0
Parcels that Overlap	:	2
Cities and Towns	:	4
Cemeteries	:	4

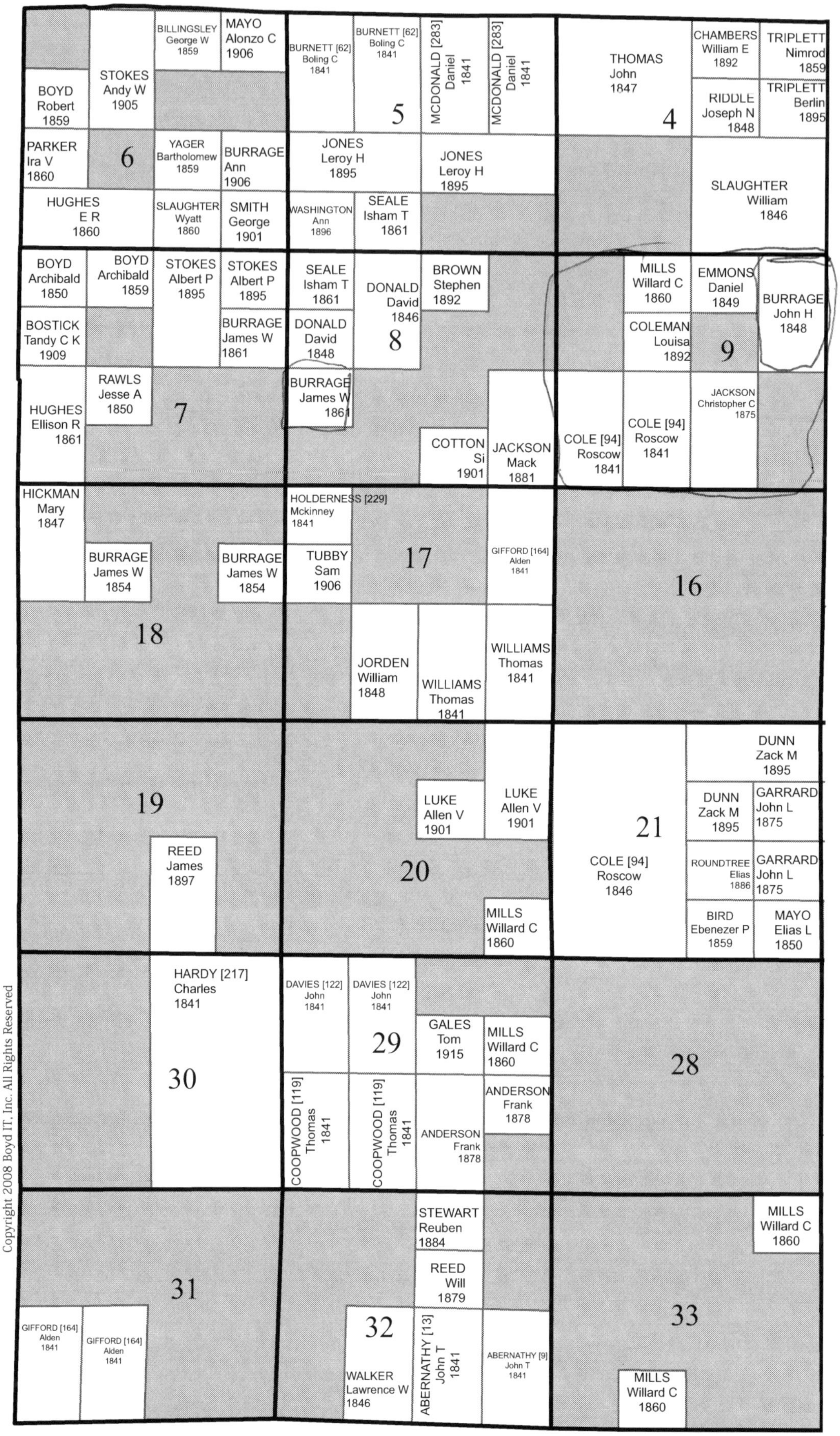

6
BOYD Robert 1859
STOKES Andy W 1905
BILLINGSLEY George W 1859
MAYO Alonzo C 1906
PARKER Ira V 1860
YAGER Bartholomew 1859
BURRAGE Ann 1906
HUGHES E R 1860
SLAUGHTER Wyatt 1860
SMITH George 1901

5
BURNETT [62] Boling C 1841
BURNETT [62] Boling C 1841
MCDONALD [283] Daniel 1841
MCDONALD [283] Daniel 1841
JONES Leroy H 1895
JONES Leroy H 1895
WASHINGTON Ann 1896
SEALE Isham T 1861

4
THOMAS John 1847
CHAMBERS William E 1892
TRIPLETT Nimrod 1859
RIDDLE Joseph N 1848
TRIPLETT Berlin 1895
SLAUGHTER William 1846

7
BOYD Archibald 1850
BOYD Archibald 1859
STOKES Albert P 1895
STOKES Albert P 1895
BOSTICK Tandy C K 1909
BURRAGE James W 1861
RAWLS Jesse A 1850
HUGHES Ellison R 1861

8
SEALE Isham T 1861
DONALD David 1846
BROWN Stephen 1892
DONALD David 1848
BURRAGE James W 1861
COTTON Si 1901
JACKSON Mack 1881

9
MILLS Willard C 1860
EMMONS Daniel 1849
BURRAGE John H 1848
COLEMAN Louisa 1892
JACKSON Christopher C 1875
COLE [94] Roscow 1841
COLE [94] Roscow 1841

18
HICKMAN Mary 1847
BURRAGE James W 1854
BURRAGE James W 1854

17
HOLDERNESS [229] Mckinney 1841
TUBBY Sam 1906
GIFFORD [164] Alden 1841
JORDEN William 1848
WILLIAMS Thomas 1841
WILLIAMS Thomas 1841

16

19
REED James 1897

20
LUKE Allen V 1901
LUKE Allen V 1901
MILLS Willard C 1860

21
DUNN Zack M 1895
DUNN Zack M 1895
GARRARD John L 1875
COLE [94] Roscow 1846
ROUNDTREE Elias 1886
GARRARD John L 1875
BIRD Ebenezer P 1859
MAYO Elias L 1850

30
HARDY [217] Charles 1841

29
DAVIES [122] John 1841
DAVIES [122] John 1841
GALES Tom 1915
MILLS Willard C 1860
COOPWOOD [119] Thomas 1841
COOPWOOD [119] Thomas 1841
ANDERSON Frank 1878
ANDERSON Frank 1878

28

31
GIFFORD [164] Alden 1841
GIFFORD [164] Alden 1841

32
STEWART Reuben 1884
REED Will 1879
WALKER Lawrence W 1846
ABERNATHY [13] John T 1841
ABERNATHY [9] John T 1841

33
MILLS Willard C 1860
MILLS Willard C 1860

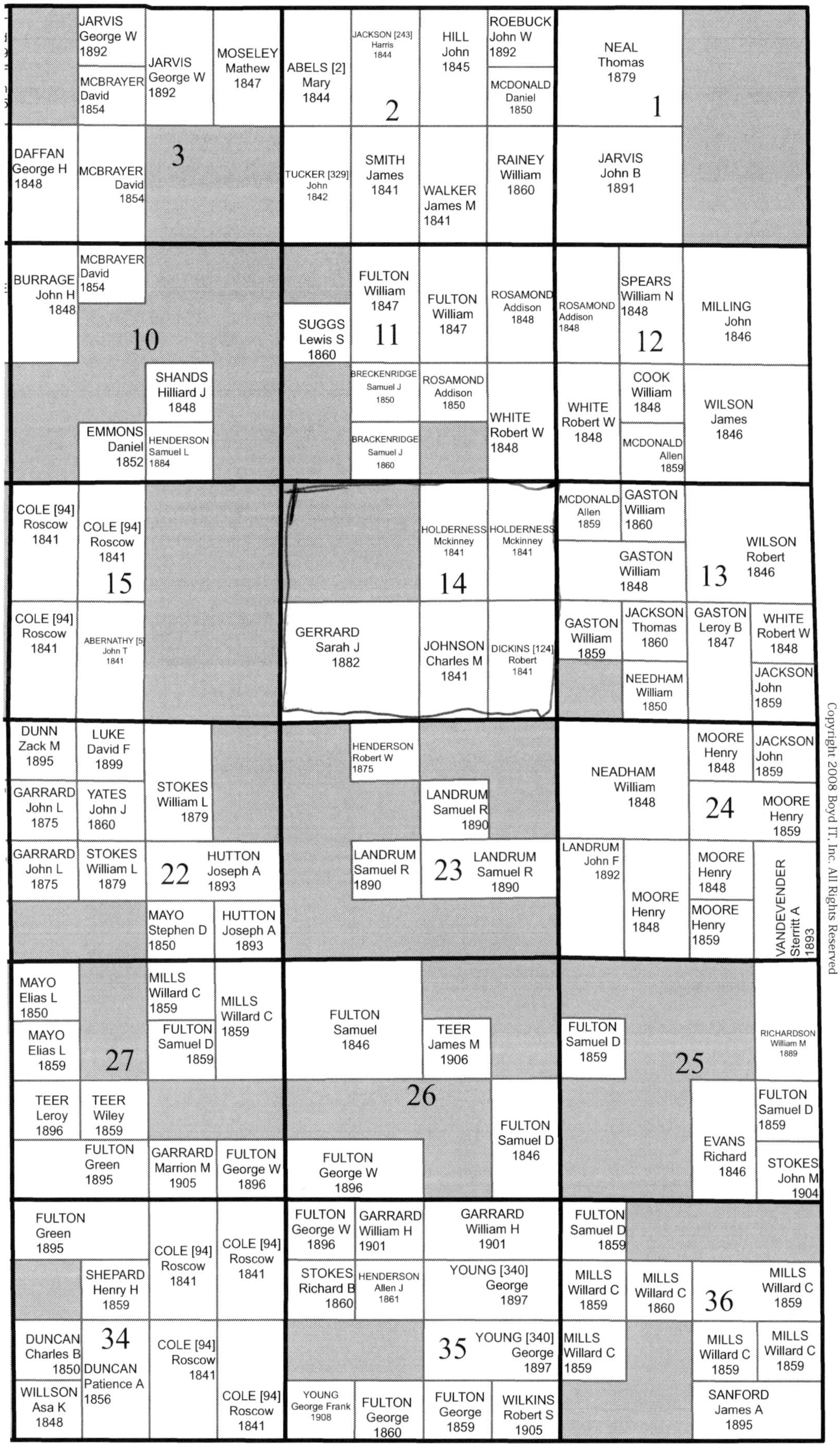

JARVIS George W 1892
MCBRAYER David 1854
JARVIS George W 1892
MOSELEY Mathew 1847
DAFFAN George H 1848
MCBRAYER David 1854
3

ABELS [2] Mary 1844
JACKSON [243] Harris 1844
HILL John 1845
ROEBUCK John W 1892
MCDONALD Daniel 1850
2
TUCKER [329] John 1842
SMITH James 1841
WALKER James M 1841
RAINEY William 1860

NEAL Thomas 1879
1
JARVIS John B 1891

BURRAGE John H 1848
MCBRAYER David 1854
10
SHANDS Hilliard J 1848
EMMONS Daniel 1852
HENDERSON Samuel L 1884

SUGGS Lewis S 1860
FULTON William 1847
FULTON William 1847
ROSAMOND Addison 1848
11
BRECKENRIDGE Samuel J 1850
ROSAMOND Addison 1850
BRACKENRIDGE Samuel J 1860
WHITE Robert W 1848

ROSAMOND Addison 1848
SPEARS William N 1848
12
MILLING John 1846
WHITE Robert W 1848
COOK William 1848
MCDONALD Allen 1859
WILSON James 1846

COLE [94] Roscow 1841
COLE [94] Roscow 1841
15
COLE [94] Roscow 1841
ABERNATHY [5] John T 1841

HOLDERNESS Mckinney 1841
HOLDERNESS Mckinney 1841
14
GERRARD Sarah J 1882
JOHNSON Charles M 1841
DICKINS [124] Robert 1841

MCDONALD Allen 1859
GASTON William 1860
GASTON William 1848
13
WILSON Robert 1846
GASTON William 1859
JACKSON Thomas 1860
GASTON Leroy B 1847
WHITE Robert W 1848
NEEDHAM William 1850
JACKSON John 1859

DUNN Zack M 1895
LUKE David F 1899
GARRARD John L 1875
YATES John J 1860
STOKES William L 1879
GARRARD John L 1875
STOKES William L 1879
22
HUTTON Joseph A 1893
MAYO Stephen D 1850
HUTTON Joseph A 1893

HENDERSON Robert W 1875
LANDRUM Samuel R 1890
LANDRUM Samuel R 1890
23
LANDRUM Samuel R 1890

NEADHAM William 1848
MOORE Henry 1848
JACKSON John 1859
24
MOORE Henry 1859
LANDRUM John F 1892
MOORE Henry 1848
MOORE Henry 1848
MOORE Henry 1859
VANDEVENDER Sterritt A 1893

MAYO Elias L 1850
MAYO Elias L 1859
27
MILLS Willard C 1859
MILLS Willard C 1859
FULTON Samuel D 1859
TEER Leroy 1896
TEER Wiley 1859
FULTON Green 1895
GARRARD Marrion M 1905
FULTON George W 1896

FULTON Samuel 1846
TEER James M 1906
26
FULTON Samuel D 1846
FULTON George W 1896

FULTON Samuel D 1859
25
RICHARDSON William M 1889
FULTON Samuel D 1859
EVANS Richard 1846
STOKES John M 1904

FULTON Green 1895
COLE [94] Roscow 1841
COLE [94] Roscow 1841
SHEPARD Henry H 1859
DUNCAN Charles B 1850
34
DUNCAN Patience A 1856
COLE [94] Roscow 1841
WILLSON Asa K 1848
COLE [94] Roscow 1841

FULTON George W 1896
GARRARD William H 1901
GARRARD William H 1901
STOKES Richard B 1860
HENDERSON Allen J 1861
YOUNG [340] George 1897
35
YOUNG [340] George 1897
YOUNG George Frank 1908
FULTON George 1860
FULTON George 1859
WILKINS Robert S 1905

FULTON Samuel D 1859
MILLS Willard C 1859
MILLS Willard C 1860
36
MILLS Willard C 1859
MILLS Willard C 1859
MILLS Willard C 1859
MILLS Willard C 1859
SANFORD James A 1895

Helpful Hints

1. This Map's INDEX can be found on the preceding pages.
2. Refer to Map "C" to see where this Township lies within Kemper County, Mississippi.
3. Numbers within square brackets [ ] denote a multi-patentee land parcel (multi-owner). Refer to Appendix "C" for a full list of members in this group.
4. Areas that look to be crowded with Patentees usually indicate multiple sales of the same parcel (Re-issues) or Overlapping parcels. See this Township's Index for an explanation of these and other circumstances that might explain "odd" groupings of Patentees on this map.

Legend

Patent Boundary

Section Boundary

No Patents Found (or Outside County)

1., 2., 3., ... Lot Numbers (when beside a name)

[ ] Group Number (see Appendix "C")

Scale: Section = 1 mile X 1 mile (generally, with some exceptions)

Road Map

T12-N R14-E
Choctaw Meridian

Map Group 1

Cities & Towns

Coy
Lynville
Preston
Prince Chapel

Cemeteries

Dry Creek Cemetery
Pleasant Springs Cemetery
Pleasant Springs Church Cemetery
Shepard Grove Cemetery

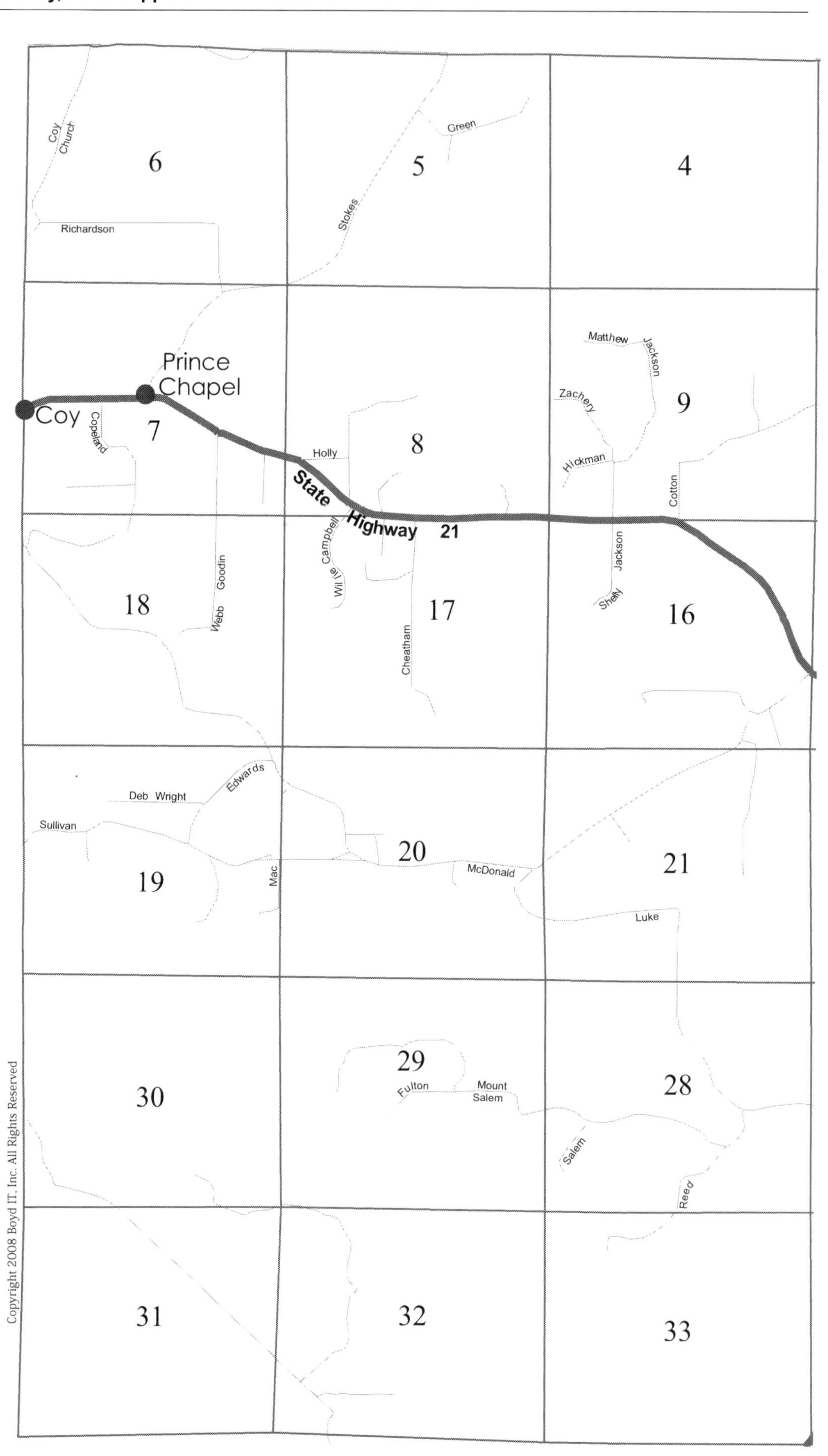

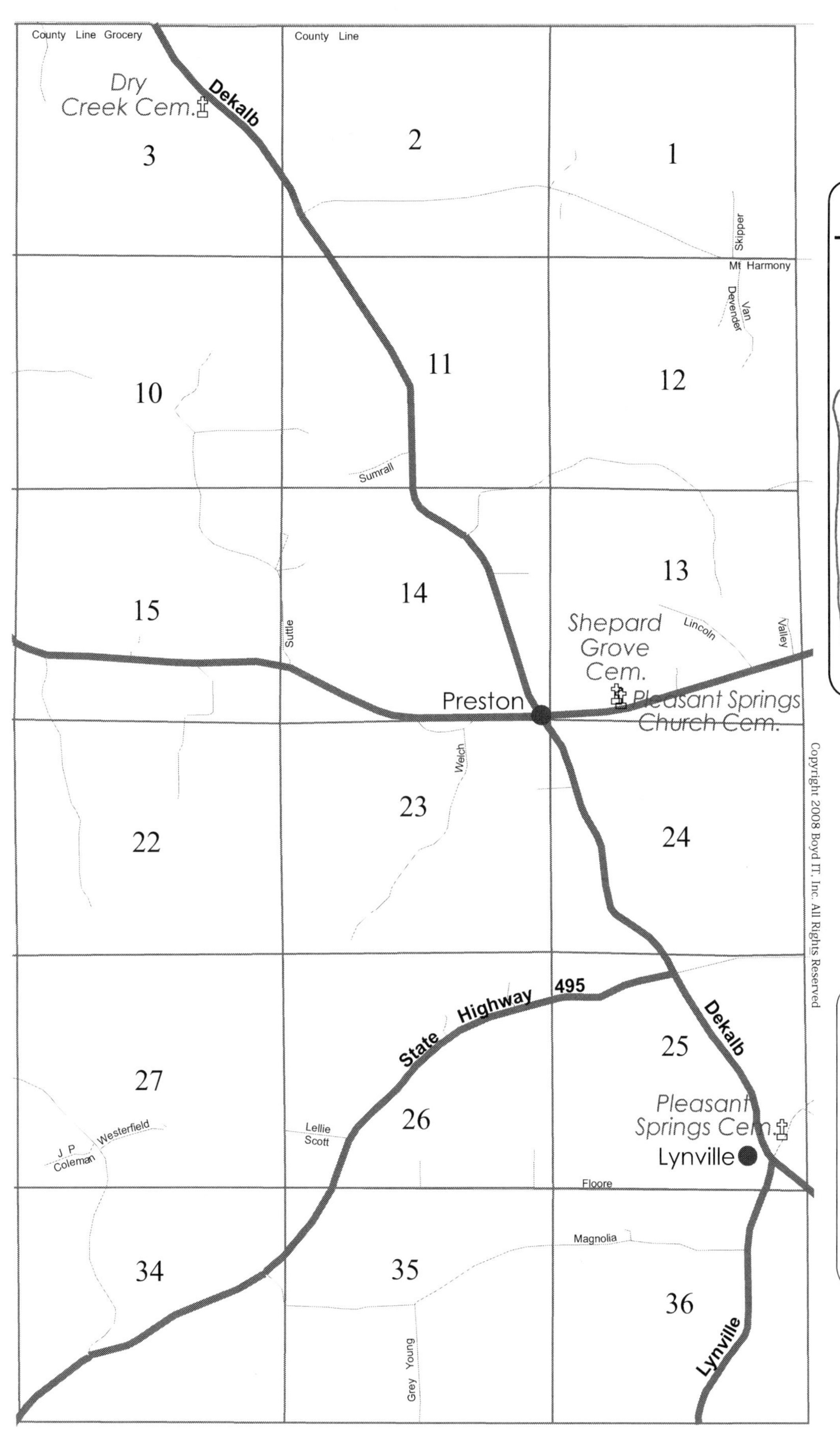

Helpful Hints

1. This road map has a number of uses, but primarily it is to help you: a) find the present location of land owned by your ancestors (at least the general area), b) find cemeteries and city-centers, and c) estimate the route/roads used by Census-takers & tax-assessors.
2. If you plan to travel to Kemper County to locate cemeteries or land parcels, please pick up a modern travel map for the area before you do. Mapping old land parcels on modern maps is not as exact a science as you might think. Just the slightest variations in public land survey coordinates, estimates of parcel boundaries, or road-map deviations can greatly alter a map's representation of how a road either does or doesn't cross a particular parcel of land.

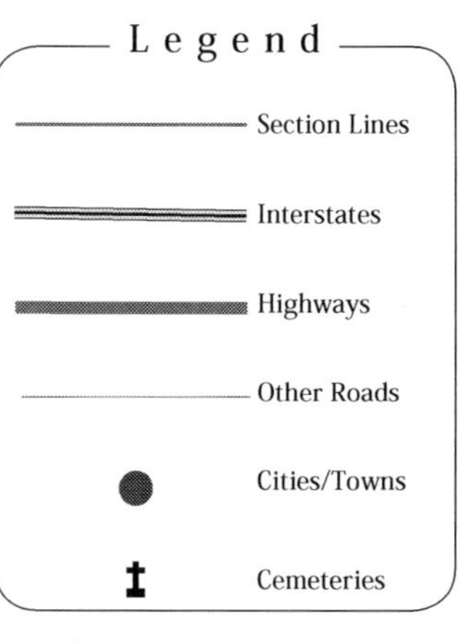

Scale: Section = 1 mile X 1 mile
(generally, with some exceptions)

Historical Map

T12-N R14-E
Choctaw Meridian

Map Group 1

Cities & Towns

Coy
Lynville
Preston
Prince Chapel

Cemeteries

Dry Creek Cemetery
Pleasant Springs Cemetery
Pleasant Springs Church Cemetery
Shepard Grove Cemetery

6 5 4
Prince Chapel
Coy 7 8 9
18 17 16
19 20 21
30 29 28
Bogue Chitto Creek
31 32 33
Cow Creek

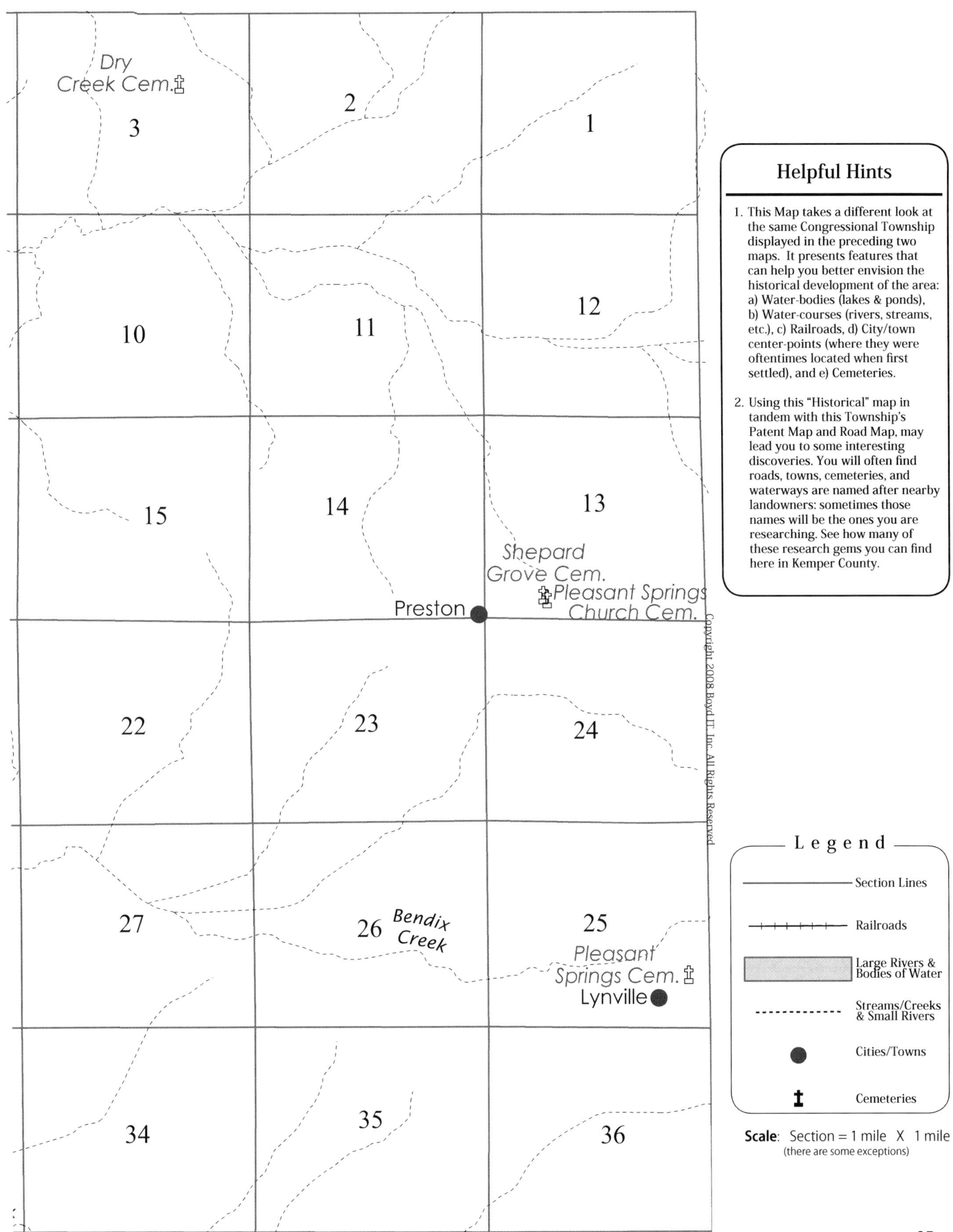

Helpful Hints

1. This Map takes a different look at the same Congressional Township displayed in the preceding two maps. It presents features that can help you better envision the historical development of the area: a) Water-bodies (lakes & ponds), b) Water-courses (rivers, streams, etc.), c) Railroads, d) City/town center-points (where they were oftentimes located when first settled), and e) Cemeteries.
2. Using this "Historical" map in tandem with this Township's Patent Map and Road Map, may lead you to some interesting discoveries. You will often find roads, towns, cemeteries, and waterways are named after nearby landowners: sometimes those names will be the ones you are researching. See how many of these research gems you can find here in Kemper County.

Map Group 2: Index to Land Patents

Township 12-North Range 15-East (Choctaw)

After you locate an individual in this Index, take note of the Section and Section Part then proceed to the Land Patent map on the pages immediately following. You should have no difficulty locating the corresponding parcel of land.

The "For More Info" Column will lead you to more information about the underlying Patents. See the *Legend* at right, and the "How to Use this Book" chapter, for more information.

LEGEND

"For More Info . . . " column

A = Authority (Legislative Act, See Appendix "A")
B = Block or Lot (location in Section unknown)
C = Cancelled Patent
F = Fractional Section
G = Group (Multi-Patentee Patent, see Appendix "C")
V = Overlaps another Parcel
R = Re-Issued (Parcel patented more than once)

(A & G items require you to look in the Appendixes referred to above. All other Letter-designations followed by a number require you to locate line-items in this index that possess the ID number found after the letter).

ID	Individual in Patent	Sec.	Sec. Part	Date Issued	Other Counties	For More Info . . .
340	ABERNATHY, John T	21	E½NW	1841-02-27		A1 G6
338	" "	21	E½SE	1841-02-27		A1 G10
341	" "	21	W½NW	1841-02-27		A1 G6
339	" "	21	W½SE	1841-02-27		A1 G10
318	ADCOCK, John	24	NENE	1859-10-01		A1
319	" "	24	NWSE	1859-10-01		A1
251	ALLEN, Daniel	5	E½NW	1841-02-27		A1
252	" "	5	W½NW	1841-02-27		A1
257	BARNES, Dempsey	4	7	1860-10-01		A1
320	BARTLETT, John	29	E½NE	1841-02-27		A1 G31
321	" "	32	E½SE	1841-02-27		A1 G31
322	" "	33	NE	1841-02-27		A1 G31
323	" "	33	W½SW	1841-02-27		A1 G31
427	BROADWAY, William	6	E½SE	1841-02-27		A1 G54
281	BUCHANNAN, Henry	24	NW	1841-02-27		A1 G58
282	BUCHANNON, Henry	13	E½SW	1841-02-27		A1 G59
283	" "	13	W½SE	1841-02-27		A1 G59
243	BURNETT, Boling C	11	E½SE	1844-09-10		A1 G64
342	BYRD, John W	6	NE	1841-02-01		A1
343	BYRN, John W	33	E½SW	1841-02-27		A1 G74
344	" "	33	W½SE	1841-02-27		A1 G74
345	" "	34	E½SE	1841-02-27		A1 G74
346	" "	34	W½SE	1841-02-27		A1 G74
429	CALHOUN, William C	2	S½SW	1860-05-01		A1
428	" "	2	N½SW	1860-10-01		A1
262	CARLISLE, Edward K	32	W½NE	1841-02-27		A1 G79
417	CATES, Thomas P	4	10	1850-12-05		A1
418	" "	4	8	1850-12-05		A1
280	CLARK, Gilbert	4	15	1860-10-01		A1 G88
280	CLARK, John	4	15	1860-10-01		A1 G88
280	CLARK, William	4	15	1860-10-01		A1 G88
236	CLEMENT, Benjamin	31	E½SE	1841-02-27		A1
237	" "	31	W½NE	1841-02-27		A1
238	" "	31	W½SE	1841-02-27		A1
433	COLBERT, William	10	SE	1841-02-27		A1
434	" "	15	E½NW	1841-02-27		A1
435	" "	15	NE	1841-02-27		A1
436	" "	3	NW	1844-06-05		A1 G91
327	COLGLAZER, John	29	W½NE	1841-02-27		A1 G98
288	COOK, Henry R	31	S½SW	1902-01-17		A2
347	COOK, John W	31	NESW	1895-05-11		A2
365	COOK, Nelson	27	NWNE	1848-09-01		A1
362	COOKE, Naomi L	24	NWSW	1860-05-01		A1
348	COOLEDGE, Jonathan	5	E½SW	1841-02-27		A1 G100
350	" "	5	W½SW	1841-02-27		A1 G101
349	" "	8	W½SW	1841-02-27		A1 G102

ID	Individual in Patent	Sec.	Sec. Part	Date Issued	Other Counties	For More Info . . .
351	COOLIDGE, Jonathan	8	NW	1843-02-01		A1
352	" "	8	SE	1850-12-05		A1
353	" "	8	SENE	1850-12-05		A1
404	COOPWOOD, Thomas	10	E½NE	1841-02-27		A1 G111
405	" "	10	W½NE	1841-02-27		A1 G111
406	" "	11	E½NW	1841-02-27		A1 G111
399	" "	11	W½NE	1841-02-27		A1 G113
407	" "	11	W½NW	1841-02-27		A1 G111
327	" "	29	W½NE	1841-02-27		A1 G98
402	" "	32	E½NW	1841-02-27		A1 G105
403	" "	32	W½NW	1841-02-27		A1 G105
408	" "	33	E½NW	1841-02-27		A1 G111
409	" "	33	E½SE	1841-02-27		A1 G111
398	" "	33	W½NW	1841-02-27		A1
400	" "	36	E½NW	1841-02-27		A1 G106
401	" "	36	W½NW	1841-02-27		A1 G112
378	CRAIN, Robert Bruce	30	SESW	1920-12-10		A2
262	DADE, Henry C	32	W½NE	1841-02-27		A1 G79
371	DAVIS, Ralph C	3	SE	1850-12-05		A1
372	" "	3	SENE	1850-12-05		A1
340	DICKINS, Robert	21	E½NW	1841-02-27		A1 G6
341	" "	21	W½NW	1841-02-27		A1 G6
402	" "	32	E½NW	1841-02-27		A1 G105
403	" "	32	W½NW	1841-02-27		A1 G105
442	DODSON, William R	28	SENE	1848-09-01		A1
360	DREWRY, Littleton	20	NWSE	1860-05-01		A1
299	ECKFORD, James	26	W½NW	1841-02-27		A1
300	" "	26	W½SW	1841-02-27		A1
420	EDWARDS, Will	30	NWSE	1890-08-16		A2
421	" "	30	S½SE	1890-08-16		A2
272	EGGERTON, George	23	W½SW	1844-09-10		A1 G138
301	ELLIOT, James	23	E½NE	1841-02-27		A1
302	" "	23	W½NE	1841-02-27		A1
303	" "	25	E½SE	1841-02-27		A1
305	" "	36	E½NE	1841-02-27		A1 G140
400	" "	36	E½NW	1841-02-27		A1 G106
304	" "	36	SE	1841-02-27		A1
306	" "	36	W½NE	1841-02-27		A1 G140
307	ELLIOTT, James	35	NE	1841-02-27		A1
308	" "	36	NWSW	1841-02-27		A1 G144
328	ESTELL, John	6	W½SW	1841-02-27		A1 G146
273	FAIN, George H	20	NENE	1850-12-05		A1
274	" "	20	SENE	1854-03-15		A1
359	FLOORE, Lewis J	10	NENW	1896-12-14		A2
437	FLOORE, William H	10	SENW	1854-03-15		A1
268	FLORD, Ephraim	2	SENE	1856-04-01		A1
234	GAY, Arthur	6	E½SW	1844-09-10		A1 G160
235	" "	6	W½SE	1844-09-10		A1 G160
436	GRAHAM, Christiana	3	NW	1844-06-05		A1 G91
436	GRAHAM, George J	3	NW	1844-06-05		A1 G91
376	GRANT, Reuben H	10	SW	1841-02-27		A1 G170
320	" "	29	E½NE	1841-02-27		A1 G31
321	" "	32	E½SE	1841-02-27		A1 G31
322	" "	33	NE	1841-02-27		A1 G31
323	" "	33	W½SW	1841-02-27		A1 G31
240	GUINN, Bennett M	30	N½NW	1906-06-30		A2
241	" "	30	SENW	1906-06-30		A2
244	HAGGARD, Burrel J	22	NENE	1854-03-15		A1
245	HAILLY, Charles	27	SWNW	1849-12-01		A1
329	HARDEMAN, John	15	E½SW	1841-02-27		A1
330	HARDIMAN, John	15	W½SW	1841-02-27		A1
376	HARRIS, Robert E	10	SW	1841-02-27		A1 G170
308	HARRIS, Thompson	36	NWSW	1841-02-27		A1 G144
277	HAYNES, George P	9	SENE	1850-12-05		A1
331	HAYNES, John	2	SE	1846-09-01		A1
305	HOLDERNESS, Mckinney	36	E½NE	1841-02-27		A1 G140
306	" "	36	W½NE	1841-02-27		A1 G140
328	" "	6	W½SW	1841-02-27		A1 G146
338	HOLDERNESS, Mckinney T	21	E½SE	1841-02-27		A1 G10
339	" "	21	W½SE	1841-02-27		A1 G10
239	HUGHES, Benjamin J	21	NE	1841-02-01		A1 G236
272	HUNDLEY, Cecilius J	23	W½SW	1844-09-10		A1 G138
284	HUNDLEY, Henry J	24	E½SW	1841-02-27		A1

ID	Individual in Patent	Sec.	Sec. Part	Date Issued	Other Counties	For More Info . . .
285	HUNDLEY, Henry J (Cont'd)	24	SWSE	1841-02-27		A1
286	" "	25	E½NW	1841-02-27		A1
287	" "	25	W½NE	1841-02-27		A1
316	HUNDLEY, Joel	34	E½NW	1841-02-01		A1 G238
317	" "	34	W½NE	1841-02-01		A1 G238
314	" "	26	E½NE	1841-02-27		A1
315	" "	26	W½NE	1841-02-27		A1
374	HUNDLEY, Renard A	23	NESW	1841-02-27		A1
375	" "	23	NWSE	1841-02-27		A1
272	HUNDLEY, Solomon M	23	W½SW	1844-09-10		A1 G138
384	" "	26	NWSE	1844-09-10		A1
438	HUNT, William	5	E½NE	1841-02-25		A1
439	" "	5	W½NE	1841-05-24		A1
348	JACKSON, Andrew	5	E½SW	1841-02-27		A1 G100
228	" "	7	W½NW	1841-02-27		A1 G242
332	JACKSON, John	18	SWSW	1859-10-01		A1
361	JACKSON, Mary	18	SESW	1860-05-01		A1
410	JACKSON, Thomas	19	E½NW	1860-05-01		A1
411	" "	19	NWNW	1860-05-01		A1
412	" "	19	SWNW	1860-05-01		A1
261	JARVIS, Edmond P	22	NW	1848-09-01		A1
267	JARVIS, Elizabeth	30	W½NE	1878-06-24		A2
278	JARVIS, George W	10	NWNW	1849-12-01		A1
246	JOHNSON, Charles M	11	W½SE	1841-02-27		A1
247	" "	25	W½SW	1841-02-27		A1
239	JORDEN, Henry A	21	NE	1841-02-01		A1 G236
275	KEAHEY, George J	15	W½NW	1841-02-27		A1
276	KEAKY, George J	9	E½SE	1841-02-27		A1
270	KEENAN, Francis	29	E½NW	1841-02-27		A1 G258
271	" "	29	W½NW	1841-02-27		A1 G258
324	LAMPLEY, John C	28	SWSW	1849-12-01		A1
325	" "	32	NWSE	1850-12-02		A1
326	LAMPLY, John C	32	NESW	1860-05-01		A1
350	LANG, William	5	W½SW	1841-02-27		A1 G101
364	LITTLE, Neill	2	NW	1841-02-01		A1
413	MABRY, Thomas	26	E½NW	1841-02-27		A1
414	" "	26	E½SW	1841-02-27		A1
385	MARSHALL, Solomon	15	SE	1841-02-27		A1
386	" "	25	W½NW	1841-02-27		A1
387	" "	29	E½SE	1841-02-27		A1
388	" "	29	W½SE	1841-02-27		A1
389	" "	32	E½NE	1841-02-27		A1
343	" "	33	E½SW	1841-02-27		A1 G74
344	" "	33	W½SE	1841-02-27		A1 G74
390	" "	34	E½NE	1841-02-27		A1
345	" "	34	E½SE	1841-02-27		A1 G74
391	" "	34	W½NW	1841-02-27		A1
346	" "	34	W½SE	1841-02-27		A1 G74
392	" "	36	E½SW	1841-02-27		A1
415	MAYBRY, Thomas	26	E½SE	1841-02-27		A1
416	" "	26	SWSE	1841-02-27		A1
293	MCAFEE, Hugh M	18	NENW	1854-03-15		A1
294	" "	18	NWSW	1860-05-01		A1
295	" "	18	SENW	1860-05-01		A1
229	MCARTHUR, Archibald	12	E½SW	1841-02-01		A1
230	" "	13	NWNE	1841-02-27		A1
231	" "	14	E½NE	1841-02-27		A1
232	" "	14	SWNE	1841-02-27		A1
259	MCARTHUR, Dugald	20	E½NW	1846-09-01		A1
260	" "	28	NENW	1848-09-01		A1
258	" "	18	SESE	1860-05-01		A1
289	MCARTHUR, Hiram	20	SESE	1860-05-01		A1
290	" "	20	SWSW	1860-05-01		A1
255	MCBRAYER, David	22	E½SW	1854-03-15		A1
333	MCCRIMON, John	24	E½SE	1859-10-01		A1
334	" "	24	SENE	1859-10-01		A1
335	" "	24	SWNE	1859-10-01		A1
219	MCSIVEEN, Alexander	20	NESW	1850-12-05		A1
220	" "	28	E½SW	1850-12-05		A1
221	" "	28	NWSW	1850-12-05		A1
423	MILLS, Willard C	22	NWNE	1854-03-15		A1
425	" "	22	W½SE	1856-04-01		A1
422	" "	22	NESE	1859-10-01		A1

ID	Individual in Patent	Sec.	Sec. Part	Date Issued	Other Counties	For More Info . . .
424	MILLS, Willard C (Cont'd)	22	SESE	1859-10-01		A1
426	" "	8	NENE	1861-01-01		A1
393	MISSISSIPPI, State Of	12	SWNW	1909-05-14		A3
394	" "	32	NWSW	1909-05-14		A3
395	" "	32	SWSE	1909-05-14		A3
404	MOODY, Washington	10	E½NE	1841-02-27		A1 G111
405	" "	10	W½NE	1841-02-27		A1 G111
406	" "	11	E½NW	1841-02-27		A1 G111
407	" "	11	W½NW	1841-02-27		A1 G111
408	" "	33	E½NW	1841-02-27		A1 G111
409	" "	33	E½SE	1841-02-27		A1 G111
243	" "	11	E½SE	1844-09-10		A1 G64
215	MOORE, Albert	29	NESW	1849-12-01		A1
264	MOORE, Elbert	29	NWSW	1850-12-05		A1
366	MOORE, Perry	11	E½NE	1841-02-27		A1
367	" "	12	W½SW	1856-04-01		A1
368	" "	14	SE	1860-05-01		A1
382	MOORE, Samuel	12	NWNW	1849-12-01		A1
383	MOORE, Silas	12	E½NW	1846-09-01		A1
441	MOORE, William	12	SE	1848-09-01		A1
214	NAIL, Absalom L	24	SWSW	1859-10-01		A1
336	NEAL, John	18	W½NE	1846-09-01		A1
337	" "	18	W½SE	1846-09-01		A1
440	NEAL, William M	18	NESW	1854-03-15		A1
296	NICHOLSON, Jack	20	W½NE	1891-06-30		A2
266	NUNN, Elisha F	6	E½NW	1860-05-01		A1
327	OREILLY, Edmond	29	W½NE	1841-02-27		A1 G98
327	OREILLY, Nicholas	29	W½NE	1841-02-27		A1 G98
401	" "	36	W½NW	1841-02-27		A1 G112
263	PACE, Edwin	30	NENE	1856-04-01		A1
270	PACE, Edwind	29	E½NW	1841-02-27		A1 G258
271	" "	29	W½NW	1841-02-27		A1 G258
222	PALMER, Alexander	9	SESW	1849-12-01		A1
223	" "	9	SWSW	1850-12-05		A1
227	PALMER, Alsa C	19	E½SW	1899-05-31		A2
311	PALMER, James	8	E½SW	1846-09-01		A1
309	" "	20	SESW	1860-05-01		A1
310	" "	30	NESE	1860-05-01		A1
356	PALMER, Laura A	20	NWSW	1901-03-23		A2
212	PARKER, Abram	10	SWNW	1849-12-01		A1
213	" "	4	9	1917-04-23		A1
377	PARKER, Richard	3	SW	1850-12-05		A1
397	PEARL, Sylvester	13	E½SE	1841-02-27		A1
282	" "	13	E½SW	1841-02-27		A1 G59
283	" "	13	W½SE	1841-02-27		A1 G59
281	" "	24	NW	1841-02-27		A1 G58
216	PEDEN, Alexander B	30	N½SW	1893-04-12		A2
217	" "	30	SWSW	1893-04-12		A2
218	" "	31	NWNW	1893-04-12		A2
399	PFISTER, Amandtus S	11	W½NE	1841-02-27		A1 G113
349	PHARMER, Calvin	8	W½SW	1841-02-27		A1 G102
363	PICKETT, Nathaniel M	20	SWSE	1881-06-23		A1
291	RICHARDSON, Hugh B	18	NESE	1859-10-01		A1
292	" "	30	SWNW	1875-11-20		A2
355	RIDDLE, Joseph N	18	W½NW	1848-09-01		A1 G315
443	ROBINSON, William	35	SW	1841-02-01		A1
313	SANFORD, Jessee H	20	NESE	1892-05-31		A2
256	SHEPHERD, David W	36	SWSW	1885-04-04		A2
234	SHIRLEY, Nathaniel	6	E½SW	1844-09-10		A1 G160
235	" "	6	W½SE	1844-09-10		A1 G160
253	SMALL, Daniel	28	W½NW	1846-09-01		A1
312	STEEL, James	2	NENE	1856-04-01		A1
224	STEWART, Alexander	14	W½NW	1859-10-01		A1
225	" "	14	W½SW	1859-10-01		A1
379	STEWART, Robert E	14	NENW	1845-01-21		A1
380	" "	14	NWNE	1845-01-21		A1
358	STOKES, Leoin	31	NWSW	1860-05-01		A1
369	STOKES, Pinkney R	31	SENW	1859-10-01		A1
370	" "	31	SWNW	1859-10-01		A1
419	STOKES, Thomas	31	NENW	1850-12-05		A1
354	THOMAS, Joseph M	12	NE	1846-09-01		A1
430	THOMAS, William C	14	E½SW	1841-02-27		A1
431	" "	14	SENW	1841-02-27		A1

ID	Individual in Patent	Sec.	Sec. Part	Date Issued	Other Counties	For More Info . . .
432	THOMAS, William C (Cont'd)	23	NW	1841-02-27		A1
381	TOAL, Robert E	8	W½NE	1861-01-01		A1
228	VANDEAVENDER, Christopher	7	W½NW	1841-02-27		A1 G242
248	VANDERVANDER, Christopher	7	E½NW	1841-02-27		A1
250	VANDEVANDER, Christopher	7	SE	1841-02-27		A1 G331
249	" "	7	SW	1841-02-27		A1
250	VANDEVANDER, Hiram	7	SE	1841-02-27		A1 G331
297	VANDEVANDER, Jacob	7	NE	1841-02-01		A1
427	" "	6	E½SE	1841-02-27		A1 G54
298	" "	9	W½SE	1846-09-01		A1
373	VANDEVANDER, Ralph T	18	E½NE	1846-09-01		A1
396	VANDEVENDER, Sterritt A	19	W½SW	1893-12-21		A2
357	WALKER, Lawrence W	1	E½SE	1841-02-27		A1
279	WATKINS, George W	24	NWNE	1892-04-29		A2
254	WATSON, Daniel	30	SENE	1860-05-01		A1
316	WATSON, Edwin H	34	E½NW	1841-02-01		A1 G238
317	" "	34	W½NE	1841-02-01		A1 G238
226	WATTERS, Alexander	20	W½NW	1848-12-01		A1
355	WHITE, Robert W	18	W½NW	1848-09-01		A1 G315
239	WHITEHEAD, James	21	NE	1841-02-01		A1 G236
233	WHITFIELD, Archimedes M	31	E½NE	1843-02-01		A1 G337 R242
242	WHITFIELD, Boaz	31	E½NE	1841-02-27		A1 C R233
233	" "	31	E½NE	1843-02-01		A1 G337 R242
265	WILLIAMS, Elbert	22	SWSW	1850-12-05		A1
269	WILSON, Ezekiel B	32	S½SW	1883-04-30		A2

Patent Map

T12-N R15-E
Choctaw Meridian

Map Group 2

Township Statistics

Parcels Mapped	:	232
Number of Patents	:	207
Number of Individuals	:	154
Patentees Identified	:	142
Number of Surnames	:	113
Multi-Patentee Parcels	:	52
Oldest Patent Date	:	2/1/1841
Most Recent Patent	:	12/10/1920
Block/Lot Parcels	:	5
Parcels Re - Issued	:	1
Parcels that Overlap	:	0
Cities and Towns	:	1
Cemeteries	:	3

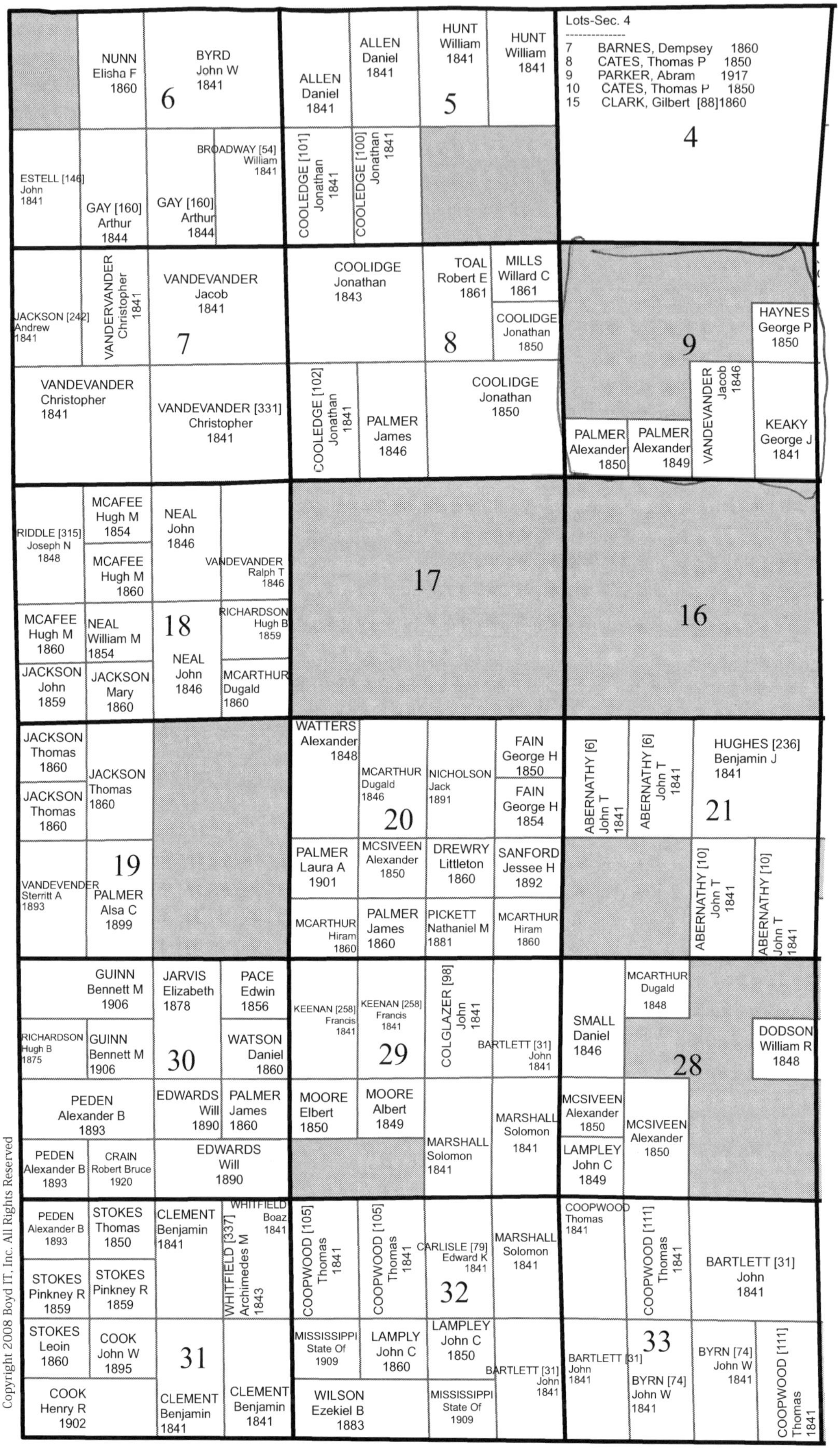

NUNN Elisha F 1860
BYRD John W 1841
6
ESTELL [146] John 1841
GAY [160] Arthur 1844
GAY [160] Arthur 1844
BROADWAY [54] William 1841

ALLEN Daniel 1841
ALLEN Daniel 1841
HUNT William 1841
HUNT William 1841
5
COOLEDGE [101] Jonathan 1841
COOLEDGE [100] Jonathan 1841

Lots-Sec. 4
7 BARNES, Dempsey 1860
8 CATES, Thomas P 1850
9 PARKER, Abram 1917
10 CATES, Thomas P 1850
15 CLARK, Gilbert [88]1860
4

JACKSON [242] Andrew 1841
VANDERVANDER Christopher 1841
VANDEVANDER Jacob 1841
7
VANDEVANDER Christopher 1841
VANDEVANDER [331] Christopher 1841

COOLIDGE Jonathan 1843
TOAL Robert E 1861
MILLS Willard C 1861
COOLIDGE Jonathan 1850
8
COOLEDGE [102] Jonathan 1841
PALMER James 1846
COOLIDGE Jonathan 1850

HAYNES George P 1850
9
VANDEVANDER Jacob 1846
PALMER Alexander 1850
PALMER Alexander 1849
KEAKY George J 1841

RIDDLE [315] Joseph N 1848
MCAFEE Hugh M 1854
MCAFEE Hugh M 1860
NEAL John 1846
VANDEVANDER Ralph T 1846
MCAFEE Hugh M 1860
NEAL William M 1854
18
NEAL John 1846
RICHARDSON Hugh B 1859
JACKSON John 1859
JACKSON Mary 1860
MCARTHUR Dugald 1860

17

16

JACKSON Thomas 1860
JACKSON Thomas 1860
JACKSON Thomas 1860
19
VANDEVENDER Sterritt A 1893
PALMER Alsa C 1899

WATTERS Alexander 1848
MCARTHUR Dugald 1846
NICHOLSON Jack 1891
FAIN George H 1850
FAIN George H 1854
20
PALMER Laura A 1901
MCSIVEEN Alexander 1850
DREWRY Littleton 1860
SANFORD Jessee H 1892
MCARTHUR Hiram 1860
PALMER James 1860
PICKETT Nathaniel M 1881
MCARTHUR Hiram 1860

ABERNATHY [6] John T 1841
ABERNATHY [6] John T 1841
HUGHES [236] Benjamin J 1841
21
ABERNATHY [10] John T 1841
ABERNATHY [10] John T 1841

GUINN Bennett M 1906
JARVIS Elizabeth 1878
PACE Edwin 1856
RICHARDSON Hugh B 1875
GUINN Bennett M 1906
30
WATSON Daniel 1860
PEDEN Alexander B 1893
EDWARDS Will 1890
PALMER James 1860
PEDEN Alexander B 1893
CRAIN Robert Bruce 1920
EDWARDS Will 1890

KEENAN [258] Francis 1841
KEENAN [258] Francis 1841
29
COLGLAZER [98] John 1841
BARTLETT [31] John 1841
MOORE Elbert 1850
MOORE Albert 1849
MARSHALL Solomon 1841
MARSHALL Solomon 1841

MCARTHUR Dugald 1848
SMALL Daniel 1846
DODSON William R 1848
28
MCSIVEEN Alexander 1850
MCSIVEEN Alexander 1850
LAMPLEY John C 1849

PEDEN Alexander B 1893
STOKES Thomas 1850
CLEMENT Benjamin 1841
WHITFIELD Boaz 1841
WHITFIELD [337] Archimedes M 1843
STOKES Pinkney R 1859
STOKES Pinkney R 1859
STOKES Leoin 1860
COOK John W 1895
31
COOK Henry R 1902
CLEMENT Benjamin 1841
CLEMENT Benjamin 1841

COOPWOOD [105] Thomas 1841
COOPWOOD [105] Thomas 1841
CARLISLE [79] Edward K 1841
MARSHALL Solomon 1841
32
MISSISSIPPI State Of 1909
LAMPLY John C 1860
LAMPLEY John C 1850
BARTLETT [31] John 1841
WILSON Ezekiel B 1883
MISSISSIPPI State Of 1909

COOPWOOD Thomas 1841
COOPWOOD [111] Thomas 1841
BARTLETT [31] John 1841
33
BARTLETT [31] John 1841
BYRN [74] John W 1841
BYRN [74] John W 1841
COOPWOOD [111] Thomas 1841

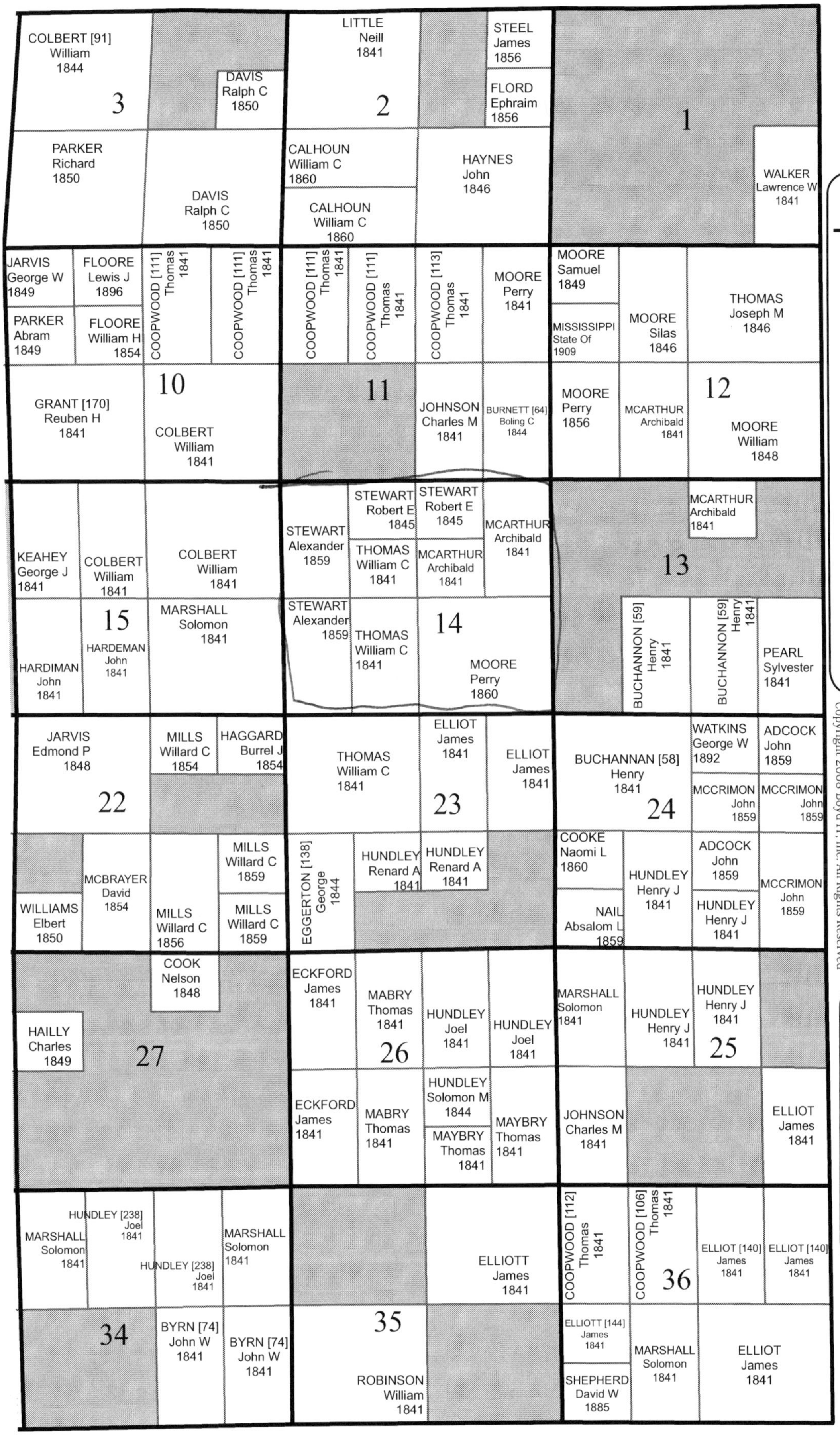

3
COLBERT [91] William 1844
DAVIS Ralph C 1850
PARKER Richard 1850
DAVIS Ralph C 1850

2
LITTLE Neill 1841
STEEL James 1856
FLORD Ephraim 1856
CALHOUN William C 1860
CALHOUN William C 1860
HAYNES John 1846

1
WALKER Lawrence W 1841

10
JARVIS George W 1849
FLOORE Lewis J 1896
PARKER Abram 1849
FLOORE William H 1854
COOPWOOD [111] Thomas 1841
COOPWOOD [111] Thomas 1841
GRANT [170] Reuben H 1841
COLBERT William 1841

11
COOPWOOD [111] Thomas 1841
COOPWOOD [111] Thomas 1841
COOPWOOD [113] Thomas 1841
MOORE Perry 1841
JOHNSON Charles M 1841
BURNETT [64] Boling C 1844

12
MOORE Samuel 1849
MISSISSIPPI State Of 1909
MOORE Silas 1846
THOMAS Joseph M 1846
MOORE Perry 1856
MCARTHUR Archibald 1841
MOORE William 1848

15
KEAHEY George J 1841
COLBERT William 1841
COLBERT William 1841
HARDIMAN John 1841
HARDEMAN John 1841
MARSHALL Solomon 1841

14
STEWART Alexander 1859
STEWART Robert E 1845
STEWART Robert E 1845
MCARTHUR Archibald 1841
THOMAS William C 1841
MCARTHUR Archibald 1841
STEWART Alexander 1859
THOMAS William C 1841
MOORE Perry 1860

13
MCARTHUR Archibald 1841
BUCHANNON [59] Henry 1841
BUCHANNON [59] Henry 1841
PEARL Sylvester 1841

22
JARVIS Edmond P 1848
MILLS Willard C 1854
HAGGARD Burrel J 1854
MCBRAYER David 1854
MILLS Willard C 1859
WILLIAMS Elbert 1850
MILLS Willard C 1856
MILLS Willard C 1859

23
THOMAS William C 1841
ELLIOT James 1841
ELLIOT James 1841
EGGERTON [138] George 1844
HUNDLEY Renard A 1841
HUNDLEY Renard A 1841

24
BUCHANNAN [58] Henry 1841
WATKINS George W 1892
ADCOCK John 1859
MCCRIMON John 1859
MCCRIMON John 1859
COOKE Naomi L 1860
HUNDLEY Henry J 1841
ADCOCK John 1859
MCCRIMON John 1859
NAIL Absalom L 1859
HUNDLEY Henry J 1841

27
COOK Nelson 1848
HAILLY Charles 1849

26
ECKFORD James 1841
MABRY Thomas 1841
HUNDLEY Joel 1841
HUNDLEY Joel 1841
ECKFORD James 1841
MABRY Thomas 1841
HUNDLEY Solomon M 1844
MAYBRY Thomas 1841
MAYBRY Thomas 1841

25
MARSHALL Solomon 1841
HUNDLEY Henry J 1841
HUNDLEY Henry J 1841
JOHNSON Charles M 1841
ELLIOT James 1841

34
HUNDLEY [238] Joel 1841
MARSHALL Solomon 1841
MARSHALL Solomon 1841
HUNDLEY [238] Joel 1841
BYRN [74] John W 1841
BYRN [74] John W 1841

35
ELLIOTT James 1841
ROBINSON William 1841

36
COOPWOOD [112] Thomas 1841
COOPWOOD [106] Thomas 1841
ELLIOT [140] James 1841
ELLIOT [140] James 1841
ELLIOTT [144] James 1841
MARSHALL Solomon 1841
ELLIOT James 1841
SHEPHERD David W 1885

Helpful Hints

1. This Map's INDEX can be found on the preceding pages.
2. Refer to Map "C" to see where this Township lies within Kemper County, Mississippi.
3. Numbers within square brackets [ ] denote a multi-patentee land parcel (multi-owner). Refer to Appendix "C" for a full list of members in this group.
4. Areas that look to be crowded with Patentees usually indicate multiple sales of the same parcel (Re-issues) or Overlapping parcels. See this Township's Index for an explanation of these and other circumstances that might explain "odd" groupings of Patentees on this map.

Legend

Patent Boundary
Section Boundary
No Patents Found (or Outside County)
1., 2., 3., ... Lot Numbers (when beside a name)
[ ] Group Number (see Appendix "C")

Scale: Section = 1 mile X 1 mile
(generally, with some exceptions)

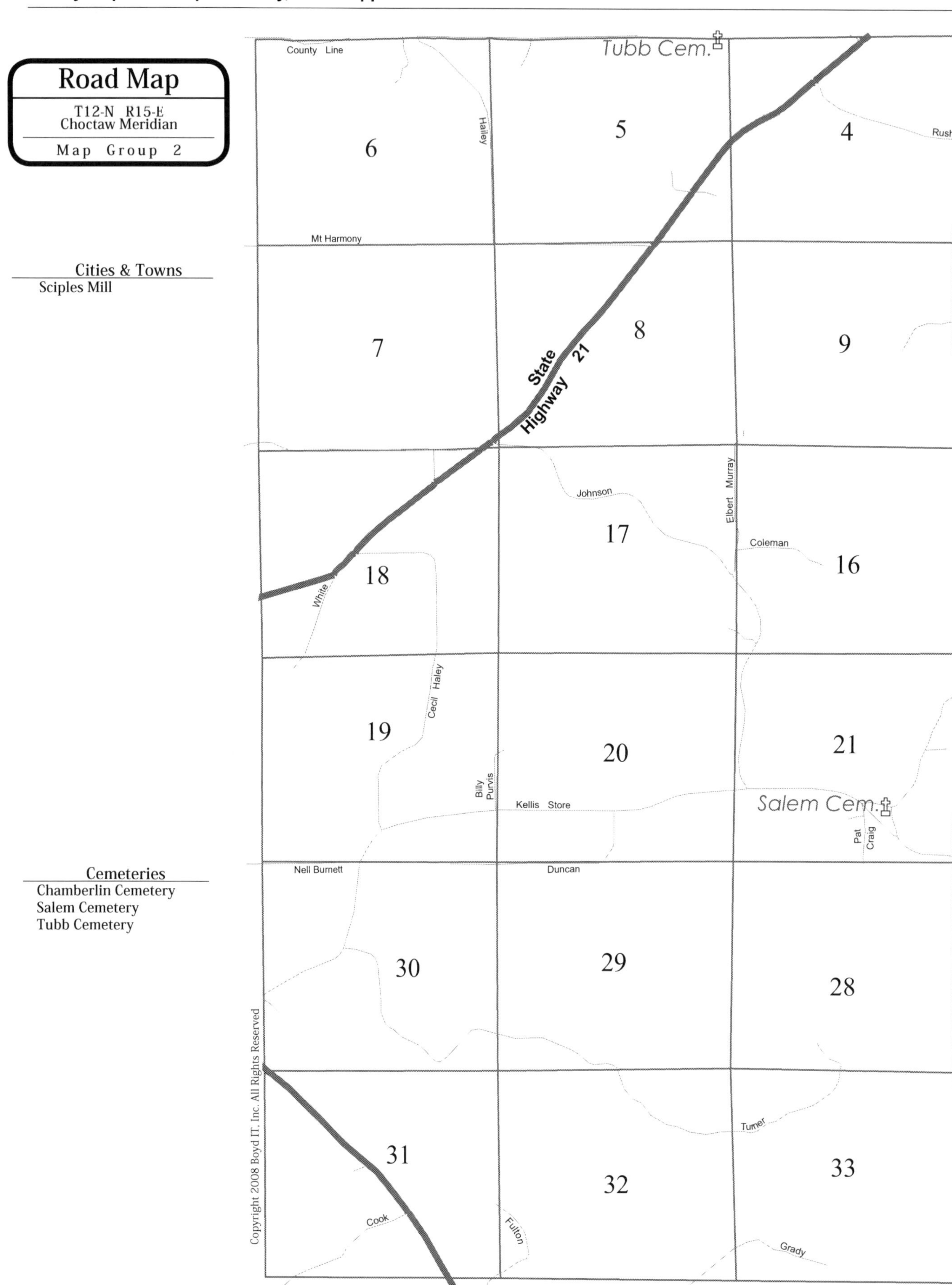
Road Map
T12-N R15-E
Choctaw Meridian
Map Group 2
Cities & Towns
Sciples Mill
Cemeteries
Chamberlin Cemetery
Salem Cemetery
Tubb Cemetery
County Line
Tubb Cem.
Halley
Rush
6
5
4
Mt Harmony
7
8
9
State Highway 21
Johnson
Elbert Murray
Coleman
17
16
18
White
Cecil Haley
19
20
21
Billy Purvis
Kellis Store
Salem Cem.
Pat Craig
Nell Burnett
Duncan
30
29
28
Turner
31
32
33
Cook
Fulton
Grady
Copyright 2008 Boyd IT, Inc. All Rights Reserved

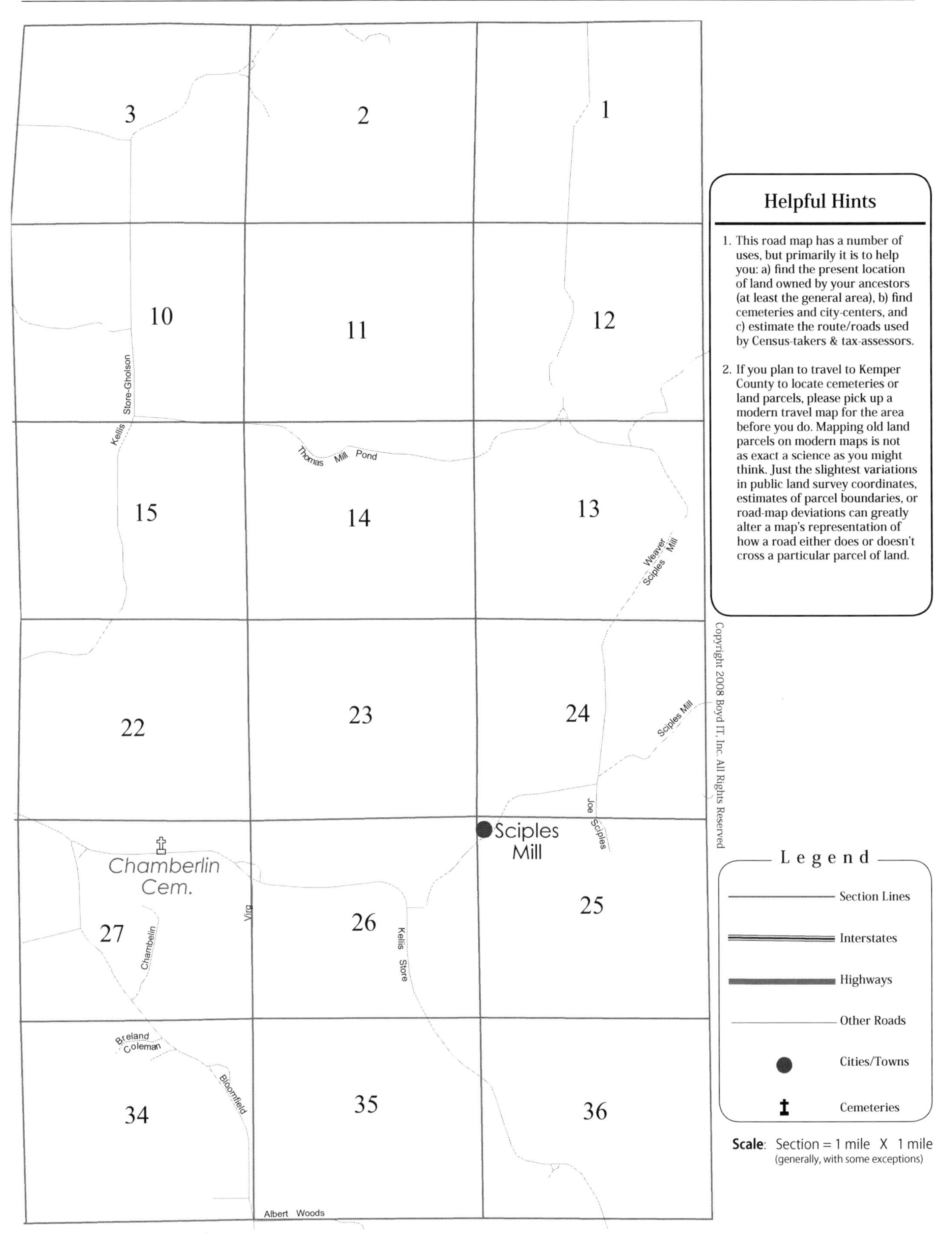
3
2
1
10
11
12
Kellis Store-Gholson
Thomas Mill Pond
15
14
13
Weaver Sciples Mill
22
23
24
Sciples Mill
Joe Sciples
Sciples Mill
Chamberlin Cem.
27
Chambelin
Virg
26
Kellis Store
25
Breland Coleman
Bloomfield
34
35
36
Albert Woods
Helpful Hints
1. This road map has a number of uses, but primarily it is to help you: a) find the present location of land owned by your ancestors (at least the general area), b) find cemeteries and city-centers, and c) estimate the route/roads used by Census-takers & tax-assessors.
2. If you plan to travel to Kemper County to locate cemeteries or land parcels, please pick up a modern travel map for the area before you do. Mapping old land parcels on modern maps is not as exact a science as you might think. Just the slightest variations in public land survey coordinates, estimates of parcel boundaries, or road-map deviations can greatly alter a map's representation of how a road either does or doesn't cross a particular parcel of land.
Copyright 2008 Boyd IT, Inc. All Rights Reserved
Legend
Section Lines
Interstates
Highways
Other Roads
Cities/Towns
Cemeteries
Scale: Section = 1 mile X 1 mile
(generally, with some exceptions)

Historical Map

T12-N R15-E
Choctaw Meridian

Map Group 2

Cities & Towns
Sciples Mill

Cemeteries
Chamberlin Cemetery
Salem Cemetery
Tubb Cemetery

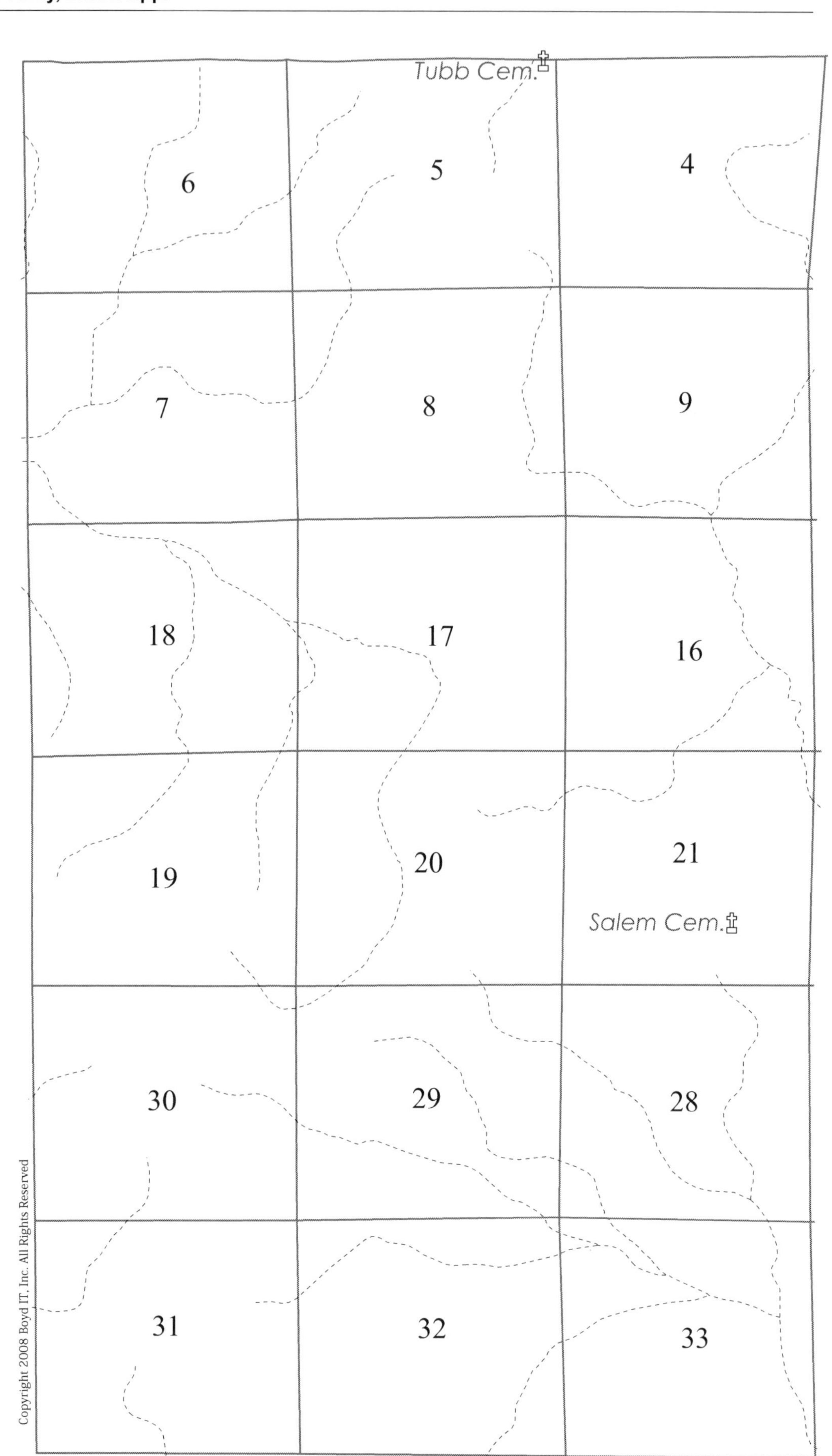

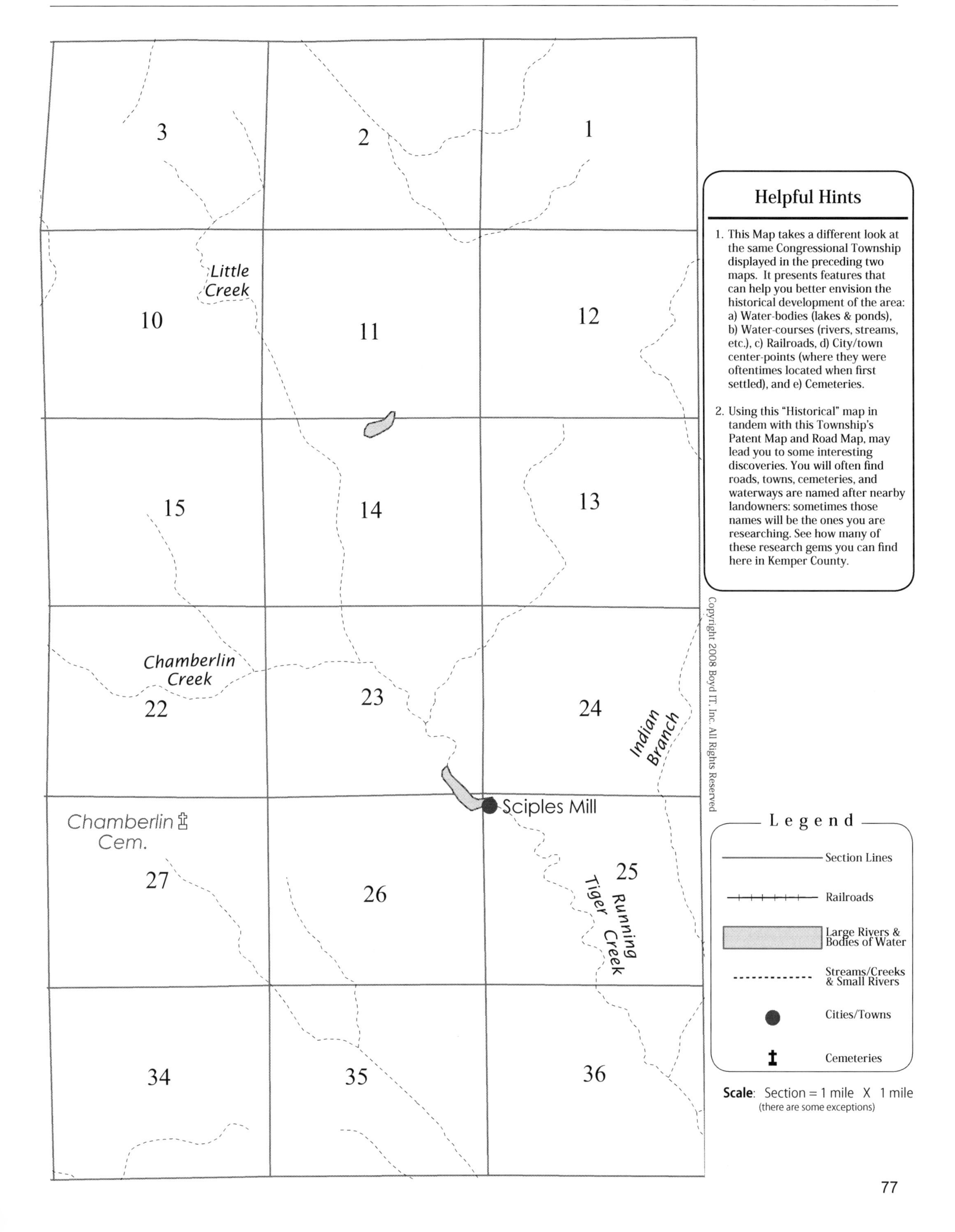
3
2
1
Little Creek
10
11
12
15
14
13
Chamberlin Creek
22
23
24
Indian Branch
Sciples Mill
Chamberlin Cem.
27
26
25
Running Tiger Creek
34
35
36
Helpful Hints
1. This Map takes a different look at the same Congressional Township displayed in the preceding two maps. It presents features that can help you better envision the historical development of the area: a) Water-bodies (lakes & ponds), b) Water-courses (rivers, streams, etc.), c) Railroads, d) City/town center-points (where they were oftentimes located when first settled), and e) Cemeteries.
2. Using this "Historical" map in tandem with this Township's Patent Map and Road Map, may lead you to some interesting discoveries. You will often find roads, towns, cemeteries, and waterways are named after nearby landowners: sometimes those names will be the ones you are researching. See how many of these research gems you can find here in Kemper County.
Legend
Section Lines
Railroads
Large Rivers & Bodies of Water
Streams/Creeks & Small Rivers
Cities/Towns
Cemeteries
Scale: Section = 1 mile X 1 mile
(there are some exceptions)

Map Group 3: Index to Land Patents

Township 12-North Range 16-East (Choctaw)

After you locate an individual in this Index, take note of the Section and Section Part then proceed to the Land Patent map on the pages immediately following. You should have no difficulty locating the corresponding parcel of land.

The "For More Info" Column will lead you to more information about the underlying Patents. See the *Legend* at right, and the "How to Use this Book" chapter, for more information.

LEGEND

"For More Info . . . " column

A = Authority (Legislative Act, See Appendix "A")
B = Block or Lot (location in Section unknown)
C = Cancelled Patent
F = Fractional Section
G = Group (Multi-Patentee Patent, see Appendix "C")
V = Overlaps another Parcel
R = Re-Issued (Parcel patented more than once)

(A & G items require you to look in the Appendixes referred to above. All other Letter-designations followed by a number require you to locate line-items in this index that possess the ID number found after the letter).

ID	Individual in Patent	Sec.	Sec Part	Date Issued	Other Counties	For More Info . . .
533	ADCOCK, Henry	18	SWNW	1849-12-01		A1
532	" "	18	NWSW	1850-12-05		A1
531	" "	18	NWNW	1859-10-01		A1
534	" "	18	SWSW	1859-10-01		A1
541	ADCOCK, Henry L	28	NWSW	1849-12-01		A1
542	" "	29	NENE	1849-12-01		A1
543	" "	29	NWNE	1849-12-01		A1
544	" "	29	SENE	1849-12-01		A1
566	ADCOCK, John	31	W½SW	1850-12-05		A1
445	BECK, Abner	33	W½SE	1841-02-27		A1
444	" "	33	NESW	1850-12-02		A1
610	BENNETT, Louvenia	34	NENE	1913-11-29		A2 G36
547	BETHANY, Hilliard T	26	NWSW	1906-06-21		A2
548	" "	26	SWSE	1906-06-21		A2
577	BETHANY, John H	26	NWNE	1860-05-01		A1
576	" "	26	NESW	1860-10-01		A1
664	BETHANY, Thomas N	22	SENW	1841-02-27		A1
665	" "	26	NWNW	1848-09-01		A1
666	" "	26	SENW	1848-09-01		A1
667	" "	26	SWNW	1860-05-01		A1
682	BETHANY, William D	26	SESW	1913-05-08		A2
692	BETHANY, William W	22	SWNE	1860-10-01		A1
522	BLUE, George W	18	E½SW	1905-03-30		A2
629	BOYKIN, Redmon	36	E½SE	1897-05-07		A2
614	BUCHANAN, Mary	7	NW	1846-09-01		A1
486	BURNETT, Boling C	15	E½SW	1841-02-27		A1 G66
487	" "	15	W½SW	1841-02-27		A1 G66
490	" "	32	E½SW	1841-02-27		A1 G60
491	" "	32	W½SE	1841-02-27		A1 G60
488	" "	8	E½SE	1841-02-27		A1 G61
489	" "	8	W½SE	1841-02-27		A1 G61
492	" "	9	W½SW	1841-02-27		A1 G64
637	BUTTERWORTH, Samuel F	10	E½SE	1841-02-27		A1 G72
638	" "	11	W½SW	1841-02-27		A1 G72
636	" "	17	W½SW	1841-02-27		A1 G73
523	CALHOUN, George W	6	E½NE	1847-04-01		A1
668	CATES, Thomas P	6	SENW	1850-12-05		A1
527	CHANCELOR, Harrison Jackson	6	NENW	1920-07-14		A2
528	" "	6	W½NW	1920-07-14		A2
496	CHANEY, Charles P	34	SENW	1854-03-15		A1
495	" "	34	NENW	1859-10-01		A1
677	CLEARMAN, Will	1	NW	1901-06-08		A2
475	COLEMAN, Allen	3	SENW	1889-01-12		A2
476	" "	3	SWNE	1889-01-12		A2
499	COLEMAN, Dave	3	NWSW	1885-07-27		A2
500	" "	3	SWNW	1885-07-27		A2

ID	Individual in Patent	Sec.	Sec. Part	Date Issued	Other Counties	For More Info . . .
516	COLEMAN, George	3	S½SE	1883-09-15		A2
555	COLEMAN, Isaiah	10	SENE	1849-12-01		A1
556	" "	4	NESW	1849-12-01		A1
557	" "	4	NWSE	1849-12-01		A1
554	" "	10	NWSW	1850-12-05		A1
573	COLGLAZER, John	24	E½SW	1841-02-27		A1 G98
574	" "	24	W½NE	1841-02-27		A1 G98
610	CONN, Louvenia	34	NENE	1913-11-29		A2 G36
637	COOPWOOD, Thomas	10	E½SE	1841-02-27		A1 G72
638	" "	11	W½SW	1841-02-27		A1 G72
651	" "	13	E½SW	1841-02-27		A1 G118
652	" "	13	W½SE	1841-02-27		A1 G118
655	" "	21	E½NW	1841-02-27		A1 G114
656	" "	22	E½SE	1841-02-27		A1 G114
657	" "	22	E½SW	1841-02-27		A1 G114
658	" "	22	W½SE	1841-02-27		A1 G114
659	" "	22	W½SW	1841-02-27		A1 G114
573	" "	24	E½SW	1841-02-27		A1 G98
574	" "	24	W½NE	1841-02-27		A1 G98
653	" "	24	W½SW	1841-02-27		A1 G104
660	" "	27	E½SW	1841-02-27		A1 G120
661	" "	27	W½SW	1841-02-27		A1 G120
662	" "	28	E½SE	1841-02-27		A1 G120
663	" "	28	W½SE	1841-02-27		A1 G120
648	" "	33	E½NE	1841-02-27		A1
649	" "	33	E½SE	1841-02-27		A1
650	" "	33	W½NE	1841-02-27		A1
654	" "	7	W½SW	1841-02-27		A1 G115
612	CORNATHORN, Manervia	34	NWSW	1906-01-30		A2
502	CRANFORD, Edmond J	21	W½SW	1848-09-01		A1
503	CRAWFORD, Edmund J	20	SWSW	1850-12-05		A1
504	" "	29	NWNW	1850-12-05		A1
671	CROOK, Walter	8	E½NW	1889-01-12		A2
672	" "	8	NWNE	1889-01-12		A2
653	DENTON, Isaac	24	W½SW	1841-02-27		A1 G104
514	DEWEESE, Fenton B	34	SENE	1859-10-01		A1
631	DICKENS, Robert	23	W½SW	1841-02-27		A1
490	DICKINS, Robert	32	E½SW	1841-02-27		A1 G60
491	" "	32	W½SE	1841-02-27		A1 G60
632	" "	32	W½SW	1841-02-27		A1 G124
505	DOOLY, Elijah	6	W½SE	1846-09-01		A1
683	DUNLAP, William	30	NENE	1859-10-01		A1
620	DYER, Otis	7	E½SW	1841-02-27		A1 G128
507	EDWARDS, Elisha	30	NESE	1859-10-01		A1
611	EDWARDS, Madison	6	NESE	1859-10-01		A1
627	EDWARDS, Raleigh	30	N½NW	1901-03-23		A2
628	" "	30	NWNE	1901-03-23		A2
561	ELLIOTT, James	36	E½NE	1841-02-27		A1 G143
562	" "	36	W½NE	1841-02-27		A1 G143
621	FELTON, Patrick	25	SESE	1848-09-01		A1
623	" "	25	W½SE	1848-09-01		A1
622	" "	25	SWNE	1849-12-01		A1
636	FERGUSON, Elijah	17	W½SW	1841-02-27		A1 G73
506	" "	18	E½SE	1841-02-27		A1 G152
639	FOWLER, Samuel	11	E½NE	1841-02-27		A1
640	" "	11	E½SE	1841-02-27		A1
641	" "	2	NW	1841-02-27		A1
642	" "	2	SW	1841-02-27		A1
449	GIFFORD, Alden	12	E½NW	1841-02-27		A1 G164
450	" "	12	E½SW	1841-02-27		A1 G164
451	" "	12	W½NW	1841-02-27		A1 G164
452	" "	12	W½SW	1841-02-27		A1 G164
453	" "	13	E½NE	1841-02-27		A1 G164 R454
454	" "	13	E½NE	1841-02-27		A1 G164 R453
455	" "	13	E½NW	1841-02-27		A1 G164
456	" "	13	E½SE	1841-02-27		A1 G164
457	" "	13	W½NW	1841-02-27		A1 G164
458	" "	13	W½SW	1841-02-27		A1 G164
459	" "	14	E½NE	1841-02-27		A1 G164
460	" "	14	E½NW	1841-02-27		A1 G164
461	" "	14	E½SE	1841-02-27		A1 G164
462	" "	14	W½NE	1841-02-27		A1 G164
463	" "	14	W½NW	1841-02-27		A1 G164

ID	Individual in Patent	Sec.	Sec. Part	Date Issued	Other Counties	For More Info . . .
464	GIFFORD, Alden (Cont'd)	14	W½SE	1841-02-27		A1 G164
465	" "	23	E½NE	1841-02-27		A1 G164
466	" "	23	W½NE	1841-02-27		A1 G164
467	" "	24	E½NW	1841-02-27		A1 G164
468	" "	24	W½NW	1841-02-27		A1 G164
449	GILCHRIST, Malcolm	12	E½NW	1841-02-27		A1 G164
450	" "	12	E½SW	1841-02-27		A1 G164
451	" "	12	W½NW	1841-02-27		A1 G164
452	" "	12	W½SW	1841-02-27		A1 G164
453	" "	13	E½NE	1841-02-27		A1 G164 R454
454	" "	13	E½NE	1841-02-27		A1 G164 R453
455	" "	13	E½NW	1841-02-27		A1 G164
456	" "	13	E½SE	1841-02-27		A1 G164
457	" "	13	W½NW	1841-02-27		A1 G164
458	" "	13	W½SW	1841-02-27		A1 G164
459	" "	14	E½NE	1841-02-27		A1 G164
460	" "	14	E½NW	1841-02-27		A1 G164
461	" "	14	E½SE	1841-02-27		A1 G164
462	" "	14	W½NE	1841-02-27		A1 G164
463	" "	14	W½NW	1841-02-27		A1 G164
464	" "	14	W½SE	1841-02-27		A1 G164
465	" "	23	E½NE	1841-02-27		A1 G164
466	" "	23	W½NE	1841-02-27		A1 G164
467	" "	24	E½NW	1841-02-27		A1 G164
468	" "	24	W½NW	1841-02-27		A1 G164
561	" "	36	E½NE	1841-02-27		A1 G143
562	" "	36	W½NE	1841-02-27		A1 G143
684	GRADY, William	11	W½NW	1910-01-20		A2
644	GRIFFIN, Solomon	20	NESW	1859-10-01		A1
597	GRIGSBY, Joseph	9	E½SW	1841-02-27		A1 G212
536	GULLY, Henry J	30	SESE	1860-05-01		A1
537	" "	30	SWSE	1860-05-01		A1
538	" "	32	E½NE	1860-05-01		A1
539	" "	32	NESE	1860-05-01		A1
540	" "	32	NWNE	1860-05-01		A1
578	HALL, John	5	NWSE	1849-12-01		A1
604	HALLFORD, Julius P	36	E½NW	1904-07-02		A2
605	" "	36	SWNW	1904-07-02		A2
567	HAMMACK, John C	28	SWNE	1860-05-01		A1
601	HAMMOCK, Julia N	20	N½NW	1876-04-01		A2
602	" "	20	NWNE	1876-04-01		A2
603	" "	20	SWNW	1876-04-01		A2
675	HARRIS, Wiley P	9	E½NW	1841-02-27		A1
597	" "	9	E½SW	1841-02-27		A1 G212
519	HASKINS, George T	20	E½NE	1894-12-17		A2
520	" "	20	SENW	1894-12-17		A2
521	" "	20	SWNE	1894-12-17		A2
632	HOLDERNESS, Mckinney	32	W½SW	1841-02-27		A1 G124
488	" "	8	E½SE	1841-02-27		A1 G61
489	" "	8	W½SE	1841-02-27		A1 G61
579	HOLLAND, John	20	NWSW	1892-05-26		A2
563	JENKINS, James H	28	E½NE	1882-05-20		A2
564	" "	28	NENW	1882-05-20		A2
565	" "	28	NWNE	1882-05-20		A2
617	JENKINS, Mary	22	SWNW	1860-05-01		A1
685	JOHNSON, William H	10	W½NE	1841-02-27		A1
686	" "	17	W½NW	1841-02-27		A1
687	" "	18	W½SE	1841-02-27		A1 G252
688	" "	9	NE	1841-02-27		A1 G252
518	KELLEY, George S	1	SE	1911-06-22		A1
690	KILLIN, William	34	E½SW	1841-02-27		A1
598	LACY, Joseph H	26	NWSE	1848-09-01		A1
599	" "	26	SWNE	1848-09-01		A1
568	LAMPLEY, John C	30	NWSE	1859-10-01		A1
569	" "	30	SWNW	1859-10-01		A1
570	" "	32	SENW	1859-10-01		A1
571	" "	32	SWNE	1859-10-01		A1
572	" "	32	W½NW	1859-10-01		A1
515	LENTON, Floyd	23	E½NW	1906-03-16		A1
691	LEWIS, William M	25	E½SW	1848-09-01		A1
678	LOVE, William A	30	NESW	1856-04-01		A1
679	" "	30	NWSW	1859-10-01		A1
680	" "	30	SESW	1859-10-01		A1

ID	Individual in Patent	Sec.	Sec. Part	Date Issued	Other Counties	For More Info . . .
559	MADISON, James A	34	SESE	1902-07-03		A2 G277
559	MADISON, Narcissa M	34	SESE	1902-07-03		A2 G277
681	MADISON, William A	23	E½SE	1906-06-30		A2
580	MALONE, John	5	SWSW	1848-09-01		A1
581	" "	8	NWNW	1848-09-01		A1
582	" "	8	SWNW	1850-12-05		A1
630	MARS, Robert A	36	W½SE	1860-05-01		A1
595	MARSHALL, Joseph A	35	NWSW	1841-02-27		A1
596	" "	35	SESW	1841-02-27		A1
645	MARSHALL, Solomon	9	W½SE	1841-02-27		A1 G279
583	MATHEWS, John	24	E½NE	1841-02-27		A1
584	" "	24	E½SE	1841-02-27		A1
585	" "	24	W½SE	1841-02-27		A1
446	MAURY, Abraham	3	NWNW	1890-08-16		A2
498	MAURY, Dan	3	E½SW	1890-08-16		A2
517	MAURY, George	3	N½SE	1885-07-27		A2
529	MAURY, Harrison	6	W½NE	1889-01-12		A2
694	MAURY, Zack	3	NENW	1890-03-28		A2
695	" "	3	NWNE	1890-03-28		A2
483	MCARTHUR, Archibald	5	W½NE	1848-09-01		A1
477	MCCRAY, Allen	10	NWNW	1841-02-27		A1
478	" "	9	NESE	1841-02-27		A1
687	MCCRORY, Allen	18	W½SE	1841-02-27		A1 G252
688	" "	9	NE	1841-02-27		A1 G252
645	" "	9	W½SE	1841-02-27		A1 G279
479	" "	15	W½NW	1848-09-01		A1
508	MCDONALD, Elizabeth	36	SW	1881-05-10		A2
480	MCINTYRE, Angus	4	SWNE	1841-02-27		A1
482	" "	5	E½NE	1841-02-27		A1 G292
481	" "	9	NWNW	1841-02-27		A1
482	MCKELVIN, Benjamin A	5	E½NE	1841-02-27		A1 G292
497	MCLAURIN, Christopher C	20	NWSE	1892-06-15		A2
474	MCNEES, Alice C	18	E½NW	1920-07-19		A1
618	MCSWEAN, Nancy A	28	SWSW	1860-05-01		A1
646	MISSISSIPPI, State Of	1	NWSW	1909-05-14		A3
647	" "	23	NWSE	1909-05-14		A3
620	MOODY, Washington	7	E½SW	1841-02-27		A1 G128
492	" "	9	W½SW	1841-02-27		A1 G64
586	MOORE, John	5	NWNW	1850-12-05		A1
600	MORSE, Joshua H	31	NE	1850-12-05		A1
643	MURRY, Samuel L	28	E½SW	1848-09-01		A1
689	MURRY, William H	26	NESE	1848-09-01		A1
693	MURRY, Wilson	21	SWNW	1849-12-01		A1
512	NASH, Ezekiel	7	E½SE	1841-02-27		A1 G301
513	" "	8	E½SW	1841-02-27		A1 G301
506	NASH, Orsamus L	18	E½SE	1841-02-27		A1 G152
512	" "	7	E½SE	1841-02-27		A1 G301
513	" "	8	E½SW	1841-02-27		A1 G301
535	NEAL, Henry E	7	NE	1846-09-01		A1
525	NESTER, Guilford S	8	E½NE	1906-10-15		A2
526	" "	8	SWNE	1906-10-15		A2
545	NEWELL, Henry	18	NE	1841-02-27		A1
546	" "	19	E½	1841-02-27		A1
494	NICHOLAS, Charles	1	E½SW	1882-03-04		A2
590	NICHOLAS, John	28	W½NW	1846-09-01		A1
588	" "	20	SESW	1849-12-01		A1
589	" "	21	NESW	1849-12-01		A1
587	" "	20	NESE	1860-05-01		A1
591	" "	34	NWNW	1860-05-01		A1
509	NICHOLSON, Elizabeth	3	E½NE	1890-08-16		A2
551	NICHOLSON, Isaac W	4	NESE	1850-12-02		A1
552	" "	4	SESW	1850-12-05		A1
553	" "	4	SWSE	1850-12-05		A1
550	" "	22	NWNW	1860-05-01		A1
624	NICHOLSON, Phillip	10	E½SW	1890-03-28		A2
625	" "	10	SENW	1890-03-28		A2
626	" "	10	SWSW	1890-03-28		A2
573	OREILLY, Edmond	24	E½SW	1841-02-27		A1 G98
574	" "	24	W½NE	1841-02-27		A1 G98
573	OREILLY, Nicholas	24	E½SW	1841-02-27		A1 G98
574	" "	24	W½NE	1841-02-27		A1 G98
449	ORNE, Edward	12	E½NW	1841-02-27		A1 G164
450	" "	12	E½SW	1841-02-27		A1 G164

ID	Individual in Patent	Sec.	Sec. Part	Date Issued	Other Counties	For More Info . . .
451	ORNE, Edward (Cont'd)	12	W½NW	1841-02-27		A1 G164
452	" "	12	W½SW	1841-02-27		A1 G164
453	" "	13	E½NE	1841-02-27		A1 G164 R454
454	" "	13	E½NE	1841-02-27		A1 G164 R453
455	" "	13	E½NW	1841-02-27		A1 G164
456	" "	13	E½SE	1841-02-27		A1 G164
457	" "	13	W½NW	1841-02-27		A1 G164
458	" "	13	W½SW	1841-02-27		A1 G164
459	" "	14	E½NE	1841-02-27		A1 G164
460	" "	14	E½NW	1841-02-27		A1 G164
461	" "	14	E½SE	1841-02-27		A1 G164
462	" "	14	W½NE	1841-02-27		A1 G164
463	" "	14	W½NW	1841-02-27		A1 G164
464	" "	14	W½SE	1841-02-27		A1 G164
465	" "	23	E½NE	1841-02-27		A1 G164
466	" "	23	W½NE	1841-02-27		A1 G164
467	" "	24	E½NW	1841-02-27		A1 G164
468	" "	24	W½NW	1841-02-27		A1 G164
615	OVERSTREET, Mary J	15	NESE	1904-12-31		A2
616	" "	15	SENE	1904-12-31		A2
447	PARKER, Abram	4	16	1849-12-01		A1 C
448	" "	4	9	1849-12-01		A1 C
619	PERMENTER, Needham	22	NENW	1850-12-05		A1
510	PERSON, Elizabeth	12	NWSE	1850-12-05		A1
511	" "	4	SESE	1850-12-05		A1
674	PERSON, Wiley C	2	S½SE	1848-09-01		A1
673	" "	1	SWSW	1850-12-05		A1
592	POLLARD, John	26	SESE	1924-02-19		A2
484	REA, Ben	34	SWNE	1891-05-20		A2
485	" "	34	W½SE	1891-05-20		A2
633	REA, Robert R	28	SENW	1905-03-30		A2
486	RICHEY, James	15	E½SW	1841-02-27		A1 G66
487	" "	15	W½SW	1841-02-27		A1 G66
655	" "	21	E½NW	1841-02-27		A1 G114
656	" "	22	E½SE	1841-02-27		A1 G114
657	" "	22	E½SW	1841-02-27		A1 G114
658	" "	22	W½SE	1841-02-27		A1 G114
659	" "	22	W½SW	1841-02-27		A1 G114
654	RUPERT, James C	7	W½SW	1841-02-27		A1 G115
470	SELLERS, Alfred	25	SENW	1860-05-01		A1
471	" "	25	SWNW	1860-05-01		A1
472	" "	36	NWNW	1860-05-01		A1
469	" "	25	NENE	1860-10-01		A1
549	SHIKLE, Hiram	25	NWSW	1848-09-01		A1
501	STENNIS, Deb	22	NWNE	1904-12-31		A2
593	STENNIS, John	22	E½NE	1904-09-28		A2
530	STEWART, Hazael	4	NW	1848-09-01		A1
486	STEWART, Hugh C	15	E½SW	1841-02-27		A1 G66
487	" "	15	W½SW	1841-02-27		A1 G66
655	" "	21	E½NW	1841-02-27		A1 G114
656	" "	22	E½SE	1841-02-27		A1 G114
657	" "	22	E½SW	1841-02-27		A1 G114
658	" "	22	W½SE	1841-02-27		A1 G114
659	" "	22	W½SW	1841-02-27		A1 G114
558	STEWART, Isaiah	27	NENE	1841-02-27		A1
473	SULLINS, Alfred	25	SWSW	1848-09-01		A1
493	TABER, Carroll	34	NESE	1850-12-02		A1
613	TATE, Margarett M	1	NE	1905-02-13		A2
676	TEER, Wiley	6	SW	1846-12-01		A1
669	TRIPLETT, Thomas	4	W½SW	1885-12-19		A2
575	TURNEY, John G	33	E½NW	1847-04-01		A1
606	WALKER, Lawrence W	11	E½NW	1841-02-27		A1
607	" "	11	E½SW	1841-02-27		A1
608	" "	11	W½NE	1841-02-27		A1
609	" "	11	W½SE	1841-02-27		A1
560	WALL, James D	34	SWSW	1860-05-01		A1
634	WALL, Robert	34	NWNE	1860-05-01		A1
635	" "	34	SWNW	1860-05-01		A1
524	WASHINGTON, George	17	NESE	1841-02-27		A1
670	WATKINS, Walter C	32	NENW	1920-07-26		A2
651	WEST, Anderson	13	E½SW	1841-02-27		A1 G118
652	" "	13	W½SE	1841-02-27		A1 G118
594	WILKS, John W	8	W½SW	1841-02-27		A1 G338

ID	Individual in Patent	Sec.	Sec. Part	Date Issued	Other Counties	For More Info . . .
594	WILSON, Henry R	8	W½SW	1841-02-27		A1 G338
660	YOUNG, Robert M	27	E½SW	1841-02-27		A1 G120
661	" "	27	W½SW	1841-02-27		A1 G120
662	" "	28	E½SE	1841-02-27		A1 G120
663	" "	28	W½SE	1841-02-27		A1 G120

Patent Map

T12-N R16-E
Choctaw Meridian

Map Group 3

Township Statistics

Parcels Mapped	:	252
Number of Patents	:	211
Number of Individuals	:	143
Patentees Identified	:	137
Number of Surnames	:	111
Multi-Patentee Parcels	:	60
Oldest Patent Date	:	2/27/1841
Most Recent Patent	:	2/19/1924
Block/Lot Parcels	:	2
Parcels Re - Issued	:	1
Parcels that Overlap	:	0
Cities and Towns	:	0
Cemeteries	:	2

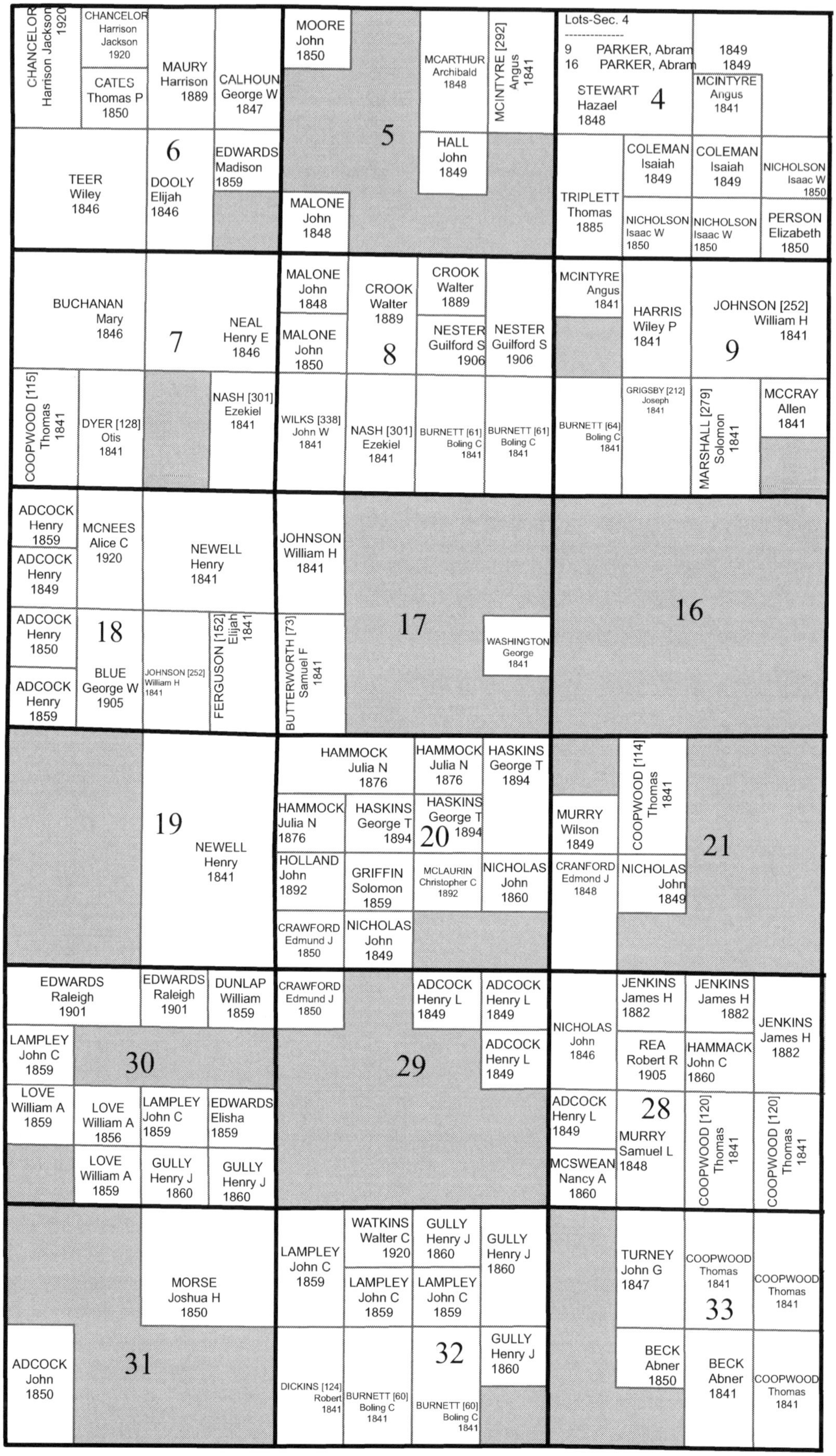

6
CHANCELOR Harrison Jackson 1920
CHANCELOR Harrison Jackson 1920
CATES Thomas P 1850
MAURY Harrison 1889
CALHOUN George W 1847
TEER Wiley 1846
DOOLY Elijah 1846
EDWARDS Madison 1859

5
MOORE John 1850
MCARTHUR Archibald 1848
MCINTYRE [292] Angus 1841
HALL John 1849
MALONE John 1848

4
Lots-Sec. 4
9 PARKER, Abram 1849
16 PARKER, Abram 1849
STEWART Hazael 1848
MCINTYRE Angus 1841
TRIPLETT Thomas 1885
COLEMAN Isaiah 1849
COLEMAN Isaiah 1849
NICHOLSON Isaac W 1850
NICHOLSON Isaac W 1850
NICHOLSON Isaac W 1850
PERSON Elizabeth 1850

7
BUCHANAN Mary 1846
NEAL Henry E 1846
COOPWOOD [115] Thomas 1841
DYER [128] Otis 1841
NASH [301] Ezekiel 1841

8
MALONE John 1848
CROOK Walter 1889
CROOK Walter 1889
MALONE John 1850
NESTER Guilford S 1906
NESTER Guilford S 1906
WILKS [338] John W 1841
NASH [301] Ezekiel 1841
BURNETT [61] Boling C 1841
BURNETT [61] Boling C 1841

9
MCINTYRE Angus 1841
HARRIS Wiley P 1841
JOHNSON [252] William H 1841
GRIGSBY [212] Joseph 1841
BURNETT [64] Boling C 1841
MARSHALL [279] Solomon 1841
MCCRAY Allen 1841

18
ADCOCK Henry 1859
ADCOCK Henry 1849
MCNEES Alice C 1920
NEWELL Henry 1841
ADCOCK Henry 1850
ADCOCK Henry 1859
BLUE George W 1905
JOHNSON [252] William H 1841
FERGUSON [152] Elijah 1841

17
JOHNSON William H 1841
BUTTERWORTH [73] Samuel F 1841
WASHINGTON George 1841

16

19
NEWELL Henry 1841

20
HAMMOCK Julia N 1876
HAMMOCK Julia N 1876
HASKINS George T 1894
HAMMOCK Julia N 1876
HASKINS George T 1894
HASKINS George T 1894
HOLLAND John 1892
GRIFFIN Solomon 1859
MCLAURIN Christopher C 1892
NICHOLAS John 1860
CRAWFORD Edmund J 1850
NICHOLAS John 1849

21
COOPWOOD [114] Thomas 1841
MURRY Wilson 1849
CRANFORD Edmond J 1848
NICHOLAS John 1849

30
EDWARDS Raleigh 1901
EDWARDS Raleigh 1901
DUNLAP William 1859
LAMPLEY John C 1859
LOVE William A 1859
LOVE William A 1856
LAMPLEY John C 1859
EDWARDS Elisha 1859
LOVE William A 1859
GULLY Henry J 1860
GULLY Henry J 1860

29
CRAWFORD Edmund J 1850
ADCOCK Henry L 1849
ADCOCK Henry L 1849
ADCOCK Henry L 1849

28
NICHOLAS John 1846
JENKINS James H 1882
JENKINS James H 1882
JENKINS James H 1882
REA Robert R 1905
HAMMACK John C 1860
ADCOCK Henry L 1849
MURRY Samuel L 1848
MCSWEAN Nancy A 1860
COOPWOOD [120] Thomas 1841
COOPWOOD [120] Thomas 1841

31
MORSE Joshua H 1850
ADCOCK John 1850

32
LAMPLEY John C 1859
WATKINS Walter C 1920
GULLY Henry J 1860
GULLY Henry J 1860
LAMPLEY John C 1859
LAMPLEY John C 1859
GULLY Henry J 1860
DICKINS [124] Robert 1841
BURNETT [60] Boling C 1841
BURNETT [60] Boling C 1841

33
TURNEY John G 1847
COOPWOOD Thomas 1841
COOPWOOD Thomas 1841
BECK Abner 1850
BECK Abner 1841
COOPWOOD Thomas 1841

MAURY Abraham 1890
MAURY Zack 1890
MAURY Zack 1890
NICHOLSON Elizabeth 1890
COLEMAN Dave 1885
COLEMAN Allen 1889
COLEMAN Allen 1889
COLEMAN Dave 1885
3
MAURY Dan 1890
MAURY George 1885
COLEMAN George 1883

FOWLER Samuel 1841
2
FOWLER Samuel 1841
PERSON Wiley C 1848

CLEARMAN Will 1901
TATE Margarett M 1905
1
MISSISSIPPI State Of 1909
NICHOLAS Charles 1882
PERSON Wiley C 1850
KELLEY George S 1911

MCCRAY Allen 1841
JOHNSON William H 1841
NICHOLSON Phillip 1890
COLEMAN Isaiah 1849
COLEMAN Isaiah 1850
10
NICHOLSON Phillip 1890
NICHOLSON Phillip 1890
BUTTERWORTH [72] Samuel F 1841

BUTTERWORTH [72] Samuel F 1841
GRADY William 1910
WALKER Lawrence W 1841
WALKER Lawrence W 1841
FOWLER Samuel 1841
11
WALKER Lawrence W 1841
WALKER Lawrence W 1841
FOWLER Samuel 1841

GIFFORD [164] Alden 1841
GIFFORD [164] Alden 1841
GIFFORD [164] Alden 1841
12
PERSON Elizabeth 1850
GIFFORD [164] Alden 1841

MCCRORY Allen 1848
OVERSTREET Mary J 1904
15
OVERSTREET Mary J 1904
BURNETT [66] Boling C 1841
BURNETT [66] Boling C 1841

GIFFORD [164] Alden 1841
GIFFORD [164] Alden 1841
GIFFORD [164] Alden 1841
GIFFORD [164] Alden 1841
14
GIFFORD [164] Alden 1841
GIFFORD [164] Alden 1841

GIFFORD [164] Alden 1841
GIFFORD [164] Alden 1841
13
GIFFORD [164] Alden 1841
GIFFORD [164] Alden 1841
COOPWOOD [118] Thomas 1841
COOPWOOD [118] Thomas 1841
GIFFORD [164] Alden 1841

NICHOLSON Isaac W 1860
PERMENTER Needham 1850
STENNIS Deb 1904
JENKINS Mary 1860
BETHANY Thomas N 1841
BETHANY William W 1860
STENNIS John 1904
COOPWOOD [114] Thomas 1841
COOPWOOD [114] Thomas 1841
22
COOPWOOD [114] Thomas 1841
COOPWOOD [114] Thomas 1841

LENTON Floyd 1906
GIFFORD [164] Alden 1841
GIFFORD [164] Alden 1841
23
DICKENS Robert 1841
MISSISSIPPI State Of 1909
MADISON William A 1906

GIFFORD [164] Alden 1841
GIFFORD [164] Alden 1841
24
COLGLAZER [98] John 1841
MATHEWS John 1841
COOPWOOD [104] Thomas 1841
COLGLAZER [98] John 1841
MATHEWS John 1841
MATHEWS John 1841

STEWART Isaiah 1841
27
COOPWOOD [120] Thomas 1841
COOPWOOD [120] Thomas 1841

BETHANY Thomas N 1848
BETHANY John H 1860
BETHANY Thomas N 1860
BETHANY Thomas N 1848
LACY Joseph H 1848
26
BETHANY Hilliard T 1906
BETHANY John H 1860
LACY Joseph H 1848
MURRY William H 1848
BETHANY William D 1913
BETHANY Hilliard T 1906
POLLARD John 1924

SELLERS Alfred 1860
SELLERS Alfred 1860
SELLERS Alfred 1860
FELTON Patrick 1849
SHIKLE Hiram 1848
25
LEWIS William M 1848
FELTON Patrick 1848
SULLINS Alfred 1848
FELTON Patrick 1848

NICHOLAS John 1860
CHANEY Charles P 1859
WALL Robert 1860
BENNETT [36] Louvenia 1913
WALL Robert 1860
CHANEY Charles P 1854
REA Ben 1891
DEWEESE Fenton B 1859
CORNATHORN Manervia 1906
34
REA Ben 1891
TABER Carroll 1850
WALL James D 1860
KILLIN William 1841
MADISON [277] James A 1902

35
MARSHALL Joseph A 1841
MARSHALL Joseph A 1841

SELLERS Alfred 1860
HALLFORD Julius P 1904
ELLIOTT [143] James 1841
ELLIOTT [143] James 1841
HALLFORD Julius P 1904
36
MCDONALD Elizabeth 1881
MARS Robert A 1860
BOYKIN Redmon 1897

Helpful Hints

1. This Map's INDEX can be found on the preceding pages.
2. Refer to Map "C" to see where this Township lies within Kemper County, Mississippi.
3. Numbers within square brackets [ ] denote a multi-patentee land parcel (multi-owner). Refer to Appendix "C" for a full list of members in this group.
4. Areas that look to be crowded with Patentees usually indicate multiple sales of the same parcel (Re-issues) or Overlapping parcels. See this Township's Index for an explanation of these and other circumstances that might explain "odd" groupings of Patentees on this map.

Legend

(thin line)	Patent Boundary
(thick line)	Section Boundary
(shaded)	No Patents Found (or Outside County)
1., 2., 3., ...	Lot Numbers (when beside a name)
[ ]	Group Number (see Appendix "C")

Scale: Section = 1 mile X 1 mile (generally, with some exceptions)

Road Map

T12-N R16-E
Choctaw Meridian

Map Group 3

Cities & Towns

None

Cemeteries

Spring Hill Cemetery
Van Devender Cemetery

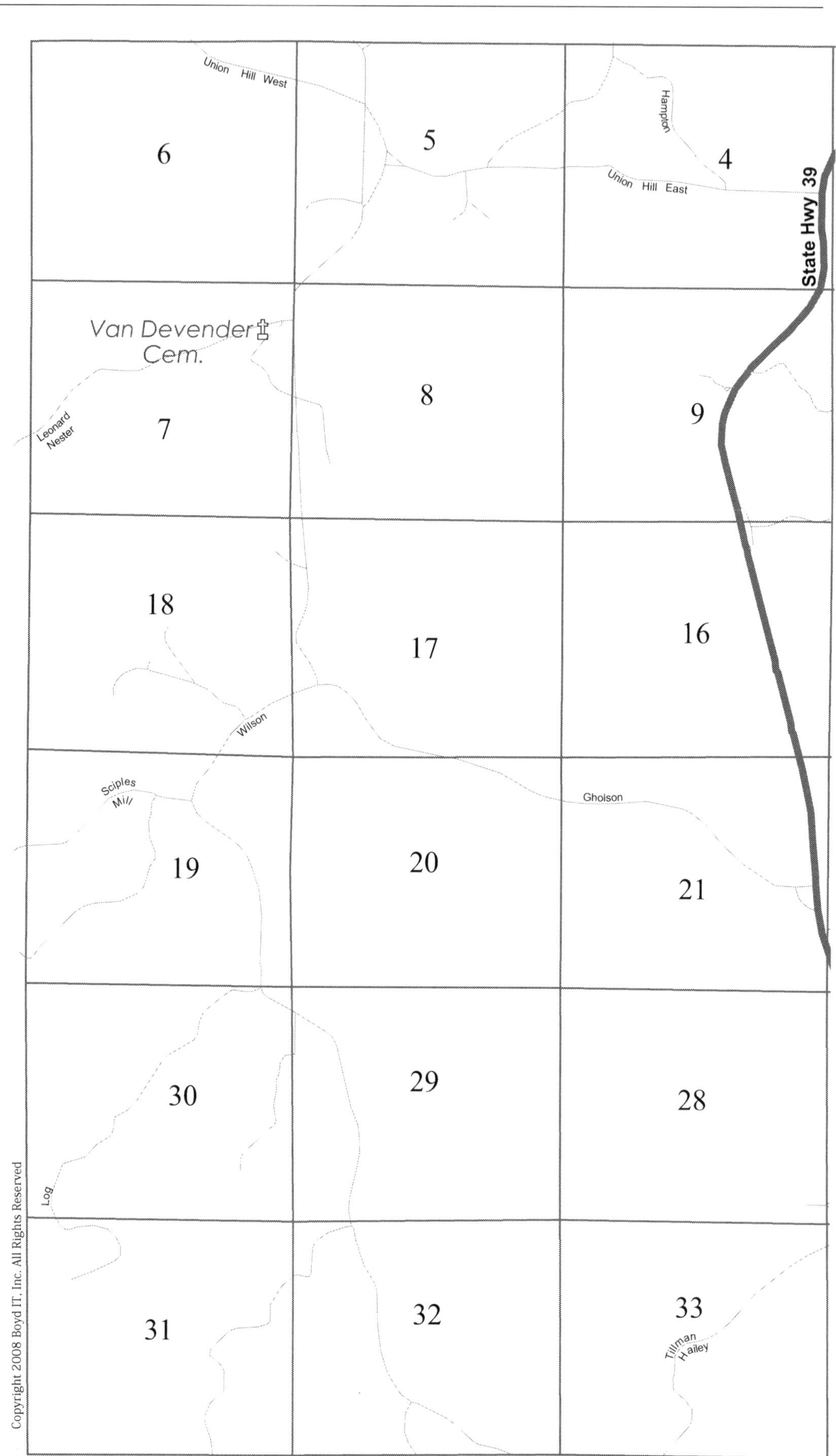

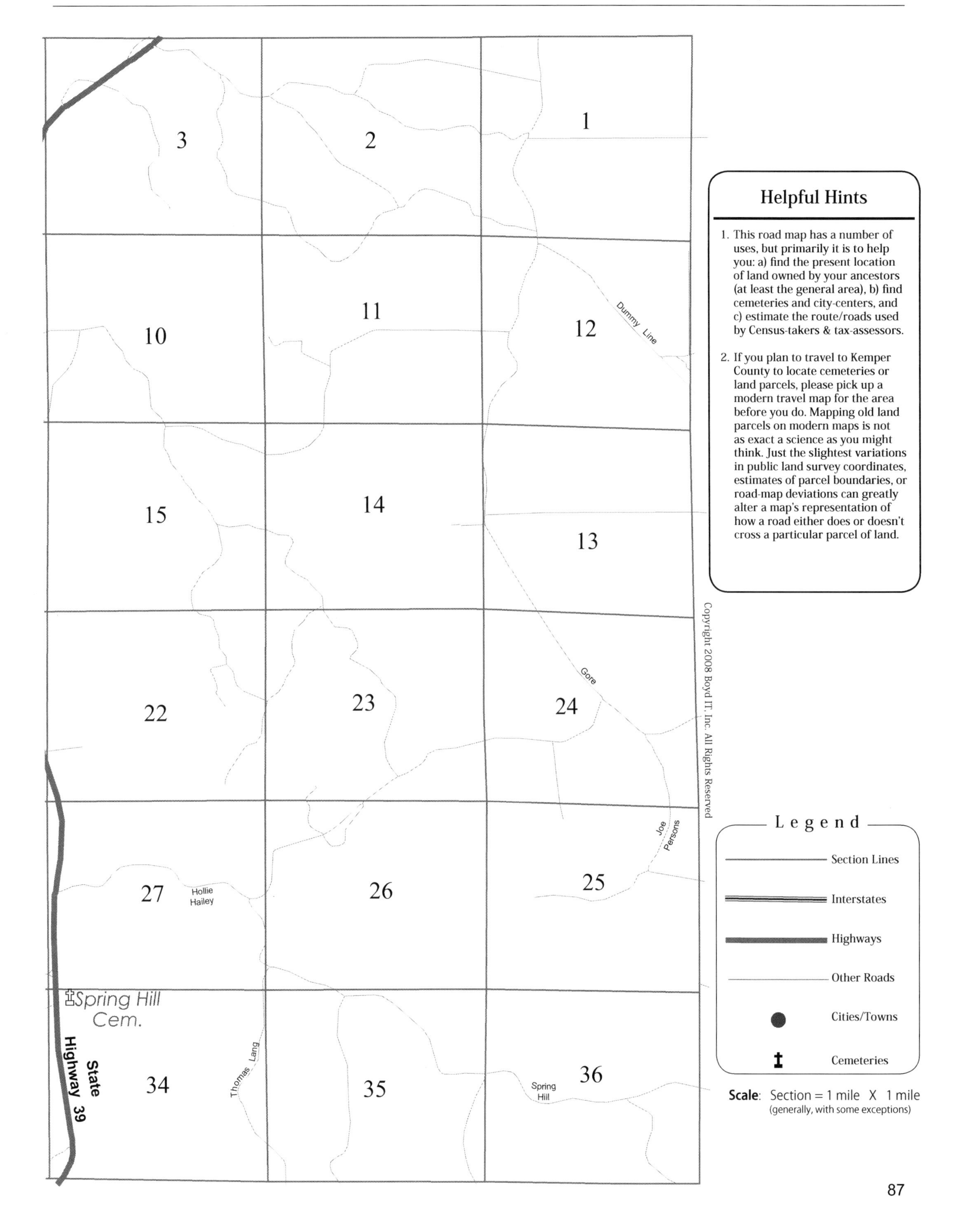

Helpful Hints

1. This road map has a number of uses, but primarily it is to help you: a) find the present location of land owned by your ancestors (at least the general area), b) find cemeteries and city-centers, and c) estimate the route/roads used by Census-takers & tax-assessors.

2. If you plan to travel to Kemper County to locate cemeteries or land parcels, please pick up a modern travel map for the area before you do. Mapping old land parcels on modern maps is not as exact a science as you might think. Just the slightest variations in public land survey coordinates, estimates of parcel boundaries, or road-map deviations can greatly alter a map's representation of how a road either does or doesn't cross a particular parcel of land.

Scale: Section = 1 mile X 1 mile (generally, with some exceptions)

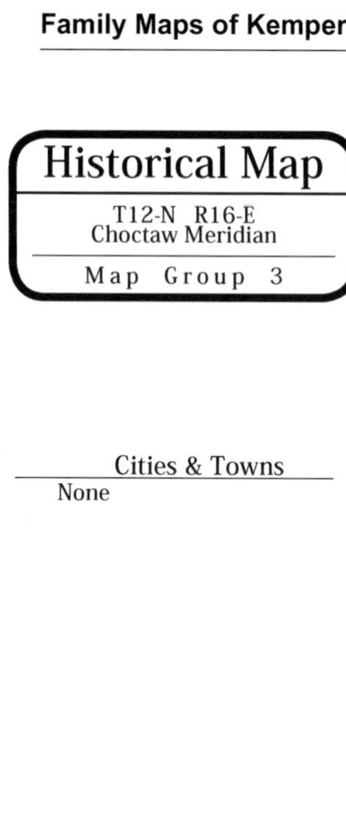

Cities & Towns

None

Cemeteries

Spring Hill Cemetery
Van Devender Cemetery

6
5
4
Van Devender Cem.
7
8
9
Indian Branch
18
17
16
19
20
Straight Creek
21
30
29
28
31
32
33

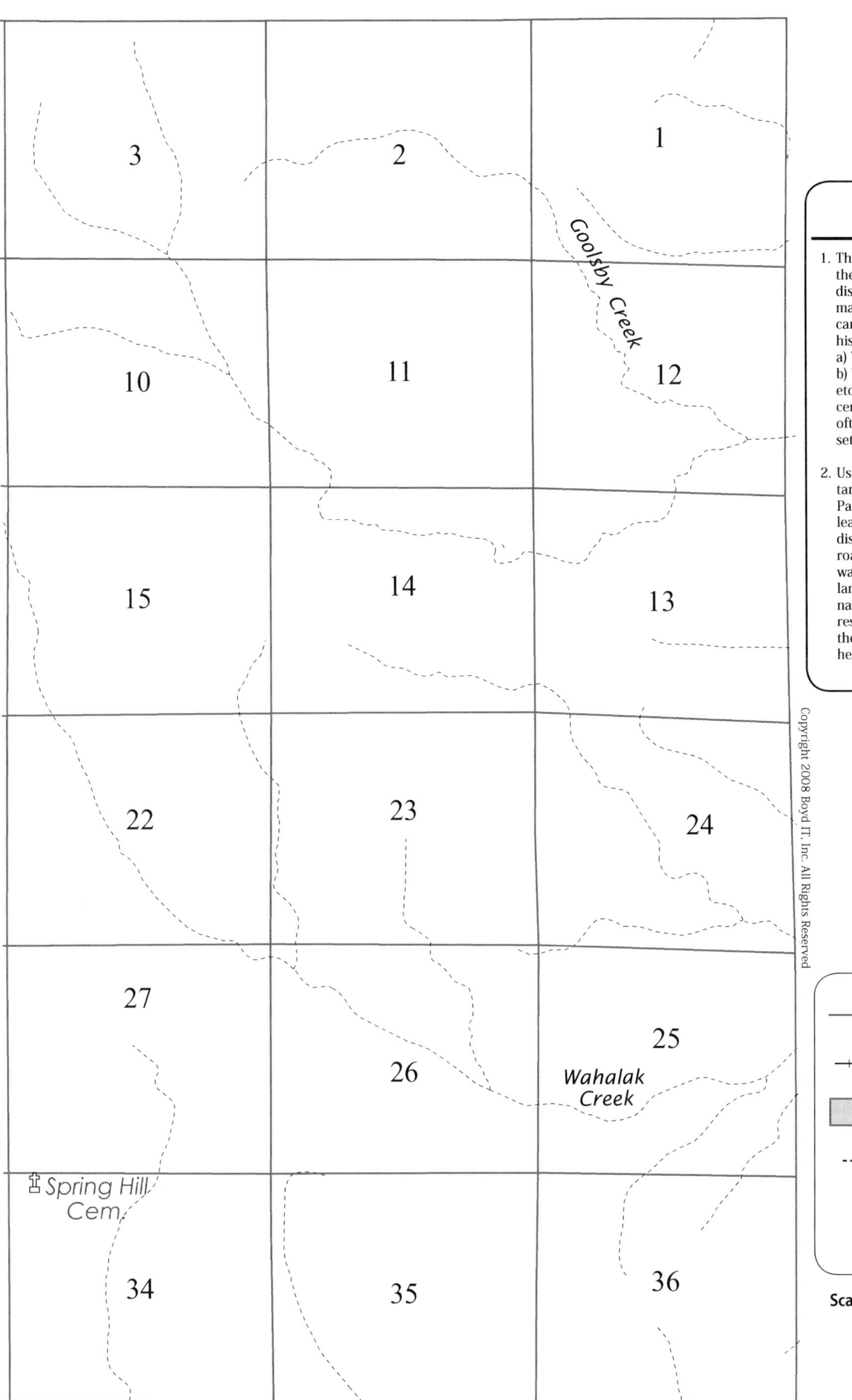

Helpful Hints

1. This Map takes a different look at the same Congressional Township displayed in the preceding two maps. It presents features that can help you better envision the historical development of the area: a) Water-bodies (lakes & ponds), b) Water-courses (rivers, streams, etc.), c) Railroads, d) City/town center-points (where they were oftentimes located when first settled), and e) Cemeteries.

2. Using this "Historical" map in tandem with this Township's Patent Map and Road Map, may lead you to some interesting discoveries. You will often find roads, towns, cemeteries, and waterways are named after nearby landowners: sometimes those names will be the ones you are researching. See how many of these research gems you can find here in Kemper County.

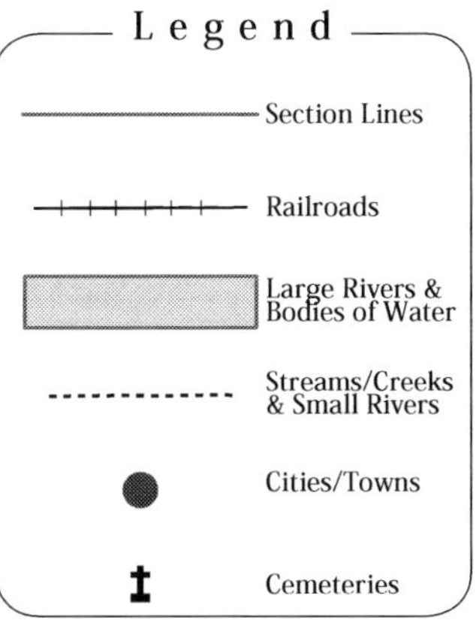

Scale: Section = 1 mile X 1 mile
(there are some exceptions)

Map Group 4: Index to Land Patents

Township 12-North Range 17-East (Choctaw)

After you locate an individual in this Index, take note of the Section and Section Part then proceed to the Land Patent map on the pages immediately following. You should have no difficulty locating the corresponding parcel of land.

The "For More Info" Column will lead you to more information about the underlying Patents. See the *Legend* at right, and the "How to Use this Book" chapter, for more information.

LEGEND

"For More Info . . . " column

A = Authority (Legislative Act, See Appendix "A")
B = Block or Lot (location in Section unknown)
C = Cancelled Patent
F = Fractional Section
G = Group (Multi-Patentee Patent, see Appendix "C")
V = Overlaps another Parcel
R = Re-Issued (Parcel patented more than once)

(A & G items require you to look in the Appendixes referred to above. All other Letter-designations followed by a number require you to locate line-items in this index that possess the ID number found after the letter).

ID	Individual in Patent	Sec.	Sec. Part	Date Issued	Other Counties	For More Info . . .
723	ADAMS, Irvin	22		1841-02-27		A1 G15 C R722
719	" "	6	N½	1841-02-27		A1
720	" "	6	SE	1841-02-27		A1
721	" "	6	W½SW	1841-02-27		A1
722	" "	22		1860-08-15		A1 G16 R723
724	ADAMS, Irvine	6	E½SW	1841-02-27		A1 G17
746	ADCOCK, John	31	W½NW	1841-02-27		A1
700	ANDERSON, Alexander	30	SW	1841-02-27		A1
737	BARNES, James	20	E½NE	1841-02-27		A1 G29
738	" "	20	W½NE	1841-02-27		A1 G29
739	" "	21	W½NW	1841-02-27		A1 G29
855	BARNES, William	15	W½SE	1841-02-27		A1
715	BASKIN, George P	29	SE	1841-02-27		A1
791	CADE, Reuben S	11	E½SW	1846-09-01		A1
793	CALVART, Robert	31	E½SE	1841-02-27		A1
794	" "	32	W½SW	1841-02-27		A1
857	CALVART, William	32	NE	1841-02-27		A1
858	" "	32	SE	1841-02-27		A1
795	CALVERT, Robert	32	NW	1841-02-27		A1
701	COLEMAN, Benjamin	23	N½E½SE	1841-02-27		A1
702	" "	24	E½SE	1841-02-27		A1
703	" "	24	E½SW	1841-02-27		A1
704	" "	24	N½W½SW	1841-02-27		A1
705	" "	24	W½SE	1841-02-27		A1
755	COLEMAN, John R	10	W½NE	1841-02-27		A1
717	DICKSON, Henry	25	E½NW	1892-04-29		A2
789	DUNCAN, Patience A	3	W½NW	1854-03-15		A1
740	EDMONDS, James N	35	W½NW	1913-05-08		A2
762	ELLIOTT, Jonathan	1	N½NW	1841-02-01		A1 G145
761	" "	4	NW	1841-02-27		A1
859	FLEMMING, William H	3	N½SW	1838-06-01		A1 G153
860	" "	3	W½SE	1838-06-01		A1 G153
861	" "	4	NE	1838-06-01		A1 G153
862	" "	4	S½	1838-06-01		A1 G153
863	" "	5		1838-06-01		A1 G153
864	" "	9	E½	1838-06-01		A1 G153
865	" "	9	E½NW	1838-06-01		A1 G153
770	GILCHRIST, Malcolm	2	E½NW	1841-02-27		A1 G166
741	GOODWIN, Jarod	31	E½NE	1892-03-17		A2
819	GRAHAM, Thomas	31	W½NE	1841-02-27		A1
718	GRAY, Henry S	19	W½NW	1890-05-20		A2
768	GRIGSBY, Joseph	10	SE	1841-02-27		A1 G210
708	HAIR, Ellen	35	E½NW	1912-02-01		A2
747	HAIR, John	35	W½NE	1914-02-10		A2
748	HALL, John	31	S½E½SW	1841-02-27		A1
749	" "	31	S½W½SE	1841-02-27		A1

ID	Individual in Patent	Sec.	Sec. Part	Date Issued	Other Counties	For More Info . . .
769	HARDIN, Kiziah E	31	E½NW	1912-06-14		A2
768	HARRIS, Robert E	10	SE	1841-02-27		A1 G210
768	HARRIS, Wiley P	10	SE	1841-02-27		A1 G210
803	HUBBARD, Samuel	20	SW	1841-02-27		A1 G233
797	" "	21	S½	1841-02-27		A1 G234
798	" "	26	SW	1841-02-27		A1 G234
799	" "	27		1841-02-27		A1 G234
800	" "	29	NE	1841-02-27		A1 G234
801	" "	33	S½	1841-02-27		A1 G234
802	" "	34	SW	1841-02-27		A1 G234
804	" "	35	E½SW	1841-02-27		A1 G233
805	" "	35	W½SE	1841-02-27		A1 G233
806	" "	36	E½SW	1841-02-27		A1 G233
807	" "	36	W½SE	1841-02-27		A1 G233
762	JENKINS, William	1	N½NW	1841-02-01		A1 G145
874	" "	1	S½NW	1841-02-01		A1 G246
866	" "	1	E½SE	1841-02-27		A1
867	" "	1	E½SW	1841-02-27		A1
868	" "	1	W½SW	1841-02-27		A1
869	" "	11	E½NE	1841-02-27		A1
870	" "	11	E½SE	1841-02-27		A1
871	" "	13	W½NW	1841-02-27		A1
872	" "	2	NESE	1841-02-27		A1
873	" "	2	W½SW	1841-02-27		A1
854	JENKINS, William B	11	W½SE	1846-09-01		A1
750	JOHNSON, John	32	E½SW	1841-02-27		A1
859	JUDSON, Charles	3	N½SW	1838-06-01		A1 G153
860	" "	3	W½SE	1838-06-01		A1 G153
861	" "	4	NE	1838-06-01		A1 G153
862	" "	4	S½	1838-06-01		A1 G153
863	" "	5		1838-06-01		A1 G153
864	" "	9	E½	1838-06-01		A1 G153
865	" "	9	E½NW	1838-06-01		A1 G153
714	KNAPP, Frederick	15	SW	1844-06-05		A1 G260
771	LEWIS, Moses	12	E½NE	1841-02-27		A1
772	" "	12	E½NW	1841-02-27		A1
773	" "	12	E½SW	1841-02-27		A1
774	" "	12	W½NE	1841-02-27		A1
775	" "	12	W½NW	1841-02-27		A1
776	" "	12	W½SW	1841-02-27		A1
777	" "	13	E½SW	1841-02-27		A1
778	" "	13	W½NE	1841-02-27		A1
779	" "	13	W½SE	1841-02-27		A1
780	" "	15	E½NE	1841-02-27		A1
781	" "	15	W½NE	1841-02-27		A1
737	" "	20	E½NE	1841-02-27		A1 G29
738	" "	20	W½NE	1841-02-27		A1 G29
739	" "	21	W½NW	1841-02-27		A1 G29
782	" "	24	E½NW	1841-02-27		A1
783	" "	24	W½NE	1841-02-27		A1
784	" "	24	W½NW	1841-02-27		A1
785	" "	30	E½NE	1841-02-27		A1
786	" "	30	E½NW	1841-02-27		A1
787	" "	30	W½NE	1841-02-27		A1
788	" "	30	W½NW	1841-02-27		A1
803	LEWIS, Rufus G	20	SW	1841-02-27		A1 G233
797	" "	21	S½	1841-02-27		A1 G234
798	" "	26	SW	1841-02-27		A1 G234
799	" "	27		1841-02-27		A1 G234
800	" "	29	NE	1841-02-27		A1 G234
801	" "	33	S½	1841-02-27		A1 G234
802	" "	34	SW	1841-02-27		A1 G234
804	" "	35	E½SW	1841-02-27		A1 G233
805	" "	35	W½SE	1841-02-27		A1 G233
806	" "	36	E½SW	1841-02-27		A1 G233
807	" "	36	W½SE	1841-02-27		A1 G233
875	LEWIS, William M	20	SE	1841-02-27		A1
803	" "	20	SW	1841-02-27		A1 G233
804	" "	35	E½SW	1841-02-27		A1 G233
805	" "	35	W½SE	1841-02-27		A1 G233
806	" "	36	E½SW	1841-02-27		A1 G233
807	" "	36	W½SE	1841-02-27		A1 G233
808	LILES, Samuel	13	E½NE	1841-02-27		A1 G270

ID	Individual in Patent	Sec.	Sec. Part	Date Issued	Other Counties	For More Info . . .
752	LOFTIN, John	14	N½W½SE	1841-02-27		A1
753	" "	14	S½E½NE	1841-02-27		A1
754	" "	14	W½NE	1841-02-27		A1
751	" "	14	E½SE	1844-06-05		A1
874	MASSEY, David	1	S½NW	1841-02-01		A1 G246
706	MCALISTER, Collin	2	NE	1841-02-01		A1
770	MCALLISTER, Collin	2	E½NW	1841-02-27		A1 G166
709	MINNIECE, Emma	23	SESE	1915-06-25		A2 G295
816	MISSISSIPPI, State Of	23	SW	1909-05-14		A3
745	MURRAY, Jesse W	19	E½NW	1892-03-23		A2
725	NICHOLSON, Isaac	15	E½SE	1841-02-27		A1
726	NICHOLSON, Isaac W	11	E½NW	1841-02-27		A1
727	" "	11	W½NE	1841-02-27		A1
728	" "	14	NENE	1841-02-27		A1
729	" "	14	NW	1841-02-27		A1
730	" "	14	S½W½SE	1841-02-27		A1
731	" "	14	SW	1841-02-27		A1
734	" "	19	S½	1841-02-27		A1 G304
735	" "	19	W½NE	1841-02-27		A1 G304
732	" "	23	N½	1841-02-27		A1
733	" "	23	W½SE	1841-02-27		A1
736	" "	29	NW	1841-02-27		A1 G304
723	PEARL, Sylvester	22		1841-02-27		A1 G15 C R722
724	" "	6	E½SW	1841-02-27		A1 G17
852	PERSON, Wiley C	10	W½	1841-02-27		A1
853	" "	15	NW	1841-02-27		A1
817	ROBERTS, Thomas G	21	E½NW	1841-02-27		A1
818	" "	21	NE	1841-02-27		A1
709	RORY, Emma Minniece	23	SESE	1915-06-25		A2 G295
809	ROWE, Shadrach	25	N½NE	1841-02-27		A1
734	ROWE, Shadrack	19	S½	1841-02-27		A1 G304
735	" "	19	W½NE	1841-02-27		A1 G304
810	" "	25	S½E½NE	1841-02-27		A1
811	" "	25	W½SE	1841-02-27		A1
736	" "	29	NW	1841-02-27		A1 G304
812	" "	36	E½NW	1841-02-27		A1
813	" "	36	W½NE	1841-02-27		A1
756	RUPERT, John	12	E½SE	1841-02-27		A1
808	" "	13	E½NE	1841-02-27		A1 G270
758	" "	13	E½NW	1841-02-27		A1
759	" "	13	E½SE	1841-02-27		A1
760	" "	24	E½NE	1841-02-27		A1
757	" "	12	W½SE	1845-01-21		A1
742	SANDERS, Jeremiah	25	E½SE	1841-02-27		A1
743	" "	25	SWNE	1841-02-27		A1
710	SCOTT, Francis T	35	E½NE	1841-02-27		A1
711	" "	35	E½SE	1841-02-27		A1
712	" "	36	W½NW	1841-02-27		A1
713	" "	36	W½SW	1841-02-27		A1
764	SCUDDAY, Joseph B	25	W½NW	1841-02-27		A1
765	" "	26	E½NE	1841-02-27		A1
766	" "	26	E½SE	1841-02-27		A1
767	" "	26	SWSE	1841-02-27		A1
763	" "	25	SW	1844-09-10		A1
707	STEDE, Elihu R	33	N½	1841-02-27		A1
792	STEEL, Richard G	28		1841-02-27		A1
696	STEELE, Abner A	34	E½SE	1841-02-27		A1
697	" "	35	W½SW	1841-02-27		A1
698	" "	36	E½NE	1841-02-27		A1
699	" "	36	E½SE	1841-02-27		A1
803	TAPPAN, John	20	SW	1841-02-27		A1 G233
797	" "	21	S½	1841-02-27		A1 G234
798	" "	26	SW	1841-02-27		A1 G234
799	" "	27		1841-02-27		A1 G234
800	" "	29	NE	1841-02-27		A1 G234
801	" "	33	S½	1841-02-27		A1 G234
802	" "	34	SW	1841-02-27		A1 G234
804	" "	35	E½SW	1841-02-27		A1 G233
805	" "	35	W½SE	1841-02-27		A1 G233
806	" "	36	E½SW	1841-02-27		A1 G233
807	" "	36	W½SE	1841-02-27		A1 G233
856	TAYLOR, William C	13	W½SW	1841-02-27		A1
716	THOMAS, Gilford	29	N½SW	1906-10-18		A1

ID	Individual in Patent	Sec.	Sec. Part	Date Issued	Other Counties	For More Info . . .
744	THOMAS, Jeremiah	31	W½SW	1841-02-27		A1
796	THOMAS, Ruth J	29	S½SW	1913-09-17		A2
714	VAUGHAN, James	15	SW	1844-06-05		A1 G260
723	WEIR, Andrew	22		1841-02-27		A1 G15 C R722
722	" "	22		1860-08-15		A1 G16 R723
723	WEIR, Robert	22		1841-02-27		A1 G15 C R722
724	" "	6	E½SW	1841-02-27		A1 G17
790	WHITE, Raleigh	2	W½NW	1841-02-27		A1
814	WHITLEY, Simon D	31	NESW	1841-02-27		A1
815	" "	31	NWSE	1841-02-27		A1
820	WILLIAMS, Thomas	10	E½NE	1841-02-27		A1
821	" "	11	W½NW	1841-02-27		A1
822	" "	11	W½SW	1841-02-27		A1
823	" "	17		1841-02-27		A1
824	" "	18	E½NE	1841-02-27		A1
825	" "	18	E½SE	1841-02-27		A1
826	" "	18	W½SE	1841-02-27		A1
827	" "	19	E½NE	1841-02-27		A1
828	" "	2	E½SW	1841-02-27		A1
829	" "	2	W½SE	1841-02-27		A1
830	" "	20	E½NW	1841-02-27		A1
831	" "	20	W½NW	1841-02-27		A1
832	" "	3	E½SE	1841-02-27		A1
833	" "	7	E½NE	1841-02-27		A1
834	" "	7	E½NW	1841-02-27		A1
835	" "	7	E½SE	1841-02-27		A1
836	" "	7	E½SW	1841-02-27		A1
837	" "	7	W½NE	1841-02-27		A1
838	" "	7	W½NW	1841-02-27		A1
839	" "	7	W½SE	1841-02-27		A1
840	" "	7	W½SW	1841-02-27		A1
841	" "	8	E½NE	1841-02-27		A1
842	" "	8	E½NW	1841-02-27		A1
843	" "	8	E½SE	1841-02-27		A1
844	" "	8	E½SW	1841-02-27		A1
845	" "	8	W½NE	1841-02-27		A1
846	" "	8	W½NW	1841-02-27		A1
847	" "	8	W½SE	1841-02-27		A1
848	" "	8	W½SW	1841-02-27		A1
849	" "	9	E½SW	1841-02-27		A1
850	" "	9	W½NW	1841-02-27		A1
851	" "	9	W½SW	1841-02-27		A1

Patent Map

T12-N R17-E
Choctaw Meridian

Map Group 4

Township Statistics

Parcels Mapped	:	180
Number of Patents	:	160
Number of Individuals	:	72
Patentees Identified	:	66
Number of Surnames	:	58
Multi-Patentee Parcels	:	34
Oldest Patent Date	:	6/1/1838
Most Recent Patent	:	6/25/1915
Block/Lot Parcels	:	0
Parcels Re - Issued	:	1
Parcels that Overlap	:	0
Cities and Towns	:	1
Cemeteries	:	4

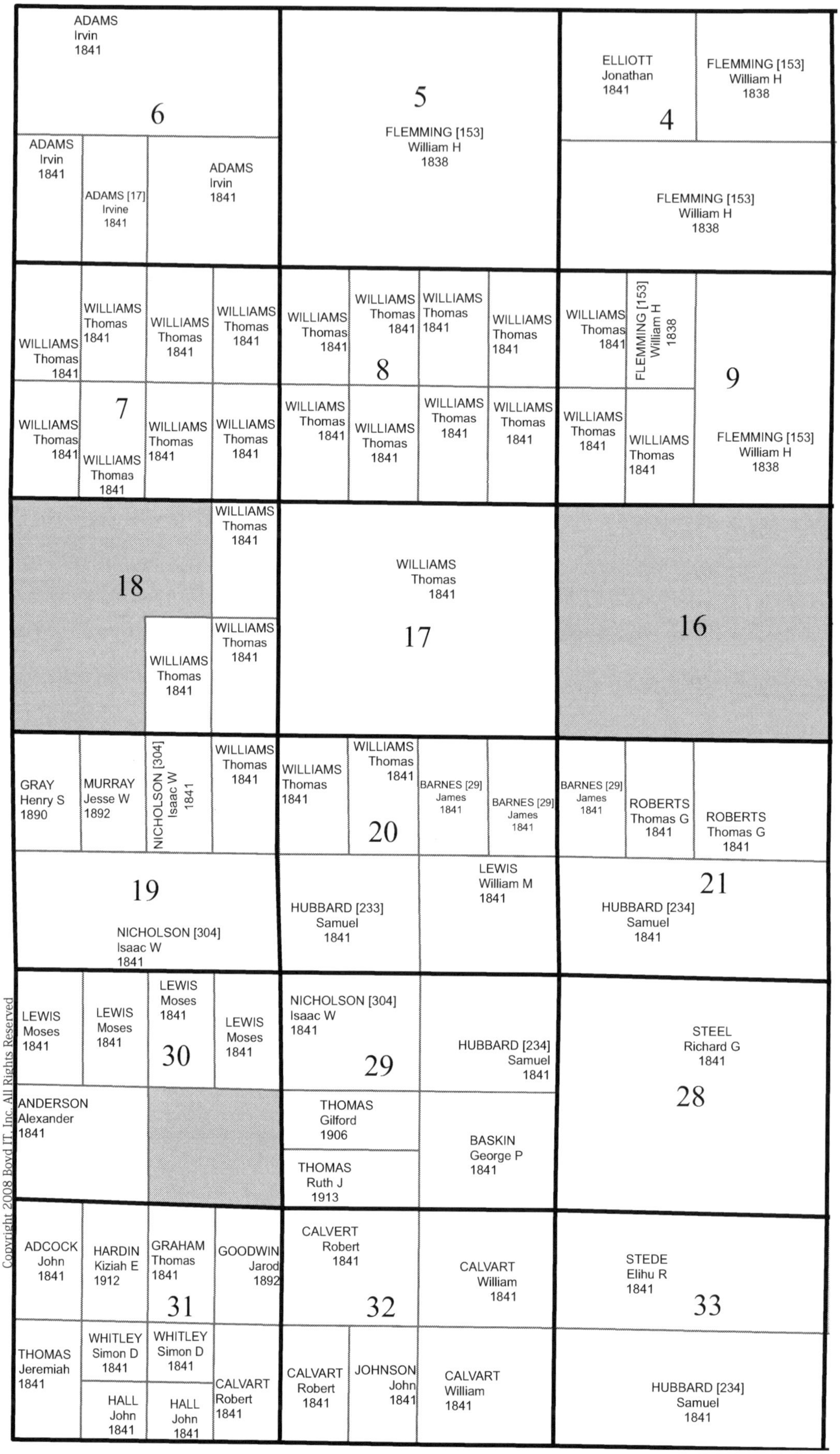

6
ADAMS Irvin 1841
ADAMS Irvin 1841
ADAMS [17] Irvine 1841
ADAMS Irvin 1841

5
FLEMMING [153] William H 1838

4
ELLIOTT Jonathan 1841
FLEMMING [153] William H 1838
FLEMMING [153] William H 1838

7
WILLIAMS Thomas 1841
WILLIAMS Thomas 1841
WILLIAMS Thomas 1841
WILLIAMS Thomas 1841
WILLIAMS Thomas 1841
WILLIAMS Thomas 1841
WILLIAMS Thomas 1841
WILLIAMS Thomas 1841

8
WILLIAMS Thomas 1841
WILLIAMS Thomas 1841
WILLIAMS Thomas 1841
WILLIAMS Thomas 1841
WILLIAMS Thomas 1841
WILLIAMS Thomas 1841
WILLIAMS Thomas 1841
WILLIAMS Thomas 1841

9
WILLIAMS Thomas 1841
FLEMMING [153] William H 1838
WILLIAMS Thomas 1841
WILLIAMS Thomas 1841
FLEMMING [153] William H 1838

18
WILLIAMS Thomas 1841
WILLIAMS Thomas 1841
WILLIAMS Thomas 1841

17
WILLIAMS Thomas 1841

16

19
GRAY Henry S 1890
MURRAY Jesse W 1892
NICHOLSON [304] Isaac W 1841
WILLIAMS Thomas 1841
NICHOLSON [304] Isaac W 1841

20
WILLIAMS Thomas 1841
WILLIAMS Thomas 1841
BARNES [29] James 1841
BARNES [29] James 1841
HUBBARD [233] Samuel 1841
LEWIS William M 1841

21
BARNES [29] James 1841
ROBERTS Thomas G 1841
ROBERTS Thomas G 1841
HUBBARD [234] Samuel 1841

30
LEWIS Moses 1841
LEWIS Moses 1841
LEWIS Moses 1841
LEWIS Moses 1841
ANDERSON Alexander 1841

29
NICHOLSON [304] Isaac W 1841
HUBBARD [234] Samuel 1841
THOMAS Gilford 1906
THOMAS Ruth J 1913
BASKIN George P 1841

28
STEEL Richard G 1841

31
ADCOCK John 1841
HARDIN Kiziah E 1912
GRAHAM Thomas 1841
GOODWIN Jarod 1892
THOMAS Jeremiah 1841
WHITLEY Simon D 1841
WHITLEY Simon D 1841
HALL John 1841
HALL John 1841
CALVART Robert 1841

32
CALVERT Robert 1841
CALVART William 1841
CALVART Robert 1841
JOHNSON John 1841
CALVART William 1841

33
STEDE Elihu R 1841
HUBBARD [234] Samuel 1841

3
DUNCAN Patience A 1854
FLEMMING [153] William H 1838
FLEMMING [153] William H 1838
WILLIAMS Thomas 1841

2
WHITE Raleigh 1841
GILCHRIST [166] Malcolm 1841
MCALISTER Collin 1841
JENKINS William 1841
WILLIAMS Thomas 1841
JENKINS William 1841
WILLIAMS Thomas 1841

1
ELLIOTT [145] Jonathan 1841
JENKINS [246] William 1841
JENKINS William 1841
JENKINS William 1841
JENKINS William 1841

10
COLEMAN John R 1841
WILLIAMS Thomas 1841
PERSON Wiley C 1841
GRIGSBY [210] Joseph 1841

11
WILLIAMS Thomas 1841
NICHOLSON Isaac W 1841
NICHOLSON Isaac W 1841
JENKINS William 1841
WILLIAMS Thomas 1841
CADE Reuben S 1846
JENKINS William B 1846
JENKINS William 1841

12
LEWIS Moses 1841
LEWIS Moses 1841
LEWIS Moses 1841
LEWIS Moses 1841
LEWIS Moses 1841
LEWIS Moses 1841
RUPERT John 1845
RUPERT John 1841

15
PERSON Wiley C 1841
LEWIS Moses 1841
LEWIS Moses 1841
KNAPP [260] Frederick 1844
BARNES William 1841
NICHOLSON Isaac 1841

14
NICHOLSON Isaac W 1841
LOFTIN John 1841
NICHOLSON Isaac W 1841
LOFTIN John 1841
NICHOLSON Isaac W 1841
LOFTIN John 1841
NICHOLSON Isaac W 1841
LOFTIN John 1844

13
JENKINS William 1841
RUPERT John 1841
LEWIS Moses 1841
LILES [270] Samuel 1841
TAYLOR William C 1841
LEWIS Moses 1841
LEWIS Moses 1841
RUPERT John 1841

22
ADAMS [15] Irvin 1841
ADAMS [16] Irvin 1860

23
NICHOLSON Isaac W 1841
MISSISSIPPI State Of 1909
NICHOLSON Isaac W 1841
COLEMAN Benjamin 1841
MINNIECE [295] Emma 1915

24
LEWIS Moses 1841
LEWIS Moses 1841
LEWIS Moses 1841
RUPERT John 1841
COLEMAN Benjamin 1841
COLEMAN Benjamin 1841
COLEMAN Benjamin 1841
COLEMAN Benjamin 1841

27
HUBBARD [234] Samuel 1841

26
SCUDDAY Joseph B 1841
HUBBARD [234] Samuel 1841
SCUDDAY Joseph B 1841
SCUDDAY Joseph B 1841

25
SCUDDAY Joseph B 1841
DICKSON Henry 1892
ROWE Shadrach 1841
SANDERS Jeremiah 1841
ROWE Shadrack 1841
SCUDDAY Joseph B 1844
ROWE Shadrack 1841
SANDERS Jeremiah 1841

34
HUBBARD [234] Samuel 1841
STEELE Abner A 1841

35
EDMONDS James N 1913
HAIR Ellen 1912
SCOTT Francis T 1841
HAIR John 1914
STEELE Abner A 1841
HUBBARD [233] Samuel 1841
HUBBARD [233] Samuel 1841
SCOTT Francis T 1841

36
SCOTT Francis T 1841
ROWE Shadrack 1841
ROWE Shadrack 1841
STEELE Abner A 1841
SCOTT Francis T 1841
HUBBARD [233] Samuel 1841
HUBBARD [233] Samuel 1841
STEELE Abner A 1841

Helpful Hints

1. This Map's INDEX can be found on the preceding pages.
2. Refer to Map "C" to see where this Township lies within Kemper County, Mississippi.
3. Numbers within square brackets [ ] denote a multi-patentee land parcel (multi-owner). Refer to Appendix "C" for a full list of members in this group.
4. Areas that look to be crowded with Patentees usually indicate multiple sales of the same parcel (Re-issues) or Overlapping parcels. See this Township's Index for an explanation of these and other circumstances that might explain "odd" groupings of Patentees on this map.

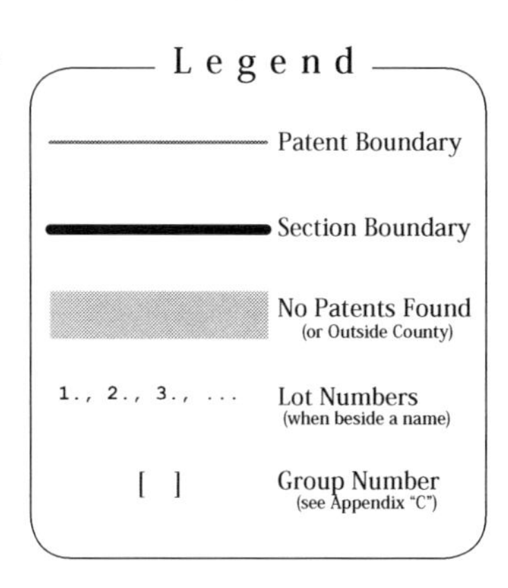

Scale: Section = 1 mile X 1 mile
(generally, with some exceptions)

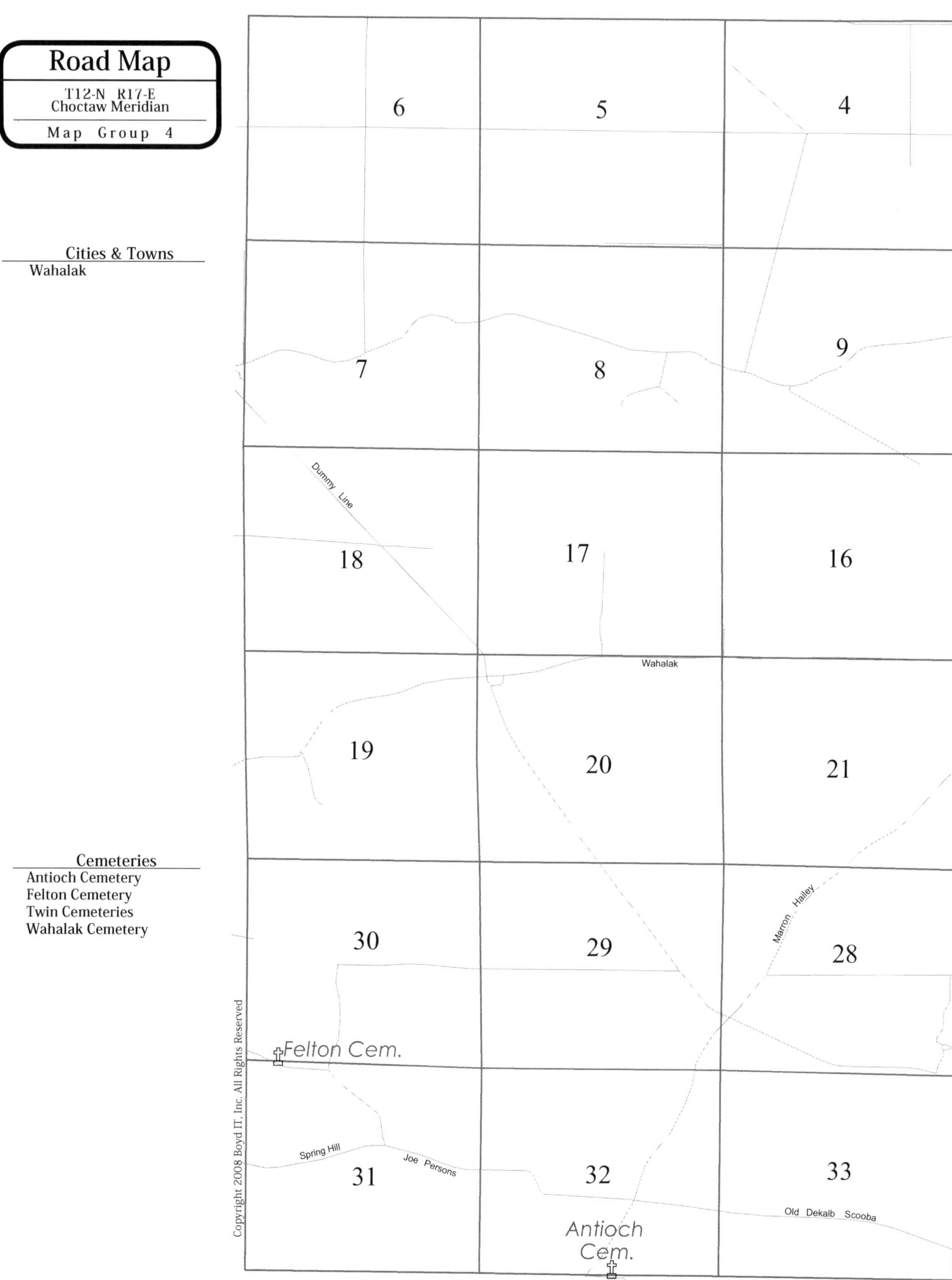
Road Map
T12-N R17-E
Choctaw Meridian
Map Group 4
Cities & Towns
Wahalak
Cemeteries
Antioch Cemetery
Felton Cemetery
Twin Cemeteries
Wahalak Cemetery
6
5
4
7
8
9
18
17
16
19
20
21
30
29
28
31
32
33
Dummy Line
Wahalak
Marron Hailey
Felton Cem.
Spring Hill
Joe Persons
Old Dekalb Scooba
Antioch Cem.

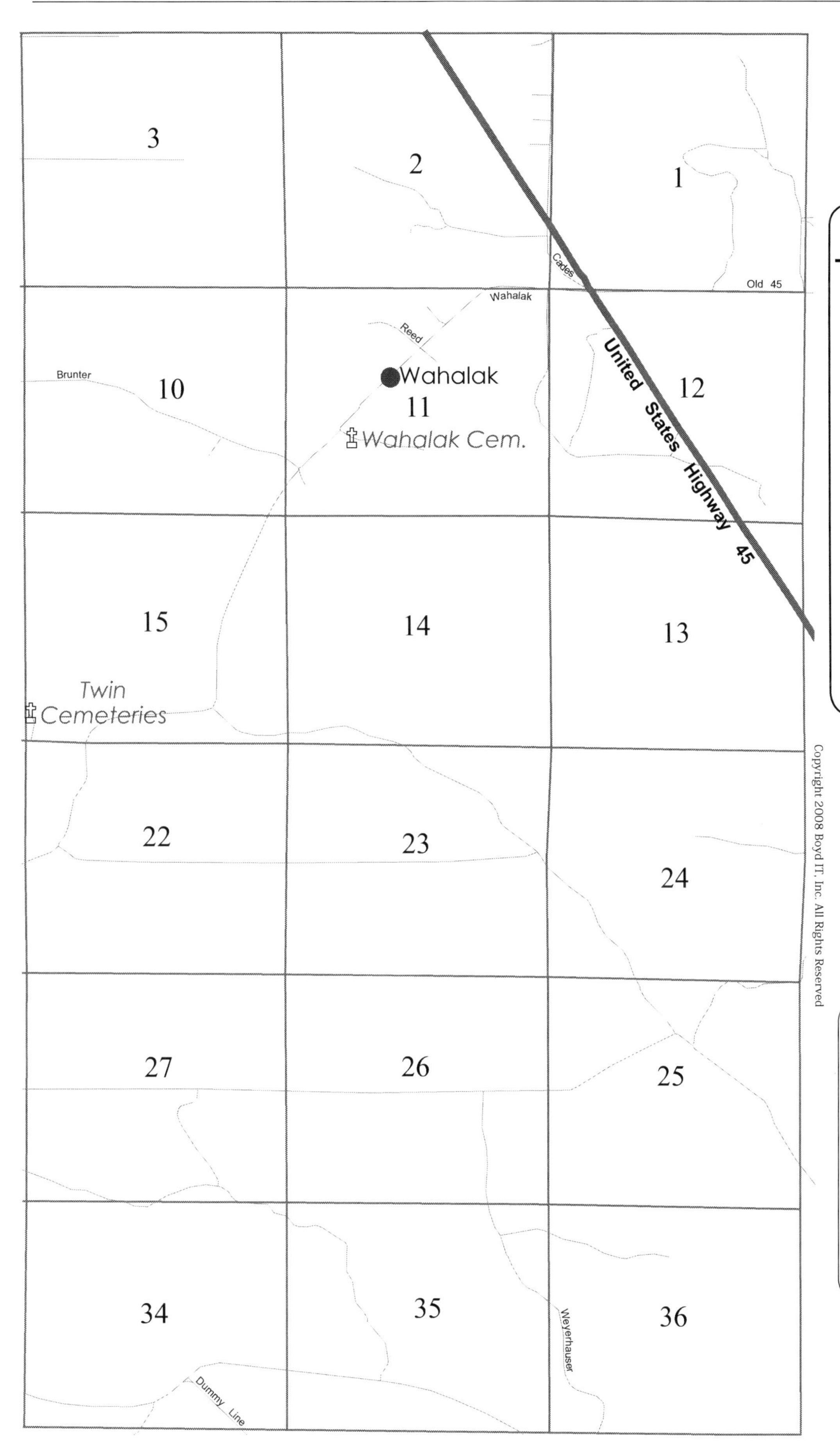

Helpful Hints

1. This road map has a number of uses, but primarily it is to help you: a) find the present location of land owned by your ancestors (at least the general area), b) find cemeteries and city-centers, and c) estimate the route/roads used by Census-takers & tax-assessors.

2. If you plan to travel to Kemper County to locate cemeteries or land parcels, please pick up a modern travel map for the area before you do. Mapping old land parcels on modern maps is not as exact a science as you might think. Just the slightest variations in public land survey coordinates, estimates of parcel boundaries, or road-map deviations can greatly alter a map's representation of how a road either does or doesn't cross a particular parcel of land.

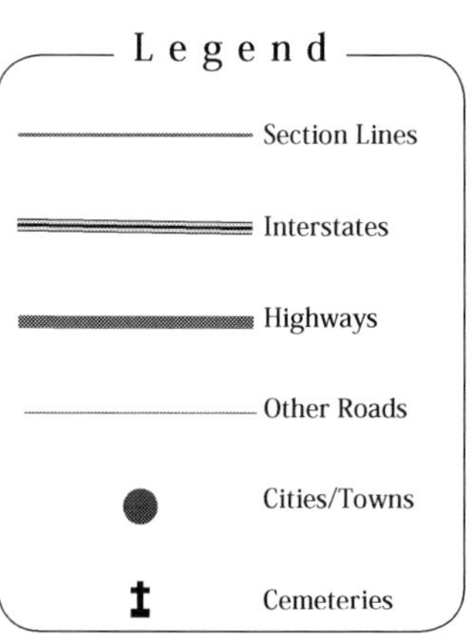

Scale: Section = 1 mile X 1 mile
(generally, with some exceptions)

Historical Map

T12-N R17-E
Choctaw Meridian

Map Group 4

Cities & Towns
Wahalak

Cemeteries
Antioch Cemetery
Felton Cemetery
Twin Cemeteries
Wahalak Cemetery

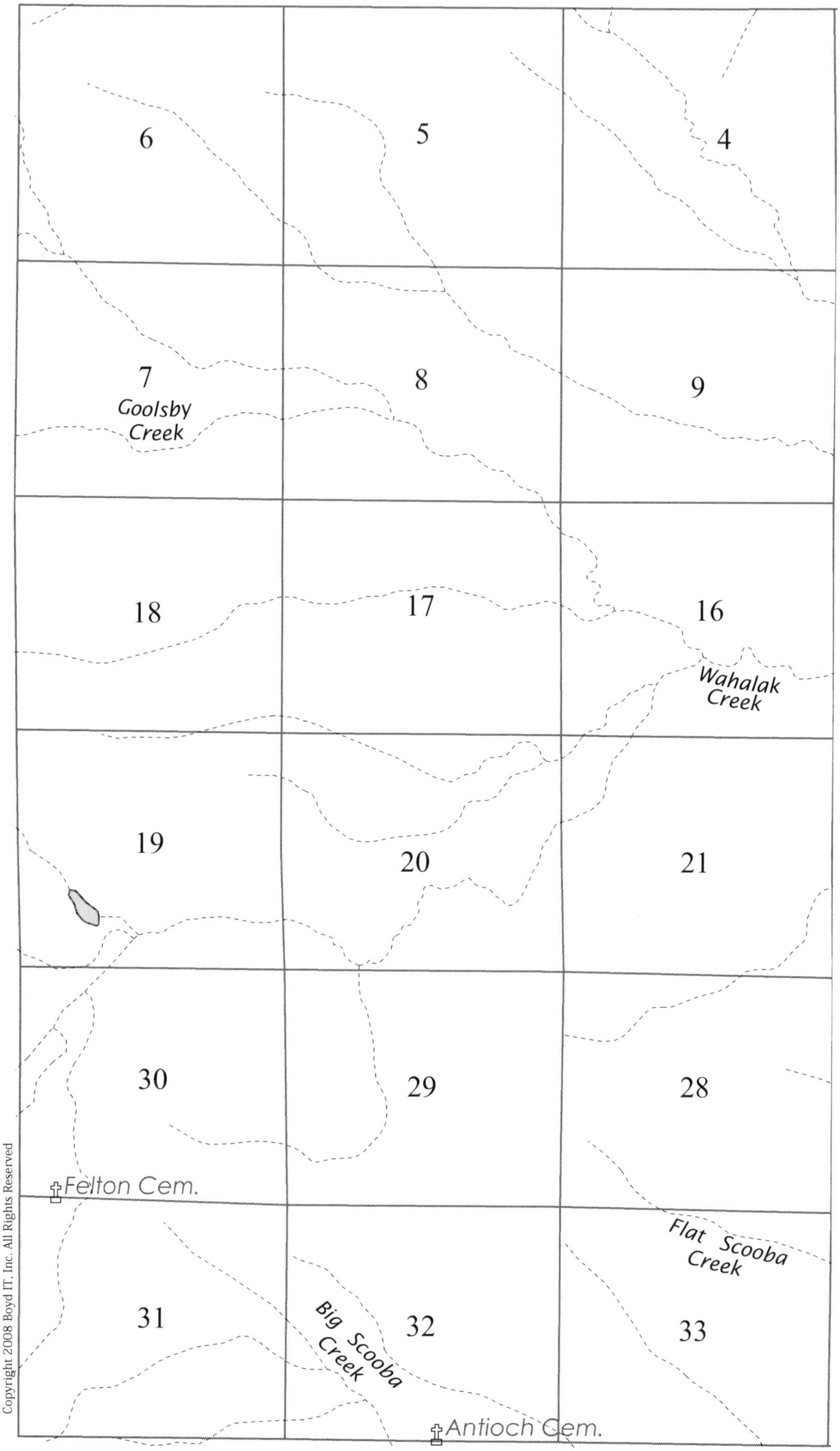

6
5
4
7
Goolsby Creek
8
9
18
17
16
Wahalak Creek
19
20
21
30
29
28
Felton Cem.
31
Big Scooba Creek
32
Flat Scooba Creek
33
Antioch Cem.

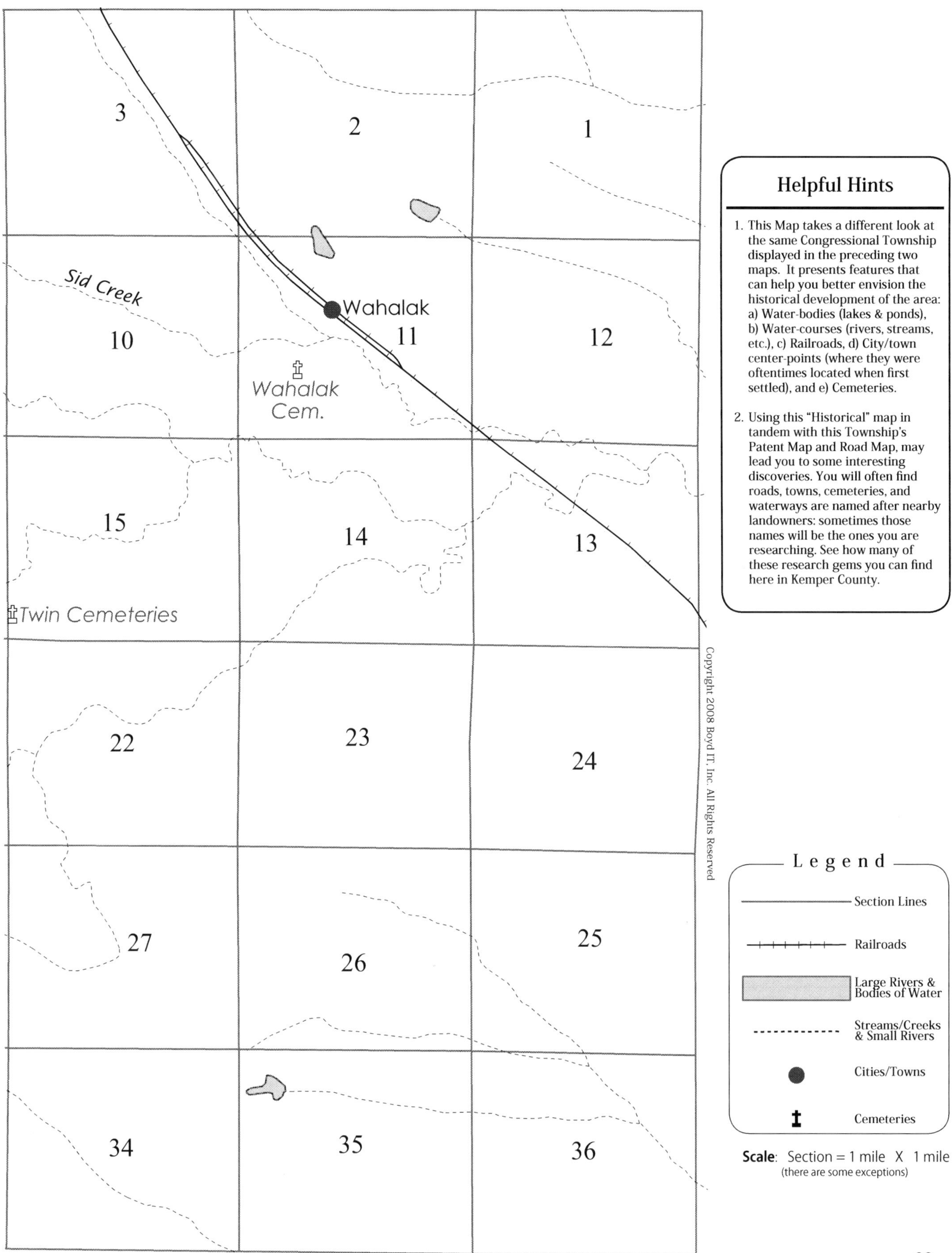
3
2
1
Sid Creek
10
Wahalak
11
12
Wahalak Cem.
15
14
13
Twin Cemeteries
22
23
24
27
26
25
34
35
36
Copyright 2008 Boyd IT, Inc. All Rights Reserved
Helpful Hints
1. This Map takes a different look at the same Congressional Township displayed in the preceding two maps. It presents features that can help you better envision the historical development of the area: a) Water-bodies (lakes & ponds), b) Water-courses (rivers, streams, etc.), c) Railroads, d) City/town center-points (where they were oftentimes located when first settled), and e) Cemeteries.
2. Using this "Historical" map in tandem with this Township's Patent Map and Road Map, may lead you to some interesting discoveries. You will often find roads, towns, cemeteries, and waterways are named after nearby landowners: sometimes those names will be the ones you are researching. See how many of these research gems you can find here in Kemper County.
Legend
Section Lines
Railroads
Large Rivers & Bodies of Water
Streams/Creeks & Small Rivers
Cities/Towns
Cemeteries
Scale: Section = 1 mile X 1 mile
(there are some exceptions)

Map Group 5: Index to Land Patents

Township 12-North Range 18-East (Choctaw)

After you locate an individual in this Index, take note of the Section and Section Part then proceed to the Land Patent map on the pages immediately following. You should have no difficulty locating the corresponding parcel of land.

The "For More Info" Column will lead you to more information about the underlying Patents. See the *Legend* at right, and the "How to Use this Book" chapter, for more information.

LEGEND

"For More Info . . . " column

A = Authority (Legislative Act, See Appendix "A")
B = Block or Lot (location in Section unknown)
C = Cancelled Patent
F = Fractional Section
G = Group (Multi-Patentee Patent, see Appendix "C")
V = Overlaps another Parcel
R = Re-Issued (Parcel patented more than once)

(A & G items require you to look in the Appendixes referred to above. All other Letter-designations followed by a number require you to locate line-items in this index that possess the ID number found after the letter).

ID	Individual in Patent	Sec.	Sec. Part	Date Issued	Other Counties	For More Info . . .
960	ADAMS, Howell C	1	SENW	1841-02-27		A1
961	" "	1	SWNE	1841-02-27		A1
962	" "	1	W½SE	1841-02-27		A1
1044	ADAMS, Robert E	13	E½NE	1841-02-27		A1
980	ALLEN, John	17	W½NE	1845-12-01		A1 G20
945	ANDERSON, Garrison	1	S½E½NE	1841-02-27		A1
1026	ANDERSON, Joshua	5	E½SE	1841-02-01		A1
1030	" "	9	E½NW	1841-02-01		A1
1027	" "	8	E½NW	1841-02-27		A1
1028	" "	8	E½SE	1841-02-27		A1
1032	" "	8	W½NE	1841-02-27		A1 G24
1029	" "	8	W½SE	1841-02-27		A1
1031	" "	9	W½NW	1841-02-27		A1
880	BENNETT, Anthony	36	E½SE	1841-02-27		A1 G35
1047	BOUGHTON, Samuel	2	NESE	1841-02-27		A1
981	BROOM, John	9	E½NE	1841-02-27		A1
1097	BROWNLEE, William R	17	W½NW	1841-02-27		A1 G56
1032	BURFOOT, Mitchell	8	W½NE	1841-02-27		A1 G24
1036	BURFORD, Mitchell	5	W½SE	1841-02-01		A1
1037	" "	8	E½NE	1841-02-01		A1
1098	BUTLER, Winfield M	23	NE	1841-02-27		A1
931	CAMPBELL, Duncan A	6	NW	0000-00-00		A1 C R932
932	" "	6	NW	1844-09-10		A1 R931
976	CAROTHERS, James N	10	SE	1841-02-01		A1
992	CARTER, John R	17	E½SE	1841-02-27		A1
934	CATES, Ephraim	1	N½W½NW	1841-02-27		A1
935	" "	1	S½E½SW	1841-02-27		A1
936	" "	12	E½NE	1841-02-27		A1
937	" "	12	E½NW	1841-02-27		A1
938	" "	2	E½NE	1841-02-27		A1
939	" "	2	W½NE	1841-02-27		A1
1025	CATES, Joseph	4	E½NW	1841-02-01		A1
885	COLEMAN, Benjamin	9	E½SW	1841-02-27		A1 G97
886	" "	9	W½SE	1841-02-27		A1 G97
883	" "	23	E½NW	1911-09-18		A1
884	" "	23	W½SW	1911-09-18		A1
966	DANIEL, Isham	32	E½NE	1841-02-27		A1
967	" "	32	E½SE	1841-02-27		A1
1086	DEW, Warren	1	NESW	1884-12-30		A2
889	DOBBS, Charles	14	W½NW	1841-02-27		A1 G125
1011	EARLE, Joseph B	19	E½SW	1841-02-27		A1 G133
1012	" "	19	W½SW	1841-02-27		A1 G133
1014	" "	26	E½NW	1841-02-27		A1 G132
1015	" "	26	E½SE	1841-02-27		A1 G132
1016	" "	26	E½SW	1841-02-27		A1 G132
1017	" "	26	W½NE	1841-02-27		A1 G132

ID	Individual in Patent	Sec.	Sec. Part	Date Issued	Other Counties	For More Info . . .
1018	EARLE, Joseph B (Cont'd)	26	W½SE	1841-02-27		A1 G132
1013	" "	26	W½SW	1841-02-27		A1 G133
1009	" "	20	E½SW	1844-09-10		A1
1020	" "	20	W½SW	1844-09-10		A1 G131
1019	" "	26	E½NE	1844-12-10		A1 G129
1008	" "	19	W½SE	1845-01-21		A1
1010	" "	20	W½NW	1845-01-21		A1
1084	ETHRIDGE, Thomas W	1	SWNW	1882-05-10		A1
959	EVERETT, Horace	31	E½SW	1854-03-15		A1
888	FELTS, Caswell	14	NE	1841-02-27		A1 G149
1048	FELTS, Samuel D	35	SE	1841-02-27		A1 G150
973	FLETCHER, James	5	W½NE	1844-09-10		A1
948	GAINES, George S	29	E½NW	1841-02-27		A1 G159
949	" "	29	E½SW	1841-02-27		A1 G159
950	" "	29	W½NW	1841-02-27		A1 G159
951	" "	29	W½SW	1841-02-27		A1 G159
952	" "	30	E½SE	1841-02-27		A1 G159
953	" "	30	W½SE	1841-02-27		A1 G159
948	GLOVER, Allen	29	E½NW	1841-02-27		A1 G159
949	" "	29	E½SW	1841-02-27		A1 G159
950	" "	29	W½NW	1841-02-27		A1 G159
951	" "	29	W½SW	1841-02-27		A1 G159
952	" "	30	E½SE	1841-02-27		A1 G159
953	" "	30	W½SE	1841-02-27		A1 G159
1056	GOODE, Sidney M	21	E½SW	1841-02-01		A1
1063	" "	22	SW	1841-02-01		A1 G168
1057	" "	21	W½SW	1841-02-27		A1
1058	" "	27	W½NW	1841-02-27		A1
1059	" "	28	E½NE	1841-02-27		A1
1060	" "	28	W½NE	1841-02-27		A1
1061	" "	32	E½NW	1841-02-27		A1
1062	" "	32	W½NE	1841-02-27		A1
1088	GOODE, William	21	SE	1841-02-27		A1
897	GREEN, Daniel	12	E½SW	1841-02-27		A1 G172
903	" "	24	E½NW	1841-02-27		A1 G174
904	" "	24	E½SE	1841-02-27		A1 G174
907	" "	24	W½NW	1841-02-27		A1 G177
905	" "	24	W½SE	1841-02-27		A1 G174
899	" "	25	E½SW	1841-02-27		A1 G171
906	" "	25	W½NE	1841-02-27		A1 G174
898	" "	35	E½NE	1841-02-27		A1 G175
896	" "	35	W½NE	1841-02-27		A1 G176
900	" "	36	E½SW	1841-02-27		A1 G178
901	" "	36	W½NE	1841-02-27		A1 G178
902	" "	36	W½SW	1841-02-27		A1 G178
893	" "	7	E½NW	1841-02-27		A1
894	" "	7	W½NE	1841-02-27		A1
895	" "	7	W½NW	1841-02-27		A1
908	GREENE, Daniel	12	W½SW	1841-02-27		A1 G187
909	" "	13	E½NW	1841-02-27		A1 G187
919	" "	13	E½SE	1841-02-27		A1 G188
910	" "	13	E½SW	1841-02-27		A1 G187
911	" "	13	W½NW	1841-02-27		A1 G187
920	" "	13	W½SE	1841-02-27		A1 G188
912	" "	17	E½NE	1841-02-27		A1 G194
924	" "	17	E½SW	1841-02-27		A1 G192
921	" "	25	E½NE	1841-02-27		A1 G189
913	" "	25	E½NW	1841-02-27		A1 G181
914	" "	25	W½NW	1841-02-27		A1 G181
915	" "	25	W½SW	1841-02-27		A1 G181
948	" "	29	E½NW	1841-02-27		A1 G159
949	" "	29	E½SW	1841-02-27		A1 G159
950	" "	29	W½NW	1841-02-27		A1 G159
951	" "	29	W½SW	1841-02-27		A1 G159
952	" "	30	E½SE	1841-02-27		A1 G159
953	" "	30	W½SE	1841-02-27		A1 G159
916	" "	36	E½NW	1841-02-27		A1 G197
917	" "	36	W½NW	1841-02-27		A1 G197
918	" "	36	W½SE	1841-02-27		A1 G197
922	" "	6	E½SE	1841-02-27		A1 G184
923	" "	6	W½SE	1841-02-27		A1 G184
925	" "	7	E½NE	1841-02-27		A1 G196
926	" "	9	W½NE	1841-02-27		A1 G195

ID	Individual in Patent	Sec.	Sec. Part	Date Issued	Other Counties	For More Info . . .
1043	GRIFFIN, Richard	11	W½NW	1841-02-27		A1 G204
957	GRIGGS, Green	26	W½NW	1841-02-27		A1 G208
958	" "	27	E½NE	1841-02-27		A1 G208
955	GRIGGS, Green B	23	W½SE	1841-02-27		A1 G207
956	" "	35	E½NW	1841-02-27		A1 G207
1048	HARRIS, Buckner	35	SE	1841-02-27		A1 G150
979	HILLHOUSE, Jesse S	17	W½SE	1841-02-27		A1 G225
983	HOLMES, John	35	W½NW	1841-02-27		A1
984	HOMES, John	34	NE	1841-02-27		A1
1049	HUBBARD, Samuel	31	E½NE	1841-02-27		A1 G234
1051	" "	31	SE	1841-02-27		A1 G233
1052	" "	32	SW	1841-02-27		A1 G233
1050	" "	32	W½NW	1841-02-27		A1 G234
1095	JENKINS, William	6	W½SW	1841-02-01		A1 G246
1092	" "	6	E½NE	1841-02-27		A1
1093	" "	6	E½SW	1841-02-27		A1
1094	" "	6	W½NE	1841-02-27		A1
957	JINCKS, William	26	W½NW	1841-02-27		A1 G208
958	" "	27	E½NE	1841-02-27		A1 G208
929	JOHNSON, David	28	SW	1841-02-27		A1 G247
974	JOHNSON, James	20	SE	1846-01-15		A1 G248
885	JOHNSON, Warren B	9	E½SW	1841-02-27		A1 G97
886	" "	9	W½SE	1841-02-27		A1 G97
1087	JONES, William F	23	E½SE	1841-02-27		A1
1083	KING, Thomas P	1	E½SE	1841-02-27		A1
1034	KYLE, Margaret	15	E½SE	1841-02-27		A1
913	LAKE, James	25	E½NW	1841-02-27		A1 G181
899	" "	25	E½SW	1841-02-27		A1 G171
914	" "	25	W½NW	1841-02-27		A1 G181
915	" "	25	W½SW	1841-02-27		A1 G181
1019	" "	26	E½NE	1844-12-10		A1 G129
1049	LEWIS, Rufus G	31	E½NE	1841-02-27		A1 G234
1051	" "	31	SE	1841-02-27		A1 G233
1052	" "	32	SW	1841-02-27		A1 G233
1050	" "	32	W½NW	1841-02-27		A1 G234
1051	LEWIS, William M	31	SE	1841-02-27		A1 G233
1052	" "	32	SW	1841-02-27		A1 G233
985	LLOYD, John	34	NW	1841-02-27		A1 G273
930	LYLE, David	14	SE	1841-02-27		A1 G276
1035	MADDEN, Martin	11	SW	1841-02-27		A1
986	MALONE, John	4	SE	1841-02-01		A1
987	" "	5	E½NW	1841-02-27		A1
988	" "	5	E½SW	1841-02-27		A1
989	" "	5	W½NW	1841-02-27		A1
990	" "	5	W½SW	1841-02-27		A1
922	" "	6	E½SE	1841-02-27		A1 G184
923	" "	6	W½SE	1841-02-27		A1 G184
991	" "	8	E½SW	1841-02-27		A1 G278
1038	MALONE, Nancy	4	SW	1841-02-27		A1
1095	MASSEY, David	6	W½SW	1841-02-01		A1 G246
975	MCCALEBB, James	2	NWSE	1841-02-27		A1
1096	MCCLURG, William	10	NE	1841-02-27		A1
1079	MCGEE, Thomas	11	E½NE	1841-02-27		A1 G289
1082	" "	11	E½NW	1841-02-27		A1 G286
1077	" "	11	E½SE	1841-02-27		A1 G288
1080	" "	11	W½NE	1841-02-27		A1 G289
1078	" "	11	W½SE	1841-02-27		A1 G288
1081	" "	12	W½NW	1841-02-27		A1 G289
1064	" "	32	W½SE	1841-02-27		A1
1065	" "	33	E½SE	1841-02-27		A1
1066	" "	33	E½SW	1841-02-27		A1
1076	" "	33	NE	1841-02-27		A1 G284
1067	" "	33	W½NW	1841-02-27		A1
1068	" "	33	W½SE	1841-02-27		A1
1069	" "	33	W½SW	1841-02-27		A1
1070	" "	34	E½SE	1841-02-27		A1
1071	" "	34	E½SW	1841-02-27		A1
985	" "	34	NW	1841-02-27		A1 G273
1072	" "	34	W½SE	1841-02-27		A1
1073	" "	34	W½SW	1841-02-27		A1
1074	" "	35	E½SW	1841-02-27		A1 G285
1075	" "	35	W½SW	1841-02-27		A1 G285
891	MCLAUGHLIN, Charles	28	E½SE	1841-02-27		A1 G294

ID	Individual in Patent	Sec.	Sec. Part	Date Issued	Other Counties	For More Info . . .
890	MCLAUGHLIN, Charles (Cont'd)	33	E½NW	1841-02-27		A1
946	MCLAUGHLIN, George	27	E½SW	1841-02-27		A1
947	" "	27	W½SW	1841-02-27		A1
964	NICHOLSON, Isaac W	22	E½NE	1841-02-27		A1
965	" "	23	W½NW	1841-02-27		A1
876	PEARCE, Aaron	14	E½NW	1841-02-27		A1
881	PETTIS, Anthony W	13	W½NE	1841-02-27		A1
897	PETTUS, Alice T	12	E½SW	1841-02-27		A1 G172
877	" "	12	SE	1841-02-27		A1
908	" "	12	W½SW	1841-02-27		A1 G187
909	" "	13	E½NW	1841-02-27		A1 G187
910	" "	13	E½SW	1841-02-27		A1 G187
911	" "	13	W½NW	1841-02-27		A1 G187
933	PIERCE, Eli	9	W½SW	1841-02-27		A1
887	POOL, Benjamin	28	NW	1841-02-27		A1 G311
878	POPE, Allen	25	E½SE	1841-02-27		A1
879	" "	25	W½SE	1841-02-27		A1
1089	POWE, William H	36	E½NE	1841-02-27		A1
882	PRUIT, Archibald	15	E½NE	1841-02-01		A1
963	QUARLES, Hubbard	4	E½NE	1841-02-01		A1
887	RILEY, Peter	28	NW	1841-02-27		A1 G311
1039	" "	29	E½NE	1841-02-27		A1 G317
919	ROGERS, John D	13	E½SE	1841-02-27		A1 G188
920	" "	13	W½SE	1841-02-27		A1 G188
903	" "	24	E½NW	1841-02-27		A1 G174
904	" "	24	E½SE	1841-02-27		A1 G174
982	" "	24	NE	1841-02-27		A1
905	" "	24	W½SE	1841-02-27		A1 G174
921	" "	25	E½NE	1841-02-27		A1 G189
906	" "	25	W½NE	1841-02-27		A1 G174
919	ROGERS, Lewin	13	E½SE	1841-02-27		A1 G188
920	" "	13	W½SE	1841-02-27		A1 G188
903	ROGERS, Lieuen	24	E½NW	1841-02-27		A1 G174
904	" "	24	E½SE	1841-02-27		A1 G174
905	" "	24	W½SE	1841-02-27		A1 G174
921	" "	25	E½NE	1841-02-27		A1 G189
906	" "	25	W½NE	1841-02-27		A1 G174
891	ROUNDTREE, Wright	28	E½SE	1841-02-27		A1 G294
1055	ROWE, Shadrach	14	SW	1841-02-27		A1
968	RUPERT, James C	18	SW	1841-02-27		A1
955	" "	23	W½SE	1841-02-27		A1 G207
1039	" "	29	E½NE	1841-02-27		A1 G317
969	" "	29	E½SE	1841-02-27		A1 G320
970	" "	29	W½NE	1841-02-27		A1 G320
971	" "	29	W½SE	1841-02-27		A1 G320
972	" "	30	E½NE	1841-02-27		A1 G319
956	" "	35	E½NW	1841-02-27		A1 G207
993	RUPERT, John	17	E½NW	1841-02-27		A1
924	" "	17	E½SW	1841-02-27		A1 G192
1097	" "	17	W½NW	1841-02-27		A1 G56
994	" "	17	W½SW	1841-02-27		A1
995	" "	19	E½SE	1841-02-27		A1
996	" "	19	NE	1841-02-27		A1
997	" "	19	NW	1841-02-27		A1
998	" "	20	E½NW	1841-02-27		A1
972	" "	30	E½NE	1841-02-27		A1 G319
999	" "	30	E½NW	1841-02-27		A1
1000	" "	30	E½SW	1841-02-27		A1
1001	" "	30	W½NE	1841-02-27		A1
1002	" "	30	W½NW	1841-02-27		A1
991	" "	8	E½SW	1841-02-27		A1 G278
1003	" "	8	W½NW	1841-02-27		A1
1004	" "	8	W½SW	1841-02-27		A1
1020	" "	20	W½SW	1844-09-10		A1 G131
977	SANDERS, Jeremiah	2	E½NW	1841-02-27		A1
978	" "	2	W½NW	1841-02-27		A1
969	" "	29	E½SE	1841-02-27		A1 G320
970	" "	29	W½NE	1841-02-27		A1 G320
971	" "	29	W½SE	1841-02-27		A1 G320
980	" "	17	W½NE	1845-12-01		A1 G20
974	SANDERS, Jerrimiah	20	SE	1846-01-15		A1 G248
940	SCOTT, Francis T	21	NW	1841-02-01		A1
912	" "	17	E½NE	1841-02-27		A1 G194

ID	Individual in Patent	Sec.	Sec. Part	Date Issued	Other Counties	For More Info . . .
979	SCOTT, Francis T (Cont'd)	17	W½SE	1841-02-27		A1 G225
941	" "	20	NE	1841-02-27		A1 G321
941	SCOTT, William T	20	NE	1841-02-27		A1 G321
1021	SCUDDAY, Joseph B	30	W½SW	1841-02-27		A1
1063	SCUDDY, Joseph B	22	SW	1841-02-01		A1 G168
1022	" "	27	E½NW	1841-02-01		A1
1023	" "	31	E½NW	1841-02-27		A1
1024	" "	31	W½NE	1841-02-27		A1
927	SESSIONS, Daniel	23	E½SW	1911-09-18		A1
928	" "	28	W½SE	1912-02-05		A1
1053	SHAW, Samuel	13	W½SW	1841-02-27		A1
930	SMYTH, John B	14	SE	1841-02-27		A1 G276
1014	SPENCER, Hezekiah G	26	E½NW	1841-02-27		A1 G132
1015	" "	26	E½SE	1841-02-27		A1 G132
1016	" "	26	E½SW	1841-02-27		A1 G132
1017	" "	26	W½NE	1841-02-27		A1 G132
1018	" "	26	W½SE	1841-02-27		A1 G132
898	" "	35	E½NE	1841-02-27		A1 G175
1076	SPINKS, Enoch	33	NE	1841-02-27		A1 G284
888	STEELE, Abner A	14	NE	1841-02-27		A1 G149
1011	" "	19	E½SW	1841-02-27		A1 G133
1012	" "	19	W½SW	1841-02-27		A1 G133
1013	" "	26	W½SW	1841-02-27		A1 G133
1074	" "	35	E½SW	1841-02-27		A1 G285
896	" "	35	W½NE	1841-02-27		A1 G176
1075	" "	35	W½SW	1841-02-27		A1 G285
1043	STEELE, Griffin	11	W½NW	1841-02-27		A1 G204
1042	STEELE, Richard G	10	NW	1841-02-27		A1
1082	" "	11	E½NW	1841-02-27		A1 G286
907	" "	24	W½NW	1841-02-27		A1 G177
926	" "	9	W½NE	1841-02-27		A1 G195
1033	STOVALL, Lewis	4	W½NE	1841-02-01		A1
1049	TAPPAN, John	31	E½NE	1841-02-27		A1 G234
1051	" "	31	SE	1841-02-27		A1 G233
1052	" "	32	SW	1841-02-27		A1 G233
1050	" "	32	W½NW	1841-02-27		A1 G234
942	THOMAS, Francis	3	NW	1841-02-27		A1
943	" "	4	W½NW	1841-02-27		A1
944	" "	5	E½NE	1841-02-27		A1
1040	THURMOND, Powhattan B	7	E½SW	1841-02-27		A1
1041	" "	7	W½SW	1841-02-27		A1
925	THURMOND, Powhatten B	7	E½NE	1841-02-27		A1 G196
1090	WADE, William H	7	E½SE	1841-02-27		A1
1091	" "	7	W½SE	1841-02-27		A1
1048	WEIR, Adolphus G	35	SE	1841-02-27		A1 G150
1077	WELSH, George	11	E½SE	1841-02-27		A1 G288
1078	" "	11	W½SE	1841-02-27		A1 G288
889	" "	14	W½NW	1841-02-27		A1 G125
954	" "	2	SW	1841-02-27		A1
1005	WELSH, John V	1	W½SW	1841-02-27		A1
1079	" "	11	E½NE	1841-02-27		A1 G289
1080	" "	11	W½NE	1841-02-27		A1 G289
1081	" "	12	W½NW	1841-02-27		A1 G289
1006	" "	3	NE	1844-12-10		A1
1007	WELSH, John W	2	S½SE	1841-02-27		A1
1045	WHITE, Robert	3	W½SE	1841-02-27		A1
1046	" "	3	W½SW	1841-02-27		A1
1085	WHITE, Thomas	3	E½SW	1841-02-01		A1
892	WILSON, Charles	27	E½SE	1841-02-27		A1
1054	WILSON, Samuel	3	E½SE	1841-02-01		A1
916	WINSTON, Joel W	36	E½NW	1841-02-27		A1 G197
880	" "	36	E½SE	1841-02-27		A1 G35
900	" "	36	E½SW	1841-02-27		A1 G178
901	" "	36	W½NE	1841-02-27		A1 G178
917	" "	36	W½NW	1841-02-27		A1 G197
918	" "	36	W½SE	1841-02-27		A1 G197
902	" "	36	W½SW	1841-02-27		A1 G178
929	WITHERS, Robert W	28	SW	1841-02-27		A1 G247

Patent Map

T12-N R18-E
Choctaw Meridian

Map Group 5

Township Statistics

Parcels Mapped	:	223
Number of Patents	:	217
Number of Individuals	:	111
Patentees Identified	:	122
Number of Surnames	:	88
Multi-Patentee Parcels	:	90
Oldest Patent Date	:	2/1/1841
Most Recent Patent	:	2/5/1912
Block/Lot Parcels	:	0
Parcels Re - Issued	:	1
Parcels that Overlap	:	0
Cities and Towns	:	2
Cemeteries	:	1

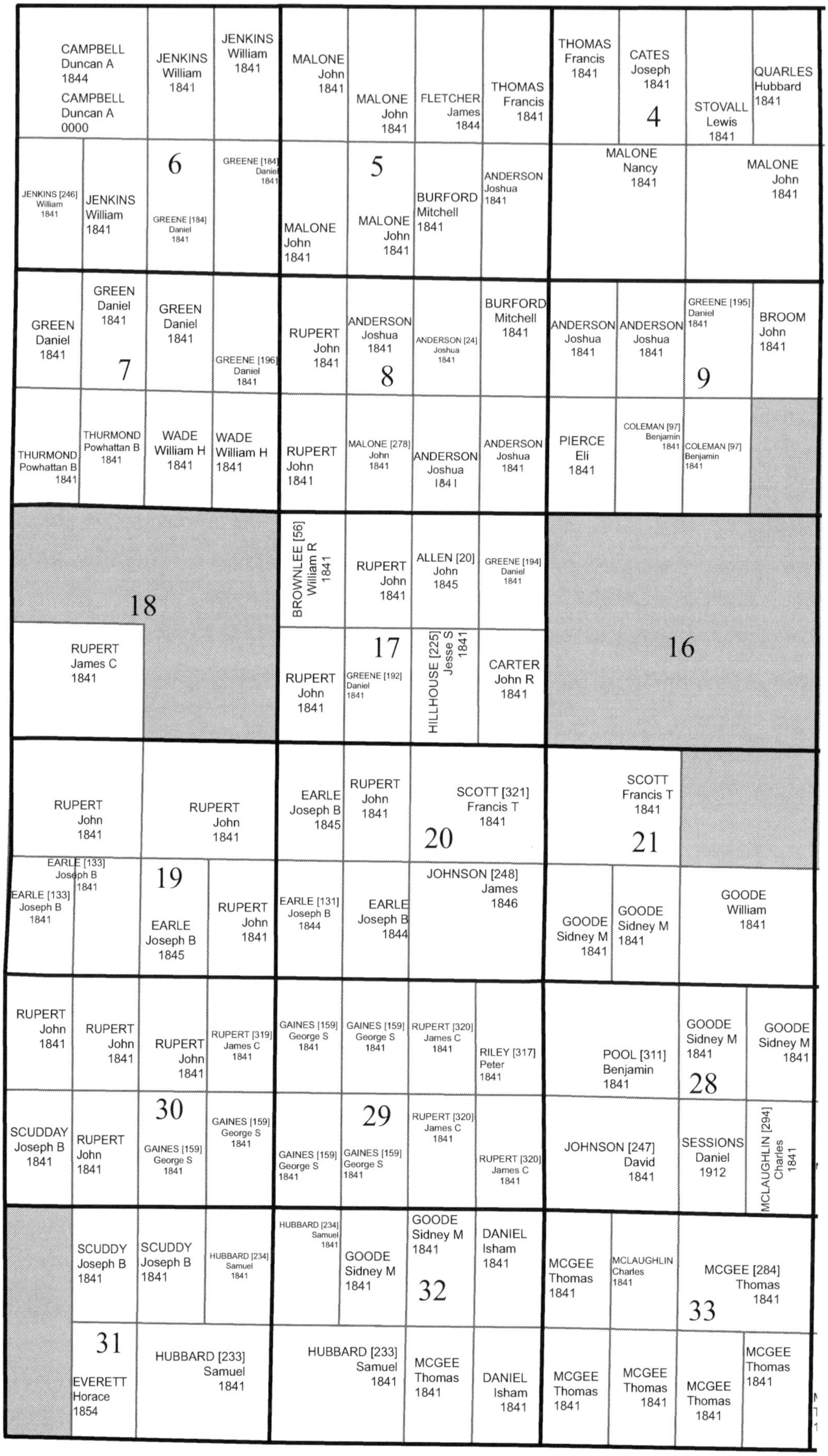

THOMAS Francis 1841
WELSH John V 1844
3
SANDERS Jeremiah 1841
SANDERS Jeremiah 1841
CATES Ephraim 1841
CATES Ephraim 1841
CATES Ephraim 1841
ETHRIDGE Thomas W 1882
ADAMS Howell C 1841
ADAMS Howell C 1841
ANDERSON Garrison 1841
WHITE Robert 1841
WHITE Thomas 1841
WHITE Robert 1841
WILSON Samuel 1841
2
WELSH George 1841
MCCALEBB James 1841
BOUGHTON Samuel 1841
WELSH John W 1841
WELSH John V 1841
DEW Warren 1884
1
ADAMS Howell C 1841
KING Thomas P 1841
CATES Ephraim 1841

STEELE Richard G 1841
10
MCCLURG William 1841
GRIFFIN [204] Richard 1841
MCGEE [286] Thomas 1841
11
MCGEE [289] Thomas 1841
MCGEE [289] Thomas 1841
MCGEE [289] Thomas 1841
CATES Ephraim 1841
CATES Ephraim 1841
CAROTHERS James N 1841
MADDEN Martin 1841
MCGEE [288] Thomas 1841
MCGEE [288] Thomas 1841
GREENE [187] Daniel 1841
GREEN [172] Daniel 1841
12
PETTUS Alice T 1841

15
PRUIT Archibald 1841
DOBBS [125] Charles 1841
PEARCE Aaron 1841
FELTS [149] Caswell 1841
GREENE [187] Daniel 1841
GREENE [187] Daniel 1841
PETTIS Anthony W 1841
ADAMS Robert E 1841
KYLE Margaret 1841
14
ROWE Shadrach 1841
LYLE [276] David 1841
SHAW Samuel 1841
GREENE [187] Daniel 1841
13
GREENE [188] Daniel 1841
GREENE [188] Daniel 1841

NICHOLSON Isaac W 1841
NICHOLSON Isaac W 1841
COLEMAN Benjamin 1911
23
BUTLER Winfield M 1841
GREEN [177] Daniel 1841
GREEN [174] Daniel 1841
24
ROGERS John D 1841
22
GOODE [168] Sidney M 1841
COLEMAN Benjamin 1911
SESSIONS Daniel 1911
GRIGGS [207] Green B 1841
JONES William F 1841
GREEN [174] Daniel 1841
GREEN [174] Daniel 1841

GOODE Sidney M 1841
SCUDDY Joseph B 1841
27
GRIGGS [208] Green 1841
GRIGGS [208] Green 1841
EARLE [132] Joseph B 1841
EARLE [132] Joseph B 1841
26
EARLE [129] Joseph B 1844
GREENE [181] Daniel 1841
GREENE [181] Daniel 1841
GREENE [189] Daniel 1841
GREEN [174] Daniel 1841
MCLAUGHLIN George 1841
MCLAUGHLIN George 1841
WILSON Charles 1841
EARLE [133] Joseph B 1841
EARLE [132] Joseph B 1841
EARLE [132] Joseph B 1841
EARLE [132] Joseph B 1841
GREENE [181] Daniel 1841
25
GREEN [174] Daniel 1841
POPE Allen 1841
POPE Allen 1841

LLOYD [273] John 1841
34
HOMES John 1841
HOLMES John 1841
GRIGGS [207] Green B 1841
GREEN [176] Daniel 1841
35
GREEN [175] Daniel 1841
GREENE [197] Daniel 1841
GREENE [197] Daniel 1841
36
GREEN [178] Daniel 1841
POWE William H 1841
MCGEE Thomas 1841
MCGEE Thomas 1841
MCGEE Thomas 1841
MCGEE Thomas 1841
MCGEE [285] Thomas 1841
MCGEE [285] Thomas 1841
FELTS [150] Samuel D 1841
GREEN [178] Daniel 1841
GREEN [178] Daniel 1841
GREENE [197] Daniel 1841
BENNETT [35] Anthony 1841

Helpful Hints

1. This Map's INDEX can be found on the preceding pages.
2. Refer to Map "C" to see where this Township lies within Kemper County, Mississippi.
3. Numbers within square brackets [ ] denote a multi-patentee land parcel (multi-owner). Refer to Appendix "C" for a full list of members in this group.
4. Areas that look to be crowded with Patentees usually indicate multiple sales of the same parcel (Re-issues) or Overlapping parcels. See this Township's Index for an explanation of these and other circumstances that might explain "odd" groupings of Patentees on this map.

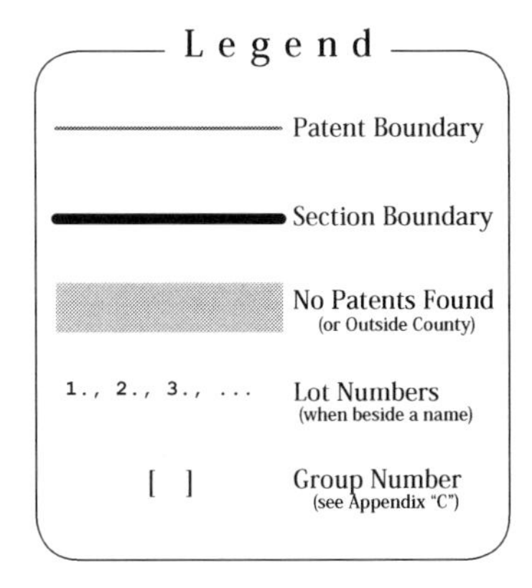

Scale: Section = 1 mile X 1 mile
(generally, with some exceptions)

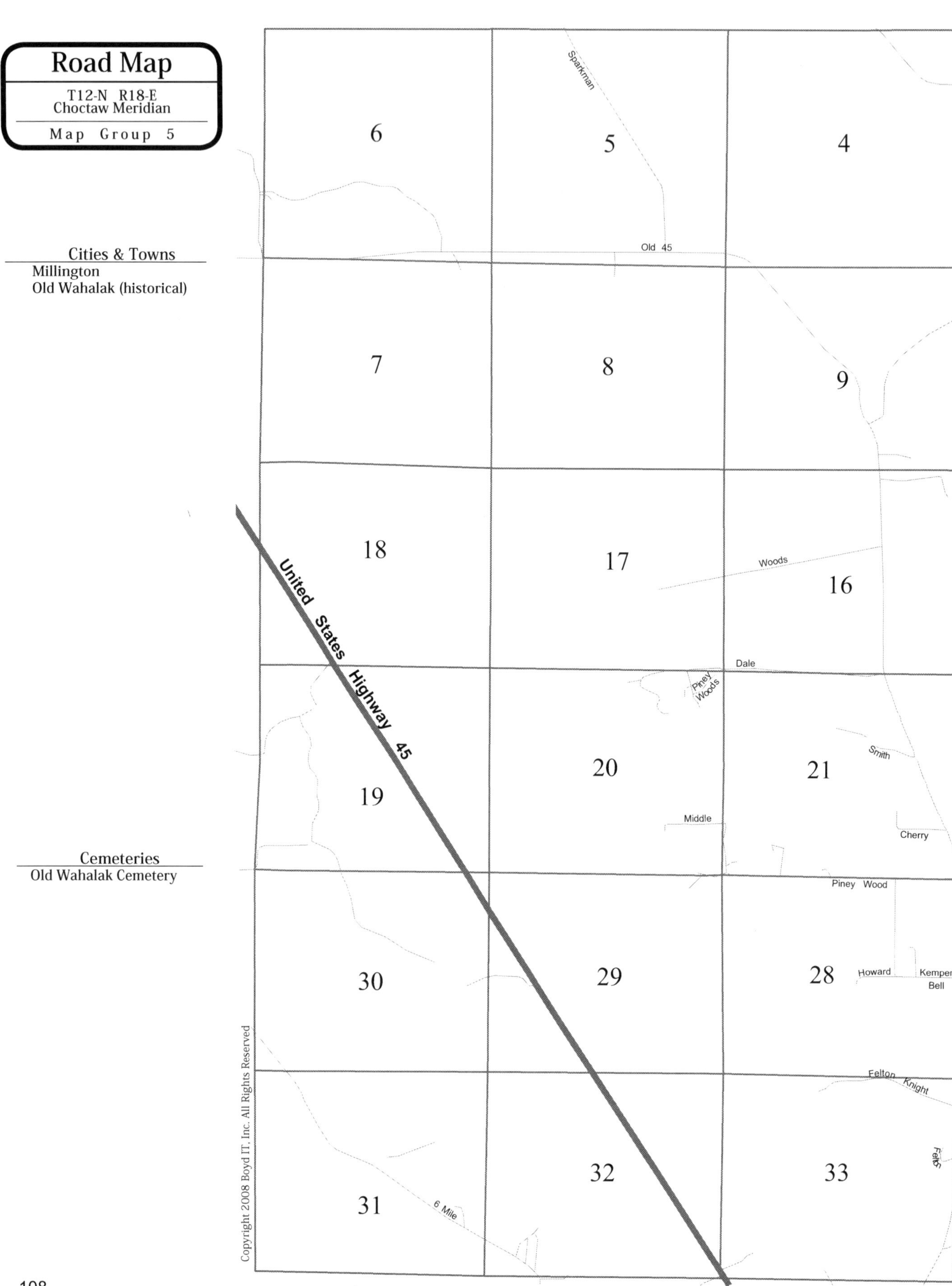
Road Map
T12-N R18-E
Choctaw Meridian
Map Group 5
Cities & Towns
Millington
Old Wahalak (historical)
Cemeteries
Old Wahalak Cemetery
6
5
4
7
8
9
18
17
16
19
20
21
30
29
28
31
32
33
Sparkman
Old 45
Woods
Dale
Piney Woods
United States Highway 45
Smith
Middle
Cherry
Piney Wood
Howard
Kemper Bell
Felton
Knight
6 Mile

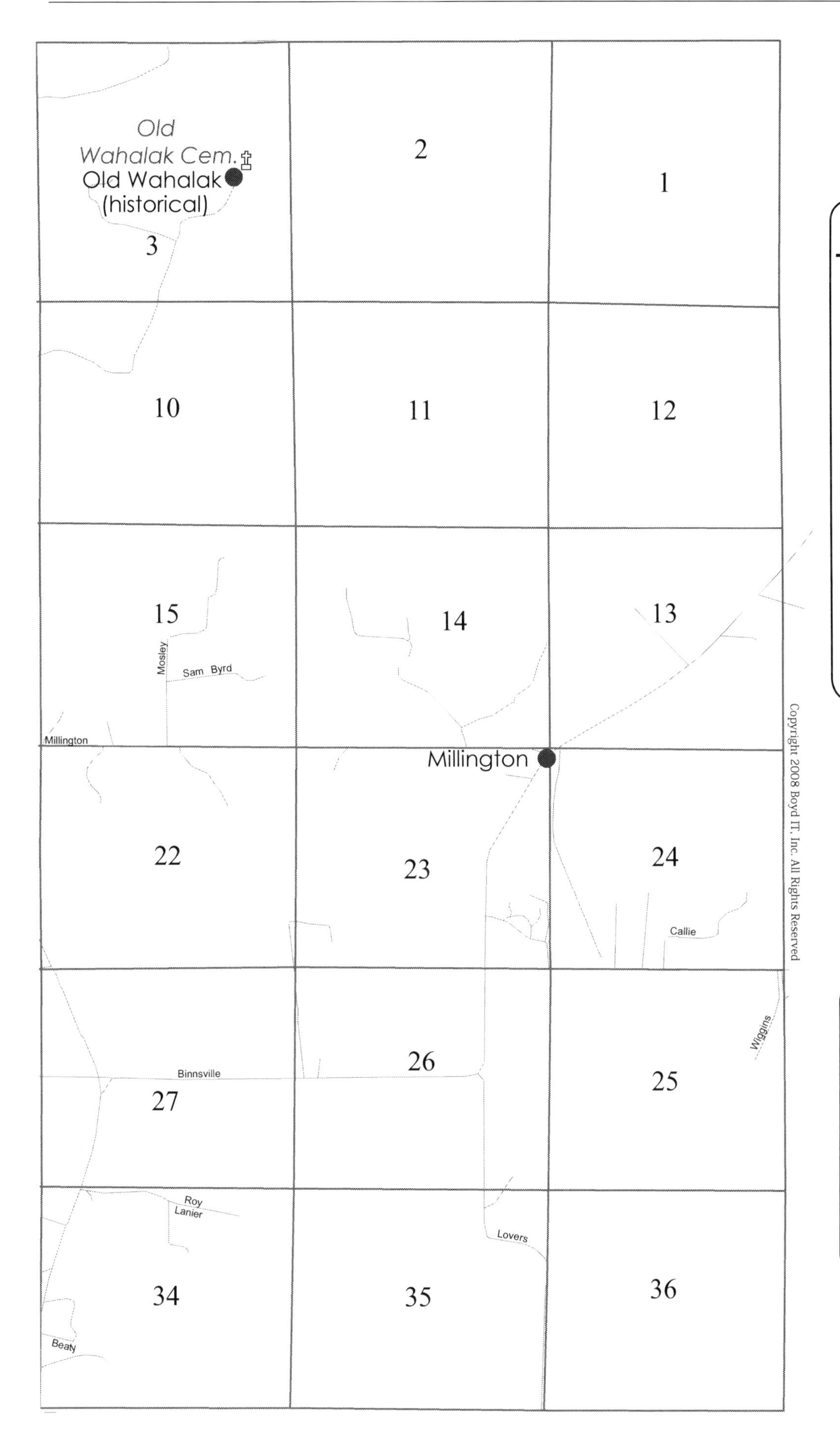

Helpful Hints

1. This road map has a number of uses, but primarily it is to help you: a) find the present location of land owned by your ancestors (at least the general area), b) find cemeteries and city-centers, and c) estimate the route/roads used by Census-takers & tax-assessors.

2. If you plan to travel to Kemper County to locate cemeteries or land parcels, please pick up a modern travel map for the area before you do. Mapping old land parcels on modern maps is not as exact a science as you might think. Just the slightest variations in public land survey coordinates, estimates of parcel boundaries, or road-map deviations can greatly alter a map's representation of how a road either does or doesn't cross a particular parcel of land.

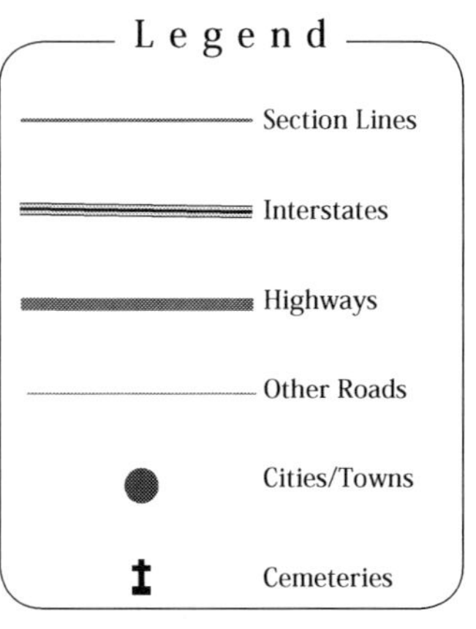

Scale: Section = 1 mile X 1 mile
(generally, with some exceptions)

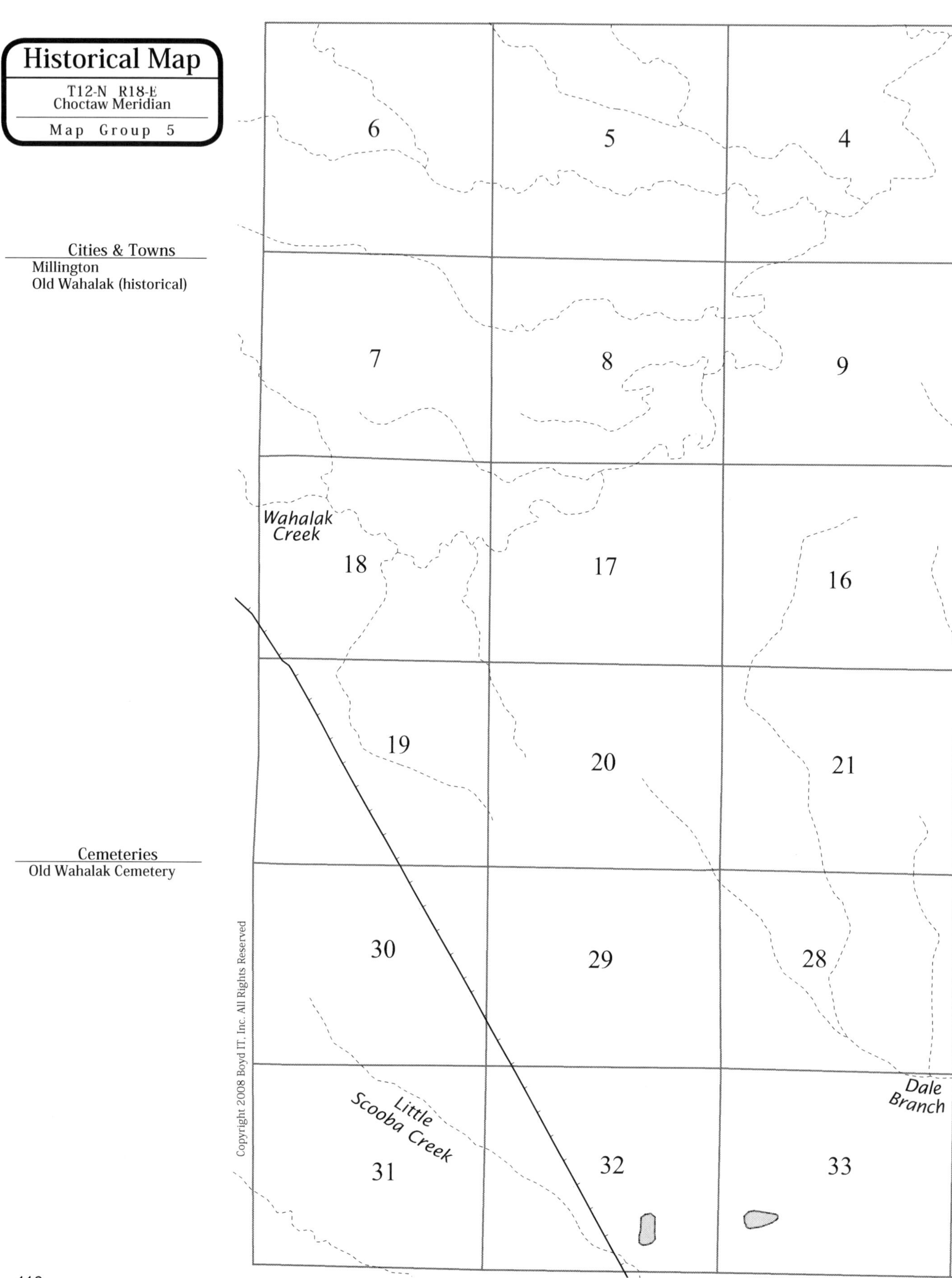
Historical Map
T12-N R18-E
Choctaw Meridian
Map Group 5
Cities & Towns
Millington
Old Wahalak (historical)
Cemeteries
Old Wahalak Cemetery
6
5
4
7
8
9
Wahalak Creek
18
17
16
19
20
21
30
29
28
Little Scooba Creek
Dale Branch
31
32
33
Copyright 2008 Boyd IT, Inc. All Rights Reserved

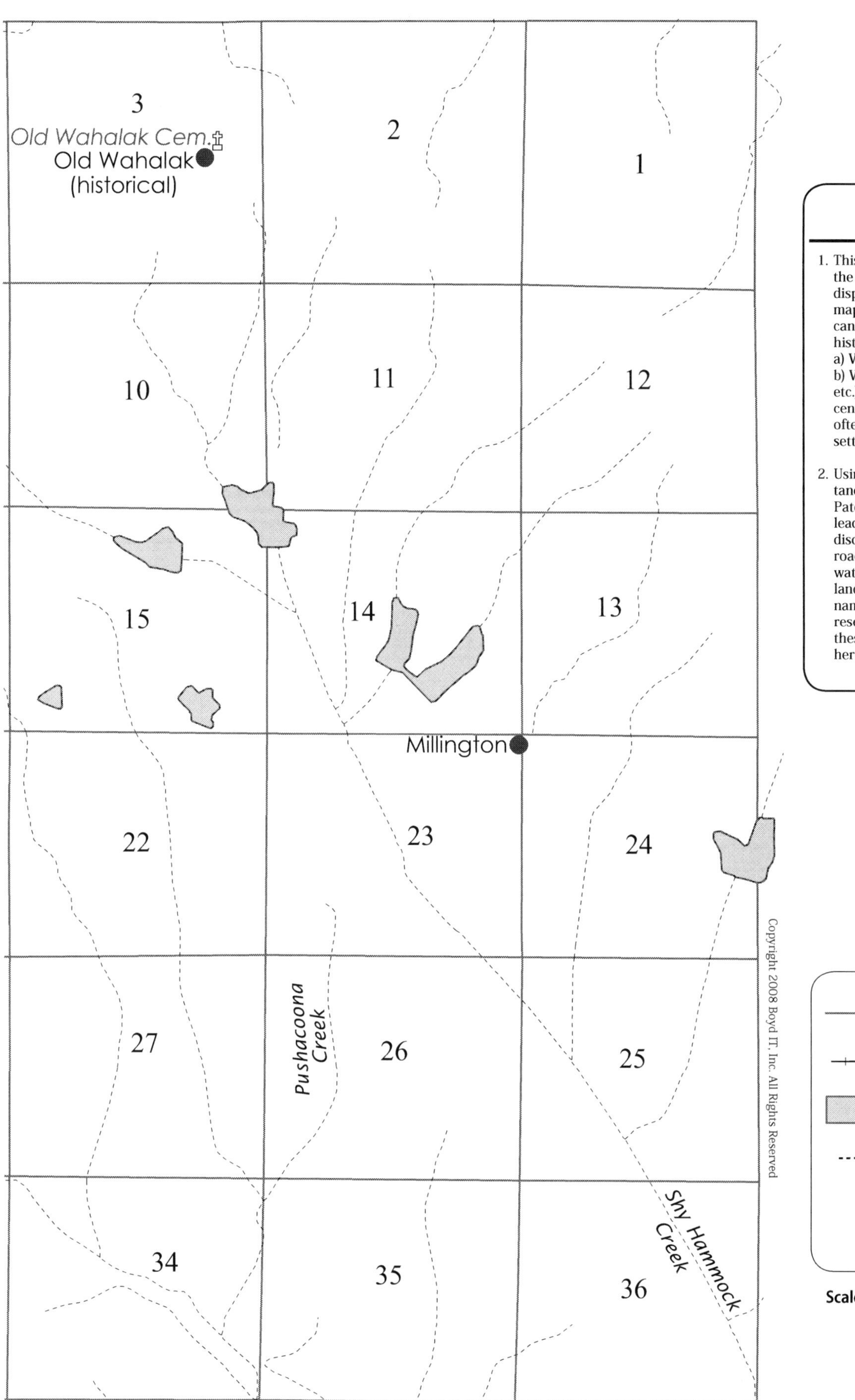

Helpful Hints

1. This Map takes a different look at the same Congressional Township displayed in the preceding two maps. It presents features that can help you better envision the historical development of the area: a) Water-bodies (lakes & ponds), b) Water-courses (rivers, streams, etc.), c) Railroads, d) City/town center-points (where they were oftentimes located when first settled), and e) Cemeteries.
2. Using this "Historical" map in tandem with this Township's Patent Map and Road Map, may lead you to some interesting discoveries. You will often find roads, towns, cemeteries, and waterways are named after nearby landowners: sometimes those names will be the ones you are researching. See how many of these research gems you can find here in Kemper County.

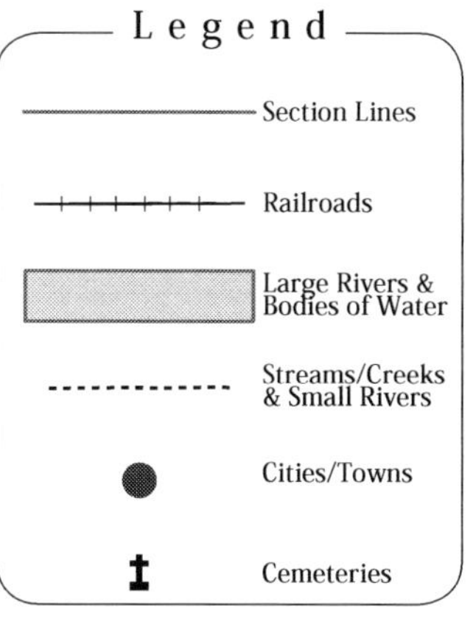

Scale: Section = 1 mile X 1 mile
(there are some exceptions)

Map Group 6: Index to Land Patents

Township 12-North Range 19-East (Choctaw)

After you locate an individual in this Index, take note of the Section and Section Part then proceed to the Land Patent map on the pages immediately following. You should have no difficulty locating the corresponding parcel of land.

The "For More Info" Column will lead you to more information about the underlying Patents. See the *Legend* at right, and the "How to Use this Book" chapter, for more information.

LEGEND

"For More Info . . . " column

A = Authority (Legislative Act, See Appendix "A")
B = Block or Lot (location in Section unknown)
C = Cancelled Patent
F = Fractional Section
G = Group (Multi-Patentee Patent, see Appendix "C")
V = Overlaps another Parcel
R = Re-Issued (Parcel patented more than once)

(A & G items require you to look in the Appendixes referred to above. All other Letter-designations followed by a number require you to locate line-items in this index that possess the ID number found after the letter).

ID	Individual in Patent	Sec.	Sec. Part	Date Issued	Other Counties	For More Info . . .
1153	BROWN, Henry	4	10	1881-08-20		A2
1149	CATES, Ephraim	6	W½NW	1841-02-27		A1
1150	" "	7	E½NW	1841-02-27		A1
1151	" "	7	W½NW	1841-02-27		A1
1212	CHARLTON, Tapley	17	NE	1841-02-27		A1 G86
1208	" "	21	2	1846-09-01		A1
1209	" "	21	3	1846-09-01		A1
1210	" "	21	4	1846-09-01		A1
1211	" "	21	5	1846-09-01		A1
1099	DUNCAN, Abraham	28	5	1846-09-01		A1
1100	" "	28	8	1846-09-01		A1
1229	FLEMMING, William H	6	E½NW	1838-06-01		A1 G153
1230	" "	6	NE	1838-06-01		A1 G153
1231	" "	6	SE	1838-06-01		A1 G153
1232	" "	6	SW	1838-06-01		A1 G153
1233	" "	9	2	1838-06-01		A1 G153
1234	" "	9	3	1838-06-01		A1 G153
1235	" "	9	4	1838-06-01		A1 G153
1236	" "	9	5	1838-06-01		A1 G153
1225	" "	5	NE	1898-12-27		A1
1226	" "	5	S½NW	1898-12-27		A1
1227	" "	5	SW	1898-12-27		A1
1228	" "	5	W½SE	1898-12-27		A1
1156	GILES, Jacob	31	E½SE	1841-02-27		A1
1157	" "	31	W½SE	1841-02-27		A1
1158	" "	31	W½SW	1841-02-27		A1
1128	GREENE, Daniel	17	E½SW	1841-02-27		A1 G186
1129	" "	17	W½SW	1841-02-27		A1 G186
1132	" "	18	E½NW	1841-02-27		A1 G182
1123	" "	18	E½SE	1841-02-27		A1 G190
1133	" "	18	W½NE	1841-02-27		A1 G182
1124	" "	18	W½SE	1841-02-27		A1 G190
1125	" "	19	E½NE	1841-02-27		A1 G190
1109	" "	19	E½NW	1841-02-27		A1
1126	" "	19	E½SE	1841-02-27		A1 G190
1110	" "	19	E½SW	1841-02-27		A1
1127	" "	19	W½NW	1841-02-27		A1 G190
1111	" "	19	W½SE	1841-02-27		A1
1112	" "	19	W½SW	1841-02-27		A1
1130	" "	21	1	1841-02-27		A1 G186
1131	" "	21	6	1841-02-27		A1 G186
1113	" "	28	1	1841-02-27		A1
1114	" "	28	2	1841-02-27		A1
1115	" "	28	3	1841-02-27		A1
1116	" "	28	4	1841-02-27		A1
1117	" "	28	6	1841-02-27		A1

ID	Individual in Patent	Sec.	Sec. Part	Date Issued	Other Counties	For More Info . . .
1118	GREENE, Daniel (Cont'd)	28	7	1841-02-27		A1
1136	" "	29	E½NW	1841-02-27		A1 G185
1137	" "	29	W½NW	1841-02-27		A1 G185
1138	" "	29	W½SW	1841-02-27		A1 G185
1139	" "	30	E½NW	1841-02-27		A1 G185
1140	" "	30	E½SE	1841-02-27		A1 G185
1120	" "	30	E½SW	1841-02-27		A1 G197
1121	" "	30	W½NW	1841-02-27		A1 G197
1141	" "	30	W½SE	1841-02-27		A1 G185
1122	" "	30	W½SW	1841-02-27		A1 G197
1142	" "	31	E½NE	1841-02-27		A1 G185
1143	" "	31	E½SW	1841-02-27		A1 G185
1144	" "	31	W½NE	1841-02-27		A1 G185
1134	" "	32	E½NE	1841-02-27		A1 G183
1135	" "	32	W½SE	1841-02-27		A1 G183
1119	" "	32	W½SW	1841-02-27		A1
1187	GRIGSBY, Joseph	21	12	1841-02-27		A1 G209
1188	" "	21	7	1841-02-27		A1 G209
1187	HARRIS, Robert E	21	12	1841-02-27		A1 G209
1188	" "	21	7	1841-02-27		A1 G209
1108	HENDERSON, Alexander	30	NE	1841-02-27		A1
1204	HUBBARD, Samuel	32	W½NE	1841-02-27		A1 G234
1205	" "	33	4	1841-02-27		A1 G234
1206	" "	33	5	1841-02-27		A1 G234
1197	" "	20	E½NE	1841-12-15		A1 G232
1199	" "	20	E½SW	1841-12-15		A1 G232
1200	" "	20	W½NW	1841-12-15		A1 G232
1201	" "	20	W½SE	1841-12-15		A1 G232
1202	" "	20	W½SW	1841-12-15		A1 G232
1203	" "	32	E½SE	1841-12-15		A1 G234
1198	" "	20	E½SE	1844-12-10		A1 G232
1229	JUDSON, Charles	6	E½NW	1838-06-01		A1 G153
1230	" "	6	NE	1838-06-01		A1 G153
1231	" "	6	SE	1838-06-01		A1 G153
1232	" "	6	SW	1838-06-01		A1 G153
1233	" "	9	2	1838-06-01		A1 G153
1234	" "	9	3	1838-06-01		A1 G153
1235	" "	9	4	1838-06-01		A1 G153
1236	" "	9	5	1838-06-01		A1 G153
1132	LEVENS, Joshua B	18	E½NW	1841-02-27		A1 G182
1133	" "	18	W½NE	1841-02-27		A1 G182
1197	LEWIS, Moses	20	E½NE	1841-12-15		A1 G232
1199	" "	20	E½SW	1841-12-15		A1 G232
1200	" "	20	W½NW	1841-12-15		A1 G232
1201	" "	20	W½SE	1841-12-15		A1 G232
1202	" "	20	W½SW	1841-12-15		A1 G232
1193	" "	29	E½SE	1842-11-01		A1 G264
1198	" "	20	E½SE	1844-12-10		A1 G232
1134	LEWIS, Rufus G	32	E½NE	1841-02-27		A1 G183
1204	" "	32	W½NE	1841-02-27		A1 G234
1135	" "	32	W½SE	1841-02-27		A1 G183
1194	" "	33	1	1841-02-27		A1 G265
1195	" "	33	2	1841-02-27		A1 G265
1196	" "	33	3	1841-02-27		A1 G265
1205	" "	33	4	1841-02-27		A1 G234
1206	" "	33	5	1841-02-27		A1 G234
1197	" "	20	E½NE	1841-12-15		A1 G232
1199	" "	20	E½SW	1841-12-15		A1 G232
1200	" "	20	W½NW	1841-12-15		A1 G232
1201	" "	20	W½SE	1841-12-15		A1 G232
1202	" "	20	W½SW	1841-12-15		A1 G232
1203	" "	32	E½SE	1841-12-15		A1 G234
1198	" "	20	E½SE	1844-12-10		A1 G232
1189	MCCASKILL, Kinnith	29	E½SW	1841-02-27		A1
1190	" "	29	W½SE	1841-02-27		A1
1191	" "	32	E½NW	1841-02-27		A1
1192	" "	32	W½NW	1841-02-27		A1
1136	MCGEE, Thomas	29	E½NW	1841-02-27		A1 G185
1219	" "	29	W½NE	1841-02-27		A1
1137	" "	29	W½NW	1841-02-27		A1 G185
1138	" "	29	W½SW	1841-02-27		A1 G185
1139	" "	30	E½NW	1841-02-27		A1 G185
1140	" "	30	E½SE	1841-02-27		A1 G185

ID	Individual in Patent	Sec.	Sec. Part	Date Issued	Other Counties	For More Info . . .
1141	MCGEE, Thomas (Cont'd)	30	W½SE	1841-02-27		A1 G185
1142	" "	31	E½NE	1841-02-27		A1 G185
1143	" "	31	E½SW	1841-02-27		A1 G185
1144	" "	31	W½NE	1841-02-27		A1 G185
1194	" "	33	1	1841-02-27		A1 G265
1195	" "	33	2	1841-02-27		A1 G265
1196	" "	33	3	1841-02-27		A1 G265
1218	" "	29	E½NE	1841-12-15		A1
1214	" "	21	10	1842-11-01		A1
1215	" "	21	11	1842-11-01		A1
1216	" "	21	8	1842-11-01		A1
1217	" "	21	9	1842-11-01		A1
1145	MCINTOSH, Daniel	4	15	1841-02-27		A1
1147	" "	5	E½SE	1841-02-27		A1
1148	" "	8	E½NE	1841-02-27		A1
1146	" "	4	4	1841-12-15		A1
1165	MCINTOSH, John P	18	E½NE	1841-02-27		A1
1166	" "	4	16	1841-02-27		A1
1167	" "	4	9	1841-02-27		A1
1168	" "	7	E½NE	1841-02-27		A1
1169	" "	7	E½SE	1841-02-27		A1
1170	" "	7	E½SW	1841-02-27		A1
1171	" "	7	W½NE	1841-02-27		A1
1172	" "	7	W½SE	1841-02-27		A1
1173	" "	9	1	1841-02-27		A1
1174	" "	9	6	1841-02-27		A1
1128	MOSELEY, John T	17	E½SW	1841-02-27		A1 G186
1129	" "	17	W½SW	1841-02-27		A1 G186
1130	" "	21	1	1841-02-27		A1 G186
1131	" "	21	6	1841-02-27		A1 G186
1175	" "	7	W½SW	1841-02-27		A1
1177	" "	8	S½E½NW	1841-02-27		A1
1178	" "	8	SE	1841-02-27		A1
1180	" "	9	S½W½SW	1841-02-27		A1
1176	" "	8	NENW	1844-09-10		A1
1179	" "	8	W½NE	1844-09-10		A1
1212	MOSELEY, William A	17	NE	1841-02-27		A1 G86
1220	" "	17	SE	1841-02-27		A1
1223	MOSELY, William A	8	E½SW	1841-02-27		A1 G299
1224	" "	8	W½NW	1841-02-27		A1 G299
1221	" "	8	W½SW	1841-02-27		A1
1222	" "	17	NW	1847-04-01		A1 G299
1181	MOSLEY, John T	20	E½NW	1841-02-27		A1 G300
1182	" "	9	11	1841-02-27		A1 G300
1183	" "	9	12	1841-02-27		A1 G300
1184	" "	9	7	1841-02-27		A1 G300
1185	" "	9	8	1841-02-27		A1 G300
1186	" "	9	9	1841-02-27		A1 G300
1181	MOSLEY, William A	20	E½NW	1841-02-27		A1 G300
1182	" "	9	11	1841-02-27		A1 G300
1183	" "	9	12	1841-02-27		A1 G300
1184	" "	9	7	1841-02-27		A1 G300
1185	" "	9	8	1841-02-27		A1 G300
1186	" "	9	9	1841-02-27		A1 G300
1161	OWEN, John	4	3	1841-02-27		A1 G306
1162	" "	4	5	1841-02-27		A1 G306
1163	" "	4	6	1841-02-27		A1 G306
1164	" "	4	7	1841-02-27		A1 G306
1101	POWE, Alexander C	4	1	1841-02-27		A1
1102	" "	4	11	1841-02-27		A1
1103	" "	4	12	1841-02-27		A1
1104	" "	4	13	1841-02-27		A1
1105	" "	4	14	1841-02-27		A1
1106	" "	4	2	1841-02-27		A1
1107	" "	4	8	1841-02-27		A1
1237	POWE, William H	31	W½NW	1841-02-27		A1
1154	QUARLES, Hubbard	5	N½E½NW	1841-02-27		A1
1155	" "	5	N½W½NW	1841-02-27		A1
1207	RIDGWAY, Sephalen	20	W½NE	1860-05-01		A1
1160	RODGERS, John D	19	W½NE	1841-02-27		A1
1123	ROGERS, John D	18	E½SE	1841-02-27		A1 G190
1124	" "	18	W½SE	1841-02-27		A1 G190
1125	" "	19	E½NE	1841-02-27		A1 G190

ID	Individual in Patent	Sec.	Sec. Part	Date Issued	Other Counties	For More Info . . .
1126	ROGERS, John D (Cont'd)	19	E½SE	1841-02-27		A1 G190
1127	" "	19	W½NW	1841-02-27		A1 G190
1123	ROGERS, Lieven	18	E½SE	1841-02-27		A1 G190
1124	" "	18	W½SE	1841-02-27		A1 G190
1125	" "	19	E½NE	1841-02-27		A1 G190
1126	" "	19	E½SE	1841-02-27		A1 G190
1127	" "	19	W½NW	1841-02-27		A1 G190
1213	ROGERS, Thomas H	18	SW	1841-02-27		A1
1223	ROSS, Michael	8	E½SW	1841-02-27		A1 G299
1224	" "	8	W½NW	1841-02-27		A1 G299
1222	" "	17	NW	1847-04-01		A1 G299
1152	SCOTT, Francis T	31	E½NW	1841-02-27		A1
1204	TAPPAN, John	32	W½NE	1841-02-27		A1 G234
1205	" "	33	4	1841-02-27		A1 G234
1206	" "	33	5	1841-02-27		A1 G234
1197	" "	20	E½NE	1841-12-15		A1 G232
1199	" "	20	E½SW	1841-12-15		A1 G232
1200	" "	20	W½NW	1841-12-15		A1 G232
1201	" "	20	W½SE	1841-12-15		A1 G232
1202	" "	20	W½SW	1841-12-15		A1 G232
1203	" "	32	E½SE	1841-12-15		A1 G234
1198	" "	20	E½SE	1844-12-10		A1 G232
1161	WEIR, Adolphus G	4	3	1841-02-27		A1 G306
1162	" "	4	5	1841-02-27		A1 G306
1163	" "	4	6	1841-02-27		A1 G306
1164	" "	4	7	1841-02-27		A1 G306
1159	WHITSETT, John C	32	E½SW	1841-02-27		A1
1193	" "	29	E½SE	1842-11-01		A1 G264
1120	WINSTON, Joel W	30	E½SW	1841-02-27		A1 G197
1121	" "	30	W½NW	1841-02-27		A1 G197
1122	" "	30	W½SW	1841-02-27		A1 G197

Patent Map

T12-N R19-E
Choctaw Meridian

Map Group 6

Township Statistics

Parcels Mapped	:	139
Number of Patents	:	103
Number of Individuals	:	39
Patentees Identified	:	39
Number of Surnames	:	32
Multi-Patentee Parcels	:	63
Oldest Patent Date	:	6/1/1838
Most Recent Patent	:	12/27/1898
Block/Lot Parcels	:	52
Parcels Re - Issued	:	0
Parcels that Overlap	:	0
Cities and Towns	:	1
Cemeteries	:	1

Note: the area contained in this map amounts to far less than a full Township. Therefore, its contents are completely on this single page (instead of a "normal" 2-page spread).

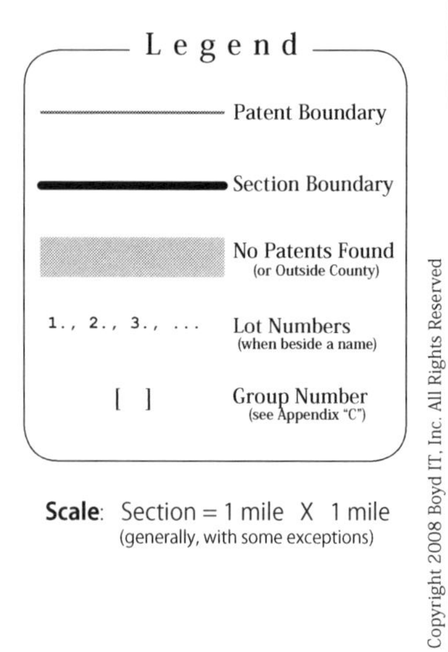

Scale: Section = 1 mile X 1 mile
(generally, with some exceptions)

6
CATES Ephraim 1841
FLEMMING [153] William H 1838
FLEMMING [153] William H 1838
FLEMMING [153] William H 1838
FLEMMING [153] William H 1838

5
QUARLES Hubbard 1841
QUARLES Hubbard 1841
FLEMMING William H 1898
FLEMMING William H 1898
FLEMMING William H 1898
FLEMMING William H 1898
MCINTOSH Daniel 1841

4
Lots-Sec. 4

1 POWE, Alexander C 1841
2 POWE, Alexander C 1841
3 OWEN, John [306]1841
4 MCINTOSH, Daniel 1841
5 OWEN, John [306]1841
6 OWEN, John [306]1841
7 OWEN, John [306]1841
8 POWE, Alexander C 1841
9 MCINTOSH, John P 1841
10 BROWN, Henry 1881
11 POWE, Alexander C 1841
12 POWE, Alexander C 1841
13 POWE, Alexander C 1841
14 POWE, Alexander C 1841
15 MCINTOSH, Daniel 1841
16 MCINTOSH, John P 1841

7
CATES Ephraim 1841
CATES Ephraim 1841
MCINTOSH John P 1841
MCINTOSH John P 1841
MOSELEY John T 1841
MCINTOSH John P 1841
MCINTOSH John P 1841
MCINTOSH John P 1841

8
MOSELY [299] William A 1841
MOSELEY John T 1844
MOSELEY John T 1841
MOSELEY John T 1844
MCINTOSH Daniel 1841
MOSELY William A 1841
MOSELY [299] William A 1841
MOSELEY John T 1841

9
Lots-Sec. 9
1 MCINTOSH, John P 1841
2 FLEMMING, Willi[153]1838
3 FLEMMING, Willi[153]1838
4 FLEMMING, Willi[153]1838
5 FLEMMING, Willi[153]1838
6 MCINTOSH, John P 1841
7 MOSLEY, John T [300]1841
8 MOSLEY, John T [300]1841
9 MOSLEY, John T [300]1841
11 MOSLEY, John T [300]1841
12 MOSLEY, John T [300]1841
MOSELEY John T 1841

18
GREENE [182] Daniel 1841
GREENE [182] Daniel 1841
MCINTOSH John P 1841
ROGERS Thomas H 1841
GREENE [190] Daniel 1841
GREENE [190] Daniel 1841

17
MOSELY [299] William A 1847
CHARLTON [86] Tapley 1841
GREENE [186] Daniel 1841
GREENE [186] Daniel 1841
MOSELEY William A 1841

16

19
GREENE [190] Daniel 1841
GREENE Daniel 1841
RODGERS John D 1841
GREENE [190] Daniel 1841
GREENE Daniel 1841
GREENE Daniel 1841
GREENE Daniel 1841
GREENE [190] Daniel 1841

20
HUBBARD [232] Samuel 1841
MOSLEY [300] John T 1841
RIDGWAY Sephalen 1860
HUBBARD [232] Samuel 1841
HUBBARD [232] Samuel 1841
HUBBARD [232] Samuel 1841
HUBBARD [232] Samuel 1841
HUBBARD [232] Samuel 1844

21
Lots-Sec. 21
1 GREENE, Daniel [186]1841
2 CHARLTON, Tapley 1846
3 CHARLTON, Tapley 1846
4 CHARLTON, Tapley 1846
5 CHARLTON, Tapley 1846
6 GREENE, Daniel [186]1841
7 GRIGSBY, Joseph[209]1841
8 MCGEE, Thomas 1842
9 MCGEE, Thomas 1842
10 MCGEE, Thomas 1842
11 MCGEE, Thomas 1842
12 GRIGSBY, Joseph[209]1841

30
GREENE [197] Daniel 1841
GREENE [185] Daniel 1841
HENDERSON Alexander 1841
GREENE [197] Daniel 1841
GREENE [197] Daniel 1841
GREENE [185] Daniel 1841
GREENE [185] Daniel 1841

29
GREENE [185] Daniel 1841
GREENE [185] Daniel 1841
MCGEE Thomas 1841
MCGEE Thomas 1841
GREENE [185] Daniel 1841
MCCASKILL Kinnith 1841
MCCASKILL Kinnith 1841
LEWIS [264] Moses 1842

28
Lots-Sec. 28
1 GREENE, Daniel 1841
2 GREENE, Daniel 1841
3 GREENE, Daniel 1841
4 GREENE, Daniel 1841
5 DUNCAN, Abraham 1846
6 GREENE, Daniel 1841
7 GREENE, Daniel 1841
8 DUNCAN, Abraham 1846

31
POWE William H 1841
SCOTT Francis T 1841
GREENE [185] Daniel 1841
GREENE [185] Daniel 1841
GILES Jacob 1841
GREENE [185] Daniel 1841
GILES Jacob 1841
GILES Jacob 1841

32
MCCASKILL Kinnith 1841
MCCASKILL Kinnith 1841
HUBBARD [234] Samuel 1841
GREENE [183] Daniel 1841
GREENE Daniel 1841
WHITSETT John C 1841
HUBBARD [234] Samuel 1841
GREENE [183] Daniel 1841

33
Lots-Sec. 33
1 LEWIS, Rufus G [265]1841
2 LEWIS, Rufus G [265]1841
3 LEWIS, Rufus G [265]1841
4 HUBBARD, Samuel[234]1841
5 HUBBARD, Samuel[234]1841

Noxubee
White Horse
6
5
4
Smith
Dunk
Binnsville
Binnsville Cem.
7
8
9
Hutcherson
Jones
Binnsville
18
17
16
Thornton
19
20
21
Sunflower
30
29
28
Giles
Cross
31
32
33
Joe Wright

Road Map

T12-N R19-E
Choctaw Meridian

Map Group 6

Note: the area contained in this map amounts to far less than a full Township. Therefore, its contents are completely on this single page (instead of a "normal" 2-page spread).

Cities & Towns

Binnsville

Cemeteries

Binnsville Cemetery

Legend

Section Lines
Interstates
Highways
Other Roads
Cities/Towns
Cemeteries

Scale: Section = 1 mile X 1 mile
(generally, with some exceptions)

Historical Map

T12-N R19-E
Choctaw Meridian

Map Group 6

Note: the area contained in this map amounts to far less than a full Township. Therefore, its contents are completely on this single page (instead of a "normal" 2-page spread).

Cities & Towns

Binnsville

Cemeteries

Binnsville Cemetery

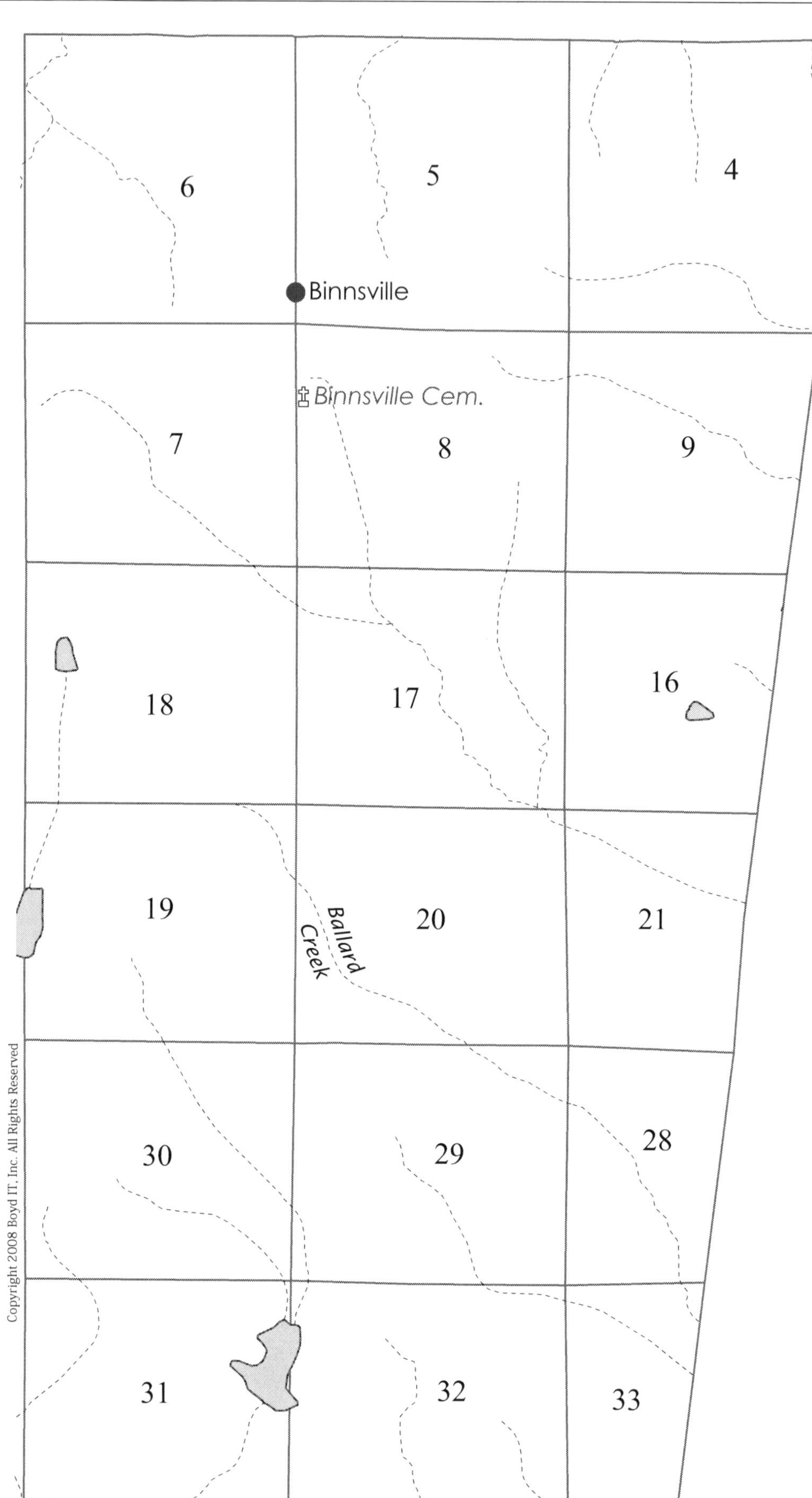

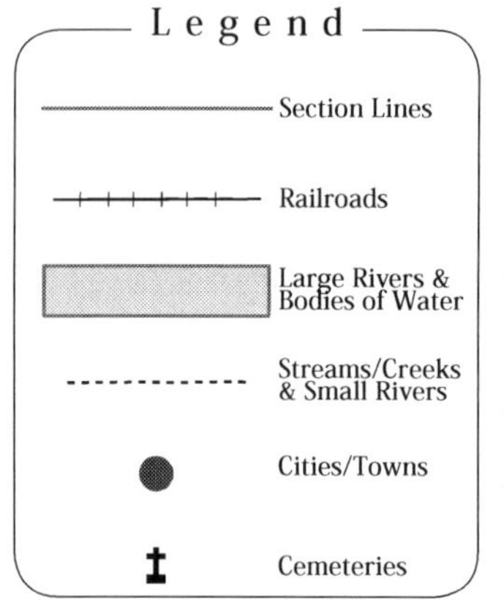

Scale: Section = 1 mile X 1 mile
(there are some exceptions)

Map Group 7: Index to Land Patents

Township 11-North Range 14-East (Choctaw)

After you locate an individual in this Index, take note of the Section and Section Part then proceed to the Land Patent map on the pages immediately following. You should have no difficulty locating the corresponding parcel of land.

The "For More Info" Column will lead you to more information about the underlying Patents. See the *Legend* at right, and the "How to Use this Book" chapter, for more information.

LEGEND

"For More Info . . . " column

- **A** = Authority (Legislative Act, See Appendix "A")
- **B** = Block or Lot (location in Section unknown)
- **C** = Cancelled Patent
- **F** = Fractional Section
- **G** = Group (Multi-Patentee Patent, see Appendix "C")
- **V** = Overlaps another Parcel
- **R** = Re-Issued (Parcel patented more than once)

(A & G items require you to look in the Appendixes referred to above. All other Letter-designations followed by a number require you to locate line-items in this index that possess the ID number found after the letter).

ID	Individual in Patent	Sec.	Sec. Part	Date Issued	Other Counties	For More Info . . .
1380	ABERCROMBIE, Oliver	36	NESE	1860-05-01		A1
1272	ANDERSON, Charles B	1	NWSW	1897-02-15		A2
1273	" "	1	SESW	1897-02-15		A2
1348	BARFOOT, John	31	SW	1844-09-10		A1
1318	BARTLETT, James	34	E½NE	1848-09-01		A1
1335	BELEW, James M	12	E½SE	1892-04-29		A2
1336	" "	12	S½NE	1892-04-29		A2
1385	BELEW, Reubin A	12	NW	1892-06-25		A2
1319	BLACKWELL, James	35	S½NE	1859-10-01		A1
1415	BOSTICK, Tandy C	10	NWNE	1854-03-15		A1
1417	" "	3	SESE	1856-04-01		A1
1416	" "	12	NWSE	1860-05-01		A1
1447	BOSTICK, William	21	NENE	1860-10-01		A1
1448	" "	22	NWNW	1860-10-01		A1
1323	BRANNING, James	14	NENE	1850-12-05		A1
1322	" "	13	W½NW	1859-10-01		A1
1325	" "	14	NWNE	1859-10-01		A1
1326	" "	14	SENE	1859-10-01		A1
1320	" "	13	E½NW	1860-05-01		A1
1321	" "	13	NWSW	1860-05-01		A1
1324	" "	14	NESE	1860-05-01		A1
1327	" "	14	SWNE	1860-05-01		A1
1409	BRANNING, Samuel A	11	SWSW	1860-10-01		A1
1468	BRANNING, William S	14	SESE	1890-06-25		A2
1469	" "	14	W½SE	1890-06-25		A2
1470	" "	23	NENE	1890-06-25		A2
1372	BROWN, Morgan D	26	NESW	1850-12-05		A1
1305	CLARK, Hugh	19	NWSE	1854-03-15		A1
1306	" "	8	E½SE	1859-10-01		A1
1375	CLARK, Nancy	26	SWSE	1856-04-01		A1
1376	" "	35	N½NE	1856-04-01		A1
1377	" "	35	NWNW	1856-04-01		A1
1337	DAVIS, James M	13	NESW	1906-06-21		A2
1397	DAVIS, Robert J	29	W½NE	1860-10-01		A1
1398	" "	33	NENW	1860-10-01		A1
1399	" "	33	NWNE	1860-10-01		A1
1463	DAVIS, William H	12	SESW	1893-12-21		A2
1464	" "	12	SWSE	1893-12-21		A2
1465	" "	12	SWSW	1895-05-11		A2
1308	DAWE, Isaac R	34	NWSW	1882-04-20		A1
1413	DAWS, Siar O	34	S½SW	1860-05-01		A1
1451	DEES, William	25	NWSW	1856-04-01		A1
1452	" "	26	NWSE	1856-04-01		A1
1453	" "	26	NWSW	1860-05-01		A1
1454	" "	26	SESE	1860-05-01		A1
1457	" "	27	NESE	1860-05-01		A1

ID	Individual in Patent	Sec.	Sec. Part	Date Issued	Other Counties	For More Info . . .
1455	DEES, William (Cont'd)	26	SWNE	1860-10-01		A1
1456	" "	26	SWNW	1861-02-01		A1
1458	DEESE, William	26	SENE	1854-03-15		A1
1459	" "	26	SENW	1854-03-15		A1
1270	DONALDS, Berry	24	NWSE	1884-12-30		A2
1271	" "	24	S½NE	1884-12-30		A2
1328	DUNN, James	9	SW	1844-09-10		A1
1349	ECHOLS, John G	30	NWSE	1856-04-01		A1
1350	" "	30	SWNE	1856-04-01		A1
1381	EDWARDS, Patrick H	13	S½SW	1888-02-25		A2
1382	" "	24	N½NW	1888-02-25		A2
1378	FOX, Nathan J	17	SWNE	1859-10-01		A1
1379	" "	17	W½SE	1859-10-01		A1
1462	FOX, William	17	NESW	1854-03-15		A1
1265	FRANKLIN, Barnet	33	SE	1844-09-10		A1
1293	FULTON, George	2	NWNW	1859-10-01		A1
1461	FULTON, William F	1	E½NE	1891-05-20		A2
1266	GERMANY, Benjamin C	21	SENE	1896-06-18		A1
1332	GERMANY, James	36	E½NW	1844-09-10		A1
1333	" "	36	W½NE	1844-09-10		A1
1351	GERMANY, John	35	W½SE	1860-05-01		A1
1281	GILLIS, Dorcey W	23	SESW	1892-06-15		A2
1282	" "	23	W½SW	1892-06-15		A2
1283	" "	26	NWNW	1892-06-15		A2
1420	GRUBBS, Thomas L	26	NENE	1906-06-21		A2
1383	GULLY, Philemon H	22	NWNE	1854-03-15		A1
1253	HANNA, Andrew	19	SESE	1860-10-01		A1
1254	" "	20	SWSW	1860-10-01		A1
1238	HARMON, Absalom T	27	NWNW	1856-04-01		A1
1239	HARMON, Absolam T	27	SWNE	1856-04-01		A1
1315	HARRISON, James A	12	NESW	1850-12-05		A1
1364	HENDERSON, Joseph C	24	S½NW	1885-05-25		A2
1365	" "	24	W½SW	1885-05-25		A2
1449	HENDERSON, William D	3	SESW	1859-10-01		A1
1450	" "	3	SWSE	1859-10-01		A1
1267	HENDRICK, Bernard G	19	NW	1848-09-01		A1 G223
1268	" "	19	W½NE	1848-09-01		A1 G223
1269	" "	20	W½NW	1848-09-01		A1 G223
1250	HENSON, Anderson	20	SENW	1854-03-15		A1
1255	HENSON, Andrew	30	NENE	1856-04-01		A1
1256	" "	31	N½NE	1856-04-01		A1
1257	" "	32	NWNW	1856-04-01		A1
1284	HENSON, Edward N	30	NWNE	1904-08-30		A2
1339	HENSON, James S	24	SWSE	1899-05-31		A2
1371	HENSON, Mary	18	E½NE	1847-08-17		A1
1392	HENSON, Richard	29	NW	1844-09-10		A1
1386	" "	20	E½SE	1856-04-01		A1
1387	" "	20	NENE	1856-04-01		A1
1388	" "	20	SENE	1856-04-01		A1
1391	" "	21	SWSW	1856-04-01		A1
1389	" "	21	NWSW	1860-10-01		A1
1390	" "	21	SWNW	1860-10-01		A1
1310	HOLT, Isham D	3	SWSW	1859-10-01		A1
1311	" "	4	SESE	1859-10-01		A1
1312	" "	9	NENE	1859-10-01		A1
1314	" "	9	SENE	1859-10-01		A1
1309	" "	10	SWNE	1860-05-01		A1
1313	" "	9	NWSE	1860-05-01		A1
1460	HOUSTON, William E	13	N½NE	1895-05-11		A2
1329	HUGHES, James F	17	NWNE	1859-10-01		A1
1475	HUGHES, William W	8	N½SW	1859-10-01		A1
1476	" "	8	S½NW	1859-10-01		A1
1477	" "	8	SWSE	1859-10-01		A1
1288	HUTTON, Francis M	17	NENW	1859-10-01		A1
1289	" "	17	SENW	1859-10-01		A1
1290	" "	19	NWSW	1859-10-01		A1
1291	" "	19	SESW	1859-10-01		A1
1292	" "	20	SWNE	1859-10-01		A1
1267	JACOWAY, Benjamin J	19	NW	1848-09-01		A1 G223
1268	" "	19	W½NE	1848-09-01		A1 G223
1269	" "	20	W½NW	1848-09-01		A1 G223
1242	JAMISON, Alexander	34	NESE	1856-04-01		A1
1418	JAMISON, Thomas	27	SW	1844-09-10		A1

ID	Individual in Patent	Sec.	Sec. Part	Date Issued	Other Counties	For More Info . . .
1419	JAMISON, Thomas (Cont'd)	34	NWNE	1850-12-05		A1
1414	JINKINS, Simon	3	NWSE	1859-10-01		A1
1412	JOHNSON, Samuel	26	NENW	1860-05-01		A1
1422	KELLEY, Tom	20	NWSE	1919-07-01		A2
1466	LEWIS, William M	33	E½NE	1848-09-01		A1
1373	LITTLE, Moses M	22	SESE	1860-10-01		A1
1374	" "	27	NENE	1860-10-01		A1
1274	MCDONALD, Daniel	10	NENE	1848-09-01		A1
1285	MCDONALD, Enoch	11	E½NW	1860-05-01		A1
1286	" "	11	NWSW	1860-05-01		A1
1287	" "	2	SESW	1860-10-01		A1
1260	MCKELLAR, Archibald	22	SW	1844-09-10		A1
1259	MCKELLAR, Archibald L	22	SWNW	1850-12-05		A1
1258	" "	22	SENW	1854-03-15		A1
1307	MCLAURIN, Hugh D	34	S½SE	1860-05-01		A1
1427	MILLS, Willard C	19	NESE	1854-03-15		A1
1428	" "	19	SWSE	1854-03-15		A1
1431	" "	25	SENE	1854-03-15		A1
1423	" "	1	NWSE	1856-04-01		A1
1424	" "	1	SESE	1856-04-01		A1
1429	" "	21	NWNW	1856-04-01		A1
1433	" "	29	S½SE	1856-04-01		A1
1434	" "	30	SENE	1856-04-01		A1
1436	" "	32	SWNE	1856-04-01		A1
1439	" "	36	NWSE	1856-04-01		A1
1426	" "	17	NENE	1859-10-01		A1
1430	" "	21	SESW	1859-10-01		A1
1432	" "	27	SENE	1859-10-01		A1
1438	" "	36	N½SW	1859-10-01		A1
1441	" "	4	N½NE	1859-10-01		A1
1442	" "	4	NESE	1859-10-01		A1
1443	" "	4	NW	1859-10-01		A1
1444	" "	4	SWNE	1859-10-01		A1
1445	" "	4	W½SE	1859-10-01		A1
1435	" "	32	SENE	1860-05-01		A1
1437	" "	32	SWSE	1860-05-01		A1
1446	" "	9	NESE	1860-05-01		A1
1425	" "	1	SWSW	1861-01-01		A1
1440	" "	36	SESW	1861-01-01		A1
1354	MOORE, John K	32	NWSE	1856-04-01		A1
1355	" "	32	NWSW	1856-04-01		A1
1352	" "	31	NESE	1860-05-01		A1
1353	" "	31	S½NE	1860-05-01		A1
1471	NORRIS, William S	10	NW	1844-09-10		A1
1410	PALMER, Samuel H	32	NESW	1860-10-01		A1
1411	" "	32	S½NW	1860-10-01		A1
1276	PEDEN, David T	22	E½NE	1859-10-01		A1
1277	" "	22	SWNE	1859-10-01		A1
1279	" "	23	NWNW	1859-10-01		A1
1278	" "	23	NENW	1860-10-01		A1
1280	" "	23	SWNW	1860-10-01		A1
1345	PEDEN, John A	15	SESW	1859-10-01		A1
1346	" "	15	SWSE	1859-10-01		A1
1347	" "	22	NENW	1859-10-01		A1
1344	" "	15	SESE	1860-05-01		A1
1343	" "	14	S½SW	1860-10-01		A1
1358	PEDEN, John R	29	SENE	1854-03-15		A1
1356	" "	28	NWNW	1856-04-01		A1
1357	" "	29	NENE	1856-04-01		A1
1361	" "	32	SWSW	1859-10-01		A1
1360	" "	31	SWSE	1860-05-01		A1
1359	" "	31	NWSE	1860-12-01		A1
1363	PEDEN, John S	29	N½SE	1859-10-01		A1
1402	PEDEN, Robert M	12	NWNE	1859-10-01		A1
1400	" "	1	SWSE	1860-05-01		A1
1401	" "	12	NENE	1860-05-01		A1
1467	PERKINS, William R	28	W½NE	1859-10-01		A1
1403	PHILLIPS, Robert	31	S½NW	1860-10-01		A1
1404	ROBBINS, Salathiel L	10	E½SE	1860-05-01		A1
1405	" "	10	NWSE	1860-05-01		A1
1407	" "	15	E½NW	1860-05-01		A1
1408	" "	15	NE	1860-05-01		A1
1406	" "	10	SWSE	1860-10-01		A1

ID	Individual in Patent	Sec.	Sec. Part	Date Issued	Other Counties	For More Info . . .
1362	ROGERS, John	1	NESW	1859-10-01		A1
1421	ROGERS, Tilmon	2	NESE	1860-05-01		A1
1240	RUTHVEN, Alexander C	23	NWNE	1899-05-31		A2
1241	RUTHVEN, Alexander G	29	SESW	1854-03-15		A1
1251	SADERFIELD, Anderson	32	NENE	1856-04-01		A1
1252	" "	33	NWNW	1856-04-01		A1
1384	SMITH, Reuben D	14	NW	1891-05-20		A2
1340	SMYTH, James S	20	NENW	1854-03-15		A1
1341	" "	20	NWNE	1854-03-15		A1
1342	" "	20	NWSW	1854-03-15		A1
1302	SPEIR, Hardy B	35	SW	1844-09-10		A1
1338	SPIER, James P	11	W½NW	1848-09-01		A1
1243	STENNIS, Alexander P	11	SENE	1856-04-01		A1
1244	" "	12	NWSW	1856-04-01		A1
1245	" "	13	E½SE	1860-05-01		A1
1246	" "	13	NWSE	1860-05-01		A1
1247	" "	13	S½NE	1860-05-01		A1
1248	" "	13	SWSE	1860-05-01		A1
1249	" "	24	N½NE	1860-05-01		A1
1303	STEWART, Hazael	2	NESW	1859-10-01		A1
1304	" "	2	S½NW	1859-10-01		A1
1334	STOVALL, James L	29	NESW	1892-06-25		A2
1367	STOVALL, Littleton B	30	NESW	1860-05-01		A1
1368	STOVALL, Littleton M	30	NENW	1859-10-01		A1
1369	" "	30	S½NW	1859-10-01		A1
1370	" "	31	N½NW	1859-10-01		A1
1478	STOVALL, Willis B	30	SESW	1860-05-01		A1
1479	STOWALL, Willis B	30	SWSE	1859-10-01		A1
1295	TERRY, Gideon	23	SWSE	1860-05-01		A1
1296	" "	24	E½SE	1860-05-01		A1
1297	" "	24	E½SW	1860-05-01		A1
1298	" "	25	N½NW	1860-05-01		A1
1299	" "	25	N½SE	1860-05-01		A1
1301	" "	26	NWNE	1860-05-01		A1
1294	" "	23	SESE	1860-10-01		A1
1300	" "	25	NWNE	1860-10-01		A1
1396	TERRY, Richard	11	SWSE	1849-12-01		A1
1395	" "	11	SWNE	1859-10-01		A1
1393	" "	11	NWSE	1860-05-01		A1
1394	" "	11	SESW	1860-05-01		A1
1275	THOMPSON, Daniel W	14	N½SW	1897-04-10		A2
1366	TODD, Lewis	4	SW	1844-09-10		A1
1261	WILSON, Asa K	26	SWSW	1850-12-05		A1
1262	" "	27	SESE	1859-10-01		A1
1263	" "	27	W½SE	1859-10-01		A1
1264	" "	34	SWNE	1861-02-01		A1
1316	YOUNG, James A	23	NESW	1895-02-21		A2
1317	" "	23	SENW	1895-02-21		A2
1330	YOUNG, James G	23	N½SE	1889-01-12		A2
1331	" "	23	S½NE	1889-01-12		A2
1472	YOUNG, William T	22	NESE	1890-02-21		A2
1473	" "	22	W½SE	1890-02-21		A2
1474	" "	27	NWNE	1890-02-21		A2

Patent Map

T11-N R14-E
Choctaw Meridian

Map Group 7

Township Statistics

Parcels Mapped	:	242
Number of Patents	:	181
Number of Individuals	:	104
Patentees Identified	:	103
Number of Surnames	:	70
Multi-Patentee Parcels	:	3
Oldest Patent Date	:	9/10/1844
Most Recent Patent	:	7/1/1919
Block/Lot Parcels	:	0
Parcels Re - Issued	:	0
Parcels that Overlap	:	0
Cities and Towns	:	4
Cemeteries	:	3

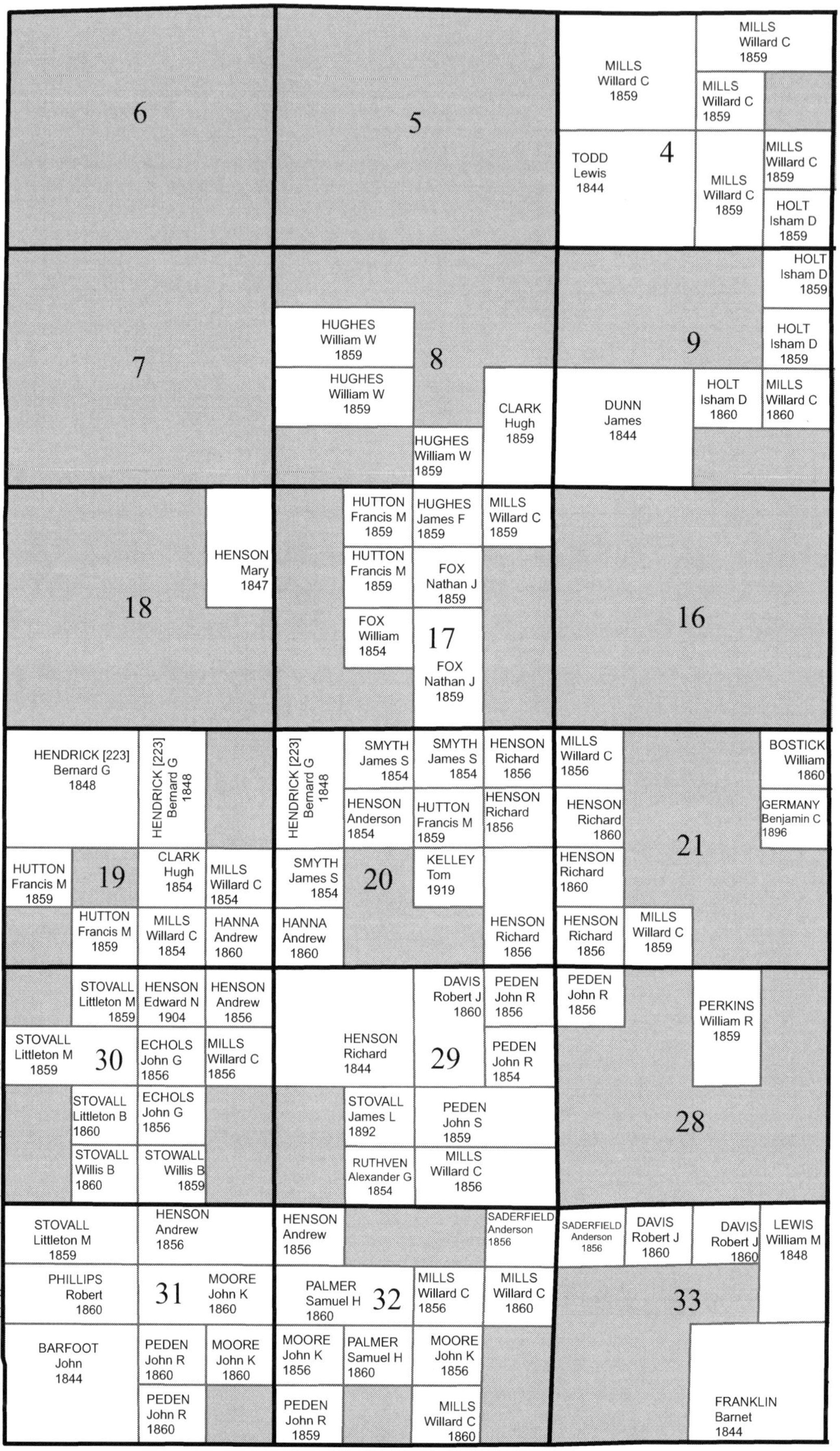

6

5

MILLS Willard C 1859
MILLS Willard C 1859
MILLS Willard C 1859
4
TODD Lewis 1844
MILLS Willard C 1859
MILLS Willard C 1859
HOLT Isham D 1859

7

HUGHES William W 1859
8
HUGHES William W 1859
CLARK Hugh 1859
HUGHES William W 1859

HOLT Isham D 1859
HOLT Isham D 1859
9
DUNN James 1844
HOLT Isham D 1860
MILLS Willard C 1860

HENSON Mary 1847
18

HUTTON Francis M 1859
HUGHES James F 1859
MILLS Willard C 1859
HUTTON Francis M 1859
FOX Nathan J 1859
FOX William 1854
17
FOX Nathan J 1859

16

HENDRICK [223] Bernard G 1848
HENDRICK [223] Bernard G 1848
HUTTON Francis M 1859
19
CLARK Hugh 1854
MILLS Willard C 1854
HUTTON Francis M 1859
MILLS Willard C 1854
HANNA Andrew 1860

HENDRICK [223] Bernard G 1848
SMYTH James S 1854
SMYTH James S 1854
HENSON Richard 1856
HENSON Anderson 1854
HUTTON Francis M 1859
HENSON Richard 1856
SMYTH James S 1854
20
KELLEY Tom 1919
HANNA Andrew 1860
HENSON Richard 1856

MILLS Willard C 1856
BOSTICK William 1860
HENSON Richard 1860
GERMANY Benjamin C 1896
21
HENSON Richard 1860
HENSON Richard 1856
MILLS Willard C 1859

STOVALL Littleton M 1859
HENSON Edward N 1904
HENSON Andrew 1856
STOVALL Littleton M 1859
30
ECHOLS John G 1856
MILLS Willard C 1856
STOVALL Littleton B 1860
ECHOLS John G 1856
STOVALL Willis B 1860
STOWALL Willis B 1859

DAVIS Robert J 1860
PEDEN John R 1856
HENSON Richard 1844
29
PEDEN John R 1854
STOVALL James L 1892
PEDEN John S 1859
RUTHVEN Alexander G 1854
MILLS Willard C 1856

PEDEN John R 1856
PERKINS William R 1859
28

STOVALL Littleton M 1859
HENSON Andrew 1856
PHILLIPS Robert 1860
31
MOORE John K 1860
BARFOOT John 1844
PEDEN John R 1860
MOORE John K 1860
PEDEN John R 1860

HENSON Andrew 1856
SADERFIELD Anderson 1856
PALMER Samuel H 1860
32
MILLS Willard C 1856
MILLS Willard C 1860
MOORE John K 1856
PALMER Samuel H 1860
MOORE John K 1856
PEDEN John R 1859
MILLS Willard C 1860

SADERFIELD Anderson 1856
DAVIS Robert J 1860
DAVIS Robert J 1860
LEWIS William M 1848
33
FRANKLIN Barnet 1844

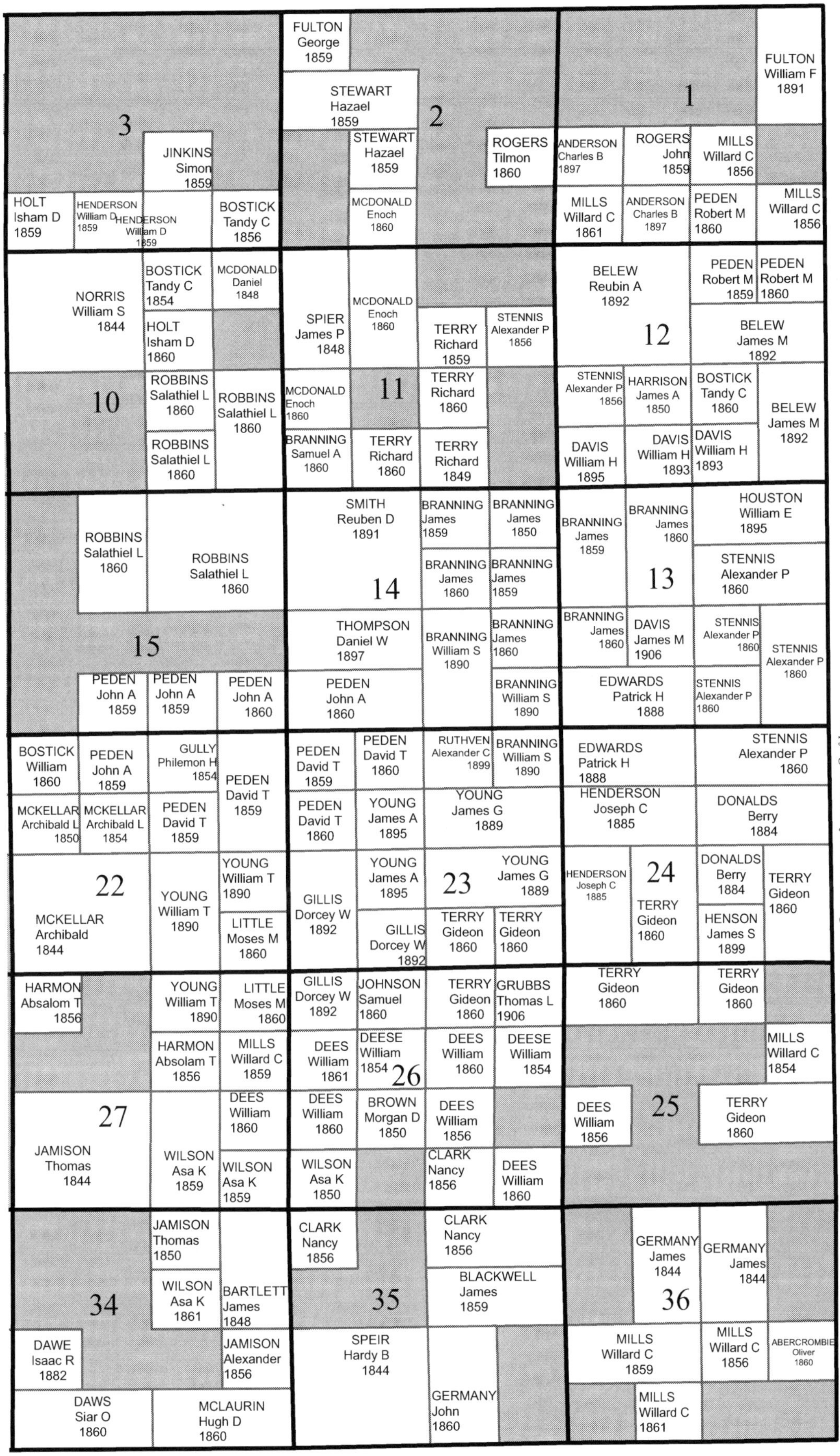

Helpful Hints

1. This Map's INDEX can be found on the preceding pages.
2. Refer to Map "C" to see where this Township lies within Kemper County, Mississippi.
3. Numbers within square brackets [ ] denote a multi-patentee land parcel (multi-owner). Refer to Appendix "C" for a full list of members in this group.
4. Areas that look to be crowded with Patentees usually indicate multiple sales of the same parcel (Re-issues) or Overlapping parcels. See this Township's Index for an explanation of these and other circumstances that might explain "odd" groupings of Patentees on this map.

Legend

- Patent Boundary
- Section Boundary
- No Patents Found (or Outside County)
- 1., 2., 3., ... Lot Numbers (when beside a name)
- [ ] Group Number (see Appendix "C")

Scale: Section = 1 mile X 1 mile (generally, with some exceptions)

Road Map

T11-N R14-E
Choctaw Meridian

Map Group 7

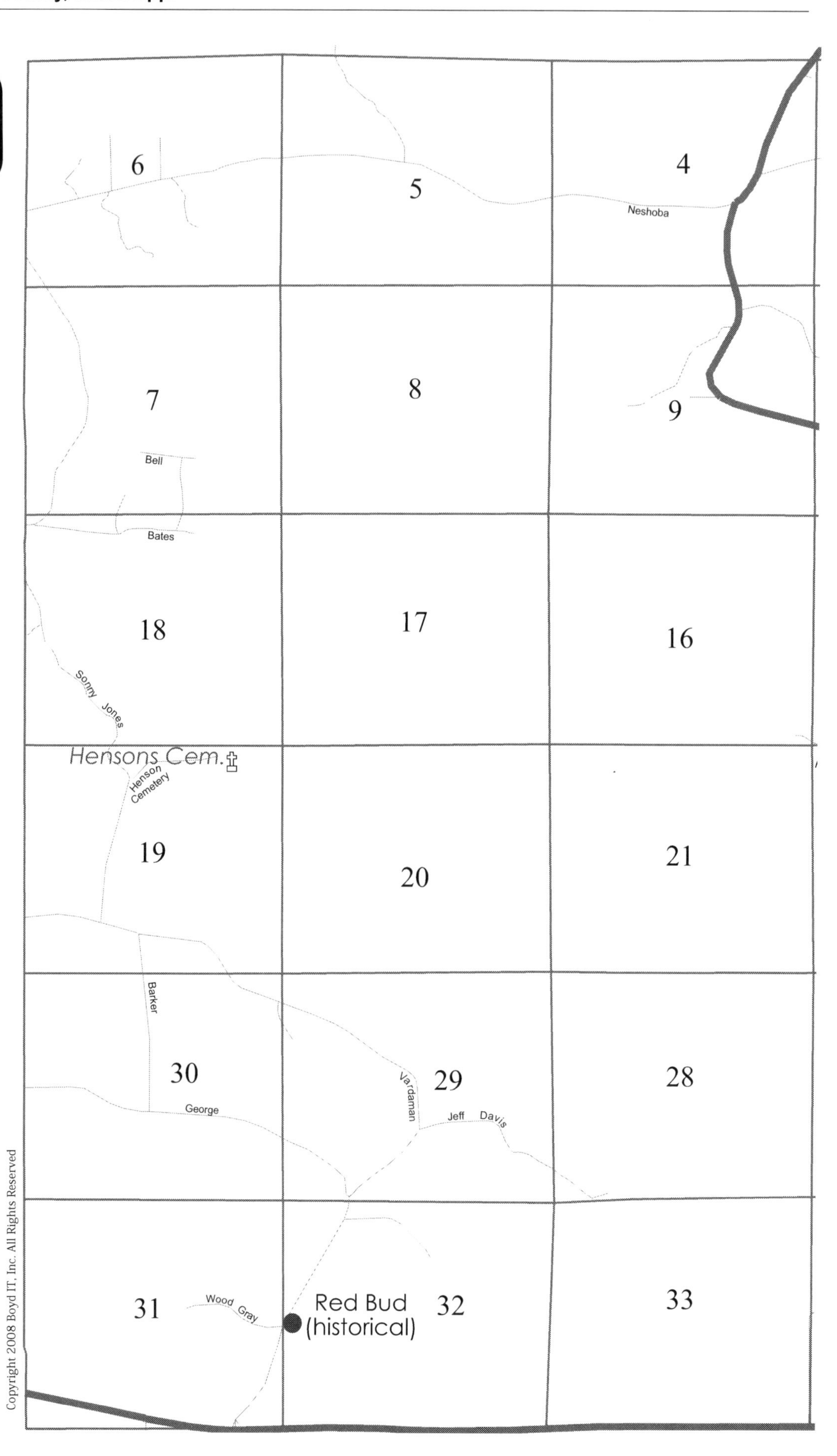

Cities & Towns

- Bluff Springs
- Cleveland
- Cow Creek (historical)
- Red Bud (historical)

Cemeteries

- Bluff Springs Cemetery
- Hensons Cemetery
- Shepherd Cemetery

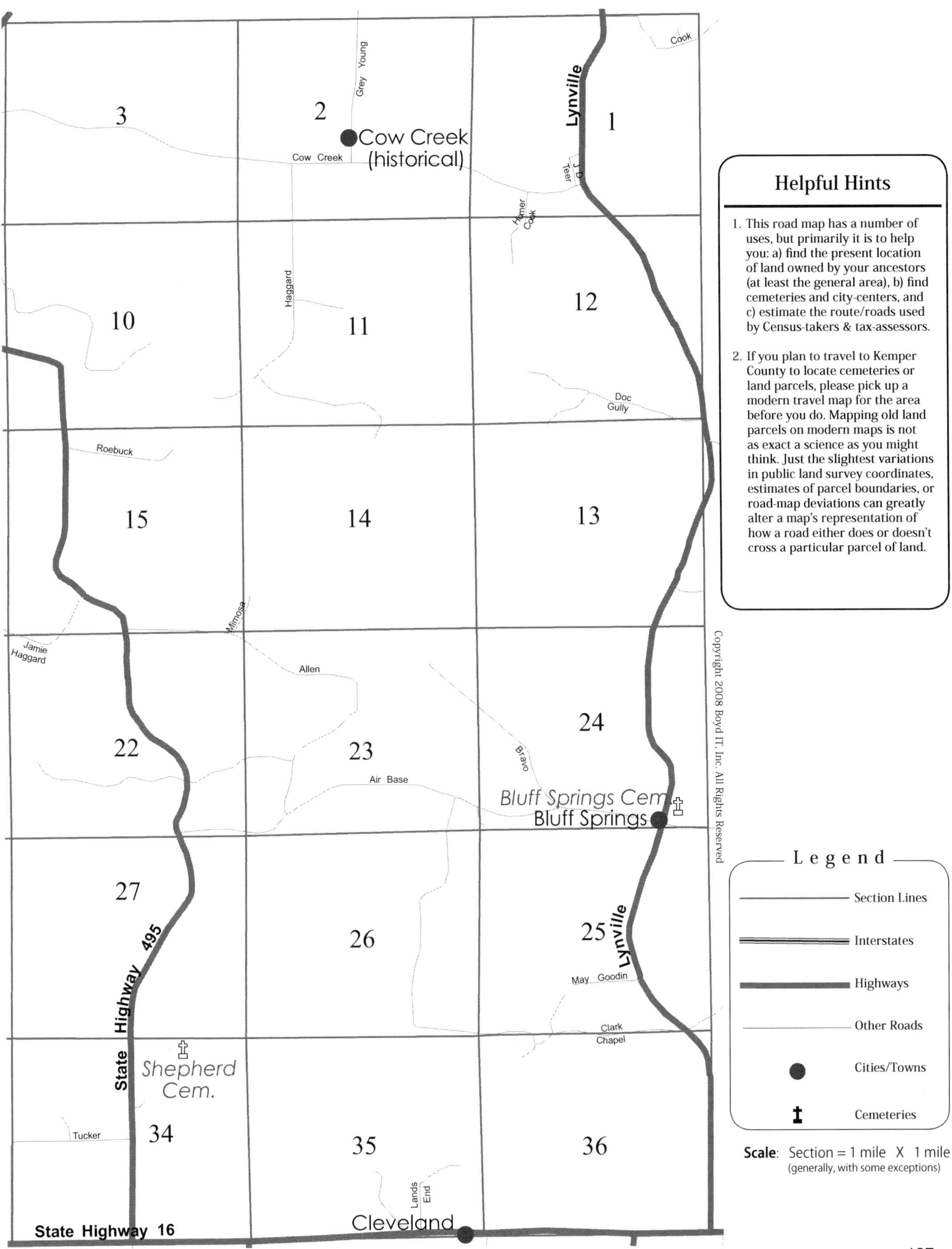

Helpful Hints

1. This road map has a number of uses, but primarily it is to help you: a) find the present location of land owned by your ancestors (at least the general area), b) find cemeteries and city-centers, and c) estimate the route/roads used by Census-takers & tax-assessors.
2. If you plan to travel to Kemper County to locate cemeteries or land parcels, please pick up a modern travel map for the area before you do. Mapping old land parcels on modern maps is not as exact a science as you might think. Just the slightest variations in public land survey coordinates, estimates of parcel boundaries, or road-map deviations can greatly alter a map's representation of how a road either does or doesn't cross a particular parcel of land.

Legend

- Section Lines
- Interstates
- Highways
- Other Roads
- Cities/Towns
- Cemeteries

Scale: Section = 1 mile X 1 mile
(generally, with some exceptions)

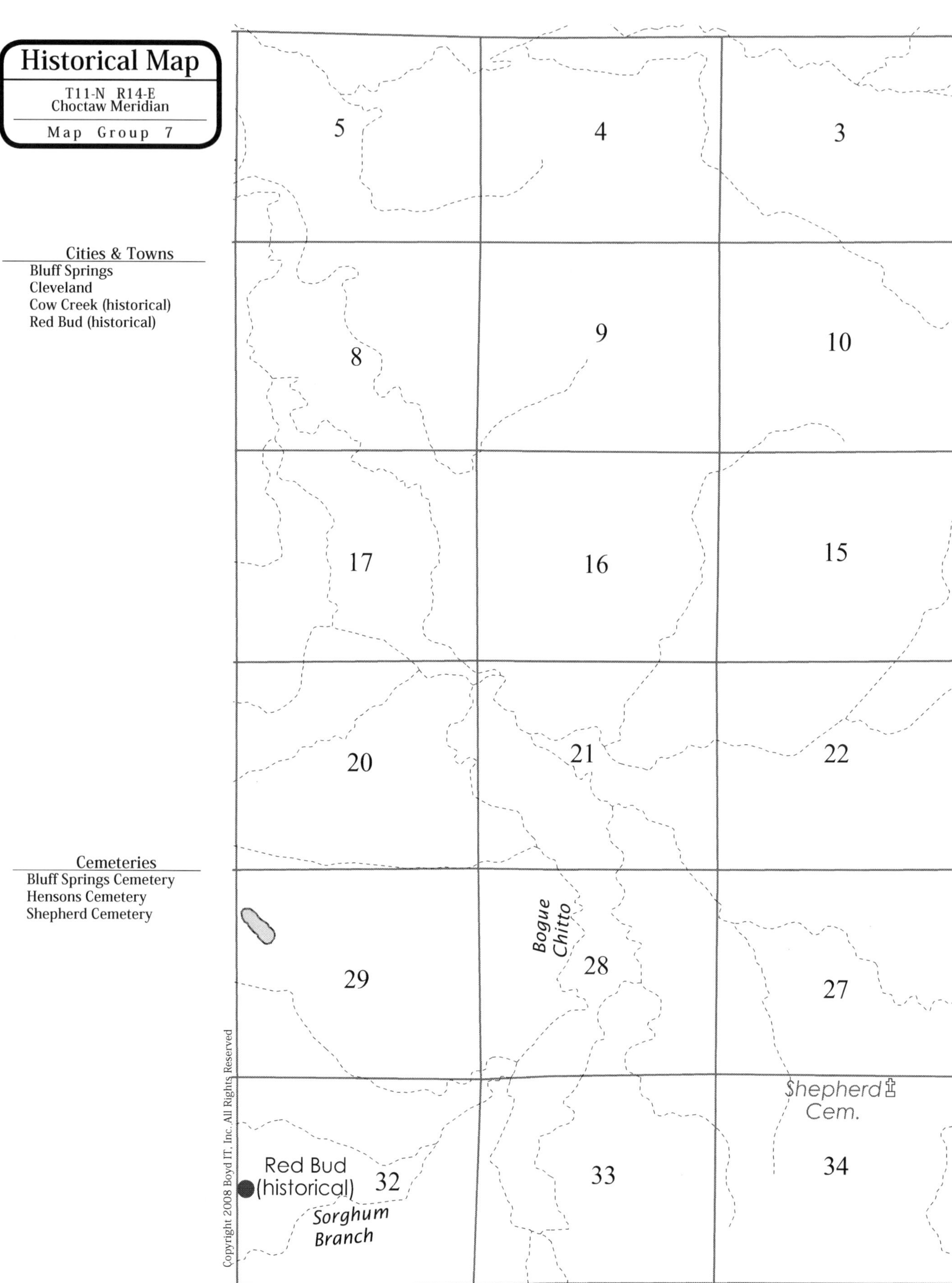
Historical Map
T11-N R14-E
Choctaw Meridian
Map Group 7
Cities & Towns
Bluff Springs
Cleveland
Cow Creek (historical)
Red Bud (historical)
Cemeteries
Bluff Springs Cemetery
Hensons Cemetery
Shepherd Cemetery
5
4
3
8
9
10
17
16
15
20
21
22
29
28
27
32
33
34
Bogue Chitto
Shepherd Cem.
Red Bud (historical)
Sorghum Branch
Copyright 2008 Boyd IT, Inc. All Rights Reserved

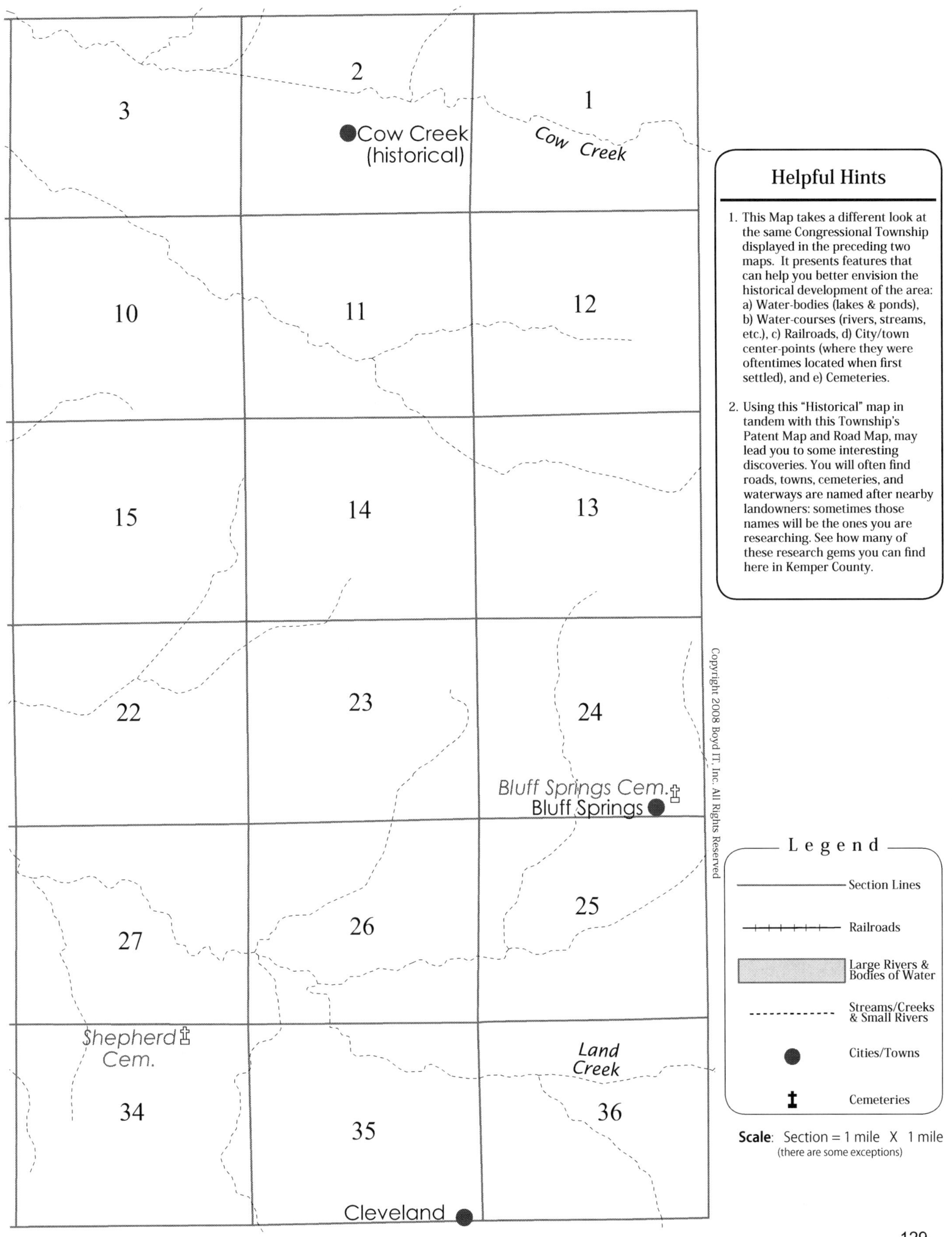

Helpful Hints

1. This Map takes a different look at the same Congressional Township displayed in the preceding two maps. It presents features that can help you better envision the historical development of the area: a) Water-bodies (lakes & ponds), b) Water-courses (rivers, streams, etc.), c) Railroads, d) City/town center-points (where they were oftentimes located when first settled), and e) Cemeteries.

2. Using this "Historical" map in tandem with this Township's Patent Map and Road Map, may lead you to some interesting discoveries. You will often find roads, towns, cemeteries, and waterways are named after nearby landowners: sometimes those names will be the ones you are researching. See how many of these research gems you can find here in Kemper County.

Map Group 8: Index to Land Patents

Township 11-North Range 15-East (Choctaw)

After you locate an individual in this Index, take note of the Section and Section Part then proceed to the Land Patent map on the pages immediately following. You should have no difficulty locating the corresponding parcel of land.

The "For More Info" Column will lead you to more information about the underlying Patents. See the *Legend* at right, and the "How to Use this Book" chapter, for more information.

LEGEND

"For More Info . . . " column

A = Authority (Legislative Act, See Appendix "A")
B = Block or Lot (location in Section unknown)
C = Cancelled Patent
F = Fractional Section
G = Group (Multi-Patentee Patent, see Appendix "C")
V = Overlaps another Parcel
R = Re-Issued (Parcel patented more than once)

(A & G items require you to look in the Appendixes referred to above. All other Letter-designations followed by a number require you to locate line-items in this index that possess the ID number found after the letter).

ID	Individual in Patent	Sec.	Sec. Part	Date Issued	Other Counties	For More Info . . .
1587	ADAMS, James	31	NESE	1884-12-30		A2
1588	" "	31	SENE	1884-12-30		A2
1544	ANDERSON, Edmon W	30	N½SW	1876-02-01		A2
1547	ANDERSON, Edward W	30	SENW	1882-06-01		A1
1624	ANDERSON, John	2	NWSW	1892-06-15		A2
1529	BAREFIELD, David	20	NESW	1856-04-01		A1
1531	" "	20	SWSW	1856-04-01		A1
1532	" "	29	NENE	1856-04-01		A1
1530	" "	20	SESW	1860-05-01		A1
1533	" "	29	SENE	1860-05-01		A1
1602	BARFIELD, James G	29	NWNW	1885-12-19		A2
1592	BARTLETT, James	14	SWSW	1848-09-01		A1 G30
1589	" "	4	SWSW	1848-09-01		A1
1590	" "	5	SESE	1848-09-01		A1
1591	" "	9	NWNW	1848-09-01		A1
1760	BAUGHMAN, Zackariah T	6	N½NE	1893-02-28		A2
1692	BISHOP, Robert W	6	S½SW	1902-02-12		A2
1693	" "	7	N½NW	1902-02-12		A2
1746	BLACKWELL, William J	32	SWNW	1883-07-10		A2
1581	BRITTAIN, Henson G	36	NWSE	1854-03-15		A1
1582	" "	36	SESE	1859-10-01		A1
1584	BRITTAIN, Horatio G	36	E½NW	1849-12-01		A1
1747	BURTON, William J	19	NESW	1889-11-23		A2
1748	" "	19	SENW	1889-11-23		A2
1510	CAMPBELL, Archibald D	27	SESE	1854-03-15		A1
1511	" "	34	N½NW	1856-04-01		A1
1513	" "	34	NWNE	1856-04-01		A1
1509	" "	27	E½SW	1859-10-01		A1
1512	" "	34	NENE	1859-10-01		A1
1514	" "	34	S½NE	1860-05-01		A1
1623	CAMPBELL, John A	27	NWSW	1892-06-25		A2
1668	CAMPBELL, Martha	26	SWSE	1892-09-27		A2
1687	CAMPBELL, Robert	27	SENW	1848-09-01		A1
1605	CAVANAH, James H	17	SW	1846-09-01		A1
1606	CAVANAH, James R	17	E½NE	1848-09-01		A1 G85
1525	CHANEY, Charles P	13	SWSE	1850-12-05		A1
1486	CLARK, Alexander	14	E½NE	1859-10-01		A1
1666	CLARK, Malcom	31	NWSW	1860-05-01		A1
1618	CLEMENT, Jesse	15	SE	1844-09-10		A1
1686	COLE, Peter H	34	SESW	1859-10-01		A1
1526	COLEMAN, Charles P	2	NW	1844-09-10		A1
1580	COOK, Henry R	6	NENW	1902-01-17		A2
1638	COWSAR, John F	9	SWSW	1850-12-02		A1
1637	" "	9	SESW	1859-10-01		A1
1639	COWSER, John F	9	N½SW	1848-09-01		A1
1578	DONALD, Henry	17	SWNW	1892-07-25		A2

ID	Individual in Patent	Sec.	Sec. Part	Date Issued	Other Counties	For More Info . . .
1579	DONALD, Henry (Cont'd)	18	S½NE	1892-07-25		A2
1586	EARNEST, Isham C	24	SW	1844-09-10		A1
1548	EDWARDS, Elisha	12	NENE	1860-05-01		A1
1681	ELLIS, Oliver	2	NENE	1859-10-01		A1
1682	" "	2	NESE	1859-10-01		A1
1683	" "	2	SENE	1859-10-01		A1
1684	" "	2	SWSE	1860-05-01		A1
1685	" "	2	W½NE	1860-05-01		A1
1516	FALKNER, Asa	30	E½SE	1879-12-15		A2
1517	" "	30	SESW	1879-12-15		A2
1518	" "	30	SWSE	1879-12-15		A2
1740	FALKNER, William F	30	SWSW	1889-01-12		A2
1667	FOX, Mally	14	NENW	1849-12-01		A1
1641	FULLER, John M	20	SENE	1891-08-19		A2
1741	FULTON, William F	6	W½NW	1891-05-20		A2
1642	GIBSON, John M	31	E½SW	1844-09-10		A1
1643	" "	31	W½SE	1844-09-10		A1
1555	GOYNE, Erasmus C	34	SWSW	1850-12-05		A1
1603	GRIFFITH, James	24	SENW	1859-10-01		A1
1604	" "	24	W½NE	1859-10-01		A1
1659	GULLY, John W	36	NENE	1850-12-05		A1
1660	" "	36	NESE	1856-04-01		A1
1698	GULLY, Samuel K	36	W½NW	1854-03-15		A1
1697	" "	35	NWNW	1860-05-01		A1
1701	GULLY, Samuel R	25	SWSE	1849-12-01		A1
1549	HARGROVE, Elizabeth	28	NWSW	1849-12-01		A1
1550	HENDERSON, Ellis	17	E½NW	1846-09-01		A1
1551	" "	17	W½NE	1846-09-01		A1
1553	" "	8	SESW	1850-12-02		A1
1552	" "	7	NESE	1850-12-05		A1
1554	" "	8	SWSE	1856-04-01		A1
1745	HITCHCOCK, William	8	N½SW	1895-11-11		A2
1625	HOLTON, John B	22	SESE	1856-04-01		A1
1626	" "	26	NWNW	1856-04-01		A1
1640	HOUSTON, John J	32	NESW	1860-10-01		A1
1611	HULL, James W	32	SENW	1856-04-01		A1
1612	" "	32	SWNE	1856-04-01		A1
1608	" "	27	SWNW	1859-10-01		A1
1609	" "	27	SWSW	1859-10-01		A1
1610	" "	29	SWSE	1860-05-01		A1
1520	JACOWAY, Benjamin J	23	W½NW	1848-09-01		A1 G244
1537	JORDAN, Dempsey	35	E½NW	1859-10-01		A1
1607	JORDAN, James T	28	N½NW	1860-05-01		A1
1628	LAMPLEY, John C	4	NWNE	1849-12-01		A1
1627	" "	3	E½SW	1850-12-02		A1
1629	" "	4	NWSE	1854-03-15		A1
1630	" "	4	SWNE	1854-03-15		A1
1631	" "	4	SWNW	1854-03-15		A1
1632	LAMPLY, John C	3	SWNW	1848-09-01		A1
1633	" "	4	E½NE	1848-09-01		A1
1502	LAND, Alonzo B	33	NESW	1859-10-01		A1
1503	" "	33	NWSE	1859-10-01		A1
1504	" "	33	SENW	1859-10-01		A1
1705	LANHAM, Solomon	23	SW	1844-09-10		A1
1689	LOVE, Robert J	35	SWSW	1849-12-01		A1
1688	" "	35	NWSW	1850-12-05		A1
1733	LOVE, William A	12	NWSW	1860-05-01		A1
1734	" "	12	SWNE	1860-05-01		A1
1735	" "	12	SWNW	1860-05-01		A1
1652	LOVELADY, John S	33	SESE	1854-03-15		A1
1651	" "	33	NESE	1859-10-01		A1
1653	" "	34	NWSW	1859-10-01		A1
1749	LOWE, William	18	SE	1844-09-10		A1 G274
1559	MADISON, Frank	8	NESE	1896-08-26		A2
1634	MASSEY, John C	5	S½NW	1891-05-20		A2
1679	MATHENY, Obadiah L	24	NENW	1860-05-01		A1
1680	" "	24	W½NW	1860-05-01		A1
1542	MCALLUM, Duncan P	28	NESE	1860-05-01		A1
1543	" "	28	SWSE	1860-05-01		A1
1515	MCBRYDE, Archibald	28	NWSE	1860-05-01		A1
1541	MCBRYDE, Duncan	28	NENE	1859-10-01		A1
1669	MCBRYDE, Mary	28	W½NE	1849-12-01		A1
1620	MCFARLAND, Jesse L	7	NWSW	1894-12-17		A2

ID	Individual in Patent	Sec.	Sec. Part	Date Issued	Other Counties	For More Info . . .
1621	MCFARLAND, Jesse L (Cont'd)	7	S½NW	1894-12-17		A2
1619	" "	7	NESW	1897-05-07		A2
1717	MCKELLAR, Walter S	32	N½NE	1892-03-23		A2
1644	MCLAURIN, John	26	NWSE	1859-10-01		A1
1645	" "	26	SWSW	1859-10-01		A1
1635	MCLAURIN, John C	34	NESW	1884-12-30		A2
1636	" "	34	SENW	1884-12-30		A2
1694	MCNEIL, Rufus L	32	NESE	1859-10-01		A1
1695	" "	32	SESE	1860-10-01		A1
1708	MCNEILL, Susanna	35	E½SE	1844-09-10		A1
1676	MCRAE, Murdock	25	SW	1844-09-10		A1
1675	" "	25	NESE	1849-12-01		A1
1677	" "	26	SENE	1859-10-01		A1
1732	MILLS, Willard C	36	W½NE	1848-09-01		A1
1722	" "	21	NW	1854-03-15		A1
1723	" "	22	NW	1854-03-15		A1
1728	" "	27	SENE	1854-03-15		A1
1727	" "	26	SWNE	1856-04-01		A1
1729	" "	27	SWNE	1856-04-01		A1
1731	" "	31	SWSW	1856-04-01		A1
1718	" "	12	SENE	1859-10-01		A1
1719	" "	12	SESW	1859-10-01		A1
1721	" "	2	SESE	1859-10-01		A1
1726	" "	26	NENE	1859-10-01		A1
1720	" "	2	NESW	1860-05-01		A1
1730	" "	28	SWNW	1860-05-01		A1
1724	" "	24	SENE	1860-10-01		A1
1725	" "	24	SESE	1860-10-01		A1
1703	MOONEY, Silas M	6	S½NE	1859-10-01		A1
1704	" "	6	SESE	1859-10-01		A1
1702	MOORE, Shelby	2	SESW	1910-09-06		A2
1585	NICHOLSON, Isaac W	19	SE	1841-02-27		A1 V1561, 1558, 1706
1750	OVERSTREET, William	36	E½SW	1847-08-17		A1
1751	" "	36	SWSE	1859-10-01		A1
1521	PACE, Burrel H	22	NE	1844-09-10		A1
1505	PADEN, Andrew W	8	NWSE	1850-12-05		A1
1506	" "	8	SESE	1850-12-05		A1
1507	" "	9	NWSE	1859-10-01		A1
1508	" "	9	S½NE	1859-10-01		A1
1671	PADEN, Moses W	5	SW	1846-09-01		A1
1670	" "	5	NESE	1848-09-01		A1
1672	" "	5	W½SE	1848-09-01		A1
1673	" "	6	NESE	1850-12-05		A1
1690	PADEN, Robert M	4	E½NW	1848-09-01		A1
1691	" "	4	NWNW	1848-09-01		A1
1742	PADEN, William F	20	NENE	1850-12-05		A1
1713	PEARSON, Thomas P	10	NWNE	1848-09-01		A1
1487	PEDEN, Alexander D	10	E½SW	1859-10-01		A1
1488	" "	10	NWSE	1859-10-01		A1
1522	PEDEN, Calvin C	18	E½NW	1891-05-20		A2
1523	" "	18	NWNE	1891-05-20		A2
1524	" "	7	SWSE	1891-05-20		A2
1535	PEDEN, David W	28	SWSW	1854-03-15		A1
1534	" "	28	SESW	1859-10-01		A1
1536	" "	29	SESE	1859-10-01		A1
1567	PEDEN, Givens	22	E½SW	1844-09-10		A1
1569	" "	22	W½SE	1844-09-10		A1
1570	" "	22	W½SW	1847-08-17		A1
1568	" "	22	NESE	1854-03-15		A1
1572	" "	27	NWNE	1854-03-15		A1
1571	" "	27	NENE	1856-04-01		A1
1573	PEDEN, Givins	27	N½NW	1848-09-01		A1
1599	PEDEN, James D	3	SENE	1848-09-01		A1
1600	" "	3	SWNE	1849-12-01		A1
1601	" "	3	SWSE	1849-12-01		A1
1598	" "	3	NWSE	1850-12-05		A1
1594	" "	14	NWSW	1856-04-01		A1
1595	" "	14	SESW	1856-04-01		A1
1593	" "	14	NESW	1859-10-01		A1
1596	" "	14	W½SE	1859-10-01		A1
1597	" "	2	SWSW	1860-10-01		A1
1649	PEDEN, John	15	NWNE	1849-12-01		A1
1646	" "	10	NESE	1856-04-01		A1

ID	Individual in Patent	Sec.	Sec. Part	Date Issued	Other Counties	For More Info . . .
1648	PEDEN, John (Cont'd)	10	SWSE	1859-10-01		A1
1647	" "	10	SESE	1860-05-01		A1
1749	PEDEN, John S	18	SE	1844-09-10		A1 G274
1654	" "	20	SE	1844-09-10		A1
1657	PEDEN, John T	9	SESE	1848-09-01		A1
1658	" "	9	SWSE	1848-09-01		A1
1656	" "	9	NESE	1850-12-05		A1
1655	" "	10	NWSW	1854-03-15		A1
1674	PEDEN, Moses W	6	W½SE	1856-04-01		A1
1699	PEDEN, Samuel	17	W½SE	1843-02-01		A1
1700	" "	23	E½NW	1843-02-01		A1
1709	PEDEN, Thomas J	9	NENE	1856-04-01		A1
1716	PEDEN, Thomas W	21	SE	1844-09-10		A1
1753	PEDEN, William T	17	E½SE	1843-02-01		A1
1758	" "	23	W½SE	1843-02-01		A1
1752	" "	10	SWSW	1848-09-01		A1
1606	" "	17	E½NE	1848-09-01		A1 G85
1755	" "	20	NWNE	1860-05-01		A1
1754	" "	19	SENE	1860-10-01		A1 C R1710
1756	" "	20	S½NW	1860-10-01		A1 C
1757	" "	20	SWNE	1860-10-01		A1 C
1759	PERKINS, Wilson	28	SESE	1859-10-01		A1
1480	PHILLIPS, Aaron N	20	NWSW	1882-05-20		A2
1592	PIERCE, George	14	SWSW	1848-09-01		A1 G30
1520	" "	23	W½NW	1848-09-01		A1 G244
1560	PIERCE, George S	11	SWSW	1848-09-01		A1
1622	PORTER, Jesse	23	SWNE	1848-09-01		A1
1737	RILEY, William E	34	SESE	1856-04-01		A1
1736	" "	34	NESE	1860-05-01		A1
1738	" "	34	W½SE	1860-05-01		A1
1739	" "	35	NESW	1860-05-01		A1
1650	ROBERTS, John	24	NENE	1893-12-21		A2
1558	ROSS, Francis M	19	E½SE	1875-07-01		A2 V1585
1519	RUTHERFORD, Benjamin D	12	SE	1843-02-01		A1
1661	SADLER, John W	36	W½SW	1846-09-01		A1
1714	SCOTT, Thomas	2	NWSE	1900-10-04		A2
1706	SHEPARD, Stephen E	19	SWSE	1890-02-21		A2 V1585
1707	" "	30	N½NE	1890-02-21		A2
1665	SIMMS, Leroy H	13	NESE	1850-12-05		A1
1540	SMITH, Dixon H	33	W½SW	1859-10-01		A1
1538	" "	32	SENE	1860-05-01		A1
1539	" "	33	W½NW	1860-05-01		A1
1557	SMITH, Felix T	31	S½NW	1860-05-01		A1
1615	SMITH, Jasper N	31	SESE	1860-05-01		A1
1616	" "	32	NWSW	1860-05-01		A1
1617	" "	32	SWSW	1860-05-01		A1
1678	SPEAR, Nathaniel	12	NWNW	1859-10-01		A1
1696	SPENCE, Samuel C	35	SWNW	1893-12-21		A2
1481	STENNIS, Adam T	8	NENW	1849-12-01		A1
1483	" "	8	W½NE	1849-12-01		A1
1485	" "	9	SWNW	1849-12-01		A1
1484	" "	9	SENW	1856-04-01		A1
1482	" "	8	SENW	1860-10-01		A1
1493	STENNIS, Alexander P	19	NENE	1850-12-05		A1
1498	" "	20	NWNW	1850-12-05		A1
1499	" "	7	NWSE	1856-04-01		A1
1500	" "	7	S½NE	1856-04-01		A1
1501	" "	7	S½SW	1856-04-01		A1
1489	" "	18	NWNW	1860-05-01		A1
1490	" "	18	NWSW	1860-05-01		A1
1491	" "	18	S½SW	1860-05-01		A1
1492	" "	18	SWNW	1860-05-01		A1
1495	" "	19	NWNE	1860-05-01		A1
1496	" "	19	NWNW	1860-05-01		A1
1494	" "	19	NENW	1860-10-01		A1
1497	" "	19	SESW	1860-10-01		A1
1574	STENNIS, Hampton H	18	NESW	1892-08-01		A1
1744	STEVENSON, William H	14	W½NE	1859-10-01		A1
1743	" "	12	SWSW	1860-05-01		A1
1566	TERRY, Gideon	30	W½NW	1844-09-10		A1
1561	" "	19	NWSE	1860-05-01		A1 V1585
1564	" "	30	NWSE	1860-05-01		A1
1562	" "	19	SWSW	1860-10-01		A1

ID	Individual in Patent	Sec.	Sec. Part	Date Issued	Other Counties	For More Info . . .
1565	TERRY, Gideon (Cont'd)	30	SWNE	1860-10-01		A1
1563	" "	30	NENW	1882-08-03		A1
1715	TERRY, Thomas	21	SW	1844-09-10		A1
1711	TERRY, Thomas J	29	SWNW	1859-10-01		A1
1712	" "	30	SENE	1859-10-01		A1
1710	" "	19	SENE	1860-05-01		A1 R1754
1575	TISDALE, Hardy	33	NE	1860-05-01		A1
1576	" "	33	NENW	1860-05-01		A1
1577	" "	34	SWNW	1860-05-01		A1
1527	WATSON, Daniel	8	E½NE	1846-09-01		A1
1528	" "	9	NENW	1849-12-01		A1
1614	WATSON, James	4	SWSE	1848-09-01		A1
1613	" "	4	E½SE	1849-12-01		A1
1545	WHITE, Edward B	7	N½NE	1860-05-01		A1
1546	" "	8	W½NW	1860-05-01		A1
1662	WILLIAMSON, John	31	N½NE	1883-09-15		A2
1663	" "	31	NENW	1883-09-15		A2
1664	" "	31	SWNE	1883-09-15		A2
1556	WILSON, Ezekiel B	5	N½NW	1883-04-30		A2
1583	WOODS, Hezekiah W	25	NE	1844-09-10		A1

Patent Map

T11-N R15-E
Choctaw Meridian

Map Group 8

Township Statistics

Parcels Mapped	:	281
Number of Patents	:	225
Number of Individuals	:	131
Patentees Identified	:	131
Number of Surnames	:	91
Multi-Patentee Parcels	:	4
Oldest Patent Date	:	2/27/1841
Most Recent Patent	:	9/6/1910
Block/Lot Parcels	:	0
Parcels Re - Issued	:	1
Parcels that Overlap	:	4
Cities and Towns	:	2
Cemeteries	:	3

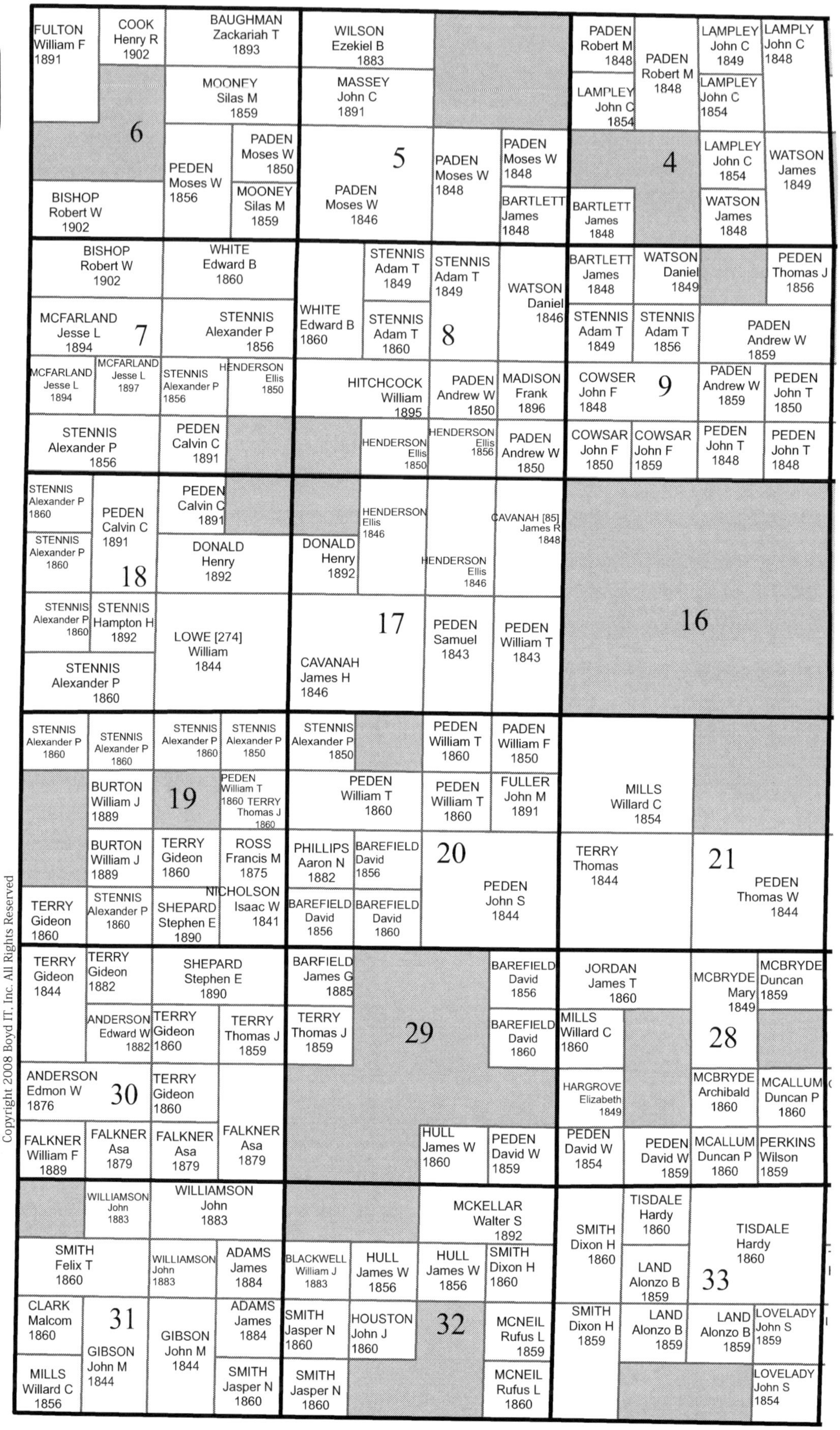

6
FULTON William F 1891
COOK Henry R 1902
BAUGHMAN Zackariah T 1893
MOONEY Silas M 1859
PADEN Moses W 1850
PEDEN Moses W 1856
MOONEY Silas M 1859
BISHOP Robert W 1902

5
WILSON Ezekiel B 1883
MASSEY John C 1891
PADEN Moses W 1846
PADEN Moses W 1848
PADEN Moses W 1848
BARTLETT James 1848

4
PADEN Robert M 1848
PADEN Robert M 1848
LAMPLEY John C 1849
LAMPLY John C 1848
LAMPLEY John C 1854
LAMPLEY John C 1854
LAMPLEY John C 1854
WATSON James 1849
BARTLETT James 1848
WATSON James 1848

7
BISHOP Robert W 1902
WHITE Edward B 1860
MCFARLAND Jesse L 1894
STENNIS Alexander P 1856
MCFARLAND Jesse L 1894
MCFARLAND Jesse L 1897
STENNIS Alexander P 1856
HENDERSON Ellis 1850
STENNIS Alexander P 1856
PEDEN Calvin C 1891

8
WHITE Edward B 1860
STENNIS Adam T 1849
STENNIS Adam T 1849
STENNIS Adam T 1860
WATSON Daniel 1846
HITCHCOCK William 1895
PADEN Andrew W 1850
MADISON Frank 1896
HENDERSON Ellis 1850
HENDERSON Ellis 1856
PADEN Andrew W 1850

9
BARTLETT James 1848
WATSON Daniel 1849
PEDEN Thomas J 1856
STENNIS Adam T 1849
STENNIS Adam T 1856
PADEN Andrew W 1859
COWSER John F 1848
PADEN Andrew W 1859
PEDEN John T 1850
COWSAR John F 1850
COWSAR John F 1859
PEDEN John T 1848
PEDEN John T 1848

18
STENNIS Alexander P 1860
PEDEN Calvin C 1891
PEDEN Calvin C 1891
STENNIS Alexander P 1860
DONALD Henry 1892
STENNIS Alexander P 1860
STENNIS Hampton H 1892
LOWE [274] William 1844
STENNIS Alexander P 1860

17
DONALD Henry 1892
HENDERSON Ellis 1846
CAVANAH [85] James R 1848
HENDERSON Ellis 1846
CAVANAH James H 1846
PEDEN Samuel 1843
PEDEN William T 1843

16

19
STENNIS Alexander P 1860
STENNIS Alexander P 1860
STENNIS Alexander P 1860
STENNIS Alexander P 1850
BURTON William J 1889
PEDEN William T 1860
TERRY Thomas J 1860
BURTON William J 1889
TERRY Gideon 1860
ROSS Francis M 1875
TERRY Gideon 1860
STENNIS Alexander P 1860
SHEPARD Stephen E 1890
NICHOLSON Isaac W 1841

20
STENNIS Alexander P 1850
PEDEN William T 1860
PADEN William F 1850
PEDEN William T 1860
PEDEN William T 1860
FULLER John M 1891
PHILLIPS Aaron N 1882
BAREFIELD David 1856
PEDEN John S 1844
BAREFIELD David 1856
BAREFIELD David 1860

21
MILLS Willard C 1854
TERRY Thomas 1844
PEDEN Thomas W 1844

30
TERRY Gideon 1844
TERRY Gideon 1882
SHEPARD Stephen E 1890
ANDERSON Edward W 1882
TERRY Gideon 1860
TERRY Thomas J 1859
ANDERSON Edmon W 1876
TERRY Gideon 1860
FALKNER William F 1889
FALKNER Asa 1879
FALKNER Asa 1879
FALKNER Asa 1879

29
BARFIELD James G 1885
BAREFIELD David 1856
TERRY Thomas J 1859
BAREFIELD David 1860
HULL James W 1860
PEDEN David W 1859

28
JORDAN James T 1860
MCBRYDE Mary 1849
MCBRYDE Duncan 1859
MILLS Willard C 1860
HARGROVE Elizabeth 1849
MCBRYDE Archibald 1860
MCALLUM Duncan P 1860
PEDEN David W 1854
PEDEN David W 1859
MCALLUM Duncan P 1860
PERKINS Wilson 1859

31
WILLIAMSON John 1883
WILLIAMSON John 1883
SMITH Felix T 1860
WILLIAMSON John 1883
ADAMS James 1884
CLARK Malcom 1860
ADAMS James 1884
GIBSON John M 1844
GIBSON John M 1844
MILLS Willard C 1856
SMITH Jasper N 1860

32
MCKELLAR Walter S 1892
BLACKWELL William J 1883
HULL James W 1856
HULL James W 1856
SMITH Dixon H 1860
SMITH Jasper N 1860
HOUSTON John J 1860
MCNEIL Rufus L 1859
SMITH Jasper N 1860
MCNEIL Rufus L 1860

33
SMITH Dixon H 1860
TISDALE Hardy 1860
TISDALE Hardy 1860
LAND Alonzo B 1859
SMITH Dixon H 1859
LAND Alonzo B 1859
LAND Alonzo B 1859
LOVELADY John S 1859
LOVELADY John S 1854

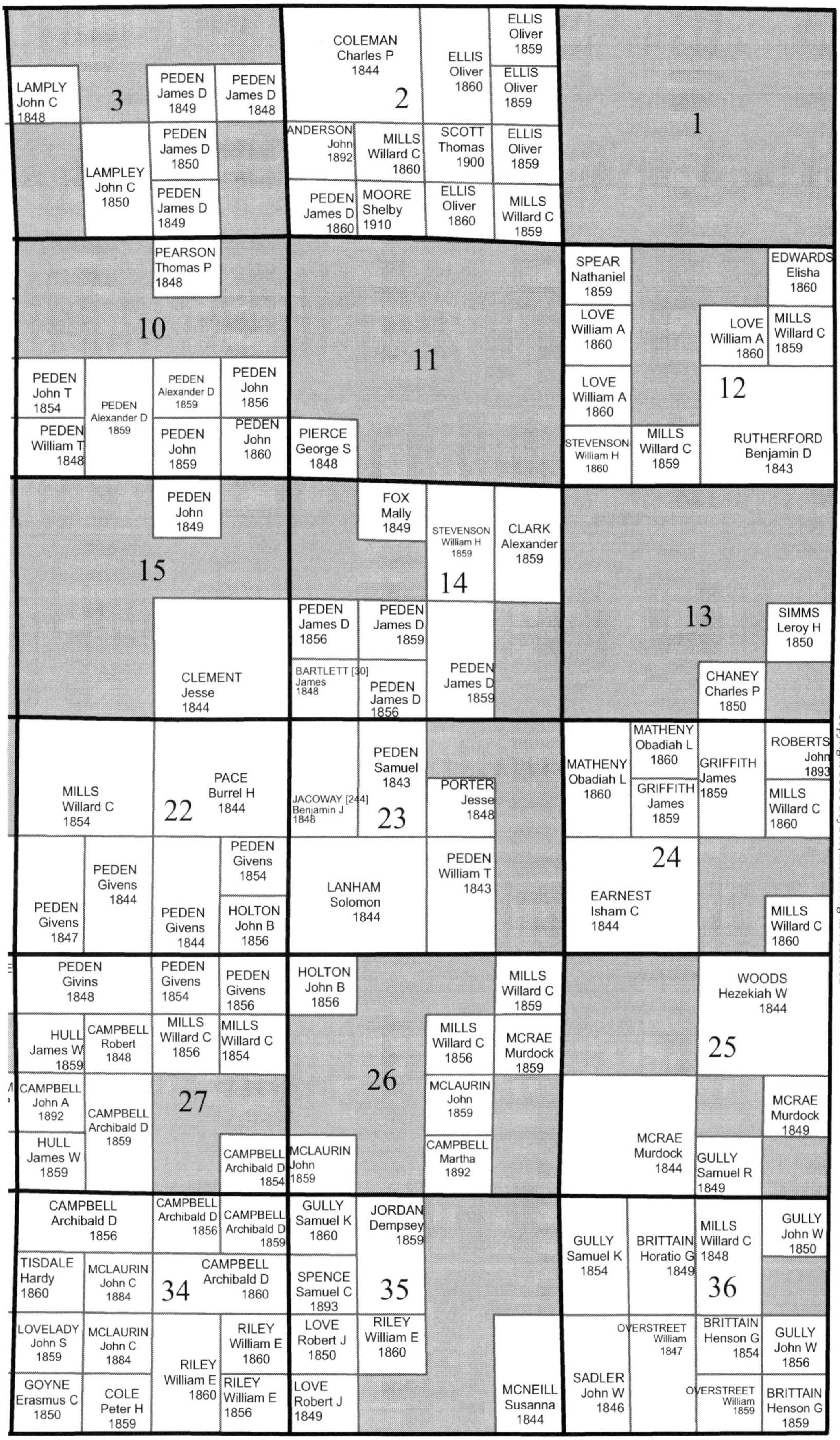

3
LAMPLY John C 1848
PEDEN James D 1849
PEDEN James D 1848
LAMPLEY John C 1850
PEDEN James D 1850
PEDEN James D 1849

2
COLEMAN Charles P 1844
ELLIS Oliver 1860
ELLIS Oliver 1859
ELLIS Oliver 1859
ANDERSON John 1892
MILLS Willard C 1860
SCOTT Thomas 1900
ELLIS Oliver 1859
PEDEN James D 1860
MOORE Shelby 1910
ELLIS Oliver 1860
MILLS Willard C 1859

1

10
PEARSON Thomas P 1848
PEDEN John T 1854
PEDEN Alexander D 1859
PEDEN Alexander D 1859
PEDEN John 1856
PEDEN William T 1848
PEDEN John 1859
PEDEN John 1860

11
PIERCE George S 1848

12
SPEAR Nathaniel 1859
EDWARDS Elisha 1860
LOVE William A 1860
LOVE William A 1860
MILLS Willard C 1859
LOVE William A 1860
STEVENSON William H 1860
MILLS Willard C 1859
RUTHERFORD Benjamin D 1843

15
PEDEN John 1849
CLEMENT Jesse 1844

14
FOX Mally 1849
STEVENSON William H 1859
CLARK Alexander 1859
PEDEN James D 1856
PEDEN James D 1859
BARTLETT [30] James 1848
PEDEN James D 1856
PEDEN James D 1859

13
SIMMS Leroy H 1850
CHANEY Charles P 1850

22
MILLS Willard C 1854
PACE Burrel H 1844
PEDEN Givens 1847
PEDEN Givens 1844
PEDEN Givens 1844
PEDEN Givens 1854
HOLTON John B 1856

23
JACOWAY [244] Benjamin J 1848
PEDEN Samuel 1843
PORTER Jesse 1848
LANHAM Solomon 1844
PEDEN William T 1843

24
MATHENY Obadiah L 1860
MATHENY Obadiah L 1860
GRIFFITH James 1859
GRIFFITH James 1859
ROBERTS John 1893
MILLS Willard C 1860
EARNEST Isham C 1844
MILLS Willard C 1860

27
PEDEN Givins 1848
PEDEN Givens 1854
PEDEN Givens 1856
HULL James W 1859
CAMPBELL Robert 1848
MILLS Willard C 1856
MILLS Willard C 1854
CAMPBELL John A 1892
CAMPBELL Archibald D 1859
HULL James W 1859
CAMPBELL Archibald D 1854

26
HOLTON John B 1856
MILLS Willard C 1859
MILLS Willard C 1856
MCRAE Murdock 1859
MCLAURIN John 1859
CAMPBELL Martha 1892
MCLAURIN John 1859

25
WOODS Hezekiah W 1844
MCRAE Murdock 1849
MCRAE Murdock 1844
GULLY Samuel R 1849

34
CAMPBELL Archibald D 1856
CAMPBELL Archibald D 1856
CAMPBELL Archibald D 1859
TISDALE Hardy 1860
MCLAURIN John C 1884
CAMPBELL Archibald D 1860
LOVELADY John S 1859
MCLAURIN John C 1884
RILEY William E 1860
RILEY William E 1860
GOYNE Erasmus C 1850
COLE Peter H 1859
RILEY William E 1856

35
GULLY Samuel K 1860
JORDAN Dempsey 1859
SPENCE Samuel C 1893
LOVE Robert J 1850
RILEY William E 1860
LOVE Robert J 1849
MCNEILL Susanna 1844

36
GULLY Samuel K 1854
BRITTAIN Horatio G 1849
MILLS Willard C 1848
GULLY John W 1850
OVERSTREET William 1847
BRITTAIN Henson G 1854
GULLY John W 1856
SADLER John W 1846
OVERSTREET William 1859
BRITTAIN Henson G 1859

Helpful Hints

1. This Map's INDEX can be found on the preceding pages.
2. Refer to Map "C" to see where this Township lies within Kemper County, Mississippi.
3. Numbers within square brackets [ ] denote a multi-patentee land parcel (multi-owner). Refer to Appendix "C" for a full list of members in this group.
4. Areas that look to be crowded with Patentees usually indicate multiple sales of the same parcel (Re-issues) or Overlapping parcels. See this Township's Index for an explanation of these and other circumstances that might explain "odd" groupings of Patentees on this map.

Legend

Patent Boundary
Section Boundary
No Patents Found (or Outside County)
1., 2., 3., ... Lot Numbers (when beside a name)
[ ] Group Number (see Appendix "C")

Scale: Section = 1 mile X 1 mile (generally, with some exceptions)

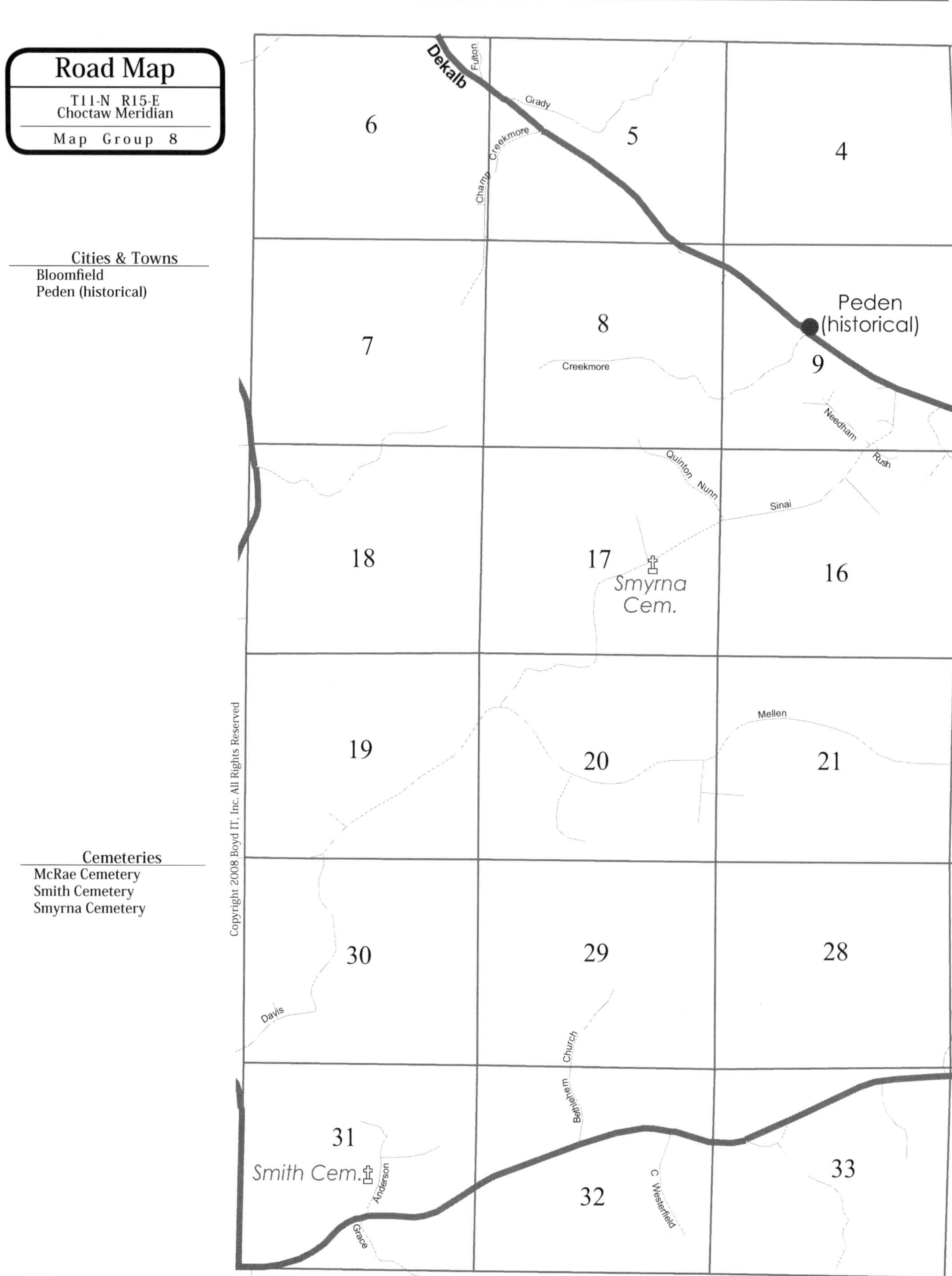
Road Map
T11-N R15-E
Choctaw Meridian
Map Group 8
Cities & Towns
Bloomfield
Peden (historical)
Cemeteries
McRae Cemetery
Smith Cemetery
Smyrna Cemetery
Copyright 2008 Boyd IT, Inc. All Rights Reserved
Dekalb
Fulton
Grady
Creekmore
Champ
Peden
(historical)
Creekmore
Needham
Rush
Quinton
Nunn
Sinai
Smyrna
Cem.
Mellen
Davis
Church
Bethlehem
Smith Cem.
Anderson
Grace
C Westerfield
6
5
4
7
8
9
18
17
16
19
20
21
30
29
28
31
32
33

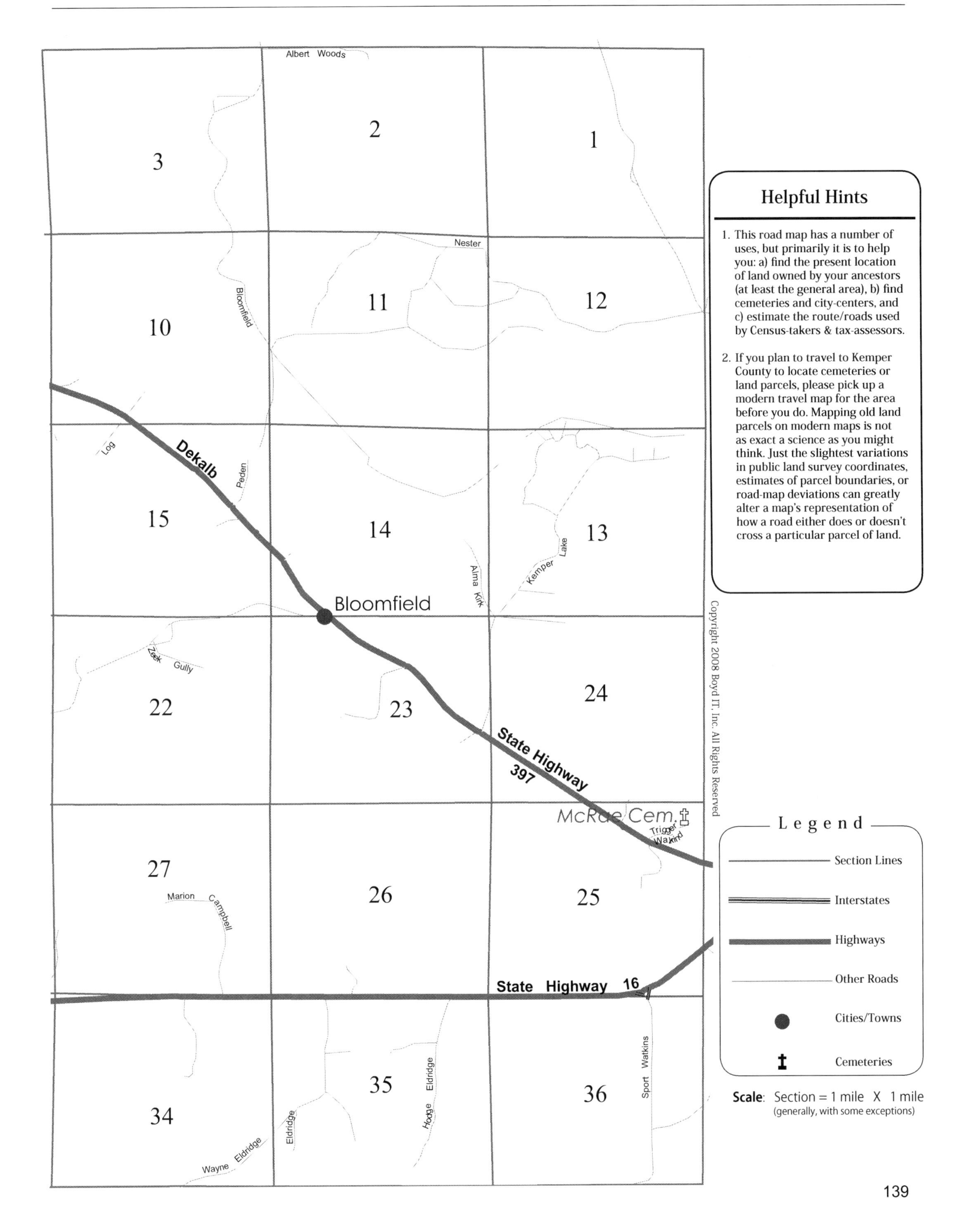

Helpful Hints

1. This road map has a number of uses, but primarily it is to help you: a) find the present location of land owned by your ancestors (at least the general area), b) find cemeteries and city-centers, and c) estimate the route/roads used by Census-takers & tax-assessors.

2. If you plan to travel to Kemper County to locate cemeteries or land parcels, please pick up a modern travel map for the area before you do. Mapping old land parcels on modern maps is not as exact a science as you might think. Just the slightest variations in public land survey coordinates, estimates of parcel boundaries, or road-map deviations can greatly alter a map's representation of how a road either does or doesn't cross a particular parcel of land.

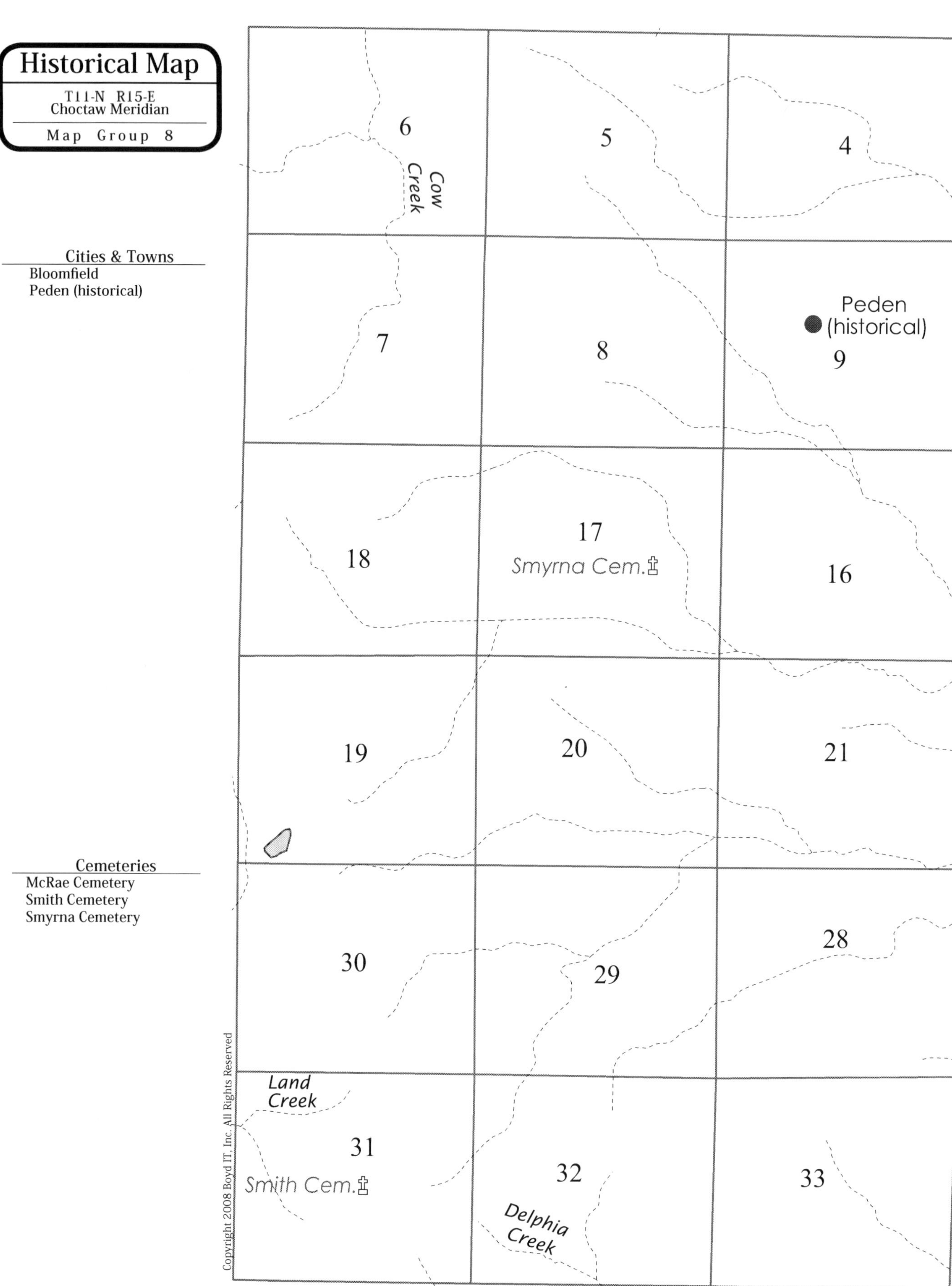
Historical Map
T11-N R15-E
Choctaw Meridian
Map Group 8
Cities & Towns
Bloomfield
Peden (historical)
Cemeteries
McRae Cemetery
Smith Cemetery
Smyrna Cemetery
6
5
4
Cow Creek
7
8
Peden (historical)
9
18
17
Smyrna Cem.
16
19
20
21
30
29
28
Land Creek
31
Smith Cem.
32
Delphia Creek
33
Copyright 2008 Boyd IT, Inc. All Rights Reserved

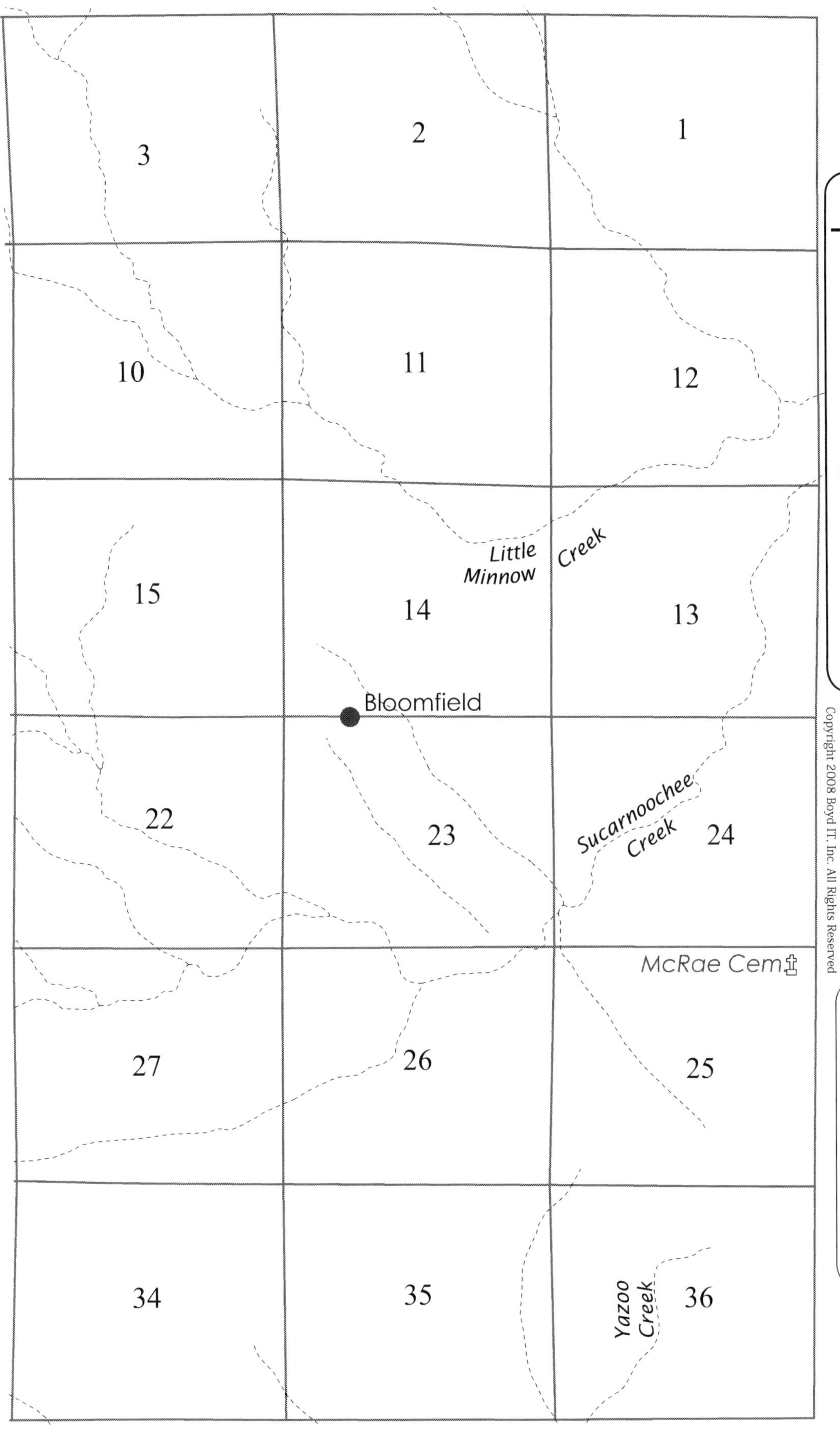

Helpful Hints

1. This Map takes a different look at the same Congressional Township displayed in the preceding two maps. It presents features that can help you better envision the historical development of the area: a) Water-bodies (lakes & ponds), b) Water-courses (rivers, streams, etc.), c) Railroads, d) City/town center-points (where they were oftentimes located when first settled), and e) Cemeteries.

2. Using this "Historical" map in tandem with this Township's Patent Map and Road Map, may lead you to some interesting discoveries. You will often find roads, towns, cemeteries, and waterways are named after nearby landowners: sometimes those names will be the ones you are researching. See how many of these research gems you can find here in Kemper County.

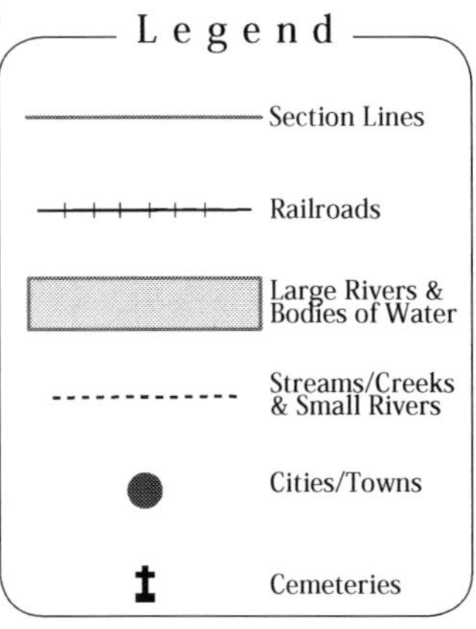

Scale: Section = 1 mile X 1 mile
(there are some exceptions)

Map Group 9: Index to Land Patents

Township 11-North Range 16-East (Choctaw)

After you locate an individual in this Index, take note of the Section and Section Part then proceed to the Land Patent map on the pages immediately following. You should have no difficulty locating the corresponding parcel of land.

The "For More Info" Column will lead you to more information about the underlying Patents. See the *Legend* at right, and the "How to Use this Book" chapter, for more information.

LEGEND

"For More Info . . . " column

A = Authority (Legislative Act, See Appendix "A")
B = Block or Lot (location in Section unknown)
C = Cancelled Patent
F = Fractional Section
G = Group (Multi-Patentee Patent, see Appendix "C")
V = Overlaps another Parcel
R = Re-Issued (Parcel patented more than once)

(A & G items require you to look in the Appendixes referred to above. All other Letter-designations followed by a number require you to locate line-items in this index that possess the ID number found after the letter).

ID	Individual in Patent	Sec.	Sec Part	Date Issued	Other Counties	For More Info . . .
1769	ALLEN, Charles	21	E½SW	1848-09-01		A1 G18
1946	ALLIS, William M	26	N½NE	1861-01-01		A1
1835	ARTHUR, John H	8	SWNW	1859-10-01		A1
1849	AVERY, Joseph C	24	E½NE	1854-03-15		A1
1773	BACON, Christopher B	10	W½NE	1848-09-01		A1 G26
1772	" "	4	NESE	1850-12-05		A1
1939	BALLARD, William J	22	NENW	1849-12-01		A1
1898	BARNES, Solomon	19	NENE	1848-09-01		A1
1903	BELANCY, Thomas L	8	NESW	1900-10-04		A2
1892	BELL, Samuel	28	SE	1848-12-01		A1
1848	BINNS, Joseph	4	NWNW	1860-05-01		A1
1813	BOHANNON, James F	17	NENE	1850-12-05		A1
1814	" "	27	NENE	1850-12-05		A1
1815	" "	34	SWNE	1850-12-05		A1
1816	BRITTAIN, James H	2	NWSW	1856-04-01		A1
1843	BRITTAIN, John R	22	SENE	1849-12-01		A1
1869	BROOKS, Nancy A	4	NWSW	1860-05-01		A1
1870	" "	4	SWNW	1860-05-01		A1
1796	BROWN, Henry	10	E½SE	1846-09-01		A1
1797	" "	10	SWSE	1856-04-01		A1
1928	BROWN, William	29	E½NW	1844-09-10		A1
1927	" "	12	SENE	1859-10-01		A1
1838	COCKRELL, John L	10	SWSW	1860-10-01		A1
1854	COLE, Lewis	36	E½SE	1844-09-10		A1 G92
1872	COLE, Peter H	31	NW	1844-09-10		A1
1852	CONNER, Joseph W	10	SESW	1860-05-01		A1
1830	COOPER, Jesse	13	SW	1844-09-10		A1 G103
1829	" "	11	SE	1846-09-01		A1
1830	CORLEY, John	13	SW	1844-09-10		A1 G103
1930	COX, William F	13	E½NW	1848-09-01		A1
1931	" "	13	W½SE	1848-09-01		A1
1902	CREEKMORE, Thomas J	6	NWNE	1881-09-17		A2
1791	DEWEESE, Fenton B	2	SWSW	1880-10-01		A1
1812	DUNLAP, James	6	NW	1844-09-10		A1 G127
1812	DUNLAP, Robert	6	NW	1844-09-10		A1 G127
1864	EDGE, Minor	10	NWNW	1849-12-01		A1
1865	" "	10	SENW	1849-12-01		A1
1867	EVANS, Moses	26	NW	1846-09-01		A1
1868	" "	27	SENE	1850-12-05		A1
1802	EVERETT, Horace	26	S½SE	1855-03-15		A1
1803	" "	36	SWSE	1855-03-15		A1
1909	FELTON, Wiley W	2	SENE	1854-03-15		A1 V1834
1910	" "	2	SWNE	1854-03-15		A1
1856	FLOURNOY, Lucy A	34	E½NE	1848-09-01		A1
1857	" "	34	NWNE	1850-12-05		A1 G154
1857	FLOURNOY, Martha C	34	NWNE	1850-12-05		A1 G154

ID	Individual in Patent	Sec.	Sec. Part	Date Issued	Other Counties	For More Info . . .
1896	FORESTER, Silas B	15	NWSW	1849-12-01		A1
1895	" "	10	NWSE	1856-04-01		A1
1897	FORRESTER, Silas B	15	SWSW	1853-04-15		A1
1932	FOX, William	34	NWNW	1848-09-01		A1
1893	GERMANY, Samuel	7	NW	1844-09-10		A1 G162
1934	GILL, William G	27	E½NW	1846-09-01		A1
1935	" "	27	W½NW	1848-09-01		A1
1933	" "	22	W½SW	1859-10-01		A1
1781	GRADY, Durham	29	SWSE	1848-09-01		A1
1805	GRADY, Jack	24	W½SW	1895-02-21		A2
1827	GRADY, Jane B	17	SWSW	1849-12-01		A1
1782	GRIFFITH, Edward	35	NW	1844-09-10		A1 G205
1876	GRIFFITH, Ralph	30	NW	1844-09-10		A1
1877	" "	35	E½SW	1844-09-10		A1 G206
1782	" "	35	NW	1844-09-10		A1 G205
1831	GULLY, Jesse E	32	E½NW	1849-12-01		A1
1929	HALLFORD, William C	2	NWNE	1911-05-03		A2
1858	HOPSON, Martin	17	NESW	1848-09-01		A1
1859	" "	17	NWSE	1848-09-01		A1
1860	" "	7	SESE	1849-12-01		A1
1861	" "	8	NWSW	1849-12-01		A1
1862	" "	8	SWSW	1850-12-02		A1
1925	HORN, William A	15	SESW	1849-12-01		A1
1938	HUGHES, William	29	NE	1844-09-10		A1
1826	HULL, James W	32	SESW	1854-03-15		A1
1817	HUNNEYCUTT, James	32	SE	1848-09-01		A1
1863	IKARD, Milton	3	SW	1846-09-01		A1
1806	IVY, James B	12	SW	1846-09-01		A1
1854	JACK, Abner M	36	E½SE	1844-09-10		A1 G92
1795	JACK, Harriet	36	SW	1844-09-10		A1
1771	JOHNSON, Charles H	32	E½NE	1846-09-01		A1
1818	JOHNSON, James	3	SWSE	1848-09-01		A1
1853	JOHNSON, Levi	10	NENW	1848-09-01		A1
1899	JOHNSON, Thomas G	33	NW	1846-09-01		A1
1943	JOHNSON, William	15	SENW	1849-12-01		A1
1798	JONES, Henry G	28	SWSW	1848-09-01		A1
1799	" "	29	SESE	1848-09-01		A1
1800	" "	9	N½NW	1848-09-01		A1
1776	KEMPER, County Of	27	SW	1841-12-15		A1 G259
1850	LACY, Joseph H	10	SENE	1854-03-15		A1
1851	" "	2	NWSE	1856-04-01		A1
1819	LANG, James M	11	SESW	1848-09-01		A1
1820	" "	12	E½SE	1854-03-15		A1
1821	" "	12	SENW	1859-10-01		A1
1822	" "	12	SWNE	1859-10-01		A1
1878	LANG, Richard W	13	W½NW	1848-09-01		A1 C
1879	" "	2	SWSE	1860-10-01		A1
1882	LANG, Robert	15	SESE	1848-09-01		A1
1883	" "	23	NENW	1848-09-01		A1
1884	" "	23	NWNW	1849-12-01		A1
1908	LANG, Wiley B	12	NWSE	1895-08-30		A2
1944	LANG, William	11	SENW	1849-12-01		A1
1936	LANG, William G	11	NESW	1848-09-01		A1
1776	LANKAM, Solomon	27	SW	1841-12-15		A1 G259
1945	LONG, William	11	SENE	1848-09-01		A1
1804	MADISON, Horrace	4	SENW	1911-01-09		A2
1947	MCCLAIN, William	9	NWSE	1849-12-01		A1
1762	MCCRORY, Allen	3	NWSE	1850-12-05		A1
1885	MCCRORY, Robert	4	SESE	1860-10-01		A1
1886	" "	4	SESW	1860-10-01		A1
1887	" "	4	SWNE	1860-10-01		A1
1888	" "	4	W½SE	1860-10-01		A1
1874	MCKELLAR, Peter	4	NWNE	1859-10-01		A1
1873	" "	4	NENW	1860-05-01		A1
1766	MCKELVIN, Benjamin A	28	E½SW	1848-09-01		A1
1777	MCLEAN, Daniel	17	SWNE	1848-09-01		A1
1778	" "	8	SESW	1860-05-01		A1
1779	" "	8	SWSE	1860-05-01		A1
1844	MCLEROY, John W	36	NWSE	1850-12-05		A1
1825	MCRAE, James	28	NE	1846-09-01		A1
1769	" "	21	E½SW	1848-09-01		A1 G18
1824	" "	21	SESE	1849-12-01		A1
1773	MILLS, Willard C	10	W½NE	1848-09-01		A1 G26

ID	Individual in Patent	Sec.	Sec. Part	Date Issued	Other Counties	For More Info . . .
1912	MILLS, Willard C (Cont'd)	22	NENE	1854-03-15		A1
1913	" "	24	E½SW	1854-03-15		A1
1914	" "	24	SENW	1854-03-15		A1
1916	" "	24	SWSE	1854-03-15		A1
1917	" "	34	SWNW	1854-03-15		A1
1918	" "	36	NENE	1854-03-15		A1
1919	" "	36	NW	1854-03-15		A1
1920	" "	36	SENE	1854-03-15		A1
1921	" "	36	SWNE	1854-03-15		A1
1922	" "	6	SWSW	1854-03-15		A1
1915	" "	24	SESE	1859-10-01		A1
1911	" "	10	SWNW	1860-05-01		A1
1923	" "	8	SENE	1860-05-01		A1
1924	" "	8	SESE	1860-05-01		A1
1832	MOORE, John A	8	SENW	1895-07-08		A2
1833	" "	8	SWNE	1895-07-08		A2
1890	MORRAH, Robert	18	E½NE	1849-12-01		A1
1889	" "	17	NESE	1850-12-02		A1
1907	MORRIS, Turner	7	NE	1844-09-10		A1
1893	" "	7	NW	1844-09-10		A1 G162
1875	NAVE, Polly	20	S½SW	1892-05-26		A2
1767	NEEL, Benjamin	4	E½NE	1846-09-01		A1
1783	NESTER, Edwin W	24	NESE	1848-09-01		A1
1765	NETTLES, Ann	34	E½NW	1846-12-01		A1
1788	ODEN, Elias	33	E½SE	1847-08-17		A1
1784	" "	11	NWNW	1848-09-01		A1
1785	" "	11	SWNE	1848-09-01		A1
1786	" "	32	W½NE	1848-09-01		A1
1787	" "	32	W½NW	1848-09-01		A1
1789	" "	33	W½SE	1848-09-01		A1
1790	" "	34	SW	1848-09-01		A1
1839	OLIVE, John	11	NENE	1849-12-01		A1
1840	" "	12	NENW	1849-12-01		A1
1764	OVERSTREET, Anderson P	9	SWNE	1850-12-05		A1
1763	" "	10	NENE	1859-10-01		A1
1841	OVERSTREET, John	4	NESW	1859-10-01		A1
1842	" "	8	NENE	1859-10-01		A1
1881	PIERCE, Robert D	30	N½SW	1848-09-01		A1
1866	PRESTON, Moses C	36	NWNE	1850-12-05		A1
1926	PRESTON, William B	26	SESW	1850-12-05		A1
1775	REY, Cornelius	13	E½SE	1846-09-01		A1
1891	RICHEY, Robert	7	W½SW	1849-12-01		A1
1904	SANDERS, Thomas	33	NE	1849-12-01		A1
1877	SCONYERS, William	35	E½SW	1844-09-10		A1 G206
1770	SCOTT, Charles C	28	NWSW	1848-09-01		A1
1792	SCOTT, Francis T	23	E½NE	1847-08-17		A1
1793	" "	35	NWSE	1848-09-01		A1
1948	SHANNON, William	14	SE	1848-09-01		A1 C
1801	SHIKLE, Hiram	2	NENW	1848-09-01		A1
1894	SIMPSON, Samuel	2	E½SE	1849-12-01		A1
1828	SMITH, Jason	18	SESE	1860-05-01		A1
1949	SMITH, William	8	NWNE	1849-12-01		A1
1807	SPEAR, James B	19	NENW	1850-12-05		A1
1900	SPEAR, Thomas G	18	NWNE	1859-10-01		A1
1901	" "	18	SWNW	1859-10-01		A1
1834	STEWARD, John F	2	E½NE	1859-10-01		A1 V1909
1905	STONE, Travis	14	NENW	1854-03-15		A1
1906	" "	14	NWNW	1860-05-01		A1
1855	STOVALL, Lewis	27	W½NE	1844-09-10		A1
1937	STUART, William H	12	W½NW	1846-09-01		A1
1774	THOMPSON, Christopher	27	SE	1844-09-10		A1
1780	TUBB, David A	3	NW	1846-09-01		A1
1823	TUCKER, James M	22	NWNW	1849-12-01		A1
1808	WALL, James B	5	E½SW	1848-09-01		A1
1809	" "	5	NWSW	1848-09-01		A1
1810	WALL, James D	5	SENW	1848-09-01		A1
1811	" "	5	SWSE	1850-12-05		A1
1761	WARREN, Aaron	29	SWSW	1848-09-01		A1
1836	WARREN, John H	30	S½SW	1892-06-15		A2
1845	WEST, John	2	W½NW	1859-10-01		A1
1880	WHITTLE, Richard	7	N½SE	1848-09-01		A1
1941	WHITTLE, William J	6	SESW	1850-12-05		A1
1942	" "	6	SWSE	1850-12-05		A1

ID	Individual in Patent	Sec.	Sec. Part	Date Issued	Other Counties	For More Info . . .
1940	WHITTLE, William J (Cont'd)	6	SESE	1860-05-01		A1
1846	WILKINSON, John	1	SENW	1849-12-01		A1
1847	" "	12	SWSE	1859-10-01		A1
1768	WILLIAMS, Benjamin	22	SESE	1850-12-05		A1
1950	WILLIAMS, William	22	W½SE	1846-09-01		A1
1794	WILLIAMSON, Frederic	6	NWSW	1859-10-01		A1
1871	WILLIAMSON, Narcissa F	6	NENE	1892-06-15		A2
1951	WILLIAMSON, William	6	N½SE	1860-05-01		A1
1952	" "	6	S½NE	1860-05-01		A1
1837	WOODSON, John J	35	SWSW	1850-12-05		A1
1954	YATES, William	32	NWSW	1848-09-01		A1
1953	" "	32	NESW	1850-12-05		A1
1955	" "	32	SWSW	1850-12-05		A1

Patent Map

T11-N R16-E
Choctaw Meridian

Map Group 9

Township Statistics

Parcels Mapped	:	195
Number of Patents	:	177
Number of Individuals	:	129
Patentees Identified	:	127
Number of Surnames	:	99
Multi-Patentee Parcels	:	10
Oldest Patent Date	:	12/15/1841
Most Recent Patent	:	5/3/1911
Block/Lot Parcels	:	0
Parcels Re - Issued	:	0
Parcels that Overlap	:	2
Cities and Towns	:	4
Cemeteries	:	3

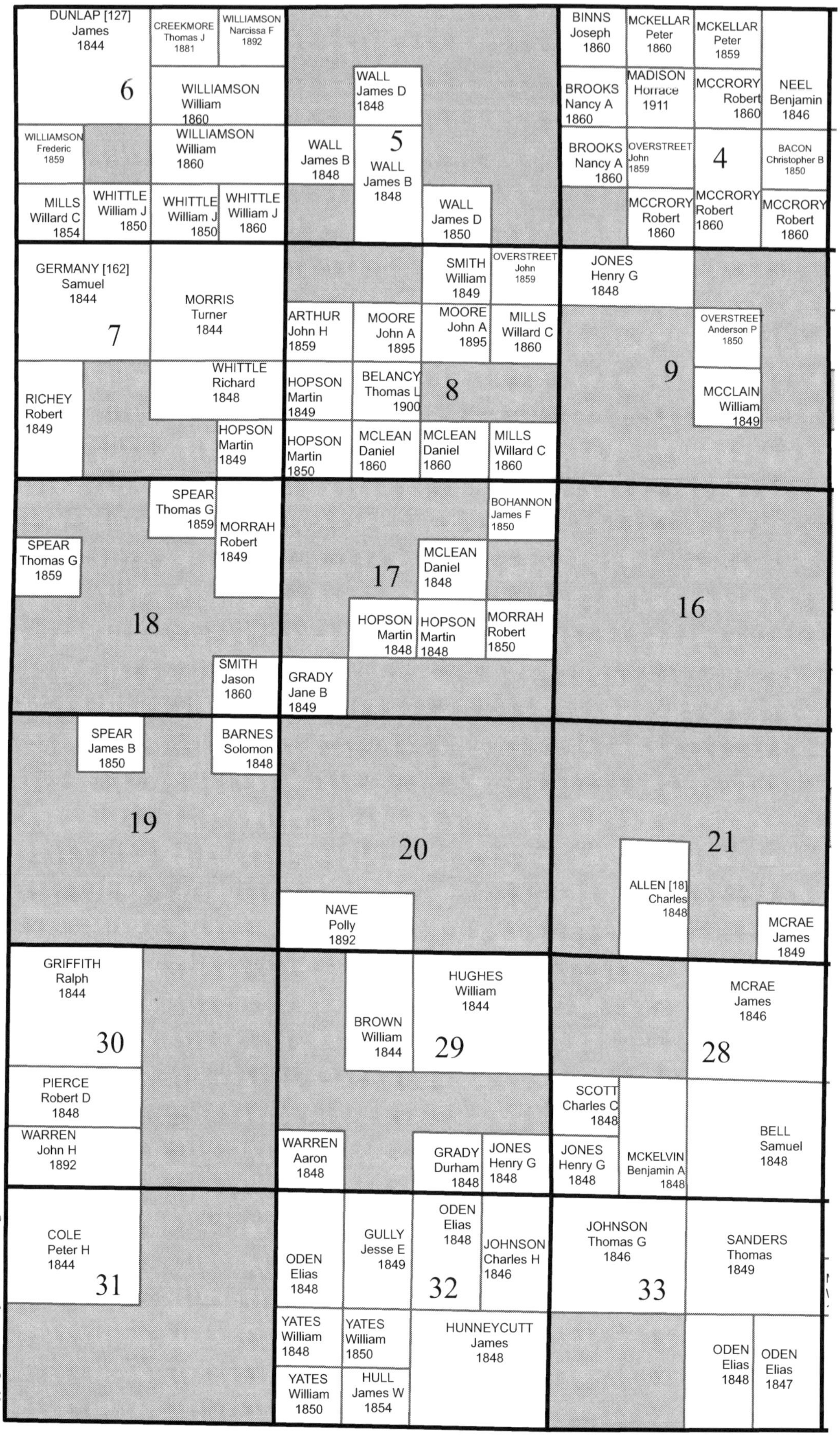

6
DUNLAP [127] James 1844
CREEKMORE Thomas J 1881
WILLIAMSON Narcissa F 1892
WILLIAMSON William 1860
WILLIAMSON Frederic 1859
WILLIAMSON William 1860
MILLS Willard C 1854
WHITTLE William J 1850
WHITTLE William J 1850
WHITTLE William J 1860

5
WALL James D 1848
WALL James B 1848
WALL James B 1848
WALL James D 1850

4
BINNS Joseph 1860
MCKELLAR Peter 1860
MCKELLAR Peter 1859
BROOKS Nancy A 1860
MADISON Horrace 1911
MCCRORY Robert 1860
NEEL Benjamin 1846
BROOKS Nancy A 1860
OVERSTREET John 1859
BACON Christopher B 1850
MCCRORY Robert 1860
MCCRORY Robert 1860
MCCRORY Robert 1860

7
GERMANY [162] Samuel 1844
MORRIS Turner 1844
WHITTLE Richard 1848
RICHEY Robert 1849
HOPSON Martin 1849

8
SMITH William 1849
OVERSTREET John 1859
ARTHUR John H 1859
MOORE John A 1895
MOORE John A 1895
MILLS Willard C 1860
HOPSON Martin 1849
BELANCY Thomas L 1900
HOPSON Martin 1850
MCLEAN Daniel 1860
MCLEAN Daniel 1860
MILLS Willard C 1860

9
JONES Henry G 1848
OVERSTREET Anderson P 1850
MCCLAIN William 1849

18
SPEAR Thomas G 1859
MORRAH Robert 1849
SPEAR Thomas G 1859
SMITH Jason 1860

17
BOHANNON James F 1850
MCLEAN Daniel 1848
HOPSON Martin 1848
HOPSON Martin 1848
MORRAH Robert 1850
GRADY Jane B 1849

16

19
SPEAR James B 1850
BARNES Solomon 1848

20
NAVE Polly 1892

21
ALLEN [18] Charles 1848
MCRAE James 1849

30
GRIFFITH Ralph 1844
PIERCE Robert D 1848
WARREN John H 1892

29
BROWN William 1844
HUGHES William 1844
WARREN Aaron 1848
GRADY Durham 1848
JONES Henry G 1848

28
MCRAE James 1846
SCOTT Charles C 1848
JONES Henry G 1848
MCKELVIN Benjamin A 1848
BELL Samuel 1848

31
COLE Peter H 1844

32
ODEN Elias 1848
GULLY Jesse E 1849
ODEN Elias 1848
JOHNSON Charles H 1846
YATES William 1848
YATES William 1850
HUNNEYCUTT James 1848
YATES William 1850
HULL James W 1854

33
JOHNSON Thomas G 1846
SANDERS Thomas 1849
ODEN Elias 1848
ODEN Elias 1847

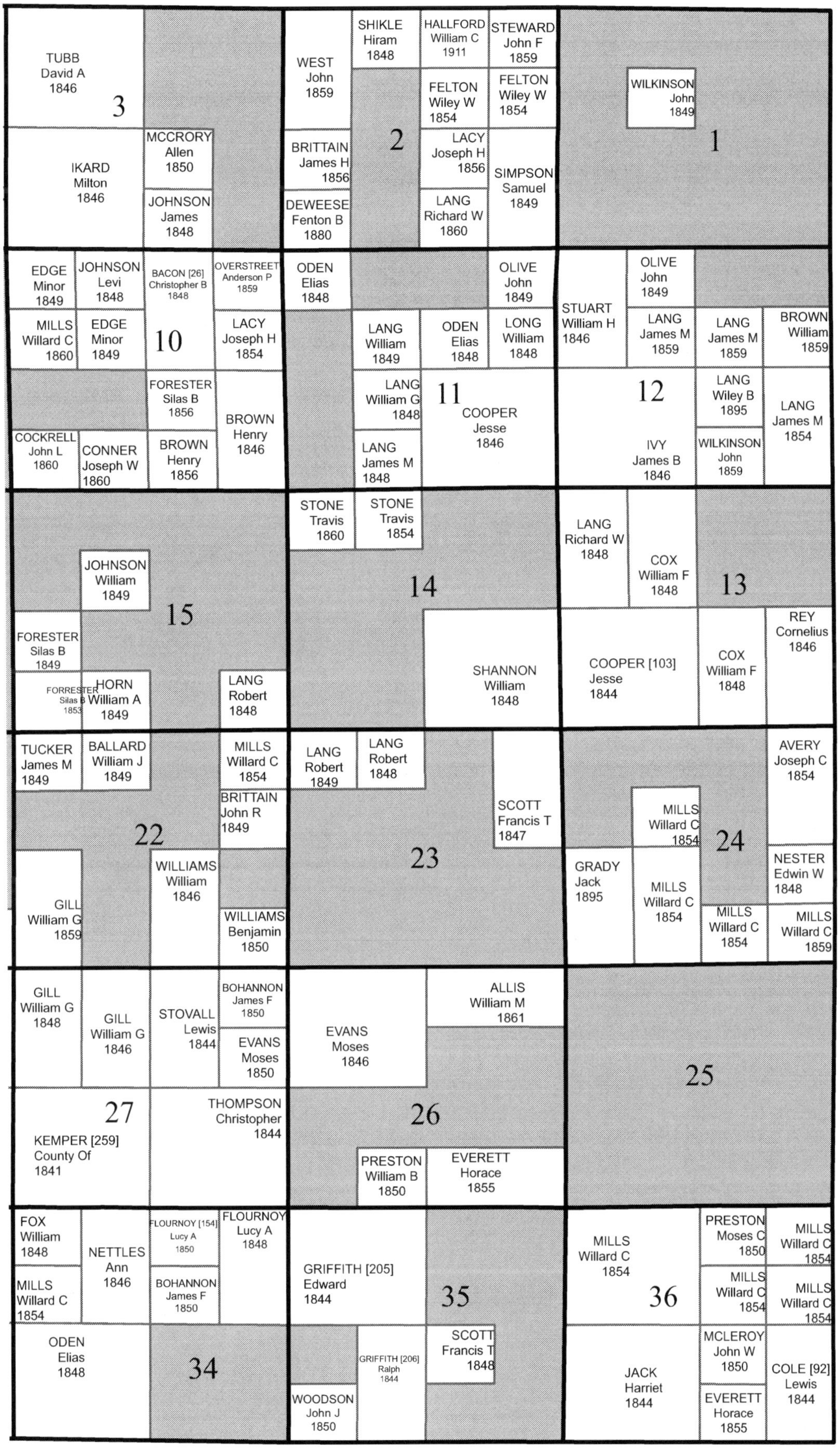

3
TUBB David A 1846
IKARD Milton 1846
MCCRORY Allen 1850
JOHNSON James 1848

2
WEST John 1859
SHIKLE Hiram 1848
HALLFORD William C 1911
STEWARD John F 1859
FELTON Wiley W 1854
FELTON Wiley W 1854
BRITTAIN James H 1856
LACY Joseph H 1856
SIMPSON Samuel 1849
DEWEESE Fenton B 1880
LANG Richard W 1860

1
WILKINSON John 1849

10
EDGE Minor 1849
JOHNSON Levi 1848
BACON [26] Christopher B 1848
OVERSTREET Anderson P 1859
MILLS Willard C 1860
EDGE Minor 1849
LACY Joseph H 1854
FORESTER Silas B 1856
BROWN Henry 1846
COCKRELL John L 1860
CONNER Joseph W 1860
BROWN Henry 1856

11
ODEN Elias 1848
OLIVE John 1849
LANG William 1849
ODEN Elias 1848
LONG William 1848
LANG William G 1848
COOPER Jesse 1846
LANG James M 1848

12
STUART William H 1846
OLIVE John 1849
LANG James M 1859
LANG James M 1859
BROWN William 1859
LANG Wiley B 1895
LANG James M 1854
IVY James B 1846
WILKINSON John 1859

15
JOHNSON William 1849
FORESTER Silas B 1849
FORRESTER Silas B 1853
HORN William A 1849
LANG Robert 1848

14
STONE Travis 1860
STONE Travis 1854
SHANNON William 1848

13
LANG Richard W 1848
COX William F 1848
REY Cornelius 1846
COOPER [103] Jesse 1844
COX William F 1848

Helpful Hints

1. This Map's INDEX can be found on the preceding pages.
2. Refer to Map "C" to see where this Township lies within Kemper County, Mississippi.
3. Numbers within square brackets [ ] denote a multi-patentee land parcel (multi-owner). Refer to Appendix "C" for a full list of members in this group.
4. Areas that look to be crowded with Patentees usually indicate multiple sales of the same parcel (Re-issues) or Overlapping parcels. See this Township's Index for an explanation of these and other circumstances that might explain "odd" groupings of Patentees on this map.

22
TUCKER James M 1849
BALLARD William J 1849
MILLS Willard C 1854
BRITTAIN John R 1849
WILLIAMS William 1846
GILL William G 1859
WILLIAMS Benjamin 1850

23
LANG Robert 1849
LANG Robert 1848
SCOTT Francis T 1847

24
AVERY Joseph C 1854
MILLS Willard C 1854
GRADY Jack 1895
MILLS Willard C 1854
NESTER Edwin W 1848
MILLS Willard C 1854
MILLS Willard C 1859

27
GILL William G 1848
GILL William G 1846
STOVALL Lewis 1844
BOHANNON James F 1850
EVANS Moses 1850
KEMPER [259] County Of 1841
THOMPSON Christopher 1844

26
EVANS Moses 1846
ALLIS William M 1861
PRESTON William B 1850
EVERETT Horace 1855

25

Legend
Patent Boundary
Section Boundary
No Patents Found (or Outside County)
1., 2., 3., ... Lot Numbers (when beside a name)
[ ] Group Number (see Appendix "C")

Scale: Section = 1 mile X 1 mile (generally, with some exceptions)

34
FOX William 1848
NETTLES Ann 1846
FLOURNOY [154] Lucy A 1850
FLOURNOY Lucy A 1848
MILLS Willard C 1854
BOHANNON James F 1850
ODEN Elias 1848

35
GRIFFITH [205] Edward 1844
GRIFFITH [206] Ralph 1844
SCOTT Francis T 1848
WOODSON John J 1850

36
MILLS Willard C 1854
PRESTON Moses C 1850
MILLS Willard C 1854
MILLS Willard C 1854
MILLS Willard C 1854
JACK Harriet 1844
MCLEROY John W 1850
COLE [92] Lewis 1844
EVERETT Horace 1855

Road Map

T11-N R16-E
Choctaw Meridian

Map Group 9

Cities & Towns

- Bogue Toocolo Chitto (historical)
- De Kalb
- East Abeika (historical)
- Holihtasha (historical)

Cemeteries

- DeKalb Cemetery
- Jerusalem Cemetery
- Pinecrest Cemetery

6
5
4
Log
Bill Jack
Wilson
Tillman Haley
Fannie Jack
Jerusalem Cem.
7
8
9
Kellis Store
Jerusalem
White
Am Legion Lake
Bogue Toocolo Chitto (historical)
Bateman Lake
18
17
16
Neely Town Road
State Highway 39
19
20
21
Watkins
Melvin Mcintosh
Otho Roberts
Rock-Knell Chocks
Baptist Springs
Birch
30
29
28
S H 397
State Highway 16
Billy Gully
McLeland
Wilson
Walnut
Oak
Philadelphia
Oak Tree
31
32
33
Welch Town Road
Jackson
Ethel Hull
Old Jackson
Avery Rush

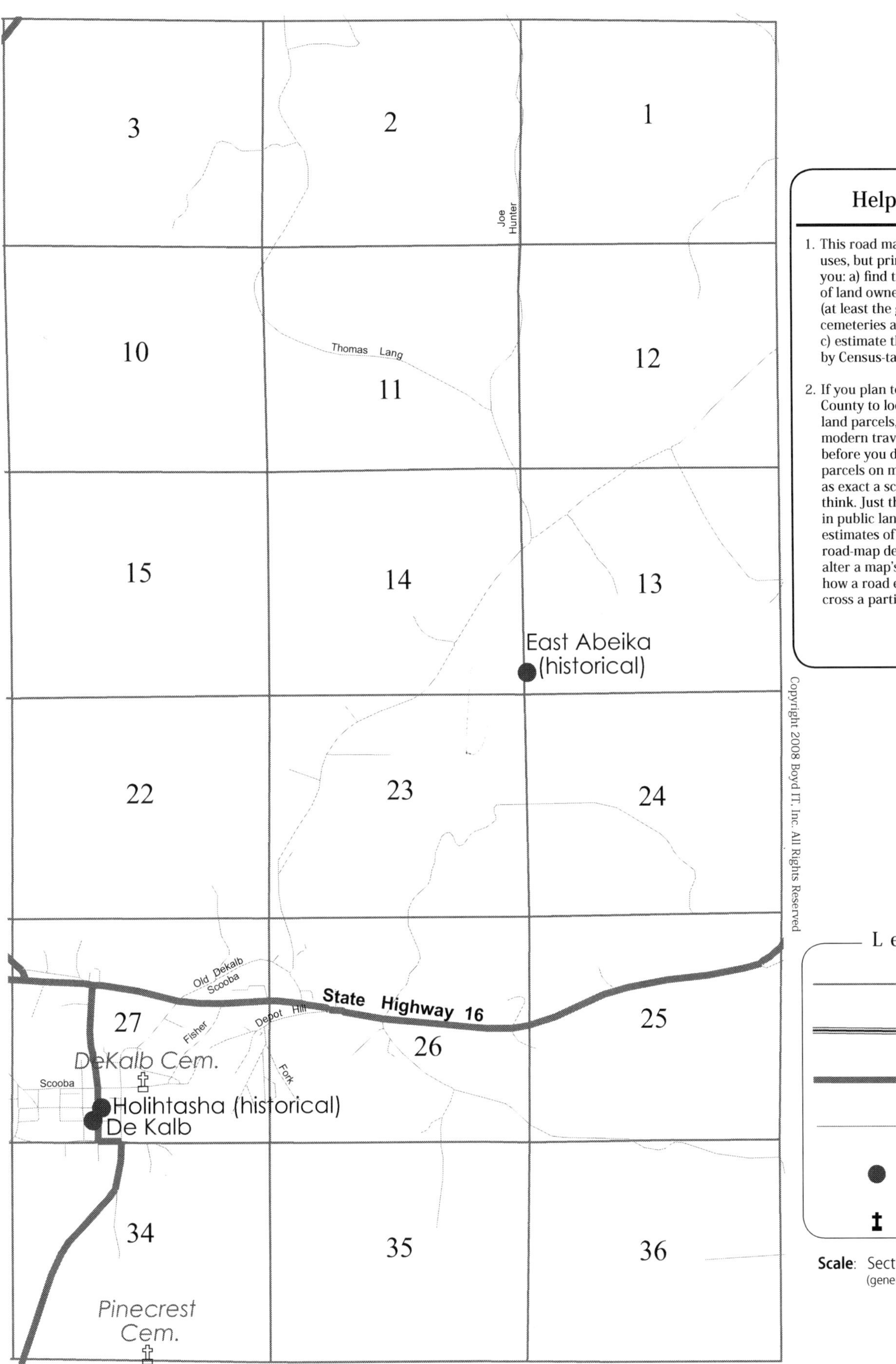

Helpful Hints

1. This road map has a number of uses, but primarily it is to help you: a) find the present location of land owned by your ancestors (at least the general area), b) find cemeteries and city-centers, and c) estimate the route/roads used by Census-takers & tax-assessors.

2. If you plan to travel to Kemper County to locate cemeteries or land parcels, please pick up a modern travel map for the area before you do. Mapping old land parcels on modern maps is not as exact a science as you might think. Just the slightest variations in public land survey coordinates, estimates of parcel boundaries, or road-map deviations can greatly alter a map's representation of how a road either does or doesn't cross a particular parcel of land.

Legend

- Section Lines
- Interstates
- Highways
- Other Roads
- Cities/Towns
- Cemeteries

Scale: Section = 1 mile X 1 mile
(generally, with some exceptions)

Historical Map

T11-N R16-E
Choctaw Meridian

Map Group 9

Cities & Towns

Bogue Toocolo Chitto (historical)
De Kalb
East Abeika (historical)
Holihtasha (historical)

Cemeteries

DeKalb Cemetery
Jerusalem Cemetery
Pinecrest Cemetery

Running Tiger Creek
6
5
4
Jerusalem Cem.
7
Bogue Toocolo Chitto (historical)
8
9
Bateman Lake
18
17
16
19
20
21
30
29
28
31
32
33
Hull Branch

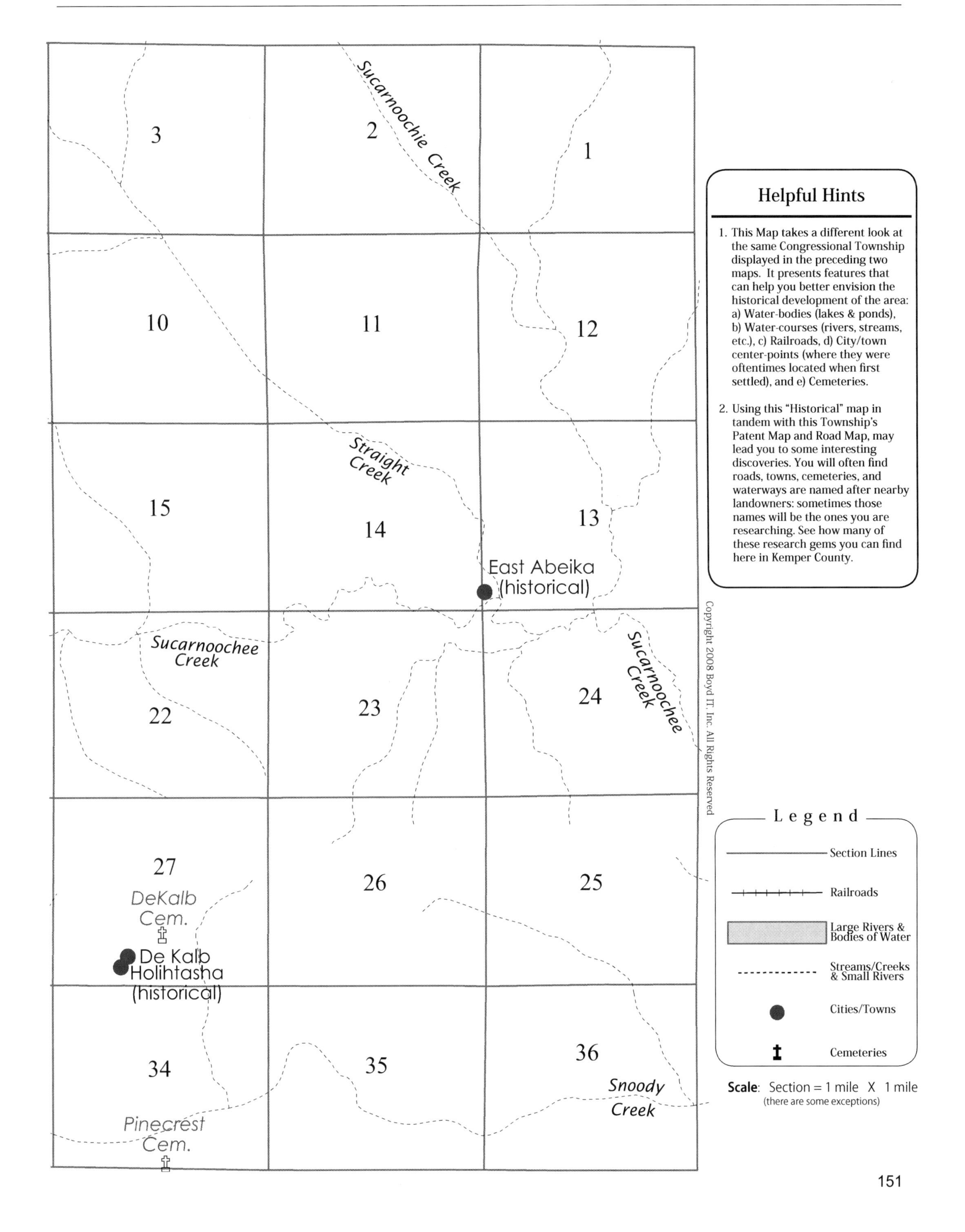

3
2
1
Sucarnoochie Creek
10
11
12
15
14
13
Straight Creek
East Abeika (historical)
Sucarnoochee Creek
22
23
24
Sucarnoochee Creek
27
26
25
DeKalb Cem.
De Kalb Holihtasha (historical)
34
35
36
Snoody Creek
Pinecrest Cem.
Helpful Hints
1. This Map takes a different look at the same Congressional Township displayed in the preceding two maps. It presents features that can help you better envision the historical development of the area: a) Water-bodies (lakes & ponds), b) Water-courses (rivers, streams, etc.), c) Railroads, d) City/town center-points (where they were oftentimes located when first settled), and e) Cemeteries.
2. Using this "Historical" map in tandem with this Township's Patent Map and Road Map, may lead you to some interesting discoveries. You will often find roads, towns, cemeteries, and waterways are named after nearby landowners: sometimes those names will be the ones you are researching. See how many of these research gems you can find here in Kemper County.
Legend
Section Lines
Railroads
Large Rivers & Bodies of Water
Streams/Creeks & Small Rivers
Cities/Towns
Cemeteries
Scale: Section = 1 mile X 1 mile
(there are some exceptions)

Map Group 10: Index to Land Patents

Township 11-North Range 17-East (Choctaw)

After you locate an individual in this Index, take note of the Section and Section Part then proceed to the Land Patent map on the pages immediately following. You should have no difficulty locating the corresponding parcel of land.

The "For More Info" Column will lead you to more information about the underlying Patents. See the *Legend* at right, and the "How to Use this Book" chapter, for more information.

LEGEND

"For More Info . . . " column

A = Authority (Legislative Act, See Appendix "A")
B = Block or Lot (location in Section unknown)
C = Cancelled Patent
F = Fractional Section
G = Group (Multi-Patentee Patent, see Appendix "C")
V = Overlaps another Parcel
R = Re-Issued (Parcel patented more than once)

(A & G items require you to look in the Appendixes referred to above. All other Letter-designations followed by a number require you to locate line-items in this index that possess the ID number found after the letter).

ID	Individual in Patent	Sec.	Sec. Part	Date Issued	Other Counties	For More Info . . .
2128	ADAMS, William C	5	SE	1841-02-27		A1
2129	" "	8	NENW	1841-02-27		A1
2130	" "	8	NWNE	1841-02-27		A1
2037	ADCOCK, John	10	E½SW	1841-02-27		A1
2038	" "	11	E½NW	1841-02-27		A1
2039	" "	11	NE	1841-02-27		A1
2040	" "	12	NW	1841-02-27		A1
2041	" "	12	W½NE	1841-02-27		A1
2089	ADCOCK, Samuel	6	W½NE	1841-02-27		A1
2074	ADCOX, Nina	8	SW	1905-12-06		A1
2051	AVERY, Joseph C	30	SENW	1854-03-15		A1
2052	" "	30	W½NW	1854-03-15		A1
2124	AYLETT, William	19	W½SW	1841-02-27		A1
2147	BASKIN, William O	1	SE	1841-02-27		A1
2148	" "	12	E½NE	1841-02-27		A1
2075	BLAKELY, Robert	7	W½NW	1841-02-27		A1 G43
2076	" "	7	W½SW	1841-02-27		A1 G43
2001	BOYD, George	31	W½NE	1841-02-27		A1
2125	BOYD, William	31	E½NE	1841-02-27		A1
2126	" "	32	E½SE	1841-02-27		A1
2127	" "	32	N½W½SW	1841-02-27		A1
1969	BRISTER, Daniel	31	NESW	1841-02-27		A1
1970	" "	31	W½SW	1841-02-27		A1
2054	BROWN, Joshua T	28	S½W½SE	1841-02-27		A1
2055	" "	28	SW	1841-02-27		A1
2056	" "	33	NE	1841-02-27		A1
2057	" "	8	E½NE	1841-02-27		A1
2116	BROWN, Shelton J	21	E½NW	1904-10-28		A1
2117	" "	21	SWNW	1904-10-28		A1
2152	BROWN, William S	21	NE	1904-10-28		A1
1962	BURTON, Andrew T	13	NW	1841-02-27		A1
1963	" "	14	E½NE	1841-02-27		A1
1971	BURTON, David	10	W½SW	1841-02-27		A1
1972	" "	15	NW	1841-02-27		A1
1973	" "	9	E½SE	1841-02-27		A1
2012	CALVART, James	5	N½	1841-02-27		A1
2029	CHERRY, James M	34	NESW	1841-02-27		A1
2030	" "	34	S½E½SW	1841-02-27		A1
2031	" "	34	W½SE	1841-02-27		A1
2044	CHERRY, John J	23	SW	1906-03-05		A2
2119	CHERRY, Thomas	33	SW	1841-02-27		A1
2120	" "	34	W½SW	1841-02-27		A1
2050	COATES, John W	18	NE	1841-02-27		A1
1960	COBB, Addison G	18	NW	1906-05-01		A2
2077	COOK, Robert	28	SWNW	1841-02-27		A1
2078	" "	29	SE	1841-02-27		A1

ID	Individual in Patent	Sec.	Sec. Part	Date Issued	Other Counties	For More Info . . .
2079	COOK, Robert (Cont'd)	32	E½NE	1841-02-27		A1
2080	" "	32	NWNE	1841-02-27		A1
2068	DILLON, Meredith T	19	W½NW	1841-02-27		A1
2004	DOZIER, Henderson	13	E½SE	1910-09-15		A2
2086	DOZIER, Sam	13	E½SW	1909-12-01		A1
2087	" "	13	W½SE	1909-12-01		A1
2053	EAKIN, Joseph R	35	N½NW	1914-03-28		A1
2013	ELLIOT, James	21	E½SE	1841-02-27		A1
2015	" "	21	E½SW	1841-02-27		A1 G142
2016	" "	21	W½SE	1841-02-27		A1 G142
2014	" "	28	E½NE	1841-02-27		A1
2017	" "	28	E½NW	1841-02-27		A1 G142
2018	" "	28	W½NE	1841-02-27		A1 G142
2019	ELLIOTT, James	20	S½	1841-02-27		A1
2020	" "	21	W½SW	1841-02-27		A1
2021	" "	28	NWNW	1841-02-27		A1
2022	" "	29	E½NW	1841-02-27		A1
2023	" "	29	NE	1841-02-27		A1
2024	" "	29	W½NW	1841-02-27		A1
2025	" "	30	NE	1841-02-27		A1
2026	" "	6	E½SE	1841-02-27		A1
2027	" "	9	SW	1841-02-27		A1
2028	" "	9	W½SE	1841-02-27		A1
2005	EVERETT, Horace	20	E½NW	1854-03-15		A1
2006	" "	20	W½NE	1854-03-15		A1
2007	" "	30	NENW	1855-03-15		A1
2064	FOWCETT, Lyle B	25	SW	1841-02-27		A1
2065	" "	26	E½	1841-02-27		A1
2066	" "	26	E½SW	1841-02-27		A1
2067	" "	36	SE	1841-02-27		A1
2011	GAY, James B	27	SW	1906-05-01		A2
2123	GOYNES, Wiley W	33	NW	1844-06-05		A1 G169
2043	HALL, John	6	E½NE	1841-02-27		A1
2090	HUBBARD, Samuel	1	E½NW	1841-02-27		A1 G233
2091	" "	1	E½SW	1841-02-27		A1 G233
2092	" "	1	NE	1841-02-27		A1 G233
2093	" "	10	NW	1841-02-27		A1 G233
2094	" "	10	W½NE	1841-02-27		A1 G233
2095	" "	11	E½SW	1841-02-27		A1 G233
2096	" "	11	SE	1841-02-27		A1 G233
2097	" "	12	S½	1841-02-27		A1 G233
2098	" "	2	SW	1841-02-27		A1 G233
2099	" "	2	W½SE	1841-02-27		A1 G233
2100	" "	3	E½NW	1841-02-27		A1 G233
2101	" "	3	E½SW	1841-02-27		A1 G233
2102	" "	3	SE	1841-02-27		A1 G233
2103	" "	3	W½NE	1841-02-27		A1 G233
2104	" "	4	W½NW	1841-02-27		A1 G233
2105	" "	4	W½SW	1841-02-27		A1 G233
2061	HUNNICUTT, Leona P	27	W½NW	1912-09-16		A2 G239
1959	JACK, Abner M	23	W½SE	1911-03-01		A1
2036	JAMES, John A	35	SE	1905-03-11		A1
2047	JOHNSON, John	7	E½NE	1841-02-27		A1
2048	" "	8	W½NW	1841-02-27		A1
2082	KENNON, Robert L	4	E½NW	1841-02-27		A1
2083	" "	4	E½SW	1841-02-27		A1
2084	" "	4	W½NE	1841-02-27		A1
2085	" "	4	W½SE	1841-02-27		A1
1956	KEY, Abel	18	W½SW	1844-06-05		A1
2049	KEY, John	18	E½SW	1844-06-05		A1
1998	LANG, Frank	6	SWNW	1904-11-30		A1
1999	" "	6	W½SW	1904-11-30		A1
2090	LEWIS, Rufus G	1	E½NW	1841-02-27		A1 G233
2091	" "	1	E½SW	1841-02-27		A1 G233
2092	" "	1	NE	1841-02-27		A1 G233
2093	" "	10	NW	1841-02-27		A1 G233
2094	" "	10	W½NE	1841-02-27		A1 G233
2095	" "	11	E½SW	1841-02-27		A1 G233
2096	" "	11	SE	1841-02-27		A1 G233
2097	" "	12	S½	1841-02-27		A1 G233
2098	" "	2	SW	1841-02-27		A1 G233
2099	" "	2	W½SE	1841-02-27		A1 G233
2100	" "	3	E½NW	1841-02-27		A1 G233

ID	Individual in Patent	Sec.	Sec. Part	Date Issued	Other Counties	For More Info . . .
2101	LEWIS, Rufus G (Cont'd)	3	E½SW	1841-02-27		A1 G233
2102	" "	3	SE	1841-02-27		A1 G233
2103	" "	3	W½NE	1841-02-27		A1 G233
2104	" "	4	W½NW	1841-02-27		A1 G233
2105	" "	4	W½SW	1841-02-27		A1 G233
2090	LEWIS, William M	1	E½NW	1841-02-27		A1 G233
2091	" "	1	E½SW	1841-02-27		A1 G233
2092	" "	1	NE	1841-02-27		A1 G233
2093	" "	10	NW	1841-02-27		A1 G233
2094	" "	10	W½NE	1841-02-27		A1 G233
2095	" "	11	E½SW	1841-02-27		A1 G233
2096	" "	11	SE	1841-02-27		A1 G233
2097	" "	12	S½	1841-02-27		A1 G233
2132	" "	13	W½SW	1841-02-27		A1
2133	" "	14	E½NW	1841-02-27		A1
2134	" "	14	E½SE	1841-02-27		A1
2135	" "	14	W½NE	1841-02-27		A1
2098	" "	2	SW	1841-02-27		A1 G233
2099	" "	2	W½SE	1841-02-27		A1 G233
2136	" "	23	E½NE	1841-02-27		A1
2137	" "	23	E½SE	1841-02-27		A1
2138	" "	24	SE	1841-02-27		A1
2139	" "	24	W½NW	1841-02-27		A1
2140	" "	24	W½SW	1841-02-27		A1
2141	" "	25	NE	1841-02-27		A1
2142	" "	25	NW	1841-02-27		A1
2143	" "	25	SE	1841-02-27		A1
2144	" "	26	W½NW	1841-02-27		A1 G269
2145	" "	27	E½NE	1841-02-27		A1 G269
2100	" "	3	E½NW	1841-02-27		A1 G233
2101	" "	3	E½SW	1841-02-27		A1 G233
2102	" "	3	SE	1841-02-27		A1 G233
2103	" "	3	W½NE	1841-02-27		A1 G233
2104	" "	4	W½NW	1841-02-27		A1 G233
2105	" "	4	W½SW	1841-02-27		A1 G233
2042	MADERSON, John E	15	W½NE	1841-02-27		A1
2033	MARS, James W	20	NENE	1905-02-13		A2
2002	MCDADE, George W	35	E½SW	1906-08-16		A1
2003	" "	35	S½NW	1906-08-16		A1
2063	MCDADE, Louis A	35	NE	1909-11-08		A2
1974	MCLAWREN, Duncan	15	E½NE	1841-02-27		A1
2081	MCMAHON, Robert G	36	W½SW	1841-02-27		A1
2121	MITCHELL, Tilman	34	E½SE	1841-02-27		A1
2122	" "	35	W½SW	1841-02-27		A1
1961	MOORE, Albert	18	W½SE	1901-03-23		A2
2062	MORRIS, Lewis	19	E½NW	1841-02-27		A1 G298
2088	NAVE, Sam	9	SENE	1920-06-25		A1
2073	NICHOLSON, Neal	8	SENW	1919-01-28		A1
2146	NOLES, William	6	E½NW	1841-02-27		A1
2123	PARKER, Isaac	33	NW	1844-06-05		A1 G169
2032	PARKER, James	33	E½SE	1841-02-01		A1
2069	PARKER, Miles	33	W½SE	1841-02-01		A1
1964	POOL, Benjamin	6	W½SE	1911-11-09		A1
1965	" "	7	W½NE	1911-11-09		A1
2149	PULLER, William P	30	NWSE	1841-02-27		A1 G313
2150	" "	30	NWSW	1841-02-27		A1 G313
2106	ROWE, Shadrach	14	E½SW	1841-02-27		A1
2107	" "	14	W½SE	1841-02-27		A1
2108	" "	14	W½SW	1841-02-27		A1
2109	" "	15	E½SW	1841-02-27		A1
2110	" "	15	SE	1841-02-27		A1
2111	" "	15	W½SW	1841-02-27		A1
2112	" "	22	NE	1841-02-27		A1
2113	" "	22	NW	1841-02-27		A1
2114	" "	23	NW	1841-02-27		A1
2115	" "	23	W½NE	1841-02-27		A1
2144	SCOTT, Christopher C	26	W½NW	1841-02-27		A1 G269
2145	" "	27	E½NE	1841-02-27		A1 G269
1975	SCOTT, Francis T	1	W½NW	1841-02-27		A1
1976	" "	1	W½SW	1841-02-27		A1
1977	" "	10	E½NE	1841-02-27		A1
1978	" "	10	E½SE	1841-02-27		A1
1979	" "	10	W½SE	1841-02-27		A1

ID	Individual in Patent	Sec.	Sec. Part	Date Issued	Other Counties	For More Info . . .
1980	SCOTT, Francis T (Cont'd)	11	W½NW	1841-02-27		A1
1981	" "	11	W½SW	1841-02-27		A1
1982	" "	2	E½SE	1841-02-27		A1
1983	" "	2	NE	1841-02-27		A1
1984	" "	29	E½SW	1841-02-27		A1
1985	" "	29	W½SW	1841-02-27		A1
1986	" "	3	W½NW	1841-02-27		A1
1987	" "	3	W½SW	1841-02-27		A1
1988	" "	30	E½SE	1841-02-27		A1
1989	" "	31	E½NW	1841-02-27		A1
1990	" "	31	N½E½SE	1841-02-27		A1
1991	" "	31	W½NW	1841-02-27		A1
1993	" "	32	E½SW	1841-02-27		A1
1994	" "	32	SWNE	1841-02-27		A1
1995	" "	32	W½NW	1841-02-27		A1
1996	" "	32	W½SE	1841-02-27		A1
1997	" "	4	E½NE	1841-02-27		A1
1992	" "	32	E½NW	1860-05-01		A1
2000	SCOTT, Frank	32	SWSW	1892-09-02		A2
2008	SMITH, Isaiah	13	NE	1841-02-27		A1
2009	" "	20	S½E½NE	1841-02-27		A1
2010	" "	21	N½W½NW	1841-02-27		A1
2015	SMITH, James L	21	E½SW	1841-02-27		A1 G142
2016	" "	21	W½SE	1841-02-27		A1 G142
2017	" "	28	E½NW	1841-02-27		A1 G142
2018	" "	28	W½NE	1841-02-27		A1 G142
1957	STEELE, Abner A	2	NW	1841-02-27		A1
1958	" "	3	E½NE	1841-02-27		A1
2070	STEPHENS, Moses	30	E½SW	1841-02-27		A1
2149	" "	30	NWSE	1841-02-27		A1 G313
2150	" "	30	NWSW	1841-02-27		A1 G313
2071	" "	30	SWSE	1841-02-27		A1
2072	" "	30	SWSW	1841-02-27		A1
2151	STEWART, William R	9	NENE	1910-12-19		A1
2090	TAPPAN, John	1	E½NW	1841-02-27		A1 G233
2091	" "	1	E½SW	1841-02-27		A1 G233
2092	" "	1	NE	1841-02-27		A1 G233
2093	" "	10	NW	1841-02-27		A1 G233
2094	" "	10	W½NE	1841-02-27		A1 G233
2095	" "	11	E½SW	1841-02-27		A1 G233
2096	" "	11	SE	1841-02-27		A1 G233
2097	" "	12	S½	1841-02-27		A1 G233
2098	" "	2	SW	1841-02-27		A1 G233
2099	" "	2	W½SE	1841-02-27		A1 G233
2100	" "	3	E½NW	1841-02-27		A1 G233
2101	" "	3	E½SW	1841-02-27		A1 G233
2102	" "	3	SE	1841-02-27		A1 G233
2103	" "	3	W½NE	1841-02-27		A1 G233
2104	" "	4	W½NW	1841-02-27		A1 G233
2105	" "	4	W½SW	1841-02-27		A1 G233
2058	TAYLOR, Josiah	36	E½SW	1841-02-27		A1
2034	THOMAS, Jeff Davis	8	SWSE	1919-10-01		A2
2035	THOMAS, Jeremiah	5	SW	1841-02-27		A1
2059	THORN, Kenedy	4	E½SE	1841-02-27		A1
2062	TUTT, James B	19	E½NW	1841-02-27		A1 G298
2153	WAIR, William	8	E½SE	1841-02-27		A1
2154	" "	9	NW	1841-02-27		A1
2075	WARD, Ebon P	7	W½NW	1841-02-27		A1 G43
2076	" "	7	W½SW	1841-02-27		A1 G43
1966	WATSON, Charles	17	W½SW	1841-02-27		A1
1967	" "	18	E½SE	1841-02-27		A1
1968	" "	20	W½NW	1841-02-27		A1
2045	WATSON, John J	27	E½NW	1905-07-13		A2
2046	" "	27	W½NE	1905-07-13		A2
2061	WATSON, Leona P	27	W½NW	1912-09-16		A2 G239
2131	WATSON, William D	27	SE	1906-05-01		A2
2118	WHITLEY, Simon D	6	NWNW	1841-02-27		A1
2060	WHITTLE, Lawson N	17	NENE	1911-03-01		A1
2155	WIER, William	9	W½NE	1841-02-27		A1

Patent Map

T11-N R17-E
Choctaw Meridian

Map Group 10

Township Statistics

Parcels Mapped	:	200
Number of Patents	:	155
Number of Individuals	:	86
Patentees Identified	:	80
Number of Surnames	:	66
Multi-Patentee Parcels	:	29
Oldest Patent Date	:	2/1/1841
Most Recent Patent	:	6/25/1920
Block/Lot Parcels	:	0
Parcels Re - Issued	:	0
Parcels that Overlap	:	0
Cities and Towns	:	3
Cemeteries	:	1

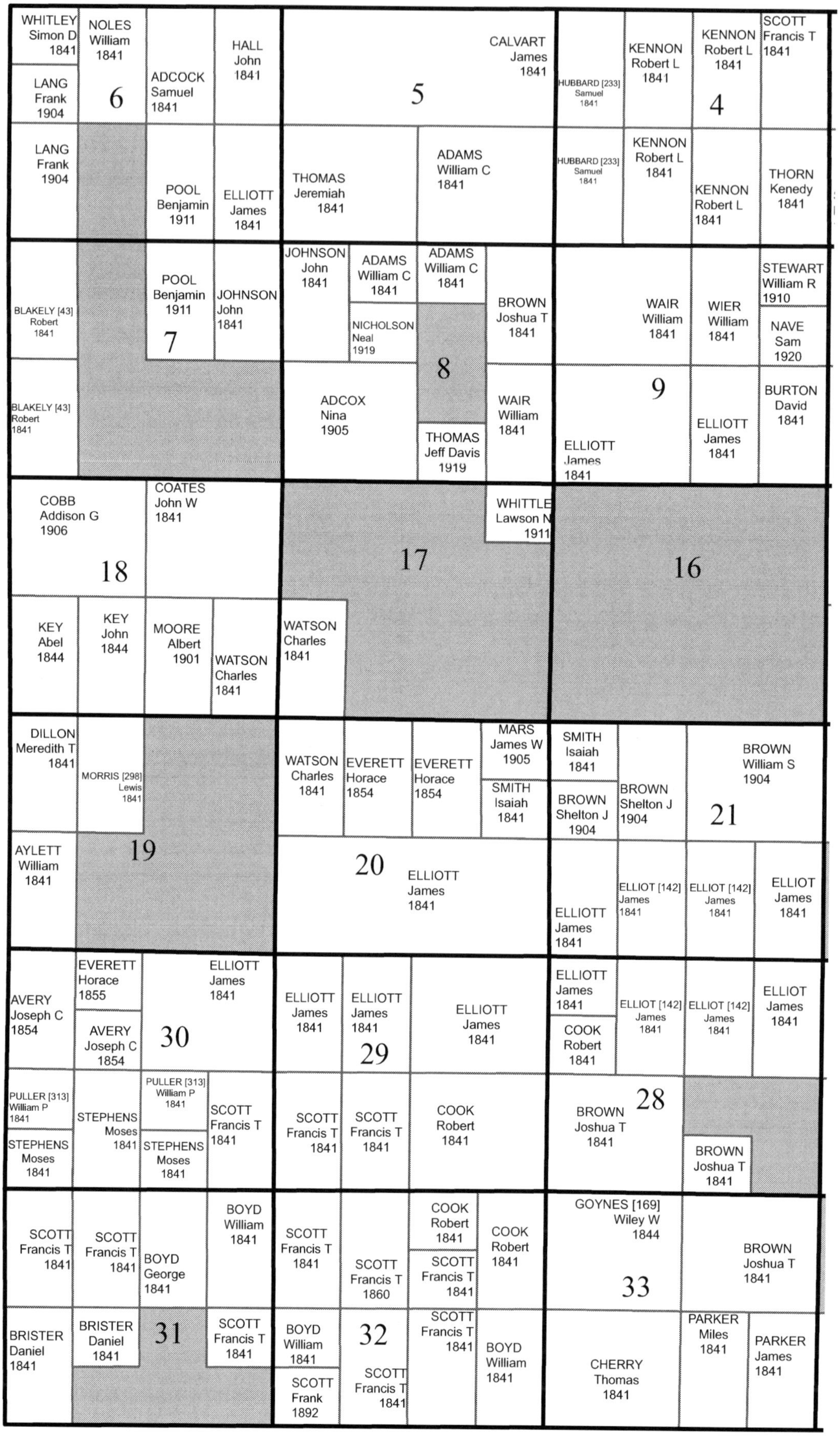

6
WHITLEY Simon D 1841
NOLES William 1841
ADCOCK Samuel 1841
HALL John 1841
LANG Frank 1904
LANG Frank 1904
POOL Benjamin 1911
ELLIOTT James 1841

5
CALVART James 1841
THOMAS Jeremiah 1841
ADAMS William C 1841

4
HUBBARD [233] Samuel 1841
KENNON Robert L 1841
KENNON Robert L 1841
SCOTT Francis T 1841
HUBBARD [233] Samuel 1841
KENNON Robert L 1841
KENNON Robert L 1841
THORN Kenedy 1841

7
BLAKELY [43] Robert 1841
POOL Benjamin 1911
JOHNSON John 1841
BLAKELY [43] Robert 1841

8
JOHNSON John 1841
ADAMS William C 1841
ADAMS William C 1841
NICHOLSON Neal 1919
BROWN Joshua T 1841
ADCOX Nina 1905
THOMAS Jeff Davis 1919
WAIR William 1841

9
WAIR William 1841
WIER William 1841
STEWART William R 1910
NAVE Sam 1920
ELLIOTT James 1841
ELLIOTT James 1841
BURTON David 1841

18
COBB Addison G 1906
COATES John W 1841
KEY Abel 1844
KEY John 1844
MOORE Albert 1901
WATSON Charles 1841

17
WHITTLE Lawson N 1911
WATSON Charles 1841

16

19
DILLON Meredith T 1841
MORRIS [298] Lewis 1841
AYLETT William 1841

20
WATSON Charles 1841
EVERETT Horace 1854
EVERETT Horace 1854
MARS James W 1905
SMITH Isaiah 1841
ELLIOTT James 1841

21
SMITH Isaiah 1841
BROWN Shelton J 1904
BROWN Shelton J 1904
BROWN William S 1904
ELLIOTT James 1841
ELLIOT [142] James 1841
ELLIOT [142] James 1841
ELLIOT James 1841

30
AVERY Joseph C 1854
EVERETT Horace 1855
AVERY Joseph C 1854
ELLIOTT James 1841
PULLER [313] William P 1841
STEPHENS Moses 1841
PULLER [313] William P 1841
STEPHENS Moses 1841
STEPHENS Moses 1841
SCOTT Francis T 1841

29
ELLIOTT James 1841
ELLIOTT James 1841
ELLIOTT James 1841
SCOTT Francis T 1841
SCOTT Francis T 1841
COOK Robert 1841

28
ELLIOTT James 1841
COOK Robert 1841
ELLIOT [142] James 1841
ELLIOT [142] James 1841
ELLIOT James 1841
BROWN Joshua T 1841
BROWN Joshua T 1841

31
SCOTT Francis T 1841
SCOTT Francis T 1841
BOYD George 1841
BOYD William 1841
BRISTER Daniel 1841
BRISTER Daniel 1841
SCOTT Francis T 1841

32
SCOTT Francis T 1841
SCOTT Francis T 1860
COOK Robert 1841
SCOTT Francis T 1841
COOK Robert 1841
BOYD William 1841
SCOTT Frank 1892
SCOTT Francis T 1841
SCOTT Francis T 1841
BOYD William 1841

33
GOYNES [169] Wiley W 1844
BROWN Joshua T 1841
CHERRY Thomas 1841
PARKER Miles 1841
PARKER James 1841

3
SCOTT Francis T 1841
HUBBARD [233] Samuel 1841
HUBBARD [233] Samuel 1841
STEELE Abner A 1841
SCOTT Francis T 1841
HUBBARD [233] Samuel 1841
HUBBARD [233] Samuel 1841

2
STEELE Abner A 1841
SCOTT Francis T 1841
HUBBARD [233] Samuel 1841
HUBBARD [233] Samuel 1841
SCOTT Francis T 1841

1
SCOTT Francis T 1841
HUBBARD [233] Samuel 1841
HUBBARD [233] Samuel 1841
SCOTT Francis T 1841
HUBBARD [233] Samuel 1841
BASKIN William O 1841

10
HUBBARD [233] Samuel 1841
HUBBARD [233] Samuel 1841
SCOTT Francis T 1841
BURTON David 1841
ADCOCK John 1841
SCOTT Francis T 1841
SCOTT Francis T 1841

11
SCOTT Francis T 1841
ADCOCK John 1841
ADCOCK John 1841
SCOTT Francis T 1841
HUBBARD [233] Samuel 1841
HUBBARD [233] Samuel 1841

12
ADCOCK John 1841
ADCOCK John 1841
BASKIN William O 1841
HUBBARD [233] Samuel 1841

15
BURTON David 1841
MADERSON John E 1841
MCLAWREN Duncan 1841
ROWE Shadrach 1841
ROWE Shadrach 1841
ROWE Shadrach 1841

14
LEWIS William M 1841
LEWIS William M 1841
BURTON Andrew T 1841
ROWE Shadrach 1841
ROWE Shadrach 1841
LEWIS William M 1841
ROWE Shadrach 1841

13
BURTON Andrew T 1841
SMITH Isaiah 1841
LEWIS William M 1841
DOZIER Sam 1909
DOZIER Sam 1909
DOZIER Henderson 1910

22
ROWE Shadrach 1841
ROWE Shadrach 1841

23
ROWE Shadrach 1841
LEWIS William M 1841
ROWE Shadrach 1841
CHERRY John J 1906
JACK Abner M 1911
LEWIS William M 1841

24
LEWIS William M 1841
LEWIS William M 1841
LEWIS William M 1841

27
HUNNICUTT [239] Leona P 1912
WATSON John J 1905
WATSON John J 1905
LEWIS [269] William M 1841
GAY James B 1906
WATSON William D 1906

26
LEWIS [269] William M 1841
FOWCETT Lyle B 1841
FOWCETT Lyle B 1841

25
LEWIS William M 1841
LEWIS William M 1841
FOWCETT Lyle B 1841
LEWIS William M 1841

34
CHERRY Thomas 1841
CHERRY James M 1841
CHERRY James M 1841
CHERRY James M 1841
MITCHELL Tilman 1841

35
EAKIN Joseph R 1914
MCDADE George W 1906
MCDADE Louis A 1909
MITCHELL Tilman 1841
MCDADE George W 1906
JAMES John A 1905

36
MCMAHON Robert G 1841
TAYLOR Josiah 1841
FOWCETT Lyle B 1841

Helpful Hints

1. This Map's INDEX can be found on the preceding pages.
2. Refer to Map "C" to see where this Township lies within Kemper County, Mississippi.
3. Numbers within square brackets [ ] denote a multi-patentee land parcel (multi-owner). Refer to Appendix "C" for a full list of members in this group.
4. Areas that look to be crowded with Patentees usually indicate multiple sales of the same parcel (Re-issues) or Overlapping parcels. See this Township's Index for an explanation of these and other circumstances that might explain "odd" groupings of Patentees on this map.

Legend

Patent Boundary

Section Boundary

No Patents Found (or Outside County)

1., 2., 3., ... Lot Numbers (when beside a name)

[ ] Group Number (see Appendix "C")

Scale: Section = 1 mile X 1 mile (generally, with some exceptions)

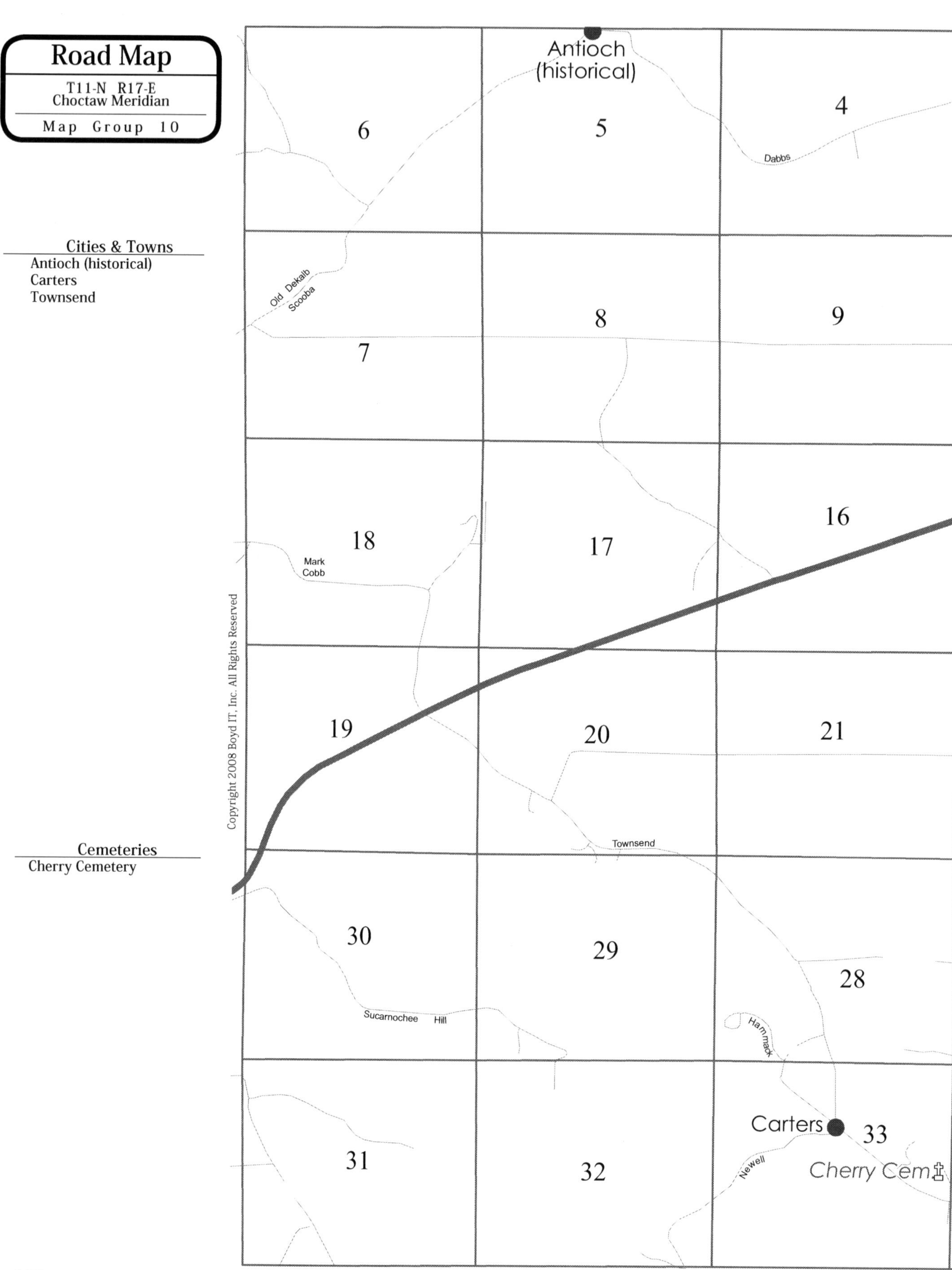
Road Map
T11-N R17-E
Choctaw Meridian
Map Group 10
Cities & Towns
Antioch (historical)
Carters
Townsend
Cemeteries
Cherry Cemetery
Antioch
(historical)
6
5
4
Dabbs
Old Dekalb
Scooba
7
8
9
18
Mark
Cobb
17
16
19
20
21
Townsend
30
29
28
Sucarnochee
Hill
Hammack
31
32
Carters
33
Newell
Cherry Cem

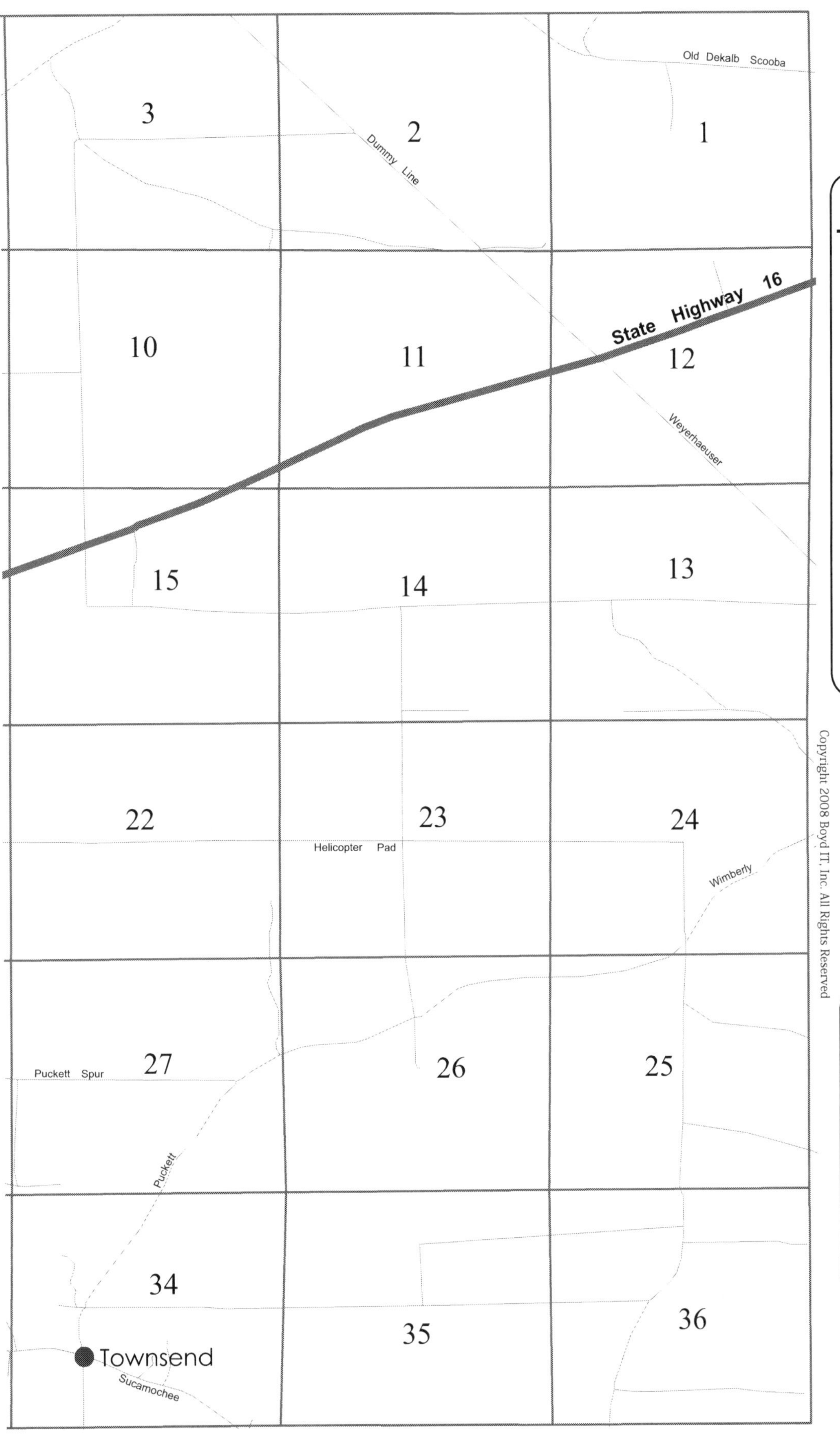

Helpful Hints

1. This road map has a number of uses, but primarily it is to help you: a) find the present location of land owned by your ancestors (at least the general area), b) find cemeteries and city-centers, and c) estimate the route/roads used by Census-takers & tax-assessors.

2. If you plan to travel to Kemper County to locate cemeteries or land parcels, please pick up a modern travel map for the area before you do. Mapping old land parcels on modern maps is not as exact a science as you might think. Just the slightest variations in public land survey coordinates, estimates of parcel boundaries, or road-map deviations can greatly alter a map's representation of how a road either does or doesn't cross a particular parcel of land.

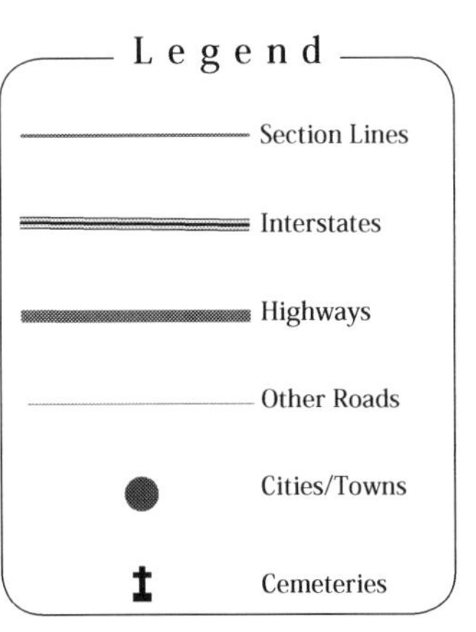

Scale: Section = 1 mile X 1 mile
(generally, with some exceptions)

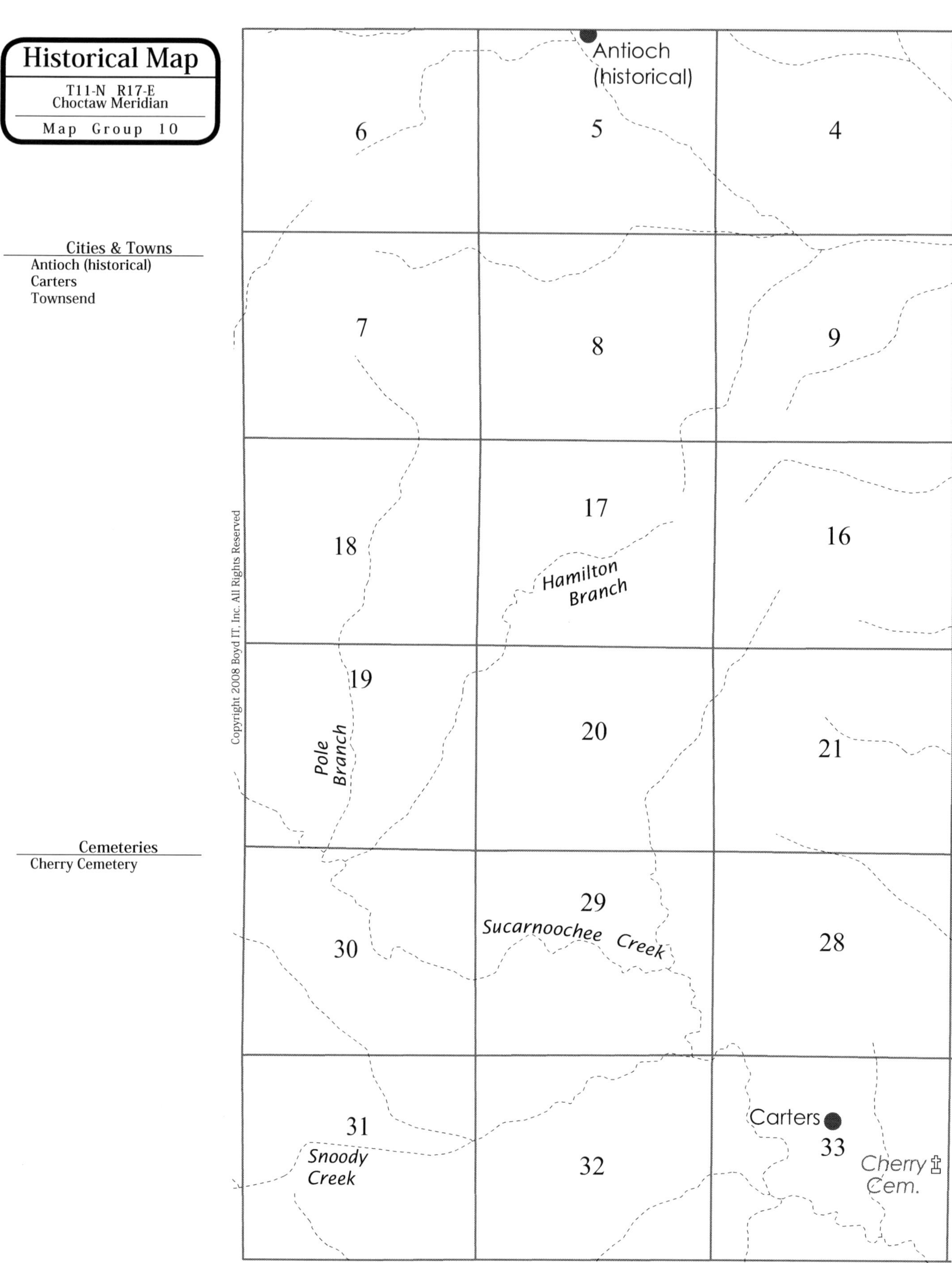
Historical Map
T11-N R17-E
Choctaw Meridian
Map Group 10
Cities & Towns
Antioch (historical)
Carters
Townsend
Cemeteries
Cherry Cemetery
Copyright 2008 Boyd IT, Inc. All Rights Reserved
Antioch (historical)
6
5
4
7
8
9
18
17
16
Hamilton Branch
19
20
21
Pole Branch
30
29
28
Sucarnoochee Creek
31
32
33
Snoody Creek
Carters
Cherry Cem.

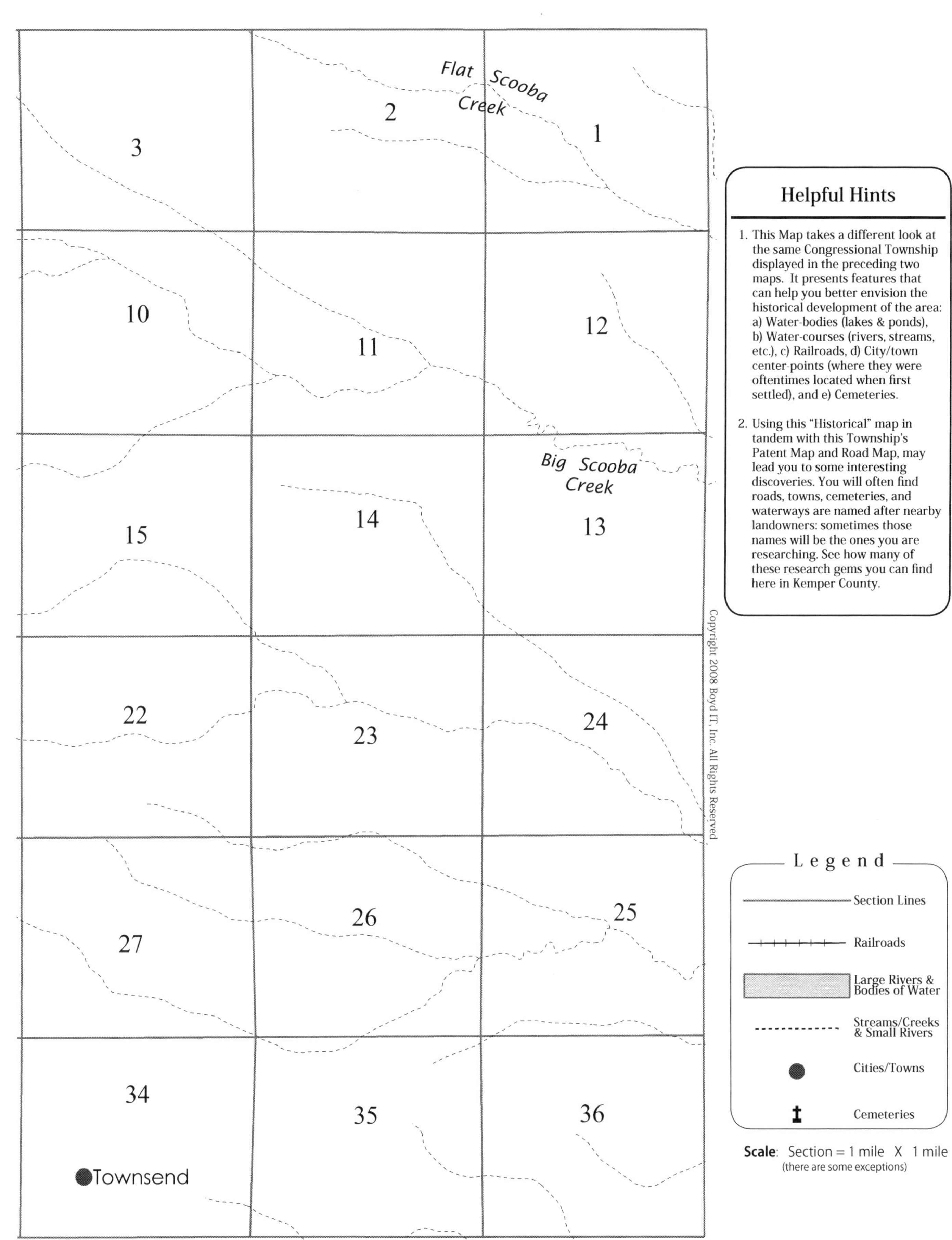
Flat Scooba Creek
3
2
1
10
11
12
Big Scooba Creek
15
14
13
22
23
24
27
26
25
34
35
36
Townsend
Helpful Hints
1. This Map takes a different look at the same Congressional Township displayed in the preceding two maps. It presents features that can help you better envision the historical development of the area: a) Water-bodies (lakes & ponds), b) Water-courses (rivers, streams, etc.), c) Railroads, d) City/town center-points (where they were oftentimes located when first settled), and e) Cemeteries.
2. Using this "Historical" map in tandem with this Township's Patent Map and Road Map, may lead you to some interesting discoveries. You will often find roads, towns, cemeteries, and waterways are named after nearby landowners: sometimes those names will be the ones you are researching. See how many of these research gems you can find here in Kemper County.
Legend
Section Lines
Railroads
Large Rivers & Bodies of Water
Streams/Creeks & Small Rivers
Cities/Towns
Cemeteries
Scale: Section = 1 mile X 1 mile
(there are some exceptions)

Map Group 11: Index to Land Patents

Township 11-North Range 18-East (Choctaw)

After you locate an individual in this Index, take note of the Section and Section Part then proceed to the Land Patent map on the pages immediately following. You should have no difficulty locating the corresponding parcel of land.

The "For More Info" Column will lead you to more information about the underlying Patents. See the *Legend* at right, and the "How to Use this Book" chapter, for more information.

LEGEND

"For More Info . . . " column

A = Authority (Legislative Act, See Appendix "A")
B = Block or Lot (location in Section unknown)
C = Cancelled Patent
F = Fractional Section
G = Group (Multi-Patentee Patent, see Appendix "C")
V = Overlaps another Parcel
R = Re-Issued (Parcel patented more than once)

(A & G items require you to look in the Appendixes referred to above. All other Letter-designations followed by a number require you to locate line-items in this index that possess the ID number found after the letter).

ID	Individual in Patent	Sec.	Sec. Part	Date Issued	Other Counties	For More Info . . .
2158	ABERCROMBIE, Albert R	17	NENW	1905-10-19		A2
2263	ABERCROMBIE, Lizzie M	17	NWSW	1905-12-30		A2
2264	" "	17	S½SW	1905-12-30		A2
2353	ADAMS, William C	1	NW	1841-02-27		A1
2218	ARCHIBALD, James H	7	E½NW	1841-02-27		A1
2260	AVERY, Joseph C	27	SESW	1854-03-15		A1
2259	" "	21	W½SE	1858-07-15		A1
2258	BARNETT, Joseph	34	SW	1841-02-27		A1
2159	BENNETT, Anthony	36	W½SE	1843-02-01		A1 G34
2184	BESTER, Daniel P	3	E½SE	1841-02-27		A1 G38
2185	" "	3	E½SW	1841-02-27		A1 G38
2186	" "	3	W½SE	1841-02-27		A1 G38
2187	" "	3	W½SW	1841-02-27		A1 G38
2188	" "	4	E½SE	1841-02-27		A1 G38
2182	" "	4	W½SW	1841-02-27		A1
2183	" "	5	E½SE	1841-02-27		A1
2202	CALLAHAN, Henry	19	SE	1901-12-17		A2 G76
2201	" "	19	NW	1906-05-01		A2
2233	CALLAHAN, John	19	NE	1906-05-01		A2
2202	CALLAHAN, Mary	19	SE	1901-12-17		A2 G76
2162	CAMRON, Benjamin	22	W½NW	1841-02-27		A1
2163	CANNON, Benjamin	10	W½SE	1841-02-27		A1
2164	" "	15	E½NW	1841-02-27		A1
2165	" "	15	N½E½SW	1841-02-27		A1
2166	" "	15	N½W½SE	1841-02-27		A1
2167	" "	15	W½NE	1841-02-27		A1
2168	" "	15	W½SW	1841-02-27		A1
2195	CANNON, George W	13	SW	1841-02-01		A1
2196	" "	21	SW	1841-02-27		A1
2197	" "	26	W½NW	1841-02-27		A1
2198	" "	26	W½SW	1841-02-27		A1
2199	" "	28	E½NW	1841-02-27		A1
2200	" "	29	E½NE	1841-02-27		A1
2361	CANNON, William	12	E½SE	1841-02-27		A1 G78
2354	" "	13	E½NW	1841-02-27		A1
2355	" "	13	E½SE	1841-02-27		A1
2356	" "	13	W½NE	1841-02-27		A1
2357	" "	13	W½NW	1841-02-27		A1
2358	" "	13	W½SE	1841-02-27		A1
2359	" "	14	E½SE	1841-02-27		A1
2360	" "	24	E½NE	1841-02-27		A1
2169	CARTER, Clark	11	E½NE	1841-02-01		A1
2175	" "	12	W½NW	1841-02-01		A1
2170	" "	11	E½SE	1841-02-27		A1
2171	" "	11	W½NE	1841-02-27		A1
2172	" "	11	W½NW	1841-02-27		A1

ID	Individual in Patent	Sec.	Sec. Part	Date Issued	Other Counties	For More Info . . .
2361	CARTER, Clark (Cont'd)	12	E½SE	1841-02-27		A1 G78
2173	" "	12	E½SW	1841-02-27		A1
2174	" "	12	W½NE	1841-02-27		A1
2176	" "	12	W½SE	1841-02-27		A1
2177	" "	12	W½SW	1841-02-27		A1
2178	" "	2	E½SE	1841-02-27		A1
2179	" "	2	W½SE	1841-02-27		A1
2294	CHISOLM, Richard P	33	E½SW	1841-02-27		A1
2295	" "	33	SWSW	1841-02-27		A1
2217	CRAWFORD, James	30	NE	1841-02-27		A1
2285	CROCKER, Nathaniel	35	E½SW	1841-02-27		A1
2286	CROKER, Nathaniel	35	E½NW	1841-02-27		A1
2236	CULPEPPER, John	17	W½NE	1841-02-27		A1
2234	" "	17	N½E½SW	1843-02-01		A1
2235	" "	17	S½E½NW	1843-02-01		A1
2211	DANIEL, Isham	5	E½NE	1841-02-27		A1
2212	" "	5	W½	1841-02-27		A1
2213	" "	5	W½SE	1841-02-27		A1
2214	" "	6	E½NE	1841-02-27		A1
2215	" "	9	E½SW	1841-02-27		A1
2216	" "	9	NW	1841-02-27		A1
2318	DARNAL, Thomas	34	E½NE	1841-02-27		A1
2319	" "	35	W½NW	1841-02-27		A1
2296	DARNALL, Samuel B	36	S½W½NW	1841-02-27		A1
2297	" "	36	SW	1841-02-27		A1
2320	DARNALL, Thomas	34	E½SE	1841-02-27		A1
2321	" "	34	W½SE	1841-02-27		A1
2322	" "	35	W½SW	1841-02-27		A1
2157	DOZIER, Albert	29	NWSW	1910-03-17		A2
2261	DOZIER, Judy	29	E½SW	1908-08-17		A2 G126
2261	DOZIER, Robert	29	E½SW	1908-08-17		A2 G126
2244	EARL, Joseph B	1	W½SE	1845-01-21		A1
2256	EARLE, Joseph B	2	E½NE	1840-02-13		A1 G136
2257	" "	2	W½NE	1840-02-13		A1 G136
2251	" "	1	W½SW	1841-02-27		A1 G135
2248	" "	10	E½NE	1841-02-27		A1 G129
2249	" "	10	E½SE	1841-02-27		A1 G129
2250	" "	10	W½NE	1841-02-27		A1 G129
2252	" "	11	E½SW	1841-02-27		A1 G130
2253	" "	11	W½SE	1841-02-27		A1 G130
2254	" "	11	W½SW	1841-02-27		A1 G130
2246	" "	2	E½SW	1841-02-27		A1 G134
2247	" "	2	W½SW	1841-02-27		A1 G134
2255	" "	3	E½NE	1841-02-27		A1 G130
2245	" "	12	E½NW	1845-01-21		A1
2298	FELTS, Samuel D	2	NW	1841-02-01		A1
2303	" "	17	E½NE	1841-02-27		A1 G151
2299	" "	20	E½NE	1841-02-27		A1
2300	" "	7	NENE	1841-02-27		A1 C
2304	" "	8	N½	1841-02-27		A1 G151
2301	" "	9	E½SE	1841-02-27		A1
2302	" "	9	W½SE	1841-02-27		A1
2305	" "	9	W½SW	1841-02-27		A1 G151
2306	FELTZ, Samuel D	18	N½	1841-02-27		A1
2364	FOX, William	25	E½NW	1841-02-27		A1 G157
2363	" "	25	W½NE	1841-02-27		A1 G158
2180	GREEN, Daniel	13	E½NE	1841-02-27		A1
2181	" "	36	E½SE	1841-02-27		A1 G173
2365	GREENLEES, William	33	SE	1844-09-10		A1
2307	HUBBARD, Samuel	1	E½SW	1841-02-27		A1 G232
2308	" "	14	E½NE	1841-02-27		A1 G232
2309	" "	6	NW	1841-02-27		A1 G233
2310	" "	6	W½NE	1841-02-27		A1 G233
2311	" "	6	W½SW	1841-02-27		A1 G233
2314	" "	8	S½	1841-02-27		A1 G233
2312	" "	7	E½NE	1844-09-10		A1 G233
2313	" "	7	S½	1844-09-10		A1 G233
2267	JACKSON, Mathew	14	E½SW	1841-02-27		A1
2268	" "	14	W½NW	1841-02-27		A1
2269	" "	14	W½SE	1841-02-27		A1
2270	" "	14	W½SW	1841-02-27		A1
2271	" "	15	E½NE	1841-02-27		A1
2272	JACKSON, Matthew	14	E½NW	1841-02-27		A1

ID	Individual in Patent	Sec.	Sec. Part	Date Issued	Other Counties	For More Info . . .
2273	JACKSON, Matthew (Cont'd)	14	W½NE	1841-02-27		A1
2292	JACKSON, Quam	27	N½NE	1904-12-31		A2
2293	" "	27	NENW	1904-12-31		A2
2367	JINCKS, William	4	E½NW	1841-02-27		A1
2219	JOHNSON, James	4	W½NW	1841-02-27		A1
2303	JOHNSON, Warren B	17	E½NE	1841-02-27		A1 G151
2304	" "	8	N½	1841-02-27		A1 G151
2305	" "	9	W½SW	1841-02-27		A1 G151
2193	JONES, Gabriel	15	W½NW	1841-02-27		A1
2194	" "	17	SE	1845-12-01		A1 G257
2205	JONES, Henry P	21	NW	1841-02-27		A1
2206	" "	21	W½NE	1841-02-27		A1
2226	JONES, Jesse	31	S½E½SW	1841-02-27		A1
2227	" "	31	W½SW	1841-02-27		A1
2291	JONES, Philip	19	E½SW	1911-11-13		A2
2373	JONES, Zad	27	SENW	1905-02-13		A2
2374	" "	27	SWNE	1905-02-13		A2
2248	LAKE, James	10	E½NE	1841-02-27		A1 G129
2220	" "	10	E½NW	1841-02-27		A1 G262
2249	" "	10	E½SE	1841-02-27		A1 G129
2250	" "	10	W½NE	1841-02-27		A1 G129
2221	" "	10	W½NW	1841-02-27		A1 G262
2307	LEWIS, Moses	1	E½SW	1841-02-27		A1 G232
2308	" "	14	E½NE	1841-02-27		A1 G232
2307	LEWIS, Rufus G	1	E½SW	1841-02-27		A1 G232
2308	" "	14	E½NE	1841-02-27		A1 G232
2309	" "	6	NW	1841-02-27		A1 G233
2310	" "	6	W½NE	1841-02-27		A1 G233
2311	" "	6	W½SW	1841-02-27		A1 G233
2314	" "	8	S½	1841-02-27		A1 G233
2312	" "	7	E½NE	1844-09-10		A1 G233
2313	" "	7	S½	1844-09-10		A1 G233
2309	LEWIS, William M	6	NW	1841-02-27		A1 G233
2310	" "	6	W½NE	1841-02-27		A1 G233
2311	" "	6	W½SW	1841-02-27		A1 G233
2314	" "	8	S½	1841-02-27		A1 G233
2312	" "	7	E½NE	1844-09-10		A1 G233
2313	" "	7	S½	1844-09-10		A1 G233
2368	" "	35	NWNE	1860-05-01		A1
2203	LIPSCOMB, Henry	21	NESE	1905-03-30		A2
2204	" "	21	SENE	1905-03-30		A2
2369	MADISON, William	6	E½SW	1841-02-27		A1
2370	" "	6	SE	1841-02-27		A1
2220	MCGEE, Thomas	10	E½NW	1841-02-27		A1 G262
2221	" "	10	W½NW	1841-02-27		A1 G262
2252	" "	11	E½SW	1841-02-27		A1 G130
2253	" "	11	W½SE	1841-02-27		A1 G130
2254	" "	11	W½SW	1841-02-27		A1 G130
2325	" "	23	NE	1841-02-27		A1
2344	" "	23	W½NW	1841-02-27		A1 G290
2345	" "	24	E½NW	1841-02-27		A1 G287
2327	" "	24	E½SE	1841-02-27		A1
2346	" "	24	E½SW	1841-02-27		A1 G287
2328	" "	24	W½NE	1841-02-27		A1
2329	" "	24	W½NW	1841-02-27		A1
2347	" "	24	W½SE	1841-02-27		A1 G287
2330	" "	24	W½SW	1841-02-27		A1
2348	" "	25	E½NE	1841-02-27		A1 G287
2364	" "	25	E½NW	1841-02-27		A1 G157
2349	" "	25	E½SE	1841-02-27		A1 G287
2350	" "	25	E½SW	1841-02-27		A1 G287
2351	" "	25	W½SE	1841-02-27		A1 G287
2331	" "	25	W½SW	1841-02-27		A1
2332	" "	26	E½NW	1841-02-27		A1
2333	" "	26	E½SE	1841-02-27		A1 R2334
2334	" "	26	E½SE	1841-02-27		A1 R2333
2335	" "	26	E½SW	1841-02-27		A1
2336	" "	26	W½NE	1841-02-27		A1
2337	" "	26	W½SE	1841-02-27		A1
2255	" "	3	E½NE	1841-02-27		A1 G130
2338	" "	3	E½NW	1841-02-27		A1
2184	" "	3	E½SE	1841-02-27		A1 G38
2185	" "	3	E½SW	1841-02-27		A1 G38

ID	Individual in Patent	Sec.	Sec. Part	Date Issued	Other Counties	For More Info . . .
2339	MCGEE, Thomas (Cont'd)	3	W½NE	1841-02-27		A1
2340	" "	3	W½NW	1841-02-27		A1
2186	" "	3	W½SE	1841-02-27		A1 G38
2187	" "	3	W½SW	1841-02-27		A1 G38
2341	" "	4	E½NE	1841-02-27		A1
2188	" "	4	E½SE	1841-02-27		A1 G38
2342	" "	4	W½NE	1841-02-27		A1
2343	" "	5	W½NE	1841-02-27		A1
2323	" "	23	E½SE	1842-11-01		A1
2324	" "	23	E½SW	1842-11-01		A1
2326	" "	23	W½SE	1842-11-01		A1
2237	MCNEILL, John	31	SE	1841-02-27		A1
2238	" "	32	S½W½SW	1841-02-27		A1
2316	MISSISSIPPI, State Of	27	SENE	1909-05-14		A3
2317	" "	31	NESW	1909-05-14		A3
2207	NICHOLSON, Isaac W	1	E½NE	1841-02-27		A1
2208	" "	1	E½SE	1841-02-27		A1
2209	" "	1	W½NE	1841-02-27		A1
2210	" "	12	E½NE	1841-02-27		A1
2239	NORRISS, John N	17	W½NW	1841-02-27		A1
2240	" "	18	NESE	1841-02-27		A1
2241	" "	20	E½SW	1841-02-27		A1
2242	" "	20	W½SE	1841-02-27		A1
2160	OLIVE, Anthony	29	NW	1841-02-27		A1
2194	" "	17	SE	1845-12-01		A1 G257
2243	OLIVE, John	21	NENE	1844-09-10		A1
2287	PERRY, Nathaniel H	27	W½NW	1841-02-27		A1
2288	" "	27	W½SW	1841-02-27		A1
2289	" "	28	E½NE	1841-02-27		A1
2290	" "	28	E½SE	1841-02-27		A1
2159	PICKETT, James	36	W½SE	1843-02-01		A1 G34
2265	POWELL, Martin	10	E½SW	1841-02-27		A1 G312
2222	PUCKETT, James	36	E½NW	1841-02-27		A1
2181	" "	36	E½SE	1841-02-27		A1 G173
2161	RENCHER, Arran	21	SESE	1916-03-20		A2
2315	RIDGWAY, Sephalen	35	NENE	1860-05-01		A1
2352	ROBINSON, Tom	29	W½NE	1914-06-19		A2
2362	SANDFORD, William D	32	SESE	1843-02-01		A1
2274	SAYRE, Milton	30	SE	1841-02-27		A1
2275	" "	30	W½	1841-02-27		A1
2276	" "	31	N½	1841-02-27		A1
2281	" "	33	N½	1841-02-27		A1
2282	" "	33	NWSW	1841-02-27		A1
2283	" "	34	NW	1841-02-27		A1
2284	" "	34	W½NE	1841-02-27		A1
2277	" "	32	N½	1844-09-10		A1
2278	" "	32	N½SW	1844-09-10		A1
2279	" "	32	NESE	1844-09-10		A1
2280	" "	32	W½SE	1844-09-10		A1
2190	SCOTT, Francis T	4	E½SW	1841-02-27		A1
2191	" "	4	W½SE	1841-02-27		A1
2192	" "	9	NE	1841-02-27		A1
2156	STEELE, Abner A	7	W½NE	1841-02-27		A1
2371	STEELE, William	7	W½NW	1841-02-27		A1
2262	STOVALL, Lewis	25	W½NW	1841-02-01		A1
2307	TAPPAN, John	1	E½SW	1841-02-27		A1 G232
2308	" "	14	E½NE	1841-02-27		A1 G232
2309	" "	6	NW	1841-02-27		A1 G233
2310	" "	6	W½NE	1841-02-27		A1 G233
2311	" "	6	W½SW	1841-02-27		A1 G233
2314	" "	8	S½	1841-02-27		A1 G233
2312	" "	7	E½NE	1844-09-10		A1 G233
2313	" "	7	S½	1844-09-10		A1 G233
2363	TART, Thomas E	25	W½NE	1841-02-27		A1 G158
2345	TARTT, Thomas E	24	E½NW	1841-02-27		A1 G287
2346	" "	24	E½SW	1841-02-27		A1 G287
2347	" "	24	W½SE	1841-02-27		A1 G287
2348	" "	25	E½NE	1841-02-27		A1 G287
2349	" "	25	E½SE	1841-02-27		A1 G287
2350	" "	25	E½SW	1841-02-27		A1 G287
2351	" "	25	W½SE	1841-02-27		A1 G287
2266	ULMER, Mary	36	NE	1841-02-27		A1 G330
2266	ULMER, Richard	36	NE	1841-02-27		A1 G330

ID	Individual in Patent	Sec.	Sec. Part	Date Issued	Other Counties	For More Info . . .
2224	WALTON, Jason	35	S½NE	1841-02-27		A1
2225	WATSON, Jason	35	SE	1841-02-27		A1
2223	WEST, James	29	S½SE	1906-05-01		A1
2246	WHITFIELD, Boaz	2	E½SW	1841-02-27		A1 G134
2247	" "	2	W½SW	1841-02-27		A1 G134
2265	WHITSETT, John C	10	E½SW	1841-02-27		A1 G312
2228	" "	10	W½SW	1841-02-27		A1
2229	" "	15	E½SE	1841-02-27		A1
2230	" "	22	E½NE	1841-02-27		A1
2231	" "	23	E½NW	1841-02-27		A1
2232	" "	23	W½SW	1841-02-27		A1
2372	WIGGINS, Willie	29	SWSW	1912-04-18		A2
2189	WIMBERLY, Eli W	19	W½SW	1904-10-17		A2
2251	WINSTON, Joel W	1	W½SW	1841-02-27		A1 G135
2344	" "	23	W½NW	1841-02-27		A1 G290
2256	WINSTON, William	2	E½NE	1840-02-13		A1 G136
2257	" "	2	W½NE	1840-02-13		A1 G136
2366	WINSTON, William H	11	E½NW	1841-02-27		A1

Patent Map

T11-N R18-E
Choctaw Meridian

Map Group 11

Township Statistics

Parcels Mapped	:	219
Number of Patents	:	189
Number of Individuals	:	88
Patentees Identified	:	90
Number of Surnames	:	66
Multi-Patentee Parcels	:	48
Oldest Patent Date	:	2/13/1840
Most Recent Patent	:	3/20/1916
Block/Lot Parcels	:	0
Parcels Re - Issued	:	1
Parcels that Overlap	:	0
Cities and Towns	:	4
Cemeteries	:	3

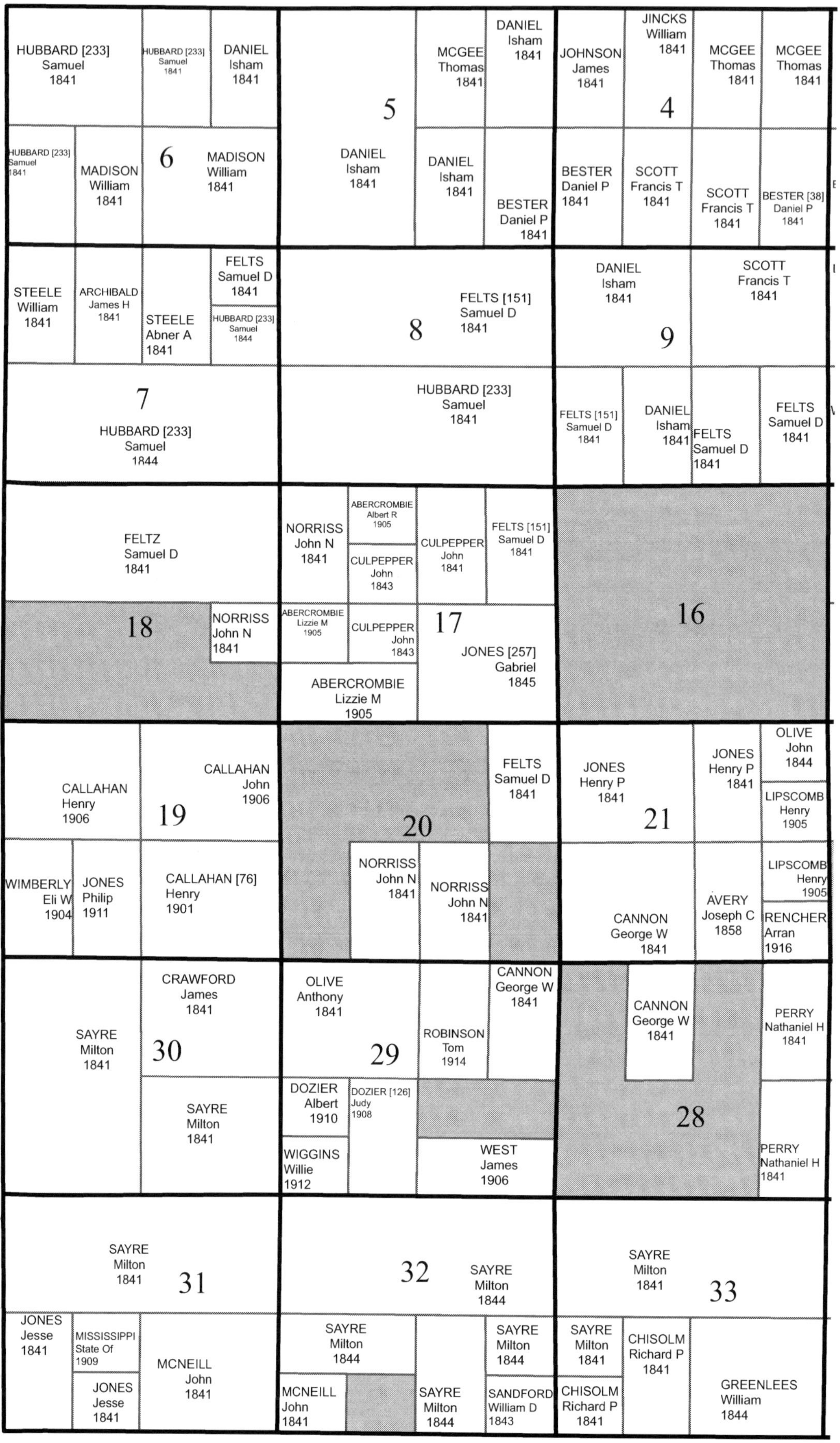

6
HUBBARD [233] Samuel 1841
HUBBARD [233] Samuel 1841
DANIEL Isham 1841
HUBBARD [233] Samuel 1841
MADISON William 1841
MADISON William 1841

5
DANIEL Isham 1841
MCGEE Thomas 1841
DANIEL Isham 1841
DANIEL Isham 1841
BESTER Daniel P 1841

4
JOHNSON James 1841
JINCKS William 1841
MCGEE Thomas 1841
MCGEE Thomas 1841
BESTER Daniel P 1841
SCOTT Francis T 1841
SCOTT Francis T 1841
BESTER [38] Daniel P 1841

7
STEELE William 1841
ARCHIBALD James H 1841
STEELE Abner A 1841
FELTS Samuel D 1841
HUBBARD [233] Samuel 1844
HUBBARD [233] Samuel 1844

8
FELTS [151] Samuel D 1841
HUBBARD [233] Samuel 1841

9
DANIEL Isham 1841
SCOTT Francis T 1841
FELTS [151] Samuel D 1841
DANIEL Isham 1841
FELTS Samuel D 1841
FELTS Samuel D 1841

18
FELTZ Samuel D 1841
NORRISS John N 1841

17
NORRISS John N 1841
ABERCROMBIE Albert R 1905
CULPEPPER John 1843
CULPEPPER John 1841
FELTS [151] Samuel D 1841
ABERCROMBIE Lizzie M 1905
CULPEPPER John 1843
JONES [257] Gabriel 1845
ABERCROMBIE Lizzie M 1905

16

19
CALLAHAN Henry 1906
CALLAHAN John 1906
WIMBERLY Eli W 1904
JONES Philip 1911
CALLAHAN [76] Henry 1901

20
FELTS Samuel D 1841
NORRISS John N 1841
NORRISS John N 1841

21
JONES Henry P 1841
JONES Henry P 1841
OLIVE John 1844
LIPSCOMB Henry 1905
LIPSCOMB Henry 1905
CANNON George W 1841
AVERY Joseph C 1858
RENCHER Arran 1916

30
SAYRE Milton 1841
CRAWFORD James 1841
SAYRE Milton 1841

29
OLIVE Anthony 1841
ROBINSON Tom 1914
CANNON George W 1841
DOZIER Albert 1910
DOZIER [126] Judy 1908
WIGGINS Willie 1912
WEST James 1906

28
CANNON George W 1841
PERRY Nathaniel H 1841
PERRY Nathaniel H 1841

31
SAYRE Milton 1841
JONES Jesse 1841
MISSISSIPPI State Of 1909
JONES Jesse 1841
MCNEILL John 1841

32
SAYRE Milton 1844
SAYRE Milton 1844
SAYRE Milton 1844
MCNEILL John 1841
SAYRE Milton 1844
SANDFORD William D 1843

33
SAYRE Milton 1841
SAYRE Milton 1841
CHISOLM Richard P 1841
CHISOLM Richard P 1841
GREENLEES William 1844

MCGEE Thomas 1841
MCGEE Thomas 1841
MCGEE Thomas 1841
EARLE [130] Joseph B 1841
FELTS Samuel D 1841
2
EARLE [136] Joseph B 1840
EARLE [136] Joseph B 1840
ADAMS William C 1841
1
NICHOLSON Isaac W 1841
NICHOLSON Isaac W 1841

3
BESTER [38] Daniel P 1841
BESTER [38] Daniel P 1841
BESTER [38] Daniel P 1841
BESTER [38] Daniel P 1841
EARLE [134] Joseph B 1841
EARLE [134] Joseph B 1841
CARTER Clark 1841
CARTER Clark 1841
EARLE [135] Joseph B 1841
HUBBARD [232] Samuel 1841
EARL Joseph B 1845
NICHOLSON Isaac W 1841

LAKE [262] James 1841
LAKE [262] James 1841
10
EARLE [129] Joseph B 1841
EARLE [129] Joseph B 1841
CARTER Clark 1841
WINSTON William H 1841
CARTER Clark 1841
11
CARTER Clark 1841
CARTER Clark 1841
EARLE Joseph B 1845
CARTER Clark 1841
NICHOLSON Isaac W 1841

WHITSETT John C 1841
POWELL [312] Martin 1841
CANNON Benjamin 1841
EARLE [129] Joseph B 1841
EARLE [130] Joseph B 1841
EARLE [130] Joseph B 1841
EARLE [130] Joseph B 1841
CARTER Clark 1841
CARTER Clark 1841
12
CARTER Clark 1841
CARTER Clark 1841
CANNON [78] William 1841

JONES Gabriel 1841
CANNON Benjamin 1841
15
CANNON Benjamin 1841
JACKSON Mathew 1841
JACKSON Mathew 1841
JACKSON Matthew 1841
JACKSON Matthew 1841
14
HUBBARD [232] Samuel 1841
CANNON William 1841
CANNON William 1841
CANNON William 1841
GREEN Daniel 1841

CANNON Benjamin 1841
CANNON Benjamin 1841
CANNON Benjamin 1841
WHITSETT John C 1841
JACKSON Mathew 1841
JACKSON Mathew 1841
JACKSON Mathew 1841
CANNON William 1841
CANNON George W 1841
13
CANNON William 1841
CANNON William 1841

CAMRON Benjamin 1841
22
WHITSETT John C 1841
MCGEE [290] Thomas 1841
WHITSETT John C 1841
23
MCGEE Thomas 1841
MCGEE Thomas 1841
MCGEE [287] Thomas 1841
24
MCGEE Thomas 1841
CANNON William 1841

WHITSETT John C 1841
MCGEE Thomas 1842
MCGEE Thomas 1842
MCGEE Thomas 1842
MCGEE Thomas 1841
MCGEE [287] Thomas 1841
MCGEE [287] Thomas 1841
MCGEE Thomas 1841

JACKSON Quam 1904
JACKSON Quam 1904
PERRY Nathaniel H 1841
JONES Zad 1905
JONES Zad 1905
MISSISSIPPI State Of 1909
CANNON George W 1841
MCGEE Thomas 1841
MCGEE Thomas 1841
26
STOVALL Lewis 1841
FOX [157] William 1841
FOX [158] William 1841
MCGEE [287] Thomas 1841

27
PERRY Nathaniel H 1841
AVERY Joseph C 1854
CANNON George W 1841
MCGEE Thomas 1841
MCGEE Thomas 1841
MCGEE Thomas 1841
MCGEE Thomas 1841
25
MCGEE [287] Thomas 1841
MCGEE [287] Thomas 1841
MCGEE [287] Thomas 1841

SAYRE Milton 1841
SAYRE Milton 1841
34
DARNAL Thomas 1841
DARNAL Thomas 1841
CROKER Nathaniel 1841
LEWIS William M 1860
RIDGWAY Sephalen 1860
WALTON Jason 1841
35
DARNALL Samuel B 1841
PUCKETT James 1841
ULMER [330] Mary 1841
36

BARNETT Joseph 1841
DARNALL Thomas 1841
DARNALL Thomas 1841
DARNALL Thomas 1841
CROCKER Nathaniel 1841
WATSON Jason 1841
DARNALL Samuel B 1841
BENNETT [34] Anthony 1843
GREEN [173] Daniel 1841

Helpful Hints

1. This Map's INDEX can be found on the preceding pages.
2. Refer to Map "C" to see where this Township lies within Kemper County, Mississippi.
3. Numbers within square brackets [ ] denote a multi-patentee land parcel (multi-owner). Refer to Appendix "C" for a full list of members in this group.
4. Areas that look to be crowded with Patentees usually indicate multiple sales of the same parcel (Re-issues) or Overlapping parcels. See this Township's Index for an explanation of these and other circumstances that might explain "odd" groupings of Patentees on this map.

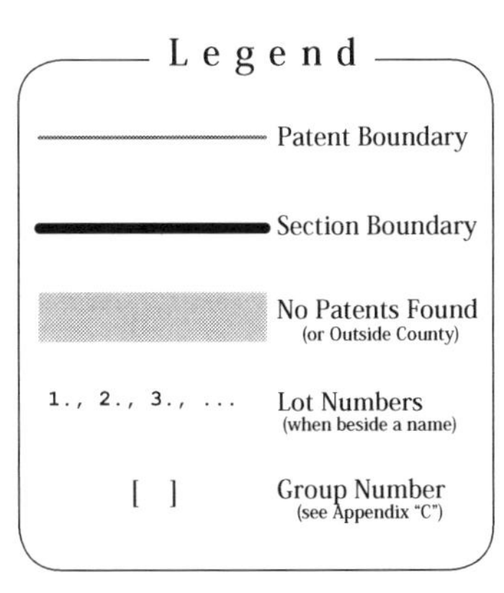

Scale: Section = 1 mile X 1 mile
(generally, with some exceptions)

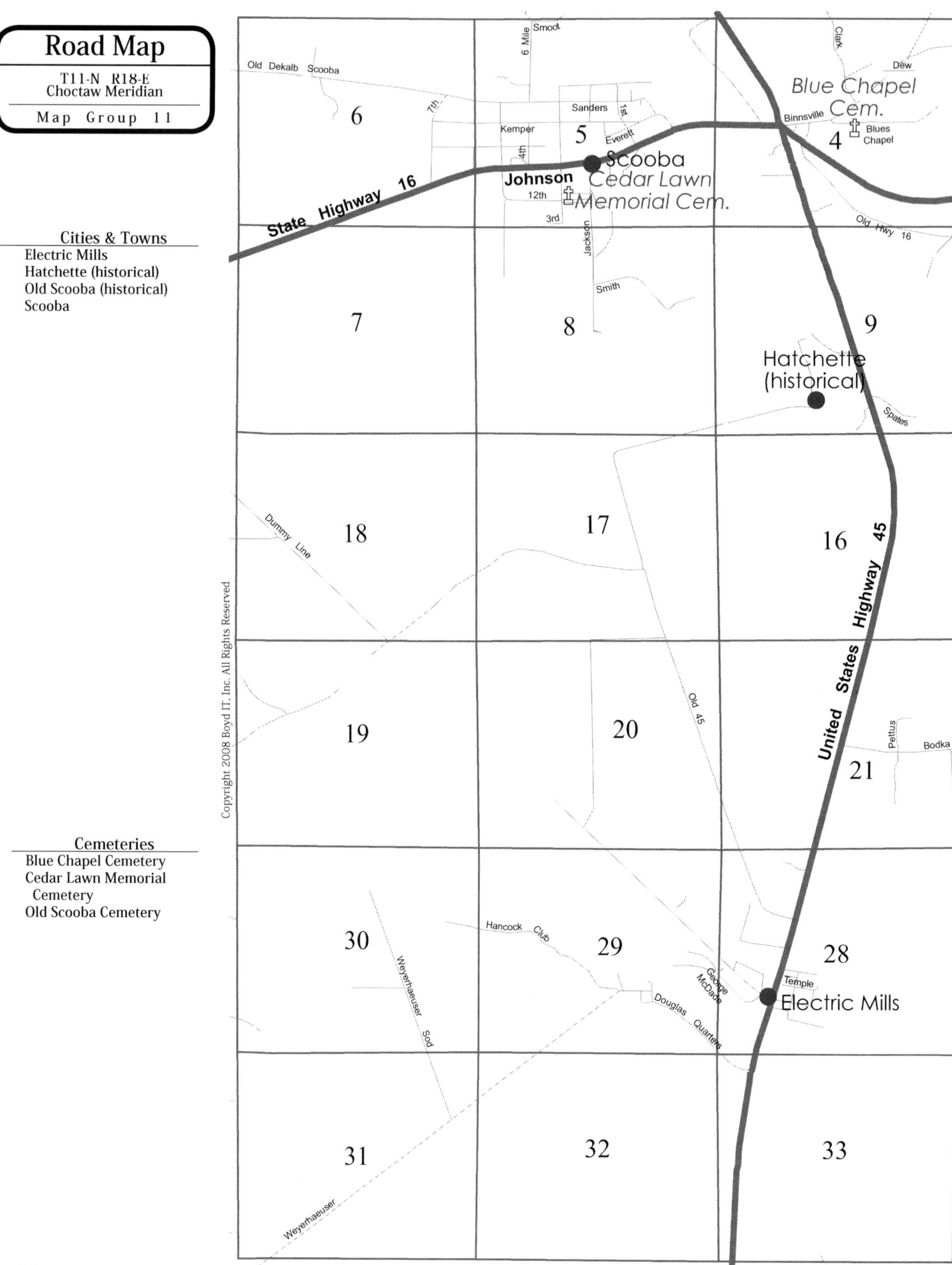
Road Map
T11-N R18-E
Choctaw Meridian
Map Group 11
Cities & Towns
Electric Mills
Hatchette (historical)
Old Scooba (historical)
Scooba
Cemeteries
Blue Chapel Cemetery
Cedar Lawn Memorial
Cemetery
Old Scooba Cemetery
Copyright 2008 Boyd IT, Inc. All Rights Reserved
6
5
4
7
8
9
18
17
16
19
20
21
30
29
28
31
32
33
Old Dekalb Scooba
6 Mile
Smoot
Clark
Dew
Blue Chapel
Cem.
7th
Sanders
1st
Binnsville
Blues
Chapel
Kemper
Everett
4th
Scooba
Johnson
Cedar Lawn
12th
Memorial Cem.
3rd
State Highway 16
Old Hwy 16
Jackson
Smith
Hatchette
(historical)
Spates
Dummy Line
United States Highway 45
Old 45
Pettus
Bodka
Hancock Club
George McDade
Temple
Electric Mills
Douglas Quarters
Weyerhaeuser Sod
Weyerhaeuser

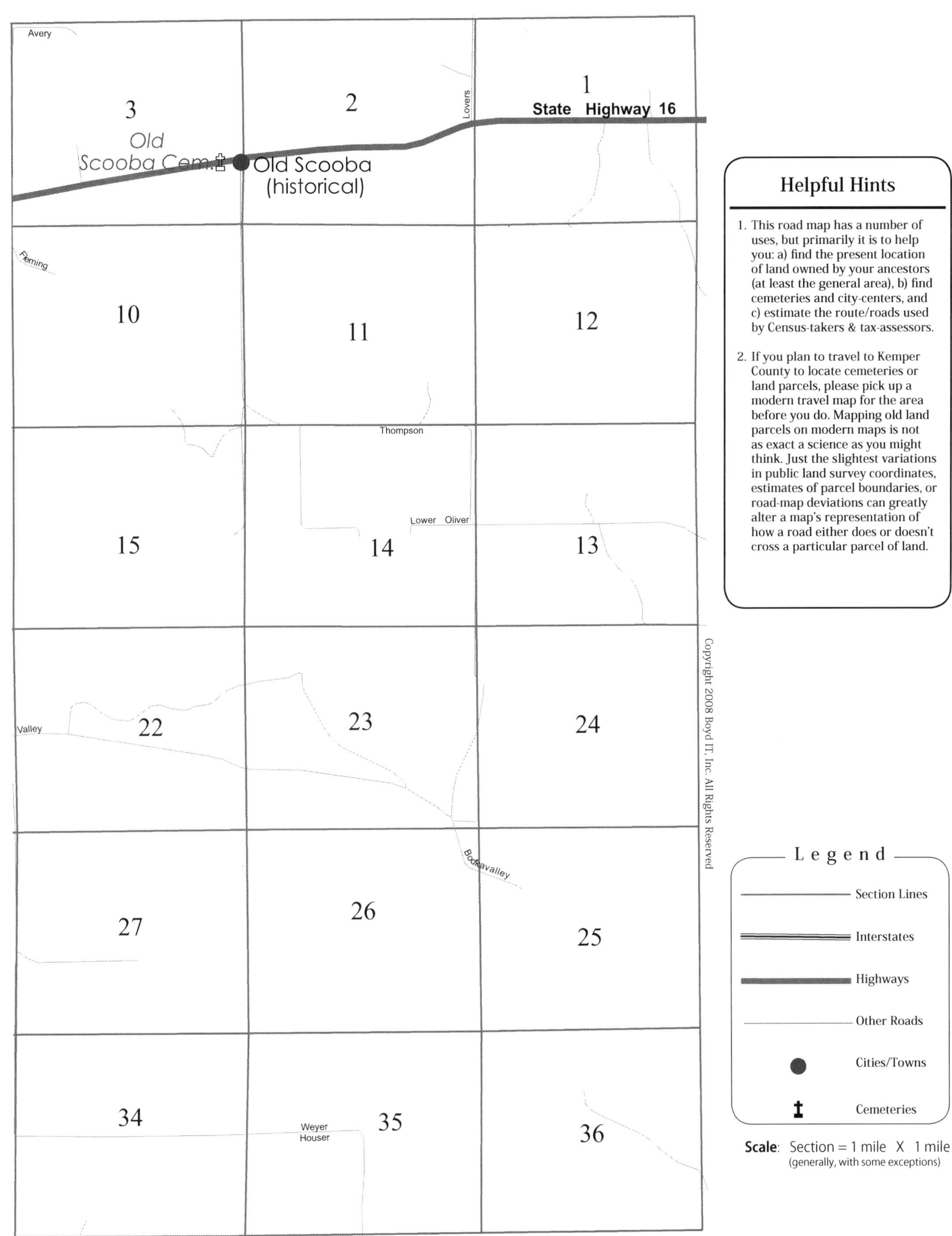

Helpful Hints

1. This road map has a number of uses, but primarily it is to help you: a) find the present location of land owned by your ancestors (at least the general area), b) find cemeteries and city-centers, and c) estimate the route/roads used by Census-takers & tax-assessors.

2. If you plan to travel to Kemper County to locate cemeteries or land parcels, please pick up a modern travel map for the area before you do. Mapping old land parcels on modern maps is not as exact a science as you might think. Just the slightest variations in public land survey coordinates, estimates of parcel boundaries, or road-map deviations can greatly alter a map's representation of how a road either does or doesn't cross a particular parcel of land.

Scale: Section = 1 mile X 1 mile
(generally, with some exceptions)

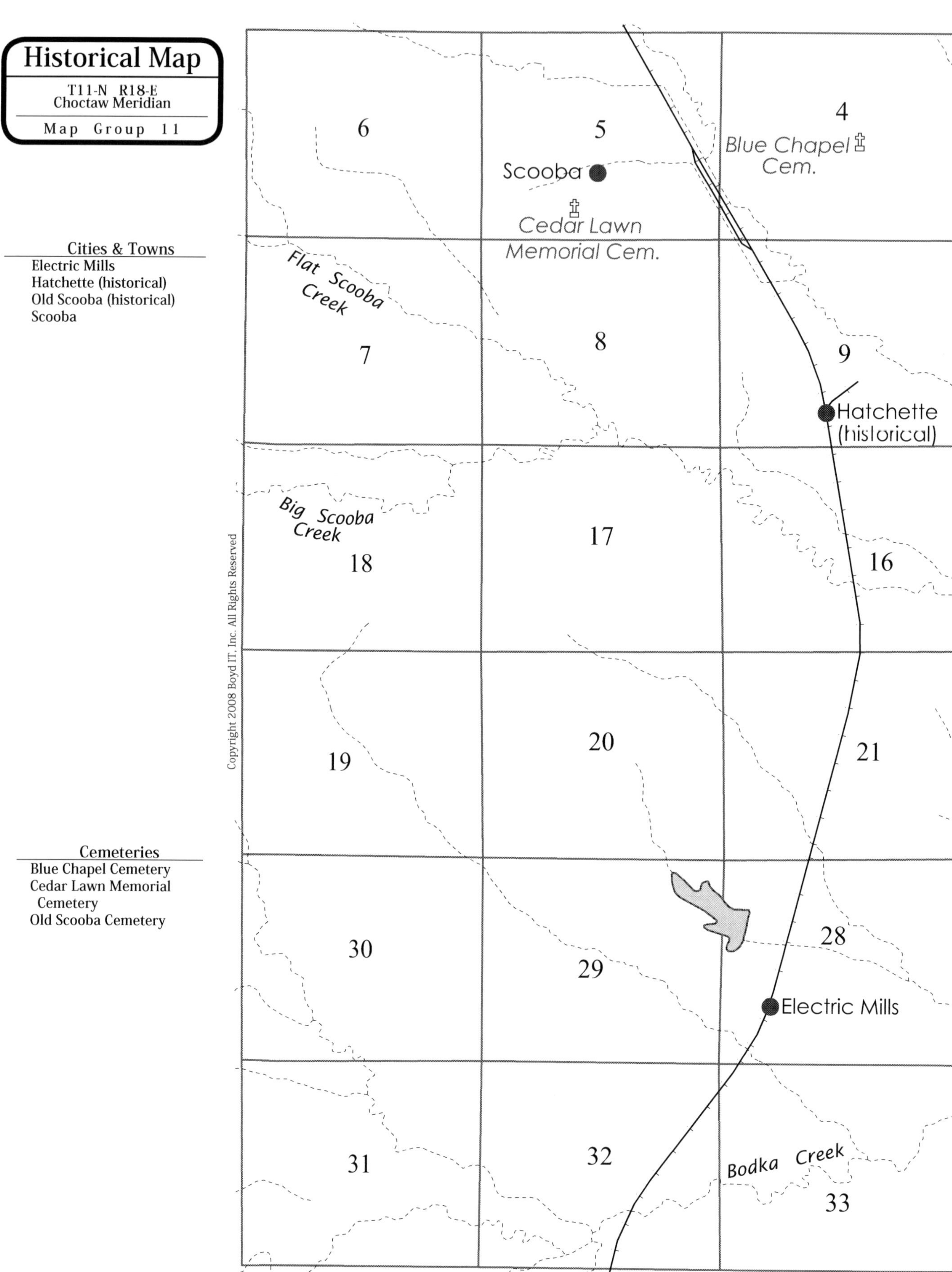
Historical Map
T11-N R18-E
Choctaw Meridian
Map Group 11
Cities & Towns
Electric Mills
Hatchette (historical)
Old Scooba (historical)
Scooba
Cemeteries
Blue Chapel Cemetery
Cedar Lawn Memorial Cemetery
Old Scooba Cemetery
Copyright 2008 Boyd IT, Inc. All Rights Reserved
6
5
4
Scooba
Blue Chapel Cem.
Cedar Lawn Memorial Cem.
Flat Scooba Creek
7
8
9
Hatchette (historical)
Big Scooba Creek
18
17
16
19
20
21
30
29
28
Electric Mills
31
32
Bodka Creek
33

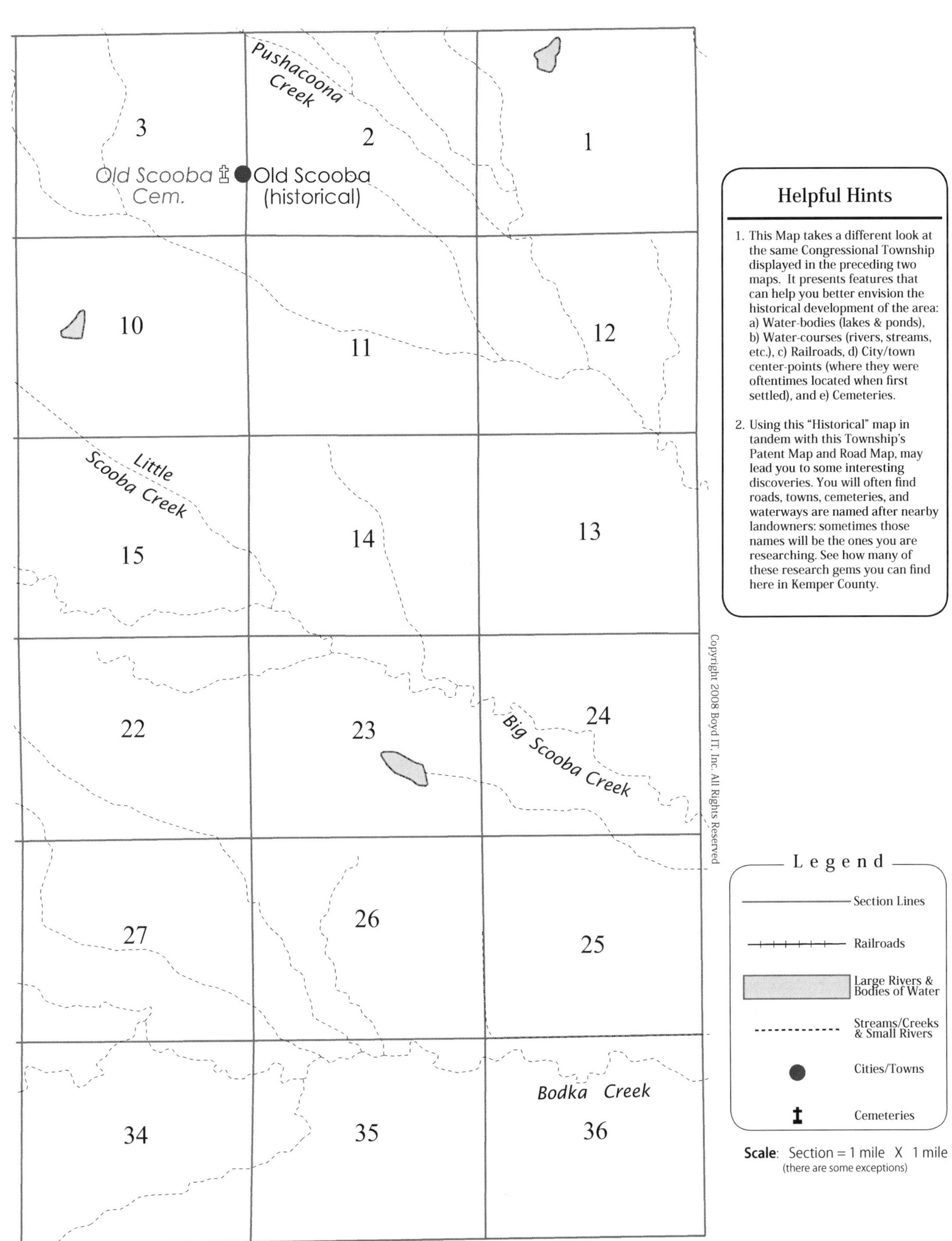

Helpful Hints

1. This Map takes a different look at the same Congressional Township displayed in the preceding two maps. It presents features that can help you better envision the historical development of the area: a) Water-bodies (lakes & ponds), b) Water-courses (rivers, streams, etc.), c) Railroads, d) City/town center-points (where they were oftentimes located when first settled), and e) Cemeteries.
2. Using this "Historical" map in tandem with this Township's Patent Map and Road Map, may lead you to some interesting discoveries. You will often find roads, towns, cemeteries, and waterways are named after nearby landowners: sometimes those names will be the ones you are researching. See how many of these research gems you can find here in Kemper County.

Legend

- Section Lines
- Railroads
- Large Rivers & Bodies of Water
- Streams/Creeks & Small Rivers
- Cities/Towns
- Cemeteries

Scale: Section = 1 mile X 1 mile
(there are some exceptions)

Map Group 12: Index to Land Patents

Township 11-North Range 19-East (Choctaw)

After you locate an individual in this Index, take note of the Section and Section Part then proceed to the Land Patent map on the pages immediately following. You should have no difficulty locating the corresponding parcel of land.

The "For More Info" Column will lead you to more information about the underlying Patents. See the *Legend* at right, and the "How to Use this Book" chapter, for more information.

LEGEND

"For More Info . . . " column

A = Authority (Legislative Act, See Appendix "A")
B = Block or Lot (location in Section unknown)
C = Cancelled Patent
F = Fractional Section
G = Group (Multi-Patentee Patent, see Appendix "C")
V = Overlaps another Parcel
R = Re-Issued (Parcel patented more than once)

(A & G items require you to look in the Appendixes referred to above. All other Letter-designations followed by a number require you to locate line-items in this index that possess the ID number found after the letter).

ID	Individual in Patent	Sec.	Sec. Part	Date Issued	Other Counties	For More Info . . .
2430	BARNETT, Joseph	29	10	1841-02-27		A1
2431	" "	29	11	1841-02-27		A1
2432	" "	29	12	1841-02-27		A1
2433	" "	29	13	1841-02-27		A1
2434	" "	29	14	1841-02-27		A1
2435	" "	29	15	1841-02-27		A1
2436	" "	29	4	1841-02-27		A1
2437	" "	29	5	1841-02-27		A1
2438	" "	30	E½NE	1841-02-27		A1
2439	" "	30	E½SE	1841-02-27		A1
2440	" "	31	E½NE	1841-02-27		A1
2441	" "	31	E½SW	1841-02-27		A1
2442	" "	31	W½NE	1841-02-27		A1
2443	" "	31	W½SW	1841-02-27		A1
2444	" "	32	3	1841-02-27		A1
2445	" "	32	4	1841-02-27		A1
2446	" "	32	SW	1841-02-27		A1
2400	BATES, Henry	20	1	1841-02-27		A1
2401	" "	20	8	1841-02-27		A1
2375	BENNETT, Anthony	32	12	1841-02-27		A1 G33
2376	" "	32	7	1841-02-27		A1 G33
2424	BENTON, John	30	W½	1841-02-27		A1 G37
2425	" "	30	W½SE	1841-02-27		A1 G37
2421	BLANTON, James A	18	SE	1841-02-27		A1
2423	" "	19	E½NE	1841-02-27		A1 G44
2422	" "	19	W½NE	1841-02-27		A1
2454	BORDEN, Joseph	5	E½NE	1841-02-27		A1 G46
2455	" "	5	E½SE	1841-02-27		A1 G46
2456	" "	5	E½SW	1841-02-27		A1 G46
2457	" "	5	W½SE	1841-02-27		A1 G46
2458	" "	5	W½SW	1841-02-27		A1 G46
2462	" "	8	E½NE	1841-02-27		A1 G47
2447	" "	8	E½NW	1841-02-27		A1
2448	" "	8	E½SE	1841-02-27		A1
2449	" "	8	E½SW	1841-02-27		A1
2450	" "	8	W½NE	1841-02-27		A1
2451	" "	8	W½NW	1841-02-27		A1
2452	" "	8	W½SE	1841-02-27		A1
2453	" "	8	W½SW	1841-02-27		A1
2459	" "	9	1	1841-02-27		A1 G46
2460	" "	9	2	1841-02-27		A1 G46
2461	" "	9	3	1841-02-27		A1 G46
2395	CANNON, George W	7	W½NW	1841-02-27		A1 G77
2479	CANNON, William	18	E½SW	1841-02-27		A1
2480	" "	18	W½SW	1841-02-27		A1
2481	" "	19	E½NW	1841-02-27		A1

ID	Individual in Patent	Sec.	Sec. Part	Date Issued	Other Counties	For More Info . . .
2482	CANNON, William (Cont'd)	19	W½NW	1841-02-27		A1
2395	" "	7	W½NW	1841-02-27		A1 G77
2465	ELLINGTON, Richard D	17	NE	1914-11-18		A2
2416	GILES, Jacob	5	E½NW	1841-02-27		A1
2417	" "	5	W½NW	1841-02-27		A1
2418	" "	6	E½NW	1841-02-27		A1
2419	" "	6	NE	1841-02-27		A1
2420	" "	6	W½NW	1841-02-27		A1
2483	GILES, William	4	1	1841-02-27		A1
2484	" "	4	2	1841-02-27		A1
2375	GREENE, Daniel	32	12	1841-02-27		A1 G33
2376	" "	32	7	1841-02-27		A1 G33
2389	" "	4	3	1841-02-27		A1
2390	" "	4	4	1841-02-27		A1
2454	" "	5	E½NE	1841-02-27		A1 G46
2455	" "	5	E½SE	1841-02-27		A1 G46
2456	" "	5	E½SW	1841-02-27		A1 G46
2393	" "	5	W½NE	1841-02-27		A1 G185
2457	" "	5	W½SE	1841-02-27		A1 G46
2458	" "	5	W½SW	1841-02-27		A1 G46
2391	" "	6	E½SW	1841-02-27		A1
2394	" "	6	W½SW	1841-02-27		A1 G185
2392	" "	7	E½SW	1841-02-27		A1
2459	" "	9	1	1841-02-27		A1 G46
2460	" "	9	2	1841-02-27		A1 G46
2461	" "	9	3	1841-02-27		A1 G46
2396	HARPER, George W	19	SW	1841-02-27		A1
2424	" "	30	W½	1841-02-27		A1 G37
2425	" "	30	W½SE	1841-02-27		A1 G37
2397	" "	31	E½NW	1841-02-27		A1
2398	" "	31	NWNW	1841-02-27		A1
2462	HARRISON, Simmons	8	E½NE	1841-02-27		A1 G47
2472	HUBBARD, Samuel	32	1	1841-02-27		A1 G232
2473	" "	32	2	1841-02-27		A1 G232
2474	" "	32	5	1841-02-27		A1 G232
2475	" "	32	6	1841-02-27		A1 G232
2476	" "	6	E½SE	1841-02-27		A1 G232
2477	" "	7	E½NW	1841-02-27		A1 G232
2478	" "	7	W½SW	1841-02-27		A1 G232
2399	JOYNER, Giles J	17	E½SE	1918-04-11		A2
2464	KOONCE, Michael	6	W½SE	1844-09-10		A1 G261
2377	LACY, Austin	17	E½NW	1841-02-27		A1
2378	" "	20	10	1841-02-27		A1
2379	" "	20	11	1841-02-27		A1
2380	" "	20	14	1841-02-27		A1
2381	" "	20	15	1841-02-27		A1
2382	" "	20	16	1841-02-27		A1
2383	" "	20	9	1841-02-27		A1
2468	LACY, Samuel B	29	2	1841-02-27		A1
2469	" "	29	3	1841-02-27		A1
2470	" "	29	6	1841-02-27		A1
2471	" "	29	7	1841-02-27		A1
2472	LEWIS, Moses	32	1	1841-02-27		A1 G232
2473	" "	32	2	1841-02-27		A1 G232
2474	" "	32	5	1841-02-27		A1 G232
2475	" "	32	6	1841-02-27		A1 G232
2476	" "	6	E½SE	1841-02-27		A1 G232
2477	" "	7	E½NW	1841-02-27		A1 G232
2478	" "	7	W½SW	1841-02-27		A1 G232
2472	LEWIS, Rufus G	32	1	1841-02-27		A1 G232
2473	" "	32	2	1841-02-27		A1 G232
2474	" "	32	5	1841-02-27		A1 G232
2475	" "	32	6	1841-02-27		A1 G232
2476	" "	6	E½SE	1841-02-27		A1 G232
2477	" "	7	E½NW	1841-02-27		A1 G232
2478	" "	7	W½SW	1841-02-27		A1 G232
2393	MCGEE, Thomas	5	W½NE	1841-02-27		A1 G185
2394	" "	6	W½SW	1841-02-27		A1 G185
2402	NICHOLSON, Isaac W	17	E½SW	1841-02-27		A1
2403	" "	17	N½W½SW	1841-02-27		A1
2404	" "	17	S½W½SW	1841-02-27		A1
2405	" "	17	W½NW	1841-02-27		A1
2406	" "	17	W½SE	1841-02-27		A1

ID	Individual in Patent	Sec.	Sec. Part	Date Issued	Other Counties	For More Info . . .
2407	NICHOLSON, Isaac W (Cont'd)	18	NE	1841-02-27		A1
2408	" "	18	NW	1841-02-27		A1
2409	" "	20	4	1841-02-27		A1
2410	" "	20	5	1841-02-27		A1
2411	" "	30	W½NE	1841-02-27		A1
2412	" "	7	E½NE	1841-02-27		A1
2413	" "	7	E½SE	1841-02-27		A1
2414	" "	7	W½NE	1841-02-27		A1
2415	" "	7	W½SE	1841-02-27		A1
2423	ROGERS, John	19	E½NE	1841-02-27		A1 G44
2472	TAPPAN, John	32	1	1841-02-27		A1 G232
2473	" "	32	2	1841-02-27		A1 G232
2474	" "	32	5	1841-02-27		A1 G232
2475	" "	32	6	1841-02-27		A1 G232
2476	" "	6	E½SE	1841-02-27		A1 G232
2477	" "	7	E½NW	1841-02-27		A1 G232
2478	" "	7	W½SW	1841-02-27		A1 G232
2463	ULMER, Mary	31	W½SE	1841-02-27		A1
2466	ULMER, Richard	31	E½SE	1841-02-27		A1
2467	ULMORE, Richard	31	S½W½NW	1841-02-27		A1
2384	WHITE, Bushrod W	20	2	1841-02-27		A1
2385	" "	20	3	1841-02-27		A1
2386	" "	20	6	1841-02-27		A1
2387	" "	20	7	1841-02-27		A1
2388	" "	20	W½SW	1841-02-27		A1
2426	WHITSETT, John C	29	1	1841-02-27		A1
2427	" "	29	16	1841-02-27		A1
2428	" "	29	8	1841-02-27		A1
2429	" "	29	9	1841-02-27		A1
2464	WILLIAMS, Jeptha	6	W½SE	1844-09-10		A1 G261

GILES Jacob 1841
GILES Jacob 1841
GILES Jacob 1841
6
GREENE Daniel 1841
GREENE [185] Daniel 1841
KOONCE [261] Michael 1844
HUBBARD [232] Samuel 1841

GILES Jacob 1841
GILES Jacob 1841
GREENE [185] Daniel 1841
BORDEN [46] Joseph 1841
5
BORDEN [46] Joseph 1841
BORDEN [46] Joseph 1841
BORDEN [46] Joseph 1841
BORDEN [46] Joseph 1841

4
Lots-Sec. 4
1 GILES, William 1841
2 GILES, William 1841
3 GREENE, Daniel 1841
4 GREENE, Daniel 1841

HUBBARD [232] Samuel 1841
CANNON [77] George W 1841
NICHOLSON Isaac W 1841
NICHOLSON Isaac W 1841
7
GREENE Daniel 1841
HUBBARD [232] Samuel 1841
NICHOLSON Isaac W 1841
NICHOLSON Isaac W 1841

BORDEN Joseph 1841
BORDEN Joseph 1841
BORDEN Joseph 1841
BORDEN [47] Joseph 1841
8
BORDEN Joseph 1841
BORDEN Joseph 1841
BORDEN Joseph 1841
BORDEN Joseph 1841

9
Lots-Sec. 9
1 BORDEN, Joseph [46]1841
2 BORDEN, Joseph [46]1841
3 BORDEN, Joseph [46]1841

NICHOLSON Isaac W 1841
NICHOLSON Isaac W 1841
18
CANNON William 1841
CANNON William 1841
BLANTON James A 1841

NICHOLSON Isaac W 1841
LACY Austin 1841
17
ELLINGTON Richard D 1914
NICHOLSON Isaac W 1841
NICHOLSON Isaac W 1841
NICHOLSON Isaac W 1841
NICHOLSON Isaac W 1841
JOYNER Giles J 1918

16

BLANTON [44] James A 1841
CANNON William 1841
CANNON William 1841
19
BLANTON James A 1841
HARPER George W 1841

20
WHITE Bushrod W 1841
Lots-Sec. 20
1 BATES, Henry 1841
2 WHITE, Bushrod W 1841
3 WHITE, Bushrod W 1841
4 NICHOLSON, Isaac W 1841
5 NICHOLSON, Isaac W 1841
6 WHITE, Bushrod W 1841
7 WHITE, Bushrod W 1841
8 BATES, Henry 1841
9 LACY, Austin 1841
10 LACY, Austin 1841
11 LACY, Austin 1841
14 LACY, Austin 1841
15 LACY, Austin 1841
16 LACY, Austin 1841

NICHOLSON Isaac W 1841
BARNETT Joseph 1841
30
BENTON [37] John 1841
BARNETT Joseph 1841
BENTON [37] John 1841

Lots-Sec. 29
1 WHITSETT, John C 1841
2 LACY, Samuel B 1841
3 LACY, Samuel B 1841
4 BARNETT, Joseph 1841
5 BARNETT, Joseph 1841
6 LACY, Samuel B 1841
7 LACY, Samuel B 1841
8 WHITSETT, John C 1841
9 WHITSETT, John C 1841
10 BARNETT, Joseph 1841
11 BARNETT, Joseph 1841
12 BARNETT, Joseph 1841
13 BARNETT, Joseph 1841
14 BARNETT, Joseph 1841
15 BARNETT, Joseph 1841
16 WHITSETT, John C 1841
29

HARPER George W 1841
ULMORE Richard 1841
HARPER George W 1841
BARNETT Joseph 1841
BARNETT Joseph 1841
31
BARNETT Joseph 1841
BARNETT Joseph 1841
ULMER Mary 1841
ULMER Richard 1841

Lots-Sec. 32
1 HUBBARD, Samuel[232]1841
2 HUBBARD, Samuel[232]1841
3 BARNETT, Joseph 1841
4 BARNETT, Joseph 1841
5 HUBBARD, Samuel[232]1841
6 HUBBARD, Samuel[232]1841
7 BENNETT, Anthony[33]1841
12 BENNETT, Anthony[33]1841
BARNETT Joseph 1841
32

Patent Map

T11-N R19-E
Choctaw Meridian

Map Group 12

Township Statistics

Parcels Mapped	:	110
Number of Patents	:	77
Number of Individuals	:	31
Patentees Identified	:	28
Number of Surnames	:	26
Multi-Patentee Parcels	:	25
Oldest Patent Date	:	2/27/1841
Most Recent Patent	:	4/11/1918
Block/Lot Parcels	:	45
Parcels Re - Issued	:	0
Parcels that Overlap	:	0
Cities and Towns	:	1
Cemeteries	:	1

Note: the area contained in this map amounts to far less than a full Township. Therefore, its contents are completely on this single page (instead of a "normal" 2-page spread).

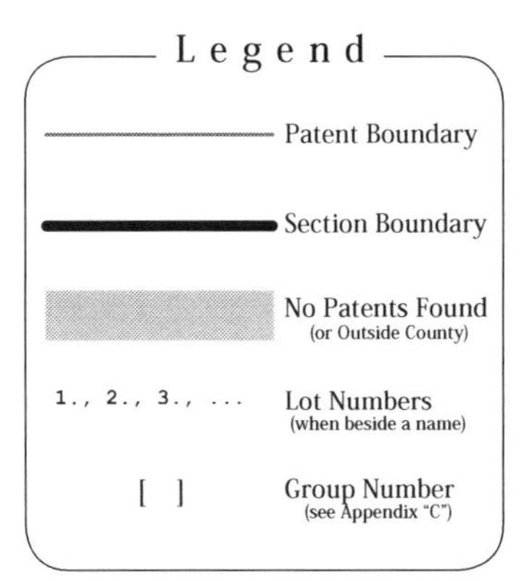

Scale: Section = 1 mile X 1 mile
(generally, with some exceptions)

Road Map

T11-N R19-E
Choctaw Meridian

Map Group 12

Note: the area contained in this map amounts to far less than a full Township. Therefore, its contents are completely on this single page (instead of a "normal" 2-page spread).

Cities & Towns

Giles

Cemeteries

Giles Cemetery

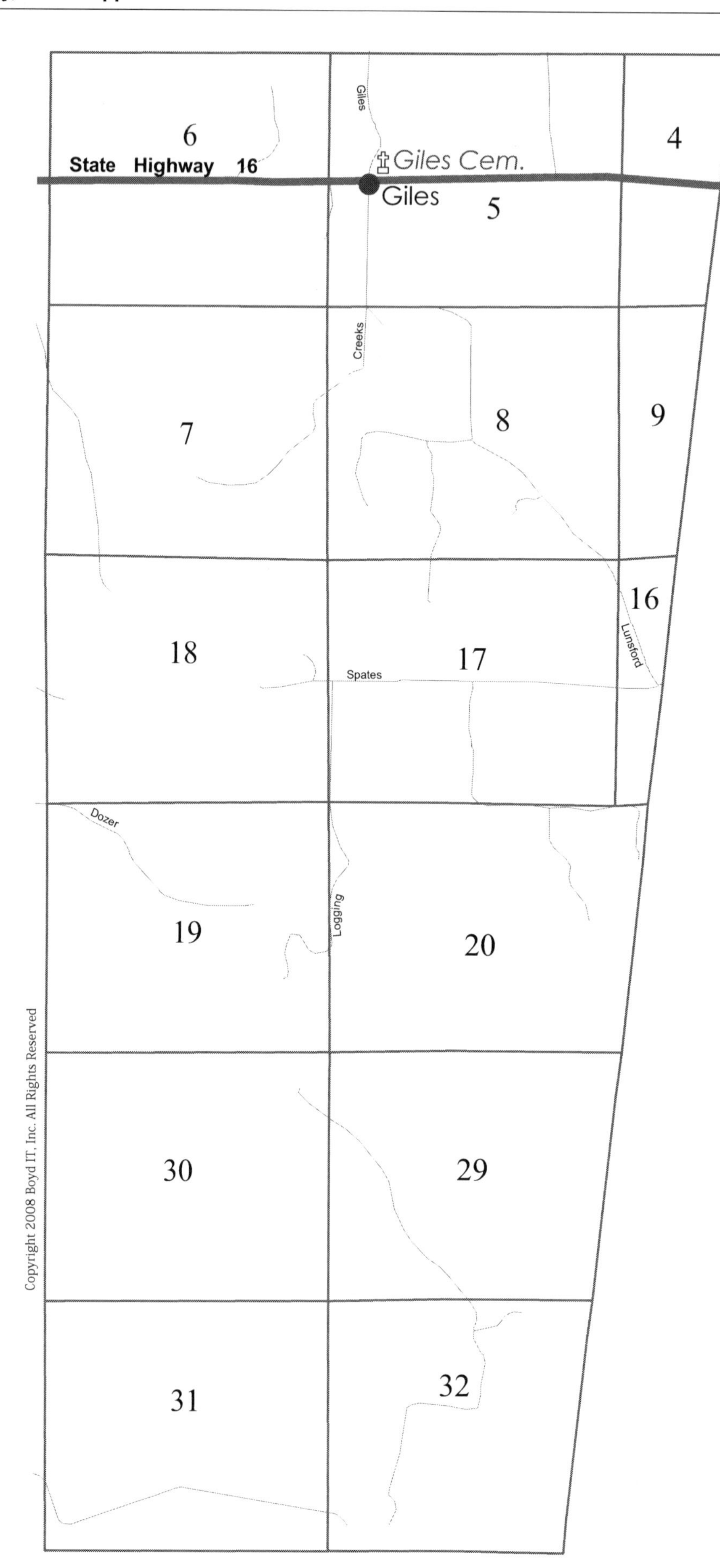

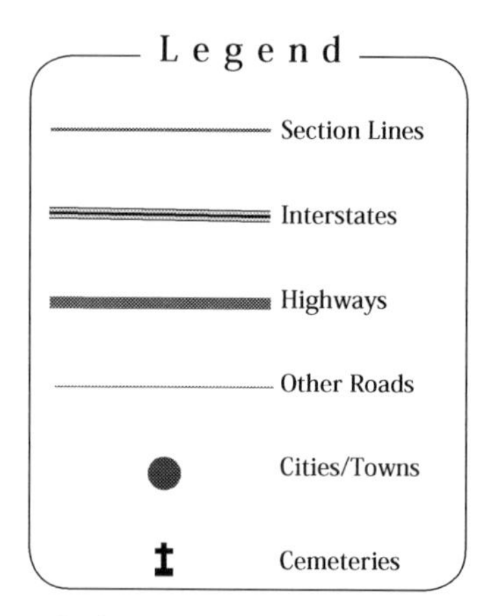

Scale: Section = 1 mile X 1 mile
(generally, with some exceptions)

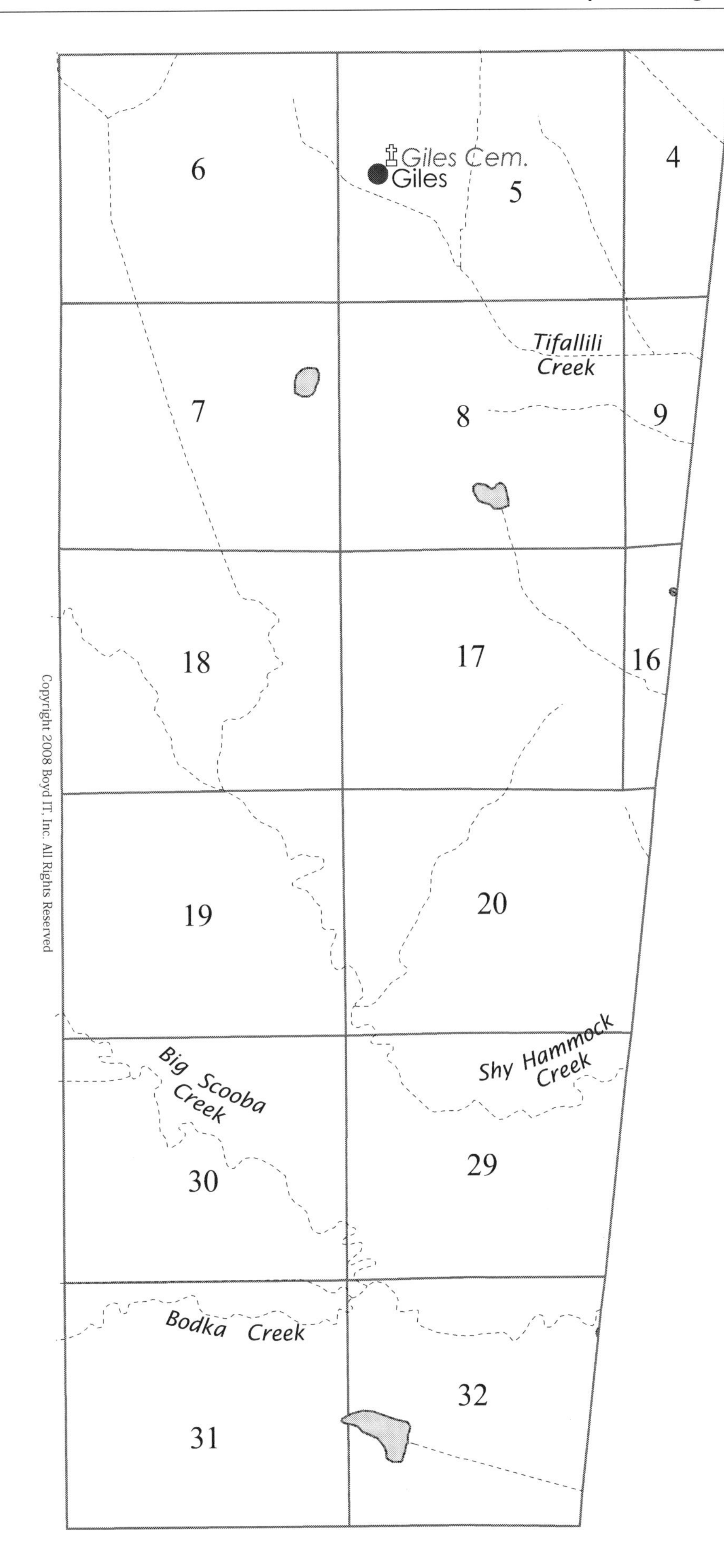

Historical Map

T11-N R19-E
Choctaw Meridian

Map Group 12

Note: the area contained in this map amounts to far less than a full Township. Therefore, its contents are completely on this single page (instead of a "normal" 2-page spread).

Cities & Towns

Giles

Cemeteries

Giles Cemetery

Legend

- Section Lines
- Railroads
- Large Rivers & Bodies of Water
- Streams/Creeks & Small Rivers
- Cities/Towns
- Cemeteries

Scale: Section = 1 mile X 1 mile
(there are some exceptions)

Map Group 13: Index to Land Patents

Township 10-North Range 14-East (Choctaw)

After you locate an individual in this Index, take note of the Section and Section Part then proceed to the Land Patent map on the pages immediately following. You should have no difficulty locating the corresponding parcel of land.

The "For More Info" Column will lead you to more information about the underlying Patents. See the *Legend* at right, and the "How to Use this Book" chapter, for more information.

LEGEND

"For More Info . . . " column

A = Authority (Legislative Act, See Appendix "A")
B = Block or Lot (location in Section unknown)
C = Cancelled Patent
F = Fractional Section
G = Group (Multi-Patentee Patent, see Appendix "C")
V = Overlaps another Parcel
R = Re-Issued (Parcel patented more than once)

(A & G items require you to look in the Appendixes referred to above. All other Letter-designations followed by a number require you to locate line-items in this index that possess the ID number found after the letter).

ID	Individual in Patent	Sec.	Sec. Part	Date Issued	Other Counties	For More Info . . .
2626	ABERNATHY, John T	19	E½SW	1841-02-27		A1 G7
2627	" "	19	W½NW	1841-02-27		A1 G7
2628	" "	21	W½SE	1841-02-27		A1 G3
2629	" "	28	W½NE	1841-02-27		A1 G3
2602	ALDERMAN, John	19	NWSW	1856-04-01		A1
2508	ALLEN, Charles	32	E½NW	1848-09-01		A1
2646	ALLEN, Margaret	32	NESW	1860-05-01		A1
2647	" "	32	NWNE	1860-05-01		A1
2648	" "	32	NWSE	1860-05-01		A1
2506	ANDERSON, Burbin	12	E½SW	1841-02-27		A1
2507	" "	12	W½SE	1841-02-27		A1
2559	ANDERSON, Hartford	14	SESW	1860-05-01		A1
2560	" "	14	SWSW	1860-10-01		A1
2568	ANDERSON, James B	7	S½NE	1892-06-15		A2
2609	ANDERSON, John E	24	E½NE	1841-02-27		A1
2610	" "	24	E½SE	1841-02-27		A1
2611	" "	24	W½NE	1841-02-27		A1
2612	" "	24	W½SE	1841-02-27		A1
2681	ANDERSON, Sina	10	E½SE	1841-02-27		A1
2682	" "	14	W½NW	1841-02-27		A1
2554	BATES, Francis M	20	SENE	1854-03-15		A1
2687	BEVIL, Thomas L	10	E½NE	1841-02-27		A1
2688	" "	21	E½SE	1841-02-27		A1
2689	" "	21	E½SW	1841-02-27		A1
2690	" "	21	W½SW	1841-02-27		A1
2691	" "	27	E½SE	1841-02-27		A1
2692	" "	27	E½SW	1841-02-27		A1
2693	" "	28	E½NW	1841-02-27		A1
2694	" "	28	E½SE	1841-02-27		A1
2695	" "	28	W½NW	1841-02-27		A1
2696	" "	28	W½SW	1841-02-27		A1
2697	" "	29	E½NE	1841-02-27		A1
2698	" "	34	E½NE	1841-02-27		A1
2699	" "	34	E½SE	1841-02-27		A1
2700	" "	35	W½SW	1841-02-27		A1 R2625
2701	" "	9	E½SW	1841-02-27		A1
2702	" "	9	W½SE	1841-02-27		A1
2703	" "	9	W½SW	1841-02-27		A1
2628	BEVILL, Thomas L	21	W½SE	1841-02-27		A1 G3
2629	" "	28	W½NE	1841-02-27		A1 G3
2704	" "	28	E½SW	1844-07-31		A1 G40
2677	BOBO, Simpson	15	E½SE	1841-02-27		A1
2678	" "	30	E½SW	1841-02-27		A1
2679	" "	31	NW	1841-12-15		A1
2680	" "	31	W½NE	1841-12-15		A1
2603	BONNER, John	14	E½NW	1841-02-27		A1 G45

ID	Individual in Patent	Sec.	Sec. Part	Date Issued	Other Counties	For More Info . . .
2496	BOUNDS, Benjamin	32	SENE	1881-08-20		A2
2618	BOUNDS, John R	12	NWNE	1906-05-01		A2
2664	BOUNDS, Robert P	22	NWNW	1896-12-01		A1
2651	BOZEMAN, Nancy C	29	W½NE	1895-05-11		A2 G52
2651	BOZEMAN, Thomas C	29	W½NE	1895-05-11		A2 G52
2634	BRICKELL, Joseph J	30	W½NW	1841-02-27		A1 G53
2635	" "	31	SW	1841-02-27		A1 G53
2500	BURNETT, Boling C	29	W½SW	1841-02-27		A1
2501	" "	30	E½SE	1841-02-27		A1
2502	" "	30	W½SE	1841-02-27		A1
2503	" "	31	E½NE	1841-02-27		A1
2504	" "	34	E½NW	1841-02-27		A1 G67
2505	" "	34	W½NW	1841-02-27		A1 G67
2571	CAMPBELL, James	26	SWSW	1894-12-17		A2
2555	CARMICHAEL, George W	14	SE	1879-05-06		A2
2650	CARTER, Meshac	2	E½NW	1841-02-27		A1
2653	CARTER, Neshach	3	E½NE	1841-02-27		A1
2654	" "	3	W½NE	1841-02-27		A1
2563	CHIPMAN, Hezekiah	14	NESW	1841-02-27		A1
2564	" "	8	NWNE	1860-05-01		A1
2513	CLARK, Daniel	1	SWNE	1856-04-01		A1
2512	" "	1	SENE	1859-10-01		A1
2511	CLARK, Daniel A	1	E½SE	1846-09-01		A1
2514	CLARK, Daniel D	1	W½SE	1848-09-01		A1
2652	CLARK, Nancy	12	SWNE	1860-05-01		A1
2665	COLE, Roscow	11	SE	1841-02-27		A1 G96
2730	COLE, William T	12	NWNW	1860-10-01		A1
2731	" "	12	S½NW	1860-10-01		A1
2660	CRENSHAW, Plesant	21	SWNW	1854-03-15		A1
2572	CULBERTSON, James	26	NWSW	1859-10-01		A1
2497	DARNALL, Benjamin F	19	SWSW	1885-04-04		A2
2674	DARNALL, Scheharrizad	21	SENE	1854-03-15		A1
2673	" "	21	NENE	1860-10-01		A1
2675	" "	21	SWNE	1860-10-01		A1
2729	DARNALL, William J	21	NWNE	1849-12-01		A1
2604	DAVIES, John	27	E½NW	1841-02-27		A1
2605	" "	27	W½NW	1841-02-27		A1 G122
2606	" "	27	W½SW	1841-02-27		A1 G122
2607	" "	28	E½NE	1841-02-27		A1 G122
2608	" "	28	W½SE	1841-02-27		A1 G122
2552	DAVIS, Fielding	2	E½SE	1841-02-27		A1
2553	" "	2	W½SE	1841-02-27		A1
2676	DAWS, Siaroutley	10	SENW	1849-12-01		A1
2683	DAWS, Sira O	10	NENW	1859-10-01		A1
2666	DOLBEAR, Rufus	10	E½SW	1841-02-27		A1
2667	" "	10	W½NW	1841-02-27		A1 R2528
2668	" "	15	W½SE	1841-02-27		A1
2669	" "	36	NW	1841-02-27		A1
2657	DYER, Otis	27	W½NE	1841-02-27		A1
2605	" "	27	W½NW	1841-02-27		A1 G122
2606	" "	27	W½SW	1841-02-27		A1 G122
2607	" "	28	E½NE	1841-02-27		A1 G122
2608	" "	28	W½SE	1841-02-27		A1 G122
2617	EAKES, John M	6	S½NE	1896-07-11		A2
2613	EAKS, John H	6	S½SW	1906-06-16		A2
2633	EASON, Jonathan T	23	NWSE	1854-03-15		A1
2712	EKES, Timothy	6	S½NW	1854-03-15		A1
2710	" "	5	NWSW	1860-10-01		A1
2711	" "	6	NESW	1860-10-01		A1
2575	ELLIOT, James	1	SW	1841-02-27		A1 G141
2576	" "	19	E½SE	1841-02-27		A1 G139
2626	" "	19	E½SW	1841-02-27		A1 G7
2627	" "	19	W½NW	1841-02-27		A1 G7
2577	" "	19	W½SE	1841-02-27		A1 G139
2573	" "	29	E½SE	1841-02-27		A1
2578	" "	30	E½NW	1841-02-27		A1 G139
2574	" "	4	E½SE	1841-02-27		A1
2639	FAUCETT, Lyle B	25	SE	1841-02-27		A1
2640	" "	25	W½NW	1841-02-27		A1
2550	FOWLER, Ezra R	26	NESW	1859-10-01		A1
2551	" "	32	NENE	1860-10-01		A1
2726	FRANKLIN, William E	6	NWSE	1901-03-23		A2
2576	GILCHRIST, Malcolm	19	E½SE	1841-02-27		A1 G139

ID	Individual in Patent	Sec.	Sec. Part	Date Issued	Other Counties	For More Info . . .
2577	GILCHRIST, Malcolm (Cont'd)	19	W½SE	1841-02-27		A1 G139
2641	" "	29	E½SW	1841-02-27		A1 G167
2642	" "	29	W½NW	1841-02-27		A1 G167
2578	" "	30	E½NW	1841-02-27		A1 G139
2643	" "	31	E½SE	1841-02-27		A1 G165
2644	" "	31	W½SE	1841-02-27		A1 G165
2520	GREENE, Daniel	4	E½SW	1840-03-02		A1 G193
2522	" "	4	W½SW	1840-03-02		A1 G193
2523	" "	9	E½NW	1840-03-02		A1 G193
2524	" "	9	W½NW	1840-03-02		A1 G193
2528	" "	10	W½NW	1841-02-27		A1 G179 R2667
2529	" "	11	W½NE	1841-02-27		A1 G179
2527	" "	11	W½SW	1841-02-27		A1 G180
2517	" "	13	W½SE	1841-02-27		A1
2530	" "	15	E½NW	1841-02-27		A1 G179
2531	" "	15	E½SW	1841-02-27		A1 G179
2532	" "	15	W½NE	1841-02-27		A1 G179
2533	" "	15	W½NW	1841-02-27		A1 G179
2534	" "	15	W½SW	1841-02-27		A1 G179
2518	" "	20	E½SE	1841-02-27		A1
2519	" "	20	W½SE	1841-02-27		A1
2535	" "	3	E½SE	1841-02-27		A1 G179
2536	" "	3	E½SW	1841-02-27		A1 G179
2537	" "	3	W½SE	1841-02-27		A1 G179
2538	" "	3	W½SW	1841-02-27		A1 G179
2643	" "	31	E½SE	1841-02-27		A1 G165
2644	" "	31	W½SE	1841-02-27		A1 G165
2525	" "	34	E½SW	1841-02-27		A1 G191
2539	" "	34	W½SE	1841-02-27		A1 G179
2526	" "	34	W½SW	1841-02-27		A1 G191
2540	" "	9	E½NE	1841-02-27		A1 G179
2541	" "	9	E½SE	1841-02-27		A1 G179
2704	" "	28	E½SW	1844-07-31		A1 G40
2521	" "	4	W½SE	1844-09-10		A1 G193
2597	GRIFFIN, Jesse	5	SWSE	1854-03-15		A1
2595	" "	5	NESE	1860-05-01		A1
2596	" "	5	NWSE	1860-05-01		A1
2649	GROCE, Martin	2	E½NE	1841-02-27		A1
2659	GULLY, Philemon H	5	NENE	1860-10-01		A1
2727	HAGGARD, William E	12	E½SE	1893-12-19		A2
2728	" "	12	SENE	1893-12-19		A2
2603	HANLEY, James	14	E½NW	1841-02-27		A1 G45
2495	HARDY, Bemon B	14	NENE	1888-12-29		A1
2561	HARDY, Henry H	12	W½SW	1888-12-29		A1
2515	HARPER, Daniel E	24	E½SW	1841-02-27		A1
2516	" "	25	NE	1841-02-27		A1
2556	HARPER, George W	11	E½SW	1841-02-27		A1
2557	" "	13	W½NW	1841-02-27		A1
2732	HENDON, William T	32	NESE	1898-07-12		A2
2488	HICKS, Andrew J	8	S½SW	1860-05-01		A1
2490	HODGES, Armstrong J	13	E½NW	1841-02-27		A1 G227
2491	" "	13	E½SE	1841-02-27		A1 G227
2492	" "	13	E½SW	1841-02-27		A1 G227
2493	" "	13	W½SW	1841-02-27		A1 G227
2494	" "	36	E½	1841-02-27		A1 G227
2528	HUBBARD, Samuel	10	W½NW	1841-02-27		A1 G179 R2667
2529	" "	11	W½NE	1841-02-27		A1 G179
2530	" "	15	E½NW	1841-02-27		A1 G179
2531	" "	15	E½SW	1841-02-27		A1 G179
2532	" "	15	W½NE	1841-02-27		A1 G179
2533	" "	15	W½NW	1841-02-27		A1 G179
2534	" "	15	W½SW	1841-02-27		A1 G179
2672	" "	3	E½NW	1841-02-27		A1 G234
2535	" "	3	E½SE	1841-02-27		A1 G179
2536	" "	3	E½SW	1841-02-27		A1 G179
2537	" "	3	W½SE	1841-02-27		A1 G179
2538	" "	3	W½SW	1841-02-27		A1 G179
2539	" "	34	W½SE	1841-02-27		A1 G179
2540	" "	9	E½NE	1841-02-27		A1 G179
2541	" "	9	E½SE	1841-02-27		A1 G179
2671	" "	10	W½SE	1841-12-15		A1 G234
2734	HUMPHRIES, William W	22	E½SW	1841-02-27		A1 G237
2735	" "	22	SE	1841-02-27		A1 G237

ID	Individual in Patent	Sec.	Sec. Part	Date Issued	Other Counties	For More Info . . .
2586	HUTCHINS, James L	11	E½NW	1841-02-27		A1 G241
2587	" "	11	W½NW	1841-02-27		A1 G241
2588	" "	2	E½SW	1841-02-27		A1 G241
2582	" "	3	W½NW	1841-02-27		A1
2583	" "	4	E½NE	1841-02-27		A1
2584	" "	4	W½NE	1841-02-27		A1
2585	" "	9	W½NE	1841-02-27		A1
2586	HUTCHINS, Washington P	11	E½NW	1841-02-27		A1 G241
2587	" "	11	W½NW	1841-02-27		A1 G241
2588	" "	2	E½SW	1841-02-27		A1 G241
2489	JACKSON, Andrew	30	NE	1841-02-27		A1
2621	JEMISON, John S	11	E½NE	1841-02-27		A1
2622	" "	2	W½SW	1841-02-27		A1
2623	" "	27	W½SE	1841-02-27		A1
2624	" "	35	E½SW	1841-02-27		A1
2625	" "	35	W½SW	1841-02-27		A1 R2700
2527	JENKINS, John H	11	W½SW	1841-02-27		A1 G180
2614	" "	15	E½NE	1841-02-27		A1
2685	JOHNSON, Squire C	8	NWNW	1860-10-01		A1
2684	LANHAN, Solomon	34	W½NE	1841-02-27		A1
2637	LATHAM, Lorenzo	24	E½NW	1841-02-27		A1
2638	" "	24	W½NW	1841-02-27		A1
2528	LEWIS, Rufus G	10	W½NW	1841-02-27		A1 G179 R2667
2529	" "	11	W½NE	1841-02-27		A1 G179
2530	" "	15	E½NW	1841-02-27		A1 G179
2531	" "	15	E½SW	1841-02-27		A1 G179
2532	" "	15	W½NE	1841-02-27		A1 G179
2533	" "	15	W½NW	1841-02-27		A1 G179
2534	" "	15	W½SW	1841-02-27		A1 G179
2670	" "	22	W½SW	1841-02-27		A1 G268
2672	" "	3	E½NW	1841-02-27		A1 G234
2535	" "	3	E½SE	1841-02-27		A1 G179
2536	" "	3	E½SW	1841-02-27		A1 G179
2537	" "	3	W½SE	1841-02-27		A1 G179
2538	" "	3	W½SW	1841-02-27		A1 G179
2539	" "	34	W½SE	1841-02-27		A1 G179
2540	" "	9	E½NE	1841-02-27		A1 G179
2541	" "	9	E½SE	1841-02-27		A1 G179
2671	" "	10	W½SE	1841-12-15		A1 G234
2714	LOVELADY, West D	22	SENE	1854-03-15		A1
2616	LOVEN, John	8	NENW	1854-03-15		A1
2636	LYLE, Joseph	22	NENE	1849-12-01		A1
2566	MAYFIELD, Isaac	7	NWNW	1859-10-01		A1
2543	MCALLUM, Duncan P	26	SESW	1859-10-01		A1
2589	MCDONALD, James	14	SENE	1841-02-27		A1
2590	" "	14	W½NE	1841-02-27		A1
2600	MCFARLAND, John A	22	SENW	1897-11-01		A2
2591	MCGOWEN, James	4	E½NW	1841-02-27		A1 G291
2592	" "	4	W½NW	1841-02-27		A1 G291
2591	MCGOWEN, Samuel	4	E½NW	1841-02-27		A1 G291
2592	" "	4	W½NW	1841-02-27		A1 G291
2645	MCINTYRE, Malcolm L	36	SW	1841-02-27		A1
2601	MCKELLAR, John A	23	NE	1841-02-27		A1
2565	MCKINNEY, Hughey W	8	SESE	1854-03-15		A1
2663	MCKINNEY, Robert	5	SWSW	1854-03-15		A1
2686	MCKINNEY, Thomas J	18	NWNE	1854-03-15		A1
2733	MCKINNEY, William T	6	E½SE	1894-02-10		A2
2615	MCMAHON, John J	19	E½NW	1841-02-27		A1
2634	" "	30	W½NW	1841-02-27		A1 G53
2635	" "	31	SW	1841-02-27		A1 G53
2661	MCMAHON, Robert G	24	W½SW	1841-02-27		A1
2662	" "	25	NENW	1841-02-27		A1
2485	MCRIGHT, Anderson W	33	NENE	1848-09-01		A1
2486	" "	33	NWNE	1848-09-01		A1
2658	MIETT, Peter	23	NESE	1841-02-27		A1
2720	MILLS, Willard C	22	W½NE	1856-04-01		A1
2718	" "	22	NENW	1859-10-01		A1
2719	" "	22	SWNW	1859-10-01		A1
2721	" "	23	SWSE	1859-10-01		A1
2722	" "	32	SESE	1860-05-01		A1
2723	" "	32	SWSW	1860-05-01		A1
2724	" "	5	NENW	1860-05-01		A1
2716	" "	1	SWNW	1860-10-01		A1

ID	Individual in Patent	Sec.	Sec. Part	Date Issued	Other Counties	For More Info . . .
2725	MILLS, Willard C (Cont'd)	5	SESW	1860-10-01		A1
2717	" "	20	SENW	1861-01-01		A1
2593	MITCHUM, James	13	E½NE	1841-02-27		A1
2594	" "	13	W½NE	1841-02-27		A1
2713	MOODY, Washington	20	SW	1841-02-27		A1 G296
2487	MOORE, Andrew B	30	W½SW	1841-02-27		A1
2598	MOORE, Jesse T	7	N½SW	1892-04-29		A2
2599	" "	7	NWSE	1892-04-29		A2
2655	NASH, Orsamus L	23	SW	1841-02-27		A1 G302
2656	" "	23	W½NW	1841-02-27		A1 G302
2713	ONEIL, Patric	20	SW	1841-02-27		A1 G296
2734	ONEILL, Patrick	22	E½SW	1841-02-27		A1 G237
2735	" "	22	SE	1841-02-27		A1 G237
2620	PEDEN, John R	6	N½NE	1859-10-01		A1
2619	" "	5	NWNW	1860-12-01		A1
2567	PERKINS, Isaac S	7	NENW	1860-05-01		A1
2504	RUPERT, James C	34	E½NW	1841-02-27		A1 G67
2525	" "	34	E½SW	1841-02-27		A1 G191
2505	" "	34	W½NW	1841-02-27		A1 G67
2526	" "	34	W½SW	1841-02-27		A1 G191
2569	" "	35	E½	1841-02-27		A1
2570	" "	35	E½NW	1841-02-27		A1
2520	SCOTT, Christopher C	4	E½SW	1840-03-02		A1 G193
2522	" "	4	W½SW	1840-03-02		A1 G193
2523	" "	9	E½NW	1840-03-02		A1 G193
2524	" "	9	W½NW	1840-03-02		A1 G193
2509	" "	29	E½NW	1841-02-27		A1
2641	" "	29	E½SW	1841-02-27		A1 G167
2642	" "	29	W½NW	1841-02-27		A1 G167
2510	" "	29	W½SE	1841-02-27		A1
2521	" "	4	W½SE	1844-09-10		A1 G193
2549	SHIP, Ewell	26	W½SE	1841-02-27		A1
2542	SHIPP, Daniel	2	W½NE	1841-02-27		A1
2575	SHIPP, Ervel	1	SW	1841-02-27		A1 G141
2655	SMITH, James H	23	SW	1841-02-27		A1 G302
2656	" "	23	W½NW	1841-02-27		A1 G302
2580	" "	26	N½	1841-02-27		A1 G324
2581	" "	27	E½NE	1841-02-27		A1 G324
2707	SMITH, Tillotson P	25	SENW	1841-02-27		A1
2708	" "	25	SW	1841-02-27		A1
2709	" "	26	E½SE	1841-02-27		A1 G325
2709	SNEED, Peter	26	E½SE	1841-02-27		A1 G325
2498	STOCKTON, Benjamin L	20	NENW	1860-05-01		A1
2499	" "	20	SWNW	1860-05-01		A1
2528	TAPPAN, John	10	W½NW	1841-02-27		A1 G179 R2667
2529	" "	11	W½NE	1841-02-27		A1 G179
2530	" "	15	E½NW	1841-02-27		A1 G179
2531	" "	15	E½SW	1841-02-27		A1 G179
2532	" "	15	W½NE	1841-02-27		A1 G179
2533	" "	15	W½NW	1841-02-27		A1 G179
2534	" "	15	W½SW	1841-02-27		A1 G179
2672	" "	3	E½NW	1841-02-27		A1 G234
2535	" "	3	E½SE	1841-02-27		A1 G179
2536	" "	3	E½SW	1841-02-27		A1 G179
2537	" "	3	W½SE	1841-02-27		A1 G179
2538	" "	3	W½SW	1841-02-27		A1 G179
2539	" "	34	W½SE	1841-02-27		A1 G179
2540	" "	9	E½NE	1841-02-27		A1 G179
2541	" "	9	E½SE	1841-02-27		A1 G179
2671	" "	10	W½SE	1841-12-15		A1 G234
2579	TERRY, James G	5	SWNW	1882-05-10		A1
2558	THOMPSON, Granville	32	SWNE	1881-08-20		A2
2705	THORNELL, Thomas	18	NWNW	1854-03-15		A1
2706	" "	7	S½SW	1860-05-01		A1
2548	WARD, Ellen	18	NENE	1895-02-21		A2 G333
2715	WARD, Wiley P	32	NWNW	1860-05-01		A1
2548	WARD, William	18	NENE	1895-02-21		A2 G333
2544	WARREN, Edmund	10	W½SW	1841-02-27		A1
2545	" "	23	E½NW	1841-02-27		A1
2580	WESTMORELAND, Mark	26	N½	1841-02-27		A1 G324
2581	" "	27	E½NE	1841-02-27		A1 G324
2546	WHITE, Eliza	33	SENE	1850-12-02		A1
2547	" "	33	SWNE	1850-12-02		A1

ID	Individual in Patent	Sec.	Sec. Part	Date Issued	Other Counties	For More Info . . .
2630	WHITE, John W	33	SE	1847-04-01		A1
2631	" "	33	SESW	1856-04-01		A1
2632	" "	33	SWSW	1860-10-01		A1
2670	WHITSETT, John C	22	W½SW	1841-02-27		A1 G268
2562	WIGGIN, Henry T	14	NWSW	1841-02-27		A1
2665	WINSTON, William B	11	SE	1841-02-27		A1 G96
2490	" "	13	E½NW	1841-02-27		A1 G227
2491	" "	13	E½SE	1841-02-27		A1 G227
2492	" "	13	E½SW	1841-02-27		A1 G227
2493	" "	13	W½SW	1841-02-27		A1 G227
2494	" "	36	E½	1841-02-27		A1 G227

Patent Map

T10-N R14-E
Choctaw Meridian

Map Group 13

Township Statistics

Parcels Mapped	:	251
Number of Patents	:	233
Number of Individuals	:	128
Patentees Identified	:	127
Number of Surnames	:	98
Multi-Patentee Parcels	:	68
Oldest Patent Date	:	3/2/1840
Most Recent Patent	:	6/16/1906
Block/Lot Parcels	:	0
Parcels Re - Issued	:	2
Parcels that Overlap	:	0
Cities and Towns	:	3
Cemeteries	:	5

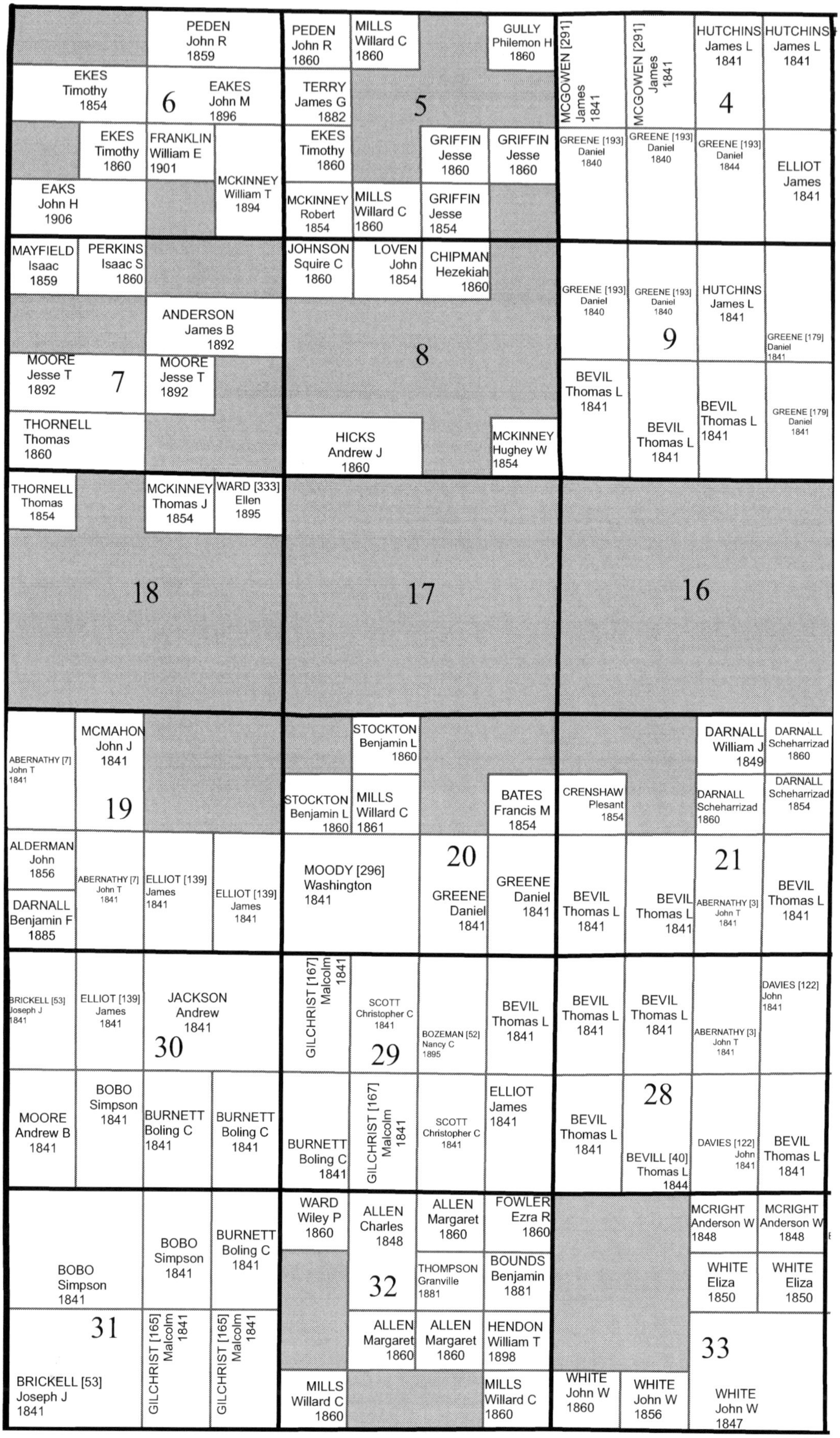

6
PEDEN John R 1859
EKES Timothy 1854
EAKES John M 1896
EKES Timothy 1860
FRANKLIN William E 1901
MCKINNEY William T 1894
EAKS John H 1906

5
PEDEN John R 1860
MILLS Willard C 1860
GULLY Philemon H 1860
TERRY James G 1882
EKES Timothy 1860
GRIFFIN Jesse 1860
GRIFFIN Jesse 1860
MCKINNEY Robert 1854
MILLS Willard C 1860
GRIFFIN Jesse 1854

4
MCGOWEN [291] James 1841
MCGOWEN [291] James 1841
HUTCHINS James L 1841
HUTCHINS James L 1841
GREENE [193] Daniel 1840
GREENE [193] Daniel 1840
GREENE [193] Daniel 1844
ELLIOT James 1841

7
MAYFIELD Isaac 1859
PERKINS Isaac S 1860
ANDERSON James B 1892
MOORE Jesse T 1892
MOORE Jesse T 1892
THORNELL Thomas 1860

8
JOHNSON Squire C 1860
LOVEN John 1854
CHIPMAN Hezekiah 1860
HICKS Andrew J 1860
MCKINNEY Hughey W 1854

9
GREENE [193] Daniel 1840
GREENE [193] Daniel 1840
HUTCHINS James L 1841
GREENE [179] Daniel 1841
BEVIL Thomas L 1841
BEVIL Thomas L 1841
BEVIL Thomas L 1841
GREENE [179] Daniel 1841

18
THORNELL Thomas 1854
MCKINNEY Thomas J 1854
WARD [333] Ellen 1895

17

16

19
ABERNATHY [7] John T 1841
MCMAHON John J 1841
ALDERMAN John 1856
DARNALL Benjamin F 1885
ABERNATHY [7] John T 1841
ELLIOT [139] James 1841
ELLIOT [139] James 1841

20
STOCKTON Benjamin L 1860
STOCKTON Benjamin L 1860
MILLS Willard C 1861
BATES Francis M 1854
MOODY [296] Washington 1841
GREENE Daniel 1841
GREENE Daniel 1841

21
DARNALL William J 1849
DARNALL Scheharrizad 1860
CRENSHAW Plesant 1854
DARNALL Scheharrizad 1860
DARNALL Scheharrizad 1854
BEVIL Thomas L 1841
BEVIL Thomas L 1841
ABERNATHY [3] John T 1841
BEVIL Thomas L 1841

30
BRICKELL [53] Joseph J 1841
ELLIOT [139] James 1841
JACKSON Andrew 1841
MOORE Andrew B 1841
BOBO Simpson 1841
BURNETT Boling C 1841
BURNETT Boling C 1841

29
GILCHRIST [167] Malcolm 1841
SCOTT Christopher C 1841
BOZEMAN [52] Nancy C 1895
BEVIL Thomas L 1841
BURNETT Boling C 1841
GILCHRIST [167] Malcolm 1841
SCOTT Christopher C 1841
ELLIOT James 1841

28
BEVIL Thomas L 1841
BEVIL Thomas L 1841
ABERNATHY [3] John T 1841
DAVIES [122] John 1841
BEVIL Thomas L 1841
BEVILL [40] Thomas L 1844
DAVIES [122] John 1841
BEVIL Thomas L 1841

31
BOBO Simpson 1841
BOBO Simpson 1841
BURNETT Boling C 1841
BRICKELL [53] Joseph J 1841
GILCHRIST [165] Malcolm 1841
GILCHRIST [165] Malcolm 1841

32
WARD Wiley P 1860
ALLEN Charles 1848
ALLEN Margaret 1860
FOWLER Ezra R 1860
THOMPSON Granville 1881
BOUNDS Benjamin 1881
ALLEN Margaret 1860
ALLEN Margaret 1860
HENDON William T 1898
MILLS Willard C 1860
MILLS Willard C 1860

33
MCRIGHT Anderson W 1848
MCRIGHT Anderson W 1848
WHITE Eliza 1850
WHITE Eliza 1850
WHITE John W 1860
WHITE John W 1856
WHITE John W 1847

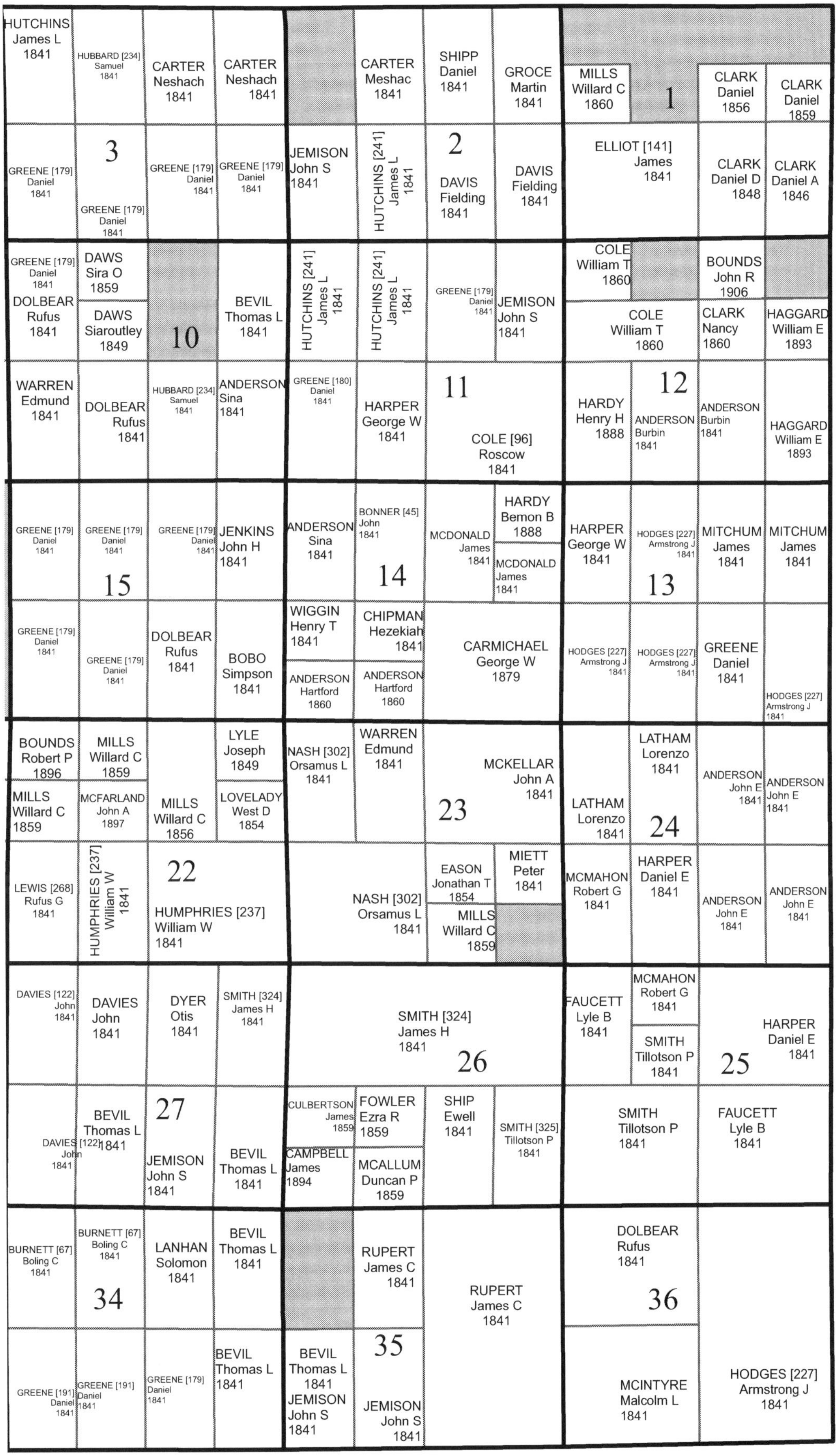

HUTCHINS James L 1841
HUBBARD [234] Samuel 1841
CARTER Neshach 1841
CARTER Neshach 1841
CARTER Meshac 1841
SHIPP Daniel 1841
GROCE Martin 1841
MILLS Willard C 1860
1
CLARK Daniel 1856
CLARK Daniel 1859
GREENE [179] Daniel 1841
3
GREENE [179] Daniel 1841
GREENE [179] Daniel 1841
GREENE [179] Daniel 1841
JEMISON John S 1841
HUTCHINS [241] James L 1841
2
DAVIS Fielding 1841
DAVIS Fielding 1841
ELLIOT [141] James 1841
CLARK Daniel D 1848
CLARK Daniel A 1846
GREENE [179] Daniel 1841
DAWS Sira O 1859
DOLBEAR Rufus 1841
DAWS Siaroutley 1849
10
BEVIL Thomas L 1841
HUTCHINS [241] James L 1841
HUTCHINS [241] James L 1841
GREENE [179] Daniel 1841
JEMISON John S 1841
COLE William T 1860
COLE William T 1860
BOUNDS John R 1906
CLARK Nancy 1860
HAGGARD William E 1893
WARREN Edmund 1841
DOLBEAR Rufus 1841
HUBBARD [234] Samuel 1841
ANDERSON Sina 1841
GREENE [180] Daniel 1841
HARPER George W 1841
11
COLE [96] Roscow 1841
HARDY Henry H 1888
12
ANDERSON Burbin 1841
ANDERSON Burbin 1841
HAGGARD William E 1893
GREENE [179] Daniel 1841
GREENE [179] Daniel 1841
15
GREENE [179] Daniel 1841
JENKINS John H 1841
ANDERSON Sina 1841
BONNER [45] John 1841
14
MCDONALD James 1841
HARDY Bemon B 1888
MCDONALD James 1841
HARPER George W 1841
HODGES [227] Armstrong J 1841
13
MITCHUM James 1841
MITCHUM James 1841
GREENE [179] Daniel 1841
GREENE [179] Daniel 1841
DOLBEAR Rufus 1841
BOBO Simpson 1841
WIGGIN Henry T 1841
CHIPMAN Hezekiah 1841
ANDERSON Hartford 1860
ANDERSON Hartford 1860
CARMICHAEL George W 1879
HODGES [227] Armstrong J 1841
HODGES [227] Armstrong J 1841
GREENE Daniel 1841
HODGES [227] Armstrong J 1841
BOUNDS Robert P 1896
MILLS Willard C 1859
MILLS Willard C 1859
MCFARLAND John A 1897
MILLS Willard C 1856
LYLE Joseph 1849
LOVELADY West D 1854
NASH [302] Orsamus L 1841
WARREN Edmund 1841
23
MCKELLAR John A 1841
LATHAM Lorenzo 1841
LATHAM Lorenzo 1841
24
ANDERSON John E 1841
ANDERSON John E 1841
LEWIS [268] Rufus G 1841
HUMPHRIES [237] William W 1841
22
HUMPHRIES [237] William W 1841
NASH [302] Orsamus L 1841
EASON Jonathan T 1854
MIETT Peter 1841
MILLS Willard C 1859
MCMAHON Robert G 1841
HARPER Daniel E 1841
ANDERSON John E 1841
ANDERSON John E 1841
DAVIES [122] John 1841
DAVIES John 1841
DYER Otis 1841
SMITH [324] James H 1841
SMITH [324] James H 1841
26
FAUCETT Lyle B 1841
MCMAHON Robert G 1841
SMITH Tillotson P 1841
25
HARPER Daniel E 1841
DAVIES [122] John 1841
BEVIL Thomas L 1841
27
JEMISON John S 1841
BEVIL Thomas L 1841
CULBERTSON James 1859
FOWLER Ezra R 1859
CAMPBELL James 1894
MCALLUM Duncan P 1859
SHIP Ewell 1841
SMITH [325] Tillotson P 1841
SMITH Tillotson P 1841
FAUCETT Lyle B 1841
BURNETT [67] Boling C 1841
BURNETT [67] Boling C 1841
34
LANHAN Solomon 1841
BEVIL Thomas L 1841
RUPERT James C 1841
RUPERT James C 1841
DOLBEAR Rufus 1841
36
GREENE [191] Daniel 1841
GREENE [191] Daniel 1841
GREENE [179] Daniel 1841
BEVIL Thomas L 1841
BEVIL Thomas L 1841
JEMISON John S 1841
35
JEMISON John S 1841
MCINTYRE Malcolm L 1841
HODGES [227] Armstrong J 1841

Helpful Hints

1. This Map's INDEX can be found on the preceding pages.
2. Refer to Map "C" to see where this Township lies within Kemper County, Mississippi.
3. Numbers within square brackets [ ] denote a multi-patentee land parcel (multi-owner). Refer to Appendix "C" for a full list of members in this group.
4. Areas that look to be crowded with Patentees usually indicate multiple sales of the same parcel (Re-issues) or Overlapping parcels. See this Township's Index for an explanation of these and other circumstances that might explain "odd" groupings of Patentees on this map.

Legend

Patent Boundary
Section Boundary
No Patents Found (or Outside County)
1., 2., 3., ... Lot Numbers (when beside a name)
[ ] Group Number (see Appendix "C")

Scale: Section = 1 mile X 1 mile (generally, with some exceptions)

Road Map

T10-N R14-E
Choctaw Meridian

Map Group 13

Cities & Towns

Darnall (historical)
Herbert (historical)
Spinks (historical)

Cemeteries

Cole Cemetery
Hopewell Cemetery
Liberty Cemetery
McDonald Cemetery
Talbert Cemetery

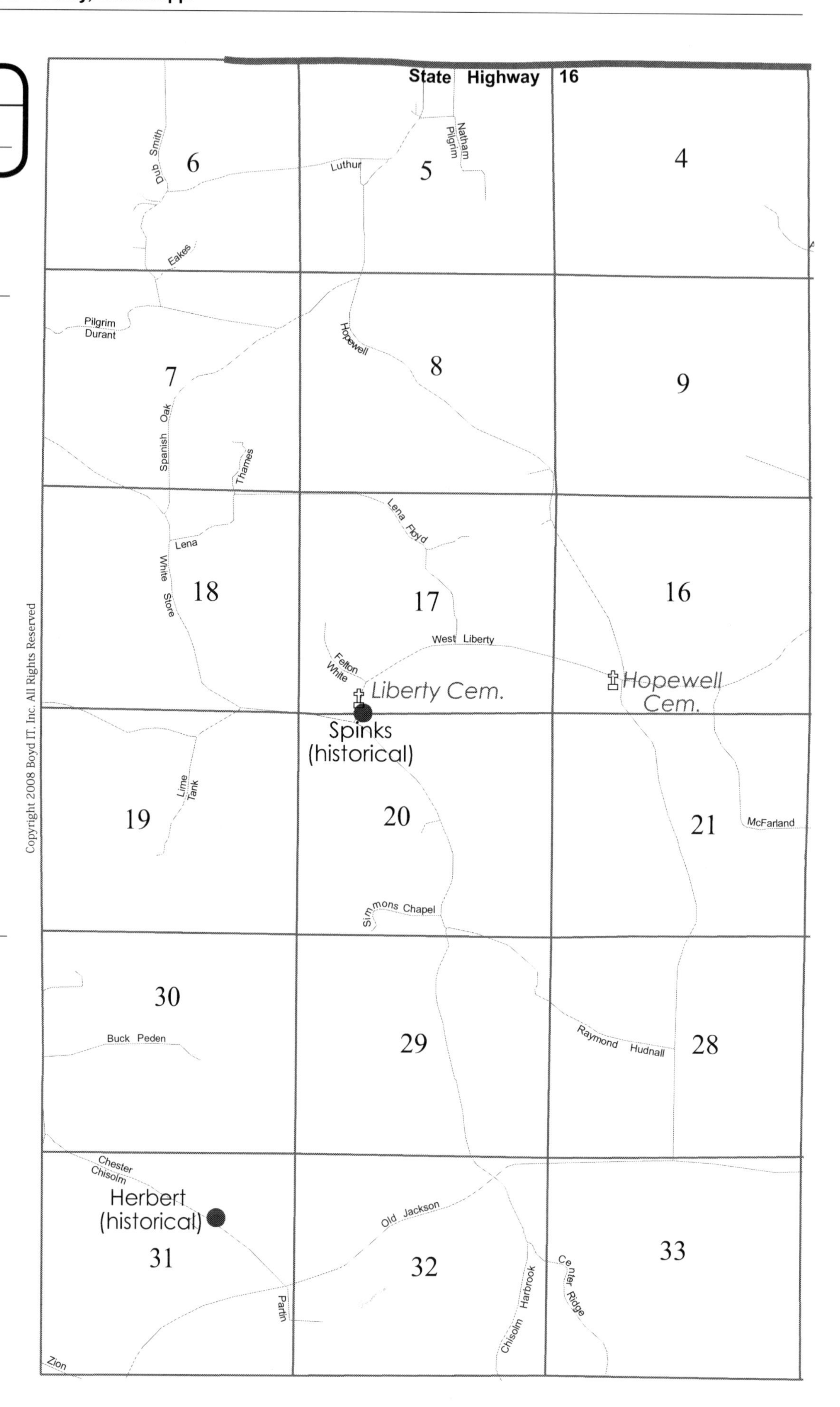

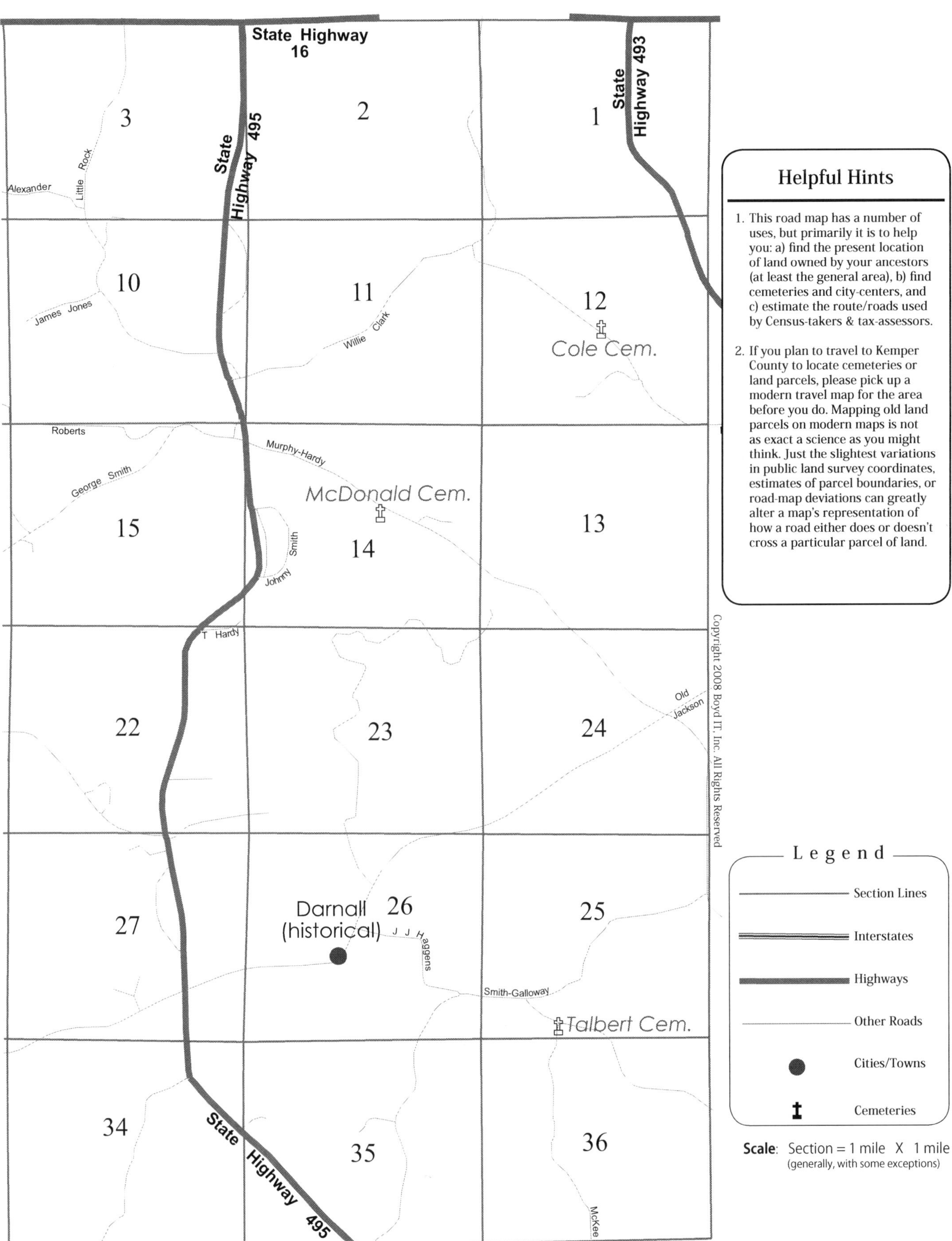
State Highway 16
State Highway 495
State Highway 493
3
2
1
Alexander
Little Rock
10
11
12
James Jones
Willie Clark
Cole Cem.
Roberts
Murphy-Hardy
George Smith
McDonald Cem.
15
14
13
Johnny Smith
T Hardy
22
23
24
Old Jackson
27
Darnall (historical)
26
25
J J Haggens
Smith-Galloway
Talbert Cem.
34
35
36
McKee
Helpful Hints
1. This road map has a number of uses, but primarily it is to help you: a) find the present location of land owned by your ancestors (at least the general area), b) find cemeteries and city-centers, and c) estimate the route/roads used by Census-takers & tax-assessors.
2. If you plan to travel to Kemper County to locate cemeteries or land parcels, please pick up a modern travel map for the area before you do. Mapping old land parcels on modern maps is not as exact a science as you might think. Just the slightest variations in public land survey coordinates, estimates of parcel boundaries, or road-map deviations can greatly alter a map's representation of how a road either does or doesn't cross a particular parcel of land.
Legend
Section Lines
Interstates
Highways
Other Roads
Cities/Towns
Cemeteries
Scale: Section = 1 mile X 1 mile
(generally, with some exceptions)

Historical Map

T10-N R14-E
Choctaw Meridian

Map Group 13

Cities & Towns
Darnall (historical)
Herbert (historical)
Spinks (historical)

Cemeteries
Cole Cemetery
Hopewell Cemetery
Liberty Cemetery
McDonald Cemetery
Talbert Cemetery

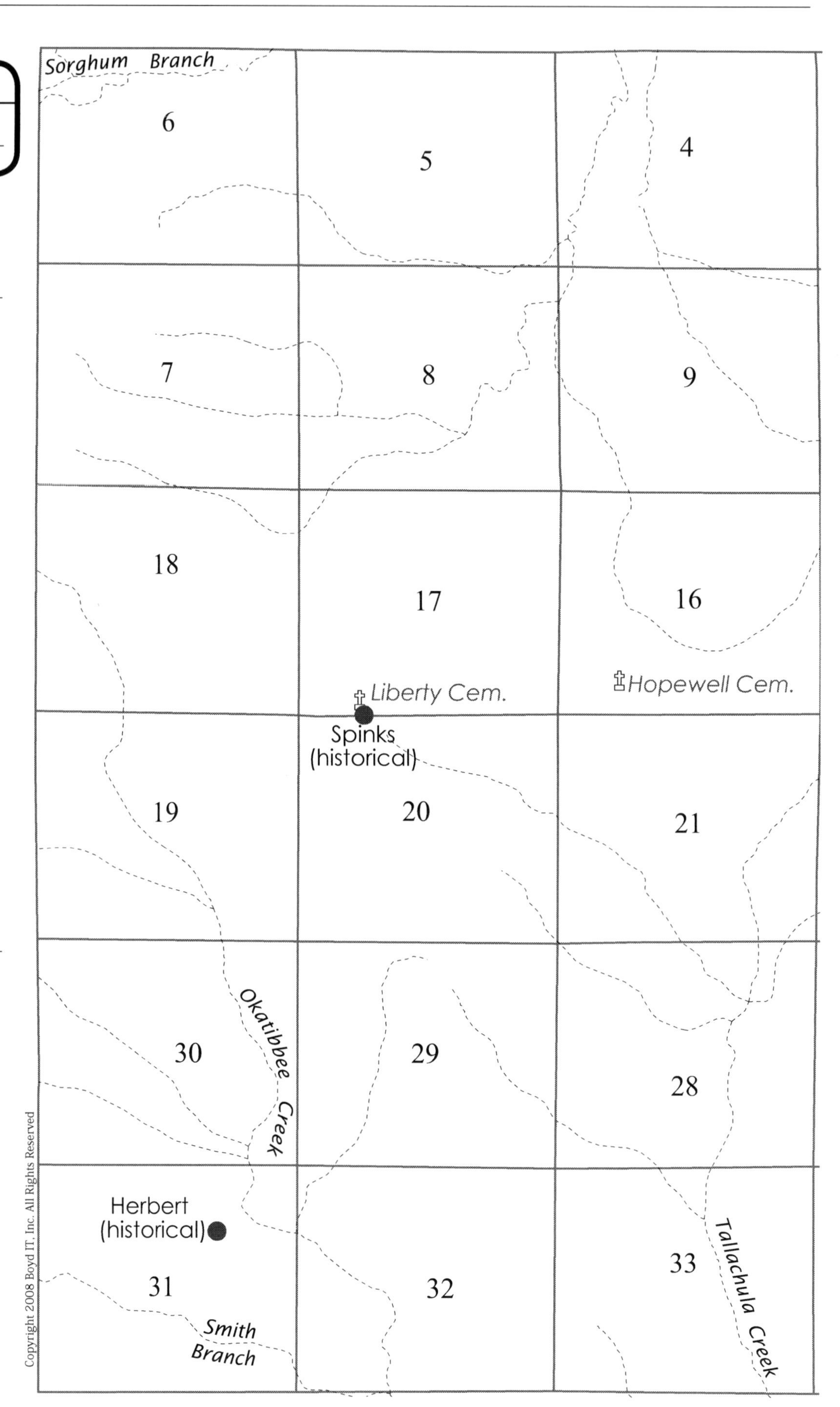

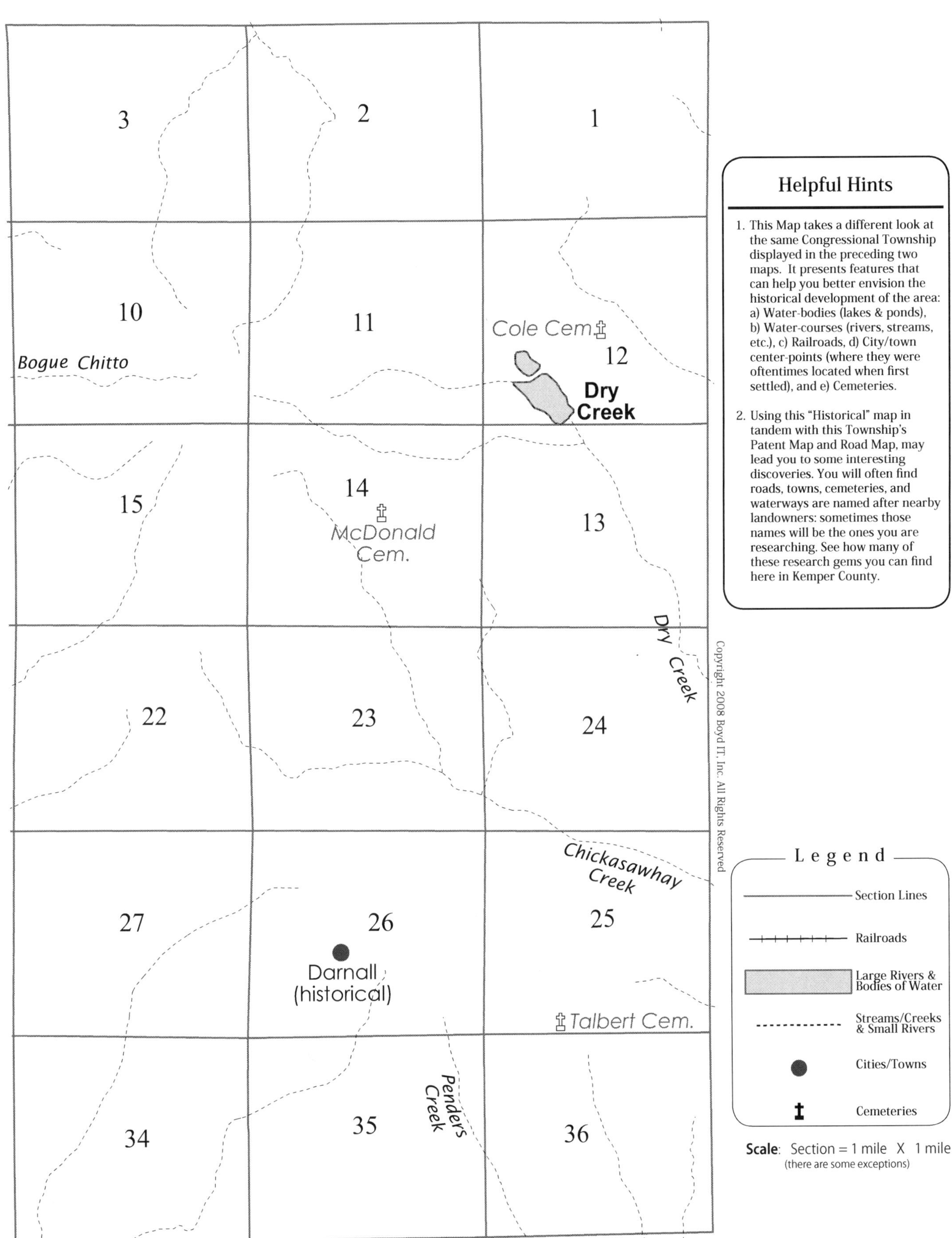

Helpful Hints

1. This Map takes a different look at the same Congressional Township displayed in the preceding two maps. It presents features that can help you better envision the historical development of the area: a) Water-bodies (lakes & ponds), b) Water-courses (rivers, streams, etc.), c) Railroads, d) City/town center-points (where they were oftentimes located when first settled), and e) Cemeteries.

2. Using this "Historical" map in tandem with this Township's Patent Map and Road Map, may lead you to some interesting discoveries. You will often find roads, towns, cemeteries, and waterways are named after nearby landowners: sometimes those names will be the ones you are researching. See how many of these research gems you can find here in Kemper County.

Legend

- Section Lines
- Railroads
- Large Rivers & Bodies of Water
- Streams/Creeks & Small Rivers
- Cities/Towns
- Cemeteries

Scale: Section = 1 mile X 1 mile
(there are some exceptions)

Map Group 14: Index to Land Patents

Township 10-North Range 15-East (Choctaw)

After you locate an individual in this Index, take note of the Section and Section Part then proceed to the Land Patent map on the pages immediately following. You should have no difficulty locating the corresponding parcel of land.

The "For More Info" Column will lead you to more information about the underlying Patents. See the *Legend* at right, and the "How to Use this Book" chapter, for more information.

LEGEND

"For More Info . . . " column

A = Authority (Legislative Act, See Appendix "A")
B = Block or Lot (location in Section unknown)
C = Cancelled Patent
F = Fractional Section
G = Group (Multi-Patentee Patent, see Appendix "C")
V = Overlaps another Parcel
R = Re-Issued (Parcel patented more than once)

(A & G items require you to look in the Appendixes referred to above. All other Letter-designations followed by a number require you to locate line-items in this index that possess the ID number found after the letter).

ID	Individual in Patent	Sec.	Sec. Part	Date Issued	Other Counties	For More Info . . .
2766	ABBERCROMBIE, Calvin	31	NW	1841-02-27		A1
2964	ABBOTT, Willis	19	E½SE	1841-02-27		A1 G1
2965	" "	19	W½SE	1841-02-27		A1 G1
2741	ABERCROMBIE, Archibald	30	SE	1848-09-01		A1
2742	" "	32	NW	1848-09-01		A1
2767	ABERCROMBIE, Calvin	29	SW	1848-09-01		A1
2820	ABERCROMBIE, Isaac	7	S½SW	1889-11-29		A1
2821	" "	7	SWSE	1889-11-29		A1
2898	ABERCROMBIE, Oliver	6	NWSW	1859-10-01		A1
2743	ABERCROMBRIE, Archibald	30	E½NE	1841-02-27		A1
2744	" "	30	W½NE	1841-02-27		A1
2745	" "	32	W½NE	1841-02-27		A1
2837	ADAMS, John A	18	NWSE	1882-05-10		A1
2839	ADAMS, John B	15	SESW	1850-12-05		A1
2840	" "	15	W½SE	1850-12-05		A1
2932	ADAMS, Thomas W	5	SESW	1854-03-15		A1
2931	" "	17	NE	1860-05-01		A1
2824	ALEXANDER, James B	22	SE	1841-02-27		A1
2823	" "	15	NW	1846-09-01		A1
2822	ALLWOOD, James	34	W½SW	1841-02-27		A1
2843	ANDERSON, John E	19	E½SW	1841-02-27		A1
2844	" "	19	W½SW	1841-02-27		A1
2845	" "	30	W½NW	1841-02-27		A1
2801	BALDWIN, Frances	8	E½NE	1841-02-27		A1
2966	BANKS, Willis	21	E½SW	1841-02-27		A1
2967	" "	21	W½SW	1841-02-27		A1
2968	" "	27	E½NW	1841-02-27		A1
2833	BOUNDS, James R	19	NWNE	1859-10-01		A1
2834	" "	19	SWNE	1859-10-01		A1
2832	" "	18	SESE	1860-05-01		A1
2831	" "	17	SWSW	1888-12-29		A1
2948	BOUNDS, William	19	E½NW	1841-02-27		A1
2949	" "	19	W½NW	1841-02-27		A1
2951	" "	29	NWSE	1856-04-01		A1
2950	" "	29	NWNW	1859-10-01		A1
2893	BROWN, Morgan D	6	W½NW	1841-02-27		A1
2763	BURNETT, Boling C	11	E½NW	1840-04-21		A1 G69
2764	" "	11	E½SE	1840-04-21		A1 G69
2765	" "	11	E½SW	1840-04-21		A1 G69
2915	BURRAGE, Rufus	5	SWSW	1888-04-05		A2
2952	CARRIEL, William	10	SWNE	1841-02-27		A1
2756	CLEMENT, Benjamin	21	E½NW	1841-02-27		A1
2757	" "	27	E½SW	1841-02-27		A1
2758	" "	30	E½NW	1841-02-27		A1
2759	" "	9	W½SW	1841-02-27		A1
2760	" "	21	W½NW	1842-03-02		A1 G90

ID	Individual in Patent	Sec.	Sec. Part	Date Issued	Other Counties	For More Info . . .
2761	CLEMENT, Benjamin (Cont'd)	27	W½SW	1842-03-02		A1 G90
2882	COATES, Madison	6	NESW	1841-02-27		A1
2900	COLE, Peter H	15	NE	1848-09-01		A1
2899	" "	14	E½NW	1850-12-05		A1
2912	COLE, Roscow	34	E½NW	1841-02-27		A1 G95
2913	" "	34	W½NW	1841-02-27		A1 G95
2841	CONELLY, John	3	E½SW	1841-02-27		A1 G99
2842	" "	3	W½SW	1841-02-27		A1 G99
2953	CONN, William	20	S½NW	1854-03-15		A1
2927	DAVIS, Thomas	27	NE	1846-09-01		A1
2739	DAWKINS, Angus	24	SE	1841-02-27		A1
2892	DAWKINS, Minor	24	NE	1841-02-27		A1
2826	ECKFORD, James	13	E½	1841-02-27		A1
2827	" "	28	SE	1841-02-27		A1
2828	ELLIOT, James	23	E½NW	1841-02-27		A1
2829	" "	23	W½NW	1841-02-27		A1
2830	" "	26	E½NE	1841-02-27		A1
2754	EVERETT, Barton C	15	NESW	1850-12-05		A1
2755	" "	15	SWSW	1850-12-05		A1
2904	FLOYD, Presley	14	W½SW	1846-12-01		A1 G155
2905	FLOYD, Presly	14	E½SW	1846-09-01		A1
2906	" "	14	W½NW	1846-09-01		A1
2923	FLOYD, Samuel K	18	NESW	1860-05-01		A1
2924	" "	18	SWSE	1860-05-01		A1
2925	" "	18	SWSW	1860-05-01		A1
2895	GOODGER, Napoleon B	30	E½SW	1841-02-27		A1
2896	" "	30	W½SW	1841-02-27		A1
2737	GRAHAM, Alexander	12	NW	1841-02-27		A1
2770	GREENE, Daniel	28	E½NE	1841-02-27		A1
2771	" "	28	E½NW	1841-02-27		A1
2772	" "	28	E½SW	1841-02-27		A1
2773	" "	28	W½NE	1841-02-27		A1
2774	" "	28	W½NW	1841-02-27		A1
2775	" "	28	W½SW	1841-02-27		A1
2776	" "	32	E½NE	1841-02-27		A1
2777	" "	33	E½NW	1841-02-27		A1
2778	" "	33	W½NW	1841-02-27		A1
2746	GRIFFIN, Archibald M	13	W½NW	1841-12-15		A1 G200
2747	" "	4	E½NW	1841-12-15		A1 G200
2902	GULLY, Philemon H	14	E½NE	1848-09-01		A1
2903	" "	14	SE	1848-09-01		A1
2954	HAGGARD, William E	7	SWNW	1893-12-19		A2
2779	HARBOUR, David	29	SWNW	1859-10-01		A1
2780	" "	29	SWSE	1859-10-01		A1
2847	HARBOUR, John	9	E½SW	1841-02-27		A1
2848	" "	9	SE	1841-02-27		A1 G216
2810	HARPER, George W	10	W½NW	1841-02-27		A1
2811	" "	13	E½SW	1841-02-27		A1
2812	" "	27	E½SE	1841-02-27		A1
2813	" "	27	W½SE	1841-02-27		A1
2959	HARREL, William	34	E½SW	1859-10-01		A1
2960	" "	34	W½SE	1859-10-01		A1
2791	HERNDON, Edward	23	W½SE	1848-09-01		A1
2781	HILLHOUSE, David	23	W½NE	1841-02-27		A1
2750	HODGES, Armstrong J	11	W½NW	1840-04-21		A1 G226
2751	" "	11	W½SW	1840-04-21		A1 G226
2752	" "	12	W½SW	1840-04-21		A1 G226
2753	" "	23	E½NE	1841-02-27		A1 G227
2746	HODGES, Philemon	13	W½NW	1841-12-15		A1 G200
2747	" "	4	E½NW	1841-12-15		A1 G200
2886	HOLDERNESS, Mckinney	12	E½SW	1840-04-21		A1 G230
2887	" "	13	W½SW	1841-02-27		A1 G231
2888	" "	24	E½NW	1841-02-27		A1 G231
2889	" "	24	E½SW	1841-02-27		A1 G231
2890	" "	24	W½NW	1841-02-27		A1 G231
2891	" "	24	W½SW	1841-02-27		A1 G231
2912	" "	34	E½NW	1841-02-27		A1 G95
2913	" "	34	W½NW	1841-02-27		A1 G95
2760	" "	21	W½NW	1842-03-02		A1 G90
2761	" "	27	W½SW	1842-03-02		A1 G90
2792	HOUSTON, Eleazar	2	SE	1850-12-05		A1
2815	HOUSTON, Henry K	2	NE	1850-12-05		A1
2920	HUBBARD, Samuel	11	W½NE	1841-12-15		A1 G234

ID	Individual in Patent	Sec.	Sec. Part	Date Issued	Other Counties	For More Info . . .
2921	HUBBARD, Samuel (Cont'd)	4	E½SE	1841-12-15		A1 G234
2922	" "	4	W½NE	1841-12-15		A1 G234
2835	HULL, James W	5	NWNW	1856-04-01		A1
2841	JACKSON, Andrew	3	E½SW	1841-02-27		A1 G99
2842	" "	3	W½SW	1841-02-27		A1 G99
2849	JAGGANS, John	36	N½NW	1841-02-27		A1
2850	JAGGERS, John	26	SW	1841-02-27		A1 G245
2855	JEMISON, John S	27	W½NW	1841-02-27		A1
2856	" "	32	E½SW	1841-02-27		A1 V2917
2857	" "	32	W½SE	1841-02-27		A1 R2918
2858	" "	32	W½SW	1841-02-27		A1
2740	JENNINGS, Ann	3	SE	1850-12-05		A1
2933	JOHNSON, Warren B	22	E½SW	1841-02-27		A1 G250
2934	" "	22	W½SW	1841-02-27		A1 G250
2964	JOHNSTON, Warren B	19	E½SE	1841-02-27		A1 G1
2965	" "	19	W½SE	1841-02-27		A1 G1
2787	JOINER, Duncan	33	E½SE	1841-02-27		A1
2788	" "	33	W½SE	1841-02-27		A1
2782	JONES, David	21	SE	1848-09-01		A1
2793	JONES, Elijah C	20	NESE	1856-04-01		A1
2794	" "	20	SESE	1860-05-01		A1
2836	JONES, James W	20	NENE	1892-06-15		A2
2786	JORDAN, Dempsey	3	NWNE	1859-10-01		A1
2955	KEELAND, William H	33	E½NE	1841-02-27		A1
2956	" "	33	W½NE	1841-02-27		A1
2783	LAUDERDALE, David	36	NE	1841-02-27		A1
2916	LEWIS, Rufus G	23	E½SE	1841-02-27		A1 G268
2920	" "	11	W½NE	1841-12-15		A1 G234
2921	" "	4	E½SE	1841-12-15		A1 G234
2922	" "	4	W½NE	1841-12-15		A1 G234
2897	LITTLE, Neill M	12	NE	1847-04-01		A1
2908	LOVE, Robert J	2	N½SW	1850-12-05		A1
2909	" "	2	SENW	1854-03-15		A1
2910	" "	2	SESW	1854-03-15		A1
2784	LYLE, David	10	SW	1841-02-27		A1 G275
2785	MCCRANIE, David	31	SW	1841-02-27		A1
2911	MCDONALD, Robert	6	NENE	1892-06-06		A1
2928	MCGEE, Thomas	32	E½SE	1841-02-27		A1
2929	" "	8	NW	1841-02-27		A1
2748	MCKELLAR, Archibald	9	E½NE	1841-02-27		A1
2749	" "	9	W½NE	1841-02-27		A1
2851	MCKELLAR, John	4	S½SW	1841-02-27		A1
2838	MCKELLAR, John A	11	E½NE	1841-02-27		A1
2957	MCLAURIN, William H	6	E½NW	1884-12-30		A2
2958	" "	6	W½NE	1884-12-30		A2
2917	MCNEAL, Rufus L	32	SESW	1861-01-01		A1 V2856
2918	" "	32	W½SE	1861-01-01		A1 R2857
2919	" "	5	NWNE	1861-01-01		A1
2784	MEYATTE, Peter	10	SW	1841-02-27		A1 G275
2937	MILLS, Willard C	2	NENW	1854-03-15		A1
2938	" "	2	SWSW	1854-03-15		A1
2939	" "	4	N½SW	1854-03-15		A1
2940	" "	4	SWNW	1854-03-15		A1
2941	" "	5	SWSE	1854-03-15		A1
2944	" "	8	NESW	1854-03-15		A1
2935	" "	18	NWSW	1856-04-01		A1
2942	" "	6	SESW	1856-04-01		A1
2936	" "	19	SENE	1859-10-01		A1
2943	" "	7	NENE	1859-10-01		A1
2945	" "	8	NWSW	1860-05-01		A1
2930	MONTAGUE, Thomas P	29	NENE	1854-03-15		A1
2961	OVERSTREET, William	1	NW	1850-12-05		A1
2962	" "	17	NWNW	1888-12-29		A1
2963	" "	8	SWSW	1888-12-29		A1
2738	PEDEN, Andrew H	15	NESE	1856-04-01		A1
2859	PEDEN, John T	4	NWSE	1854-03-15		A1
2883	PERKINS, Marcus D	7	N½SW	1892-06-15		A2
2884	" "	7	NWSE	1892-06-15		A2
2885	PERKINS, Mary O	7	NWNE	1905-02-13		A2 G309
2885	PERKINS, Silvester	7	NWNE	1905-02-13		A2 G309
2808	POLLOCK, George	34	SESE	1841-02-27		A1
2809	" "	35	SWSW	1841-02-27		A1
2825	POLLOCK, James E	25	SE	1850-12-05		A1

ID	Individual in Patent	Sec.	Sec. Part	Date Issued	Other Counties	For More Info . . .
2914	POLLOCK, Roxanna	25	SW	1850-12-05		A1
2853	PREWITT, John	11	W½SE	1841-02-27		A1
2736	RODES, Agnes	8	W½NE	1841-02-27		A1
2907	SESSUMS, Redding	10	SE	1841-02-27		A1
2768	SKINNER, Clabourn	21	NE	1848-09-01		A1
2769	SKINNER, Claibourn	17	SWNW	1850-12-05		A1
2795	SMITH, Ephraim	22	E½NE	1841-02-27		A1
2933	" "	22	E½SW	1841-02-27		A1 G250
2796	" "	22	NW	1841-02-27		A1
2797	" "	22	W½NE	1841-02-27		A1
2934	" "	22	W½SW	1841-02-27		A1 G250
2798	" "	23	E½SW	1841-02-27		A1
2799	" "	23	W½SW	1841-02-27		A1
2800	" "	26	W½NE	1841-02-27		A1
2852	SMITH, John P	9	NW	1841-02-27		A1
2848	SMITH, Reuben	9	SE	1841-02-27		A1 G216
2806	SNEAD, Garland	10	E½NW	1841-02-27		A1
2807	" "	8	SE	1841-02-27		A1
2901	SNEAD, Peter	6	SE	1841-02-27		A1
2860	SORSBY, John T	31	E½NE	1841-02-27		A1
2861	" "	31	E½SE	1841-02-27		A1
2862	" "	31	W½NE	1841-02-27		A1
2863	" "	31	W½SE	1841-02-27		A1
2850	STEEL, Lemuel G	26	SW	1841-02-27		A1 G245
2870	" "	26	NW	1848-09-01		A1
2871	STEELE, Lemuel G	26	E½SE	1841-02-27		A1
2872	" "	26	W½SE	1841-02-27		A1
2873	" "	34	NESE	1860-05-01		A1
2874	" "	36	S½NW	1860-05-01		A1
2875	" "	36	SW	1860-05-01		A1
2876	STEELE, Lemuel J	34	NE	1841-02-27		A1
2877	" "	35	E½SW	1841-02-27		A1
2878	" "	35	NWSW	1841-02-27		A1
2926	STEELE, Samuel	35	N½	1841-02-27		A1 G326
2880	STOVALL, Lewis	33	E½SW	1841-02-27		A1 G327
2881	" "	33	W½SW	1841-02-27		A1 G327
2946	SWARENGIN, William B	7	E½SE	1882-08-03		A2
2947	" "	7	S½NE	1882-08-03		A2
2802	SWEARINGEN, Francis B	5	SWNW	1860-05-01		A1
2803	" "	6	SENE	1860-05-01		A1
2880	SWEARINGEN, Morgan	33	E½SW	1841-02-27		A1 G327
2881	" "	33	W½SW	1841-02-27		A1 G327
2920	TAPPAN, John	11	W½NE	1841-12-15		A1 G234
2921	" "	4	E½SE	1841-12-15		A1 G234
2922	" "	4	W½NE	1841-12-15		A1 G234
2865	TERRY, John	5	NWSE	1856-04-01		A1
2864	" "	5	NESW	1859-10-01		A1
2867	" "	8	SESW	1860-05-01		A1
2866	" "	5	SWNE	1861-01-01		A1
2814	TISDALE, Hardy	4	SWSE	1859-10-01		A1
2894	TODD, Moses S	20	NWNE	1850-12-05		A1
2854	WALKER, John R	36	S½SE	1899-04-17		A2
2763	WALTHALL, Madison	11	E½NW	1840-04-21		A1 G69
2764	" "	11	E½SE	1840-04-21		A1 G69
2765	" "	11	E½SW	1840-04-21		A1 G69
2750	" "	11	W½NW	1840-04-21		A1 G226
2751	" "	11	W½SW	1840-04-21		A1 G226
2886	" "	12	E½SW	1840-04-21		A1 G230
2752	" "	12	W½SW	1840-04-21		A1 G226
2790	WARREN, Edmund	6	SWSW	1841-02-27		A1
2789	WARRIN, Edmond	18	NW	1841-02-27		A1
2879	WATKINS, Leven C	25	NE	1848-09-01		A1
2816	WHITE, Henry	10	E½NE	1841-02-27		A1
2817	" "	10	NWNE	1841-02-27		A1
2869	WHITE, John	29	NESE	1849-12-01		A1
2868	" "	25	NW	1850-12-05		A1
2904	WHITE, Rebecca	14	W½SW	1846-12-01		A1 G155
2926	WHITFIELD, Boaz	35	N½	1841-02-27		A1 G326
2762	" "	4	E½NE	1841-02-27		A1
2804	WHITFIELD, Gains	3	E½NW	1841-02-27		A1
2805	" "	3	W½NW	1841-02-27		A1
2916	WHITSETT, John C	23	E½SE	1841-02-27		A1 G268
2846	WILLIAMS, John F	18	SESW	1854-03-15		A1

ID	Individual in Patent	Sec.	Sec. Part	Date Issued	Other Counties	For More Info . . .
2819	WILSON, Hilliard	20	SWNE	1850-12-05		A1
2818	" "	17	SWSE	1856-04-01		A1
2887	WINSTON, William B	13	W½SW	1841-02-27		A1 G231
2753	" "	23	E½NE	1841-02-27		A1 G227
2888	" "	24	E½NW	1841-02-27		A1 G231
2889	" "	24	E½SW	1841-02-27		A1 G231
2890	" "	24	W½NW	1841-02-27		A1 G231
2891	" "	24	W½SW	1841-02-27		A1 G231

Patent Map

T10-N R15-E
Choctaw Meridian

Map Group 14

Township Statistics

Parcels Mapped	233
Number of Patents	212
Number of Individuals	130
Patentees Identified	122
Number of Surnames	98
Multi-Patentee Parcels	37
Oldest Patent Date	4/21/1840
Most Recent Patent	2/13/1905
Block/Lot Parcels	0
Parcels Re - Issued	1
Parcels that Overlap	2
Cities and Towns	4
Cemeteries	4

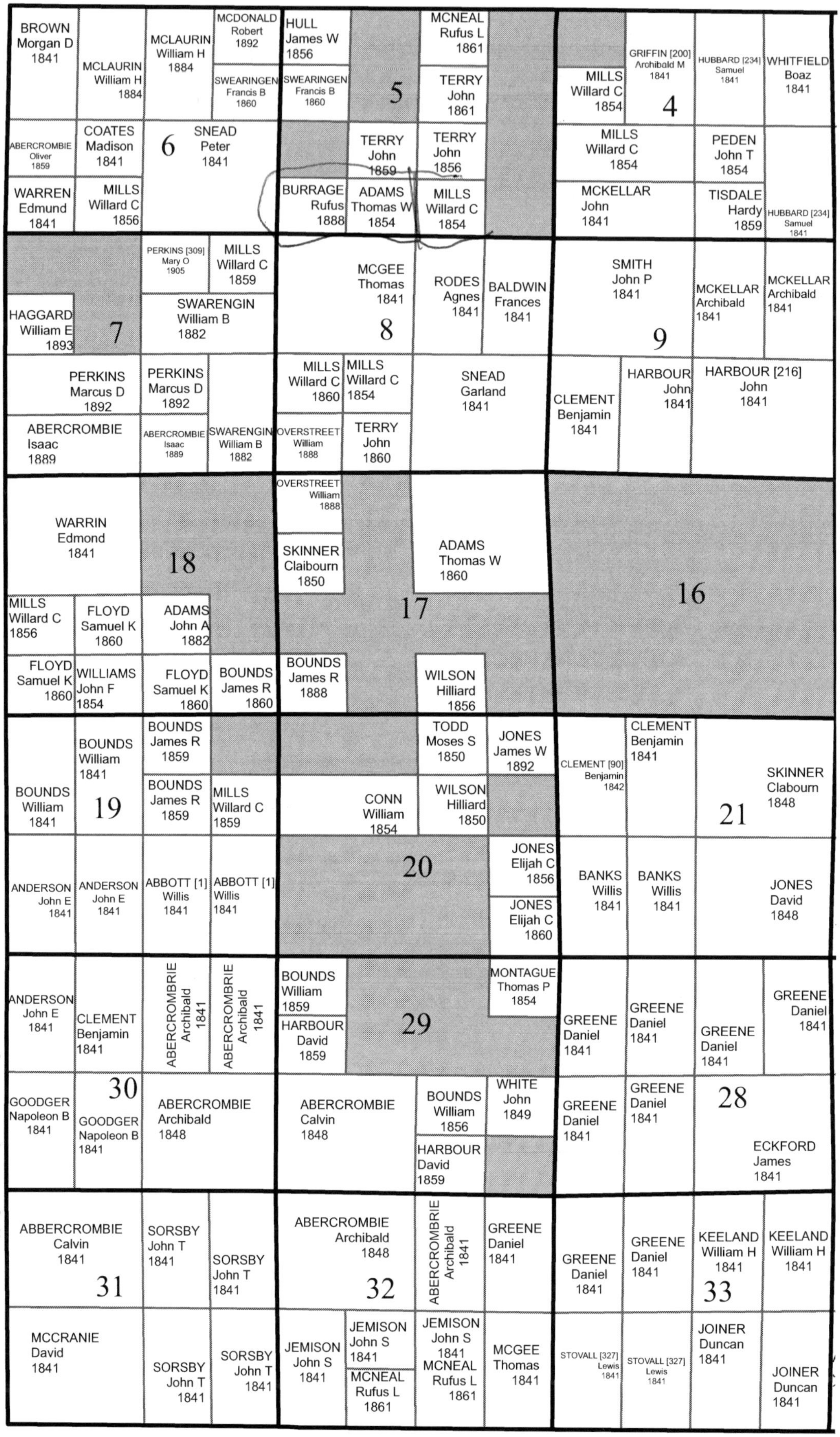

WHITFIELD Gains 1841
WHITFIELD Gains 1841
JORDAN Dempsey 1859
MILLS Willard C 1854
LOVE Robert J 1854
HOUSTON Henry K 1850
2
OVERSTREET William 1850
1
CONELLY [99] John 1841
CONELLY [99] John 1841
3
JENNINGS Ann 1850
LOVE Robert J 1850
MILLS Willard C 1854
LOVE Robert J 1854
HOUSTON Eleazar 1850

HARPER George W 1841
SNEAD Garland 1841
WHITE Henry 1841
CARRIEL William 1841
WHITE Henry 1841
HODGES [226] Armstrong J 1840
BURNETT [69] Boling C 1840
HUBBARD [234] Samuel 1841
MCKELLAR John A 1841
11
GRAHAM Alexander 1841
LITTLE Neill M 1847
12
10
LYLE [275] David 1841
SESSUMS Redding 1841
HODGES [226] Armstrong J 1840
BURNETT [69] Boling C 1840
PREWITT John 1841
BURNETT [69] Boling C 1840
HODGES [226] Armstrong J 1840
HOLDERNESS [230] Mckinney 1840

ALEXANDER James B 1846
15
COLE Peter H 1848
FLOYD Presly 1846
COLE Peter H 1850
GULLY Philemon H 1848
GRIFFIN [200] Archibald M 1841
ECKFORD James 1841
EVERETT Barton C 1850
ADAMS John B 1850
PEDEN Andrew H 1856
EVERETT Barton C 1850
ADAMS John B 1850
FLOYD [155] Presley 1846
14
FLOYD Presly 1846
GULLY Philemon H 1848
HOLDERNESS [231] Mckinney 1841
13
HARPER George W 1841

SMITH Ephraim 1841
22
SMITH Ephraim 1841
SMITH Ephraim 1841
ELLIOT James 1841
ELLIOT James 1841
23
HILLHOUSE David 1841
HODGES [227] Armstrong J 1841
HOLDERNESS [231] Mckinney 1841
HOLDERNESS [231] Mckinney 1841
DAWKINS Minor 1841
24
JOHNSON [250] Warren B 1841
JOHNSON [250] Warren B 1841
ALEXANDER James B 1841
SMITH Ephraim 1841
SMITH Ephraim 1841
HERNDON Edward 1848
LEWIS [268] Rufus G 1841
HOLDERNESS [231] Mckinney 1841
HOLDERNESS [231] Mckinney 1841
DAWKINS Angus 1841

JEMISON John S 1841
BANKS Willis 1841
27
DAVIS Thomas 1846
STEEL Lemuel G 1848
26
SMITH Ephraim 1841
ELLIOT James 1841
WHITE John 1850
WATKINS Leven C 1848
25
CLEMENT [90] Benjamin 1842
CLEMENT Benjamin 1841
HARPER George W 1841
HARPER George W 1841
JAGGERS [245] John 1841
STEELE Lemuel G 1841
STEELE Lemuel G 1841
POLLOCK Roxanna 1850
POLLOCK James E 1850

COLE [95] Roscow 1841
COLE [95] Roscow 1841
STEELE Lemuel J 1841
34
STEELE [326] Samuel 1841
35
JAGGANS John 1841
STEELE Lemuel G 1860
LAUDERDALE David 1841
ALLWOOD James 1841
HARREL William 1859
HARREL William 1859
STEELE Lemuel G 1860
POLLOCK George 1841
STEELE Lemuel J 1841
POLLOCK George 1841
STEELE Lemuel J 1841
36
STEELE Lemuel G 1860
WALKER John R 1899

Helpful Hints

1. This Map's INDEX can be found on the preceding pages.
2. Refer to Map "C" to see where this Township lies within Kemper County, Mississippi.
3. Numbers within square brackets [ ] denote a multi-patentee land parcel (multi-owner). Refer to Appendix "C" for a full list of members in this group.
4. Areas that look to be crowded with Patentees usually indicate multiple sales of the same parcel (Re-issues) or Overlapping parcels. See this Township's Index for an explanation of these and other circumstances that might explain "odd" groupings of Patentees on this map.

Legend

Patent Boundary
Section Boundary
No Patents Found (or Outside County)
1., 2., 3., ... Lot Numbers (when beside a name)
[ ] Group Number (see Appendix "C")

Scale: Section = 1 mile X 1 mile (generally, with some exceptions)

Road Map

T10-N R15-E
Choctaw Meridian

Map Group 14

Cities & Towns

Ayanabi (historical)
East Coongetto (historical)
Haanka Ullah (historical)
Moscow

Cemeteries

New Hope Cemetery
New Hope Cemetery
Shiloh Cemetery
West Kemper Cemetery

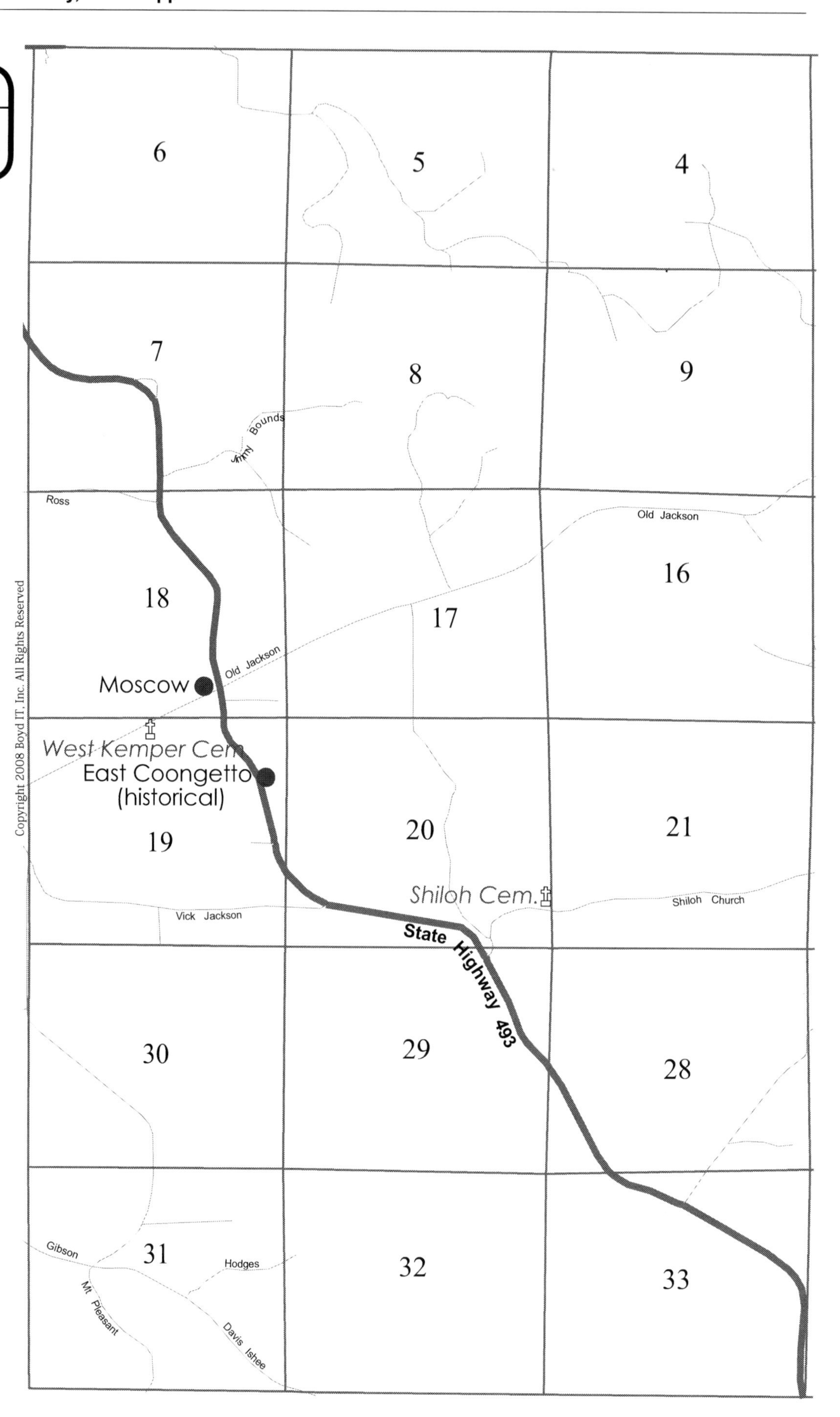

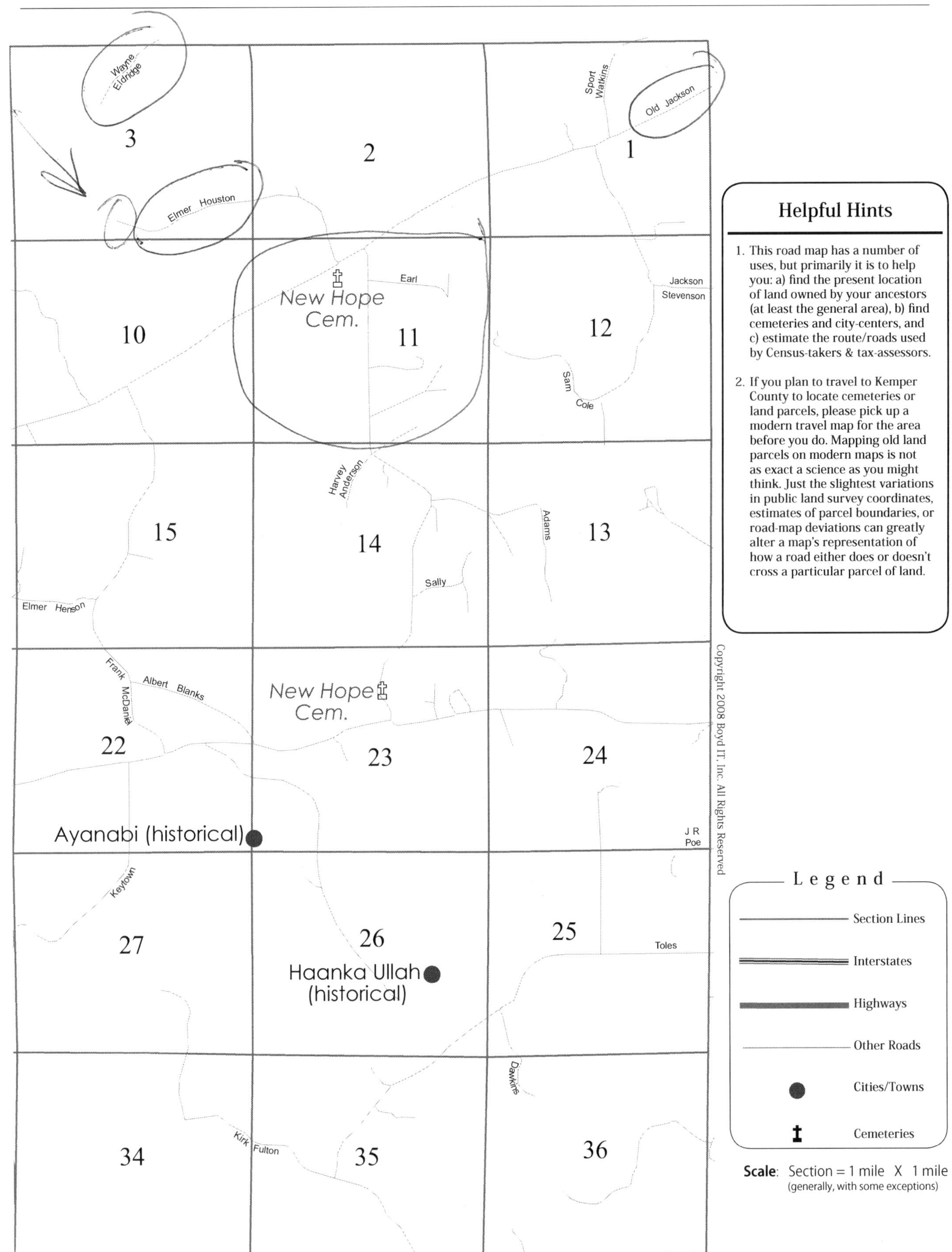

Helpful Hints

1. This road map has a number of uses, but primarily it is to help you: a) find the present location of land owned by your ancestors (at least the general area), b) find cemeteries and city-centers, and c) estimate the route/roads used by Census-takers & tax-assessors.

2. If you plan to travel to Kemper County to locate cemeteries or land parcels, please pick up a modern travel map for the area before you do. Mapping old land parcels on modern maps is not as exact a science as you might think. Just the slightest variations in public land survey coordinates, estimates of parcel boundaries, or road-map deviations can greatly alter a map's representation of how a road either does or doesn't cross a particular parcel of land.

Legend

- Section Lines
- Interstates
- Highways
- Other Roads
- Cities/Towns
- Cemeteries

Scale: Section = 1 mile X 1 mile
(generally, with some exceptions)

Historical Map

T10-N R15-E
Choctaw Meridian

Map Group 14

Cities & Towns

Ayanabi (historical)
East Coongetto (historical)
Haanka Ullah (historical)
Moscow

Cemeteries

New Hope Cemetery
New Hope Cemetery
Shiloh Cemetery
West Kemper Cemetery

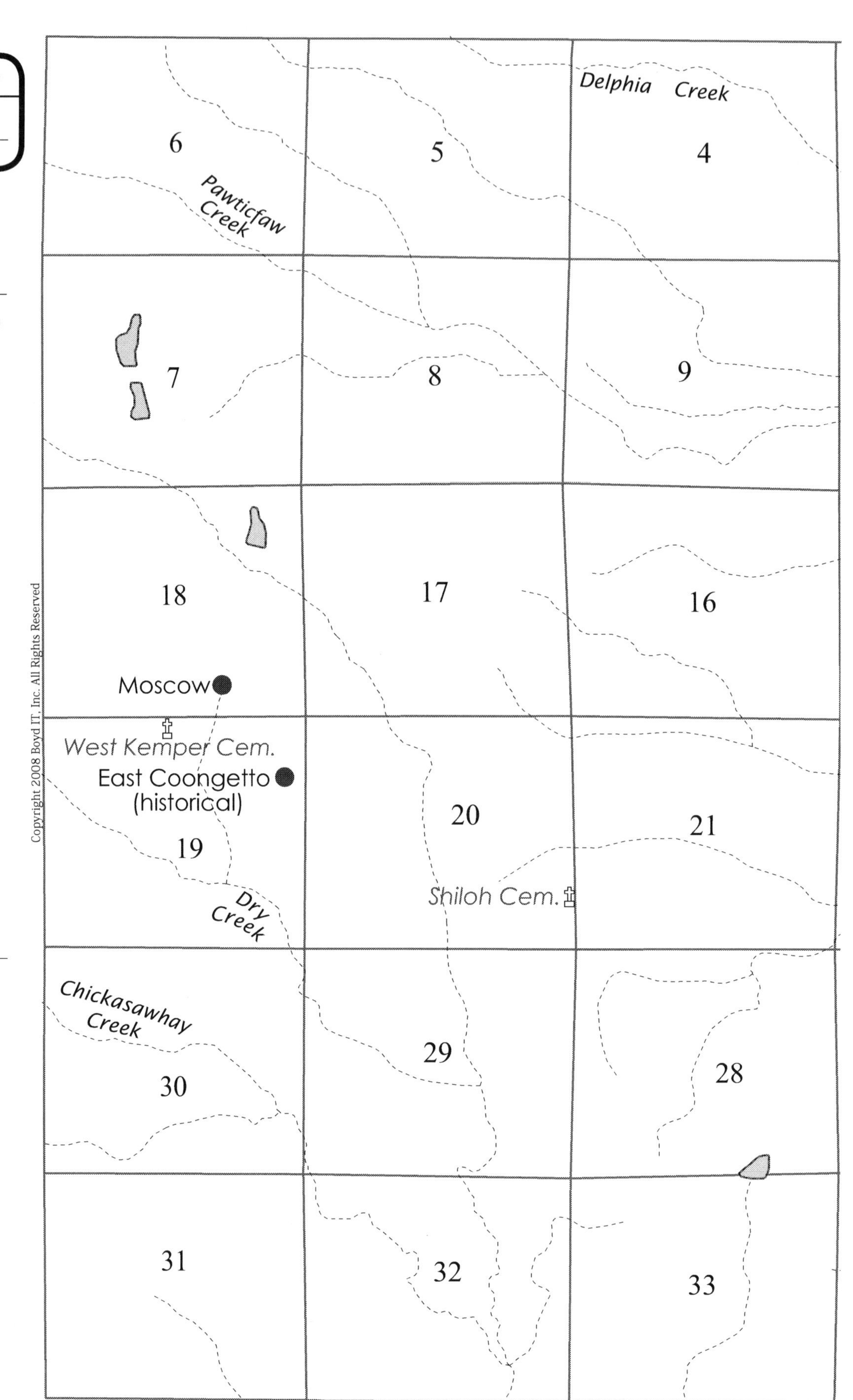

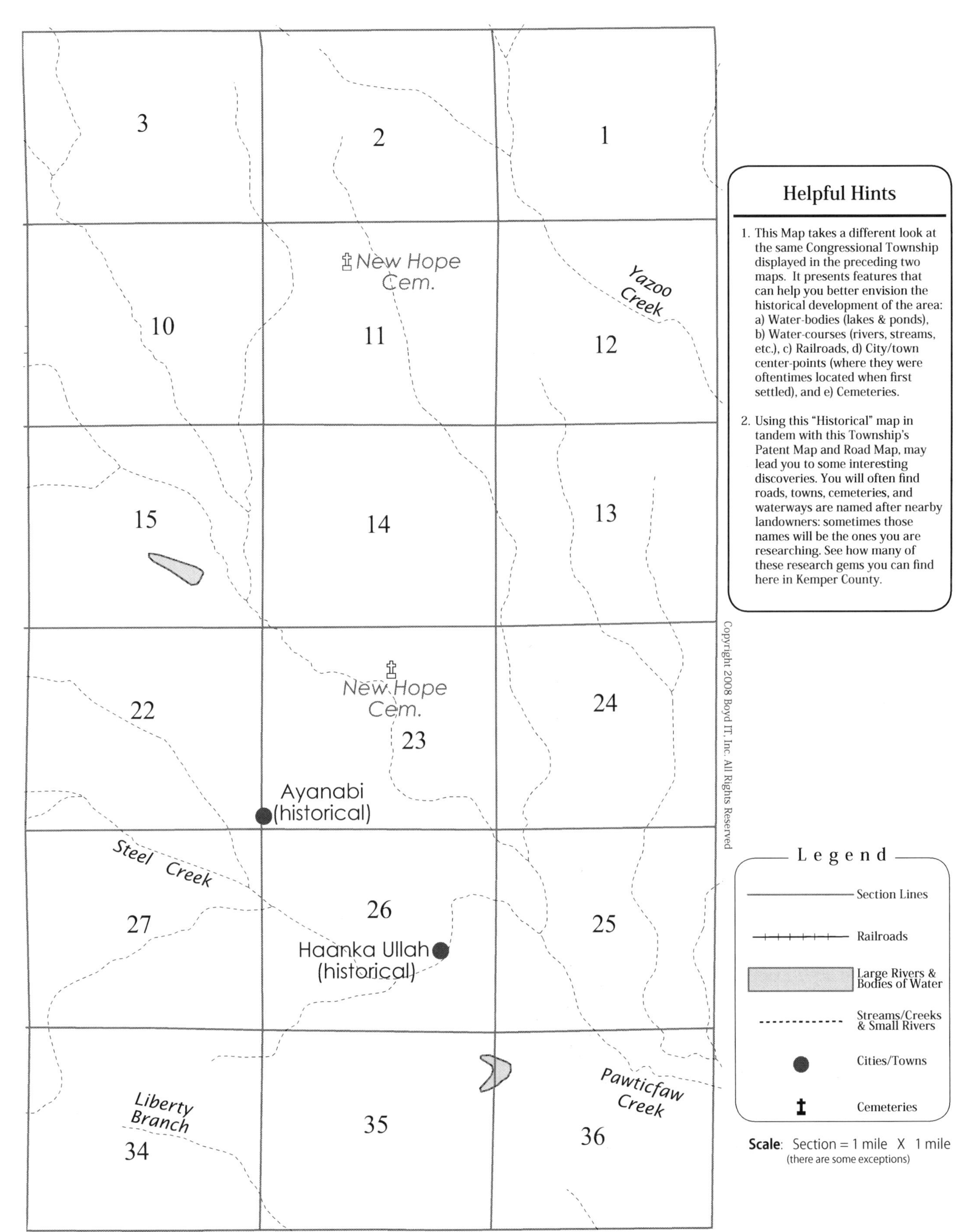

Helpful Hints

1. This Map takes a different look at the same Congressional Township displayed in the preceding two maps. It presents features that can help you better envision the historical development of the area: a) Water-bodies (lakes & ponds), b) Water-courses (rivers, streams, etc.), c) Railroads, d) City/town center-points (where they were oftentimes located when first settled), and e) Cemeteries.
2. Using this "Historical" map in tandem with this Township's Patent Map and Road Map, may lead you to some interesting discoveries. You will often find roads, towns, cemeteries, and waterways are named after nearby landowners: sometimes those names will be the ones you are researching. See how many of these research gems you can find here in Kemper County.

Scale: Section = 1 mile X 1 mile
(there are some exceptions)

Map Group 15: Index to Land Patents

Township 10-North Range 16-East (Choctaw)

After you locate an individual in this Index, take note of the Section and Section Part then proceed to the Land Patent map on the pages immediately following. You should have no difficulty locating the corresponding parcel of land.

The "For More Info" Column will lead you to more information about the underlying Patents. See the *Legend* at right, and the "How to Use this Book" chapter, for more information.

LEGEND

"For More Info . . . " column

A = Authority (Legislative Act, See Appendix "A")
B = Block or Lot (location in Section unknown)
C = Cancelled Patent
F = Fractional Section
G = Group (Multi-Patentee Patent, see Appendix "C")
V = Overlaps another Parcel
R = Re-Issued (Parcel patented more than once)

(A & G items require you to look in the Appendixes referred to above. All other Letter-designations followed by a number require you to locate line-items in this index that possess the ID number found after the letter).

ID	Individual in Patent	Sec.	Sec. Part	Date Issued	Other Counties	For More Info . . .
2977	ADAMS, Archibald C	10	NENW	1848-09-01		A1
2978	" "	10	NWNE	1848-09-01		A1
2979	" "	2	W½SW	1848-09-01		A1
3027	ADAMS, John B	25	SW	1848-09-01		A1
3171	AUTRY, Willis B	35	SE	1848-09-01		A1
3172	BANKS, Willis	20	E½SE	1841-02-27		A1
3173	" "	21	E½SW	1841-02-27		A1
3174	" "	21	W½SW	1841-02-27		A1
3175	" "	29	W½SE	1841-02-27		A1
2982	BEESON, Benjamin	35	NW	1846-12-01		A1
3026	BEESON, Joab	34	SE	1841-02-27		A1
3030	BEESON, John	35	SW	1846-12-01		A1
3070	BEESON, Jonathan	22	W½NE	1841-02-27		A1
3071	" "	26	E½SW	1841-02-27		A1
3072	" "	26	W½SE	1841-02-27		A1
3073	" "	27	E½NE	1841-02-27		A1
3004	BELL, Henry	34	NW	1848-09-01		A1
3005	" "	34	SENE	1856-04-01		A1
3116	BENNET, Thomas	10	SWNE	1841-02-27		A1
3024	BREAZEALE, Jefferson	9	NENE	1841-02-27		A1
2997	BROWN, Ervin	33	SE	1846-09-01		A1
2994	CAMPBELL, Duncan A	10	NWNW	1848-09-01		A1
2973	CLARK, Albert	21	SE	1841-02-27		A1
3036	CLARK, John	22	NWNW	1841-02-27		A1
3038	" "	27	NW	1841-02-27		A1
3037	" "	22	W½SW	1844-12-10		A1
3144	CLARK, Wiett	28	NE	1841-02-27		A1
3093	COLE, Peter H	18	SENE	1841-02-27		A1
3094	" "	8	NE	1841-02-27		A1
3095	" "	8	NESE	1841-02-27		A1
3096	" "	9	NWSE	1841-02-27		A1
3097	" "	9	SW	1841-02-27		A1
3117	COOPWOOD, Thomas	10	E½SE	1841-02-27		A1
3118	" "	21	E½NW	1841-02-27		A1 G114
3119	" "	3	E½NE	1841-02-27		A1 G114
3081	CRAWFORD, Mastin D	10	SENE	1853-03-15		A1
3130	CRAWFORD, Wade H	34	SW	1841-02-27		A1
3063	DAVIS, John R	19	NWSW	1850-12-05		A1
3109	DAWKINS, Samuel F	20	NW	1841-02-27		A1
3016	DEGGES, James B	11	SWSW	1850-12-05		A1
3129	ESKRIDGE, Thomas P	24	W½NE	1841-02-27		A1
2972	FEW, Agnes	18	SESW	1850-12-05		A1
3006	GEORGE, Henry	3	E½SE	1850-12-05		A1
3007	" "	3	E½SW	1850-12-05		A1
3123	GEWIN, Thomas	35	E½NE	1848-09-01		A1
3124	" "	36	E½NW	1848-09-01		A1

ID	Individual in Patent	Sec.	Sec. Part	Date Issued	Other Counties	For More Info . . .
3126	GEWIN, Thomas (Cont'd)	36	W½NE	1848-09-01		A1
3125	" "	36	NWSW	1850-12-05		A1
3145	GOYNES, Wiley W	24	W½SE	1841-02-27		A1
3018	GRACE, James H	24	NENE	1860-05-01		A1
2995	GRADY, Durham	7	NW	1848-09-01		A1
3077	GRAY, Leslie	13	S½SW	1841-02-27		A1
2991	GREENE, Daniel	28	E½SW	1841-02-27		A1
2992	" "	28	W½SW	1841-02-27		A1
3008	GREGORY, Henry	10	NENE	1848-09-01		A1
3010	" "	15	SW	1848-09-01		A1 G199
3009	" "	3	W½SW	1848-09-01		A1
3157	GUNTER, William	19	SENE	1849-12-01		A1
3039	HALL, John	10	E½SW	1841-02-27		A1
3040	" "	10	W½SE	1841-02-27		A1
3041	" "	11	E½SW	1841-02-27		A1
3042	" "	11	W½SE	1841-02-27		A1
3043	" "	12	SW	1841-02-27		A1
3044	" "	15	E½NE	1841-02-27		A1
3045	" "	15	W½NE	1841-02-27		A1
3047	" "	4	SE	1841-02-27		A1
3049	" "	4	W½NW	1845-01-21		A1
3046	" "	19	SWSW	1849-12-01		A1
3048	" "	4	SESW	1849-12-01		A1
3127	HAMPTON, Thomas H	1	W½SW	1860-05-01		A1
3128	" "	8	NESW	1860-05-01		A1
2976	HARRELL, Alfred G	33	W½SW	1841-02-27		A1 G218
2975	" "	31	E½NW	1848-08-14		A1
2983	HARRELL, Bogan C	12	SESE	1861-01-01		A1
3050	HARRELL, John	32	SE	1841-02-27		A1
3028	HARRELL, John B	30	E½SW	1841-02-27		A1 V3021
3029	" "	33	E½SW	1841-02-27		A1 G219
2986	HARRIS, Calvin T	15	NENW	1848-09-01		A1
2987	" "	15	SENW	1850-12-05		A1
3079	HIGGINBOTHAM, Linsey	18	NENE	1841-02-27		A1
3080	" "	18	W½NE	1841-02-27		A1
2985	HOLMES, Burwell	34	NENE	1854-03-15		A1
3131	HUDSON, Walter	2	SWNE	1848-09-01		A1
3023	HULL, James W	6	SENE	1859-10-01		A1
3055	HUNNICUTT, John L	12	NESE	1875-07-01		A2
3065	JEMISON, John S	20	W½SW	1841-02-27		A1
3066	" "	26	E½NW	1841-02-27		A1
3067	" "	26	E½SE	1841-02-27		A1
3068	" "	26	W½NW	1841-02-27		A1
2990	JOHNSON, Charles H	14	SWNE	1841-02-27		A1
2988	" "	13	NENW	1845-01-21		A1
2989	" "	14	NWNE	1845-01-21		A1 R3115
3052	JOHNSON, John	11	E½NE	1841-02-27		A1
3053	" "	12	E½NW	1841-02-27		A1
3054	" "	2	E½SE	1841-02-27		A1
3120	JOHNSON, Thomas G	15	SESE	1841-02-27		A1
3122	" "	20	NE	1841-02-27		A1 G249
3121	" "	22	SWNW	1841-02-27		A1
3132	JOHNSON, Warren B	14	E½NE	1841-02-27		A1
3133	" "	14	SW	1841-02-27		A1
3134	" "	14	SWNW	1841-02-27		A1
3135	" "	14	W½SE	1841-02-27		A1
3136	" "	15	NESE	1841-02-27		A1
3138	" "	15	W½SE	1841-02-27		A1
3140	" "	20	E½SW	1841-02-27		A1 G251
3141	" "	20	W½SE	1841-02-27		A1 G251
3139	" "	23	NWNW	1841-02-27		A1
3137	" "	15	W½NW	1845-01-21		A1
3142	JOHNSTON, Warren B	21	W½NW	1841-02-27		A1 G253
3101	KENNON, Robert L	28	E½SE	1841-02-27		A1
3102	" "	28	W½SE	1841-02-27		A1
2971	KEY, Abel	24	SWSW	1859-10-01		A1
3020	MARR, James	24	E½NW	1841-02-27		A1
3010	MARS, James	15	SW	1848-09-01		A1 G199
3075	MARSHALL, Joseph A	4	NE	1841-02-27		A1
3062	MATHEWS, John	32	E½SW	1841-02-27		A1
3110	MAYNOR, Samuel H	26	W½SW	1841-02-27		A1
3143	MCDONALD, Washington I	12	SENE	1861-07-01		A1
3076	MCKAY, Kennith	27	SW	1846-12-01		A1

ID	Individual in Patent	Sec.	Sec. Part	Date Issued	Other Counties	For More Info . . .
3056	MEEKS, John L	10	NWSW	1846-09-01		A1
3057	" "	10	SWNW	1848-09-01		A1
3058	" "	9	NESE	1849-12-01		A1
3059	" "	9	SENE	1849-12-01		A1
3012	MIDDLEBROOKS, Ibzan	17	SW	1841-02-27		A1
3013	" "	8	SESE	1841-02-27		A1
3014	" "	8	W½SE	1841-02-27		A1
3146	MILLS, Willard C	14	E½NW	1848-09-01		A1
3151	" "	23	NWSW	1848-09-01		A1
3152	" "	24	NWNW	1848-09-01		A1
3149	" "	2	E½SW	1854-03-15		A1
3150	" "	2	W½SE	1854-03-15		A1
3148	" "	18	SWNW	1856-04-01		A1 V3147
3147	" "	18	S½NW	1859-10-01		A1 V3148
3153	" "	6	NENE	1859-10-01		A1
3114	MISSISSIPPI, State Of	12	NENE	1909-05-14		A3
3115	" "	14	NWNE	1909-05-14		A3 R2989
3103	MORROW, Robert	21	NE	1848-09-01		A1
3104	" "	22	NENE	1848-09-01		A1
3105	" "	22	SESE	1848-09-01		A1
3106	" "	9	SESE	1848-09-01		A1
3107	" "	9	SWNE	1848-09-01		A1
3051	MULDROW, John J	33	NE	1847-04-01		A1
2998	NASH, Ezekiel	27	W½NE	1841-02-27		A1 G301
2999	" "	32	W½SW	1841-02-27		A1 G301
2998	NASH, Orsamus L	27	W½NE	1841-02-27		A1 G301
2999	" "	32	W½SW	1841-02-27		A1 G301
2974	NICHOLSON, Alexander G	28	NW	1848-09-01		A1
3002	NORDEN, Hardy	11	NESE	1841-02-27		A1
3108	OWENS, Robert	19	NENE	1849-12-01		A1
3170	PARKER, William	24	SENE	1859-10-01		A1
3021	POLLOCK, James	30	SW	1846-09-01		A1 V3028
3154	POOL, Willey	35	W½NE	1848-09-01		A1
3118	RICHEY, James	21	E½NW	1841-02-27		A1 G114
3119	" "	3	E½NE	1841-02-27		A1 G114
2984	RIGBY, Bryant	29	E½SE	1841-02-27		A1 G316
2981	ROACH, Bedford C	24	NWSW	1848-09-01		A1
3064	ROBERTS, John	29	NW	1848-09-01		A1
3019	ROGERS, James M	18	NESW	1849-12-01		A1
3060	ROSS, John M	36	SWSW	1896-12-14		A2
3061	" "	36	W½NW	1896-12-14		A2
3082	ROSS, Michael	24	E½SE	1841-02-27		A1
3084	" "	33	E½NW	1841-02-27		A1
3029	" "	33	E½SW	1841-02-27		A1 G219
3085	" "	33	W½NW	1841-02-27		A1
2976	" "	33	W½SW	1841-02-27		A1 G218
3083	" "	31	SE	1846-09-01		A1
3086	RUSH, Miles J	6	NWNE	1859-10-01		A1
3112	RUSH, Simeon	10	SWSW	1859-10-01		A1
3156	RUSH, William C	27	SE	1846-12-01		A1
3155	" "	22	E½SW	1850-12-02		A1
3158	RUSH, William H	6	W½SE	1856-04-01		A1
2993	RUSSELL, David M	36	NENE	1859-10-01		A1
3078	SADLER, Levi	31	NE	1846-09-01		A1
3113	SADLER, Smith	32	NW	1841-02-27		A1
2980	SHARP, Basil	25	NE	1850-12-02		A1
2996	SHUMATE, Eli T	36	E½SW	1850-12-05		A1
3074	SHUMATE, Jonathan G	36	SE	1848-12-01		A1
3022	SIMS, James	24	SWNW	1848-09-01		A1
3025	SINCLAIR, Jennie	6	NESE	1891-06-30		A2
3000	SNEAD, Garland	3	NW	1841-02-27		A1
3001	" "	3	W½SE	1841-02-27		A1
3098	SNEAD, Peter	5	NENW	1841-02-27		A1
3099	" "	5	NWNE	1841-02-27		A1
3011	STARLING, Herbert	6	SWNE	1854-03-15		A1
3118	STEWART, Hugh C	21	E½NW	1841-02-27		A1 G114
3119	" "	3	E½NE	1841-02-27		A1 G114
3159	STUART, William H	4	NESW	1849-12-01		A1
3160	" "	4	W½SW	1849-12-01		A1
3031	THOMAS, John C	2	NW	1841-02-27		A1
3015	TINDALL, James A	23	SENE	1841-02-27		A1
3003	TUBBS, Harriet	30	W½SE	1848-09-01		A1
3111	TURNER, Samuel S	36	SENE	1850-12-05		A1

ID	Individual in Patent	Sec.	Sec. Part	Date Issued	Other Counties	For More Info . . .
3142	VAUGHAN, Malinda	21	W½NW	1841-02-27		A1 G253
2969	WARREN, Aaron	23	SWNW	1841-02-27		A1
2970	" "	34	W½NE	1846-12-01		A1
3017	WARREN, James C	7	SW	1848-09-01		A1
3032	WARREN, John C	32	E½NE	1841-02-27		A1
3033	" "	32	W½NE	1841-02-27		A1
3034	" "	9	NENW	1841-02-27		A1
3035	" "	9	NWNE	1841-02-27		A1
3087	WARREN, Moses	17	NW	1846-09-01		A1
3088	" "	17	NWNE	1849-12-01		A1
3091	" "	8	SESW	1849-12-01		A1
3092	" "	8	SWSW	1849-12-01		A1
3089	" "	18	NENW	1859-10-01		A1
3090	" "	8	NWSW	1860-05-01		A1
3100	WARREN, Reuben	25	NW	1848-09-01		A1
3161	WARREN, William H	22	E½NW	1841-02-27		A1
3162	" "	22	NESE	1841-02-27		A1
3163	" "	22	SENE	1841-02-27		A1
3164	" "	22	W½SE	1841-02-27		A1
3165	" "	23	E½NW	1841-02-27		A1
3166	" "	23	W½NE	1841-02-27		A1
3167	" "	26	E½NE	1841-02-27		A1
3168	" "	26	W½NE	1841-02-27		A1
2984	" "	29	E½SE	1841-02-27		A1 G316
3169	" "	29	NE	1841-02-27		A1
3140	WELSH, James	20	E½SW	1841-02-27		A1 G251
3141	" "	20	W½SE	1841-02-27		A1 G251
3122	WHITE, Dorset	20	NE	1841-02-27		A1 G249
3069	WHITE, John	3	W½NE	1841-02-27		A1

Patent Map

T10-N R16-E
Choctaw Meridian

Map Group 15

Township Statistics

Parcels Mapped	:	207
Number of Patents	:	186
Number of Individuals	:	113
Patentees Identified	:	112
Number of Surnames	:	86
Multi-Patentee Parcels	:	12
Oldest Patent Date	:	2/27/1841
Most Recent Patent	:	5/14/1909
Block/Lot Parcels	:	0
Parcels Re - Issued	:	1
Parcels that Overlap	:	4
Cities and Towns	:	3
Cemeteries	:	3

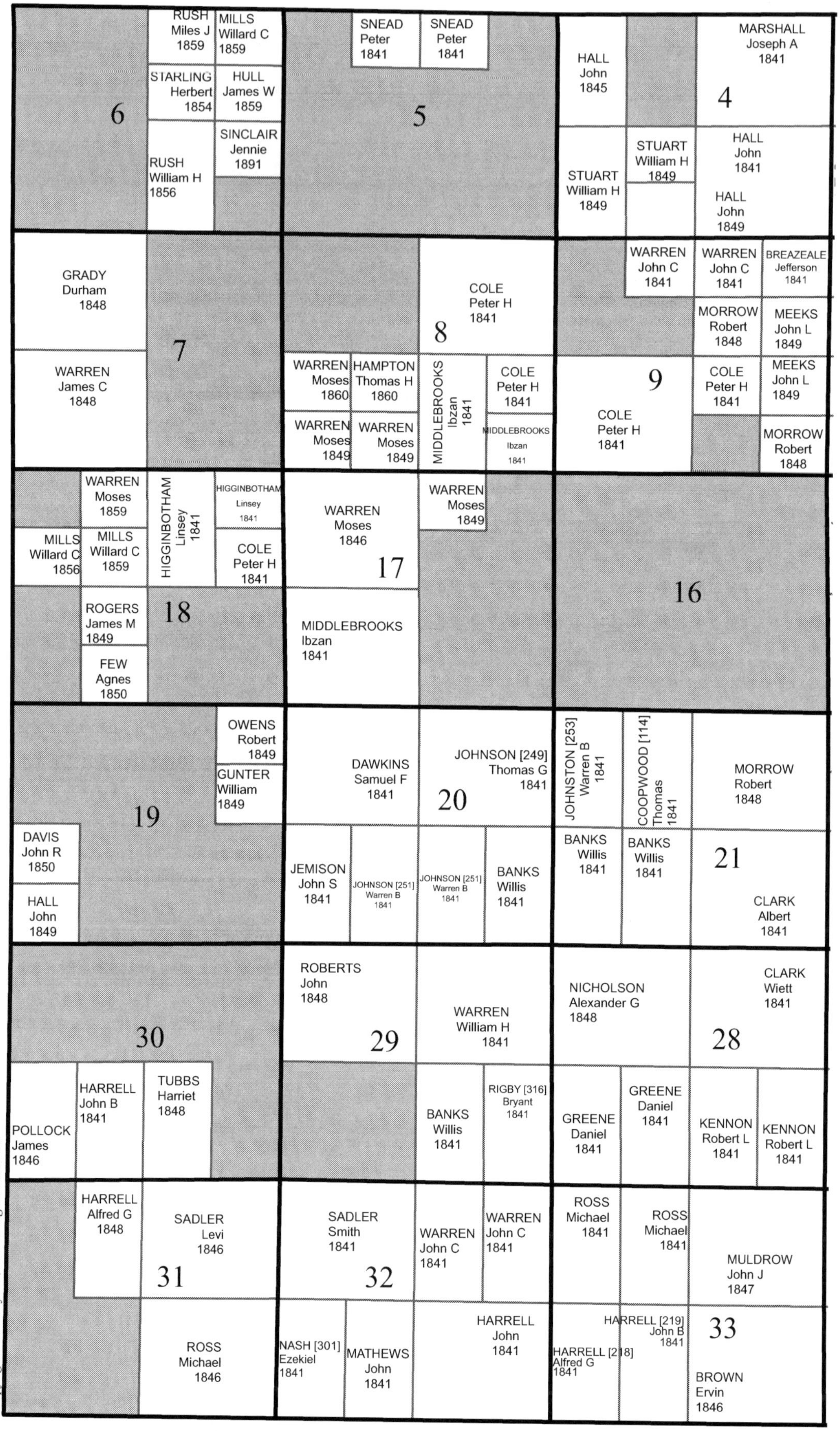

6
RUSH Miles J 1859
MILLS Willard C 1859
STARLING Herbert 1854
HULL James W 1859
SINCLAIR Jennie 1891
RUSH William H 1856

5
SNEAD Peter 1841
SNEAD Peter 1841

4
HALL John 1845
MARSHALL Joseph A 1841
STUART William H 1849
STUART William H 1849
HALL John 1841
HALL John 1849

7
GRADY Durham 1848
WARREN James C 1848

8
COLE Peter H 1841
WARREN Moses 1860
HAMPTON Thomas H 1860
MIDDLEBROOKS Ibzan 1841
COLE Peter H 1841
WARREN Moses 1849
WARREN Moses 1849
MIDDLEBROOKS Ibzan 1841

9
WARREN John C 1841
WARREN John C 1841
BREAZEALE Jefferson 1841
MORROW Robert 1848
MEEKS John L 1849
COLE Peter H 1841
MEEKS John L 1849
COLE Peter H 1841
MORROW Robert 1848

18
WARREN Moses 1859
HIGGINBOTHAM Linsey 1841
HIGGINBOTHAM Linsey 1841
MILLS Willard C 1856
MILLS Willard C 1859
COLE Peter H 1841
ROGERS James M 1849
FEW Agnes 1850

17
WARREN Moses 1846
WARREN Moses 1849
MIDDLEBROOKS Ibzan 1841

16

19
OWENS Robert 1849
GUNTER William 1849
DAVIS John R 1850
HALL John 1849

20
DAWKINS Samuel F 1841
JOHNSON [249] Thomas G 1841
JEMISON John S 1841
JOHNSON [251] Warren B 1841
JOHNSON [251] Warren B 1841
BANKS Willis 1841

21
JOHNSTON [253] Warren B 1841
COOPWOOD [114] Thomas 1841
MORROW Robert 1848
BANKS Willis 1841
BANKS Willis 1841
CLARK Albert 1841

30
HARRELL John B 1841
TUBBS Harriet 1848
POLLOCK James 1846

29
ROBERTS John 1848
WARREN William H 1841
BANKS Willis 1841
RIGBY [316] Bryant 1841

28
NICHOLSON Alexander G 1848
CLARK Wiett 1841
GREENE Daniel 1841
GREENE Daniel 1841
KENNON Robert L 1841
KENNON Robert L 1841

31
HARRELL Alfred G 1848
SADLER Levi 1846
ROSS Michael 1846

32
SADLER Smith 1841
WARREN John C 1841
WARREN John C 1841
NASH [301] Ezekiel 1841
MATHEWS John 1841
HARRELL John 1841

33
ROSS Michael 1841
ROSS Michael 1841
MULDROW John J 1847
HARRELL [219] John B 1841
HARRELL [218] Alfred G 1841
BROWN Ervin 1846

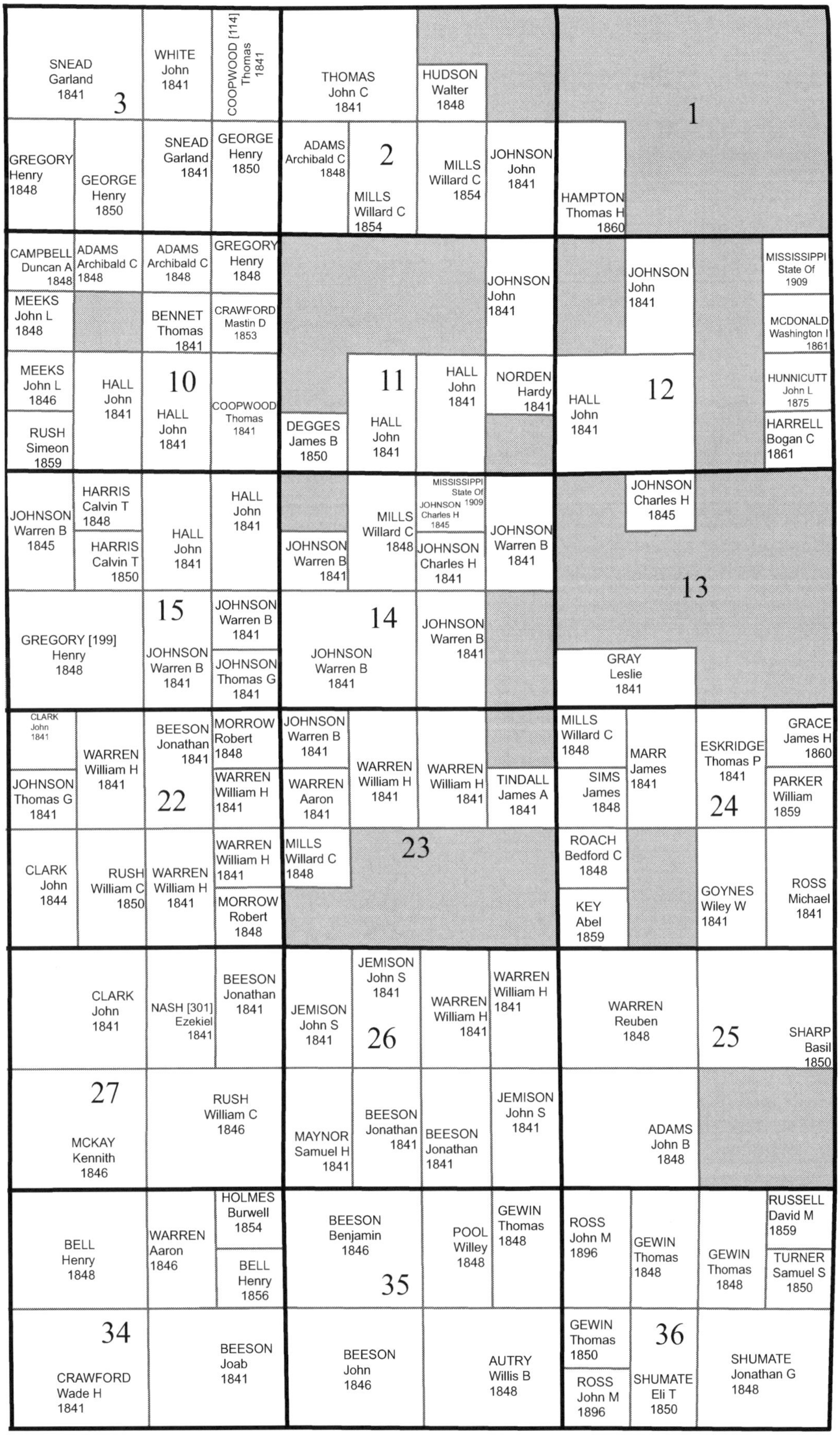

Helpful Hints

1. This Map's INDEX can be found on the preceding pages.
2. Refer to Map "C" to see where this Township lies within Kemper County, Mississippi.
3. Numbers within square brackets [ ] denote a multi-patentee land parcel (multi-owner). Refer to Appendix "C" for a full list of members in this group.
4. Areas that look to be crowded with Patentees usually indicate multiple sales of the same parcel (Re-issues) or Overlapping parcels. See this Township's Index for an explanation of these and other circumstances that might explain "odd" groupings of Patentees on this map.

Legend

- Patent Boundary
- Section Boundary
- No Patents Found (or Outside County)
- 1., 2., 3., ... Lot Numbers (when beside a name)
- [ ] Group Number (see Appendix "C")

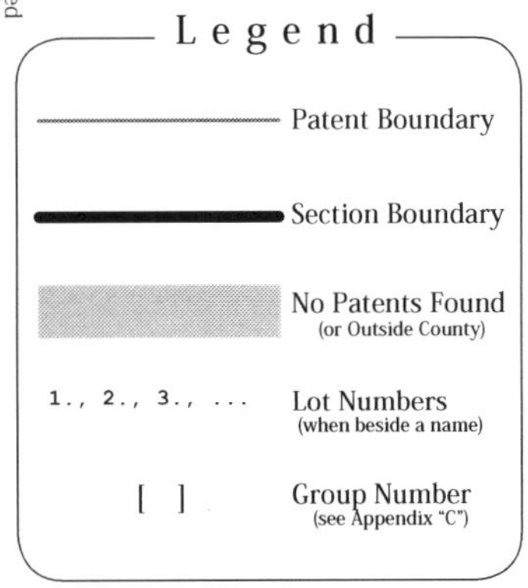

Scale: Section = 1 mile X 1 mile (generally, with some exceptions)

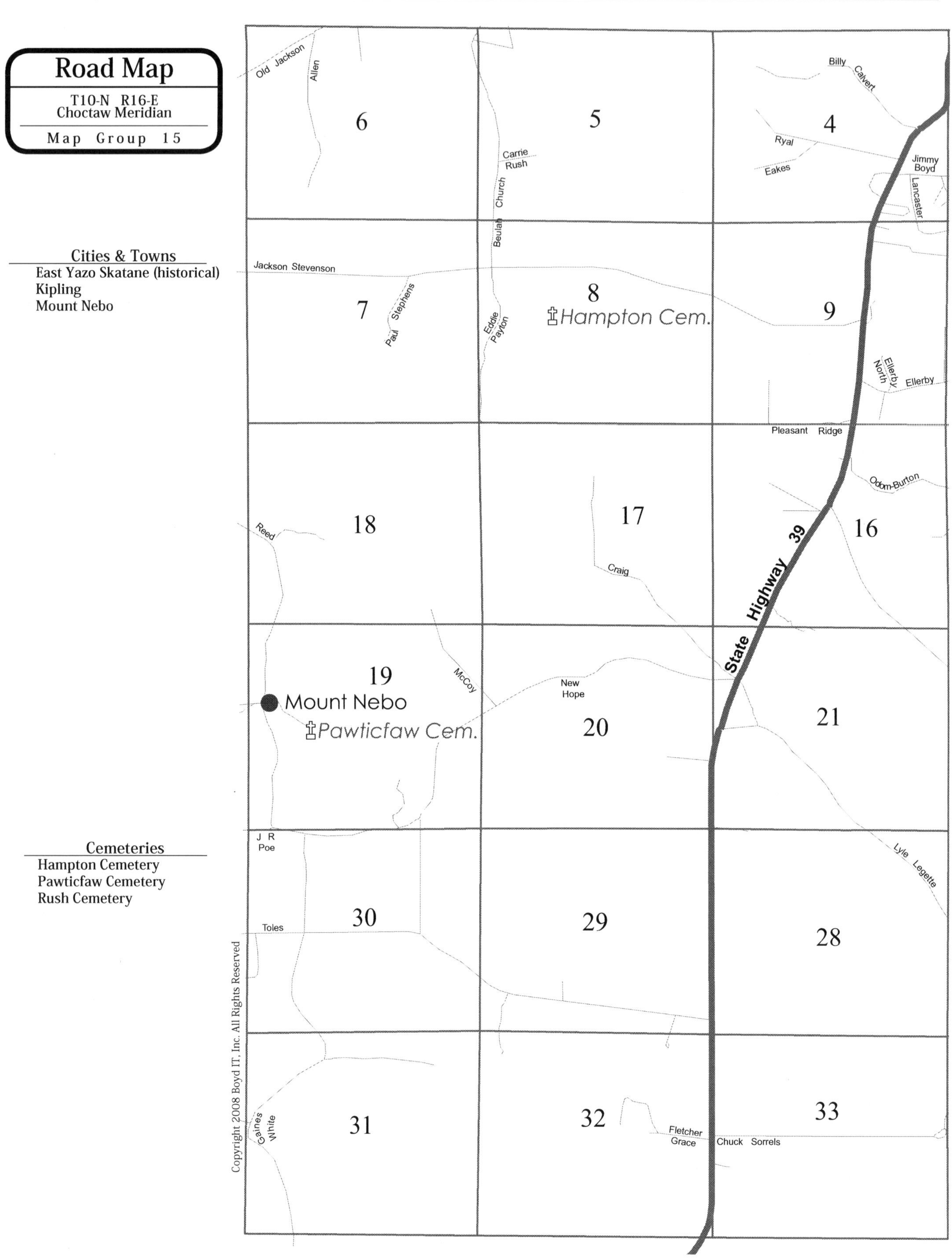
Road Map
T10-N R16-E
Choctaw Meridian
Map Group 15
Cities & Towns
East Yazo Skatane (historical)
Kipling
Mount Nebo
Cemeteries
Hampton Cemetery
Pawticfaw Cemetery
Rush Cemetery
6
5
4
7
8
9
18
17
16
19
20
21
30
29
28
31
32
33
Old Jackson
Allen
Carrie Rush
Beulah Church
Billy Calvert
Ryal
Eakes
Jimmy Boyd
Lancaster
Jackson Stevenson
Paul Stephens
Eddie Payton
Hampton Cem.
Ellerby North
Ellerby
Pleasant Ridge
Odom-Burton
Reed
Craig
State Highway 39
McCoy
New Hope
Mount Nebo
Pawticfaw Cem.
J R Poe
Toles
Lyle Legette
Gaines White
Fletcher Grace
Chuck Sorrels
Copyright 2008 Boyd IT, Inc. All Rights Reserved

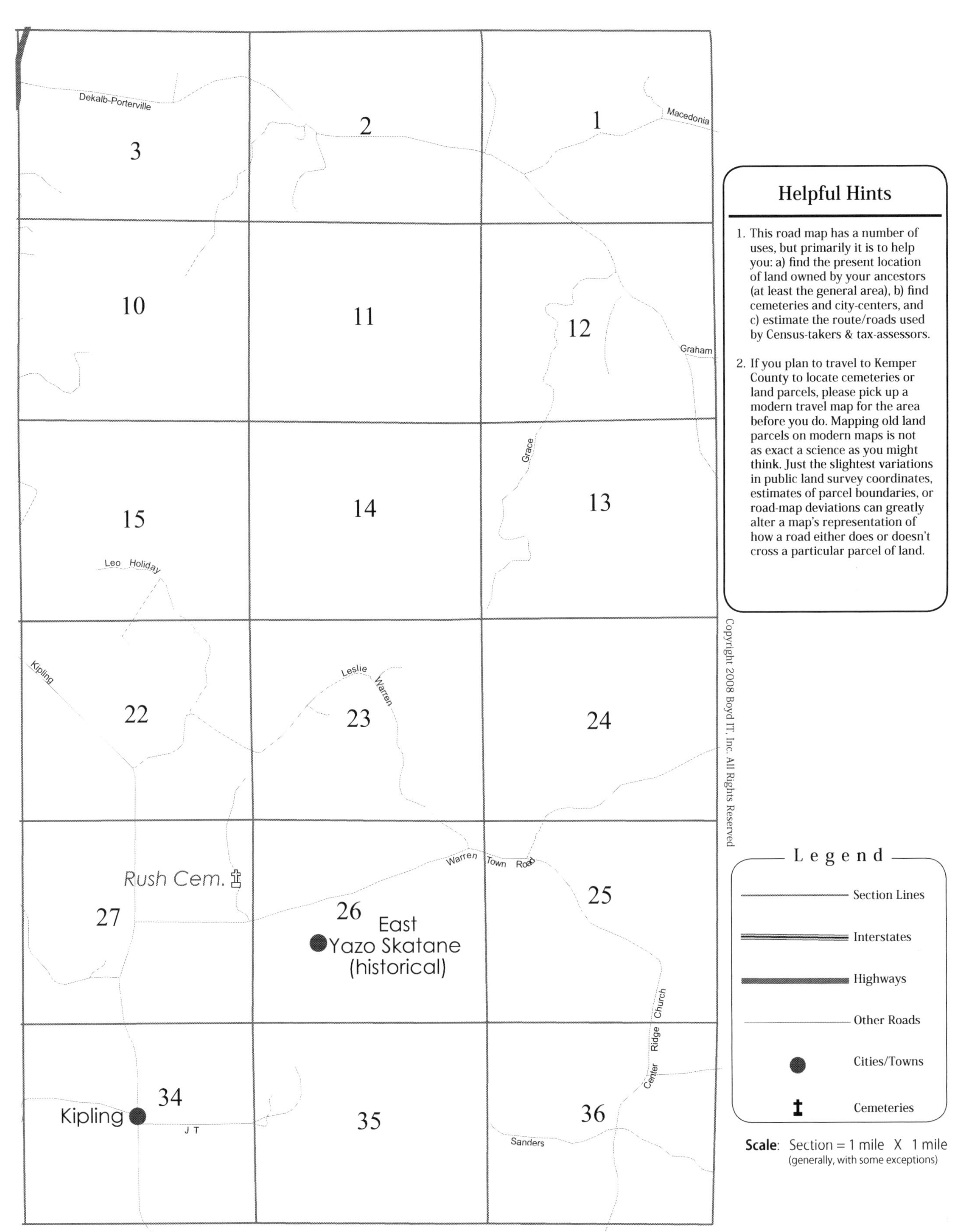
Dekalb-Porterville
3
2
1
Macedonia
10
11
12
Graham
Grace
15
14
13
Leo Holiday
Kipling
Leslie
Warren
22
23
24
Rush Cem.
27
Warren Town Road
26
East
Yazo Skatane
(historical)
25
Church
Ridge
Center
34
Kipling
J T
35
36
Sanders
Helpful Hints
1. This road map has a number of uses, but primarily it is to help you: a) find the present location of land owned by your ancestors (at least the general area), b) find cemeteries and city-centers, and c) estimate the route/roads used by Census-takers & tax-assessors.
2. If you plan to travel to Kemper County to locate cemeteries or land parcels, please pick up a modern travel map for the area before you do. Mapping old land parcels on modern maps is not as exact a science as you might think. Just the slightest variations in public land survey coordinates, estimates of parcel boundaries, or road-map deviations can greatly alter a map's representation of how a road either does or doesn't cross a particular parcel of land.
Copyright 2008 Boyd IT, Inc. All Rights Reserved
Legend
Section Lines
Interstates
Highways
Other Roads
Cities/Towns
Cemeteries
Scale: Section = 1 mile X 1 mile
(generally, with some exceptions)

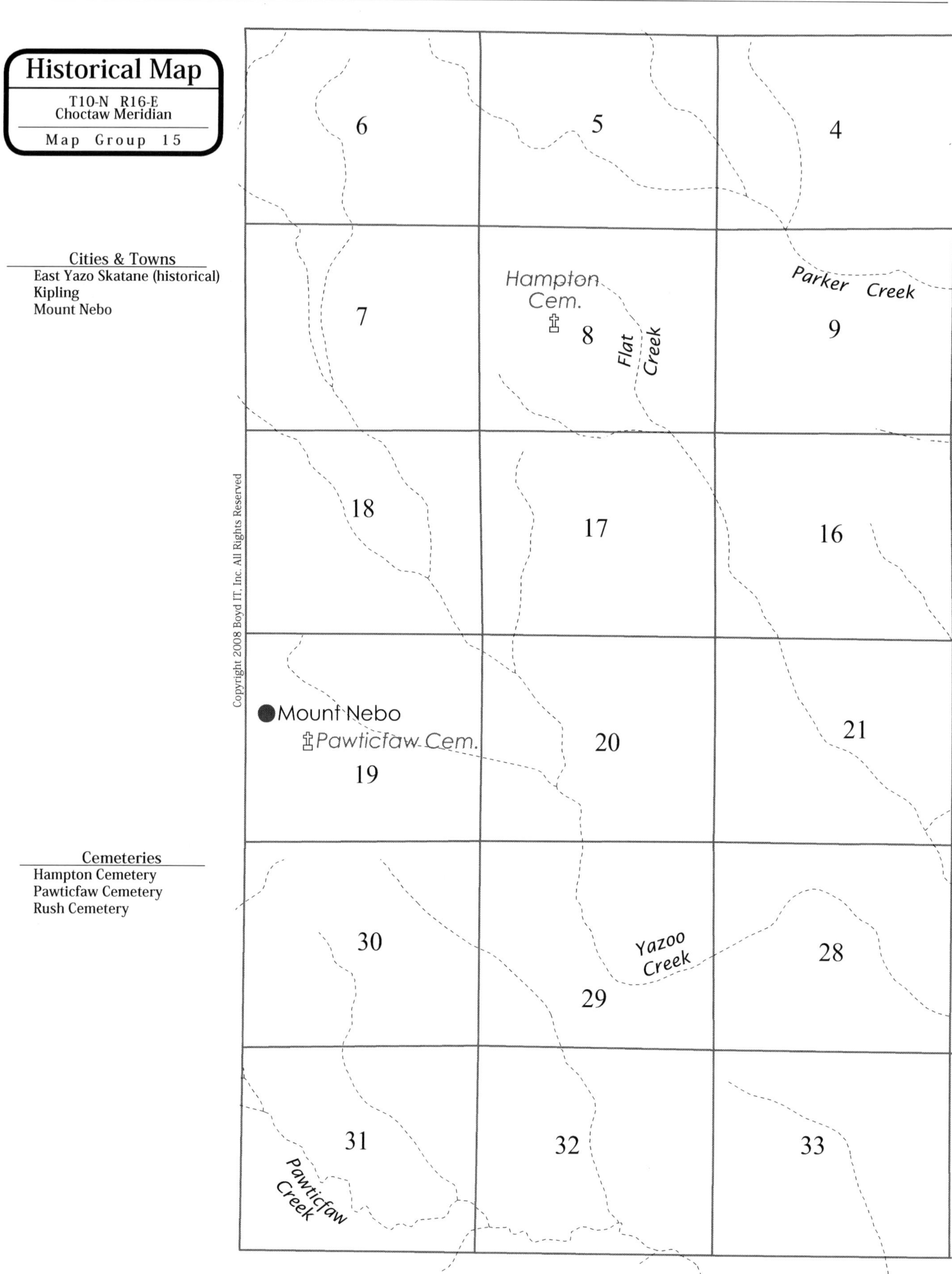
Historical Map
T10-N R16-E
Choctaw Meridian
Map Group 15
Cities & Towns
East Yazo Skatane (historical)
Kipling
Mount Nebo
Cemeteries
Hampton Cemetery
Pawticfaw Cemetery
Rush Cemetery
6
5
4
7
Hampton Cem.
8
Flat Creek
Parker Creek
9
18
17
16
Mount Nebo
Pawticfaw Cem.
19
20
21
30
Yazoo Creek
29
28
31
Pawticfaw Creek
32
33
Copyright 2008 Boyd IT, Inc. All Rights Reserved

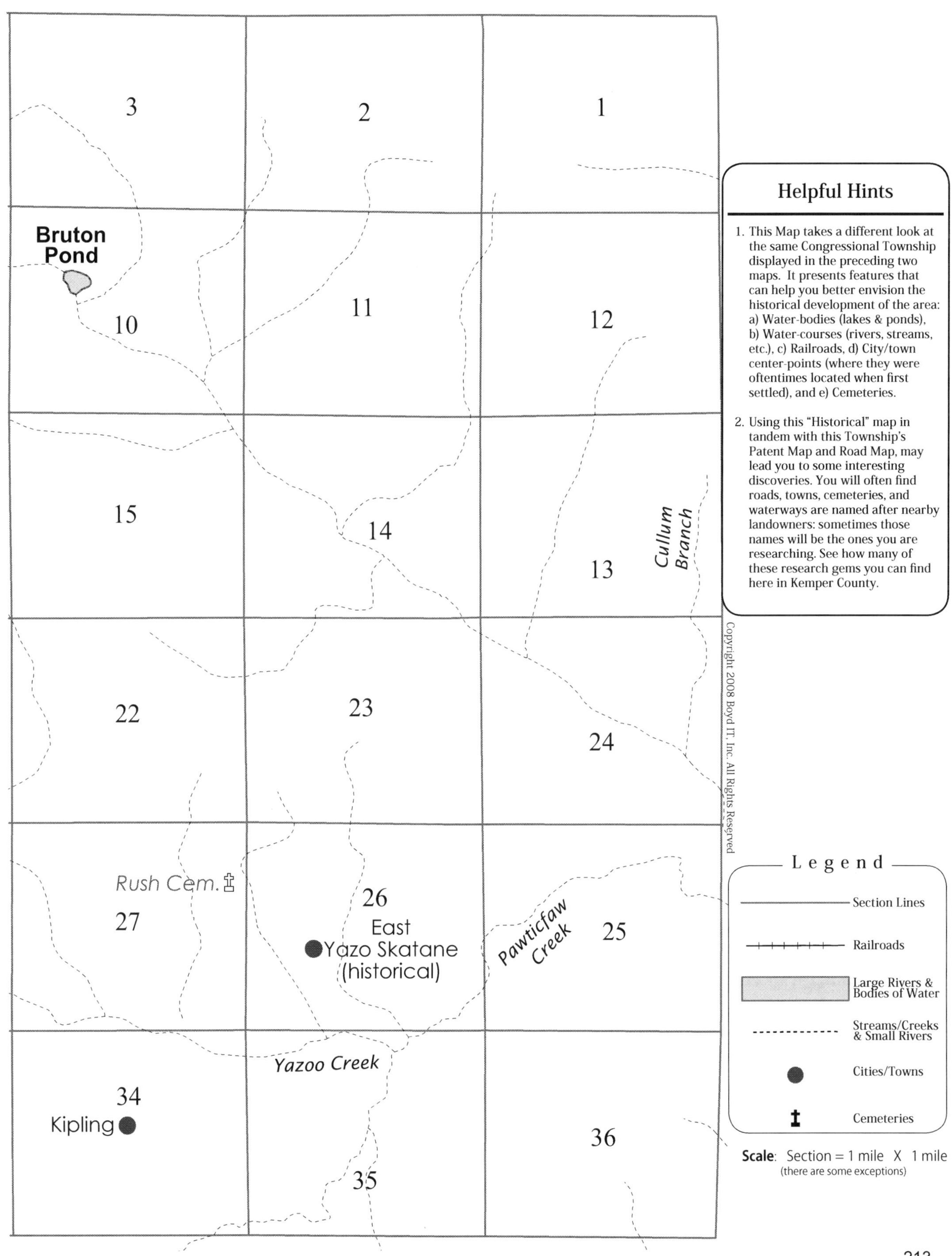

3
2
1
Bruton Pond
10
11
12
15
14
13
Cullum Branch
22
23
24
Rush Cem.
27
26
East Yazo Skatane (historical)
Pawticfaw Creek
25
Yazoo Creek
34
Kipling
35
36
Helpful Hints
1. This Map takes a different look at the same Congressional Township displayed in the preceding two maps. It presents features that can help you better envision the historical development of the area: a) Water-bodies (lakes & ponds), b) Water-courses (rivers, streams, etc.), c) Railroads, d) City/town center-points (where they were oftentimes located when first settled), and e) Cemeteries.
2. Using this "Historical" map in tandem with this Township's Patent Map and Road Map, may lead you to some interesting discoveries. You will often find roads, towns, cemeteries, and waterways are named after nearby landowners: sometimes those names will be the ones you are researching. See how many of these research gems you can find here in Kemper County.
Copyright 2008 Boyd IT, Inc. All Rights Reserved
Legend
Section Lines
Railroads
Large Rivers & Bodies of Water
Streams/Creeks & Small Rivers
Cities/Towns
Cemeteries
Scale: Section = 1 mile X 1 mile
(there are some exceptions)

Map Group 16: Index to Land Patents

Township 10-North Range 17-East (Choctaw)

After you locate an individual in this Index, take note of the Section and Section Part then proceed to the Land Patent map on the pages immediately following. You should have no difficulty locating the corresponding parcel of land.

The "For More Info" Column will lead you to more information about the underlying Patents. See the *Legend* at right, and the "How to Use this Book" chapter, for more information.

LEGEND

"For More Info . . . " column

A = Authority (Legislative Act, See Appendix "A")
B = Block or Lot (location in Section unknown)
C = Cancelled Patent
F = Fractional Section
G = Group (Multi-Patentee Patent, see Appendix "C")
V = Overlaps another Parcel
R = Re-Issued (Parcel patented more than once)

(A & G items require you to look in the Appendixes referred to above. All other Letter-designations followed by a number require you to locate line-items in this index that possess the ID number found after the letter).

ID	Individual in Patent	Sec.	Sec. Part	Date Issued	Other Counties	For More Info . . .
3268	AVERY, Joseph C	35	NWSE	1854-03-15		A1
3293	BETSILL, Robert G	17	NENE	1883-09-15		A2
3248	BOYD, James	5	SESW	1841-02-27		A1
3331	BOYD, William	5	SWSE	1841-02-27		A1
3338	BROWNLEE, William R	27	SW	1912-02-05		A1 G57
3188	BURNETT, Boling C	2	E½SW	1841-02-27		A1
3189	" "	2	W½SE	1841-02-27		A1
3190	" "	28	E½SW	1841-02-27		A1 G65
3210	CARLISLE, Edward K	30	E½NE	1841-02-27		A1 G81
3211	" "	30	E½SW	1841-02-27		A1 G81
3212	" "	30	W½SE	1841-02-27		A1 G81
3213	" "	8	E½NE	1841-02-27		A1 G80
3214	" "	9	W½NW	1841-02-27		A1 G80
3209	CHERRY, Edward	5	E½SE	1875-07-01		A2
3240	CHERRY, Glisson	3	E½SW	1846-12-01		A1
3241	" "	3	W½SE	1846-12-01		A1
3177	CLEMENT, Abraham	9	SWNE	1841-02-27		A1
3318	COOPWOOD, Thomas	32	E½SE	1846-12-01		A1 G116
3319	" "	32	E½SW	1846-12-01		A1 G116
3320	" "	32	W½SE	1846-12-01		A1 G116
3321	" "	32	W½SW	1846-12-01		A1 G116
3207	COWAN, David S	1	NW	1841-02-27		A1
3208	" "	2	NE	1841-02-27		A1
3286	CULLUM, Peter P	31	NESE	1849-12-01		A1
3287	" "	31	NESW	1849-12-01		A1
3288	" "	31	SENW	1850-12-05		A1
3289	" "	31	SESW	1850-12-05		A1
3249	CUNNINGHAM, James M	33	SESE	1854-03-15		A1
3250	" "	35	SWNE	1859-10-01		A1
3273	DAVIDSON, Joshua	10	E½NE	1841-02-27		A1
3274	" "	10	E½SE	1841-02-27		A1
3196	DEAN, Clem	30	E½SE	1906-06-21		A2
3262	EAKIN, John	3	W½SW	1890-08-16		A2
3258	EDMONDSON, James W	6	SESE	1841-02-27		A1
3322	ESKRIDGE, Thomas P	8	E½SW	1841-02-27		A1
3314	EVANS, Solomon	10	W½SW	1841-02-27		A1
3315	" "	9	SE	1841-02-27		A1
3332	EVANS, William	17	W½NE	1841-02-27		A1
3213	" "	8	E½NE	1841-02-27		A1 G80
3333	" "	8	NENW	1841-02-27		A1
3334	" "	8	SENW	1841-02-27		A1
3335	" "	8	SWNE	1841-02-27		A1
3214	" "	9	W½NW	1841-02-27		A1 G80
3247	EVERETT, Horace	11	W½	1854-03-15		A1
3244	FOOTE, Hezekiah W	8	SE	1841-02-27		A1 G156
3245	" "	9	E½NW	1841-02-27		A1 G156

ID	Individual in Patent	Sec.	Sec. Part	Date Issued	Other Counties	For More Info . . .
3246	FOOTE, Hezekiah W (Cont'd)	9	SW	1841-02-27		A1 G156
3264	GENTRY, John M	28	NE	1841-02-27		A1 G161
3235	GRAHAM, George W	8	W½NW	1893-04-12		A2
3276	GRAY, Leslie	17	E½NW	1841-02-27		A1
3277	" "	19	SW	1841-02-27		A1
3278	" "	30	E½NW	1841-02-27		A1
3291	GRAY, Pulaski	6	S½SW	1859-10-01		A1
3290	" "	6	N½SW	1860-10-01		A1
3200	GREENE, Daniel	26	E½SW	1841-02-27		A1 G198
3201	" "	26	W½SW	1841-02-27		A1 G198
3202	" "	28	W½NW	1841-02-27		A1 G198
3203	" "	34	E½SE	1841-02-27		A1 G198
3204	" "	34	W½SE	1841-02-27		A1 G198
3198	" "	11	W½NE	1841-12-15		A1 G179
3199	" "	11	W½SE	1841-12-15		A1 G179
3205	" "	35	E½SW	1844-09-10		A1 G198
3271	GRIGSBY, Joseph	23	W½SW	1841-02-27		A1 G211
3272	" "	34	E½SW	1841-02-27		A1 G213
3269	" "	1	SE	1896-08-15		A1
3270	" "	23	N½	1896-08-15		A1
3236	HARPER, George W	19	E½SE	1841-02-27		A1
3237	" "	19	W½NE	1841-02-27		A1
3238	" "	19	W½SE	1841-02-27		A1
3239	" "	30	W½NW	1841-02-27		A1
3187	HARRELL, Bogan C	18	SWNW	1861-01-01		A1
3271	HARRIS, Robert E	23	W½SW	1841-02-27		A1 G211
3219	HAWES, Ezekiel	31	W½SE	1841-02-27		A1
3316	HAWES, Stephen V	32	E½NW	1846-09-01		A1
3301	HUBBARD, Samuel	1	W½SW	1841-12-15		A1 G234
3198	" "	11	W½NE	1841-12-15		A1 G179
3199	" "	11	W½SE	1841-12-15		A1 G179
3302	" "	2	E½NW	1841-12-15		A1 G234
3303	" "	2	E½SE	1841-12-15		A1 G234
3304	" "	27	E½NE	1841-12-15		A1 G234
3305	" "	3	E½SE	1841-12-15		A1 G234
3306	" "	4	NE	1846-12-01		A1 G234 R3294
3327	HUDSON, Walter	18	E½NE	1841-02-27		A1
3328	" "	18	NWNE	1841-02-27		A1
3279	HUNNICUTT, Madison	12	SW	1848-09-01		A1
3244	HUNTINGTON, Elisha	8	SE	1841-02-27		A1 G156
3245	" "	9	E½NW	1841-02-27		A1 G156
3246	" "	9	SW	1841-02-27		A1 G156
3336	HUSBANDS, William	27	SE	1841-02-27		A1
3210	JEMISON, John S	30	E½NE	1841-02-27		A1 G81
3211	" "	30	E½SW	1841-02-27		A1 G81
3212	" "	30	W½SE	1841-02-27		A1 G81
3182	JONES, Alfred	35	NW	1841-02-27		A1 G254
3191	JONES, Britain	28	E½NW	1841-02-27		A1
3192	" "	34	NE	1841-02-27		A1 G255
3193	JONES, Burnell	26	E½NW	1841-02-27		A1
3194	" "	26	W½NW	1841-02-27		A1
3220	JONES, Ezekiel	20	E½SW	1841-02-27		A1
3242	JONES, H C	6	NWNW	1860-05-01		A1
3280	LEACH, Mango P	18	NWSE	1859-10-01		A1
3298	LEWIS, Rufus G	20	W½SE	1841-02-27		A1 G268
3295	" "	27	NW	1841-02-27		A1 G266
3296	" "	30	W½SW	1841-02-27		A1 G266
3301	" "	1	W½SW	1841-12-15		A1 G234
3198	" "	11	W½NE	1841-12-15		A1 G179
3199	" "	11	W½SE	1841-12-15		A1 G179
3302	" "	2	E½NW	1841-12-15		A1 G234
3303	" "	2	E½SE	1841-12-15		A1 G234
3304	" "	27	E½NE	1841-12-15		A1 G234
3305	" "	3	E½SE	1841-12-15		A1 G234
3294	" "	4	NE	1843-02-01		A1 C R3306
3297	" "	22	E½NE	1844-09-10		A1 G267
3306	" "	4	NE	1846-12-01		A1 G234 R3294
3263	LITTLE, John	6	S½NW	1875-07-01		A2
3232	LONG, Gabriel	18	NWNW	1841-02-27		A1
3284	MATHENY, Obadiah	34	SWSW	1850-12-05		A1
3285	MATHENY, Obediah	23	SESE	1860-05-01		A1
3178	MATTHEWS, Adison	22	SE	1841-02-27		A1
3179	" "	22	W½NE	1841-02-27		A1

ID	Individual in Patent	Sec.	Sec. Part	Date Issued	Other Counties	For More Info . . .
3251	MCCOY, James N	32	W½NW	1859-10-01		A1
3180	MCDADE, Albert	6	W½SE	1904-09-28		A2
3183	MCDADE, Andrew A	9	SENE	1898-09-28		A2
3184	MCDADE, Averilla	17	SENE	1895-08-30		A2
3259	MCDADE, Jane	6	NESE	1884-12-30		A2
3313	MCDONALD, Sarah J	5	S½NE	1895-06-28		A2
3326	MCLENDON, Wade	33	NESE	1895-11-05		A2
3206	MCMILLAN, Daniel	30	W½NE	1841-02-27		A1
3329	MILLS, Willard C	33	SWSE	1854-03-15		A1
3330	" "	35	SWSE	1854-03-15		A1
3324	MITCHEL, Tilman	10	W½NE	1841-02-27		A1
3325	" "	3	W½NE	1841-02-27		A1
3323	MITCHELL, Tilghman	3	E½NE	1841-02-27		A1
3260	MOORE, John D	22	E½SW	1841-02-27		A1
3261	" "	22	E½NW	1841-12-10		A1 G297
3221	NASH, Ezekiel	1	E½SW	1841-02-27		A1 G301
3222	" "	11	E½NE	1841-02-27		A1 G301
3223	" "	11	E½SE	1841-02-27		A1 G301
3224	" "	12	E½NE	1841-02-27		A1 G301
3225	" "	12	E½NW	1841-02-27		A1 G301
3226	" "	12	W½NE	1841-02-27		A1 G301
3227	" "	12	W½NW	1841-02-27		A1 G301
3221	NASH, Orsamus L	1	E½SW	1841-02-27		A1 G301
3222	" "	11	E½NE	1841-02-27		A1 G301
3223	" "	11	E½SE	1841-02-27		A1 G301
3224	" "	12	E½NE	1841-02-27		A1 G301
3225	" "	12	E½NW	1841-02-27		A1 G301
3226	" "	12	W½NE	1841-02-27		A1 G301
3227	" "	12	W½NW	1841-02-27		A1 G301
3292	NAYLOR, Richmond	27	SWNE	1904-12-31		A2
3197	NEWELL, D E	9	N½NE	1875-11-01		A2
3264	NEWTON, Matthew A	28	NE	1841-02-27		A1 G161
3181	ODEN, Alexander	17	E½SW	1848-12-01		A1
3215	ODEN, Elias	17	SWSE	1841-02-27		A1
3216	" "	20	E½NE	1841-02-27		A1
3217	" "	20	E½SE	1841-02-27		A1
3218	" "	20	W½NE	1841-02-27		A1
3234	ODEN, George	21	SW	1841-02-27		A1
3195	ODOM, Charles	27	NWNE	1860-05-01		A1
3190	PAGE, Elijah	28	E½SW	1841-02-27		A1 G65
3257	PARKER, James S	18	SWSE	1861-01-01		A1
3337	PARKER, William J	18	E½NW	1860-05-01		A1
3192	PENNINGTON, Lawrence	34	NE	1841-02-27		A1 G255
3275	" "	35	W½SW	1841-02-27		A1 G308
3261	POPE, Tripp	22	E½NW	1841-12-10		A1 G297
3252	REYNOLDS, James	18	E½SE	1841-02-27		A1
3253	" "	19	E½NE	1841-02-27		A1
3254	" "	20	SENW	1841-02-27		A1
3255	" "	20	W½NW	1841-02-27		A1
3256	" "	20	W½SW	1841-02-27		A1
3299	RIGBY, Russell	28	SE	1846-12-01		A1
3300	" "	33	SENW	1850-12-05		A1
3243	ROBERTSON, Henry	35	E½SE	1850-12-05		A1
3186	ROSS, Benjamin S	18	SWNE	1861-02-01		A1
3295	SANDERS, Jesse P	27	NW	1841-02-27		A1 G266
3296	" "	30	W½SW	1841-02-27		A1 G266
3297	SAUNDERS, Jesse P	22	E½NE	1844-09-10		A1 G267
3176	SCOTT, Aaron	6	NENW	1881-08-20		A2
3229	SCOTT, Francis T	7	E½SE	1841-02-27		A1
3230	" "	7	W½SE	1841-02-27		A1
3228	" "	7	E½NW	1844-09-10		A1
3281	SCOTT, Nathan	6	NE	1888-02-25		A2
3267	SHUMATE, Jonathan G	31	SWSW	1848-09-01		A1
3266	" "	31	NWSW	1850-12-05		A1
3265	SINCLAIR, John O	33	E½SW	1860-10-01		A1
3185	SPEED, Benjamin B	8	W½SW	1841-02-27		A1
3301	TAPPAN, John	1	W½SW	1841-12-15		A1 G234
3198	" "	11	W½NE	1841-12-15		A1 G179
3199	" "	11	W½SE	1841-12-15		A1 G179
3302	" "	2	E½NW	1841-12-15		A1 G234
3303	" "	2	E½SE	1841-12-15		A1 G234
3304	" "	27	E½NE	1841-12-15		A1 G234
3305	" "	3	E½SE	1841-12-15		A1 G234

ID	Individual in Patent	Sec.	Sec. Part	Date Issued	Other Counties	For More Info . . .
3306	TAPPAN, John (Cont'd)	4	NE	1846-12-01		A1 G234 R3294
3231	TOWNSEND, Frank	5	N1/2NE	1892-01-20		A2
3307	TOWNSEND, Samuel	3	NW	1860-10-01		A1
3317	VAN HAWES, STEPHEN	29	SESW	1845-01-21		A1
3338	WALTER, Henry	27	SW	1912-02-05		A1 G57
3282	WARE, Nimrod W	1	E1/2NE	1841-02-27		A1 G334
3283	" "	1	W1/2NE	1841-02-27		A1 G334
3318	WATTERS, Stacey B	32	E1/2SE	1846-12-01		A1 G116
3319	" "	32	E1/2SW	1846-12-01		A1 G116
3320	" "	32	W1/2SE	1846-12-01		A1 G116
3321	" "	32	W1/2SW	1846-12-01		A1 G116
3233	WELSH, George L	33	NWSE	1860-05-01		A1
3298	WHITSETT, John C	20	W1/2SE	1841-02-27		A1 G268
3282	WILLIAMS, Benjamin	1	E1/2NE	1841-02-27		A1 G334
3283	" "	1	W1/2NE	1841-02-27		A1 G334
3308	YOUNG, Samuel	23	E1/2SW	1841-02-27		A1
3271	" "	23	W1/2SW	1841-02-27		A1 G211
3200	" "	26	E1/2SW	1841-02-27		A1 G198
3309	" "	26	SE	1841-02-27		A1
3201	" "	26	W1/2SW	1841-02-27		A1 G198
3202	" "	28	W1/2NW	1841-02-27		A1 G198
3310	" "	29	E1/2NE	1841-02-27		A1
3311	" "	29	E1/2SE	1841-02-27		A1
3203	" "	34	E1/2SE	1841-02-27		A1 G198
3272	" "	34	E1/2SW	1841-02-27		A1 G213
3204	" "	34	W1/2SE	1841-02-27		A1 G198
3182	" "	35	NW	1841-02-27		A1 G254
3275	" "	35	W1/2SW	1841-02-27		A1 G308
3312	" "	29	W1/2SE	1841-12-15		A1
3205	" "	35	E1/2SW	1844-09-10		A1 G198

Patent Map

T10-N R17-E
Choctaw Meridian

Map Group 16

Township Statistics

Parcels Mapped	:	163
Number of Patents	:	159
Number of Individuals	:	101
Patentees Identified	:	97
Number of Surnames	:	81
Multi-Patentee Parcels	:	48
Oldest Patent Date	:	2/27/1841
Most Recent Patent	:	2/5/1912
Block/Lot Parcels	:	0
Parcels Re - Issued	:	1
Parcels that Overlap	:	0
Cities and Towns	:	5
Cemeteries	:	5

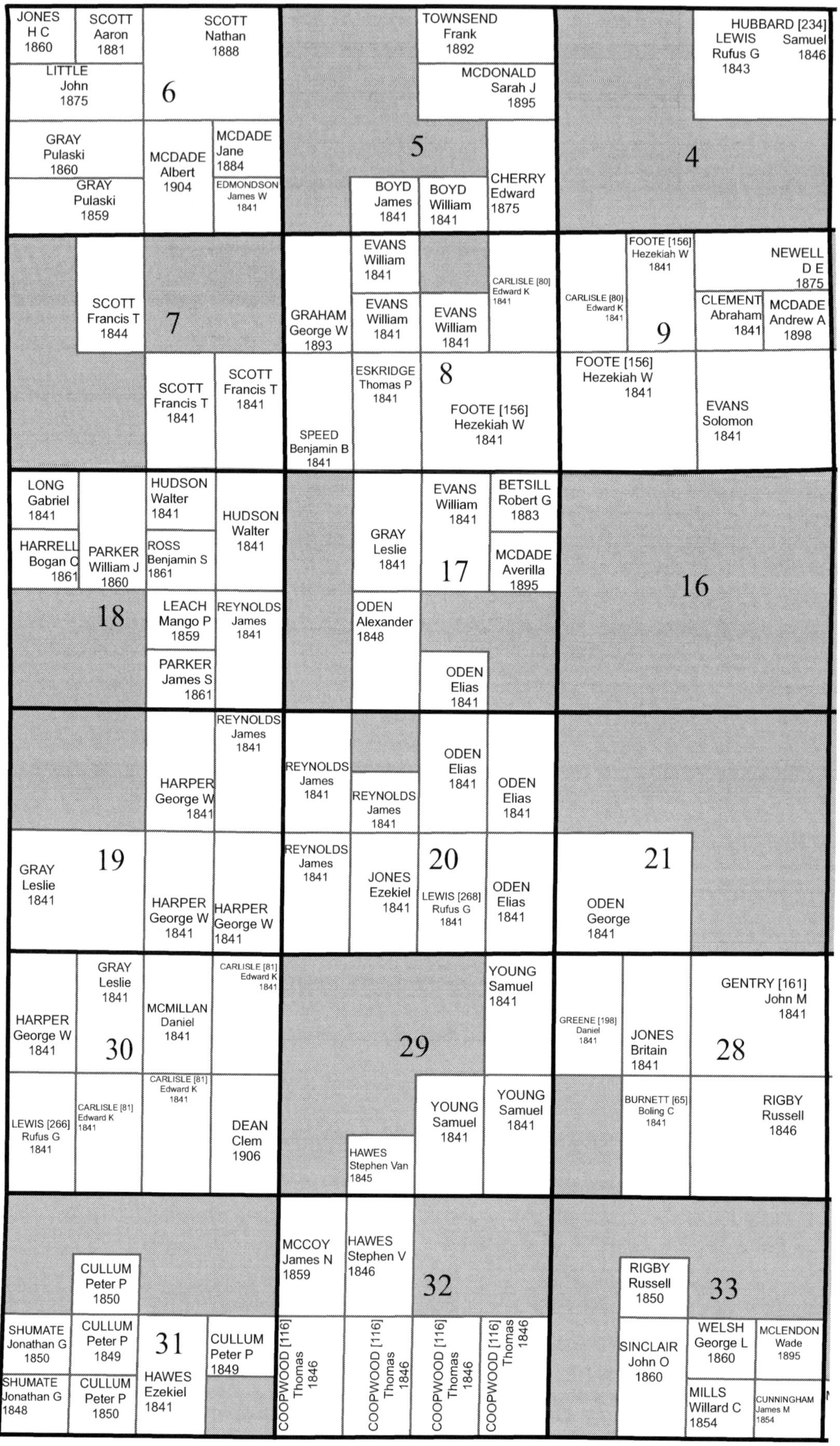

6
JONES H C 1860
SCOTT Aaron 1881
SCOTT Nathan 1888
LITTLE John 1875
GRAY Pulaski 1860
GRAY Pulaski 1859
MCDADE Albert 1904
MCDADE Jane 1884
EDMONDSON James W 1841

5
TOWNSEND Frank 1892
MCDONALD Sarah J 1895
BOYD James 1841
BOYD William 1841
CHERRY Edward 1875

4
HUBBARD [234]
LEWIS Rufus G 1843
Samuel 1846

7
SCOTT Francis T 1844
SCOTT Francis T 1841
SCOTT Francis T 1841

8
EVANS William 1841
CARLISLE [80] Edward K 1841
GRAHAM George W 1893
EVANS William 1841
EVANS William 1841
ESKRIDGE Thomas P 1841
SPEED Benjamin B 1841
FOOTE [156] Hezekiah W 1841

9
FOOTE [156] Hezekiah W 1841
NEWELL D E 1875
CARLISLE [80] Edward K 1841
CLEMENT Abraham 1841
MCDADE Andrew A 1898
FOOTE [156] Hezekiah W 1841
EVANS Solomon 1841

18
LONG Gabriel 1841
HUDSON Walter 1841
HUDSON Walter 1841
HARRELL Bogan C 1861
PARKER William J 1860
ROSS Benjamin S 1861
LEACH Mango P 1859
REYNOLDS James 1841
PARKER James S 1861

17
EVANS William 1841
BETSILL Robert G 1883
GRAY Leslie 1841
MCDADE Averilla 1895
ODEN Alexander 1848
ODEN Elias 1841

16

19
REYNOLDS James 1841
HARPER George W 1841
GRAY Leslie 1841
HARPER George W 1841
HARPER George W 1841

20
REYNOLDS James 1841
REYNOLDS James 1841
ODEN Elias 1841
ODEN Elias 1841
REYNOLDS James 1841
JONES Ezekiel 1841
LEWIS [268] Rufus G 1841
ODEN Elias 1841

21
ODEN George 1841

30
GRAY Leslie 1841
CARLISLE [81] Edward K 1841
HARPER George W 1841
MCMILLAN Daniel 1841
CARLISLE [81] Edward K 1841
LEWIS [266] Rufus G 1841
CARLISLE [81] Edward K 1841
DEAN Clem 1906

29
YOUNG Samuel 1841
YOUNG Samuel 1841
YOUNG Samuel 1841
HAWES Stephen Van 1845

28
GREENE [198] Daniel 1841
JONES Britain 1841
GENTRY [161] John M 1841
BURNETT [65] Boling C 1841
RIGBY Russell 1846

31
CULLUM Peter P 1850
SHUMATE Jonathan G 1850
CULLUM Peter P 1849
CULLUM Peter P 1849
SHUMATE Jonathan G 1848
CULLUM Peter P 1850
HAWES Ezekiel 1841

32
MCCOY James N 1859
HAWES Stephen V 1846
COOPWOOD [116] Thomas 1846
COOPWOOD [116] Thomas 1846
COOPWOOD [116] Thomas 1846
COOPWOOD [116] Thomas 1846

33
RIGBY Russell 1850
SINCLAIR John O 1860
WELSH George L 1860
MCLENDON Wade 1895
MILLS Willard C 1854
CUNNINGHAM James M 1854

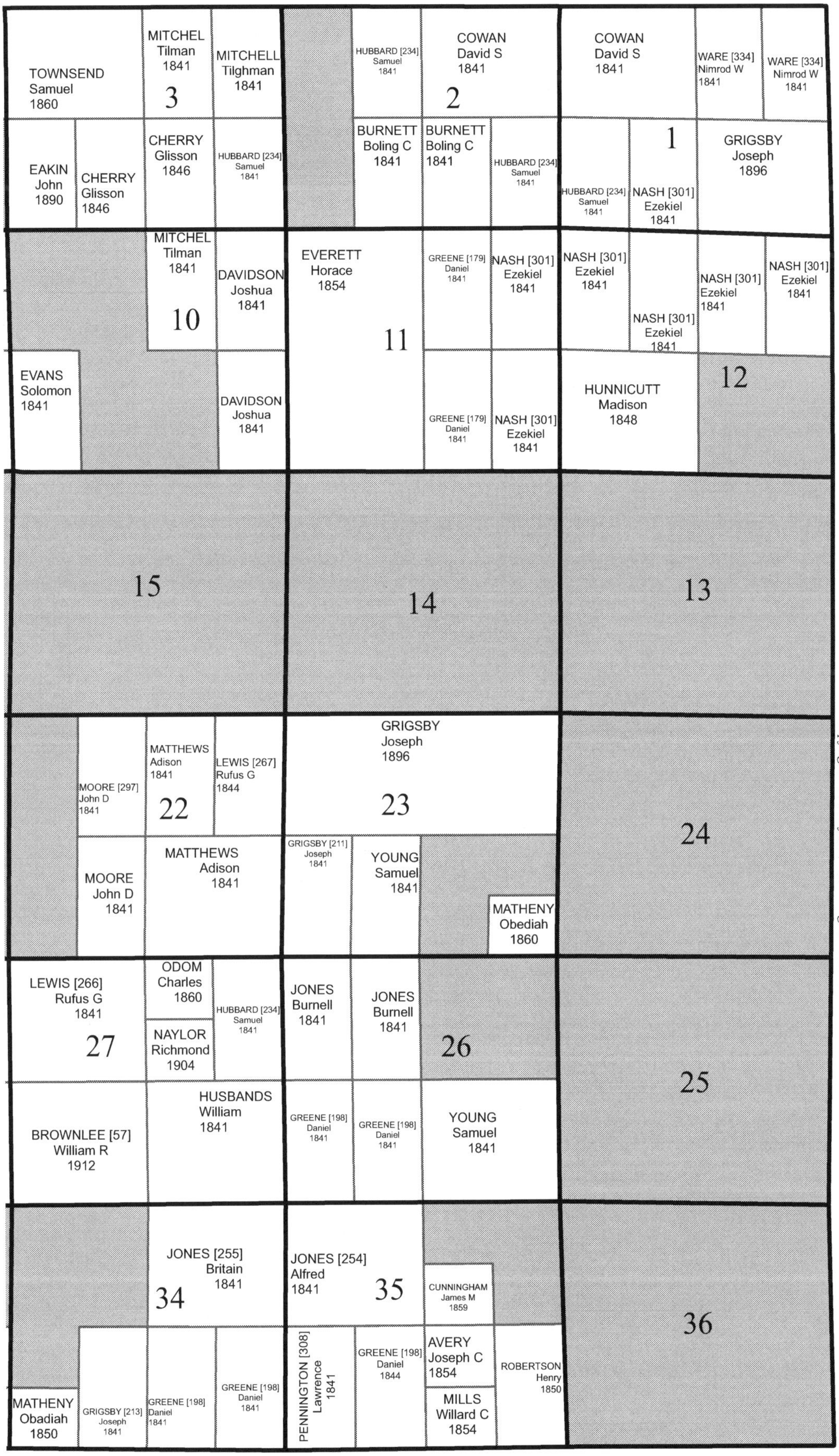

TOWNSEND Samuel 1860
MITCHEL Tilman 1841
MITCHELL Tilghman 1841
3
EAKIN John 1890
CHERRY Glisson 1846
CHERRY Glisson 1846
HUBBARD [234] Samuel 1841

HUBBARD [234] Samuel 1841
COWAN David S 1841
2
BURNETT Boling C 1841
BURNETT Boling C 1841
HUBBARD [234] Samuel 1841

COWAN David S 1841
WARE [334] Nimrod W 1841
WARE [334] Nimrod W 1841
1
GRIGSBY Joseph 1896
HUBBARD [234] Samuel 1841
NASH [301] Ezekiel 1841

MITCHEL Tilman 1841
DAVIDSON Joshua 1841
10
EVANS Solomon 1841
DAVIDSON Joshua 1841

EVERETT Horace 1854
GREENE [179] Daniel 1841
NASH [301] Ezekiel 1841
11
GREENE [179] Daniel 1841
NASH [301] Ezekiel 1841

NASH [301] Ezekiel 1841
NASH [301] Ezekiel 1841
NASH [301] Ezekiel 1841
NASH [301] Ezekiel 1841
12
HUNNICUTT Madison 1848

15
14
13

MATTHEWS Adison 1841
LEWIS [267] Rufus G 1844
MOORE [297] John D 1841
22
MOORE John D 1841
MATTHEWS Adison 1841

GRIGSBY Joseph 1896
23
GRIGSBY [211] Joseph 1841
YOUNG Samuel 1841
MATHENY Obediah 1860

24

LEWIS [266] Rufus G 1841
ODOM Charles 1860
HUBBARD [234] Samuel 1841
NAYLOR Richmond 1904
27
BROWNLEE [57] William R 1912
HUSBANDS William 1841

JONES Burnell 1841
JONES Burnell 1841
26
GREENE [198] Daniel 1841
GREENE [198] Daniel 1841
YOUNG Samuel 1841

25

JONES [255] Britain 1841
34
MATHENY Obadiah 1850
GRIGSBY [213] Joseph 1841
GREENE [198] Daniel 1841
GREENE [198] Daniel 1841

JONES [254] Alfred 1841
35
CUNNINGHAM James M 1859
PENNINGTON [308] Lawrence 1841
GREENE [198] Daniel 1844
AVERY Joseph C 1854
ROBERTSON Henry 1850
MILLS Willard C 1854

36

Helpful Hints

1. This Map's INDEX can be found on the preceding pages.
2. Refer to Map "C" to see where this Township lies within Kemper County, Mississippi.
3. Numbers within square brackets [ ] denote a multi-patentee land parcel (multi-owner). Refer to Appendix "C" for a full list of members in this group.
4. Areas that look to be crowded with Patentees usually indicate multiple sales of the same parcel (Re-issues) or Overlapping parcels. See this Township's Index for an explanation of these and other circumstances that might explain "odd" groupings of Patentees on this map.

Legend

Patent Boundary

Section Boundary

No Patents Found (or Outside County)

1., 2., 3., ... Lot Numbers (when beside a name)

[ ] Group Number (see Appendix "C")

Scale: Section = 1 mile X 1 mile (generally, with some exceptions)

Road Map

T10-N R17-E
Choctaw Meridian

Map Group 16

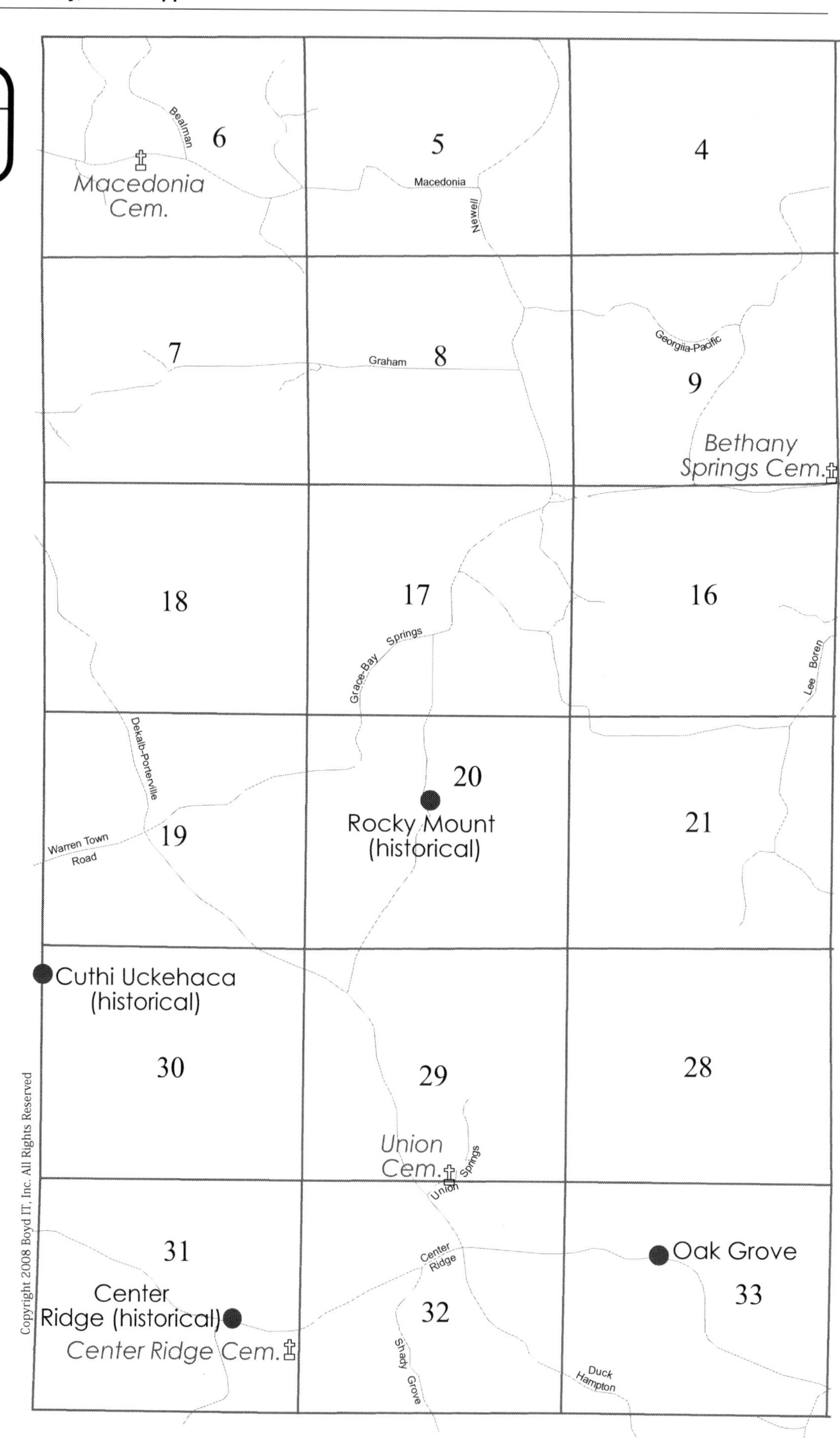

Cities & Towns

Akron
Center Ridge (historical)
Cuthi Uckehaca (historical)
Oak Grove
Rocky Mount (historical)

Cemeteries

Bethany Springs Cemetery
Center Ridge Cemetery
Chapel Hill Cemetery
Macedonia Cemetery
Union Cemetery

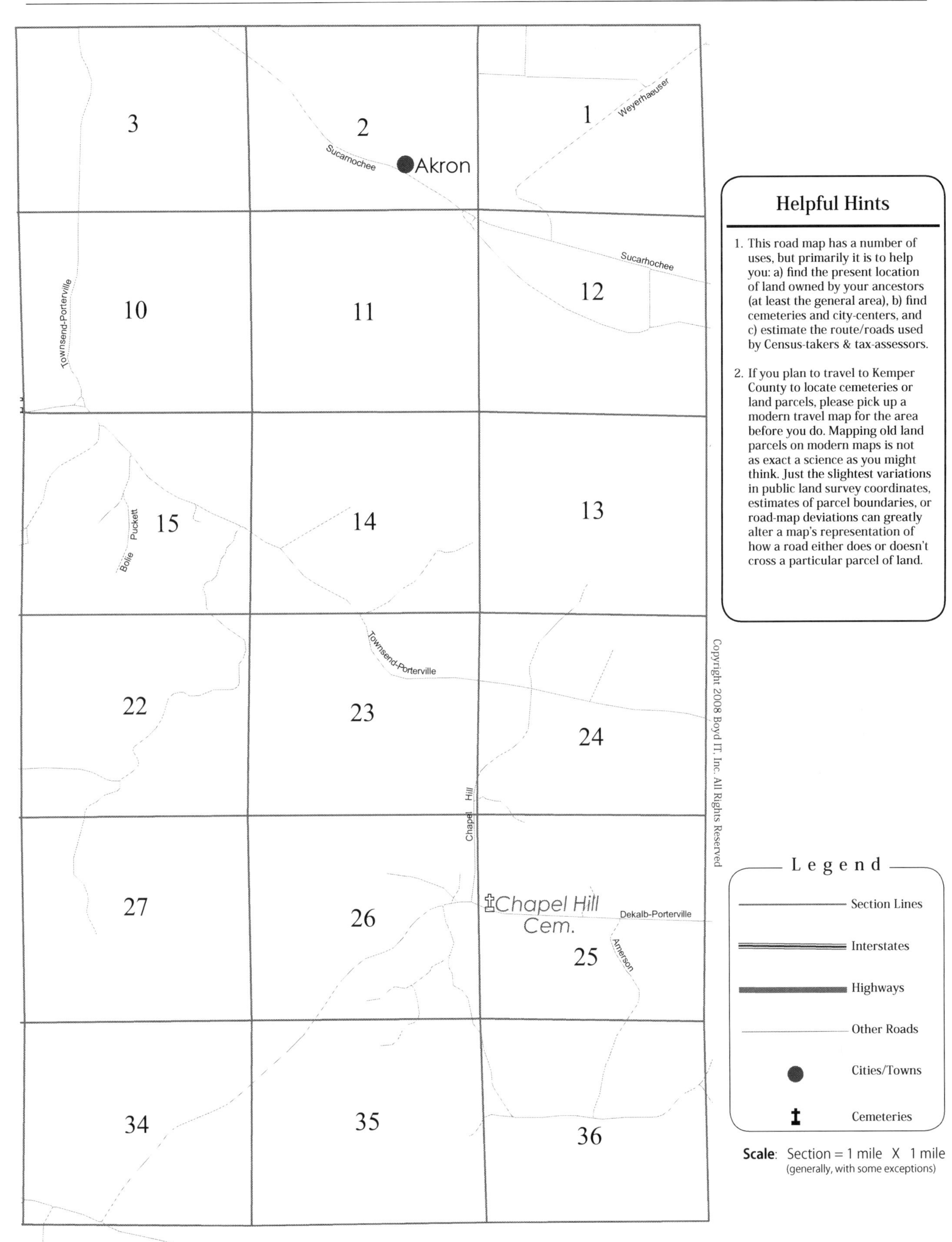
3
2
1
Weyerhaeuser
Sucarnochee
Akron
10
11
12
Sucarhochee
Townsend-Porterville
15
14
13
Puckett
Bolie
22
23
24
Townsend-Porterville
Chapel Hill
27
26
25
Chapel Hill Cem.
Dekalb-Porterville
Amerson
34
35
36
Copyright 2008 Boyd IT, Inc. All Rights Reserved
Helpful Hints
1. This road map has a number of uses, but primarily it is to help you: a) find the present location of land owned by your ancestors (at least the general area), b) find cemeteries and city-centers, and c) estimate the route/roads used by Census-takers & tax-assessors.
2. If you plan to travel to Kemper County to locate cemeteries or land parcels, please pick up a modern travel map for the area before you do. Mapping old land parcels on modern maps is not as exact a science as you might think. Just the slightest variations in public land survey coordinates, estimates of parcel boundaries, or road-map deviations can greatly alter a map's representation of how a road either does or doesn't cross a particular parcel of land.
Legend
Section Lines
Interstates
Highways
Other Roads
Cities/Towns
Cemeteries
Scale: Section = 1 mile X 1 mile
(generally, with some exceptions)

Historical Map

T10-N R17-E
Choctaw Meridian

Map Group 16

Cities & Towns
- Akron
- Center Ridge (historical)
- Cuthi Uckehaca (historical)
- Oak Grove
- Rocky Mount (historical)

Cemeteries
- Bethany Springs Cemetery
- Center Ridge Cemetery
- Chapel Hill Cemetery
- Macedonia Cemetery
- Union Cemetery

6
Macedonia Cem.
5
4
7
Poole Branch
8
9
Bethany Springs Cem.
18
17
16
19
Rocky Mount (historical)
20
Little Ross Branch
21
Cuthi Uckehaca (historical)
30
29
28
Union Cem.
Center Ridge (historical)
31
Center Ridge Cem.
32
Oak Grove
33

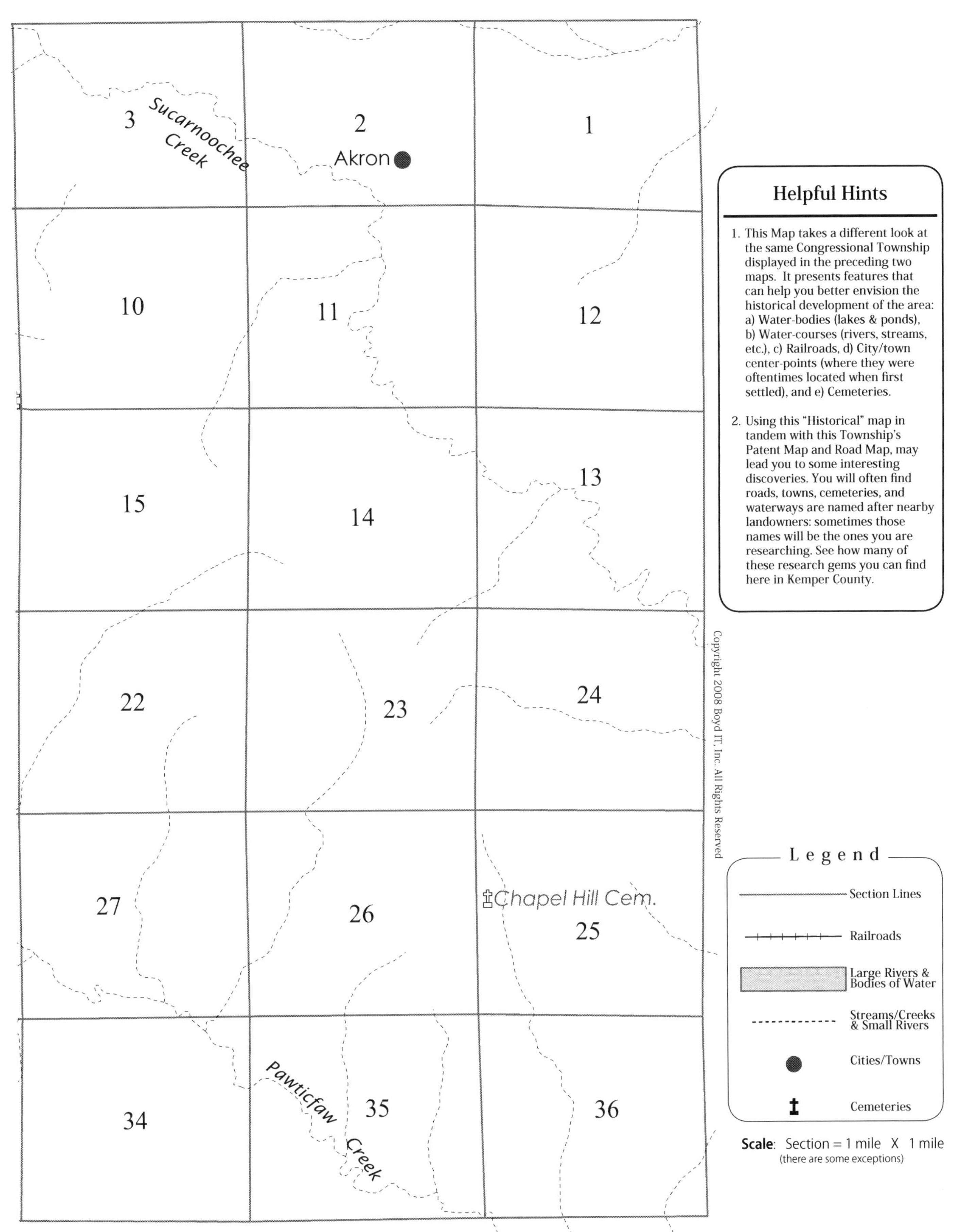

3
Sucarnoochee Creek
2
Akron
1
10
11
12
15
14
13
22
23
24
27
26
Chapel Hill Cem.
25
34
Pawticfaw Creek
35
36
Copyright 2008 Boyd IT, Inc. All Rights Reserved
Helpful Hints
1. This Map takes a different look at the same Congressional Township displayed in the preceding two maps. It presents features that can help you better envision the historical development of the area: a) Water-bodies (lakes & ponds), b) Water-courses (rivers, streams, etc.), c) Railroads, d) City/town center-points (where they were oftentimes located when first settled), and e) Cemeteries.
2. Using this "Historical" map in tandem with this Township's Patent Map and Road Map, may lead you to some interesting discoveries. You will often find roads, towns, cemeteries, and waterways are named after nearby landowners: sometimes those names will be the ones you are researching. See how many of these research gems you can find here in Kemper County.
Legend
Section Lines
Railroads
Large Rivers & Bodies of Water
Streams/Creeks & Small Rivers
Cities/Towns
Cemeteries
Scale: Section = 1 mile X 1 mile
(there are some exceptions)

Map Group 17: Index to Land Patents

Township 10-North Range 18-East (Choctaw)

After you locate an individual in this Index, take note of the Section and Section Part then proceed to the Land Patent map on the pages immediately following. You should have no difficulty locating the corresponding parcel of land.

The "For More Info" Column will lead you to more information about the underlying Patents. See the *Legend* at right, and the "How to Use this Book" chapter, for more information.

LEGEND

"For More Info . . . " column

A = Authority (Legislative Act, See Appendix "A")
B = Block or Lot (location in Section unknown)
C = Cancelled Patent
F = Fractional Section
G = Group (Multi-Patentee Patent, see Appendix "C")
V = Overlaps another Parcel
R = Re-Issued (Parcel patented more than once)

(A & G items require you to locate in the Appendixes referred to above. All other Letter-designations followed by a number require you to locate line-items in this index that possess the ID number found after the letter).

ID	Individual in Patent	Sec.	Sec. Part	Date Issued	Other Counties	For More Info . . .
3349	ANDERSON, Calvin	1	SE	1848-09-01		A1
3361	ANDREWS, Ezekiel	1	NW	1860-05-01		A1
3392	AVERY, Joseph C	21	W½SW	1854-03-15		A1
3358	BARTLETT, Evanda N	7	NE	1911-06-29		A2
3403	BEVILL, Thomas L	11		1841-02-27		A1
3404	" "	23	E½NW	1841-02-27		A1
3405	" "	23	W½NW	1841-02-27		A1
3406	" "	26	E½SE	1841-02-27		A1
3407	" "	26	E½SW	1841-02-27		A1
3408	" "	26	W½SE	1841-02-27		A1
3409	" "	26	W½SW	1841-02-27		A1
3410	" "	27	E½SE	1841-02-27		A1
3411	" "	27	W½SE	1841-02-27		A1
3412	" "	27	W½SW	1841-02-27		A1
3413	" "	34	E½	1841-02-27		A1
3414	" "	35	E½NE	1841-02-27		A1
3416	" "	35	E½SE	1841-02-27		A1
3417	" "	35	SW	1841-02-27		A1
3418	" "	35	W½NE	1841-02-27		A1
3419	" "	35	W½NW	1841-02-27		A1
3420	" "	35	W½SE	1841-02-27		A1
3415	" "	35	E½NW	1844-12-15		A1
3371	BIGGS, James	33	SE	1841-12-15		A1
3375	BIRDSONG, James P	17	NE	1906-06-04		A2 G42
3383	BIRDSONG, John E	3	E½NE	1906-06-04		A2
3375	BIRDSONG, Mary S	17	NE	1906-06-04		A2 G42
3346	BURNETT, Boling C	22	NE	1841-02-27		A1
3347	" "	23	E½NE	1841-02-27		A1
3348	" "	23	W½NE	1841-02-27		A1
3426	CALVERT, William	34	W½	1841-02-27		A1
3369	CHANEY, Houston	7	E½SE	1916-11-08		A2
3390	CHANEY, John William	17	S½NW	1913-09-18		A1
3362	CHERRY, Ezekiel	12	E½NW	1848-09-01		A1
3380	DARNALL, John A	12	NE	1848-09-01		A1
3382	DELK, John	7	W½SE	1901-08-12		A2
3353	DENTON, Elijah J	15	NW	1895-10-09		A2
3359	EASON, Ezekiel A	3	W½NW	1895-12-14		A2
3360	" "	3	W½SW	1895-12-14		A2
3394	FELTON, Mary	3	NENW	1906-06-04		A2 G148
3395	" "	3	NWNE	1906-06-04		A2 G148
3394	FELTON, Thomas M	3	NENW	1906-06-04		A2 G148
3395	" "	3	NWNE	1906-06-04		A2 G148
3397	GILBERT, Oliver S	23	SW	1901-03-23		A2
3339	GRANTHAM, Adam	36	E½SE	1841-02-27		A1
3340	" "	36	W½SE	1841-02-27		A1
3351	GREENE, Daniel	27	E½SW	1841-02-27		A1

ID	Individual in Patent	Sec.	Sec. Part	Date Issued	Other Counties	For More Info . . .
3388	HALL, John W	3	NESE	1901-04-22		A2
3389	" "	3	SESE	1901-04-22		A2
3391	HENDRICKS, Jonathan H	12	SE	1848-09-01		A1
3350	HITT, Daniel F	21	SE	1901-12-04		A2
3378	HITT, Jesse M	21	E½SW	1906-05-01		A2
3421	HITT, Uriah D	21	NE	1905-12-13		A2
3372	HOLDER, James H	15	NE	1897-09-09		A2
3396	JONAS, Moses	9	NW	1897-04-02		A2
3424	JOYNER, William B	13	W½NW	1906-06-04		A2
3385	KNIGHT, John L	9	SE	1895-10-09		A2
3373	KNIGHTEN, James L	25	S½SE	1898-12-27		A2
3374	" "	25	S½SW	1898-12-27		A2
3399	LEWIS, Rufus G	33	W½SW	1841-02-27		A1 G266
3427	MATHEWS, William H	15	SE	1906-06-21		A2
3366	MCCOWN, Francis	33	E½SW	1841-02-27		A1
3367	" "	33	NE	1841-02-27		A1
3341	MCDADE, Albert B	7	NW	1910-03-21		A1
3352	MCDADE, Ed	7	SW	1898-12-27		A2
3368	MONK, Harrison	9	N½SW	1906-06-04		A2
3342	MORGAN, Benjamin S	4	5	1899-02-06		A2
3343	" "	4	8	1899-02-06		A2
3344	" "	4	9	1899-02-06		A2
3345	" "	5	NESE	1899-02-06		A2
3400	MURPHY, Sammie P	9	NE	1906-05-01		A2
3431	MURPHY, William	3	NESW	1901-03-23		A2
3432	" "	3	NWSE	1901-03-23		A2
3433	" "	3	SENW	1901-03-23		A2
3434	" "	3	SWNE	1901-03-23		A2
3376	NETHERRY, James S	1	NE	1848-09-01		A1
3428	ODOM, William H	25	N½SW	1896-12-14		A2
3429	" "	25	S½NW	1896-12-14		A2
3401	PARRISH, Solomon P	1	E½SW	1891-03-16		A2
3423	PATTON, William A	13	NE	1848-09-01		A1
3363	PEEL, Fannie E	25	N½NE	1900-11-28		A2
3364	" "	25	NWSE	1900-11-28		A2
3365	" "	25	SWNE	1900-11-28		A2
3384	RIGDON, John J	25	SENE	1912-06-27		A2
3425	RIGDON, William B	25	NESE	1913-05-21		A2
3357	ROBBINS, Emberson B	21	NW	1901-12-30		A2
3422	ROGERS, Walter Earl	17	N½NW	1912-01-22		A1
3370	SANDERS, Jacob C	13	SW	1896-12-14		A2
3399	SANDERS, Jesse P	33	W½SW	1841-02-27		A1 G266
3398	SHARP, Robert H	13	W½SE	1896-10-31		A2
3430	SHARP, William J	15	SW	1902-07-22		A1
3377	SLATON, James W	23	SE	1906-05-01		A2
3435	SLATON, William S	25	N½NW	1906-06-30		A2
3402	STRAHAN, Theodore J	13	E½SE	1914-02-06		A1
3386	TEW, John	36	E½NW	1841-02-27		A1
3387	" "	36	W½NW	1841-02-27		A1
3379	WATT, Jesse	13	E½NW	1896-12-14		A2
3381	WHITSETT, John C	22	W½	1841-02-27		A1
3354	WILLIAMS, Elizabeth	36	E½NE	1841-02-27		A1
3355	" "	36	E½SW	1841-02-27		A1
3356	" "	36	W½NE	1841-02-27		A1
3393	WILLIAMS, Joseph	36	W½SW	1841-02-27		A1

Patent Map

T10-N R18-E
Choctaw Meridian

Map Group 17

Township Statistics

Parcels Mapped	:	97
Number of Patents	:	82
Number of Individuals	:	63
Patentees Identified	:	60
Number of Surnames	:	50
Multi-Patentee Parcels	:	4
Oldest Patent Date	:	2/27/1841
Most Recent Patent	:	11/8/1916
Block/Lot Parcels	:	3
Parcels Re - Issued	:	0
Parcels that Overlap	:	0
Cities and Towns	:	4
Cemeteries	:	1

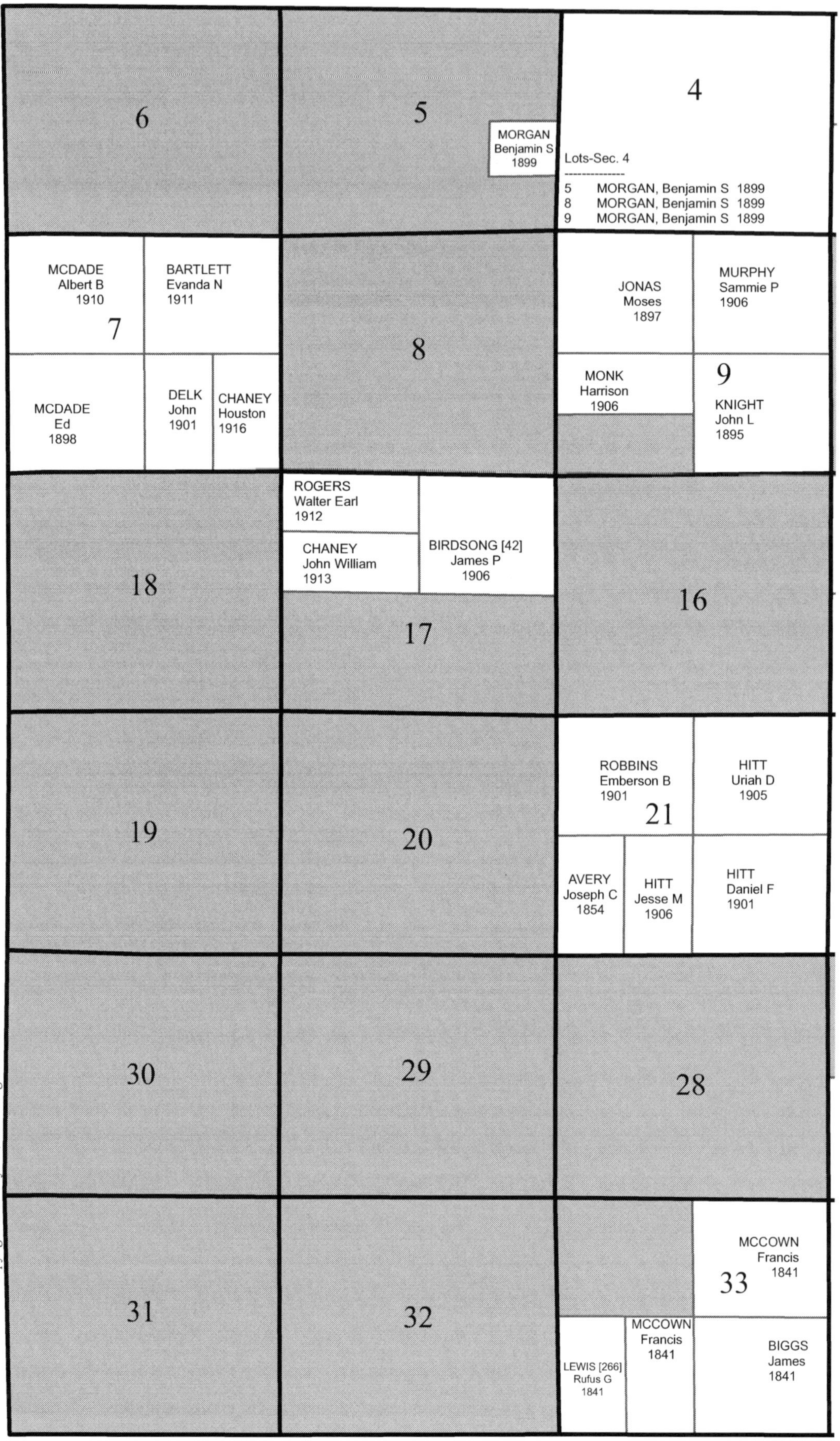

6

5

MORGAN
Benjamin S
1899

4

Lots-Sec. 4
----
5 MORGAN, Benjamin S 1899
8 MORGAN, Benjamin S 1899
9 MORGAN, Benjamin S 1899

MCDADE
Albert B
1910

BARTLETT
Evanda N
1911

7

MCDADE
Ed
1898

DELK
John
1901

CHANEY
Houston
1916

8

JONAS
Moses
1897

MURPHY
Sammie P
1906

MONK
Harrison
1906

9

KNIGHT
John L
1895

18

ROGERS
Walter Earl
1912

CHANEY
John William
1913

BIRDSONG [42]
James P
1906

17

16

19

20

ROBBINS
Emberson B
1901

21

HITT
Uriah D
1905

AVERY
Joseph C
1854

HITT
Jesse M
1906

HITT
Daniel F
1901

30

29

28

31

32

MCCOWN
Francis
1841

33

LEWIS [266]
Rufus G
1841

MCCOWN
Francis
1841

BIGGS
James
1841

3
EASON Ezekiel A 1895
FELTON [148] Mary 1906
FELTON [148] Mary 1906
BIRDSONG John E 1906
MURPHY William 1901
MURPHY William 1901
MURPHY William 1901
MURPHY William 1901
HALL John W 1901
EASON Ezekiel A 1895
HALL John W 1901

2

1
ANDREWS Ezekiel 1860
NETHERRY James S 1848
PARRISH Solomon P 1891
ANDERSON Calvin 1848

10

11
BEVILL Thomas L 1841

12
CHERRY Ezekiel 1848
DARNALL John A 1848
HENDRICKS Jonathan H 1848

15
DENTON Elijah J 1895
HOLDER James H 1897
SHARP William J 1902
MATHEWS William H 1906

14

13
JOYNER William B 1906
WATT Jesse 1896
PATTON William A 1848
SANDERS Jacob C 1896
SHARP Robert H 1896
STRAHAN Theodore J 1914

22
BURNETT Boling C 1841
WHITSETT John C 1841

23
BEVILL Thomas L 1841
BEVILL Thomas L 1841
BURNETT Boling C 1841
BURNETT Boling C 1841
GILBERT Oliver S 1901
SLATON James W 1906

24

27
BEVILL Thomas L 1841
GREENE Daniel 1841
BEVILL Thomas L 1841
BEVILL Thomas L 1841

26
BEVILL Thomas L 1841
BEVILL Thomas L 1841
BEVILL Thomas L 1841
BEVILL Thomas L 1841

25
SLATON William S 1906
PEEL Fannie E 1900
ODOM William H 1896
PEEL Fannie E 1900
RIGDON John J 1912
ODOM William H 1896
PEEL Fannie E 1900
RIGDON William B 1913
KNIGHTEN James L 1898
KNIGHTEN James L 1898

34
CALVERT William 1841
BEVILL Thomas L 1841

35
BEVILL Thomas L 1841
BEVILL Thomas L 1844
BEVILL Thomas L 1841
BEVILL Thomas L 1841
BEVILL Thomas L 1841
BEVILL Thomas L 1841
BEVILL Thomas L 1841

36
TEW John 1841
TEW John 1841
WILLIAMS Elizabeth 1841
WILLIAMS Elizabeth 1841
WILLIAMS Joseph 1841
WILLIAMS Elizabeth 1841
GRANTHAM Adam 1841
GRANTHAM Adam 1841

Helpful Hints

1. This Map's INDEX can be found on the preceding pages.
2. Refer to Map "C" to see where this Township lies within Kemper County, Mississippi.
3. Numbers within square brackets [ ] denote a multi-patentee land parcel (multi-owner). Refer to Appendix "C" for a full list of members in this group.
4. Areas that look to be crowded with Patentees usually indicate multiple sales of the same parcel (Re-issues) or Overlapping parcels. See this Township's Index for an explanation of these and other circumstances that might explain "odd" groupings of Patentees on this map.

Legend

- Patent Boundary
- Section Boundary
- No Patents Found (or Outside County)
- 1., 2., 3., ... Lot Numbers (when beside a name)
- [ ] Group Number (see Appendix "C")

Scale: Section = 1 mile X 1 mile (generally, with some exceptions)

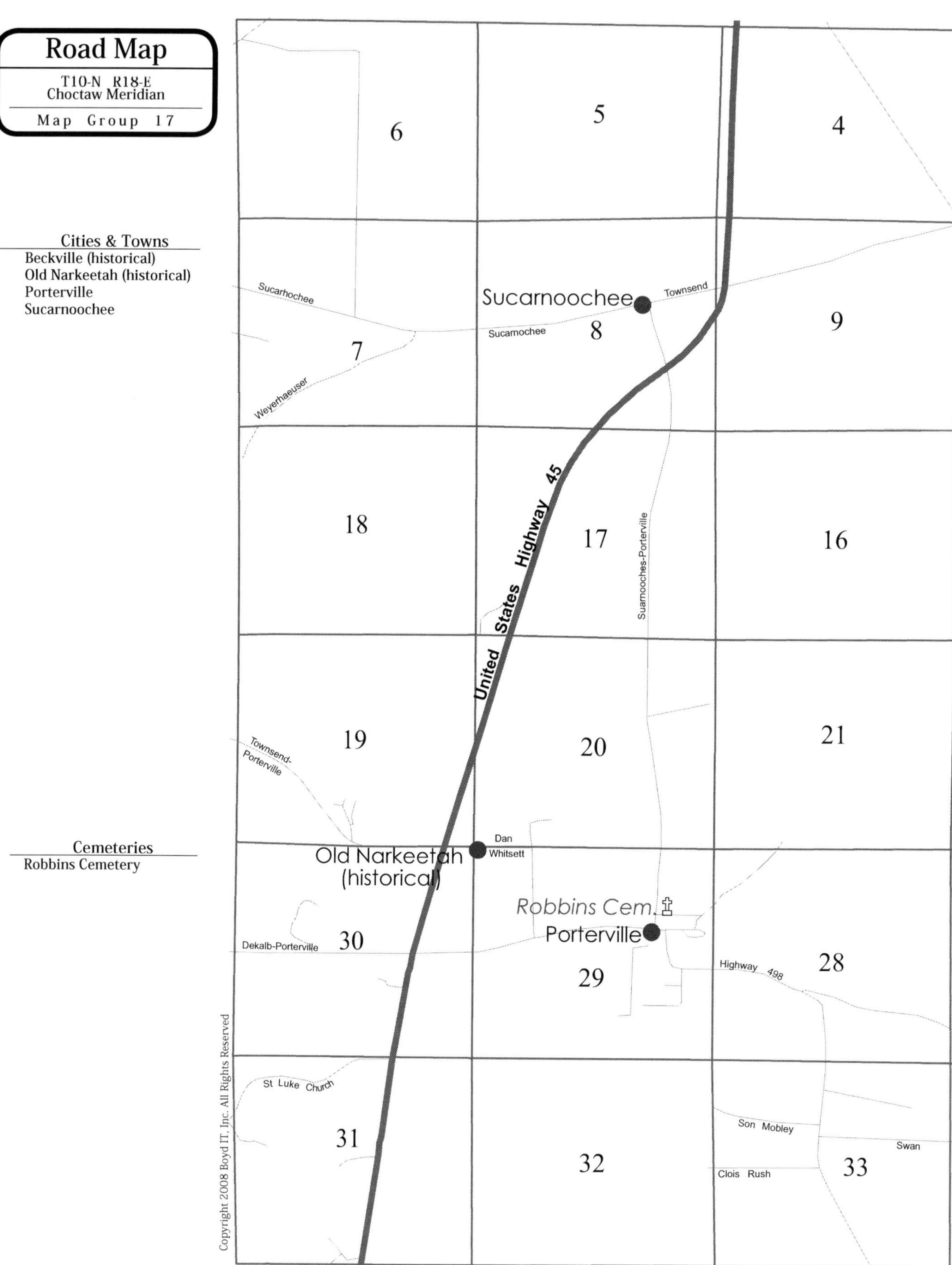
Road Map
T10-N R18-E
Choctaw Meridian
Map Group 17
Cities & Towns
Beckville (historical)
Old Narkeetah (historical)
Porterville
Sucarnoochee
Cemeteries
Robbins Cemetery
6
5
4
Sucarhochee
Sucarnoochee
Townsend
Sucarnochee
8
9
7
Weyerhaeuser
United States Highway 45
18
17
16
Suarnooches-Porterville
19
20
21
Townsend-Porterville
Dan Whitsett
Old Narkeetah (historical)
Robbins Cem.
Porterville
Dekalb-Porterville
30
29
28
Highway 498
St Luke Church
31
32
33
Son Mobley
Swan
Clois Rush
Copyright 2008 Boyd IT, Inc. All Rights Reserved

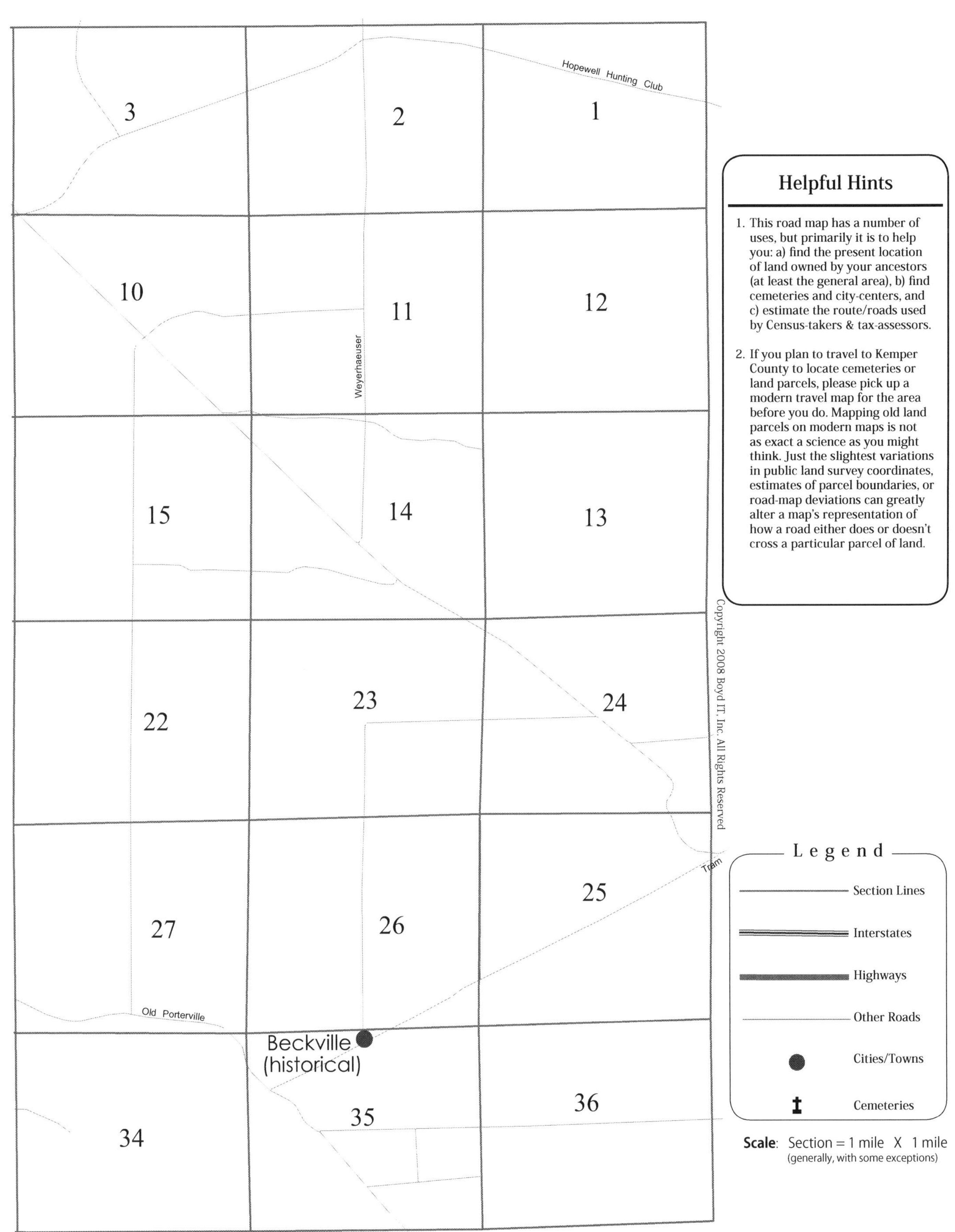

Helpful Hints

1. This road map has a number of uses, but primarily it is to help you: a) find the present location of land owned by your ancestors (at least the general area), b) find cemeteries and city-centers, and c) estimate the route/roads used by Census-takers & tax-assessors.

2. If you plan to travel to Kemper County to locate cemeteries or land parcels, please pick up a modern travel map for the area before you do. Mapping old land parcels on modern maps is not as exact a science as you might think. Just the slightest variations in public land survey coordinates, estimates of parcel boundaries, or road-map deviations can greatly alter a map's representation of how a road either does or doesn't cross a particular parcel of land.

Legend

- Section Lines
- Interstates
- Highways
- Other Roads
- Cities/Towns
- Cemeteries

Scale: Section = 1 mile X 1 mile (generally, with some exceptions)

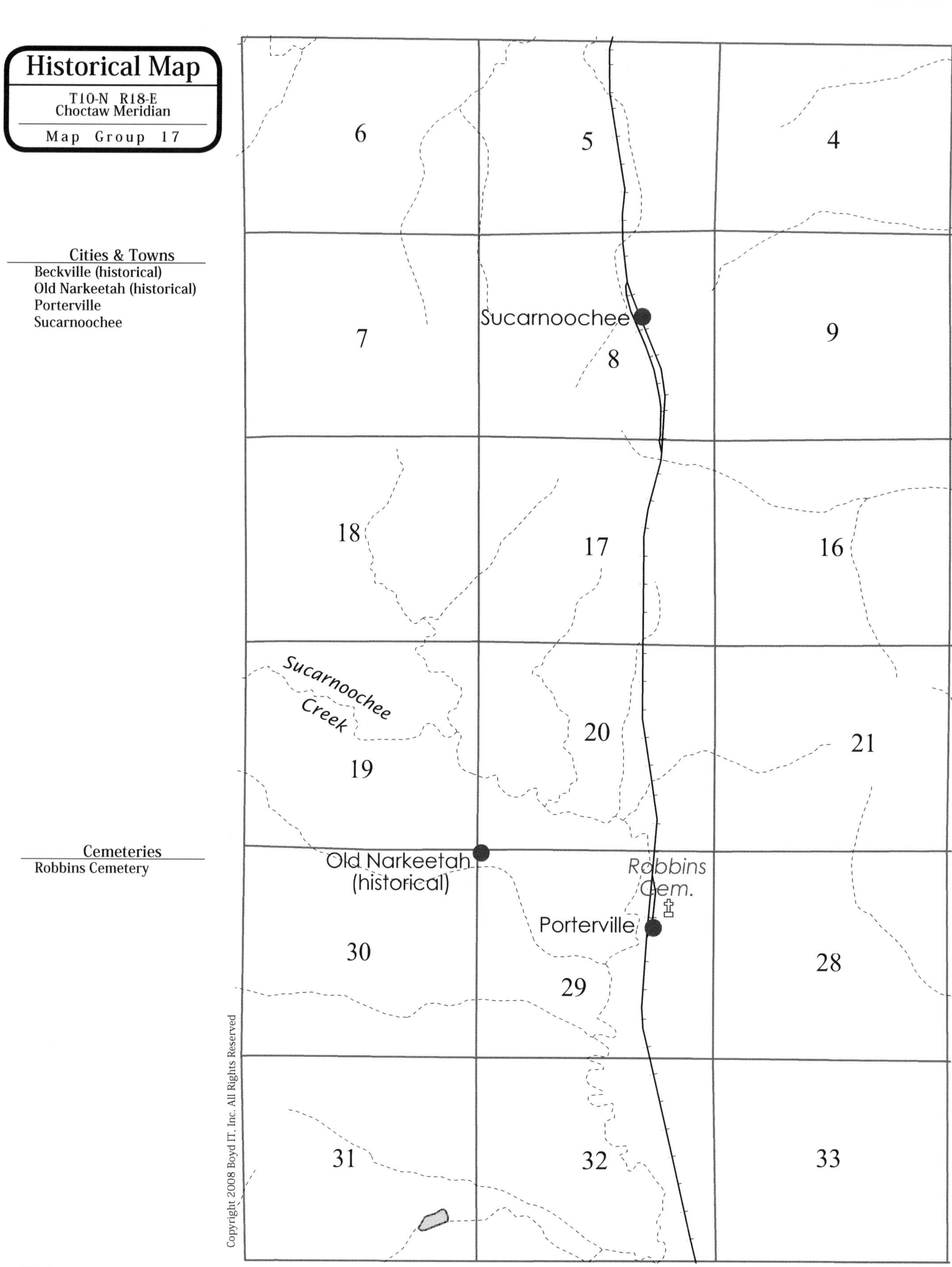
Historical Map
T10-N R18-E
Choctaw Meridian
Map Group 17
Cities & Towns
Beckville (historical)
Old Narkeetah (historical)
Porterville
Sucarnoochee
Cemeteries
Robbins Cemetery
6
5
4
7
Sucarnoochee
8
9
18
17
16
Sucarnoochee
Creek
19
20
21
Old Narkeetah
(historical)
Robbins
Cem.
Porterville
30
29
28
31
32
33
Copyright 2008 Boyd IT, Inc. All Rights Reserved

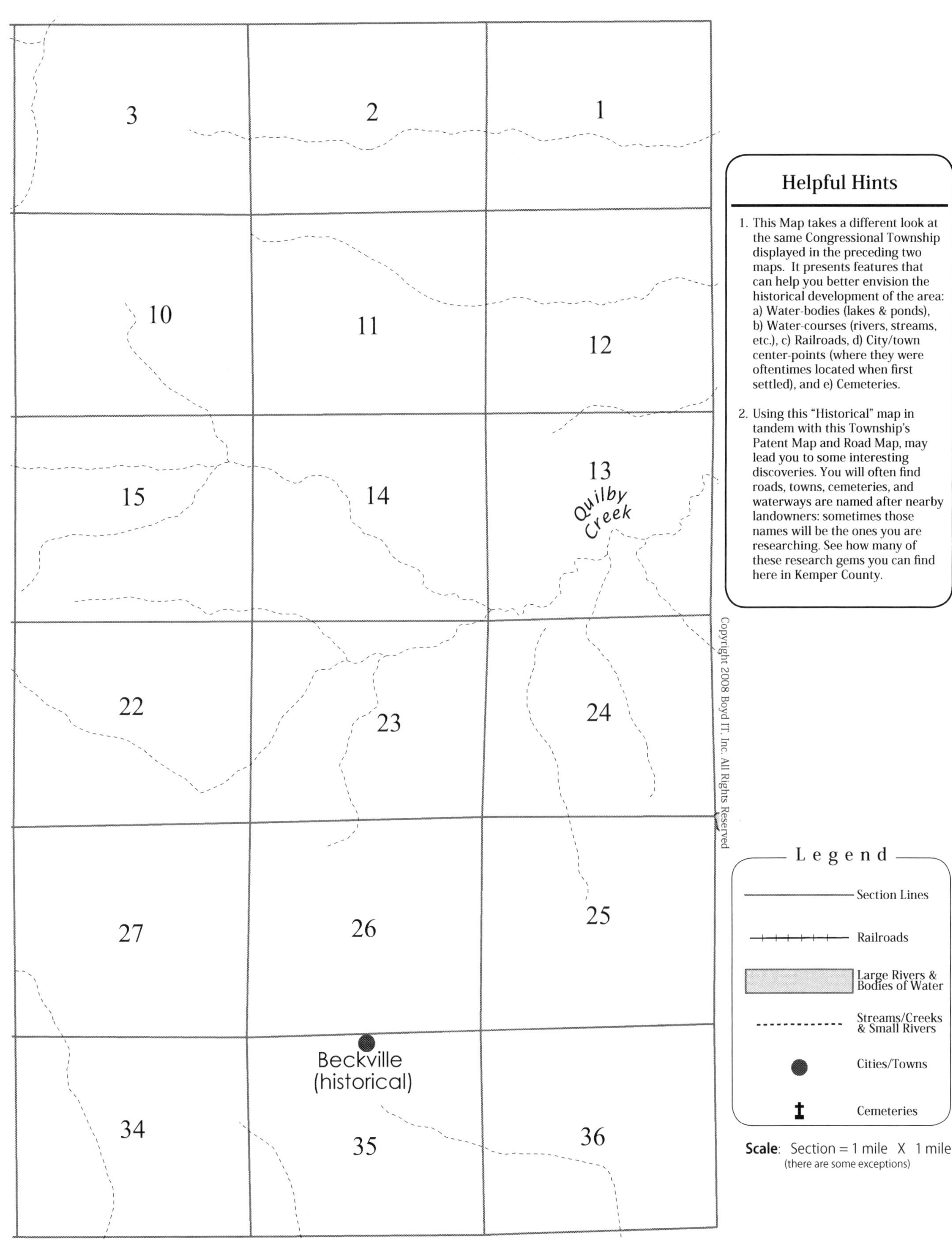

Helpful Hints

1. This Map takes a different look at the same Congressional Township displayed in the preceding two maps. It presents features that can help you better envision the historical development of the area: a) Water-bodies (lakes & ponds), b) Water-courses (rivers, streams, etc.), c) Railroads, d) City/town center-points (where they were oftentimes located when first settled), and e) Cemeteries.

2. Using this "Historical" map in tandem with this Township's Patent Map and Road Map, may lead you to some interesting discoveries. You will often find roads, towns, cemeteries, and waterways are named after nearby landowners: sometimes those names will be the ones you are researching. See how many of these research gems you can find here in Kemper County.

Legend

- Section Lines
- Railroads
- Large Rivers & Bodies of Water
- Streams/Creeks & Small Rivers
- Cities/Towns
- Cemeteries

Scale: Section = 1 mile X 1 mile
(there are some exceptions)

Map Group 18: Index to Land Patents

Township 10-North Range 19-East (Choctaw)

After you locate an individual in this Index, take note of the Section and Section Part then proceed to the Land Patent map on the pages immediately following. You should have no difficulty locating the corresponding parcel of land.

The "For More Info" Column will lead you to more information about the underlying Patents. See the *Legend* at right, and the "How to Use this Book" chapter, for more information.

LEGEND

"For More Info . . . " column

A = Authority (Legislative Act, See Appendix "A")
B = Block or Lot (location in Section unknown)
C = Cancelled Patent
F = Fractional Section
G = Group (Multi-Patentee Patent, see Appendix "C")
V = Overlaps another Parcel
R = Re-Issued (Parcel patented more than once)

(A & G items require you to look in the Appendixes referred to above. All other Letter-designations followed by a number require you to locate line-items in this index that possess the ID number found after the letter).

ID	Individual in Patent	Sec.	Sec. Part	Date Issued	Other Counties	For More Info . . .
3440	ANDERSON, Alexander	5	11	1841-02-27		A1 G22
3441	" "	5	8	1841-02-27		A1 G22
3443	" "	6	E½SE	1841-02-27		A1 G23
3442	" "	6	W½SE	1844-08-10		A1 G21
3456	ANDERSON, Hartford	6	SW	1846-12-01		A1
3454	BALDWIN, Frances	5	12	1841-07-01		A1 G27
3455	" "	5	7	1841-07-01		A1 G27
3436	BARNETT, Abigail	5	1	1846-12-01		A1
3437	" "	5	6	1846-12-01		A1
3470	BARNETT, Joseph	7	SE	1846-12-01		A1
3481	BARNETT, William	5	NW	1846-12-01		A1
3442	BARTON, John F	6	W½SE	1844-08-10		A1 G21
3468	BARTON, John J	8	S½7	1841-02-27		A1
3450	BURROUGHS, Elisha O	31	W½SW	1911-06-29		A2
3440	CARTER, John	5	11	1841-02-27		A1 G22
3441	" "	5	8	1841-02-27		A1 G22
3463	DARNALL, John A	7	W½NW	1848-09-01		A1
3478	DARNALL, Thomas	8	1	1847-04-01		A1
3479	" "	8	6	1847-04-01		A1
3482	DARNALL, William G	6	NW	1848-09-01		A1
3484	DARNALL, William J	7	NESW	1848-09-01		A1
3464	DAVIS, John B	8	2	1846-09-01		A1
3465	" "	8	3	1846-09-01		A1
3466	" "	8	4	1846-09-01		A1
3467	" "	8	5	1846-09-01		A1
3444	EVERITT, Alfred W	6	NE	1846-09-01		A1
3453	GARRISON, Ephraim	8	9	1848-09-01		A1
3474	GRACE, Morris S	29	3	1906-08-10		A2
3475	" "	29	4	1906-08-10		A2
3448	HARPER, Daniel E	17	8	1841-02-27		A1
3476	HOLCROFT, Nancy	31	NW	1906-05-01		A2
3449	JENKINS, Dominincо	8	8	1848-09-01		A1
3471	LEE, Joseph C	17	1	1909-01-25		A1
3472	" "	17	2	1909-01-25		A1
3473	MALONE, Michael	7	E½NW	1848-09-01		A1
3480	MCDANIEL, William A	31	W½NE	1906-10-15		A2
3477	MISSISSIPPI, State Of	17	7	1909-05-14		A3
3485	NEW, William	7	NE	1848-09-01		A1
3446	ODEN, Berline K	31	E½SW	1897-09-09		A2 G305
3447	" "	31	S½SE	1897-09-09		A2 G305
3446	ODEN, George W	31	E½SW	1897-09-09		A2 G305
3447	" "	31	S½SE	1897-09-09		A2 G305
3443	PAGE, Willis	6	E½SE	1841-02-27		A1 G23
3457	PARKER, James H	7	SESW	1906-06-30		A2
3458	" "	7	W½SW	1906-06-30		A2
3445	RAINER, Benjamin F	19	NW	1908-10-26		A2

ID	Individual in Patent	Sec.	Sec. Part	Date Issued	Other Counties	For More Info . . .
3438	RODES, Agnes	5	10	1841-02-27		A1 G318
3439	" "	5	9	1841-02-27		A1 G318
3483	SANDERS, William I	19	NE	1901-03-23		A2
3438	TURNER, Beloved L	5	10	1841-02-27		A1 G318
3439	" "	5	9	1841-02-27		A1 G318
3454	" "	5	12	1841-07-01		A1 G27
3455	" "	5	7	1841-07-01		A1 G27
3459	WILLIAMS, James T	17	3	1898-11-11		A2
3460	" "	17	4	1898-11-11		A2
3461	" "	17	5	1898-11-11		A2
3462	" "	17	6	1898-11-11		A2
3469	WILLIAMS, Joseph A	19	SE	1901-03-23		A2
3451	YERBY, Enoch A	31	E½NE	1906-05-01		A2
3452	" "	31	N½SE	1906-05-01		A2

Patent Map

T10-N R19-E
Choctaw Meridian

Map Group 18

Township Statistics

Parcels Mapped	:	50
Number of Patents	:	34
Number of Individuals	:	37
Patentees Identified	:	34
Number of Surnames	:	28
Multi-Patentee Parcels	:	10
Oldest Patent Date	:	2/27/1841
Most Recent Patent	:	6/29/1911
Block/Lot Parcels	:	27
Parcels Re - Issued	:	0
Parcels that Overlap	:	0
Cities and Towns	:	0
Cemeteries	:	0

Note: the area contained in this map amounts to far less than a full Township. Therefore, its contents are completely on this single page (instead of a "normal" 2-page spread).

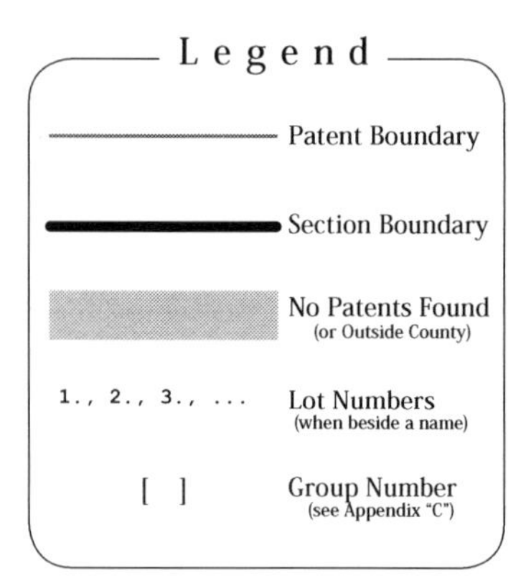

Scale: Section = 1 mile X 1 mile
(generally, with some exceptions)

DARNALL William G 1848
EVERITT Alfred W 1846
BARNETT William 1846
5
Lots-Sec. 5
1 BARNETT, Abigail 1846
6 BARNETT, Abigail 1846
7 BALDWIN, Frances[27]1841
8 ANDERSON, Alexan[22]1841
9 RODES, Agnes [318]1841
10 RODES, Agnes [318]1841
11 ANDERSON, Alexan[22]1841
12 BALDWIN, Frances[27]1841

6
ANDERSON Hartford 1846
ANDERSON [21] Alexander 1844
ANDERSON [23] Alexander 1841

DARNALL John A 1848
MALONE Michael 1848
NEW William 1848
7
DARNALL William J 1848
PARKER James H 1906
PARKER James H 1906
BARNETT Joseph 1846

Lots-Sec. 8
1 DARNALL, Thomas 1847
2 DAVIS, John B 1846
3 DAVIS, John B 1846
4 DAVIS, John B 1846
5 DAVIS, John B 1846
6 DARNALL, Thomas 1847
8 JENKINS, Domininco 1848
9 BARTON, John J 1841
9 GARRISON, Ephraim 1848
8

18

Lots-Sec. 17
1 LEE, Joseph C 1909
2 LEE, Joseph C 1909
3 WILLIAMS, James T 1898
4 WILLIAMS, James T 1898
5 WILLIAMS, James T 1898
6 WILLIAMS, James T 1898
7 MISSISSIPPI, State O1909
8 HARPER, Daniel E 1841
17

RAINER Benjamin F 1908
SANDERS William I 1901
19
WILLIAMS Joseph A 1901

20

30

Lots-Sec. 29
3 GRACE, Morris S 1906
4 GRACE, Morris S 1906
29

HOLCROFT Nancy 1906
31
MCDANIEL William A 1906
YERBY Enoch A 1906
BURROUGHS Elisha O 1911
ODEN [305] Berline K 1897
YERBY Enoch A 1906
ODEN [305] Berline K 1897

32

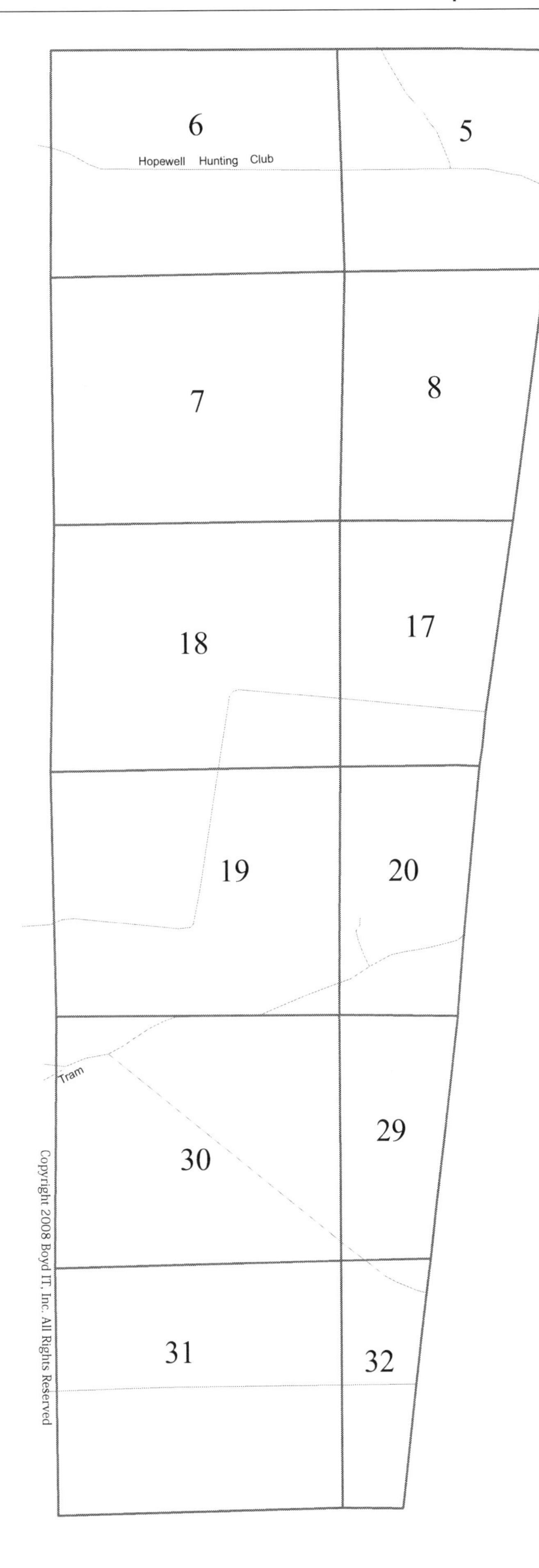

Road Map

T10-N R19-E
Choctaw Meridian

Map Group 18

Note: the area contained in this map amounts to far less than a full Township. Therefore, its contents are completely on this single page (instead of a "normal" 2-page spread).

Cities & Towns

None

Cemeteries

None

Legend

- Section Lines
- Interstates
- Highways
- Other Roads
- Cities/Towns
- Cemeteries

Scale: Section = 1 mile X 1 mile
(generally, with some exceptions)

Historical Map

T10-N R19-E
Choctaw Meridian

Map Group 18

Note: the area contained in this map amounts to far less than a full Township. Therefore, its contents are completely on this single page (instead of a "normal" 2-page spread).

Cities & Towns
None

Cemeteries
None

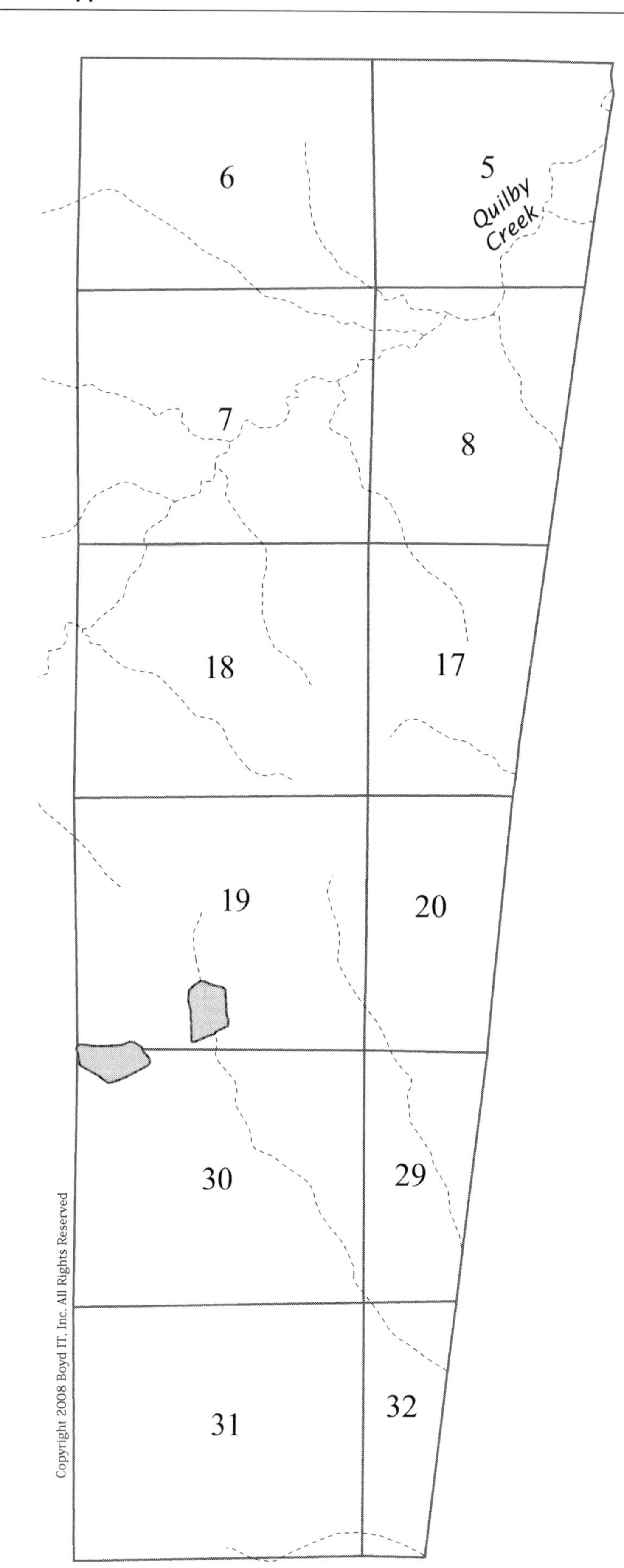

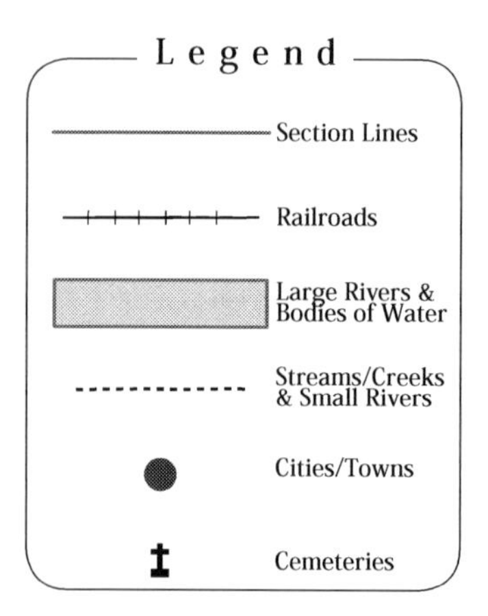

Scale: Section = 1 mile X 1 mile
(there are some exceptions)

Map Group 19: Index to Land Patents

Township 9-North Range 14-East (Choctaw)

After you locate an individual in this Index, take note of the Section and Section Part then proceed to the Land Patent map on the pages immediately following. You should have no difficulty locating the corresponding parcel of land.

The "For More Info" Column will lead you to more information about the underlying Patents. See the *Legend* at right, and the "How to Use this Book" chapter, for more information.

LEGEND

"For More Info . . . " column

A = Authority (Legislative Act, See Appendix "A")
B = Block or Lot (location in Section unknown)
C = Cancelled Patent
F = Fractional Section
G = Group (Multi-Patentee Patent, see Appendix "C")
V = Overlaps another Parcel
R = Re-Issued (Parcel patented more than once)

(A & G items require you to look in the Appendixes referred to above. All other Letter-designations followed by a number require you to locate line-items in this index that possess the ID number found after the letter).

ID	Individual in Patent	Sec.	Sec. Part	Date Issued	Other Counties	For More Info . . .
3617	ABERNATHY, John T	23	W½SE	1841-02-27		A1 G11
3616	" "	25	E½SW	1841-02-27		A1 G12
3619	" "	25	W½NW	1841-02-27		A1 G14
3620	" "	26	E½NE	1841-02-27		A1 G14
3621	" "	4	E½NW	1841-02-27		A1 G3
3614	" "	5	E½SE	1841-02-27		A1 G4
3615	" "	5	W½SE	1841-02-27		A1 G4
3618	" "	24	E½SE	1849-05-21		A1 G8
3705	BAIRD, William	33	E½NE	1841-02-27		A1
3510	BELCHER, Branch	22	SW	1841-02-27		A1 G32
3675	BEVIL, Thomas L	1	E½SW	1841-02-27		A1
3676	" "	1	W½SE	1841-02-27		A1
3677	BEVILL, Thomas L	13	E½NE	1841-02-27		A1
3678	" "	13	E½SE	1841-02-27		A1
3621	" "	4	E½NW	1841-02-27		A1 G3
3555	BOWEN, Horatio	1	W½NW	1841-02-27		A1 G51
3556	" "	1	W½SW	1841-02-27		A1 G51
3557	" "	2	SE	1841-02-27		A1 G51
3545	BOYD, Gordon D	6	NE	1860-04-02		A1
3526	BOYLS, Elisha T	31	NWNW	1856-04-01		A1
3527	" "	31	SWNW	1859-10-01		A1
3708	BOYLS, William C	30	SWSE	1854-03-15		A1
3706	" "	30	NESW	1860-05-01		A1
3707	" "	30	SESW	1860-05-01		A1
3641	BREWTON, Lecil	18	SE	1841-02-27		A1
3642	" "	18	W½SW	1841-02-27		A1
3508	BURNETT, Boling C	5	E½NE	1841-02-27		A1
3614	" "	5	E½SE	1841-02-27		A1 G4
3509	" "	5	W½NE	1841-02-27		A1
3615	" "	5	W½SE	1841-02-27		A1 G4
3488	CALVERT, Adam	21	SWNE	1854-03-15		A1
3489	" "	26	SWSE	1854-03-15		A1
3490	" "	26	SWSW	1854-03-15		A1
3491	" "	35	NWSW	1854-03-15		A1
3486	" "	21	NENW	1856-04-01		A1
3487	" "	21	SESE	1856-04-01		A1
3631	CALVERT, Joseph P	19	S½SE	1895-12-14		A2
3599	CHISOLM, John E	17	NENW	1859-10-01		A1
3679	CLARK, Thomas L	2	S½NW	1896-12-14		A2
3551	CLAY, Hillery P	4	E½NE	1854-03-15		A1
3552	" "	4	NWNE	1854-03-15		A1
3712	CLAY, William W	13	SW	1892-06-30		A2
3547	COLLUM, Harris	34	NESW	1860-05-01		A1
3548	" "	34	NWSE	1860-05-01		A1
3693	COLLUM, Wilkin	34	SESE	1841-02-27		A1
3694	" "	35	SWSW	1841-02-27		A1

ID	Individual in Patent	Sec.	Sec. Part	Date Issued	Other Counties	For More Info . . .
3492	CROWTHER, Albert W	30	W½SW	1896-11-13		A1
3595	CROWTHER, John	30	SESE	1859-10-01		A1
3592	" "	30	E½NE	1860-05-01		A1
3593	" "	30	NWSE	1860-05-01		A1
3594	" "	30	SENW	1860-05-01		A1
3596	" "	30	SWNE	1860-05-01		A1
3597	" "	30	W½NW	1860-05-01		A1
3523	DAVIS, Edwin B	36	SESE	1854-03-15		A1
3531	DUNCAN, Foster	35	NENW	1841-02-27		A1
3532	" "	35	SWSE	1843-02-01		A1
3586	DUNCAN, Jeremiah	25	E½NW	1841-02-27		A1
3587	" "	26	E½NW	1841-02-27		A1
3598	DUNKIN, John	26	SESW	1859-10-01		A1
3574	ELLIOT, James	29	E½NW	1841-02-27		A1
3575	" "	29	E½SW	1841-02-27		A1
3576	" "	29	SWSE	1841-02-27		A1
3577	" "	6	W½	1844-07-13		A1
3522	ETHRIDGE, David F	31	E½NE	1898-08-15		A2
3564	ETHRIDGE, Isaac	34	NESE	1859-10-01		A1
3565	" "	34	SWSE	1859-10-01		A1
3625	EUBANKS, John W	2	E½NE	1891-03-16		A2
3632	EVANS, Joseph S	13	SWSE	1906-09-26		A2
3647	FOSTER, Mary A	21	NWNW	1854-03-15		A1
3591	GREEN, John B	23	E½NE	1861-01-01		A1
3516	GREENE, Daniel	23	E½SE	1841-02-27		A1 G191
3517	" "	26	W½NW	1841-02-27		A1 G179
3518	" "	27	E½NE	1841-02-27		A1 G179
3514	" "	4	W½NW	1841-02-27		A1
3515	" "	4	W½SW	1841-02-27		A1
3628	GRIGSBY, Joseph	5	E½NW	1841-02-27		A1 G212
3629	" "	5	W½NW	1841-02-27		A1 G212
3578	GRISOM, James F	17	NENE	1854-03-15		A1
3561	HALL, Isaac B	25	W½SW	1860-05-01		A1
3562	" "	26	NESE	1860-05-01		A1
3563	" "	26	SWNE	1860-05-01		A1
3541	HARPER, George W	12	E½SE	1841-02-27		A1
3542	" "	12	E½SW	1841-02-27		A1
3543	" "	12	W½NE	1841-02-27		A1
3544	" "	12	W½SE	1841-02-27		A1
3628	HARRIS, Wiley P	5	E½NW	1841-02-27		A1 G212
3629	" "	5	W½NW	1841-02-27		A1 G212
3618	HENDERSON, John	24	E½SE	1849-05-21		A1 G8
3507	HENDRICK, Bernard G	21	SWSE	1850-12-05		A1
3663	HUBBARD, Samuel	18	W½NE	1841-02-27		A1 G234
3664	" "	23	W½NW	1841-02-27		A1 G234
3665	" "	23	W½SW	1841-02-27		A1 G234
3517	" "	26	W½NW	1841-02-27		A1 G179
3518	" "	27	E½NE	1841-02-27		A1 G179
3666	" "	7	E½SW	1841-02-27		A1 G234
3667	" "	7	W½SE	1841-02-27		A1 G234
3603	HUSTON, John	19	NENE	1856-04-01		A1
3605	" "	19	SWNE	1856-04-01		A1
3604	" "	19	SENE	1859-10-01		A1
3500	JACKSON, Andrew	4	E½SW	1860-05-01		A1
3610	JEMISON, John S	1	E½NE	1841-02-27		A1
3611	" "	1	E½NW	1841-02-27		A1
3612	" "	1	W½NE	1841-02-27		A1
3691	JENKINS, Wiley R	7	SENW	1854-03-15		A1
3690	" "	7	NENW	1860-05-01		A1
3513	JOHNSON, Claibourn M	2	W½NE	1901-11-16		A2
3588	JOINER, John A	31	N½SE	1910-04-11		A2
3589	" "	31	SWNE	1910-04-11		A2
3590	" "	32	NESW	1910-04-11		A2
3633	JOYNER, Joshua A	30	NENW	1884-12-30		A2
3634	" "	30	NWNE	1884-12-30		A2
3709	JOYNER, William G	31	N½SW	1899-06-28		A2
3710	" "	31	SENW	1899-06-28		A2
3622	JUMPER, John T	13	SWNW	1899-06-13		A2
3495	KING, Amos	35	SENW	1859-10-01		A1
3496	" "	36	NESW	1860-05-01		A1
3497	" "	36	SENW	1860-05-01		A1
3657	KING, Richard	26	SESE	1850-12-05		A1
3659	" "	36	W½NW	1850-12-05		A1

ID	Individual in Patent	Sec.	Sec. Part	Date Issued	Other Counties	For More Info . . .
3660	KING, Richard (Cont'd)	36	W½SW	1850-12-05		A1
3658	" "	36	SWSE	1860-05-01		A1
3643	LATHAM, Lorenzo	27	E½NW	1841-02-27		A1
3644	" "	27	W½NE	1841-02-27		A1
3645	" "	27	W½NW	1841-02-27		A1
3498	LEE, Andrew G	36	W½NE	1859-10-01		A1
3499	LEE, Andrew J	24	SWSW	1856-04-01		A1
3662	LEWIS, Rufus G	14	W½SW	1841-02-27		A1 G268
3663	" "	18	W½NE	1841-02-27		A1 G234
3664	" "	23	W½NW	1841-02-27		A1 G234
3665	" "	23	W½SW	1841-02-27		A1 G234
3517	" "	26	W½NW	1841-02-27		A1 G179
3518	" "	27	E½NE	1841-02-27		A1 G179
3666	" "	7	E½SW	1841-02-27		A1 G234
3667	" "	7	W½SE	1841-02-27		A1 G234
3600	LLOYD, John E	12	E½NE	1841-02-27		A1 G271
3558	MCDONALD, Hugh	11	SWSW	1841-02-27		A1
3559	" "	14	S½NW	1841-02-27		A1
3560	" "	7	W½SW	1841-02-27		A1
3501	MCGEHEE, Archibald	18	E½NE	1841-02-27		A1
3502	" "	18	E½NW	1841-02-27		A1
3503	" "	7	E½SE	1841-02-27		A1
3520	MCINTUSH, Daniel	18	W½NW	1841-02-27		A1
3640	MCKEE, Lawson B	22	NWNE	1850-12-05		A1
3695	MILLS, Willard C	14	NWSE	1854-03-15		A1
3700	" "	24	SESW	1854-03-15		A1
3701	" "	24	W½NW	1854-03-15		A1
3702	" "	26	NWSE	1854-03-15		A1
3696	" "	17	NESE	1856-04-01		A1
3699	" "	24	NWSE	1859-10-01		A1
3703	" "	35	NWNW	1859-10-01		A1
3697	" "	17	NWNE	1860-05-01		A1
3698	" "	2	NWNW	1860-05-01		A1
3704	" "	35	SWNW	1860-05-01		A1
3674	MISSISSIPPI, State Of	36	NENW	1909-05-14		A3
3711	MOORE, William	17	SENE	1860-05-01		A1
3713	MOORE, Willie Walter	36	SESW	1917-04-30		A2
3525	MOSLEY, Elisha	8	N½	1860-05-01		A1
3630	MULHOLLAND, Joseph	27	SESW	1860-05-01		A1
3528	NASH, Ezekiel	1	E½SE	1841-02-27		A1 G301
3528	NASH, Orsamus L	1	E½SE	1841-02-27		A1 G301
3580	ODEN, James I	13	NENW	1860-05-01		A1
3581	ODEN, James J	11	NENE	1859-10-01		A1
3582	" "	11	SENE	1860-05-01		A1
3583	" "	12	E½NW	1860-05-01		A1
3584	" "	12	W½NW	1860-05-01		A1
3608	OWEN, John	27	W½SW	1841-02-27		A1 G306
3609	" "	28	E½SE	1841-02-27		A1 G306
3601	POOL, John G	31	S½SE	1898-07-12		A2
3602	" "	31	S½SW	1898-07-12		A2
3661	POOLE, Richard P	26	NWNE	1856-04-01		A1
3668	POOLE, Samuel P	26	NWSW	1854-03-15		A1
3669	" "	27	NESE	1856-04-01		A1
3670	" "	27	SESE	1859-10-01		A1
3585	PREUIT, James	11	SE	1841-02-27		A1
3635	PREUIT, Joshua	11	E½SW	1841-02-27		A1
3636	" "	14	NE	1841-02-27		A1
3637	" "	29	NE	1841-02-27		A1
3638	" "	29	NWSE	1841-02-27		A1
3649	PREWIT, Peter	28	E½NW	1841-02-27		A1
3650	" "	28	NE	1841-02-27		A1
3651	" "	29	W½NW	1841-02-27		A1
3652	" "	29	W½SW	1841-02-27		A1
3566	PRUIT, Isaac	23	E½NW	1841-02-27		A1
3567	" "	23	E½SW	1841-02-27		A1
3568	" "	23	W½NE	1841-02-27		A1
3569	" "	29	NESE	1841-02-27		A1
3639	PRUIT, Joshua	28	NESW	1843-02-01		A1
3653	PRUITT, Peter	32	NENW	1860-10-01		A1
3654	" "	32	NESE	1860-10-01		A1
3655	" "	32	SENE	1860-10-01		A1
3656	" "	32	W½NE	1860-10-01		A1
3680	PRUITT, Thomas M	28	NWSE	1855-03-15		A1

ID	Individual in Patent	Sec.	Sec. Part	Date Issued	Other Counties	For More Info . . .
3681	PRUITT, Thomas M (Cont'd)	28	NWSW	1855-03-15		A1
3684	" "	33	NESE	1859-10-01		A1
3682	" "	28	SWSE	1860-05-01		A1
3683	" "	29	SESE	1860-05-01		A1
3685	" "	33	NW	1860-05-01		A1
3511	ROBINSON, Charles E	13	NWNE	1882-08-03		A2
3516	RUPERT, James C	23	E½SE	1841-02-27		A1 G191
3617	" "	23	W½SE	1841-02-27		A1 G11
3512	RUSHING, Charles E	8	SWSW	1860-05-01		A1
3607	SALTER, John Mark	13	SENW	1917-08-04		A2
3692	SECREST, Wiley	17	SESW	1854-03-15		A1
3521	SLATON, Daniel	33	SESW	1860-05-01		A1
3613	SMITH, John	19	NW	1841-02-27		A1
3671	SMITH, Samuel	17	SENW	1859-10-01		A1
3600	SPINKS, Enoch	12	E½NE	1841-02-27		A1 G271
3663	TAPPAN, John	18	W½NE	1841-02-27		A1 G234
3664	" "	23	W½NW	1841-02-27		A1 G234
3665	" "	23	W½SW	1841-02-27		A1 G234
3517	" "	26	W½NW	1841-02-27		A1 G179
3518	" "	27	E½NE	1841-02-27		A1 G179
3666	" "	7	E½SW	1841-02-27		A1 G234
3667	" "	7	W½SE	1841-02-27		A1 G234
3555	TAYLOR, Swepson	1	W½NW	1841-02-27		A1 G51
3556	" "	1	W½SW	1841-02-27		A1 G51
3557	" "	2	SE	1841-02-27		A1 G51
3493	THOMPSON, Alfred W	22	E½NE	1848-09-01		A1
3494	" "	22	SWNE	1848-09-01		A1
3546	TINSLEY, Green	24	E½NE	1854-03-15		A1
3549	TINSLEY, Henry G	13	NWSE	1860-05-01		A1
3550	" "	13	SWNE	1860-05-01		A1
3579	TINSLEY, James G	11	NWNE	1856-04-01		A1
3624	TINSLEY, John	18	E½SW	1841-02-27		A1
3623	" "	11	NWSW	1860-05-01		A1
3606	TINSLEY, John J	14	SWSE	1860-05-01		A1
3626	TOLES, John W	12	W½SW	1894-09-28		A2
3627	" "	13	NWNW	1894-09-28		A2
3686	TUCKER, Thomas	26	NESW	1854-03-15		A1
3687	" "	34	NENE	1859-10-01		A1
3688	" "	34	SENE	1860-05-01		A1
3533	TUTT, Gabriel H	35	E½SW	1841-02-27		A1
3616	TUTT, James B	25	E½SW	1841-02-27		A1 G12
3570	" "	25	NE	1841-02-27		A1
3571	" "	25	W½SE	1841-02-27		A1
3572	" "	35	E½SE	1841-02-27		A1
3573	" "	35	NE	1841-02-27		A1
3714	TUTT, Wilson G	35	NWSE	1844-09-10		A1
3529	VANCE, Ford Howard	33	SESE	1920-07-01		A2
3530	" "	34	S½SW	1920-07-01		A2
3534	VANCE, George	27	SWSE	1856-04-01		A1
3535	" "	33	NWNE	1856-04-01		A1
3540	" "	34	SWNW	1859-10-01		A1
3536	" "	33	SWNE	1860-05-01		A1
3537	" "	33	W½SE	1860-05-01		A1
3538	" "	34	NWNW	1860-05-01		A1
3539	" "	34	NWSW	1860-05-01		A1
3608	WEIR, Adolphus G	27	W½SW	1841-02-27		A1 G306
3609	" "	28	E½SE	1841-02-27		A1 G306
3510	WELLS, Daniel	22	SW	1841-02-27		A1 G32
3662	WHITSETT, John C	14	W½SW	1841-02-27		A1 G268
3519	WILLIAMS, Daniel M	14	E½SE	1894-02-28		A2
3504	WINDHAM, Benjamin B	11	SWNE	1854-03-15		A1
3505	" "	21	NWSE	1854-03-15		A1
3506	" "	22	SWNW	1859-10-01		A1
3524	WINDHAM, Eli	19	SW	1879-05-06		A2
3646	WINDHAM, Martha A	5	SW	1885-12-19		A2 G339
3648	WINDHAM, Paterson P	17	NWNW	1854-03-15		A1
3646	WINDHAM, S S	5	SW	1885-12-19		A2 G339
3672	WINDHAM, Samuel	21	NESE	1859-10-01		A1
3673	" "	21	SENE	1859-10-01		A1
3553	YATES, Hiram I	32	NWNW	1901-02-27		A2
3554	" "	32	S½NW	1901-02-27		A2
3619	YOUNG, Robert M	25	W½NW	1841-02-27		A1 G14
3620	" "	26	E½NE	1841-02-27		A1 G14

ID	Individual in Patent	Sec.	Sec. Part	Date Issued	Other Counties	For More Info . . .
3689	YOUNG, Thomas	14	N½NW	1841-02-27		A1

Patent Map

T9-N R14-E
Choctaw Meridian

Map Group 19

Township Statistics

Parcels Mapped	:	229
Number of Patents	:	185
Number of Individuals	:	119
Patentees Identified	:	114
Number of Surnames	:	88
Multi-Patentee Parcels	:	28
Oldest Patent Date	:	2/27/1841
Most Recent Patent	:	7/1/1920
Block/Lot Parcels	:	0
Parcels Re - Issued	:	0
Parcels that Overlap	:	0
Cities and Towns	:	3
Cemeteries	:	4

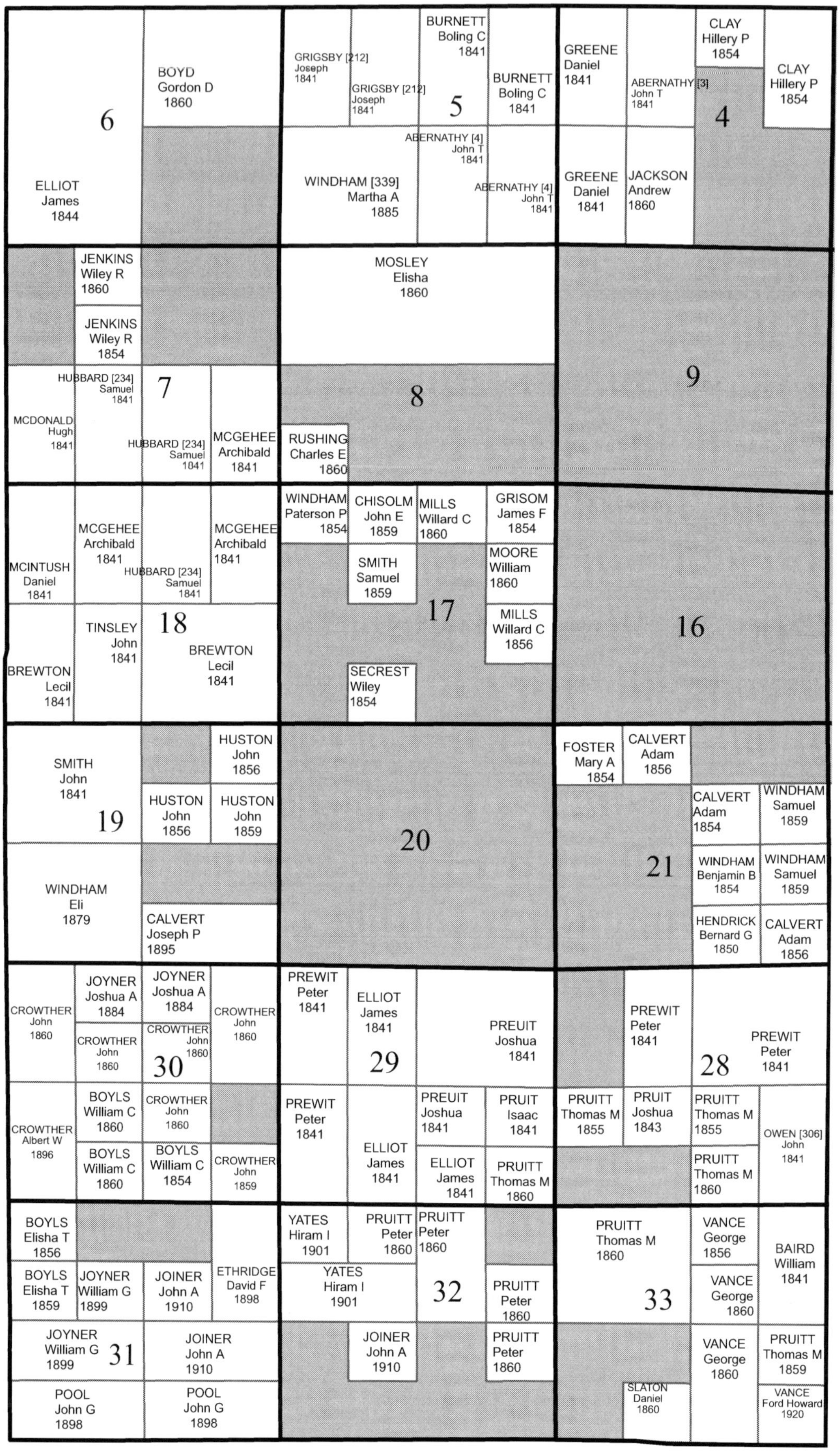

6
BOYD Gordon D 1860
ELLIOT James 1844

5
GRIGSBY [212] Joseph 1841
GRIGSBY [212] Joseph 1841
BURNETT Boling C 1841
BURNETT Boling C 1841
ABERNATHY [4] John T 1841
WINDHAM [339] Martha A 1885
ABERNATHY [4] John T 1841

4
GREENE Daniel 1841
ABERNATHY [3] John T 1841
CLAY Hillery P 1854
CLAY Hillery P 1854
GREENE Daniel 1841
JACKSON Andrew 1860

7
JENKINS Wiley R 1860
JENKINS Wiley R 1854
HUBBARD [234] Samuel 1841
MCDONALD Hugh 1841
HUBBARD [234] Samuel 1041
MCGEHEE Archibald 1841

8
MOSLEY Elisha 1860
RUSHING Charles E 1860

9

18
MCINTUSH Daniel 1841
MCGEHEE Archibald 1841
HUBBARD [234] Samuel 1841
MCGEHEE Archibald 1841
BREWTON Lecil 1841
TINSLEY John 1841
BREWTON Lecil 1841

17
WINDHAM Paterson P 1854
CHISOLM John E 1859
MILLS Willard C 1860
GRISOM James F 1854
SMITH Samuel 1859
MOORE William 1860
MILLS Willard C 1856
SECREST Wiley 1854

16

19
SMITH John 1841
HUSTON John 1856
HUSTON John 1856
HUSTON John 1859
WINDHAM Eli 1879
CALVERT Joseph P 1895

20

21
FOSTER Mary A 1854
CALVERT Adam 1856
CALVERT Adam 1854
WINDHAM Samuel 1859
WINDHAM Benjamin B 1854
WINDHAM Samuel 1859
HENDRICK Bernard G 1850
CALVERT Adam 1856

30
CROWTHER John 1860
JOYNER Joshua A 1884
JOYNER Joshua A 1884
CROWTHER John 1860
CROWTHER John 1860
CROWTHER John 1860
CROWTHER Albert W 1896
BOYLS William C 1860
CROWTHER John 1860
BOYLS William C 1860
BOYLS William C 1854
CROWTHER John 1859

29
PREWIT Peter 1841
ELLIOT James 1841
PREUIT Joshua 1841
PREWIT Peter 1841
PREUIT Joshua 1841
PRUIT Isaac 1841
ELLIOT James 1841
ELLIOT James 1841
PRUITT Thomas M 1860

28
PREWIT Peter 1841
PREWIT Peter 1841
PRUITT Thomas M 1855
PRUIT Joshua 1843
PRUITT Thomas M 1855
OWEN [306] John 1841
PRUITT Thomas M 1860

31
BOYLS Elisha T 1856
BOYLS Elisha T 1859
JOYNER William G 1899
JOINER John A 1910
ETHRIDGE David F 1898
JOYNER William G 1899
JOINER John A 1910
POOL John G 1898
POOL John G 1898

32
YATES Hiram I 1901
PRUITT Peter 1860
PRUITT Peter 1860
YATES Hiram I 1901
PRUITT Peter 1860
JOINER John A 1910
PRUITT Peter 1860

33
PRUITT Thomas M 1860
VANCE George 1856
BAIRD William 1841
VANCE George 1860
VANCE George 1860
PRUITT Thomas M 1859
SLATON Daniel 1860
VANCE Ford Howard 1920

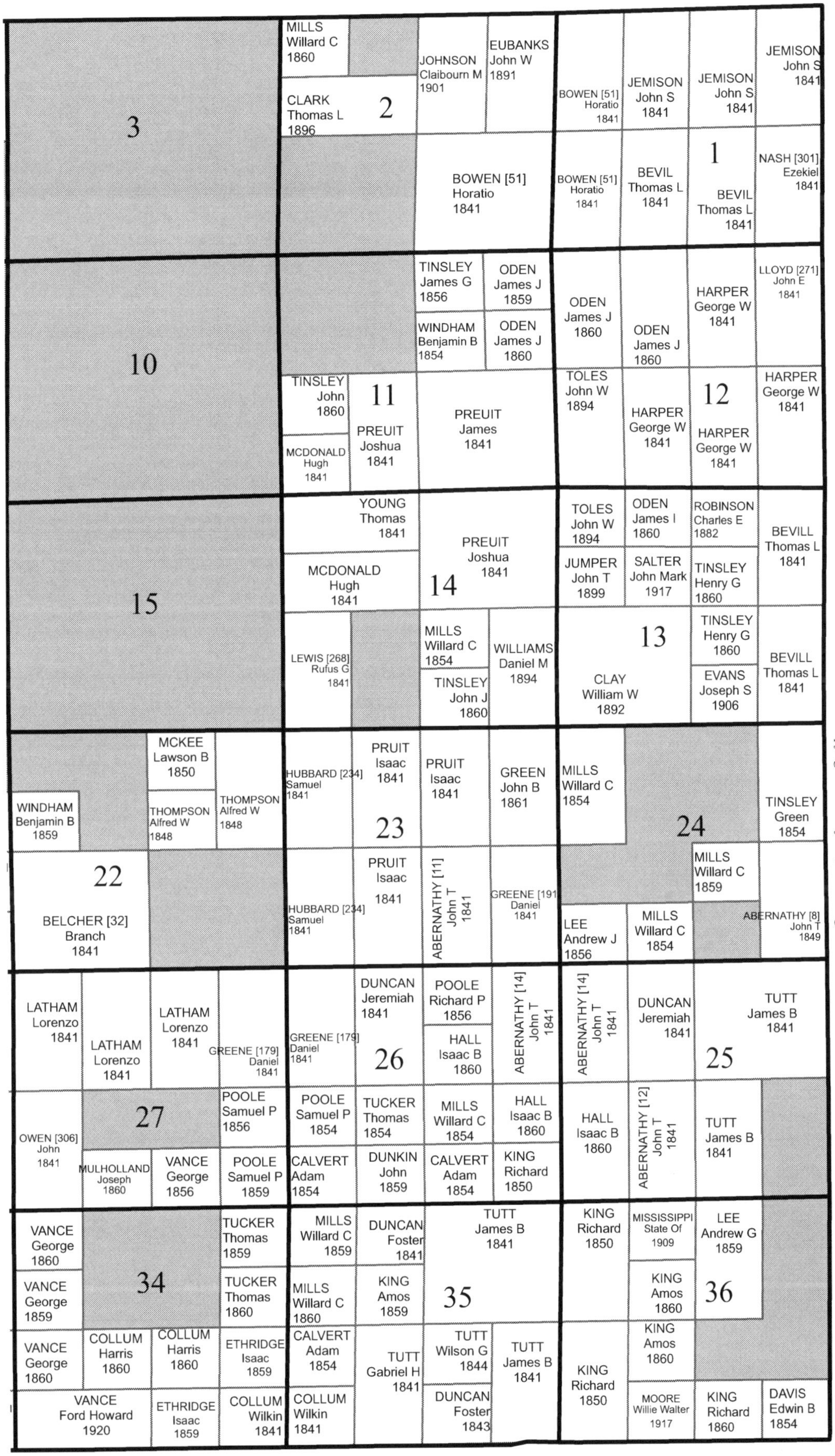

3

MILLS Willard C 1860
CLARK Thomas L 1896
2
JOHNSON Claibourn M 1901
EUBANKS John W 1891
BOWEN [51] Horatio 1841

BOWEN [51] Horatio 1841
JEMISON John S 1841
JEMISON John S 1841
JEMISON John S 1841
1
BOWEN [51] Horatio 1841
BEVIL Thomas L 1841
BEVIL Thomas L 1841
NASH [301] Ezekiel 1841

10

TINSLEY James G 1856
ODEN James J 1859
WINDHAM Benjamin B 1854
ODEN James J 1860
TINSLEY John 1860
11
MCDONALD Hugh 1841
PREUIT Joshua 1841
PREUIT James 1841

ODEN James J 1860
ODEN James J 1860
HARPER George W 1841
LLOYD [271] John E 1841
TOLES John W 1894
HARPER George W 1841
12
HARPER George W 1841
HARPER George W 1841

15

YOUNG Thomas 1841
MCDONALD Hugh 1841
PREUIT Joshua 1841
14
LEWIS [268] Rufus G 1841
MILLS Willard C 1854
TINSLEY John J 1860
WILLIAMS Daniel M 1894

TOLES John W 1894
ODEN James I 1860
ROBINSON Charles E 1882
BEVILL Thomas L 1841
JUMPER John T 1899
SALTER John Mark 1917
TINSLEY Henry G 1860
13
TINSLEY Henry G 1860
CLAY William W 1892
EVANS Joseph S 1906
BEVILL Thomas L 1841

MCKEE Lawson B 1850
WINDHAM Benjamin B 1859
THOMPSON Alfred W 1848
THOMPSON Alfred W 1848
22
BELCHER [32] Branch 1841

HUBBARD [234] Samuel 1841
PRUIT Isaac 1841
PRUIT Isaac 1841
GREEN John B 1861
23
HUBBARD [234] Samuel 1841
PRUIT Isaac 1841
ABERNATHY [11] John T 1841
GREENE [191] Daniel 1841

MILLS Willard C 1854
24
TINSLEY Green 1854
MILLS Willard C 1859
LEE Andrew J 1856
MILLS Willard C 1854
ABERNATHY [8] John T 1849

LATHAM Lorenzo 1841
LATHAM Lorenzo 1841
LATHAM Lorenzo 1841
GREENE [179] Daniel 1841
27
OWEN [306] John 1841
POOLE Samuel P 1856
MULHOLLAND Joseph 1860
VANCE George 1856
POOLE Samuel P 1859

DUNCAN Jeremiah 1841
POOLE Richard P 1856
ABERNATHY [14] John T 1841
GREENE [179] Daniel 1841
26
HALL Isaac B 1860
POOLE Samuel P 1854
TUCKER Thomas 1854
MILLS Willard C 1854
HALL Isaac B 1860
CALVERT Adam 1854
DUNKIN John 1859
CALVERT Adam 1854
KING Richard 1850

ABERNATHY [14] John T 1841
DUNCAN Jeremiah 1841
TUTT James B 1841
25
HALL Isaac B 1860
ABERNATHY [12] John T 1841
TUTT James B 1841

VANCE George 1860
TUCKER Thomas 1859
34
VANCE George 1859
TUCKER Thomas 1860
VANCE George 1860
COLLUM Harris 1860
COLLUM Harris 1860
ETHRIDGE Isaac 1859
VANCE Ford Howard 1920
ETHRIDGE Isaac 1859
COLLUM Wilkin 1841

MILLS Willard C 1859
DUNCAN Foster 1841
TUTT James B 1841
MILLS Willard C 1860
KING Amos 1859
35
CALVERT Adam 1854
TUTT Gabriel H 1841
TUTT Wilson G 1844
TUTT James B 1841
COLLUM Wilkin 1841
DUNCAN Foster 1843

KING Richard 1850
MISSISSIPPI State Of 1909
LEE Andrew G 1859
KING Amos 1860
36
KING Amos 1860
KING Richard 1850
MOORE Willie Walter 1917
KING Richard 1860
DAVIS Edwin B 1854

Helpful Hints

1. This Map's INDEX can be found on the preceding pages.
2. Refer to Map "C" to see where this Township lies within Kemper County, Mississippi.
3. Numbers within square brackets [ ] denote a multi-patentee land parcel (multi-owner). Refer to Appendix "C" for a full list of members in this group.
4. Areas that look to be crowded with Patentees usually indicate multiple sales of the same parcel (Re-issues) or Overlapping parcels. See this Township's Index for an explanation of these and other circumstances that might explain "odd" groupings of Patentees on this map.

Legend

Patent Boundary

Section Boundary

No Patents Found (or Outside County)

1., 2., 3., ... Lot Numbers (when beside a name)

[ ] Group Number (see Appendix "C")

Scale: Section = 1 mile X 1 mile (generally, with some exceptions)

Road Map

T9-N R14-E
Choctaw Meridian

Map Group 19

Cities & Towns
- Damascus
- Rio
- Texas (historical)

Cemeteries
- Chisholm Cemetery
- Damascus Cemetery
- Linwood Cemetery
- Zion Cemetery

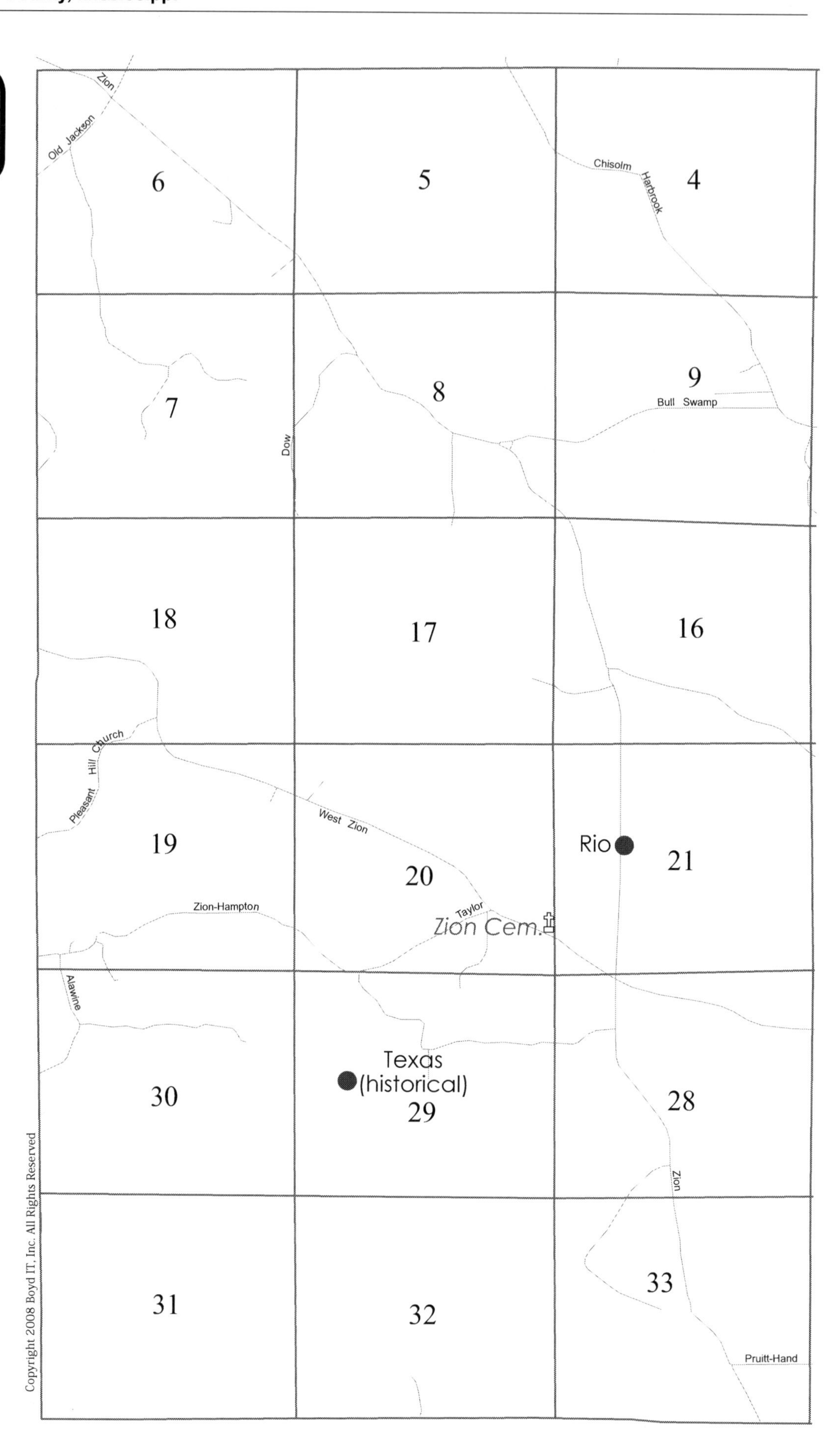

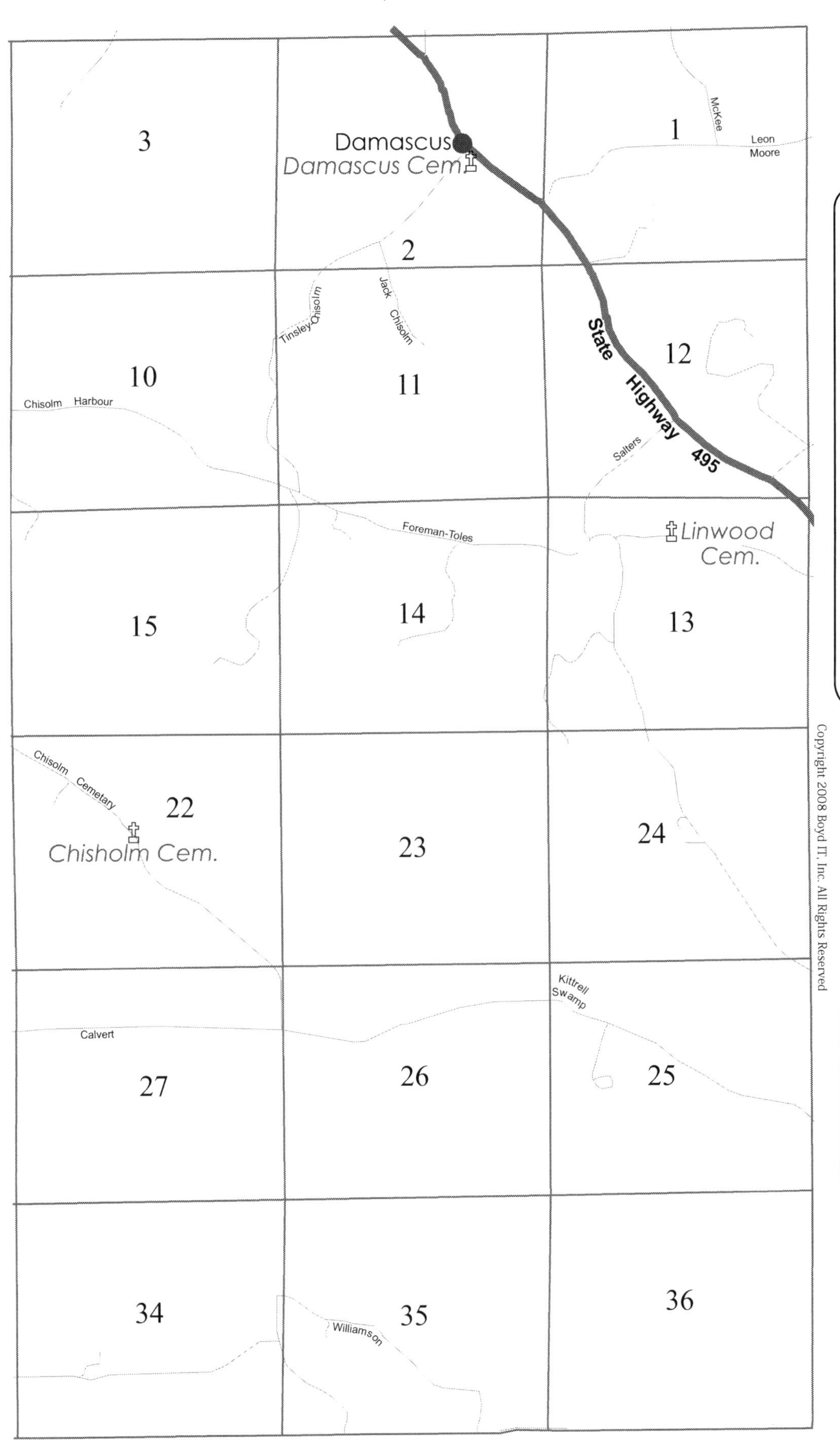

Helpful Hints

1. This road map has a number of uses, but primarily it is to help you: a) find the present location of land owned by your ancestors (at least the general area), b) find cemeteries and city-centers, and c) estimate the route/roads used by Census-takers & tax-assessors.
2. If you plan to travel to Kemper County to locate cemeteries or land parcels, please pick up a modern travel map for the area before you do. Mapping old land parcels on modern maps is not as exact a science as you might think. Just the slightest variations in public land survey coordinates, estimates of parcel boundaries, or road-map deviations can greatly alter a map's representation of how a road either does or doesn't cross a particular parcel of land.

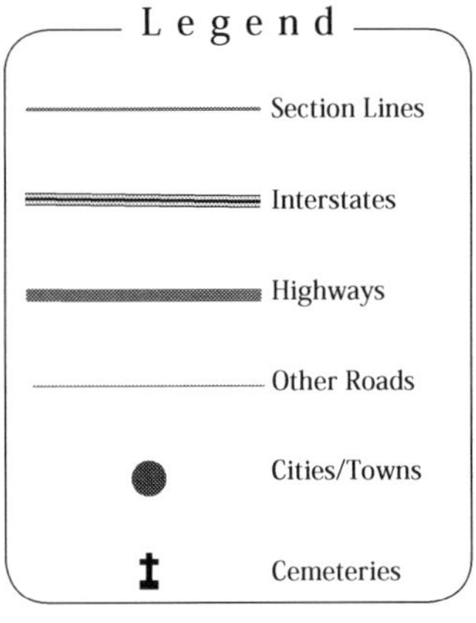

Scale: Section = 1 mile X 1 mile
(generally, with some exceptions)

Historical Map

T9-N R14-E
Choctaw Meridian

Map Group 19

Cities & Towns

- Damascus
- Rio
- Texas (historical)

Cemeteries

- Chisholm Cemetery
- Damascus Cemetery
- Linwood Cemetery
- Zion Cemetery

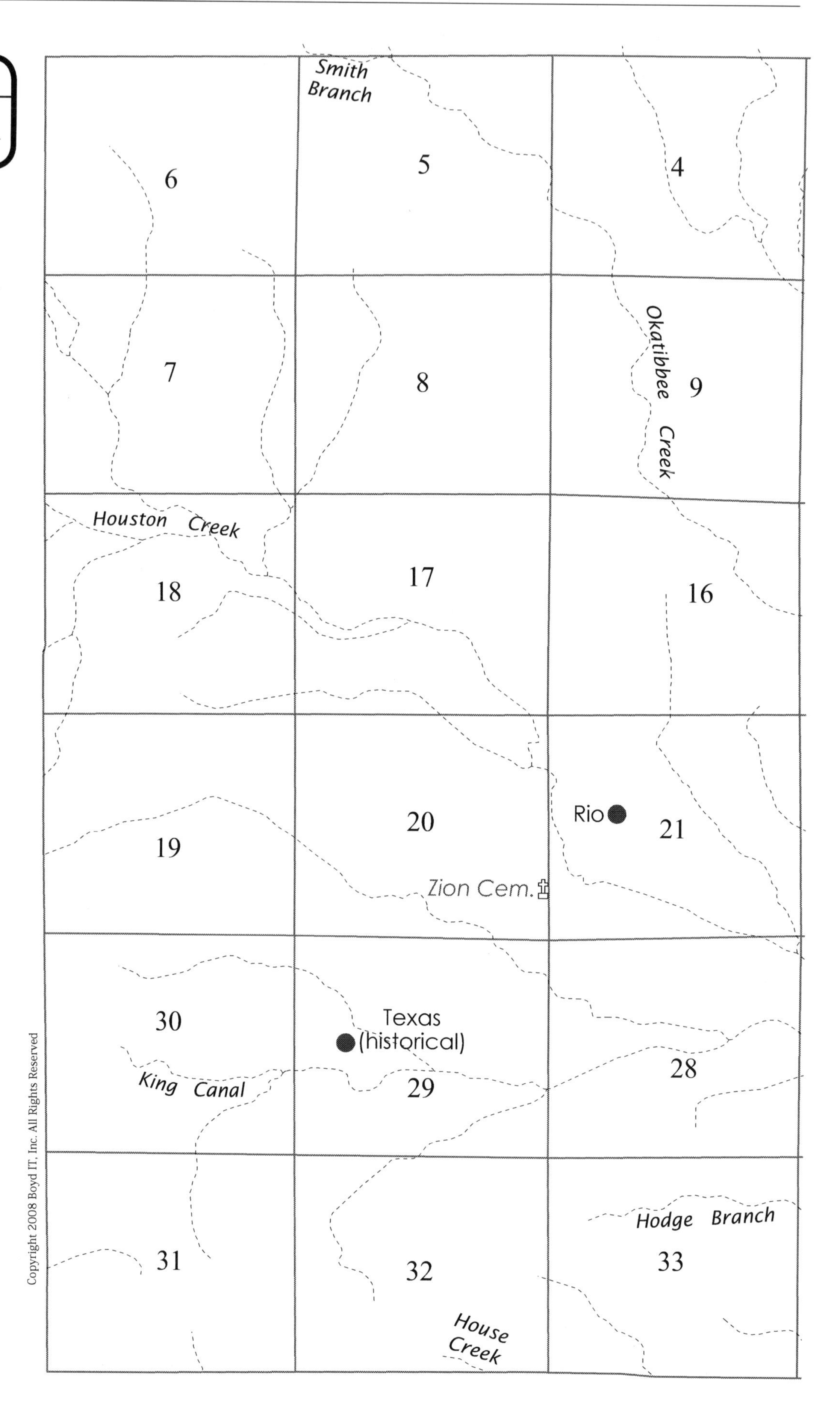

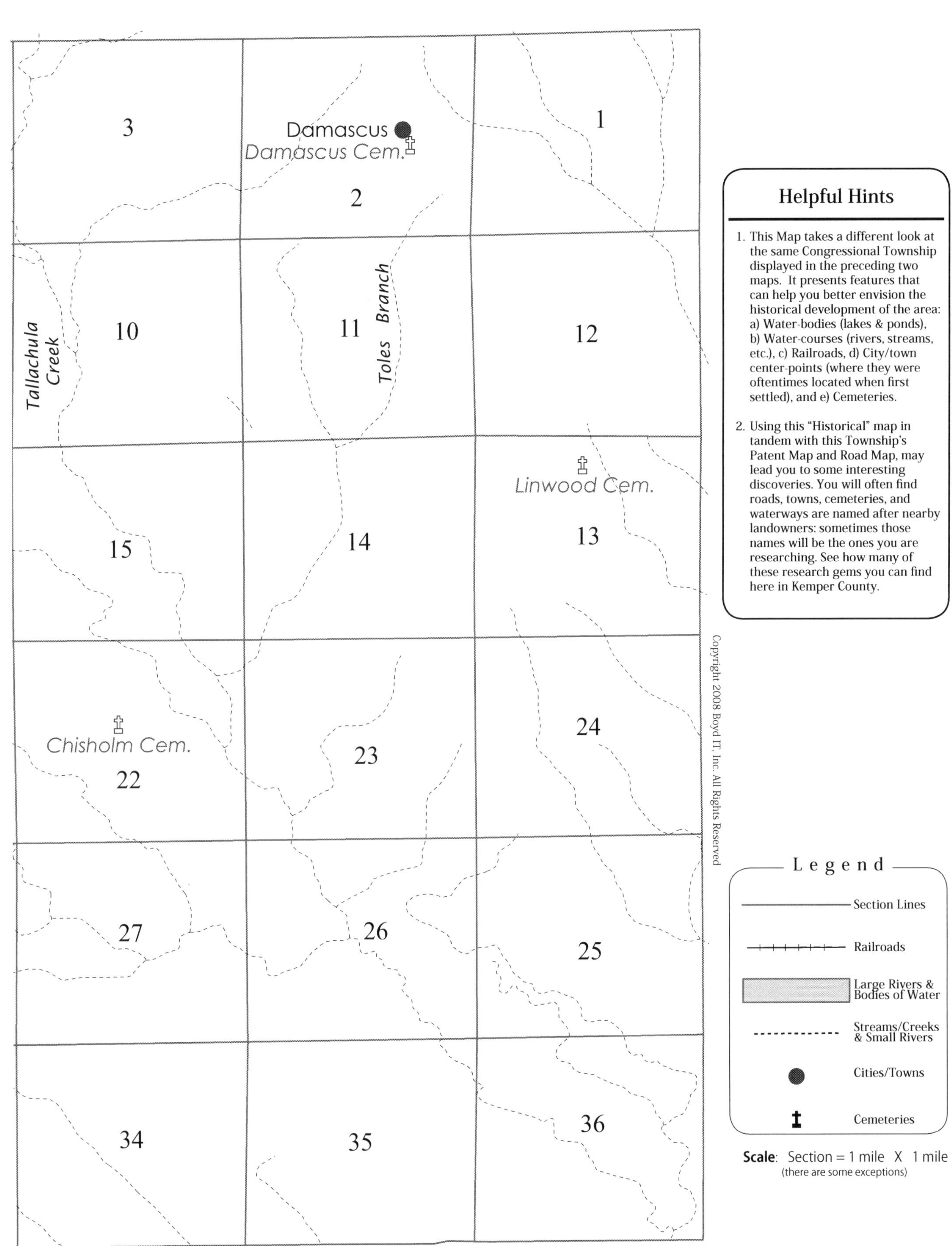

Helpful Hints

1. This Map takes a different look at the same Congressional Township displayed in the preceding two maps. It presents features that can help you better envision the historical development of the area: a) Water-bodies (lakes & ponds), b) Water-courses (rivers, streams, etc.), c) Railroads, d) City/town center-points (where they were oftentimes located when first settled), and e) Cemeteries.

2. Using this "Historical" map in tandem with this Township's Patent Map and Road Map, may lead you to some interesting discoveries. You will often find roads, towns, cemeteries, and waterways are named after nearby landowners: sometimes those names will be the ones you are researching. See how many of these research gems you can find here in Kemper County.

Scale: Section = 1 mile X 1 mile
(there are some exceptions)

Map Group 20: Index to Land Patents

Township 9-North Range 15-East (Choctaw)

After you locate an individual in this Index, take note of the Section and Section Part then proceed to the Land Patent map on the pages immediately following. You should have no difficulty locating the corresponding parcel of land.

The "For More Info" Column will lead you to more information about the underlying Patents. See the *Legend* at right, and the "How to Use this Book" chapter, for more information.

LEGEND

"For More Info . . . " column

A = Authority (Legislative Act, See Appendix "A")
B = Block or Lot (location in Section unknown)
C = Cancelled Patent
F = Fractional Section
G = Group (Multi-Patentee Patent, see Appendix "C")
V = Overlaps another Parcel
R = Re-Issued (Parcel patented more than once)

(A & G items require you to look in the Appendixes referred to above. All other Letter-designations followed by a number require you to locate line-items in this index that possess the ID number found after the letter).

ID	Individual in Patent	Sec.	Sec. Part	Date Issued	Other Counties	For More Info . . .
3721	ADAIR, Armell F	33	E½NW	1841-02-27		A1
3752	ADAIR, Ewing K	32	E½NW	1841-02-27		A1
3753	" "	32	E½SW	1841-02-27		A1
3754	" "	32	W½NE	1841-02-27		A1
3755	" "	32	W½SE	1841-02-27		A1
3777	ALLWOOD, James	3	W½NW	1841-02-27		A1
3892	AYRES, William	12	E½SW	1841-02-27		A1
3896	BANKS, Willis	28	W½SW	1841-02-27		A1
3789	BEESON, John	7	E½SW	1841-02-27		A1
3790	" "	7	W½SW	1841-02-27		A1
3879	BEVILL, Thomas L	22	E½NW	1841-02-27		A1 G41
3880	" "	7	W½SE	1841-02-27		A1 G39
3773	BROOKE, Ignatius R	34	NESE	1854-03-15		A1
3774	" "	34	SENE	1854-03-15		A1
3775	" "	34	W½NE	1854-03-15		A1
3716	CALLAWAY, Abner B	8	E½NE	1848-09-01		A1
3862	CAMPBELL, Thomas	24	NE	1846-09-01		A1
3801	COCHRAN, John H	36	SWSE	1859-10-01		A1
3846	COLE, Roscow	10	W½NW	1841-02-27		A1 G94
3847	" "	10	W½SW	1841-02-27		A1 G94
3848	" "	12	W½SW	1841-02-27		A1 G94
3849	" "	18	W½SW	1841-02-27		A1 G94 R3788
3854	" "	8	E½NW	1841-02-27		A1 G93
3850	" "	8	E½SW	1841-02-27		A1 G94
3851	" "	9	E½SE	1841-02-27		A1 G94
3852	" "	9	W½NE	1841-02-27		A1 G94
3853	" "	9	W½NW	1841-02-27		A1 G94
3868	COOPWOOD, Thomas	1	E½NW	1841-02-27		A1 G114
3869	" "	1	W½NW	1841-02-27		A1 G114
3867	" "	15	E½SW	1841-02-27		A1 G115
3875	" "	23	W½NW	1841-02-27		A1 G108
3872	" "	26	E½SE	1841-02-27		A1 G105
3863	" "	26	E½SW	1841-02-27		A1
3873	" "	26	W½SE	1841-02-27		A1 G105
3870	" "	28	E½SW	1841-02-27		A1 G114
3876	" "	33	E½SE	1841-02-27		A1 G117
3877	" "	33	W½SE	1841-02-27		A1 G117
3864	" "	35	E½SE	1841-02-27		A1
3865	" "	35	W½SE	1841-02-27		A1
3880	" "	7	W½SE	1841-02-27		A1 G39
3854	" "	8	E½NW	1841-02-27		A1 G93
3866	" "	8	W½SW	1841-02-27		A1 G109
3874	" "	9	E½NW	1841-02-27		A1 G120
3871	" "	18	E½SW	1846-08-10		A1 G107
3778	CRAWFORD, James	36	E½NW	1841-02-27		A1
3779	" "	36	NE	1841-02-27		A1

ID	Individual in Patent	Sec.	Sec. Part	Date Issued	Other Counties	For More Info . . .
3780	CRAWFORD, James (Cont'd)	36	SWNW	1841-02-27		A1
3781	" "	36	W½SW	1841-02-27		A1
3856	DAVIS, Samuel J	32	W½SW	1859-10-01		A1
3891	DAVIS, William A	31	NWNW	1849-12-01		A1
3890	" "	30	SWSW	1854-03-15		A1
3895	DAVIS, William S	31	NENW	1850-12-02		A1
3739	DEJARNAT, Elias	15	E½SE	1841-02-27		A1
3740	" "	15	W½SE	1841-02-27		A1
3855	DENNIS, Samuel	22	E½NE	1841-02-27		A1
3872	DICKINS, Robert	26	E½SE	1841-02-27		A1 G105
3873	" "	26	W½SE	1841-02-27		A1 G105
3871	ESTELL, John	18	E½SW	1846-08-10		A1 G107
3760	FLANAGIN, George B	2	SESW	1893-12-18		A2
3761	" "	2	SWNW	1893-12-18		A2
3762	" "	2	W½SW	1893-12-18		A2
3757	FOWLER, Ezra R	30	SESW	1854-03-15		A1
3875	FRANKLIN, Sidney S	23	W½NW	1841-02-27		A1 G108
3800	GALLASPY, John G	24	NW	1846-09-01		A1
3857	GAMBLE, Samuel S	18	E½NW	1841-02-27		A1
3858	" "	19	E½NW	1841-02-27		A1
3791	GREEN, John E	13	W½SE	1847-04-01		A1
3731	GREENE, Daniel	3	W½SW	1841-02-27		A1 G179
3732	" "	30	E½NW	1841-02-27		A1 G179
3733	" "	30	W½NW	1841-02-27		A1 G179
3734	" "	30	W½SE	1841-02-27		A1 G179
3729	" "	6	E½NE	1841-02-27		A1
3730	" "	7	E½SE	1841-02-27		A1
3866	" "	8	W½SW	1841-02-27		A1 G109
3723	HALE, Charles K	20	NENW	1854-03-15		A1 G214
3724	" "	20	SWNE	1854-03-15		A1 G214
3725	" "	20	SWNW	1854-03-15		A1 G214
3717	HARBOUR, Abner	8	E½SE	1848-09-01		A1
3718	" "	8	W½SE	1854-03-15		A1
3764	HARPER, George W	15	E½NW	1841-02-27		A1
3765	" "	15	W½NW	1841-02-27		A1
3766	" "	26	W½SW	1841-02-27		A1
3767	" "	3	W½SE	1841-02-27		A1
3768	" "	6	E½SW	1841-02-27		A1
3769	" "	6	W½SE	1841-02-27		A1
3770	" "	8	W½NW	1841-02-27		A1
3846	HODGES, Armstrong J	10	W½NW	1841-02-27		A1 G94
3847	" "	10	W½SW	1841-02-27		A1 G94
3848	" "	12	W½SW	1841-02-27		A1 G94
3849	" "	18	W½SW	1841-02-27		A1 G94 R3788
3879	" "	22	E½NW	1841-02-27		A1 G41
3850	" "	8	E½SW	1841-02-27		A1 G94
3851	" "	9	E½SE	1841-02-27		A1 G94
3852	" "	9	W½NE	1841-02-27		A1 G94
3853	" "	9	W½NW	1841-02-27		A1 G94
3731	HUBBARD, Samuel	3	W½SW	1841-02-27		A1 G179
3732	" "	30	E½NW	1841-02-27		A1 G179
3733	" "	30	W½NW	1841-02-27		A1 G179
3734	" "	30	W½SE	1841-02-27		A1 G179
3842	JONES, Osbon	11	SE	1848-09-01		A1
3843	" "	14	NE	1848-09-01		A1
3860	JONES, Stephen T	11	SWSW	1846-09-01		A1
3861	" "	14	NW	1846-09-01		A1
3886	JONES, Wiley C	13	NW	1848-09-01		A1
3894	JONES, William P	5	NW	1850-12-05		A1
3827	LATHAM, Lorenzo	23	E½SE	1841-02-27		A1
3828	" "	28	W½NW	1841-02-27		A1
3829	" "	30	E½NE	1841-02-27		A1
3830	" "	30	E½SE	1841-02-27		A1
3831	" "	30	W½NE	1841-02-27		A1
3832	" "	9	E½SW	1841-02-27		A1
3833	" "	9	W½SW	1841-02-27		A1
3731	LEWIS, Rufus G	3	W½SW	1841-02-27		A1 G179
3732	" "	30	E½NW	1841-02-27		A1 G179
3733	" "	30	W½NW	1841-02-27		A1 G179
3734	" "	30	W½SE	1841-02-27		A1 G179
3798	LLOYD, John E	15	W½SW	1841-02-27		A1 G272
3793	" "	25	SW	1841-02-27		A1
3794	" "	36	NWNW	1841-02-27		A1

ID	Individual in Patent	Sec.	Sec. Part	Date Issued	Other Counties	For More Info . . .
3796	LLOYD, John E (Cont'd)	7	E½NW	1841-02-27		A1
3797	" "	9	W½SE	1841-02-27		A1 G271
3795	" "	4	SE	1846-09-01		A1
3792	" "	21	SESE	1849-12-01		A1
3821	LLOYD, Joseph C	5	SE	1847-04-01		A1
3822	LOYD, Joseph C	4	SWNW	1848-09-01		A1
3803	MAJORS, John	19	E½SW	1841-02-27		A1
3804	" "	19	W½SW	1841-02-27		A1
3805	MATTHEWS, John	19	W½NW	1841-02-27		A1
3806	" "	26	W½NW	1841-02-27		A1
3807	" "	33	E½NE	1841-02-27		A1
3808	" "	33	W½NE	1841-02-27		A1
3782	MAY, James M	19	NE	1852-05-22		A1
3799	MAY, John E	17	SWSE	1849-12-01		A1
3783	MCCOWN, James	12	E½SE	1841-02-27		A1
3784	" "	12	W½SE	1841-02-27		A1
3741	MCCOY, Elijah	36	NESE	1841-02-27		A1
3881	MCGEE, Thomas	10	E½NE	1841-02-27		A1
3882	" "	10	W½NE	1841-02-27		A1
3883	" "	22	E½SE	1841-02-27		A1
3884	" "	22	W½SE	1841-02-27		A1
3885	" "	27	E½NE	1841-02-27		A1
3715	MCLELAND, Abel A	14	NESW	1850-12-05		A1
3738	MCLELAND, Elias C	25	NWNE	1850-12-05		A1
3887	MILLS, Willard C	17	SESW	1854-03-15		A1
3723	" "	20	NENW	1854-03-15		A1 G214
3724	" "	20	SWNE	1854-03-15		A1 G214
3725	" "	20	SWNW	1854-03-15		A1 G214
3888	" "	34	E½NW	1854-03-15		A1
3889	" "	34	SWNW	1854-03-15		A1
3722	MOORE, Brittan	31	E½SE	1847-04-01		A1
3742	MOSLEY, Elisha	13	E½SE	1846-09-01		A1
3756	NASH, Ezekiel	6	NW	1841-02-27		A1 G301
3756	NASH, Orsamus L	6	NW	1841-02-27		A1 G301
3809	OWEN, John	2	SE	1841-02-27		A1 G306
3820	PERKINS, John W	24	NWSW	1850-12-05		A1
3758	POLLOCK, George A	2	NESW	1859-10-01		A1
3759	" "	2	SENW	1859-10-01		A1
3785	POLLOCK, James	2	N½NW	1841-02-27		A1
3823	POSEY, Joseph	30	N½SW	1854-03-15		A1
3788	POWELL, John A	18	W½SW	1846-08-10		A1 R3849
3868	RICHEY, James	1	E½NW	1841-02-27		A1 G114
3869	" "	1	W½NW	1841-02-27		A1 G114
3870	" "	28	E½SW	1841-02-27		A1 G114
3824	ROBERTSON, Joseph	3	N½NE	1841-02-27		A1
3825	ROSS, Joseph W	10	E½SW	1890-12-20		A1
3867	RUPERT, James C	15	E½SW	1841-02-27		A1 G115
3826	SANDERSON, Joseph W	4	SW	1848-08-14		A1
3771	SKINNER, George W	12	E½NW	1885-06-12		A2
3893	SNOWDEN, William J	23	E½NE	1841-02-27		A1
3815	SORSBY, John T	6	E½SE	1841-02-27		A1
3816	" "	6	W½SW	1841-02-27		A1
3817	" "	7	E½NE	1841-02-27		A1
3818	" "	7	W½NE	1841-02-27		A1
3819	" "	7	W½NW	1841-02-27		A1
3719	SPINKS, Abraham	12	W½NE	1884-12-30		A2
3743	SPINKS, Enoch	11	NESW	1841-02-27		A1
3744	" "	11	NW	1841-02-27		A1
3745	" "	11	SESW	1841-02-27		A1
3747	" "	3	E½SW	1841-02-27		A1
3751	" "	9	E½NE	1841-02-27		A1
3797	" "	9	W½SE	1841-02-27		A1 G271
3749	" "	4	NE	1847-04-01		A1
3748	" "	4	E½NW	1848-09-01		A1
3746	" "	21	SENE	1849-12-01		A1
3750	" "	4	NWNW	1859-10-01		A1
3811	SPINKS, John	15	E½NE	1841-02-27		A1
3812	" "	15	W½NE	1841-02-27		A1
3798	" "	15	W½SW	1841-02-27		A1 G272
3813	" "	23	E½NW	1841-02-27		A1
3814	" "	23	W½NE	1841-02-27		A1
3810	" "	14	SE	1846-09-01		A1
3844	SPINKS, Peter E	13	SW	1846-09-01		A1

ID	Individual in Patent	Sec.	Sec. Part	Date Issued	Other Counties	For More Info . . .
3845	SPINKS, Peter E (Cont'd)	22	SWNE	1894-07-24		A2
3727	STEPHENSON, Charles W	32	SESE	1854-03-15		A1
3728	STEVENSON, Charles W	32	NESE	1859-10-01		A1
3868	STEWART, Hugh C	1	E½NW	1841-02-27		A1 G114
3869	" "	1	W½NW	1841-02-27		A1 G114
3870	" "	28	E½SW	1841-02-27		A1 G114
3787	STRANGE, Jesse	28	NENE	1855-03-15		A1
3731	TAPPAN, John	3	W½SW	1841-02-27		A1 G179
3732	" "	30	E½NW	1841-02-27		A1 G179
3733	" "	30	W½NW	1841-02-27		A1 G179
3734	" "	30	W½SE	1841-02-27		A1 G179
3878	TARTT, Thomas J	10	E½NW	1895-06-27		A2
3786	TREWHITT, James	32	NWNW	1859-10-01		A1
3763	TRUSSELL, George	32	SWNW	1885-07-27		A2
3834	WALTHALL, Madison	22	W½NW	1841-02-27		A1 G332
3835	" "	27	E½NW	1841-02-27		A1 G332
3836	" "	27	E½SE	1841-02-27		A1 G332
3837	" "	27	E½SW	1841-02-27		A1 G332
3838	" "	27	W½NE	1841-02-27		A1 G332
3839	" "	27	W½NW	1841-02-27		A1 G332
3840	" "	27	W½SE	1841-02-27		A1 G332
3841	" "	27	W½SW	1841-02-27		A1 G332
3876	WATTERS, Stacy B	33	E½SE	1841-02-27		A1 G117
3859	" "	33	E½SW	1841-02-27		A1
3877	" "	33	W½SE	1841-02-27		A1 G117
3809	WEIR, Adolphus G	2	SE	1841-02-27		A1 G306
3802	WELLS, John H	22	NESW	1860-05-01		A1
3720	WHITE, Andrew	1	SW	1841-02-27		A1
3735	WHITE, Dorset	1	NESE	1841-02-27		A1
3736	" "	1	SENE	1841-02-27		A1
3737	" "	1	W½SE	1841-02-27		A1
3772	WHITE, Henry	12	E½NE	1841-02-27		A1
3776	WHITE, Isaac	2	NE	1844-09-10		A1 G336
3776	WHITE, Rebecca	2	NE	1844-09-10		A1 G336
3834	WINSTON, William B	22	W½NW	1841-02-27		A1 G332
3835	" "	27	E½NW	1841-02-27		A1 G332
3836	" "	27	E½SE	1841-02-27		A1 G332
3837	" "	27	E½SW	1841-02-27		A1 G332
3838	" "	27	W½NE	1841-02-27		A1 G332
3839	" "	27	W½NW	1841-02-27		A1 G332
3840	" "	27	W½SE	1841-02-27		A1 G332
3841	" "	27	W½SW	1841-02-27		A1 G332
3726	WOLFE, Charles R	28	SWSE	1854-03-15		A1
3874	YOUNG, Robert M	9	E½NW	1841-02-27		A1 G120

Patent Map

T9-N R15-E
Choctaw Meridian

Map Group 20

Township Statistics

Parcels Mapped	182
Number of Patents	166
Number of Individuals	94
Patentees Identified	92
Number of Surnames	76
Multi-Patentee Parcels	43
Oldest Patent Date	2/27/1841
Most Recent Patent	6/27/1895
Block/Lot Parcels	0
Parcels Re - Issued	1
Parcels that Overlap	0
Cities and Towns	5
Cemeteries	4

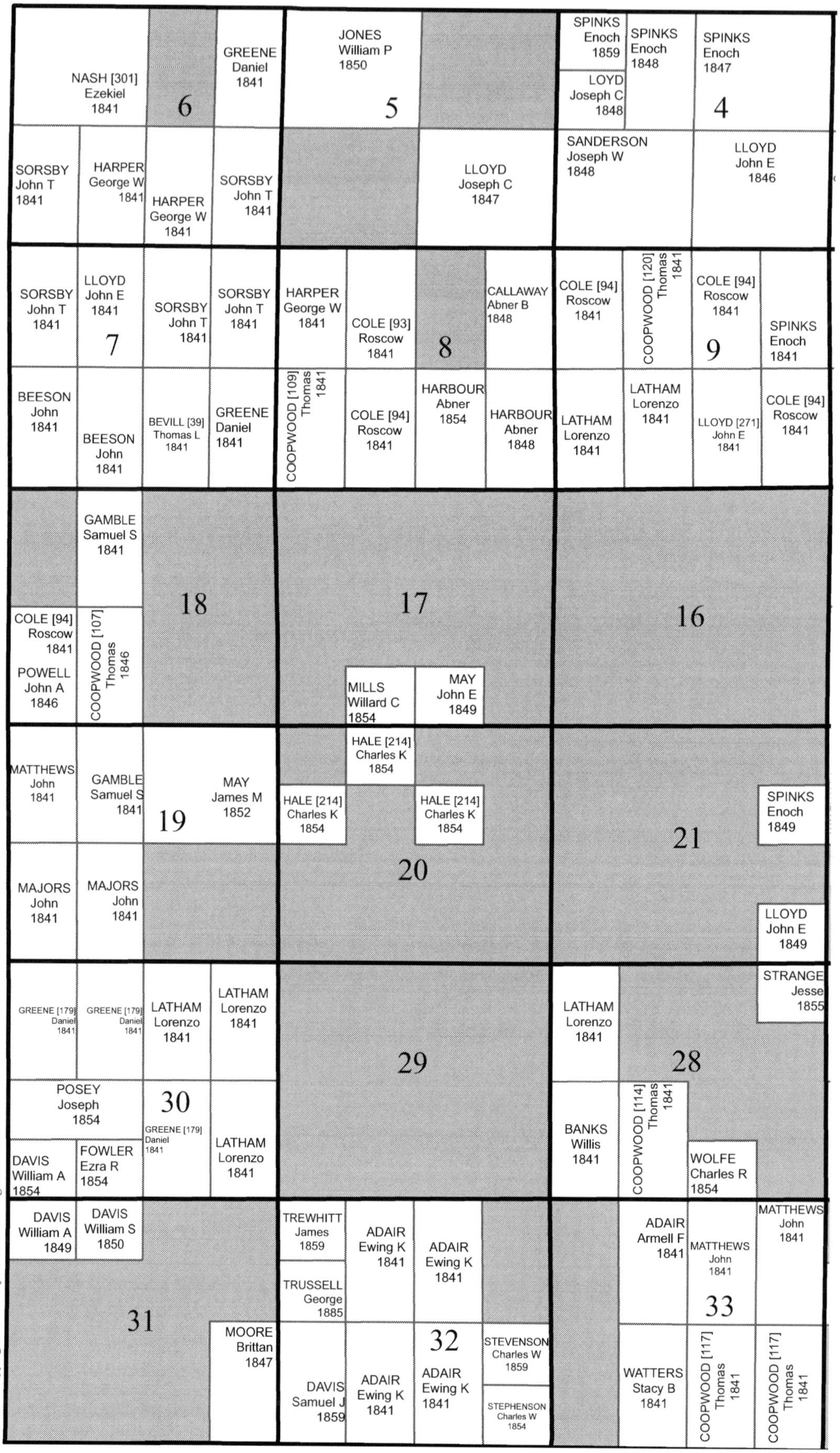

6
NASH [301] Ezekiel 1841
GREENE Daniel 1841
SORSBY John T 1841
HARPER George W 1841
HARPER George W 1841
SORSBY John T 1841

5
JONES William P 1850
LLOYD Joseph C 1847

4
SPINKS Enoch 1859
LOYD Joseph C 1848
SPINKS Enoch 1848
SPINKS Enoch 1847
SANDERSON Joseph W 1848
LLOYD John E 1846

7
SORSBY John T 1841
LLOYD John E 1841
SORSBY John T 1841
SORSBY John T 1841
BEESON John 1841
BEESON John 1841
BEVILL [39] Thomas L 1841
GREENE Daniel 1841

8
HARPER George W 1841
COLE [93] Roscow 1841
CALLAWAY Abner B 1848
COOPWOOD [109] Thomas 1841
COLE [94] Roscow 1841
HARBOUR Abner 1854
HARBOUR Abner 1848

9
COLE [94] Roscow 1841
COOPWOOD [120] Thomas 1841
COLE [94] Roscow 1841
SPINKS Enoch 1841
LATHAM Lorenzo 1841
LATHAM Lorenzo 1841
LLOYD [271] John E 1841
COLE [94] Roscow 1841

18
GAMBLE Samuel S 1841
COLE [94] Roscow 1841
POWELL John A 1846
COOPWOOD [107] Thomas 1846

17
MILLS Willard C 1854
MAY John E 1849

16

19
MATTHEWS John 1841
GAMBLE Samuel S 1841
MAY James M 1852
MAJORS John 1841
MAJORS John 1841

20
HALE [214] Charles K 1854
HALE [214] Charles K 1854
HALE [214] Charles K 1854

21
SPINKS Enoch 1849
LLOYD John E 1849

30
GREENE [179] Daniel 1841
GREENE [179] Daniel 1841
LATHAM Lorenzo 1841
LATHAM Lorenzo 1841
POSEY Joseph 1854
GREENE [179] Daniel 1841
LATHAM Lorenzo 1841
DAVIS William A 1854
FOWLER Ezra R 1854

29

28
STRANGE Jesse 1855
LATHAM Lorenzo 1841
BANKS Willis 1841
COOPWOOD [114] Thomas 1841
WOLFE Charles R 1854

31
DAVIS William A 1849
DAVIS William S 1850
MOORE Brittan 1847

32
TREWHITT James 1859
ADAIR Ewing K 1841
ADAIR Ewing K 1841
TRUSSELL George 1885
DAVIS Samuel J 1859
ADAIR Ewing K 1841
ADAIR Ewing K 1841
STEVENSON Charles W 1859
STEPHENSON Charles W 1854

33
ADAIR Armell F 1841
MATTHEWS John 1841
MATTHEWS John 1841
WATTERS Stacy B 1841
COOPWOOD [117] Thomas 1841
COOPWOOD [117] Thomas 1841

ALLWOOD James 1841
ROBERTSON Joseph 1841
3
POLLOCK James 1841
FLANAGIN George B 1893
POLLOCK George A 1859
WHITE [336] Isaac 1844
COOPWOOD [114] Thomas 1841
COOPWOOD [114] Thomas 1841
1
WHITE Dorset 1841
GREENE [179] Daniel 1841
SPINKS Enoch 1841
HARPER George W 1841
FLANAGIN George B 1893
POLLOCK George A 1859
2
FLANAGIN George B 1893
OWEN [306] John 1841
WHITE Andrew 1841
WHITE Dorset 1841
WHITE Dorset 1841

COLE [94] Roscow 1841
TARTT Thomas J 1895
MCGEE Thomas 1841
MCGEE Thomas 1841
10
SPINKS Enoch 1841
11
SKINNER George W 1885
12
SPINKS Abraham 1884
WHITE Henry 1841
COLE [94] Roscow 1841
ROSS Joseph W 1890
SPINKS Enoch 1841
JONES Stephen T 1846
SPINKS Enoch 1841
JONES Osbon 1848
COLE [94] Roscow 1841
AYRES William 1841
MCCOWN James 1841
MCCOWN James 1841

HARPER George W 1841
HARPER George W 1841
SPINKS John 1841
15
SPINKS John 1841
JONES Stephen T 1846
JONES Osbon 1848
14
JONES Wiley C 1848
13
LLOYD [272] John E 1841
COOPWOOD [115] Thomas 1841
DEJARNAT Elias 1841
DEJARNAT Elias 1841
MCLELAND Abel A 1850
SPINKS John 1846
SPINKS Peter E 1846
GREEN John E 1847
MOSLEY Elisha 1846

WALTHALL [332] Madison 1841
BEVILL [41] Thomas L 1841
SPINKS Peter E 1894
DENNIS Samuel 1841
COOPWOOD [108] Thomas 1841
SPINKS John 1841
SPINKS John 1841
SNOWDEN William J 1841
GALLASPY John G 1846
CAMPBELL Thomas 1846
WELLS John H 1860
22
MCGEE Thomas 1841
MCGEE Thomas 1841
23
LATHAM Lorenzo 1841
PERKINS John W 1850
24

WALTHALL [332] Madison 1841
WALTHALL [332] Madison 1841
27
WALTHALL [332] Madison 1841
MCGEE Thomas 1841
MATTHEWS John 1841
26
MCLELAND Elias C 1850
WALTHALL [332] Madison 1841
WALTHALL [332] Madison 1841
WALTHALL [332] Madison 1841
WALTHALL [332] Madison 1841
HARPER George W 1841
COOPWOOD Thomas 1841
COOPWOOD [105] Thomas 1841
COOPWOOD [105] Thomas 1841
25
LLOYD John E 1841

MILLS Willard C 1854
MILLS Willard C 1854
BROOKE Ignatius R 1854
BROOKE Ignatius R 1854
35
LLOYD John E 1841
CRAWFORD James 1841
CRAWFORD James 1841
CRAWFORD James 1841
36
BROOKE Ignatius R 1854
34
COOPWOOD Thomas 1841
COOPWOOD Thomas 1841
CRAWFORD James 1841
MCCOY Elijah 1841
COCHRAN John H 1859

Helpful Hints

1. This Map's INDEX can be found on the preceding pages.
2. Refer to Map "C" to see where this Township lies within Kemper County, Mississippi.
3. Numbers within square brackets [ ] denote a multi-patentee land parcel (multi-owner). Refer to Appendix "C" for a full list of members in this group.
4. Areas that look to be crowded with Patentees usually indicate multiple sales of the same parcel (Re-issues) or Overlapping parcels. See this Township's Index for an explanation of these and other circumstances that might explain "odd" groupings of Patentees on this map.

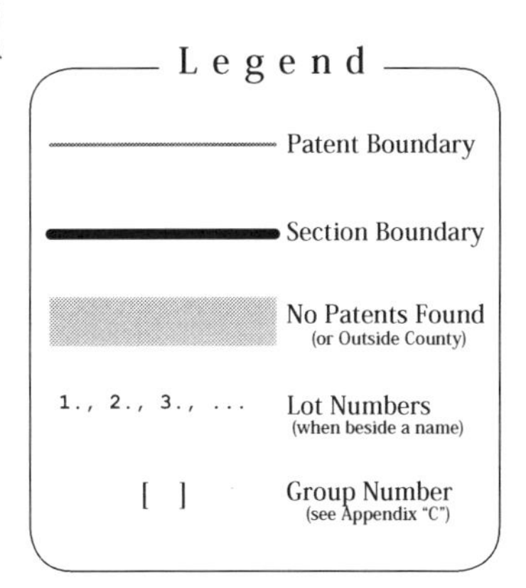

Scale: Section = 1 mile X 1 mile
(generally, with some exceptions)

Road Map

T9-N R15-E
Choctaw Meridian

Map Group 20

Cities & Towns
- Chomontakali (historical)
- Klondike
- Liberty
- Oktibbeha (historical)
- Prismatic

Cemeteries
- Klondike Cemetery
- Mount Olive Cemetery
- Mount Pleasant Cemetery
- Union Cemetery

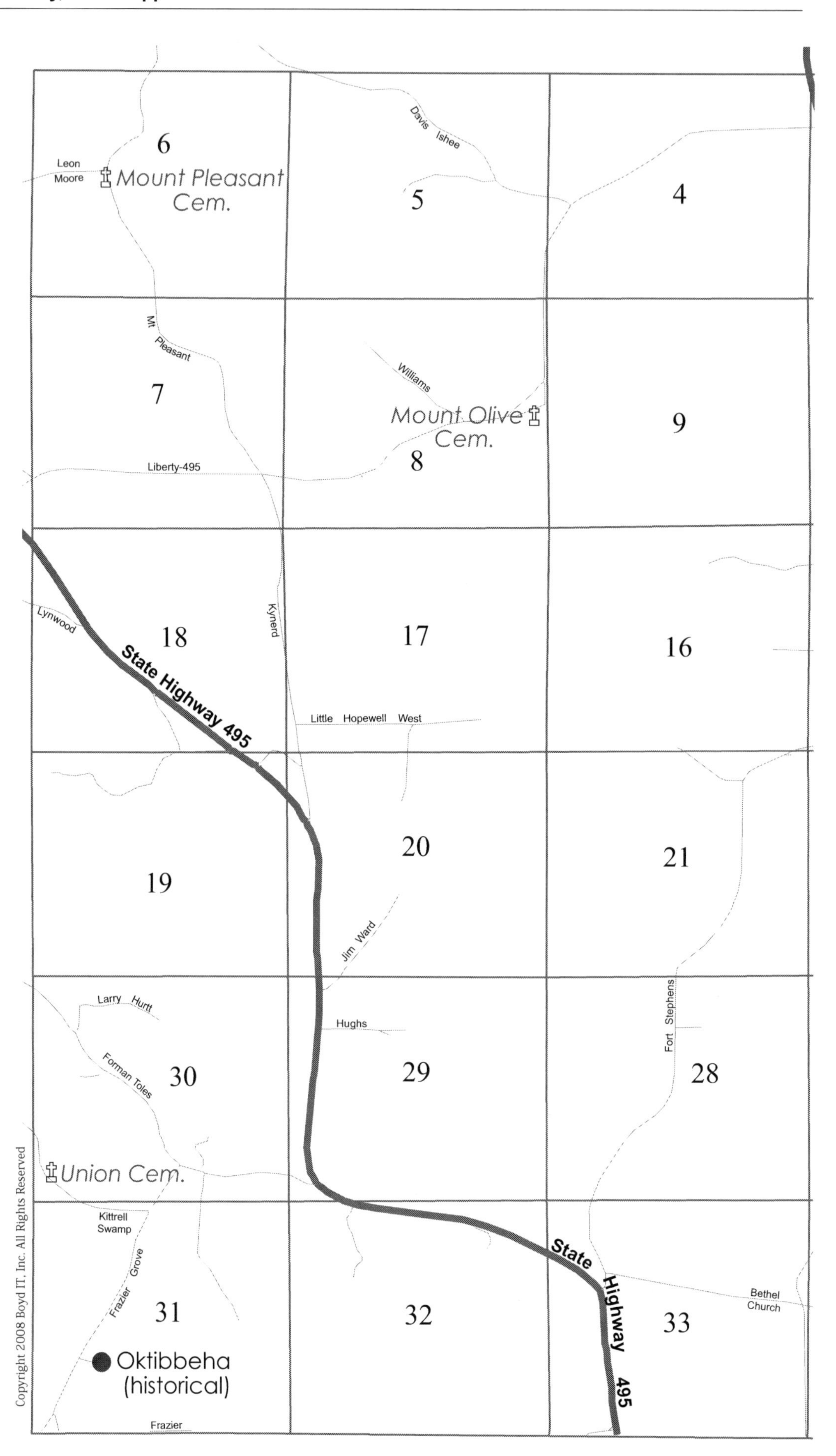

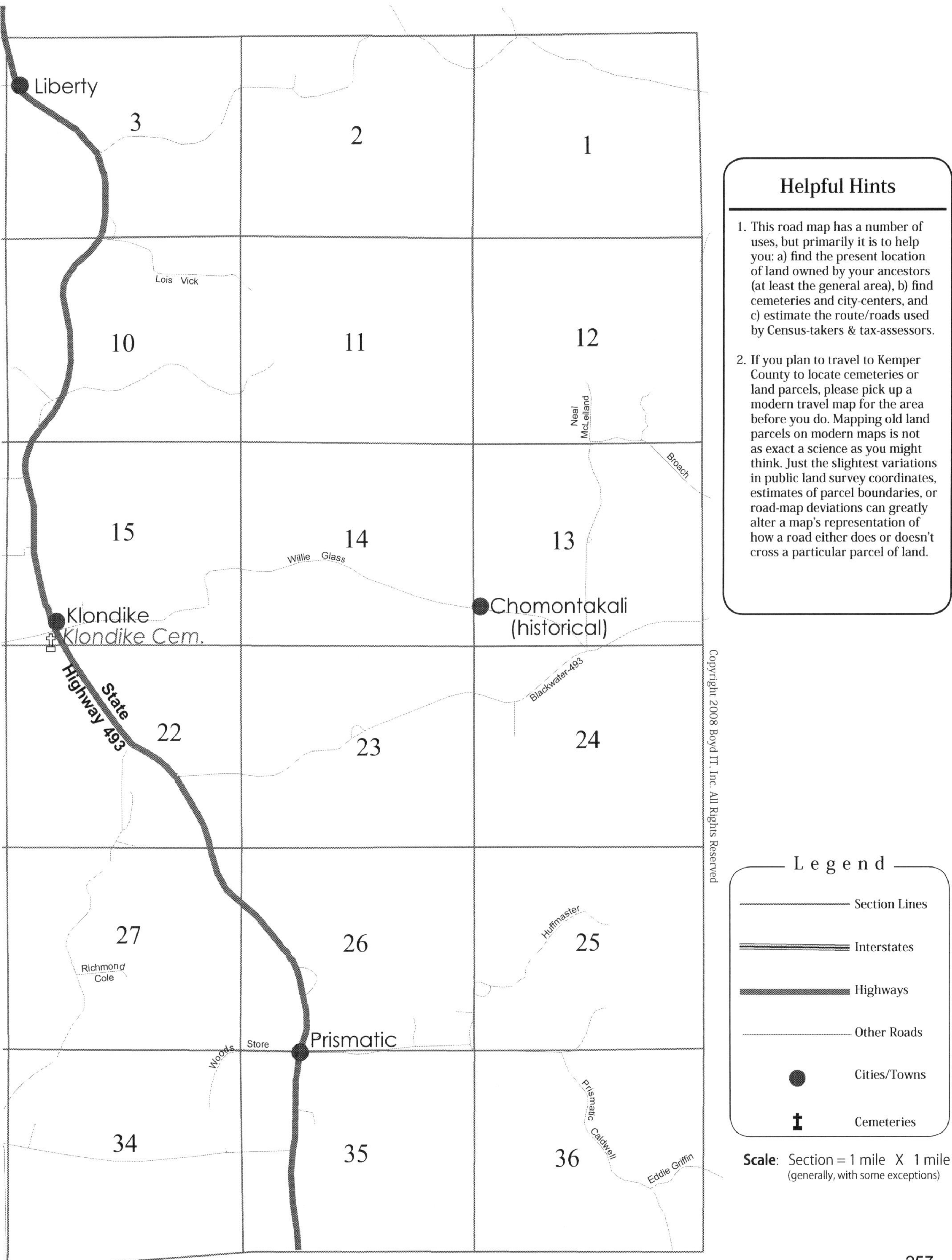
Liberty
3
2
1
Lois Vick
10
11
12
Neal McLelland
Broach
15
14
13
Willie Glass
Klondike
Klondike Cem.
Chomontakali (historical)
State Highway 493
22
23
24
Blackwater-493
27
26
25
Huffmaster
Richmond Cole
Woods
Store
Prismatic
34
35
36
Prismatic Caldwell
Eddie Griffin
Helpful Hints
1. This road map has a number of uses, but primarily it is to help you: a) find the present location of land owned by your ancestors (at least the general area), b) find cemeteries and city-centers, and c) estimate the route/roads used by Census-takers & tax-assessors.
2. If you plan to travel to Kemper County to locate cemeteries or land parcels, please pick up a modern travel map for the area before you do. Mapping old land parcels on modern maps is not as exact a science as you might think. Just the slightest variations in public land survey coordinates, estimates of parcel boundaries, or road-map deviations can greatly alter a map's representation of how a road either does or doesn't cross a particular parcel of land.
Legend
Section Lines
Interstates
Highways
Other Roads
Cities/Towns
Cemeteries
Scale: Section = 1 mile X 1 mile
(generally, with some exceptions)

Historical Map

T9-N R15-E
Choctaw Meridian

Map Group 20

Cities & Towns

- Chomontakali (historical)
- Klondike
- Liberty
- Oktibbeha (historical)
- Prismatic

Cemeteries

- Klondike Cemetery
- Mount Olive Cemetery
- Mount Pleasant Cemetery
- Union Cemetery

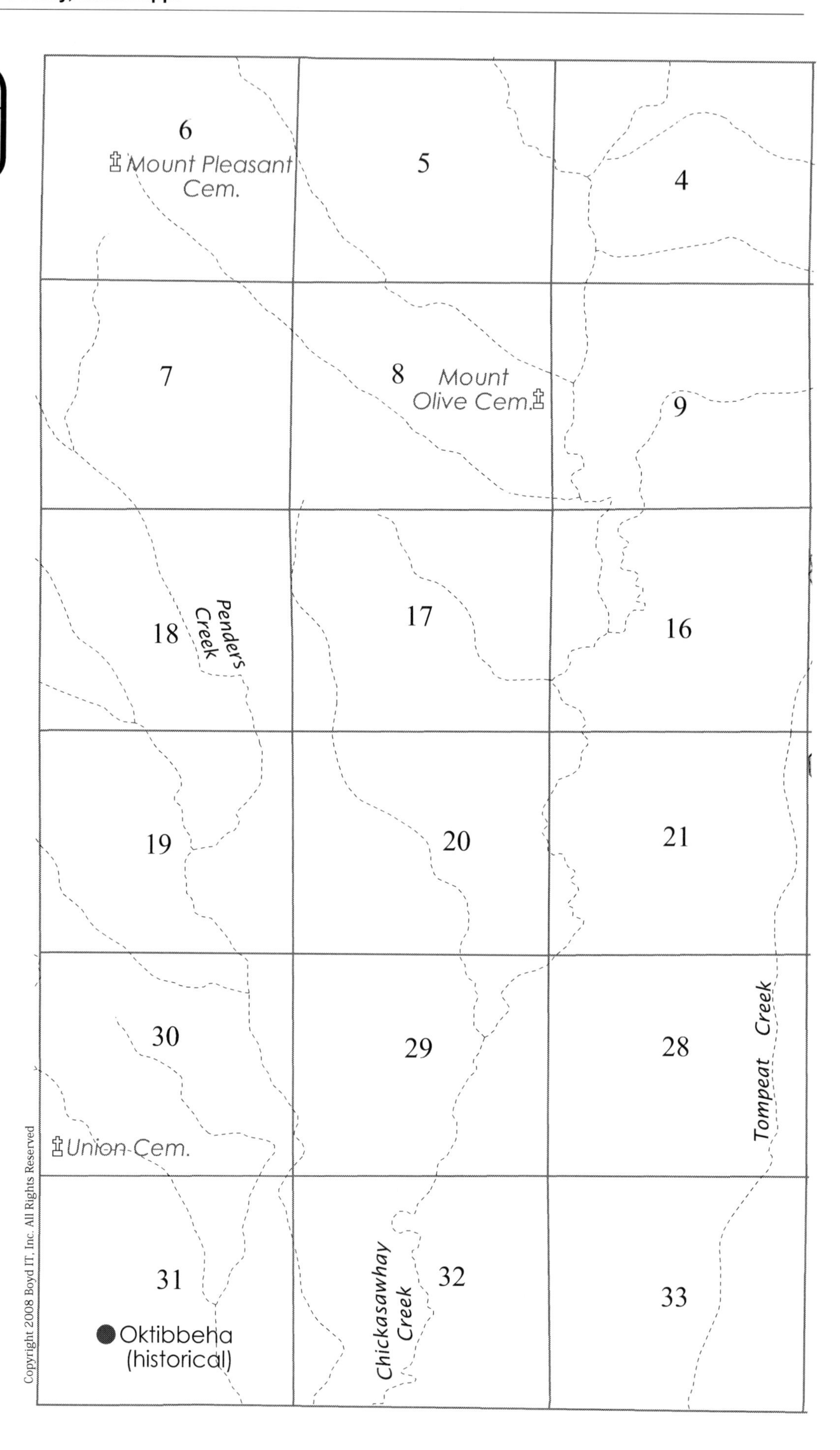

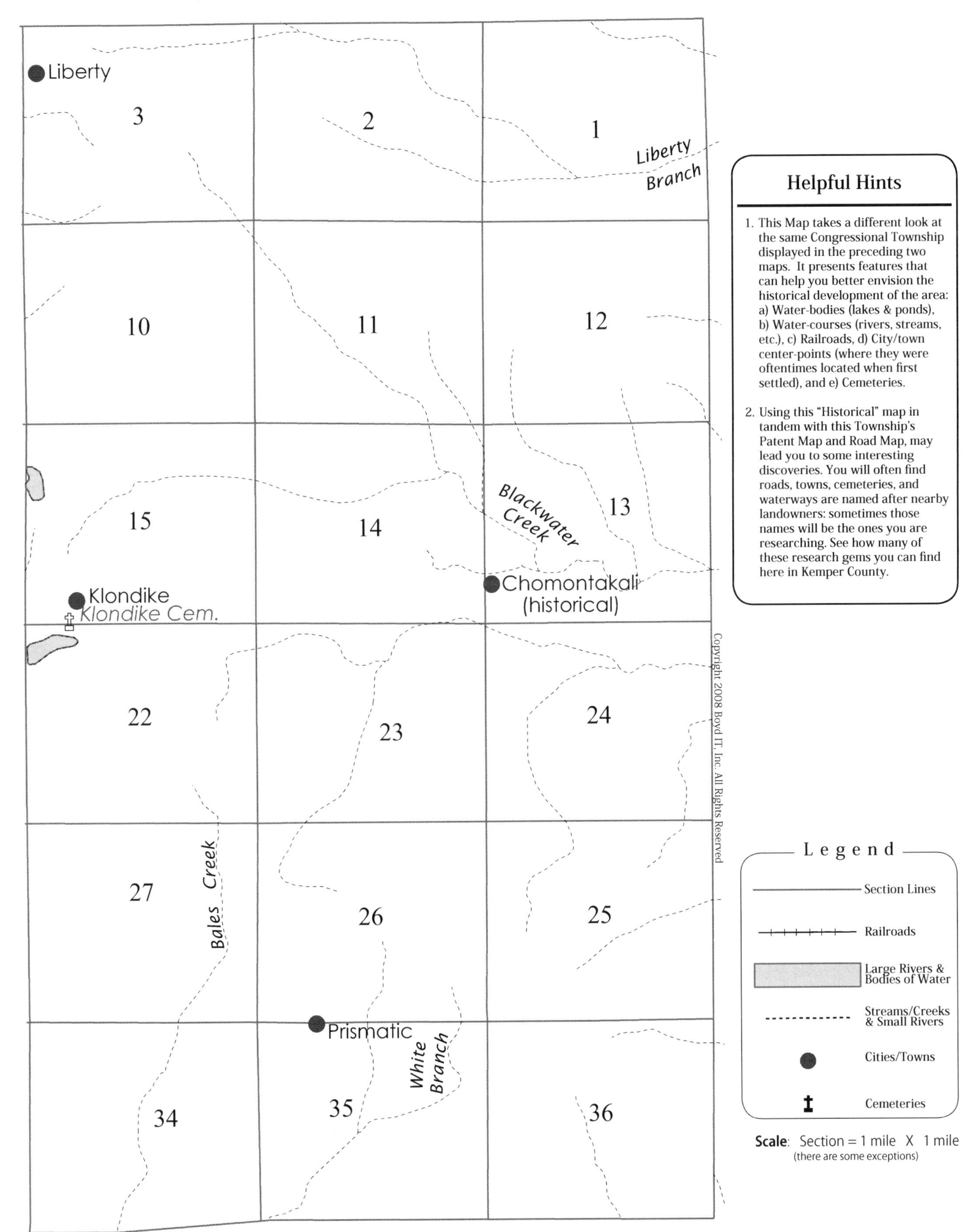
Liberty
3
2
1
Liberty Branch
10
11
12
15
14
13
Blackwater Creek
Klondike
Klondike Cem.
Chomontakali (historical)
22
23
24
27
26
25
Bales Creek
Prismatic
White Branch
34
35
36
Copyright 2008 Boyd IT, Inc. All Rights Reserved
Helpful Hints
1. This Map takes a different look at the same Congressional Township displayed in the preceding two maps. It presents features that can help you better envision the historical development of the area: a) Water-bodies (lakes & ponds), b) Water-courses (rivers, streams, etc.), c) Railroads, d) City/town center-points (where they were oftentimes located when first settled), and e) Cemeteries.
2. Using this "Historical" map in tandem with this Township's Patent Map and Road Map, may lead you to some interesting discoveries. You will often find roads, towns, cemeteries, and waterways are named after nearby landowners: sometimes those names will be the ones you are researching. See how many of these research gems you can find here in Kemper County.
Legend
Section Lines
Railroads
Large Rivers & Bodies of Water
Streams/Creeks & Small Rivers
Cities/Towns
Cemeteries
Scale: Section = 1 mile X 1 mile
(there are some exceptions)

Map Group 21: Index to Land Patents

Township 9-North Range 16-East (Choctaw)

After you locate an individual in this Index, take note of the Section and Section Part then proceed to the Land Patent map on the pages immediately following. You should have no difficulty locating the corresponding parcel of land.

The "For More Info" Column will lead you to more information about the underlying Patents. See the *Legend* at right, and the "How to Use this Book" chapter, for more information.

LEGEND

"For More Info . . . " column

A = Authority (Legislative Act, See Appendix "A")
B = Block or Lot (location in Section unknown)
C = Cancelled Patent
F = Fractional Section
G = Group (Multi-Patentee Patent, see Appendix "C")
V = Overlaps another Parcel
R = Re-Issued (Parcel patented more than once)

(A & G items require you to look in the Appendixes referred to above. All other Letter-designations followed by a number require you to locate line-items in this index that possess the ID number found after the letter).

ID	Individual in Patent	Sec.	Sec. Part	Date Issued	Other Counties	For More Info . . .
3928	AULD, Elijah M	22	SESW	1841-02-27		A1
3929	" "	27	NENW	1844-09-10		A1
3961	AULD, James A	17	E½SE	1841-02-27		A1
3962	" "	17	W½SE	1841-02-27		A1
3982	AULD, John F	21	E½NE	1841-02-27		A1
3983	" "	21	W½NE	1841-02-27		A1
3984	" "	21	W½NW	1841-02-27		A1
4056	BAREFOOT, William	8	SESE	1841-02-27		A1
3973	BARFOOT, John	8	NESE	1841-02-27		A1 G28
3974	" "	8	NWSE	1841-02-27		A1 G28
3916	BELL, Charles E	8	SWSE	1896-12-14		A2
3967	BERRYMAN, Jesse	14	SW	1846-09-01		A1
4050	BEVILL, Thomas L	3	W½NW	1841-02-27		A1 G39
3975	BOSTIAN, John	19	W½NW	1841-02-27		A1 G49
3976	" "	19	W½SW	1841-02-27		A1 G48
4028	BOSTIAN, Matthew	19	E½NW	1841-02-27		A1 G50
4027	" "	19	E½SW	1841-02-27		A1
3976	" "	19	W½SW	1841-02-27		A1 G48
3973	" "	8	NESE	1841-02-27		A1 G28
3974	" "	8	NWSE	1841-02-27		A1 G28
4057	BROADWAY, William	9	S½SW	1841-02-27		A1
3898	BROWN, Allen	8	N½NW	1895-05-11		A2
3899	BROWN, Amanda V	6	S½SE	1904-10-27		A2 G55
3900	" "	6	SESW	1904-10-27		A2 G55
3899	BROWN, David W	6	S½SE	1904-10-27		A2 G55
3900	" "	6	SESW	1904-10-27		A2 G55
3924	BROWN, Edward	5	SESW	1848-09-01		A1
3944	BROWN, Henry	8	SESW	1896-12-14		A2
4024	BROWN, Mary	20	E½NW	1848-09-01		A1
4025	" "	20	W½NE	1848-09-01		A1
4041	BROWN, Sundy	8	S½NW	1895-05-11		A2
3913	BURNETT, Boling C	2	SW	1841-02-27		A1 G68
4032	CHILDS, Morgan	8	W½NE	1841-02-27		A1 G87
4021	COATES, Madison P	25	NWSW	1841-02-27		A1
3978	COLGLAZER, John	4	E½NE	1841-02-27		A1 G98
3979	" "	4	E½NW	1841-02-27		A1 G98
3980	" "	4	W½NE	1841-02-27		A1 G98
4042	COOPWOOD, Thomas	2	W½NW	1841-02-27		A1
4048	" "	21	E½NW	1841-02-27		A1 G111
4043	" "	3	E½NE	1841-02-27		A1
4044	" "	3	E½NW	1841-02-27		A1
4045	" "	3	W½NE	1841-02-27		A1
4050	" "	3	W½NW	1841-02-27		A1 G39
3978	" "	4	E½NE	1841-02-27		A1 G98
3979	" "	4	E½NW	1841-02-27		A1 G98
3980	" "	4	W½NE	1841-02-27		A1 G98

ID	Individual in Patent	Sec.	Sec. Part	Date Issued	Other Counties	For More Info . . .
4046	COOPWOOD, Thomas (Cont'd)	4	W½NW	1841-02-27		A1 G115
4047	" "	6	W½SW	1849-05-21		A1 G110
3997	DUNCAN, John M	13	NWSW	1849-12-01		A1
4033	DYER, Otis	10	E½SW	1841-02-27		A1
4034	" "	10	NWSW	1841-02-27		A1
3918	EASTHAM, Crawford	13	E½NW	1846-12-01		A1
3981	EDWARDS, John	13	W½NW	1846-09-01		A1
3910	ESTES, Benjamin	3	E½SW	1841-02-27		A1 G147
3943	FINLEY, Harrison M	21	SW	1841-02-27		A1
3945	FLEWVELLAN, Henry	25	SWNE	1841-02-27		A1
3902	FUTRELL, Andrew J	12	SW	1848-09-01		A1
4020	GARRETT, Lumpkin J	15	E½SW	1846-12-01		A1
3963	GILLESPIE, James F	33	E½SW	1841-02-27		A1
3964	" "	33	W½SW	1841-02-27		A1
4049	GILLESPIE, Thomas	33	SWSE	1841-02-27		A1
3934	GORDON, Elkanah M	24	NWNE	1859-10-01		A1
3938	GRANT, Green W	17	E½NE	1841-02-27		A1
3939	" "	17	W½NE	1841-02-27		A1
3940	" "	7	S½SE	1841-02-27		A1
3941	" "	8	W½SW	1841-02-27		A1
3897	GREEN, Abner	3	E½SE	1841-02-27		A1
3919	GREENE, Daniel	23	W½NW	1841-02-27		A1
4036	HAGOOD, Pleasant	14	NE	1846-09-01		A1
3908	HALL, Barney	10	E½SE	1848-09-01		A1
3989	HAMBRICK, John	29	NE	1841-02-27		A1 G215
3990	HAMRICK, John	28	W½NW	1841-02-27		A1
4017	HATCH, Lemuel N	30	E½SW	1841-02-27		A1 G221
4018	" "	30	W½SE	1841-02-27		A1 G221
4019	" "	30	W½SW	1841-02-27		A1 G221
4032	" "	8	W½NE	1841-02-27		A1 G87
4047	HENDERSON, John	6	W½SW	1849-05-21		A1 G110
3994	HERRINGTON, John	20	SW	1841-02-27		A1 G224
3991	" "	26	SENW	1854-03-15		A1
3992	" "	26	SWNE	1854-03-15		A1
3993	" "	26	SWNW	1859-10-01		A1
3971	HERRINGTON, John A	26	NESE	1854-03-15		A1
3972	" "	26	SENE	1859-10-01		A1
3936	HODGE, George W	4	E½SW	1878-06-24		A2
3937	" "	4	SWSW	1878-06-24		A2
4029	HOLDERNESS, Mckinney	11	W½SW	1841-02-27		A1 G228
4038	HUBBARD, Samuel	28	E½NE	1841-02-27		A1 G235
4039	" "	28	E½NW	1841-12-15		A1 G235
4040	" "	28	W½NE	1841-12-15		A1 G235
4058	HUDNALL, William	8	NENE	1906-06-16		A2
3906	HUDNELL, Archie	6	NESW	1882-03-30		A2
3907	" "	6	NWSE	1882-03-30		A2
4004	JEMISON, John S	11	E½SE	1841-02-27		A1
4005	" "	12	E½NE	1841-02-27		A1
4006	" "	12	E½NW	1841-02-27		A1
4007	" "	12	W½NW	1841-02-27		A1
4008	" "	2	E½SE	1841-02-27		A1
4009	" "	2	W½SE	1841-02-27		A1
4061	LANG, William	14	W½NW	1841-02-27		A1
4038	LEWIS, Rufus G	28	E½NE	1841-02-27		A1 G235
4039	" "	28	E½NW	1841-12-15		A1 G235
4040	" "	28	W½NE	1841-12-15		A1 G235
4017	LINCECUM, Grant	30	E½SW	1841-02-27		A1 G221
4018	" "	30	W½SE	1841-02-27		A1 G221
4019	" "	30	W½SW	1841-02-27		A1 G221
3999	MARSHALL, John	4	E½SE	1841-02-27		A1
3909	MARTIN, Ben	20	E½NE	1896-12-14		A2
3952	MATTHEWS, Isaac	14	E½NW	1841-02-27		A1 G280
4037	MAYNOR, Samuel H	14	SE	1841-02-27		A1 G281
3949	MCCALL, Hugh H	29	W½NW	1841-02-27		A1
3950	" "	30	E½NW	1841-02-27		A1
3951	" "	30	NENE	1841-02-27		A1
3927	MCCLELAND, Elias C	19	NE	1846-09-01		A1
3977	MCCONNELL, John C	22	E½NE	1856-04-01		A1
4059	MCCONNELL, William J	20	NWNW	1850-12-05		A1
4060	" "	22	E½NW	1856-04-01		A1
3965	MCCOWN, James	7	E½SW	1841-02-27		A1
3966	" "	7	W½SW	1841-02-27		A1
3930	MCCOY, Elijah	29	NENW	1841-02-27		A1

ID	Individual in Patent	Sec.	Sec. Part	Date Issued	Other Counties	For More Info . . .
3931	MCCOY, Elijah (Cont'd)	31	SE	1841-02-27		A1
3910	MCGEE, Micajah	3	E½SW	1841-02-27		A1 G147
3952	MCKELVIN, Benjamin A	14	E½NW	1841-02-27		A1 G280
3953	MCKLEVAIN, Isaac	9	N½SW	1841-02-27		A1
3954	MCLELLAND, Isaac	18	NWNW	1895-10-09		A2
4026	MCMILLON, Matilda	35	SESE	1909-01-21		A2
3903	MCWHORTER, Andrew	35	N½SE	1895-05-11		A2
3904	" "	35	SESW	1895-05-11		A2
3905	" "	35	SWSE	1895-05-11		A2
4000	MCWOOTAN, John	17	E½NW	1841-02-27		A1
4001	" "	17	W½NW	1841-02-27		A1
4054	MILLS, Willard C	10	SENE	1860-05-01		A1
4055	" "	4	NWSW	1860-05-01		A1
4048	MOODY, Washington	21	E½NW	1841-02-27		A1 G111
3985	MOSELEY, John H	32	NWNW	1854-03-15		A1
3986	" "	32	SENW	1854-03-15		A1
4052	MOSELEY, Wiley	17	E½SW	1841-02-27		A1
4053	" "	17	W½SW	1841-02-27		A1
3932	MOSLEY, Elisha	18	W½SW	1846-09-01		A1
3988	MOSLEY, John H	32	NENW	1850-12-05		A1
3987	" "	29	E½SW	1860-05-01		A1
4035	MURPHEY, Philip R	24	SWNW	1854-03-15		A1
3911	NETTLES, Benjamin	20	E½SE	1841-02-27		A1
3912	" "	20	W½SE	1841-02-27		A1
4062	NETTLES, Zachariah	25	NESW	1841-02-27		A1 G303
3995	NEWCOMB, John L	8	NESW	1859-10-01		A1
3996	" "	8	SENE	1859-10-01		A1
3959	ODOM, Jacob	25	E½SE	1841-02-27		A1
3960	" "	25	SWNW	1848-09-01		A1
3958	" "	11	NENW	1849-12-01		A1
3978	OREILLY, Edmond	4	E½NE	1841-02-27		A1 G98
3979	" "	4	E½NW	1841-02-27		A1 G98
3980	" "	4	W½NE	1841-02-27		A1 G98
3978	OREILLY, Nicholas	4	E½NE	1841-02-27		A1 G98
3979	" "	4	E½NW	1841-02-27		A1 G98
3980	" "	4	W½NE	1841-02-27		A1 G98
4002	PARKER, John	26	NESW	1859-10-01		A1
4003	" "	26	NWSE	1859-10-01		A1
3920	PRICE, Daniel M	15	SE	1846-09-01		A1
3969	REID, Jesse	31	W½	1841-02-27		A1
3970	" "	31	W½NE	1841-02-27		A1
4029	RICHEY, James	11	W½SW	1841-02-27		A1 G228
4037	RIGBY, Bryant	14	SE	1841-02-27		A1 G281
3914	" "	9	E½SE	1841-02-27		A1
3915	" "	9	W½SE	1841-02-27		A1
3935	ROCHEL, Etherington	2	SENE	1841-02-27		A1
4030	ROSS, Michael	5	N½	1841-02-27		A1
4031	" "	6	NE	1841-02-27		A1
4046	RUPERT, James C	4	W½NW	1841-02-27		A1 G115
3901	SANDERSON, Amos	1	NWNE	1841-02-27		A1
3913	" "	2	SW	1841-02-27		A1 G68
3917	SCITZS, Christian H	23	NE	1846-12-01		A1
4037	SCITZS, Henry	14	SE	1841-02-27		A1 G281
3947	" "	23	E½NW	1841-02-27		A1
3989	" "	29	NE	1841-02-27		A1 G215
3946	SHARP, Henry R	12	SE	1847-04-01		A1
3994	SHUMATE, Daniel D	20	SW	1841-02-27		A1 G224
3926	SHUMATE, Eli T	22	W½NE	1847-04-01		A1
3925	" "	1	NENE	1850-12-05		A1
3968	SHUMATE, Jesse C	20	SWNW	1850-12-05		A1
4051	SHUMATE, Toliver	19	SE	1848-09-01		A1
3948	SITZS, Henry	15	NE	1841-02-27		A1 G323
4013	SORSBY, John T	11	E½NE	1841-02-27		A1
4014	" "	11	W½NE	1841-02-27		A1
4015	" "	11	W½SE	1841-02-27		A1
3998	STEPHENS, John M	30	SWNW	1854-03-15		A1
4029	STEWART, Hugh C	11	W½SW	1841-02-27		A1 G228
4038	TAPPAN, John	28	E½NE	1841-02-27		A1 G235
4039	" "	28	E½NW	1841-12-15		A1 G235
4040	" "	28	W½NE	1841-12-15		A1 G235
3921	WARD, David	15	E½NW	1841-02-27		A1
3933	WARD, Elisha	10	SWSW	1841-02-27		A1
4028	WARREN, Joseph M	19	E½NW	1841-02-27		A1 G50

ID	Individual in Patent	Sec.	Sec. Part	Date Issued	Other Counties	For More Info . . .
3975	WARREN, Joseph M (Cont'd)	19	W½NW	1841-02-27		A1 G49
4016	" "	28	E½SW	1841-02-27		A1
3942	WATTS, Haden	32	NE	1841-02-27		A1 G335
3942	WATTS, Sealy	32	NE	1841-02-27		A1 G335
3922	WHITE, Dorset	6	E½NW	1841-02-27		A1
3923	" "	6	W½NW	1841-02-27		A1
4062	WHITE, John S	25	NESW	1841-02-27		A1 G303
4010	" "	25	NWSE	1841-02-27		A1
4011	" "	25	SENW	1841-02-27		A1
4012	" "	25	SWSE	1841-02-27		A1
3948	WHITFIELD, Boaz	15	NE	1841-02-27		A1 G323
4038	WHITSETT, John C	28	E½NE	1841-02-27		A1 G235
4039	" "	28	E½NW	1841-12-15		A1 G235
4040	" "	28	W½NE	1841-12-15		A1 G235
4022	WITTLERS, Malachia	21	E½SE	1841-02-27		A1
4023	" "	21	W½SE	1841-02-27		A1
3955	WOOTAN, Israel	28	W½SW	1841-02-27		A1
3956	" "	29	E½SE	1841-02-27		A1
3957	" "	29	W½SE	1841-02-27		A1

Patent Map

T9-N R16-E
Choctaw Meridian

Map Group 21

Township Statistics

Parcels Mapped	:	166
Number of Patents	:	155
Number of Individuals	:	117
Patentees Identified	:	106
Number of Surnames	:	94
Multi-Patentee Parcels	:	31
Oldest Patent Date	:	2/27/1841
Most Recent Patent	:	1/21/1909
Block/Lot Parcels	:	0
Parcels Re - Issued	:	0
Parcels that Overlap	:	0
Cities and Towns	:	2
Cemeteries	:	1

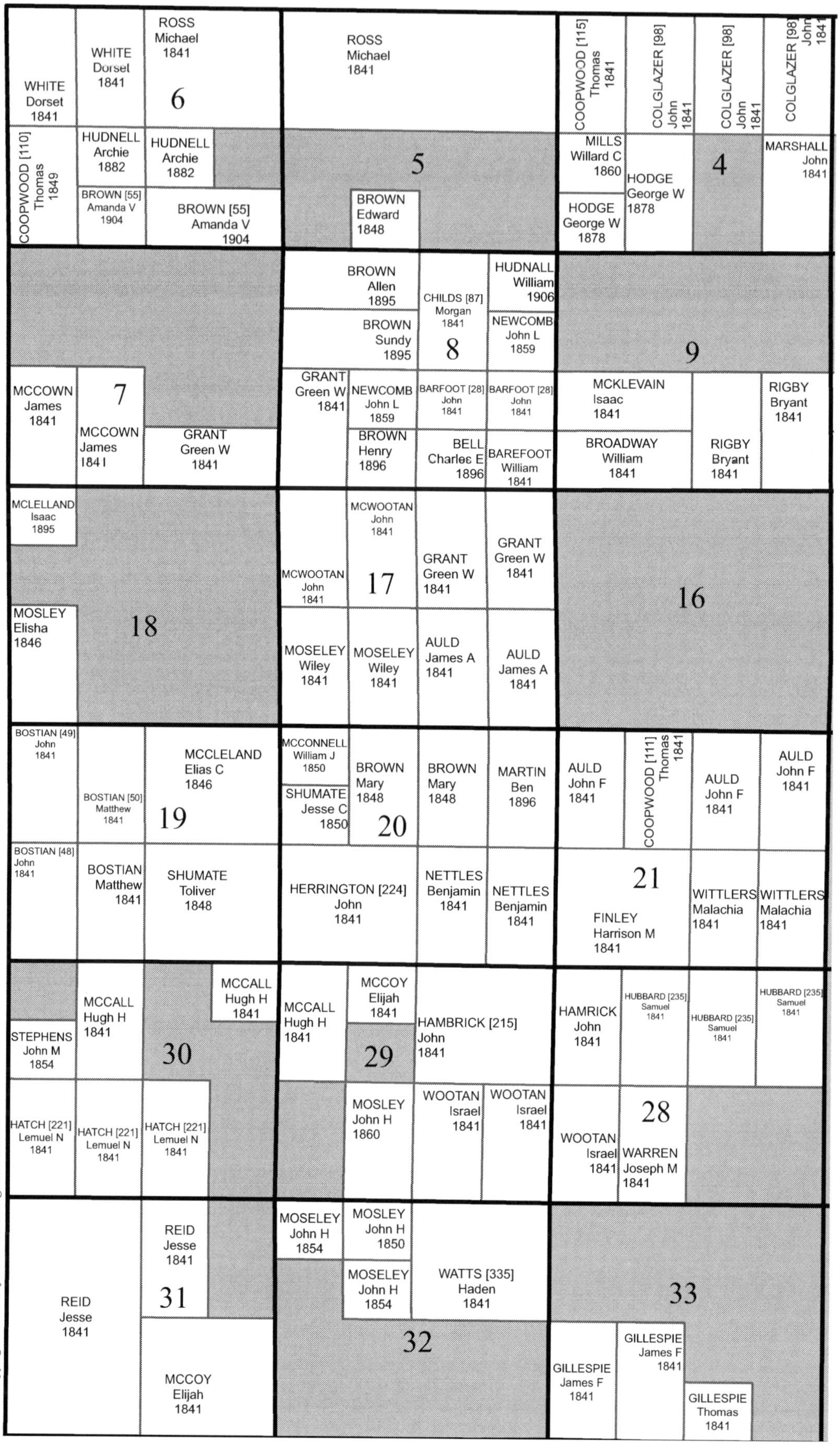

BEVILL [39] Thomas L 1841
COOPWOOD Thomas 1841
COOPWOOD Thomas 1841
COOPWOOD Thomas 1841
COOPWOOD Thomas 1841
ROCHEL Etherington 1841
SANDERSON Amos 1841
SHUMATE Eli T 1850
1
3
ESTES [147] Benjamin 1841
GREEN Abner 1841
2
BURNETT [68] Boling C 1841
JEMISON John S 1841
JEMISON John S 1841

10
MILLS Willard C 1860
DYER Otis 1841
WARD Elisha 1841
DYER Otis 1841
HALL Barney 1848
HOLDERNESS [228] Mckinney 1841
ODOM Jacob 1849
SORSBY John T 1841
11
SORSBY John T 1841
SORSBY John T 1841
JEMISON John S 1841
JEMISON John S 1841
JEMISON John S 1841
JEMISON John S 1841
12
FUTRELL Andrew J 1848
SHARP Henry R 1847

WARD David 1841
SITZS [323] Henry 1841
15
GARRETT Lumpkin J 1846
PRICE Daniel M 1846
LANG William 1841
MATTHEWS [280] Isaac 1841
HAGOOD Pleasant 1846
14
BERRYMAN Jesse 1846
MAYNOR [281] Samuel H 1841
EDWARDS John 1846
EASTHAM Crawford 1846
13
DUNCAN John M 1849

MCCONNELL William J 1856
22
SHUMATE Eli T 1847
MCCONNELL John C 1856
AULD Elijah M 1841
GREENE Daniel 1841
SCITZS Henry 1841
SCITZS Christian H 1846
23
MURPHEY Philip R 1854
GORDON Elkanah M 1859
24

AULD Elijah M 1844
27
HERRINGTON John 1859
HERRINGTON John 1854
HERRINGTON John 1854
HERRINGTON John A 1859
26
PARKER John 1859
PARKER John 1859
HERRINGTON John A 1854
ODOM Jacob 1848
WHITE John S 1841
FLEWVELLAN Henry 1841
25
COATES Madison P 1841
NETTLES [303] Zachariah 1841
WHITE John S 1841
WHITE John S 1841
ODOM Jacob 1841

34
35
MCWHORTER Andrew 1895
MCWHORTER Andrew 1895
MCWHORTER Andrew 1895
MCMILLON Matilda 1909
36

Helpful Hints

1. This Map's INDEX can be found on the preceding pages.
2. Refer to Map "C" to see where this Township lies within Kemper County, Mississippi.
3. Numbers within square brackets [ ] denote a multi-patentee land parcel (multi-owner). Refer to Appendix "C" for a full list of members in this group.
4. Areas that look to be crowded with Patentees usually indicate multiple sales of the same parcel (Re-issues) or Overlapping parcels. See this Township's Index for an explanation of these and other circumstances that might explain "odd" groupings of Patentees on this map.

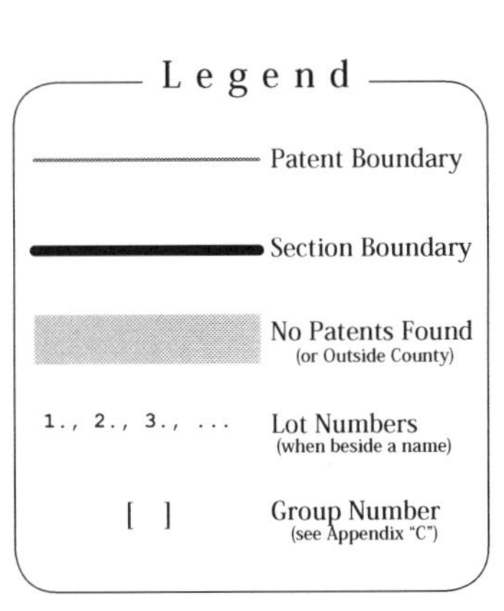

Scale: Section = 1 mile X 1 mile
(generally, with some exceptions)

Road Map

T9-N R16-E
Choctaw Meridian

Map Group 21

Cities & Towns

Blackwater
Cullum

Cemeteries

Blackwater Cemetery

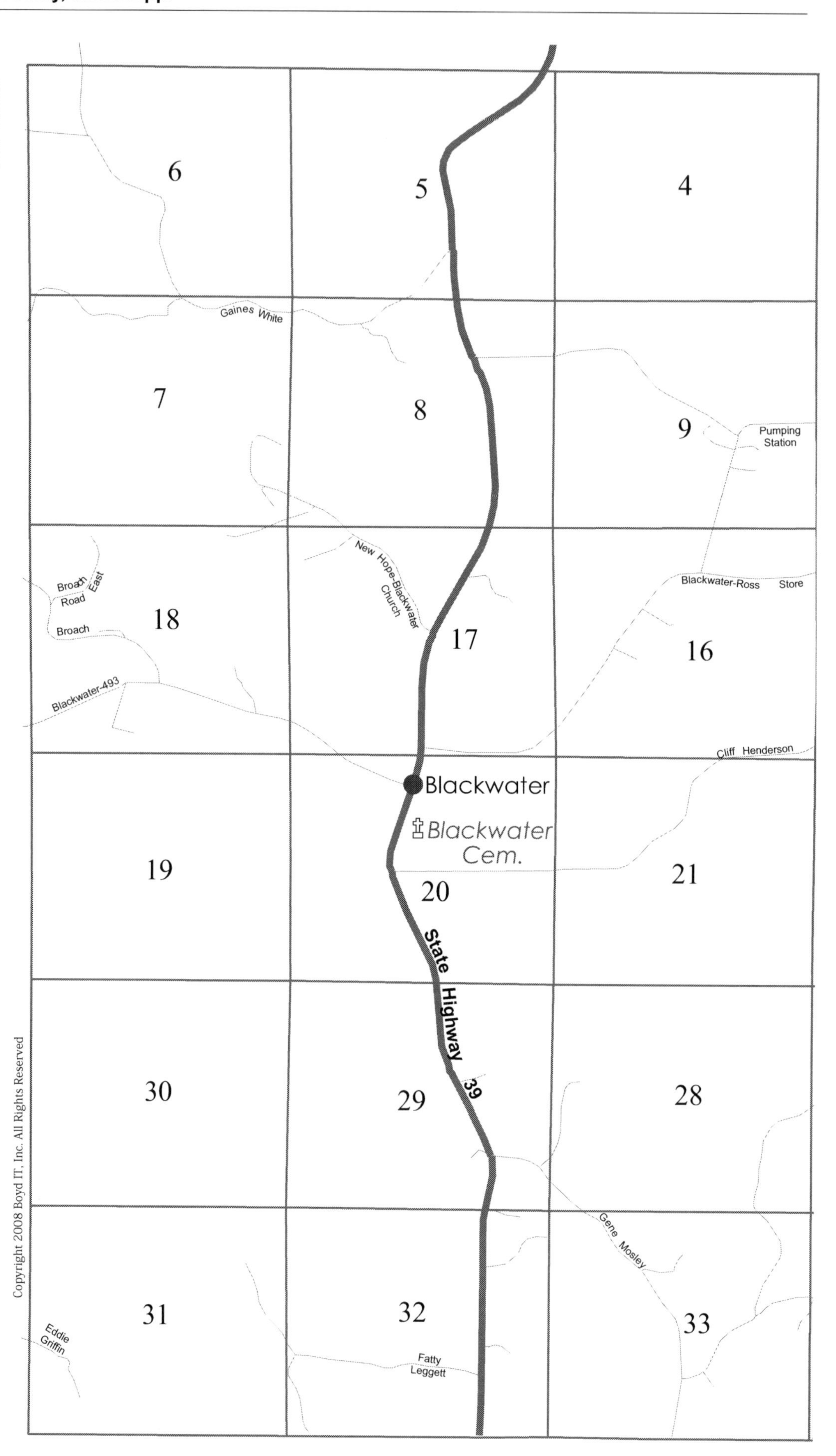

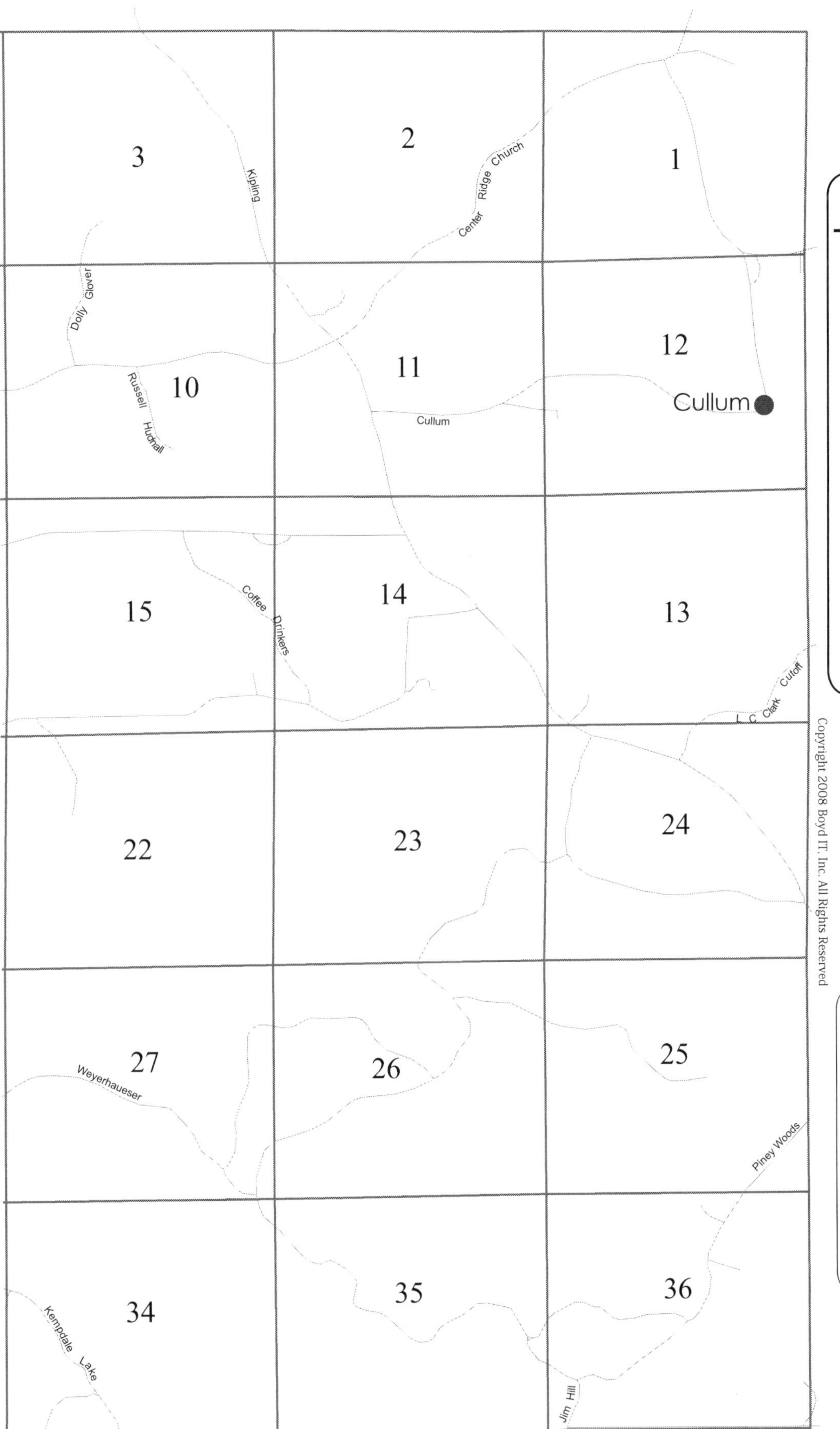

Helpful Hints

1. This road map has a number of uses, but primarily it is to help you: a) find the present location of land owned by your ancestors (at least the general area), b) find cemeteries and city-centers, and c) estimate the route/roads used by Census-takers & tax-assessors.

2. If you plan to travel to Kemper County to locate cemeteries or land parcels, please pick up a modern travel map for the area before you do. Mapping old land parcels on modern maps is not as exact a science as you might think. Just the slightest variations in public land survey coordinates, estimates of parcel boundaries, or road-map deviations can greatly alter a map's representation of how a road either does or doesn't cross a particular parcel of land.

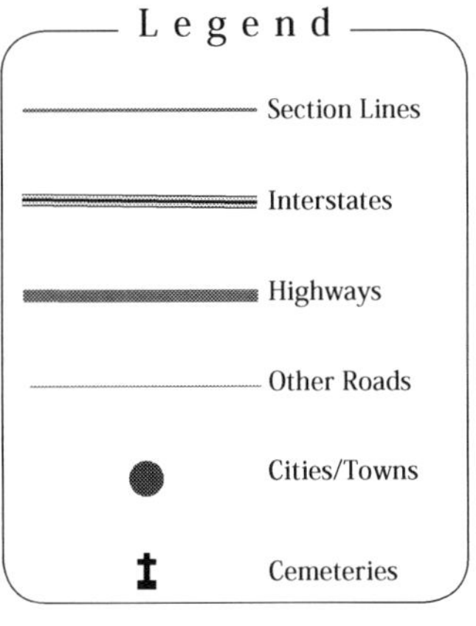

Scale: Section = 1 mile X 1 mile
(generally, with some exceptions)

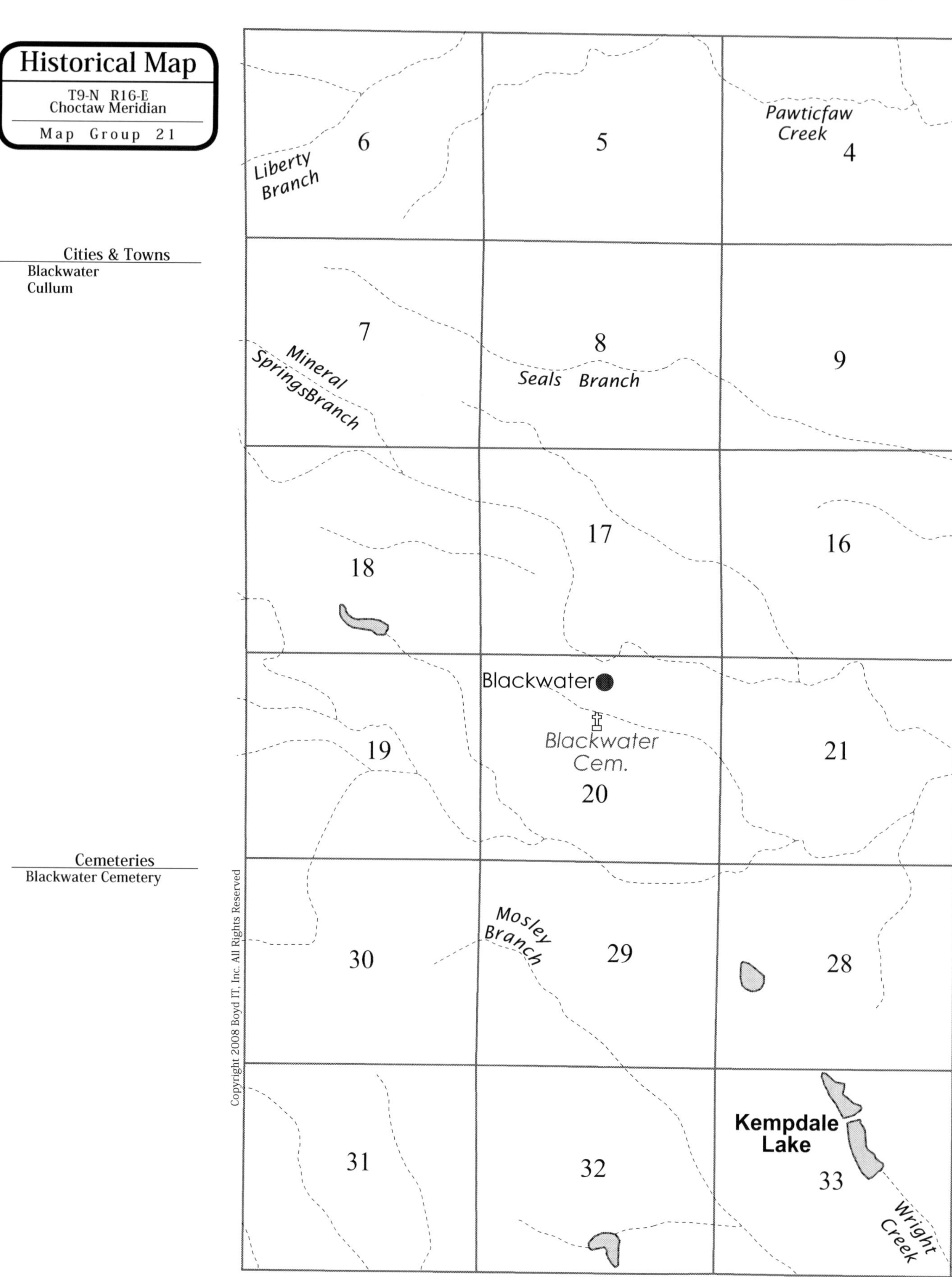
Historical Map
T9-N R16-E
Choctaw Meridian
Map Group 21
Cities & Towns
Blackwater
Cullum
Cemeteries
Blackwater Cemetery
6
5
4
Liberty Branch
Pawticfaw Creek
7
8
9
Mineral SpringsBranch
Seals Branch
18
17
16
Blackwater
Blackwater Cem.
19
20
21
30
29
28
Mosley Branch
31
32
33
Kempdale Lake
Wright Creek

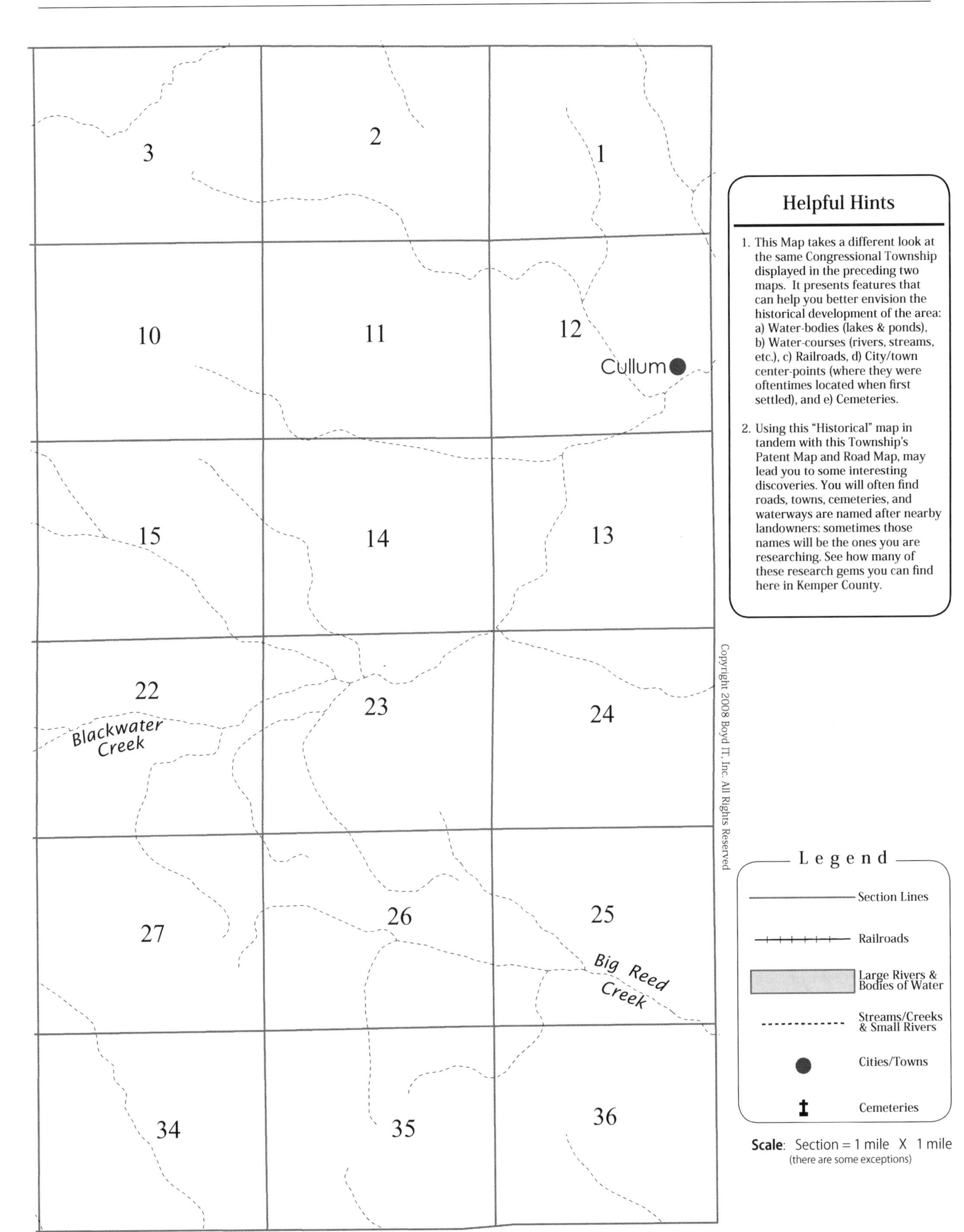
3
2
1
10
11
12
Cullum
15
14
13
22
23
24
Blackwater Creek
27
26
25
Big Reed Creek
34
35
36
Copyright 2008 Boyd IT, Inc. All Rights Reserved
Helpful Hints
1. This Map takes a different look at the same Congressional Township displayed in the preceding two maps. It presents features that can help you better envision the historical development of the area: a) Water-bodies (lakes & ponds), b) Water-courses (rivers, streams, etc.), c) Railroads, d) City/town center-points (where they were oftentimes located when first settled), and e) Cemeteries.
2. Using this "Historical" map in tandem with this Township's Patent Map and Road Map, may lead you to some interesting discoveries. You will often find roads, towns, cemeteries, and waterways are named after nearby landowners: sometimes those names will be the ones you are researching. See how many of these research gems you can find here in Kemper County.
Legend
Section Lines
Railroads
Large Rivers & Bodies of Water
Streams/Creeks & Small Rivers
Cities/Towns
Cemeteries
Scale: Section = 1 mile X 1 mile
(there are some exceptions)

Map Group 22: Index to Land Patents

Township 9-North Range 17-East (Choctaw)

After you locate an individual in this Index, take note of the Section and Section Part then proceed to the Land Patent map on the pages immediately following. You should have no difficulty locating the corresponding parcel of land.

The "For More Info" Column will lead you to more information about the underlying Patents. See the *Legend* at right, and the "How to Use this Book" chapter, for more information.

LEGEND

"For More Info . . . " column

A = Authority (Legislative Act, See Appendix "A")
B = Block or Lot (location in Section unknown)
C = Cancelled Patent
F = Fractional Section
G = Group (Multi-Patentee Patent, see Appendix "C")
V = Overlaps another Parcel
R = Re-Issued (Parcel patented more than once)

(A & G items require you to look in the Appendixes referred to above. All other Letter-designations followed by a number require you to locate line-items in this index that possess the ID number found after the letter).

ID	Individual in Patent	Sec.	Sec. Part	Date Issued	Other Counties	For More Info . . .
4135	AH, Ish Pi	15	NE	1841-02-27		A1
4233	ANDREWS, Warren	13	SW	1841-02-27		A1
4234	" "	13	W½SE	1841-02-27		A1
4067	ARCHER, Alexander	10	W½SW	1841-02-27		A1 G25
4180	ASKIN, John S	29	SENE	1860-05-01		A1
4181	" "	29	SESE	1860-05-01		A1
4090	BARFIELD, Charles	21	SW	1895-02-21		A2
4162	BOBBITT, John G	35	SENW	1859-10-01		A1
4160	" "	27	N½NW	1860-05-01		A1
4161	" "	27	NENE	1860-05-01		A1
4086	BURNETT, Boling C	15	W½SW	1841-02-27		A1 G63
4087	" "	31	E½NW	1841-02-27		A1 G70
4088	" "	31	W½NW	1841-02-27		A1 G70
4085	" "	32	E½NE	1841-02-27		A1 G71
4150	BUTCHEE, John	31	SWSW	1854-03-15		A1
4109	CALHOUN, Duncan	36	NENW	1841-02-27		A1
4153	CALHOUN, John	36	NWSE	1841-02-27		A1
4131	CARMICHAEL, Hugh	32	E½SE	1841-02-27		A1
4132	" "	32	W½SE	1841-02-27		A1
4237	CARMICHAEL, William F	21	NE	1890-06-25		A2
4065	CARRAWAY, Abram B	7	SWNW	1850-12-05		A1
4068	CARRAWAY, Alexander	7	SW	1846-12-01		A1
4154	CARTER, John	11	E½SE	1841-02-27		A1
4155	" "	14	NW	1841-02-27		A1 G83
4156	" "	7	W½SE	1841-02-27		A1 G82
4223	CLARK, Thomas B	3	SE	1901-04-22		A2
4111	COOPER, Elijah	5	SWSE	1848-09-01		A1
4112	CREER, Elijah	25	E½SE	1881-08-20		A2
4205	CROSBY, Richard	9	SW	1841-02-27		A1 G121
4129	CUBBA, Ho To	23	SWSE	1841-02-27		A1
4075	CURRIE, Archibald C	33	SWNE	1848-09-01		A1
4074	" "	29	NESE	1859-10-01		A1
4204	DAVIS, Philip W	11	SW	1841-02-27		A1 G123
4236	DUNGER, William	29	SWSE	1881-09-17		A2
4099	EASTHAM, Crawford	30	S½SW	1841-02-27		A1
4100	" "	30	W½SE	1841-02-27		A1
4158	EDWARDS, John	30	SESE	1848-09-01		A1
4159	" "	30	SWNE	1848-09-01		A1
4198	EDWARDS, Napoleon B	27	S½NW	1901-11-08		A2
4244	EDWARDS, William S	27	NESE	1881-09-17		A2
4245	" "	27	NWNE	1881-09-17		A2
4246	" "	27	S½NE	1881-09-17		A2
4204	FARMER, Thomas	11	SW	1841-02-27		A1 G123
4238	FOWLER, William	13	E½SE	1841-02-27		A1
4189	GIVAN, Joseph D	35	NESW	1859-10-01		A1
4190	" "	35	NWSE	1859-10-01		A1

ID	Individual in Patent	Sec.	Sec. Part	Date Issued	Other Counties	For More Info . . .
4191	GIVAN, Joseph D (Cont'd)	35	SWSE	1859-10-01		A1
4098	GORDON, Cornelius C	35	W½NE	1897-02-15		A2
4122	GRANT, Green W	31	E½NE	1841-02-27		A1
4123	" "	31	W½NE	1841-02-27		A1
4101	GREENE, Daniel	10	W½NW	1841-02-27		A1 G179
4076	GRIFFIN, Archibald M	11	E½NE	1841-02-27		A1
4077	" "	11	W½NE	1841-02-27		A1
4216	GRIGSBY, Solomon	10	NESE	1841-02-27		A1
4217	" "	10	W½SE	1841-02-27		A1
4070	HANNA, Andrew W	36	SWSE	1841-02-27		A1
4241	HARRIS, William H	9	SE	1841-02-01		A1 G220
4239	" "	9	E½NE	1841-02-27		A1
4240	" "	9	W½NE	1841-02-27		A1
4164	HAWS, John	6	SWSW	1841-02-27		A1
4165	HERRINGTON, John	5	SESW	1841-02-27		A1
4205	" "	9	SW	1841-02-27		A1 G121
4130	HOTAH,	23	E½SW	1841-02-27		A1
4101	HUBBARD, Samuel	10	W½NW	1841-02-27		A1 G179
4207	" "	13	NE	1841-12-15		A1 G234
4208	" "	8	NE	1841-12-15		A1 G234
4209	" "	9	NW	1841-12-15		A1 G234
4092	HUGHES, Charles	26	E½SE	1841-02-27		A1
4093	" "	26	W½SE	1841-02-27		A1
4094	HUSE, Charles	23	NWSW	1841-02-27		A1
4095	" "	25	W½SW	1841-02-27		A1
4096	" "	26	SENE	1841-02-27		A1
4182	JEMISON, John S	4	E½SE	1841-02-27		A1
4183	" "	4	W½SE	1841-02-27		A1
4125	JOHNSTON, Henry	11	SWSE	1888-12-29		A1
4069	JONES, Alfred	3	N½NE	1841-02-27		A1
4115	JONES, Ezekiel	17	NE	1841-02-27		A1 G256
4242	JONES, William	27	S½SE	1888-02-25		A2
4220	LA HO LO, TAL	15	E½SE	1841-02-27		A1
4215	LA MA, SO	14	W½NE	1841-02-27		A1
4141	LAKE, James	15	W½NW	1841-02-27		A1 G263
4140	" "	10	E½SW	1844-09-10		A1
4106	LARK, David C	33	NWNW	1850-12-05		A1
4101	LEWIS, Rufus G	10	W½NW	1841-02-27		A1 G179
4207	" "	13	NE	1841-12-15		A1 G234
4208	" "	8	NE	1841-12-15		A1 G234
4209	" "	9	NW	1841-12-15		A1 G234
4166	LOCKLIN, John	18	NWNW	1850-12-05		A1
4163	LONG, John H	6	NENW	1850-12-05		A1
4213	MA, Shoppo Ho	22	E½NE	1841-02-27		A1
4214	" "	22	E½SE	1841-02-27		A1
4103	MALLORY, Daniel	30	E½NW	1841-02-27		A1
4104	" "	30	NWNE	1841-02-27		A1
4102	" "	19	SESW	1844-09-10		A1
4142	MCCOWN, James	33	E½NE	1841-02-27		A1
4143	" "	36	E½NE	1841-02-27		A1
4144	" "	36	W½NE	1841-02-27		A1
4145	MCCOY, James N	21	NW	1901-03-23		A2
4086	MCCRANIE, Malcolm	15	W½SW	1841-02-27		A1 G63
4083	MCKELVAIN, Benjamin A	30	NWSW	1841-02-27		A1
4107	MCLENDON, Daws	5	SESE	1899-11-24		A2
4113	MCNEILL, Elizabeth	25	E½SW	1841-02-27		A1
4167	MCNEILL, John	13	NW	1841-02-27		A1
4170	" "	25	E½NW	1841-02-27		A1
4171	" "	25	W½NE	1841-02-27		A1
4168	" "	19	NESE	1848-09-01		A1
4169	" "	19	NWSW	1848-09-01		A1
4172	" "	33	SWNW	1848-09-01		A1
4212	MCPHERSON, Sarah	22	NWSW	1849-12-01		A1
4235	MILLS, Willard C	6	SENW	1854-03-15		A1
4173	MOORE, John	19	SENE	1850-12-05		A1
4178	MOORE, John R	18	NENW	1849-12-01		A1
4179	" "	18	NWNE	1849-12-01		A1
4194	MOORE, Lemuel D	17	E½NW	1848-09-01		A1
4200	MOORE, Nelson	33	E½NW	1854-03-15		A1
4133	MORRISON, Isaac	6	SESW	1885-12-19		A2
4134	MORRISON, Isah	17	E½SW	1906-09-14		A2
4110	MOSBY, Edward C	29	NWSE	1848-09-01		A1
4193	MURPHEY, Joseph R	33	E½SE	1846-12-01		A1

ID	Individual in Patent	Sec.	Sec. Part	Date Issued	Other Counties	For More Info . . .
4192	MURPHEY, Joseph R (Cont'd)	21	NESE	1848-09-01		A1
4224	MURPHEY, Thomas C	20	W½SW	1846-12-01		A1
4226	" "	29	SWSW	1849-12-01		A1
4225	" "	29	SESW	1856-04-01		A1
4151	NAYLOR, John C	29	NENE	1860-10-01		A1
4188	NAYLOR, John W	35	SESE	1905-12-13		A2
4201	NEOTLCAH,	14	E½NE	1841-02-27		A1
4202	NOATEMAH,	14	W½SW	1841-02-27		A1
4203	" "	23	W½NW	1841-02-27		A1
4136	ODOM, Jacob	28	SWSW	1848-09-01		A1
4139	" "	34	SWSE	1848-09-01		A1
4137	" "	30	NESW	1849-12-01		A1
4138	" "	34	NWSE	1849-12-01		A1
4243	ONEAL, William	25	SWNW	1841-02-27		A1
4091	PAGE, Charles G	8	SE	1846-12-01		A1
4232	PAGE, Thomas	7	E½SE	1841-02-27		A1 G307
4228	" "	7	SENW	1841-02-27		A1
4229	" "	7	SWNE	1841-02-27		A1
4230	" "	8	S½NW	1848-09-01		A1
4231	" "	8	SW	1848-12-01		A1
4067	PAGE, Willis	10	W½SW	1841-02-27		A1 G25
4141	" "	15	W½NW	1841-02-27		A1 G263
4115	" "	17	NE	1841-02-27		A1 G256
4247	" "	17	NWNW	1841-02-27		A1
4232	" "	7	E½SE	1841-02-27		A1 G307
4177	PARKER, John	27	NWSE	1905-03-30		A2
4218	PARKER, Stewart	35	N½NW	1902-07-03		A2
4126	PATRICK, Henry	6	N½SW	1850-12-05		A1
4195	PAYNE, Margaret M	4	NE	1848-09-01		A1
4219	PEARL, Sylvester	32	SW	1841-02-27		A1
4196	PEGG, Martin	28	SWSE	1841-02-27		A1
4197	" "	33	NWNE	1841-02-27		A1
4089	PHARMER, Calvin	11	NW	1841-02-27		A1 G310
4089	PHARMER, Sydney	11	NW	1841-02-27		A1 G310
4120	PRIDDY, Granvill E	25	SWSE	1856-04-01		A1
4121	PRIDDY, Granville E	25	NWSE	1859-10-01		A1
4227	RAINEY, Thomas E	27	E½SW	1889-01-12		A2
4176	RHODES, John P	10	E½NW	1841-02-27		A1 G314
4174	" "	15	E½NW	1841-02-27		A1
4175	" "	3	E½SW	1841-02-27		A1
4078	ROBERTS, Ben	17	SE	1894-12-17		A2
4147	RUSH, Jerry	23	NWSE	1892-03-17		A2
4148	" "	23	SWNE	1892-03-17		A2
4199	RUSSELL, Nathan P	23	SENW	1882-03-30		A2
4146	SANDERS, Jane	15	E½SW	1881-08-20		A2
4079	SHARP, Benet	31	NESW	1850-12-02		A1
4080	" "	31	NWSE	1850-12-02		A1
4081	" "	31	SESW	1854-03-15		A1
4082	" "	31	SWSE	1854-03-15		A1
4084	SHARP, Bennet	31	NESE	1859-10-01		A1
4124	SHARP, Groves D	27	W½SW	1898-10-04		A2 G322
4124	SHARP, Matilda A	27	W½SW	1898-10-04		A2 G322
4241	SIMMONS, John	9	SE	1841-02-01		A1 G220
4149	SKINNER, Jesse	32	NW	1841-02-27		A1
4119	SMITH, George W	23	SWSW	1860-10-01		A1
4116	STEWART, Frank	31	NWSW	1895-02-21		A2
4184	STRAIT, John	11	NWSE	1841-02-27		A1 G328
4210	STRAIT, Samuel W	35	E½NE	1841-02-27		A1
4211	" "	35	NESE	1841-02-27		A1
4185	SWIFT, John	33	E½SW	1841-02-27		A1
4186	" "	33	W½SE	1841-02-27		A1
4187	" "	33	W½SW	1841-02-27		A1
4128	TAH, Ho	25	E½NE	1841-02-27		A1
4101	TAPPAN, John	10	W½NW	1841-02-27		A1 G179
4207	" "	13	NE	1841-12-15		A1 G234
4208	" "	8	NE	1841-12-15		A1 G234
4209	" "	9	NW	1841-12-15		A1 G234
4157	TARTT, John D	25	NWNW	1881-05-10		A2
4221	TARTT, Teresa	35	SWNW	1860-05-01		A1
4222	" "	35	W½SW	1860-05-01		A1
4156	THOMAS, Page	7	W½SE	1841-02-27		A1 G82
4105	THOMPSON, Daniel T	15	W½SE	1894-02-28		A2
4114	TUBBEE, Enah	26	W½NE	1841-02-27		A1

ID	Individual in Patent	Sec.	Sec. Part	Date Issued	Other Counties	For More Info . . .
4087	WATTERS, Stacy B	31	E½NW	1841-02-27		A1 G70
4088	" "	31	W½NW	1841-02-27		A1 G70
4097	WEBB, Claiborne	35	SESW	1892-04-23		A2
4085	WEIR, Adolphus G	32	E½NE	1841-02-27		A1 G71
4066	" "	32	W½NE	1841-02-27		A1
4184	WELLS, Samuel G	11	NWSE	1841-02-27		A1 G328
4117	WHITE, Frank	5	E½NE	1895-11-11		A2
4118	" "	5	NESE	1895-11-11		A2
4176	WHITEHEAD, Gilford	10	E½NW	1841-02-27		A1 G314
4152	WHITSETT, John C	24	W½SW	1841-02-27		A1
4063	WILLIAMSON, Aaron	23	E½NE	1891-05-20		A2
4064	" "	23	E½SE	1891-05-20		A2
4073	WINN, Andrew	29	W½NE	1846-12-01		A1
4072	" "	29	E½NW	1848-09-01		A1
4071	" "	28	NWSW	1850-12-05		A1
4127	WINN, Hinchey M	28	W½NW	1846-12-01		A1
4206	WINN, Riden	31	SESE	1849-12-01		A1
4155	YOUNG, Alexander F	14	NW	1841-02-27		A1 G83
4108	YOUNG, Dozier T	23	NENW	1860-05-01		A1

Patent Map

T9-N R17-E
Choctaw Meridian

Map Group 22

Township Statistics

Parcels Mapped	:	185
Number of Patents	:	166
Number of Individuals	:	131
Patentees Identified	:	127
Number of Surnames	:	104
Multi-Patentee Parcels	:	21
Oldest Patent Date	:	2/1/1841
Most Recent Patent	:	9/14/1906
Block/Lot Parcels	:	0
Parcels Re - Issued	:	0
Parcels that Overlap	:	0
Cities and Towns	:	1
Cemeteries	:	0

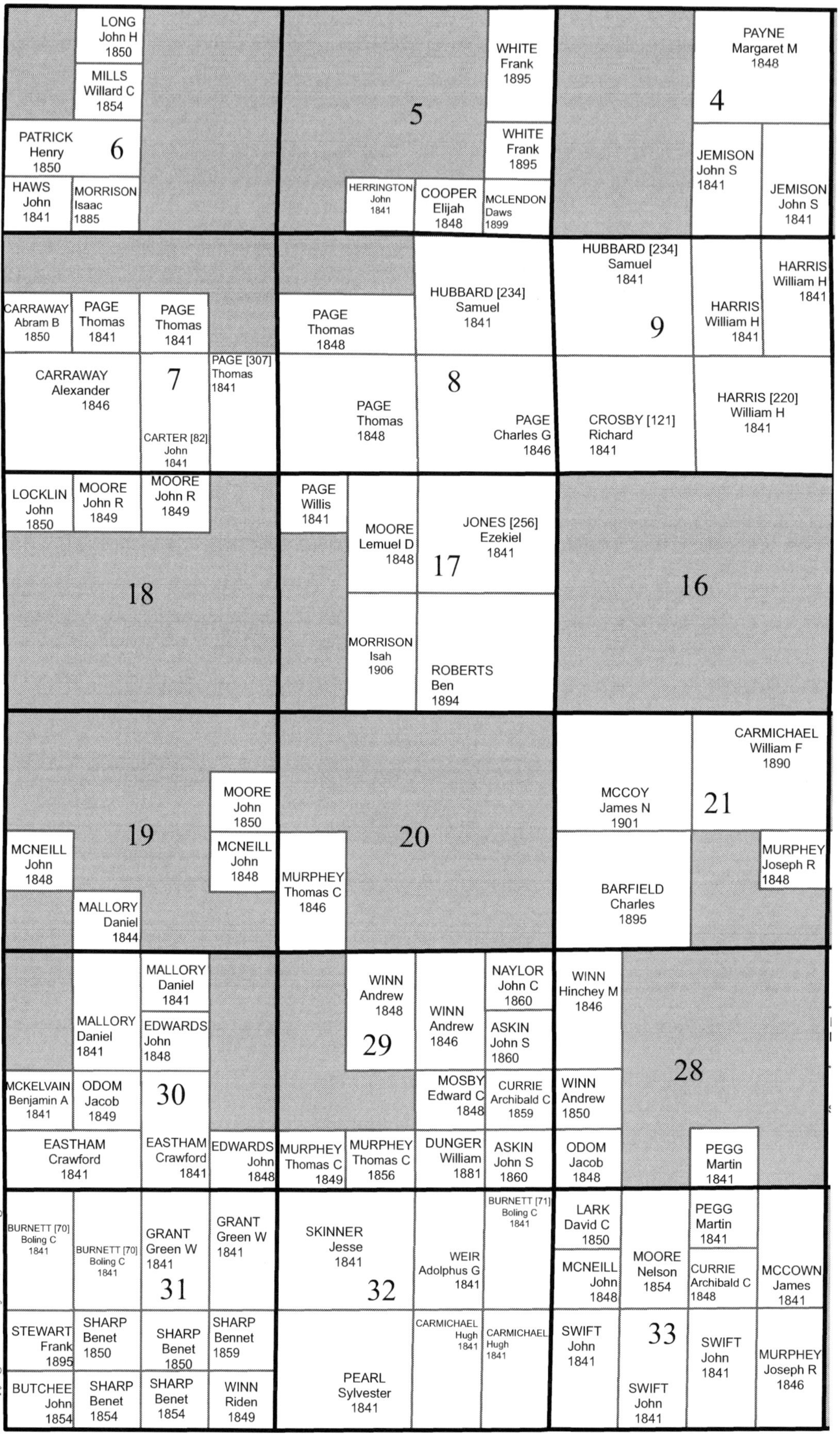

6
LONG John H 1850
MILLS Willard C 1854
PATRICK Henry 1850
HAWS John 1841
MORRISON Isaac 1885

5
WHITE Frank 1895
WHITE Frank 1895
HERRINGTON John 1841
COOPER Elijah 1848
MCLENDON Daws 1899

4
PAYNE Margaret M 1848
JEMISON John S 1841
JEMISON John S 1841

7
CARRAWAY Abram B 1850
PAGE Thomas 1841
PAGE Thomas 1841
PAGE [307] Thomas 1841
CARRAWAY Alexander 1846
CARTER [82] John 1841

8
PAGE Thomas 1848
HUBBARD [234] Samuel 1841
PAGE Thomas 1848
PAGE Charles G 1846

9
HUBBARD [234] Samuel 1841
HARRIS William H 1841
HARRIS William H 1841
HARRIS [220] William H 1841
CROSBY [121] Richard 1841

18
LOCKLIN John 1850
MOORE John R 1849
MOORE John R 1849

17
PAGE Willis 1841
MOORE Lemuel D 1848
JONES [256] Ezekiel 1841
MORRISON Isah 1906
ROBERTS Ben 1894

16

19
MOORE John 1850
MCNEILL John 1848
MCNEILL John 1848
MALLORY Daniel 1844

20
MURPHEY Thomas C 1846

21
CARMICHAEL William F 1890
MCCOY James N 1901
MURPHEY Joseph R 1848
BARFIELD Charles 1895

30
MALLORY Daniel 1841
MALLORY Daniel 1841
EDWARDS John 1848
MCKELVAIN Benjamin A 1841
ODOM Jacob 1849
EASTHAM Crawford 1841
EASTHAM Crawford 1841
EDWARDS John 1848

29
WINN Andrew 1848
WINN Andrew 1846
NAYLOR John C 1860
ASKIN John S 1860
MOSBY Edward C 1848
CURRIE Archibald C 1859
MURPHEY Thomas C 1849
MURPHEY Thomas C 1856
DUNGER William 1881
ASKIN John S 1860

28
WINN Hinchey M 1846
WINN Andrew 1850
ODOM Jacob 1848
PEGG Martin 1841

31
BURNETT [70] Boling C 1841
BURNETT [70] Boling C 1841
GRANT Green W 1841
GRANT Green W 1841
STEWART Frank 1895
SHARP Benet 1850
SHARP Benet 1850
SHARP Bennet 1859
BUTCHEE John 1854
SHARP Benet 1854
SHARP Benet 1854
WINN Riden 1849

32
SKINNER Jesse 1841
BURNETT [71] Boling C 1841
WEIR Adolphus G 1841
CARMICHAEL Hugh 1841
CARMICHAEL Hugh 1841
PEARL Sylvester 1841

33
LARK David C 1850
PEGG Martin 1841
MCNEILL John 1848
MOORE Nelson 1854
CURRIE Archibald C 1848
MCCOWN James 1841
SWIFT John 1841
SWIFT John 1841
MURPHEY Joseph R 1846
SWIFT John 1841

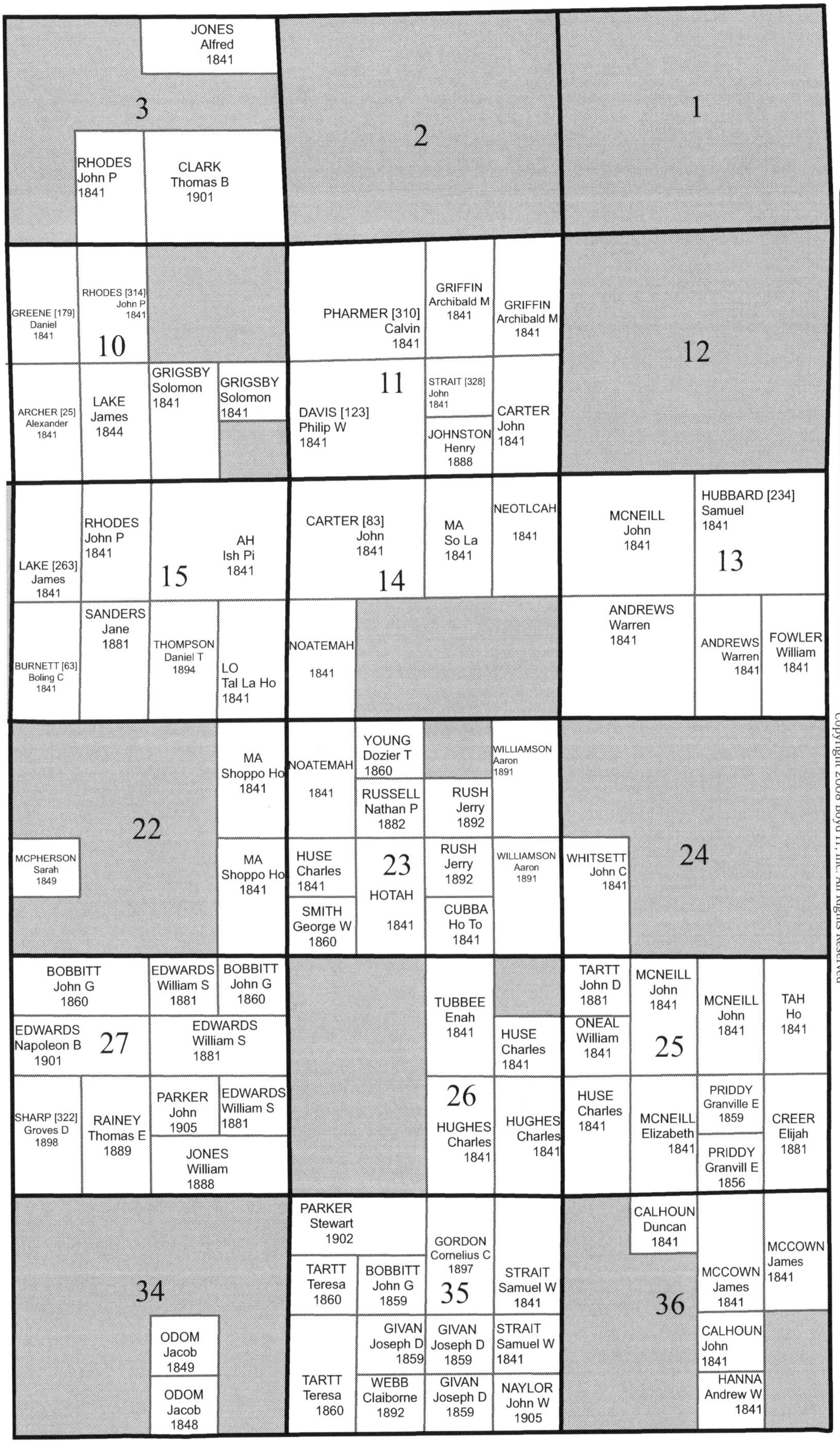

Section 3
JONES Alfred 1841
RHODES John P 1841
CLARK Thomas B 1901

Section 2

Section 1

Section 10
GREENE [179] Daniel 1841
RHODES [314] John P 1841
ARCHER [25] Alexander 1841
LAKE James 1844
GRIGSBY Solomon 1841
GRIGSBY Solomon 1841

Section 11
PHARMER [310] Calvin 1841
GRIFFIN Archibald M 1841
GRIFFIN Archibald M 1841
STRAIT [328] John 1841
DAVIS [123] Philip W 1841
JOHNSTON Henry 1888
CARTER John 1841

Section 12

Section 15
LAKE [263] James 1841
RHODES John P 1841
AH Ish Pi 1841
BURNETT [63] Boling C 1841
SANDERS Jane 1881
THOMPSON Daniel T 1894
LO Tal La Ho 1841

Section 14
CARTER [83] John 1841
MA So La 1841
NEOTLCAH 1841
NOATEMAH 1841

Section 13
MCNEILL John 1841
HUBBARD [234] Samuel 1841
ANDREWS Warren 1841
ANDREWS Warren 1841
FOWLER William 1841

Section 22
MA Shoppo Ho 1841
MCPHERSON Sarah 1849
MA Shoppo Ho 1841

Section 23
NOATEMAH 1841
YOUNG Dozier T 1860
WILLIAMSON Aaron 1891
RUSSELL Nathan P 1882
RUSH Jerry 1892
HUSE Charles 1841
RUSH Jerry 1892
WILLIAMSON Aaron 1891
HOTAH 1841
SMITH George W 1860
CUBBA Ho To 1841

Section 24
WHITSETT John C 1841

Section 27
BOBBITT John G 1860
EDWARDS William S 1881
BOBBITT John G 1860
EDWARDS Napoleon B 1901
EDWARDS William S 1881
SHARP [322] Groves D 1898
RAINEY Thomas E 1889
PARKER John 1905
EDWARDS William S 1881
JONES William 1888

Section 26
TUBBEE Enah 1841
HUSE Charles 1841
HUGHES Charles 1841
HUGHES Charles 1841

Section 25
TARTT John D 1881
ONEAL William 1841
MCNEILL John 1841
MCNEILL John 1841
TAH Ho 1841
HUSE Charles 1841
MCNEILL Elizabeth 1841
PRIDDY Granville E 1859
PRIDDY Granvill E 1856
CREER Elijah 1881

Section 34
ODOM Jacob 1849
ODOM Jacob 1848

Section 35
PARKER Stewart 1902
GORDON Cornelius C 1897
TARTT Teresa 1860
BOBBITT John G 1859
STRAIT Samuel W 1841
GIVAN Joseph D 1859
GIVAN Joseph D 1859
STRAIT Samuel W 1841
TARTT Teresa 1860
WEBB Claiborne 1892
GIVAN Joseph D 1859
NAYLOR John W 1905

Section 36
CALHOUN Duncan 1841
MCCOWN James 1841
MCCOWN James 1841
CALHOUN John 1841
HANNA Andrew W 1841

Helpful Hints

1. This Map's INDEX can be found on the preceding pages.
2. Refer to Map "C" to see where this Township lies within Kemper County, Mississippi.
3. Numbers within square brackets [ ] denote a multi-patentee land parcel (multi-owner). Refer to Appendix "C" for a full list of members in this group.
4. Areas that look to be crowded with Patentees usually indicate multiple sales of the same parcel (Re-issues) or Overlapping parcels. See this Township's Index for an explanation of these and other circumstances that might explain "odd" groupings of Patentees on this map.

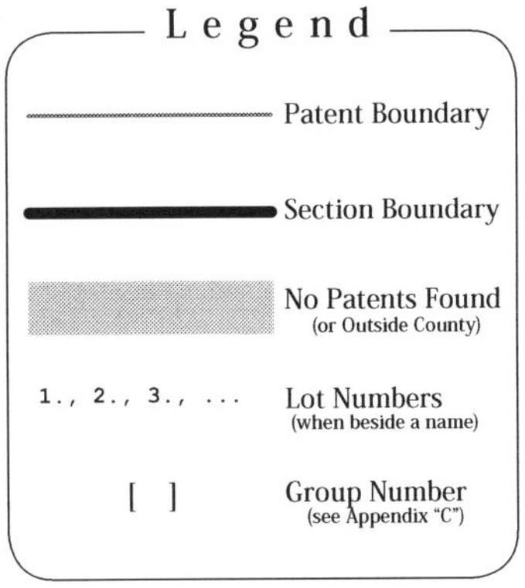

Legend

Patent Boundary
Section Boundary
No Patents Found (or Outside County)
1., 2., 3., ... Lot Numbers (when beside a name)
[ ] Group Number (see Appendix "C")

Scale: Section = 1 mile X 1 mile (generally, with some exceptions)

Road Map

T9-N R17-E
Choctaw Meridian

Map Group 22

Cities & Towns

Kemper Springs

Cemeteries

None

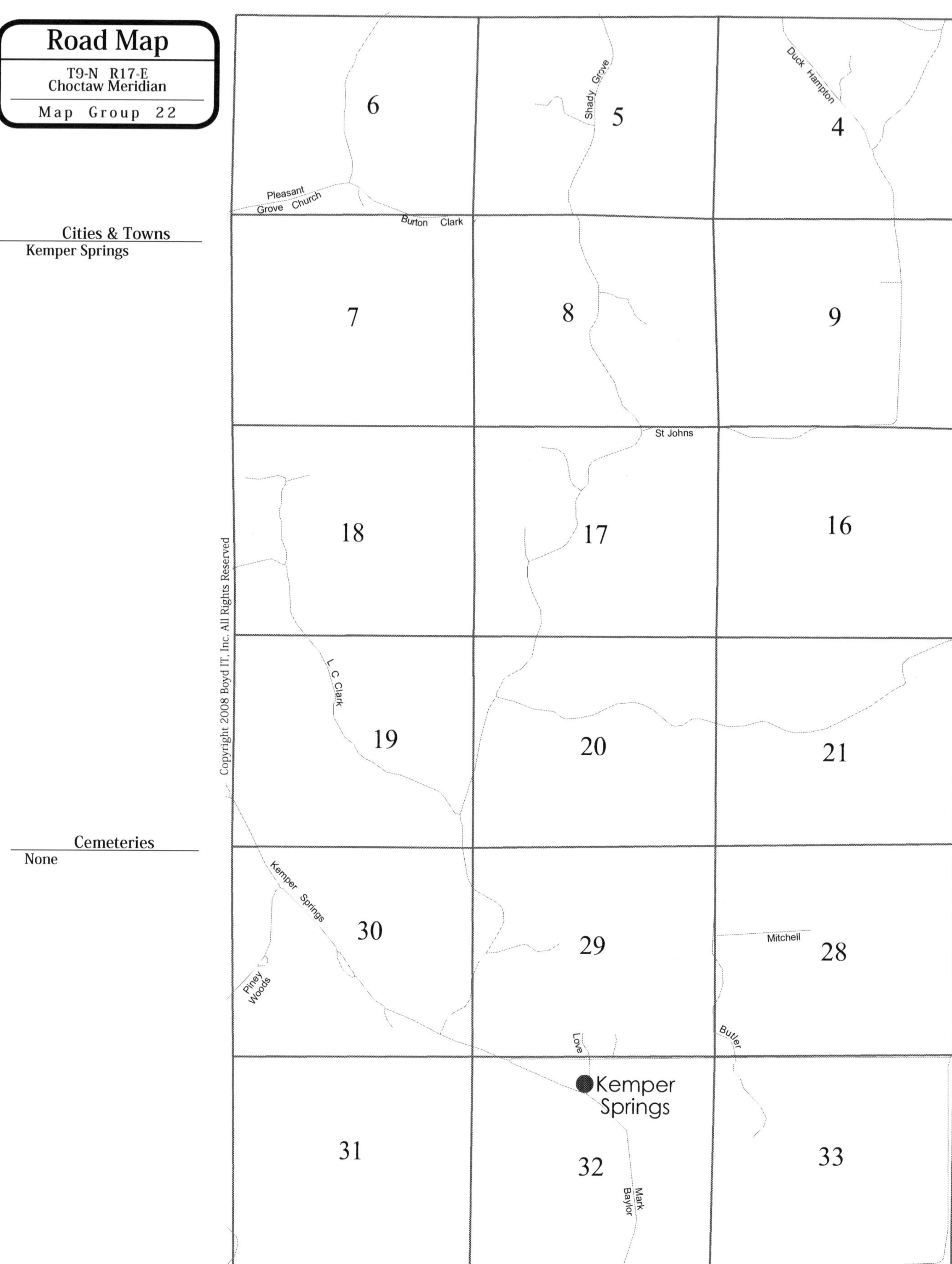

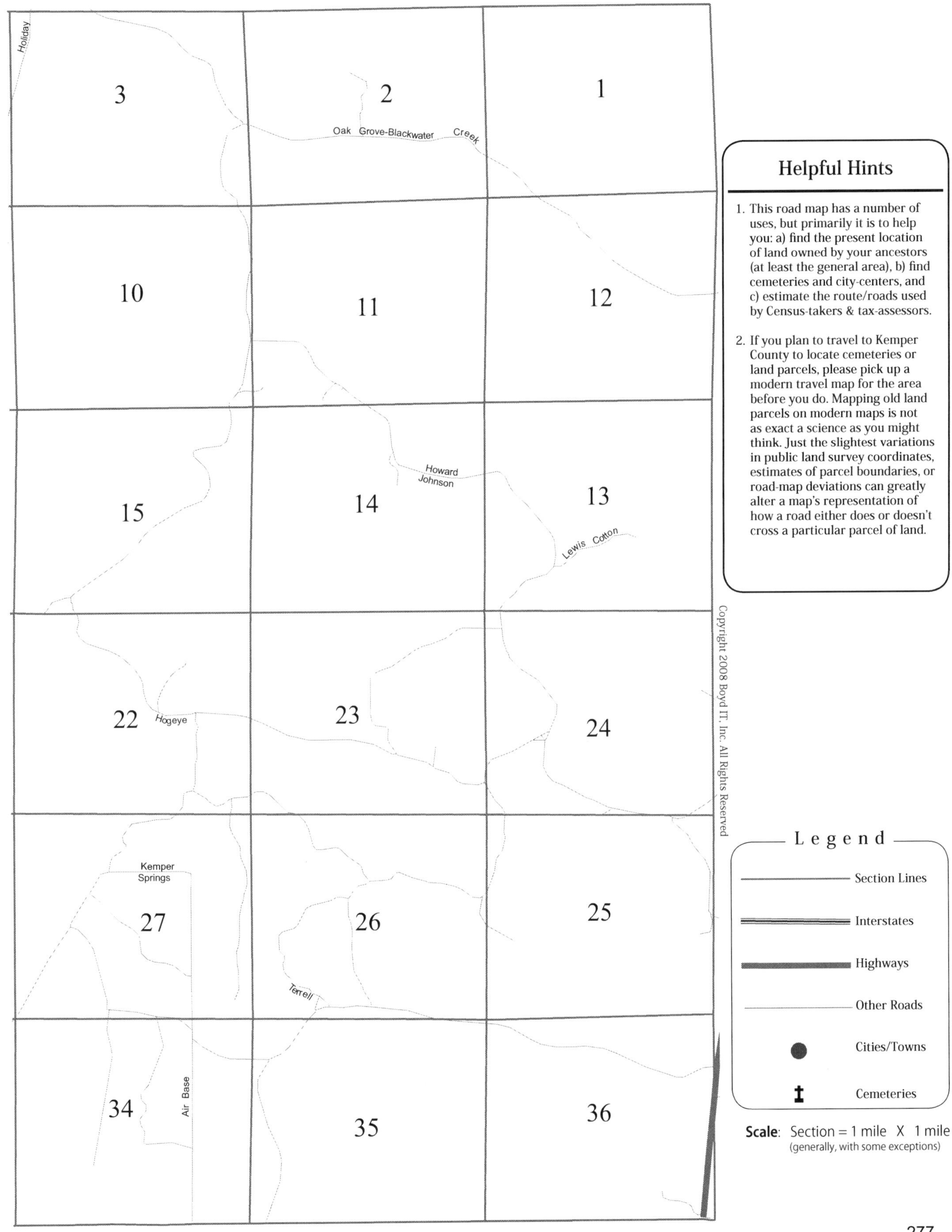
Holiday
3
2
1
Oak Grove-Blackwater Creek
10
11
12
15
14
13
Howard Johnson
Lewis Cotton
22
Hogeye
23
24
Kemper Springs
27
26
25
Terrell
34
Air Base
35
36
Helpful Hints
1. This road map has a number of uses, but primarily it is to help you: a) find the present location of land owned by your ancestors (at least the general area), b) find cemeteries and city-centers, and c) estimate the route/roads used by Census-takers & tax-assessors.
2. If you plan to travel to Kemper County to locate cemeteries or land parcels, please pick up a modern travel map for the area before you do. Mapping old land parcels on modern maps is not as exact a science as you might think. Just the slightest variations in public land survey coordinates, estimates of parcel boundaries, or road-map deviations can greatly alter a map's representation of how a road either does or doesn't cross a particular parcel of land.
Legend
Section Lines
Interstates
Highways
Other Roads
Cities/Towns
Cemeteries
Scale: Section = 1 mile X 1 mile
(generally, with some exceptions)

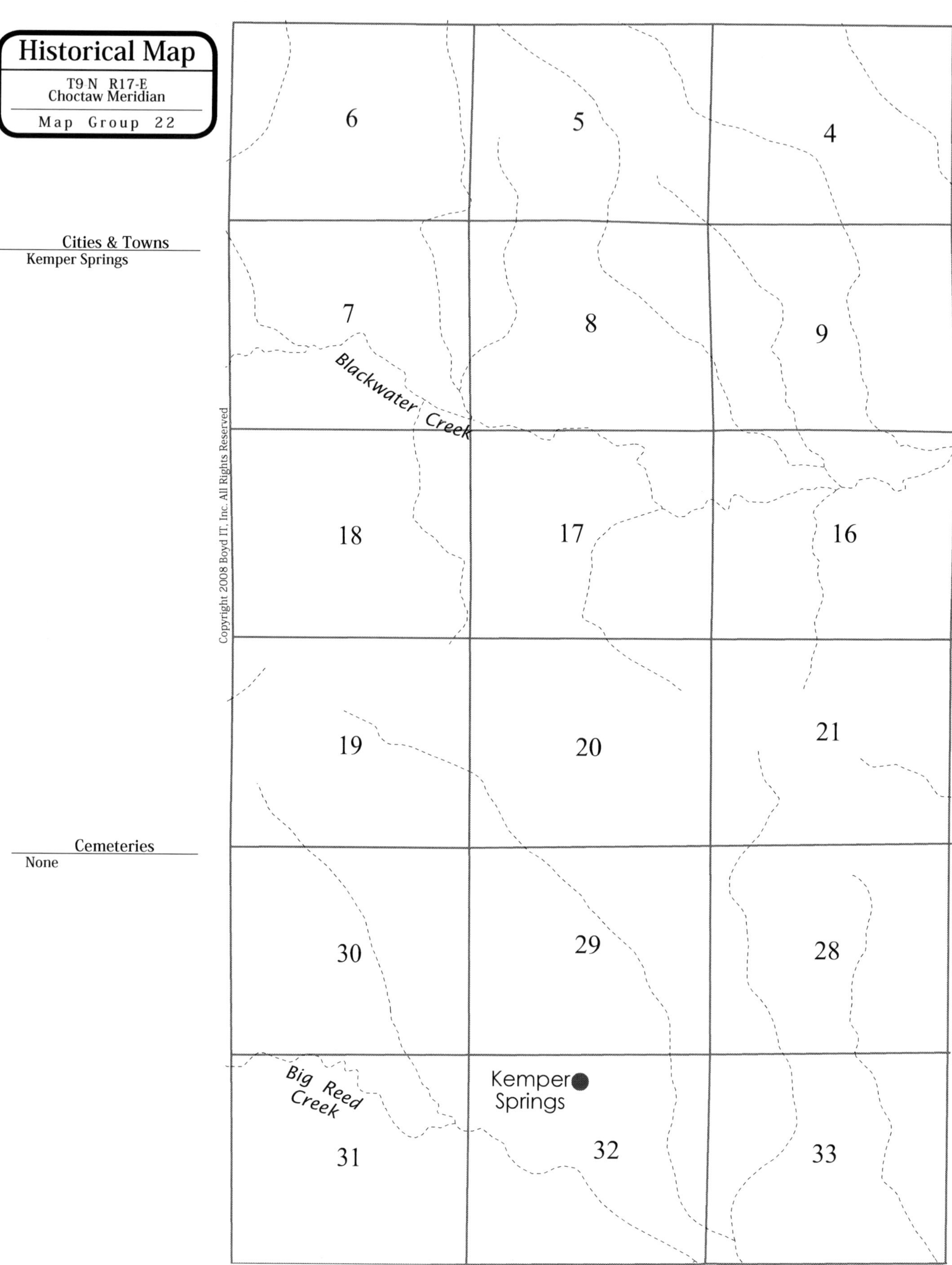
Historical Map
T9-N R17-E
Choctaw Meridian
Map Group 22
Cities & Towns
Kemper Springs
Cemeteries
None
Copyright 2008 Boyd IT, Inc. All Rights Reserved
6
5
4
7
8
9
Blackwater Creek
18
17
16
19
20
21
30
29
28
Big Reed Creek
Kemper Springs
31
32
33

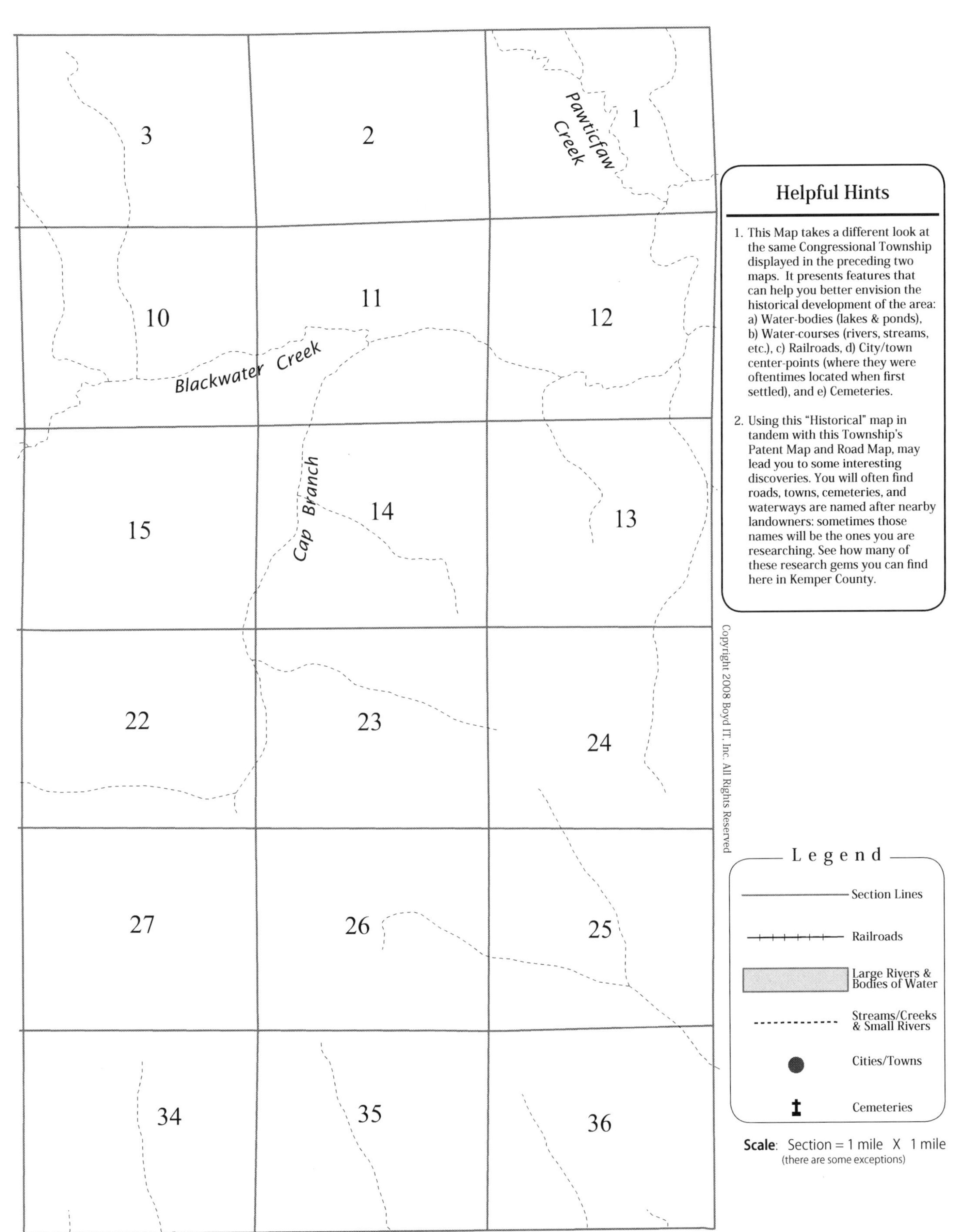

Helpful Hints

1. This Map takes a different look at the same Congressional Township displayed in the preceding two maps. It presents features that can help you better envision the historical development of the area: a) Water-bodies (lakes & ponds), b) Water-courses (rivers, streams, etc.), c) Railroads, d) City/town center-points (where they were oftentimes located when first settled), and e) Cemeteries.
2. Using this "Historical" map in tandem with this Township's Patent Map and Road Map, may lead you to some interesting discoveries. You will often find roads, towns, cemeteries, and waterways are named after nearby landowners: sometimes those names will be the ones you are researching. See how many of these research gems you can find here in Kemper County.

Scale: Section = 1 mile X 1 mile
(there are some exceptions)

Map Group 23: Index to Land Patents

Township 9-North Range 18-East (Choctaw)

After you locate an individual in this Index, take note of the Section and Section Part then proceed to the Land Patent map on the pages immediately following. You should have no difficulty locating the corresponding parcel of land.

The "For More Info" Column will lead you to more information about the underlying Patents. See the *Legend* at right, and the "How to Use this Book" chapter, for more information.

LEGEND

"For More Info . . . " column

A = Authority (Legislative Act, See Appendix "A")
B = Block or Lot (location in Section unknown)
C = Cancelled Patent
F = Fractional Section
G = Group (Multi-Patentee Patent, see Appendix "C")
V = Overlaps another Parcel
R = Re-Issued (Parcel patented more than once)

(A & G items require you to look in the Appendixes referred to above. All other Letter-designations followed by a number require you to locate line-items in this index that possess the ID number found after the letter).

ID	Individual in Patent	Sec.	Sec. Part	Date Issued	Other Counties	For More Info . . .
4335	AVERY, Joseph C	15	NW	1854-03-15		A1
4279	BANNON, Eli O	21	S½SW	1905-08-26		A2
4381	BEVILL, Thomas L	24	W½NW	1841-02-27		A1
4292	BOYD, George	21	NWSE	1890-06-25		A2
4294	" "	21	SWNE	1890-06-25		A2
4293	" "	21	NWSW	1892-05-26		A2
4295	" "	21	SWNW	1892-05-26		A2
4298	BRANTLEY, George W	15	SESW	1898-09-28		A2
4305	BRANTLEY, James	23	W½NW	1895-05-11		A2
4336	BRANTLEY, Joseph E	15	NWSE	1904-07-02		A2
4393	BRANTLEY, William B	15	S½SE	1893-12-19		A2
4349	BRIGGS, Nathan G	1	N½NE	1909-05-20		A1
4350	" "	1	N½NW	1909-05-20		A1
4291	BRODANAX, Frederick	19	NESE	1882-05-20		A2
4248	BURTON, Absalom T	25	S½NW	1894-12-17		A2
4264	BURTON, Buster	19	SESE	1912-02-01		A2
4379	BURTON, Thomas F	17	NESE	1849-12-01		A1
4382	BURTON, Thomas W	25	N½NE	1888-04-05		A2
4360	BYRN, Samuel H	22	E½NE	1841-02-27		A1 G75
4361	" "	22	E½NW	1841-02-27		A1 G75
4362	" "	22	E½SE	1841-02-27		A1 G75
4363	" "	22	E½SW	1841-02-27		A1 G75
4364	" "	22	W½NE	1841-02-27		A1 G75
4365	" "	22	W½NW	1841-02-27		A1 G75
4366	" "	22	W½SE	1841-02-27		A1 G75
4367	" "	22	W½SW	1841-02-27		A1 G75
4368	" "	27	E½NE	1841-02-27		A1 G75
4369	" "	27	E½NW	1841-02-27		A1 G75
4370	" "	27	W½NE	1841-02-27		A1 G75
4371	" "	27	W½NW	1841-02-27		A1 G75
4327	CALHOUN, John	31	NWSW	1841-02-27		A1
4296	CALVERT, George	21	SENW	1850-12-02		A1
4249	CAMPBELL, Alexander	14	NE	1912-01-25		A1
4297	CAPERS, George S	20	SW	1841-02-27		A1
4306	CARTER, James	17	W½SE	1847-04-01		A1
4328	CARTER, John	30	W½SW	1846-09-01		A1 G84
4400	CLARK, William W	25	SENE	1859-10-01		A1 G89
4322	CLAY, James T	19	SWSW	1905-12-13		A2
4380	CLAY, Thomas J	33	W½SW	1849-12-01		A1
4323	CRAWLEY, James T	17	SWNW	1856-04-01		A1
4340	CUNNINGHAM, Kevin M	19	W½SE	1889-04-23		A1
4285	DELK, Elias	35	SWSE	1856-04-01		A1
4283	DELK, Elias A	34	NESE	1848-09-01		A1
4284	" "	34	SWSE	1848-09-01		A1
4383	DELK, Vincent	33	E½SW	1841-02-27		A1
4342	DORR, Louis A	1	NESE	1856-04-01		A1 V4266

ID	Individual in Patent	Sec.	Sec. Part	Date Issued	Other Counties	For More Info . . .
4355	EDWARDS, Rigdon	27	E½SE	1841-02-27		A1 G137
4356	" "	27	W½SE	1841-02-27		A1 G137
4301	EVERETT, Horace	31	E½NW	1855-03-15		A1
4302	" "	31	E½SE	1855-03-15		A1
4303	" "	31	NE	1855-03-15		A1
4304	" "	33	NENW	1855-03-15		A1
4397	FOWLER, William	24	E½NW	1841-02-27		A1
4307	GIBBS, James	12	SW	1841-02-27		A1 G163
4299	GRANTHAM, George W	15	SWSW	1914-08-27		A2
4399	GRANTHAM, William T	23	S½SW	1901-12-17		A2
4270	GREENE, Daniel	24	W½SW	1841-12-15		A1 G179
4355	GRIFFIN, Archibald M	27	E½SE	1841-02-27		A1 G137
4256	" "	27	E½SW	1841-02-27		A1 G203
4356	" "	27	W½SE	1841-02-27		A1 G137
4252	" "	27	W½SW	1841-02-27		A1
4254	" "	33	E½SE	1841-02-27		A1
4255	" "	33	W½SE	1841-02-27		A1
4257	" "	34	E½NW	1841-02-27		A1 G202
4258	" "	34	W½NW	1841-02-27		A1 G202
4253	" "	28	E½SE	1846-12-01		A1
4308	GRISOM, James	32	NESW	1849-12-01		A1
4309	" "	32	SWSE	1849-12-01		A1
4394	GUNN, William B	25	SWNE	1850-12-05		A1
4351	HAGEWOOD, Nathaniel C	14	SW	1848-09-01		A1
4352	HAGOOD, Nathaniel C	24	E½SW	1841-02-27		A1
4269	HAMLETT, Charles R	21	NWNE	1841-02-27		A1
4334	HARPER, John W	36	W½SE	1847-04-01		A1
4333	" "	15	NESE	1860-10-01		A1
4387	HARPER, Wilkins	25	E½SE	1848-09-01		A1
4388	" "	36	E½NE	1848-09-01		A1
4259	HARRINGTON, Benjamin	30	SENW	1850-12-02		A1
4372	HARRINGTON, Samuel	29	NWSE	1850-12-02		A1
4373	" "	29	SESE	1856-04-01		A1
4325	HARVEY, Jesse	7	4	1841-01-05		A1 F
4251	HEARON, Ananias	33	E½NE	1841-02-27		A1 G222
4274	HOPSON, Dennis	23	S½SE	1896-12-14		A2
4341	HOPSON, Levi	35	NWNW	1906-06-21		A2
4360	HOUSTON, Robert F	22	E½NE	1841-02-27		A1 G75
4361	" "	22	E½NW	1841-02-27		A1 G75
4362	" "	22	E½SE	1841-02-27		A1 G75
4363	" "	22	E½SW	1841-02-27		A1 G75
4364	" "	22	W½NE	1841-02-27		A1 G75
4365	" "	22	W½NW	1841-02-27		A1 G75
4366	" "	22	W½SE	1841-02-27		A1 G75
4367	" "	22	W½SW	1841-02-27		A1 G75
4368	" "	27	E½NE	1841-02-27		A1 G75
4369	" "	27	E½NW	1841-02-27		A1 G75
4370	" "	27	W½NE	1841-02-27		A1 G75
4371	" "	27	W½NW	1841-02-27		A1 G75
4271	HUBBARD, Daniel	19	S½NE	1905-12-30		A2
4374	HUBBARD, Samuel	24	SE	1841-12-15		A1 G234
4270	" "	24	W½SW	1841-12-15		A1 G179
4348	HUDSON, Mcmillian	29	NESW	1856-04-01		A1 R4261
4286	HUNTER, Ellen	31	SWSW	1892-09-27		A2 G240
4286	JEMISON, Ellen	31	SWSW	1892-09-27		A2 G240
4343	JOHNSON, Martin L	23	E½NW	1848-09-01		A1
4346	" "	23	W½NE	1848-09-01		A1
4345	" "	23	NWSW	1854-03-15		A1
4344	" "	23	NENE	1859-10-01		A1
4401	JOHNSON, Wyatt	33	W½NE	1895-06-28		A2
4250	JONES, Allen	17	NWNW	1849-12-01		A1
4287	JONES, Ezekiel	19	NENE	1850-12-02		A1
4311	JONES, James	24	E½NE	1841-02-27		A1
4312	" "	24	W½NE	1841-02-27		A1
4310	" "	14	SWSE	1849-12-01		A1
4331	JONES, John	21	E½NE	1889-11-23		A2
4378	JONES, Starling	32	SESW	1841-02-27		A1
4265	KING, Charles C	17	NE	1848-09-01		A1
4273	KING, David R	25	W½SW	1848-09-01		A1
4260	LEVINE, Benjamin	20	W½NE	1841-02-27		A1
4313	LEWIS, James	29	NESE	1894-08-04		A2
4374	LEWIS, Rufus G	24	SE	1841-12-15		A1 G234
4270	" "	24	W½SW	1841-12-15		A1 G179

ID	Individual in Patent	Sec.	Sec. Part	Date Issued	Other Counties	For More Info . . .
4307	LEWIS, Thomas	12	SW	1841-02-27		A1 G163
4337	MCCONNELL, Jullious W	1	NWSW	1898-07-12		A2
4338	" "	1	S½NW	1898-07-12		A2
4339	" "	1	SWNE	1898-07-12		A2
4314	MCCOWN, James	20	E½NW	1841-02-27		A1
4315	" "	31	E½SW	1841-02-27		A1
4316	" "	31	W½NW	1841-02-27		A1
4317	" "	31	W½SE	1841-02-27		A1
4318	" "	34	E½NE	1841-02-27		A1 G282
4319	" "	34	W½NE	1841-02-27		A1 G282
4300	MCLAMORE, Henry	25	N½NW	1895-11-11		A2 G293
4300	MCLAMORE, Mary J	25	N½NW	1895-11-11		A2 G293
4320	MILLARD, James R	25	E½SW	1859-10-01		A1
4321	" "	25	W½SE	1859-10-01		A1
4392	MILLS, Willard C	33	SWNW	1854-03-15		A1
4389	" "	29	S½SW	1859-10-01		A1
4390	" "	33	NWNW	1859-10-01		A1
4391	" "	33	SENW	1859-10-01		A1
4359	MOORE, Sam	19	NWSW	1913-07-29		A2
4261	NEWBERRY, Benjamin	29	NESW	1856-04-01		A1 R4348
4262	" "	29	SENW	1858-07-15		A1
4272	OBANNON, David	21	S½SE	1890-06-25		A2
4400	PORTER, John C	25	SENE	1859-10-01		A1 G89
4263	ROBERTS, Berry	19	NWNE	1860-05-01		A1
4288	SCOTT, Francis T	29	NWNW	1859-10-01		A1
4289	" "	29	NWSW	1859-10-01		A1
4290	" "	29	SWSE	1860-05-01		A1
4384	SEAL, Wesley	17	SESW	1854-03-15		A1
4281	SEALE, Eli	21	NENW	1849-12-01		A1
4280	" "	17	SESE	1859-10-01		A1
4282	SEALE, Eli Y	23	NESW	1849-12-01		A1
4324	SEALE, Jarvis	17	SWSW	1859-10-01		A1
4385	SEALE, Wesley	17	N½SW	1860-05-01		A1
4386	SEALE, Wesley Y	21	NWNW	1860-10-01		A1
4329	SELBY, John H	15	NE	1848-09-01		A1
4330	" "	17	E½NW	1856-04-01		A1
4395	SELBY, William C	21	NESW	1860-10-01		A1
4251	SIGGARS, William	33	E½NE	1841-02-27		A1 G222
4332	SILLIMAN, John	35	E½SE	1875-04-20		A1
4347	SILLIMAN, Mary	35	NE	1848-09-01		A1
4375	SILLIMAN, Samuel M	35	E½NW	1854-03-15		A1
4376	" "	35	NWSE	1854-03-15		A1
4377	" "	35	SWNW	1859-10-01		A1
4396	SILLIMAN, William C	35	SW	1847-04-01		A1
4276	SIMMONS, Edward W	36	NENW	1849-12-01		A1
4277	" "	36	NWNE	1849-12-01		A1
4278	" "	36	W½NW	1849-12-01		A1
4353	SIMMONS, Nick	15	N½SW	1895-12-14		A2
4398	STANTON, William	36	SW	1847-04-01		A1
4257	STEWART, Malcolm M	34	E½NW	1841-02-27		A1 G202
4258	" "	34	W½NW	1841-02-27		A1 G202
4354	STEWART, Norman	20	SENE	1841-02-27		A1
4374	TAPPAN, John	24	SE	1841-12-15		A1 G234
4270	" "	24	W½SW	1841-12-15		A1 G179
4275	TUBBEE, E A Ka	19	W½NW	1841-02-27		A1
4256	UPCHURCH, Benjamin	27	E½SW	1841-02-27		A1 G203
4357	WALKER, Robert D	1	S½SE	1902-12-30		A2
4358	" "	1	S½SW	1902-12-30		A2
4318	WALL, James	34	E½NE	1841-02-27		A1 G282
4319	" "	34	W½NE	1841-02-27		A1 G282
4266	WARREN, Charles C	1	N½SE	1895-12-14		A2 V4342
4267	" "	1	NESW	1895-12-14		A2
4268	" "	1	SENE	1895-12-14		A2
4326	WHITSETT, John C	3	W½NW	1859-10-01		A1
4328	YOUNG, Thomas T	30	W½SW	1846-09-01		A1 G84

Patent Map

T9-N R18-E
Choctaw Meridian

Map Group 23

Township Statistics

Parcels Mapped	:	154
Number of Patents	:	134
Number of Individuals	:	108
Patentees Identified	:	99
Number of Surnames	:	74
Multi-Patentee Parcels	:	27
Oldest Patent Date	:	1/5/1841
Most Recent Patent	:	8/27/1914
Block/Lot Parcels	:	1
Parcels Re - Issued	:	1
Parcels that Overlap	:	2
Cities and Towns	:	3
Cemeteries	:	2

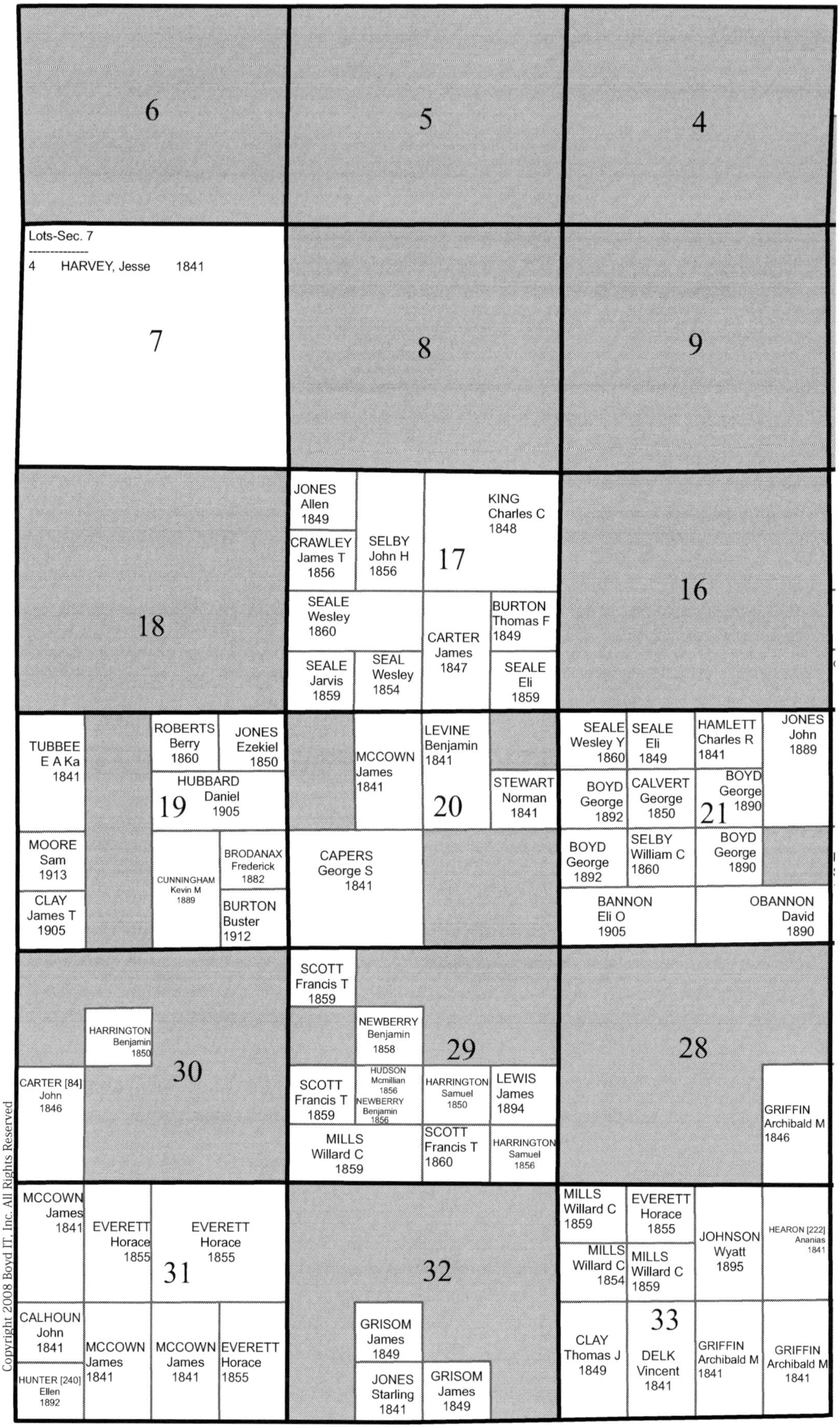

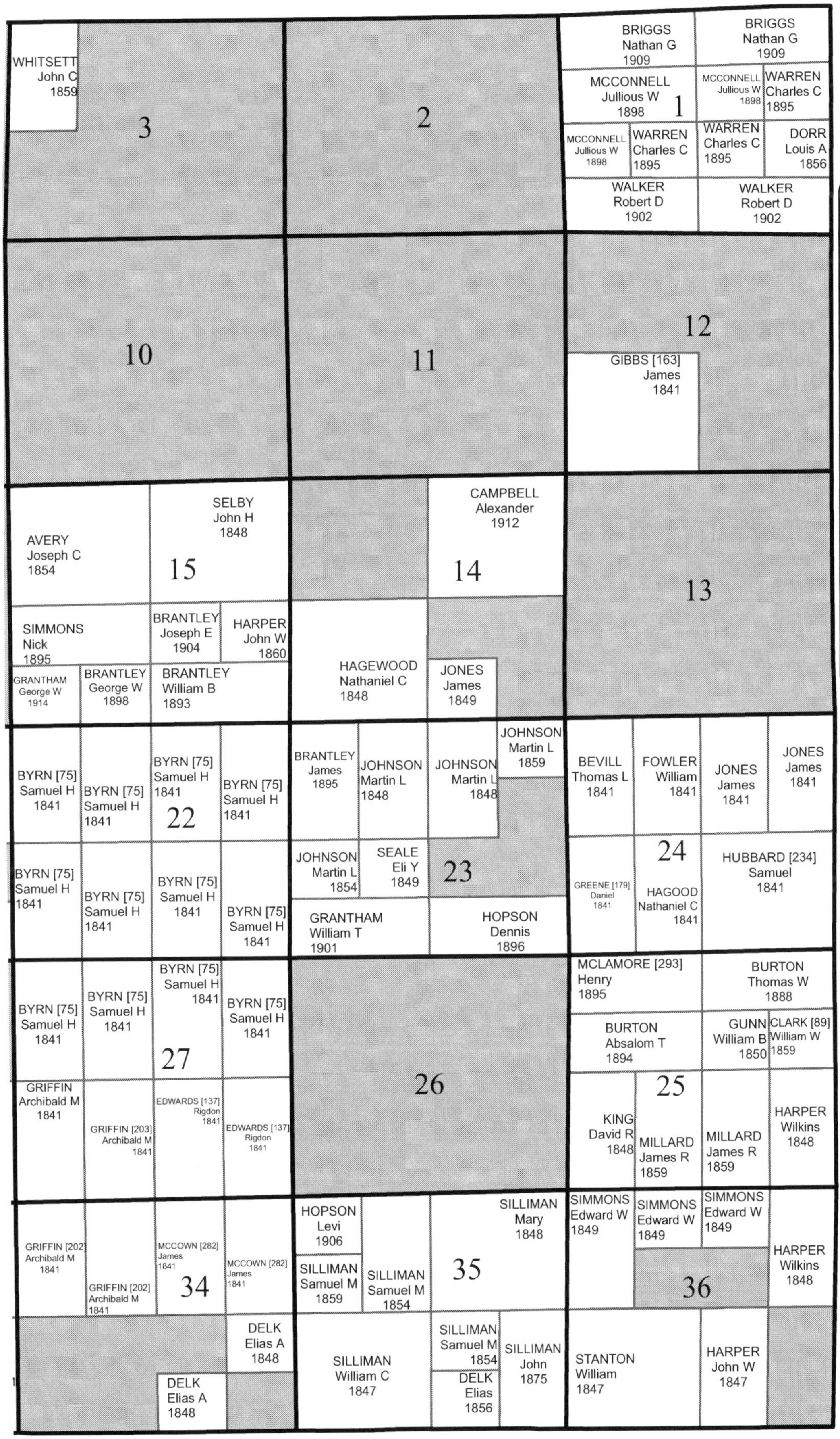

WHITSETT John C 1859
3
2
BRIGGS Nathan G 1909
BRIGGS Nathan G 1909
MCCONNELL Jullious W 1898
1
MCCONNELL Jullious W 1898
WARREN Charles C 1895
MCCONNELL Jullious W 1898
WARREN Charles C 1895
WARREN Charles C 1895
DORR Louis A 1856
WALKER Robert D 1902
WALKER Robert D 1902
10
11
12
GIBBS [163] James 1841
AVERY Joseph C 1854
SELBY John H 1848
15
14
CAMPBELL Alexander 1912
13
SIMMONS Nick 1895
BRANTLEY Joseph E 1904
HARPER John W 1860
HAGEWOOD Nathaniel C 1848
JONES James 1849
GRANTHAM George W 1914
BRANTLEY George W 1898
BRANTLEY William B 1893
BYRN [75] Samuel H 1841
BYRN [75] Samuel H 1841
BYRN [75] Samuel H 1841
22
BYRN [75] Samuel H 1841
BRANTLEY James 1895
JOHNSON Martin L 1848
JOHNSON Martin L 1848
JOHNSON Martin L 1859
BEVILL Thomas L 1841
FOWLER William 1841
JONES James 1841
JONES James 1841
BYRN [75] Samuel H 1841
BYRN [75] Samuel H 1841
BYRN [75] Samuel H 1841
BYRN [75] Samuel H 1841
JOHNSON Martin L 1854
SEALE Eli Y 1849
23
GRANTHAM William T 1901
HOPSON Dennis 1896
GREENE [179] Daniel 1841
24
HAGOOD Nathaniel C 1841
HUBBARD [234] Samuel 1841
BYRN [75] Samuel H 1841
BYRN [75] Samuel H 1841
BYRN [75] Samuel H 1841
BYRN [75] Samuel H 1841
27
26
MCLAMORE [293] Henry 1895
BURTON Thomas W 1888
BURTON Absalom T 1894
GUNN William B 1850
CLARK [89] William W 1859
GRIFFIN Archibald M 1841
GRIFFIN [203] Archibald M 1841
EDWARDS [137] Rigdon 1841
EDWARDS [137] Rigdon 1841
25
KING David R 1848
MILLARD James R 1859
MILLARD James R 1859
HARPER Wilkins 1848
GRIFFIN [202] Archibald M 1841
GRIFFIN [202] Archibald M 1841
MCCOWN [282] James 1841
34
MCCOWN [282] James 1841
HOPSON Levi 1906
SILLIMAN Mary 1848
SILLIMAN Samuel M 1859
SILLIMAN Samuel M 1854
35
SIMMONS Edward W 1849
SIMMONS Edward W 1849
SIMMONS Edward W 1849
HARPER Wilkins 1848
36
DELK Elias A 1848
DELK Elias A 1848
SILLIMAN William C 1847
SILLIMAN Samuel M 1854
DELK Elias 1856
SILLIMAN John 1875
STANTON William 1847
HARPER John W 1847

Helpful Hints

1. This Map's INDEX can be found on the preceding pages.
2. Refer to Map "C" to see where this Township lies within Kemper County, Mississippi.
3. Numbers within square brackets [ ] denote a multi-patentee land parcel (multi-owner). Refer to Appendix "C" for a full list of members in this group.
4. Areas that look to be crowded with Patentees usually indicate multiple sales of the same parcel (Re-issues) or Overlapping parcels. See this Township's Index for an explanation of these and other circumstances that might explain "odd" groupings of Patentees on this map.

Legend

- Patent Boundary
- Section Boundary
- No Patents Found (or Outside County)
- 1., 2., 3., ... Lot Numbers (when beside a name)
- [ ] Group Number (see Appendix "C")

Scale: Section = 1 mile X 1 mile (generally, with some exceptions)

Road Map

T9-N R18-E
Choctaw Meridian

Map Group 23

Cities & Towns

Enondale
Narkeeta (historical)
Tamola

Cemeteries

Enondale Cemetery
Mount Hebron Cemetery

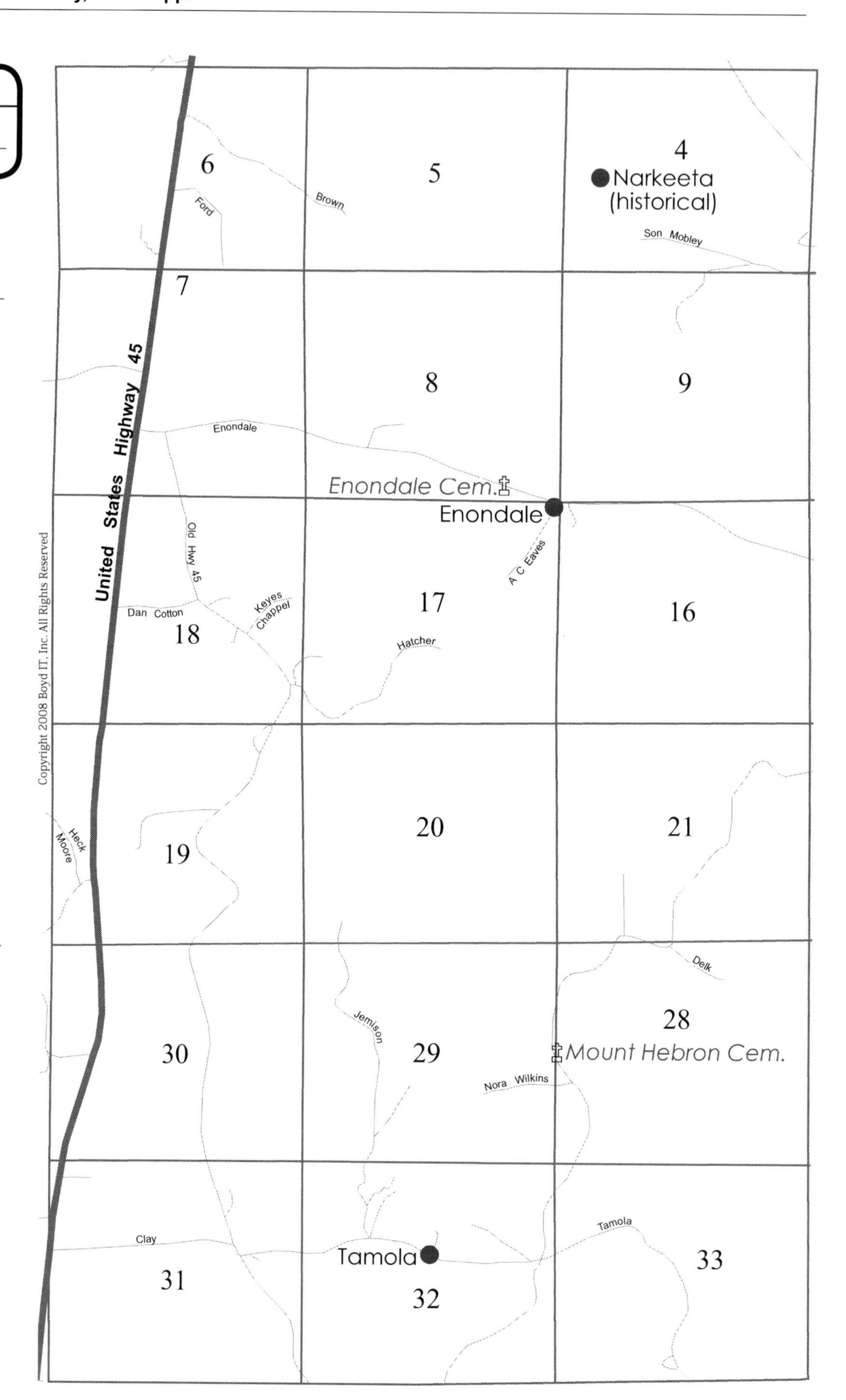

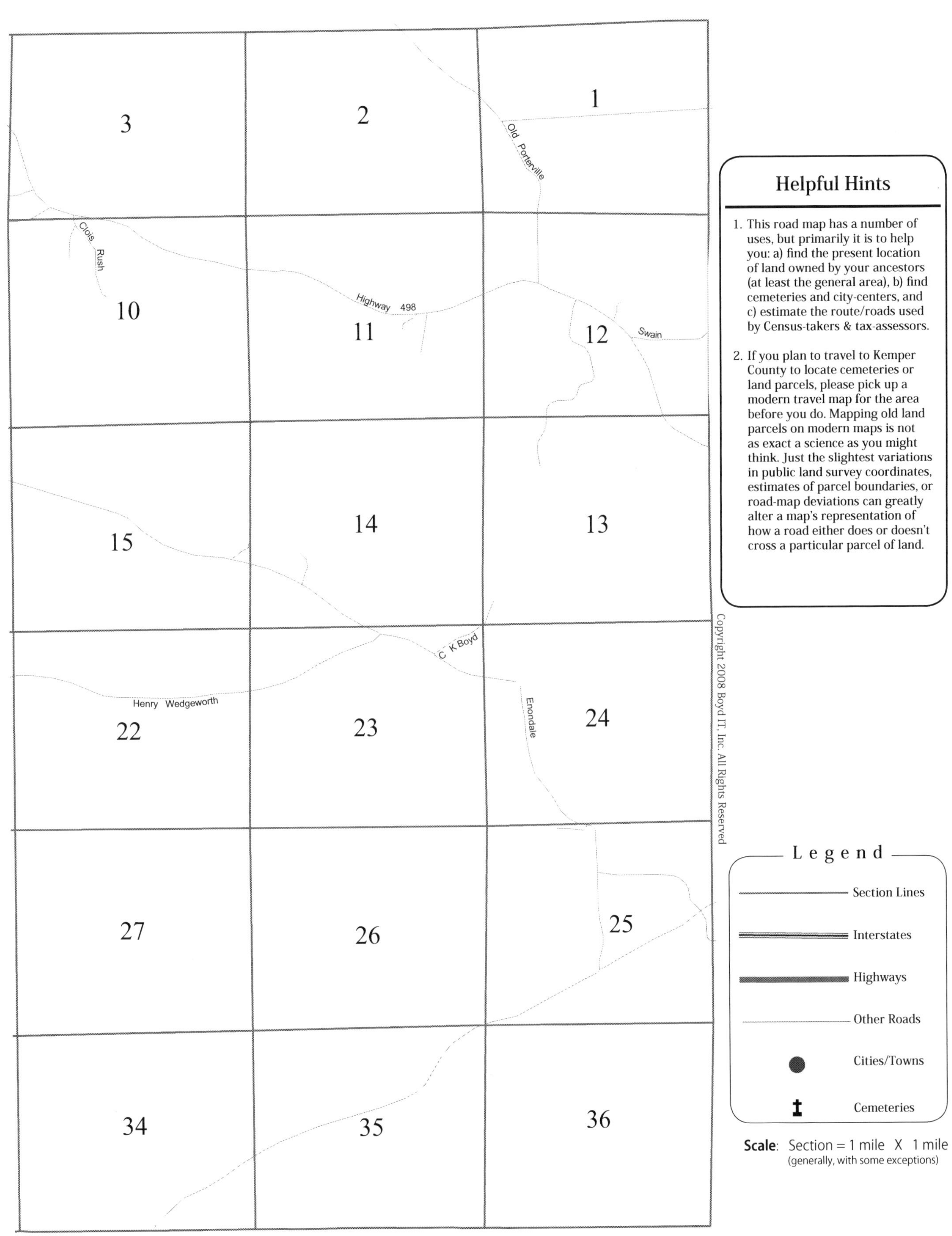

Helpful Hints

1. This road map has a number of uses, but primarily it is to help you: a) find the present location of land owned by your ancestors (at least the general area), b) find cemeteries and city-centers, and c) estimate the route/roads used by Census-takers & tax-assessors.

2. If you plan to travel to Kemper County to locate cemeteries or land parcels, please pick up a modern travel map for the area before you do. Mapping old land parcels on modern maps is not as exact a science as you might think. Just the slightest variations in public land survey coordinates, estimates of parcel boundaries, or road-map deviations can greatly alter a map's representation of how a road either does or doesn't cross a particular parcel of land.

Legend

- Section Lines
- Interstates
- Highways
- Other Roads
- Cities/Towns
- Cemeteries

Scale: Section = 1 mile X 1 mile (generally, with some exceptions)

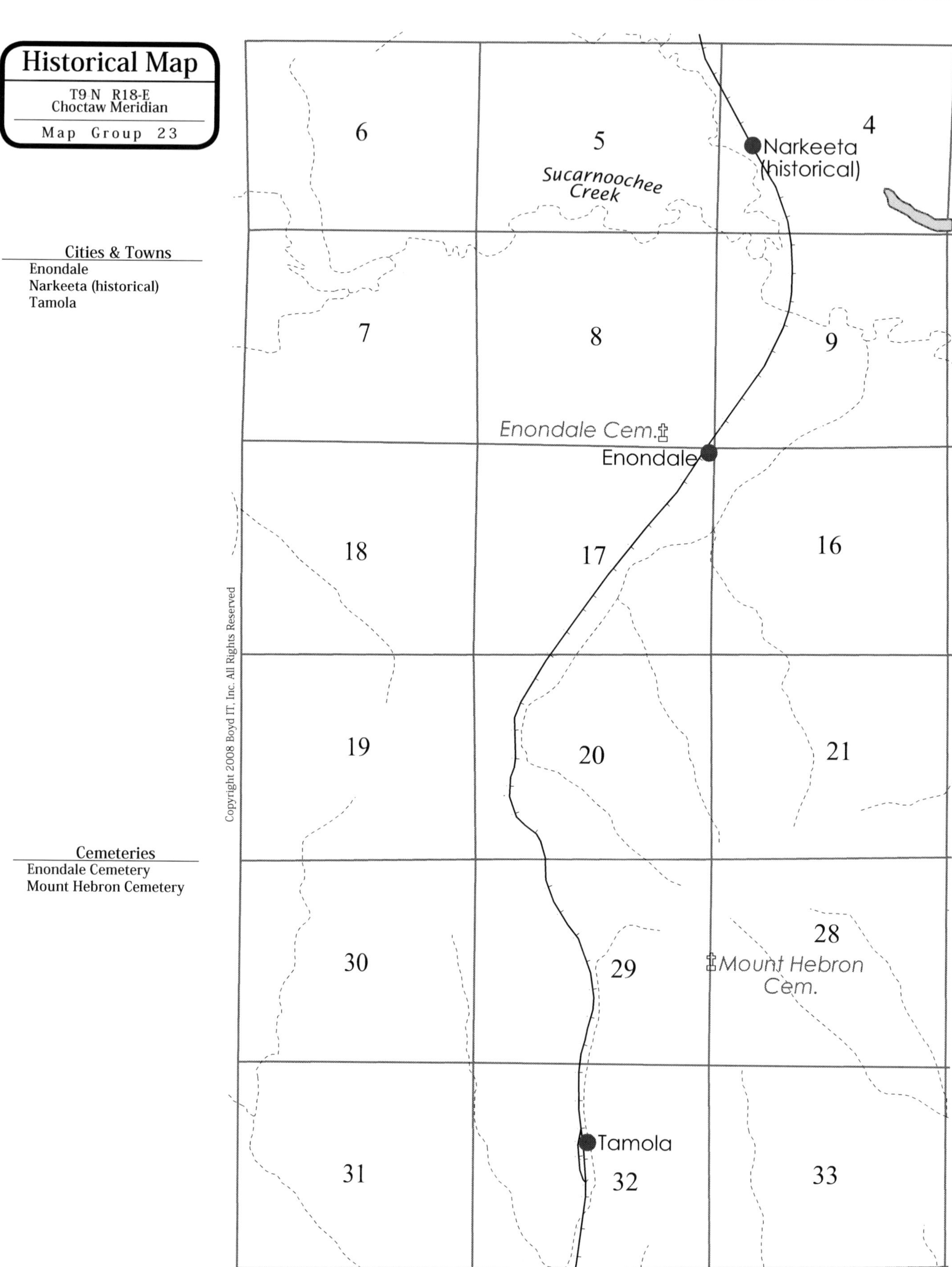
Historical Map
T9-N R18-E
Choctaw Meridian
Map Group 23
Cities & Towns
Enondale
Narkeeta (historical)
Tamola
Cemeteries
Enondale Cemetery
Mount Hebron Cemetery
6
5
4
Narkeeta (historical)
Sucarnoochee Creek
7
8
9
Enondale Cem.
Enondale
18
17
16
19
20
21
30
29
28
Mount Hebron Cem.
31
Tamola
32
33

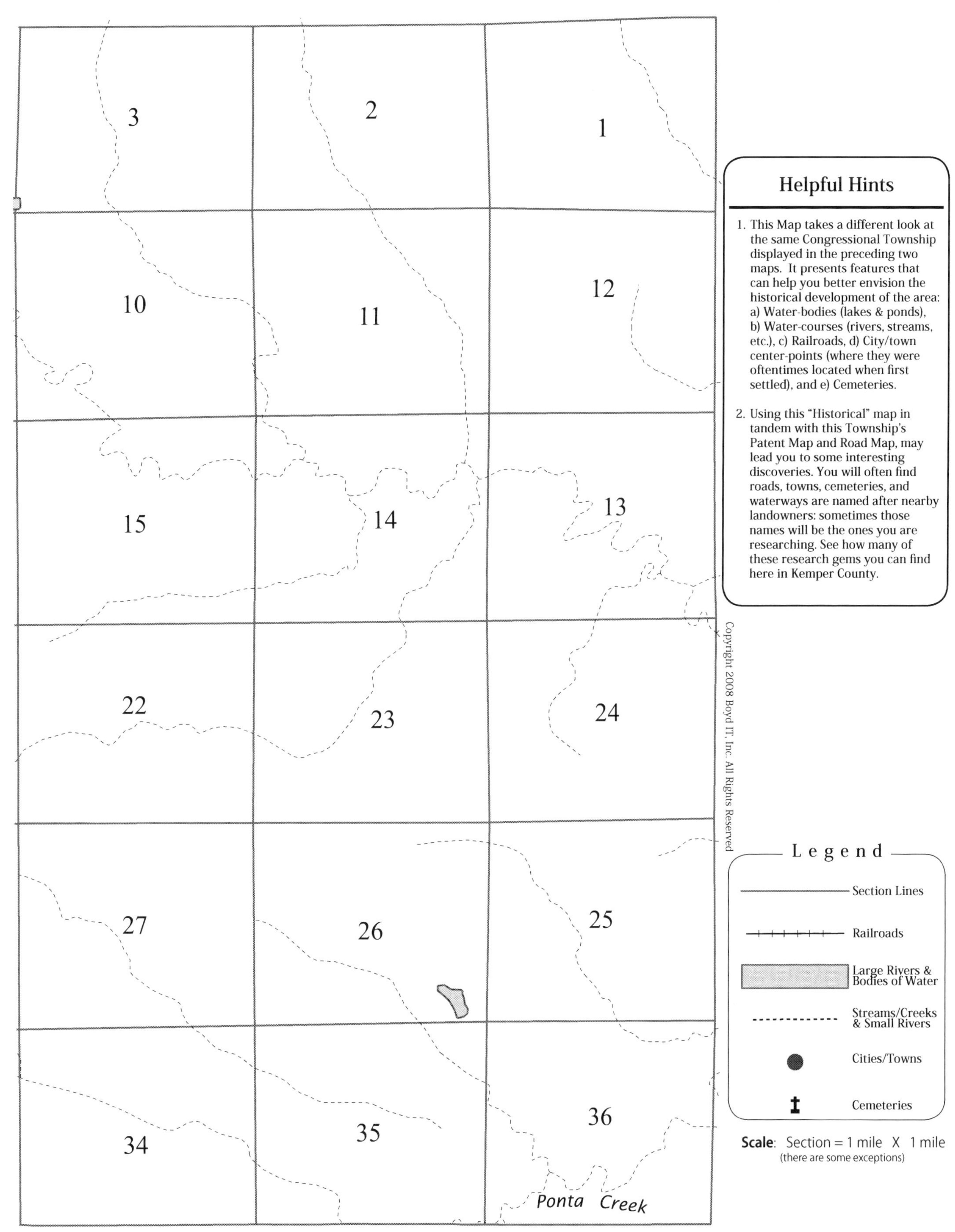

Helpful Hints

1. This Map takes a different look at the same Congressional Township displayed in the preceding two maps. It presents features that can help you better envision the historical development of the area: a) Water-bodies (lakes & ponds), b) Water-courses (rivers, streams, etc.), c) Railroads, d) City/town center-points (where they were oftentimes located when first settled), and e) Cemeteries.

2. Using this "Historical" map in tandem with this Township's Patent Map and Road Map, may lead you to some interesting discoveries. You will often find roads, towns, cemeteries, and waterways are named after nearby landowners: sometimes those names will be the ones you are researching. See how many of these research gems you can find here in Kemper County.

Map Group 24: Index to Land Patents

Township 9-North Range 19-East (Choctaw)

After you locate an individual in this Index, take note of the Section and Section Part then proceed to the Land Patent map on the pages immediately following. You should have no difficulty locating the corresponding parcel of land.

The "For More Info" Column will lead you to more information about the underlying Patents. See the *Legend* at right, and the "How to Use this Book" chapter, for more information.

LEGEND

"For More Info . . . " column

A = Authority (Legislative Act, See Appendix "A")
B = Block or Lot (location in Section unknown)
C = Cancelled Patent
F = Fractional Section
G = Group (Multi-Patentee Patent, see Appendix "C")
V = Overlaps another Parcel
R = Re-Issued (Parcel patented more than once)

(A & G items require you to look in the Appendixes referred to above. All other Letter-designations followed by a number require you to locate line-items in this index that possess the ID number found after the letter).

ID	Individual in Patent	Sec.	Sec. Part	Date Issued	Other Counties	For More Info . . .
4430	ALLEN, John	18	10	1846-03-23		A1 G19
4431	" "	18	15	1846-03-23		A1 G19
4432	" "	18	16	1846-03-23		A1 G19
4433	" "	18	9	1846-03-23		A1 G19
4418	BOYD, Gordon D	19	11	1860-04-02		A1
4419	" "	19	12	1860-04-02		A1
4442	BROWN, Robert	19	3	1841-02-27		A1
4443	" "	19	6	1841-02-27		A1
4444	" "	8		1841-02-27		A1 F
4440	" "	18	1	1846-09-01		A1
4441	" "	18	8	1846-09-01		A1
4420	BUCHANAN, Hugh Mcknight	7	SWNW	1921-06-06		A2
4455	BUTLER, William	18	3	1846-09-01		A1 F
4456	" "	18	4	1846-09-01		A1 F
4457	" "	18	5	1846-09-01		A1 F
4458	" "	18	6	1846-09-01		A1 F
4459	CLAY, William W	31	10	1841-02-27		A1
4460	" "	31	11	1841-02-27		A1
4461	" "	31	8	1841-02-27		A1
4462	" "	31	9	1841-02-27		A1
4436	DENNIS, Monroe	7	NE	1897-09-09		A2
4426	FARRAR, John A	18	11	1846-09-01		A1
4427	" "	18	12	1846-09-01		A1
4428	" "	18	13	1846-09-01		A1
4429	" "	18	14	1846-09-01		A1
4416	FREELAND, George W	30	12	1841-02-27		A1
4417	" "	30	7	1841-02-27		A1
4402	GAY, Alonzo C	7	E½SW	1891-06-30		A2
4403	" "	7	W½SE	1891-06-30		A2
4410	GREENE, Daniel	31	1	1841-02-27		A1 G179
4411	" "	31	12	1841-02-27		A1 G179
4412	" "	31	6	1841-02-27		A1 G179
4413	" "	31	7	1841-02-27		A1 G179
4434	GREENLEE, John	19	4	1841-02-27		A1
4435	" "	19	5	1841-02-27		A1
4406	GRIFFIN, Archibald M	30	1	1841-02-27		A1 G201
4404	" "	30	10	1841-02-27		A1
4407	" "	30	6	1841-02-27		A1 G201
4405	" "	30	9	1841-02-27		A1
4437	HALL, Penelope	19	14	1841-02-27		A1
4438	" "	19	8	1841-02-27		A1
4439	" "	19	9	1841-02-27		A1
4445	HODGES, Robert	19	1	1841-02-27		A1
4446	" "	19	2	1841-02-27		A1
4447	" "	19	7	1841-02-27		A1
4410	HUBBARD, Samuel	31	1	1841-02-27		A1 G179

ID	Individual in Patent	Sec.	Sec. Part	Date Issued	Other Counties	For More Info . . .
4411	HUBBARD, Samuel (Cont'd)	31	12	1841-02-27		A1 G179
4412	" "	31	6	1841-02-27		A1 G179
4413	" "	31	7	1841-02-27		A1 G179
4410	LEWIS, Rufus G	31	1	1841-02-27		A1 G179
4411	" "	31	12	1841-02-27		A1 G179
4412	" "	31	6	1841-02-27		A1 G179
4413	" "	31	7	1841-02-27		A1 G179
4450	" "	5		1841-02-27		A1 G268 F
4430	MARTIN, Joseph	18	10	1846-03-23		A1 G19
4431	" "	18	15	1846-03-23		A1 G19
4432	" "	18	16	1846-03-23		A1 G19
4433	" "	18	9	1846-03-23		A1 G19
4421	MCCOWN, James	19	10	1841-02-27		A1
4422	" "	19	13	1841-02-27		A1
4423	" "	30	2	1841-02-27		A1
4424	" "	30	5	1841-02-27		A1
4425	MCDOWELL, James P	7	W½SW	1892-07-20		A2
4408	MCMURRY, Benjamin F	7	N½NW	1895-02-21		A2
4409	" "	7	SENW	1895-02-21		A2
4414	MCQUEEN, Elizabeth W	30	11	1841-02-27		A1
4415	" "	30	8	1841-02-27		A1
4406	MULLINS, Burkley	30	1	1841-02-27		A1 G201
4407	" "	30	6	1841-02-27		A1 G201
4448	STRAITZ, Robert	30	3	1841-02-27		A1
4449	" "	30	4	1841-02-27		A1
4410	TAPPAN, John	31	1	1841-02-27		A1 G179
4411	" "	31	12	1841-02-27		A1 G179
4412	" "	31	6	1841-02-27		A1 G179
4413	" "	31	7	1841-02-27		A1 G179
4450	WHITSETT, John C	5		1841-02-27		A1 G268 F
4451	WIGGINS, Thomas	31	2	1898-09-28		A2
4452	" "	31	3	1898-09-28		A2
4453	" "	31	4	1898-09-28		A2
4454	" "	31	5	1898-09-28		A2

Patent Map

T9-N R19-E
Choctaw Meridian

Map Group 24

Township Statistics

Parcels Mapped	:	61
Number of Patents	:	30
Number of Individuals	:	27
Patentees Identified	:	23
Number of Surnames	:	27
Multi-Patentee Parcels	:	11
Oldest Patent Date	:	2/27/1841
Most Recent Patent	:	6/6/1921
Block/Lot Parcels	:	52
Parcels Re - Issued	:	0
Parcels that Overlap	:	0
Cities and Towns	:	0
Cemeteries	:	1

Note: the area contained in this map amounts to far less than a full Township. Therefore, its contents are completely on this single page (instead of a "normal" 2-page spread).

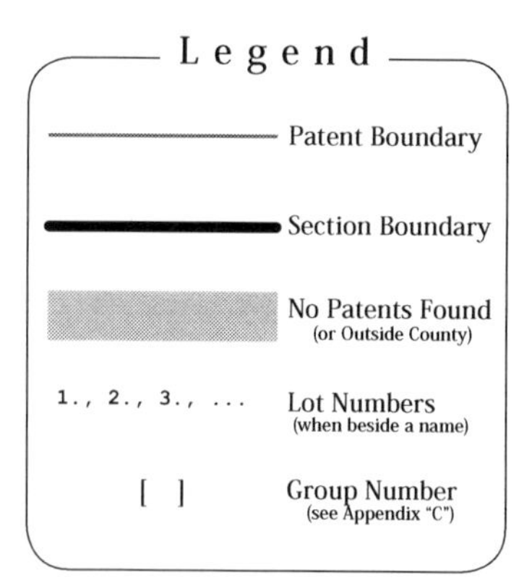

Scale: Section = 1 mile X 1 mile
(generally, with some exceptions)

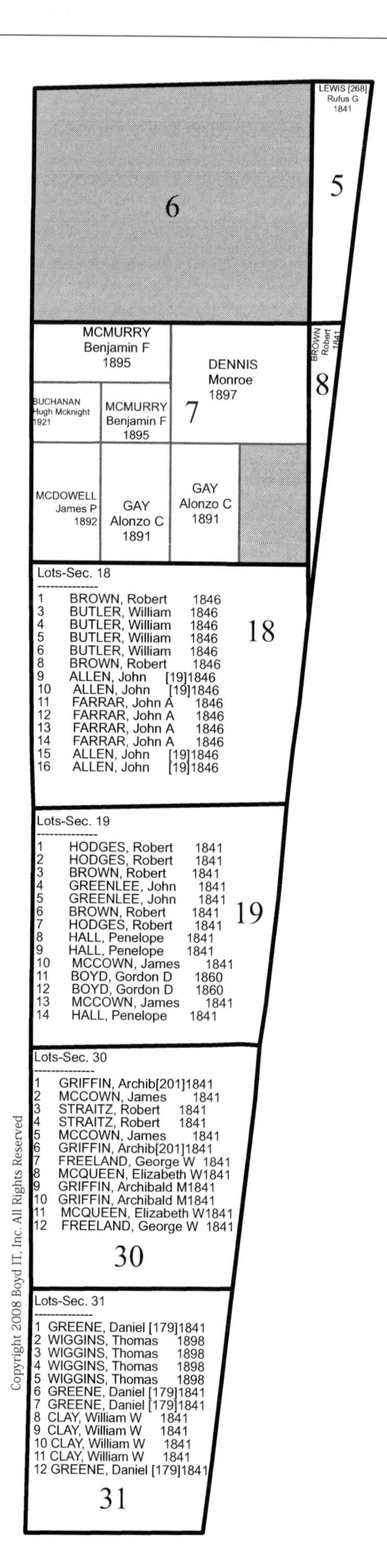

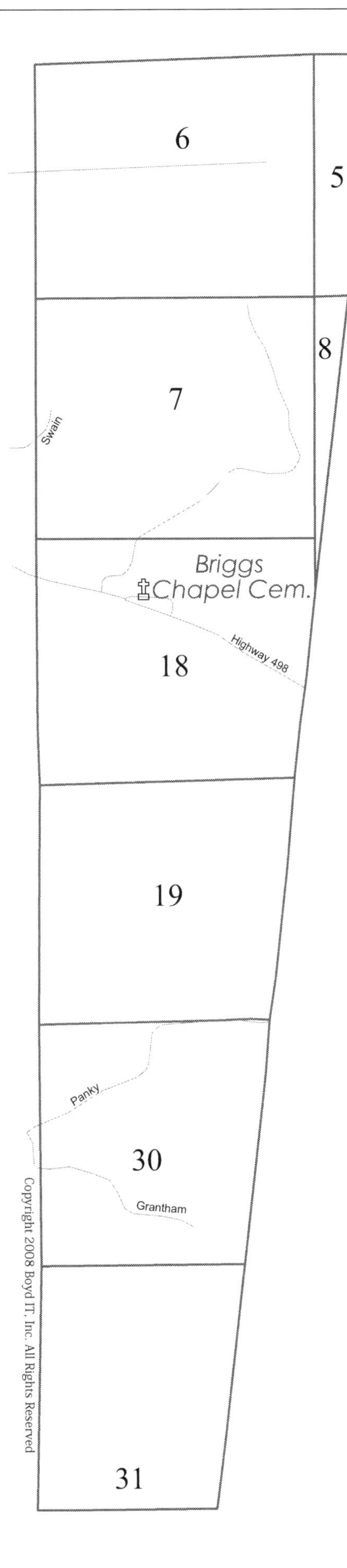

Road Map

T9-N R19-E
Choctaw Meridian

Map Group 24

Note: the area contained in this map amounts to far less than a full Township. Therefore, its contents are completely on this single page (instead of a "normal" 2-page spread).

Cities & Towns

None

Cemeteries

Briggs Chapel Cemetery

Legend

- Section Lines
- Interstates
- Highways
- Other Roads
- Cities/Towns
- Cemeteries

Scale: Section = 1 mile X 1 mile
(generally, with some exceptions)

Historical Map

T9-N R19-E
Choctaw Meridian

Map Group 24

Note: the area contained in this map amounts to far less than a full Township. Therefore, its contents are completely on this single page (instead of a "normal" 2-page spread).

Cities & Towns
None

Cemeteries
Briggs Chapel Cemetery

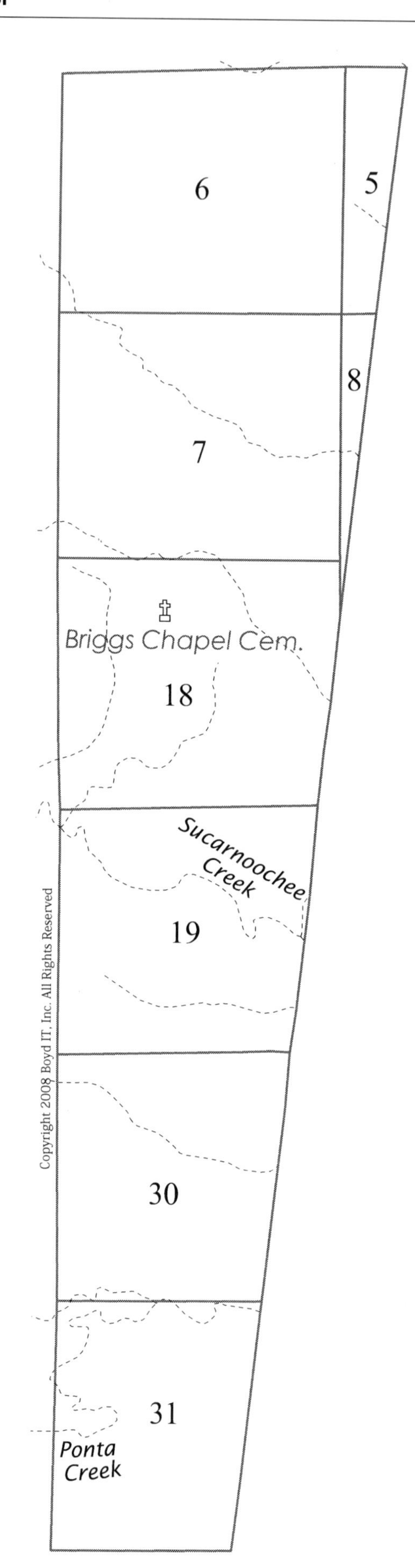

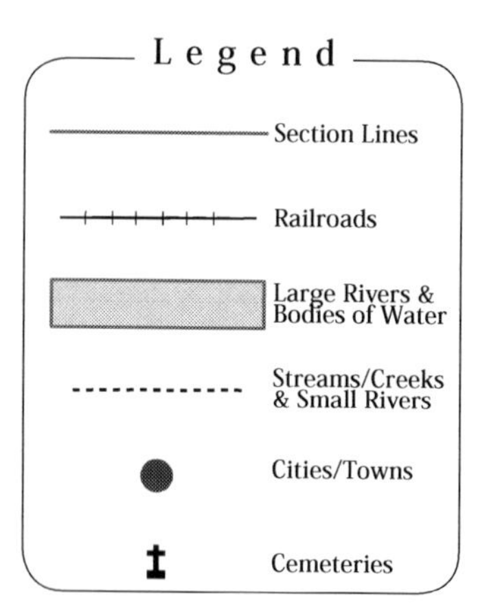

Scale: Section = 1 mile X 1 mile
(there are some exceptions)

Appendices

Appendix A - Acts of Congress Authorizing the Patents Contained in this Book

The following Acts of Congress are referred to throughout the Indexes in this book. The text of the Federal Statutes referred to below can usually be found on the web. For more information on such laws, check out the publishers's web-site at *www.arphax.com,* go to the "Research" page, and click on the "Land-Law" link.

Ref. No.	Date and Act of Congress	Number of Parcels of Land
1	April 24, 1820: Sale-Cash Entry (3 Stat. 566)	3910
2	May 20, 1862: Homestead EntryOriginal (12 Stat. 392)	540
3	September 28, 1850: Swamp Land Grant-Patent (9 Stat. 519)	12

Appendix B - Section Parts (Aliquot Parts)

The following represent the various abbreviations we have found thus far in describing the parts of a Public Land Section. Some of these are very obscure and rarely used, but we wanted to list them for just that reason. A full section is 1 square mile or 640 acres.

Section Part	Description	Acres
<none>	Full Acre (if no Section Part is listed, presumed a full Section)	640
<1-??>	A number represents a Lot Number and can be of various sizes	?
E½	East Half-Section	320
E½E½	East Half of East Half-Section	160
E½E½SE	East Half of East Half of Southeast Quarter-Section	40
E½N½	East Half of North Half-Section	160
E½NE	East Half of Northeast Quarter-Section	80
E½NENE	East Half of Northeast Quarter of Northeast Quarter-Section	20
E½NENW	East Half of Northeast Quarter of Northwest Quarter-Section	20
E½NESE	East Half of Northeast Quarter of Southeast Quarter-Section	20
E½NESW	East Half of Northeast Quarter of Southwest Quarter-Section	20
E½NW	East Half of Northwest Quarter-Section	80
E½NWNE	East Half of Northwest Quarter of Northeast Quarter-Section	20
E½NWNW	East Half of Northwest Quarter of Northwest Quarter-Section	20
E½NWSE	East Half of Northwest Quarter of Southeast Quarter-Section	20
E½NWSW	East Half of Northwest Quarter of Southwest Quarter-Section	20
E½S½	East Half of South Half-Section	160
E½SE	East Half of Southeast Quarter-Section	80
E½SENE	East Half of Southeast Quarter of Northeast Quarter-Section	20
E½SENW	East Half of Southeast Quarter of Northwest Quarter-Section	20
E½SESE	East Half of Southeast Quarter of Southeast Quarter-Section	20
E½SESW	East Half of Southeast Quarter of Southwest Quarter-Section	20
E½SW	East Half of Southwest Quarter-Section	80
E½SWNE	East Half of Southwest Quarter of Northeast Quarter-Section	20
E½SWNW	East Half of Southwest Quarter of Northwest Quarter-Section	20
E½SWSE	East Half of Southwest Quarter of Southeast Quarter-Section	20
E½SWSW	East Half of Southwest Quarter of Southwest Quarter-Section	20
E½W½	East Half of West Half-Section	160
N½	North Half-Section	320
N½E½NE	North Half of East Half of Northeast Quarter-Section	40
N½E½NW	North Half of East Half of Northwest Quarter-Section	40
N½E½SE	North Half of East Half of Southeast Quarter-Section	40
N½E½SW	North Half of East Half of Southwest Quarter-Section	40
N½N½	North Half of North Half-Section	160
N½NE	North Half of Northeast Quarter-Section	80
N½NENE	North Half of Northeast Quarter of Northeast Quarter-Section	20
N½NENW	North Half of Northeast Quarter of Northwest Quarter-Section	20
N½NESE	North Half of Northeast Quarter of Southeast Quarter-Section	20
N½NESW	North Half of Northeast Quarter of Southwest Quarter-Section	20
N½NW	North Half of Northwest Quarter-Section	80
N½NWNE	North Half of Northwest Quarter of Northeast Quarter-Section	20
N½NWNW	North Half of Northwest Quarter of Northwest Quarter-Section	20
N½NWSE	North Half of Northwest Quarter of Southeast Quarter-Section	20
N½NWSW	North Half of Northwest Quarter of Southwest Quarter-Section	20
N½S½	North Half of South Half-Section	160
N½SE	North Half of Southeast Quarter-Section	80
N½SENE	North Half of Southeast Quarter of Northeast Quarter-Section	20
N½SENW	North Half of Southeast Quarter of Northwest Quarter-Section	20
N½SESE	North Half of Southeast Quarter of Southeast Quarter-Section	20

Section Part	Description	Acres
N½SESW	North Half of Southeast Quarter of Southwest Quarter-Section	20
N½SESW	North Half of Southeast Quarter of Southwest Quarter-Section	20
N½SW	North Half of Southwest Quarter-Section	80
N½SWNE	North Half of Southwest Quarter of Northeast Quarter-Section	20
N½SWNW	North Half of Southwest Quarter of Northwest Quarter-Section	20
N½SWSE	North Half of Southwest Quarter of Southeast Quarter-Section	20
N½SWSE	North Half of Southwest Quarter of Southeast Quarter-Section	20
N½SWSW	North Half of Southwest Quarter of Southwest Quarter-Section	20
N½W½NW	North Half of West Half of Northwest Quarter-Section	40
N½W½SE	North Half of West Half of Southeast Quarter-Section	40
N½W½SW	North Half of West Half of Southwest Quarter-Section	40
NE	Northeast Quarter-Section	160
NEN½	Northeast Quarter of North Half-Section	80
NENE	Northeast Quarter of Northeast Quarter-Section	40
NENENE	Northeast Quarter of Northeast Quarter of Northeast Quarter	10
NENENW	Northeast Quarter of Northeast Quarter of Northwest Quarter	10
NENESE	Northeast Quarter of Northeast Quarter of Southeast Quarter	10
NENESW	Northeast Quarter of Northeast Quarter of Southwest Quarter	10
NENW	Northeast Quarter of Northwest Quarter-Section	40
NENWNE	Northeast Quarter of Northwest Quarter of Northeast Quarter	10
NENWNW	Northeast Quarter of Northwest Quarter of Northwest Quarter	10
NENWSE	Northeast Quarter of Northwest Quarter of Southeast Quarter	10
NENWSW	Northeast Quarter of Northwest Quarter of Southwest Quarter	10
NESE	Northeast Quarter of Southeast Quarter-Section	40
NESENE	Northeast Quarter of Southeast Quarter of Northeast Quarter	10
NESENW	Northeast Quarter of Southeast Quarter of Northwest Quarter	10
NESESE	Northeast Quarter of Southeast Quarter of Southeast Quarter	10
NESESW	Northeast Quarter of Southeast Quarter of Southwest Quarter	10
NESW	Northeast Quarter of Southwest Quarter-Section	40
NESWNE	Northeast Quarter of Southwest Quarter of Northeast Quarter	10
NESWNW	Northeast Quarter of Southwest Quarter of Northwest Quarter	10
NESWSE	Northeast Quarter of Southwest Quarter of Southeast Quarter	10
NESWSW	Northeast Quarter of Southwest Quarter of Southwest Quarter	10
NW	Northwest Quarter-Section	160
NWE½	Northwest Quarter of Eastern Half-Section	80
NWN½	Northwest Quarter of North Half-Section	80
NWNE	Northwest Quarter of Northeast Quarter-Section	40
NWNENE	Northwest Quarter of Northeast Quarter of Northeast Quarter	10
NWNENW	Northwest Quarter of Northeast Quarter of Northwest Quarter	10
NWNESE	Northwest Quarter of Northeast Quarter of Southeast Quarter	10
NWNESW	Northwest Quarter of Northeast Quarter of Southwest Quarter	10
NWNW	Northwest Quarter of Northwest Quarter-Section	40
NWNWNE	Northwest Quarter of Northwest Quarter of Northeast Quarter	10
NWNWNW	Northwest Quarter of Northwest Quarter of Northwest Quarter	10
NWNWSE	Northwest Quarter of Northwest Quarter of Southeast Quarter	10
NWNWSW	Northwest Quarter of Northwest Quarter of Southwest Quarter	10
NWSE	Northwest Quarter of Southeast Quarter-Section	40
NWSENE	Northwest Quarter of Southeast Quarter of Northeast Quarter	10
NWSENW	Northwest Quarter of Southeast Quarter of Northwest Quarter	10
NWSESE	Northwest Quarter of Southeast Quarter of Southeast Quarter	10
NWSESW	Northwest Quarter of Southeast Quarter of Southwest Quarter	10
NWSW	Northwest Quarter of Southwest Quarter-Section	40
NWSWNE	Northwest Quarter of Southwest Quarter of Northeast Quarter	10
NWSWNW	Northwest Quarter of Southwest Quarter of Northwest Quarter	10
NWSWSE	Northwest Quarter of Southwest Quarter of Southeast Quarter	10
NWSWSW	Northwest Quarter of Southwest Quarter of Southwest Quarter	10
S½	South Half-Section	320
S½E½NE	South Half of East Half of Northeast Quarter-Section	40
S½E½NW	South Half of East Half of Northwest Quarter-Section	40
S½E½SE	South Half of East Half of Southeast Quarter-Section	40

Section Part	Description	Acres
S½E½SW	South Half of East Half of Southwest Quarter-Section	40
S½N½	South Half of North Half-Section	160
S½NE	South Half of Northeast Quarter-Section	80
S½NENE	South Half of Northeast Quarter of Northeast Quarter-Section	20
S½NENW	South Half of Northeast Quarter of Northwest Quarter-Section	20
S½NESE	South Half of Northeast Quarter of Southeast Quarter-Section	20
S½NESW	South Half of Northeast Quarter of Southwest Quarter-Section	20
S½NW	South Half of Northwest Quarter-Section	80
S½NWNE	South Half of Northwest Quarter of Northeast Quarter-Section	20
S½NWNW	South Half of Northwest Quarter of Northwest Quarter-Section	20
S½NWSE	South Half of Northwest Quarter of Southeast Quarter-Section	20
S½NWSW	South Half of Northwest Quarter of Southwest Quarter-Section	20
S½S½	South Half of South Half-Section	160
S½SE	South Half of Southeast Quarter-Section	80
S½SENE	South Half of Southeast Quarter of Northeast Quarter-Section	20
S½SENW	South Half of Southeast Quarter of Northwest Quarter-Section	20
S½SESE	South Half of Southeast Quarter of Southeast Quarter-Section	20
S½SESW	South Half of Southeast Quarter of Southwest Quarter-Section	20
S½SESW	South Half of Southeast Quarter of Southwest Quarter-Section	20
S½SW	South Half of Southwest Quarter-Section	80
S½SWNE	South Half of Southwest Quarter of Northeast Quarter-Section	20
S½SWNW	South Half of Southwest Quarter of Northwest Quarter-Section	20
S½SWSE	South Half of Southwest Quarter of Southeast Quarter-Section	20
S½SWSE	South Half of Southwest Quarter of Southeast Quarter-Section	20
S½SWSW	South Half of Southwest Quarter of Southwest Quarter-Section	20
S½W½NE	South Half of West Half of Northeast Quarter-Section	40
S½W½NW	South Half of West Half of Northwest Quarter-Section	40
S½W½SE	South Half of West Half of Southeast Quarter-Section	40
S½W½SW	South Half of West Half of Southwest Quarter-Section	40
SE	Southeast Quarter Section	160
SEN½	Southeast Quarter of North Half-Section	80
SENE	Southeast Quarter of Northeast Quarter-Section	40
SENENE	Southeast Quarter of Northeast Quarter of Northeast Quarter	10
SENENW	Southeast Quarter of Northeast Quarter of Northwest Quarter	10
SENESE	Southeast Quarter of Northeast Quarter of Southeast Quarter	10
SENESW	Southeast Quarter of Northeast Quarter of Southwest Quarter	10
SENW	Southeast Quarter of Northwest Quarter-Section	40
SENWNE	Southeast Quarter of Northwest Quarter of Northeast Quarter	10
SENWNW	Southeast Quarter of Northwest Quarter of Northwest Quarter	10
SENWSE	Souteast Quarter of Northwest Quarter of Southeast Quarter	10
SENWSW	Southeast Quarter of Northwest Quarter of Southwest Quarter	10
SESE	Southeast Quarter of Southeast Quarter-Section	40
SESENE	SoutheastQuarter of Southeast Quarter of Northeast Quarter	10
SESENW	Southeast Quarter of Southeast Quarter of Northwest Quarter	10
SESESE	Southeast Quarter of Southeast Quarter of Southeast Quarter	10
SESESW	Southeast Quarter of Southeast Quarter of Southwest Quarter	10
SESW	Southeast Quarter of Southwest Quarter-Section	40
SESWNE	Southeast Quarter of Southwest Quarter of Northeast Quarter	10
SESWNW	Southeast Quarter of Southwest Quarter of Northwest Quarter	10
SESWSE	Southeast Quarter of Southwest Quarter of Southeast Quarter	10
SESWSW	Southeast Quarter of Southwest Quarter of Southwest Quarter	10
SW	Southwest Quarter-Section	160
SWNE	Southwest Quarter of Northeast Quarter-Section	40
SWNENE	Southwest Quarter of Northeast Quarter of Northeast Quarter	10
SWNENW	Southwest Quarter of Northeast Quarter of Northwest Quarter	10
SWNESE	Southwest Quarter of Northeast Quarter of Southeast Quarter	10
SWNESW	Southwest Quarter of Northeast Quarter of Southwest Quarter	10
SWNW	Southwest Quarter of Northwest Quarter-Section	40
SWNWNE	Southwest Quarter of Northwest Quarter of Northeast Quarter	10
SWNWNW	Southwest Quarter of Northwest Quarter of Northwest Quarter	10

Section Part	Description	Acres
SWNWSE	Southwest Quarter of Northwest Quarter of Southeast Quarter	10
SWNWSW	Southwest Quarter of Northwest Quarter of Southwest Quarter	10
SWSE	Southwest Quarter of Southeast Quarter-Section	40
SWSENE	Southwest Quarter of Southeast Quarter of Northeast Quarter	10
SWSENW	Southwest Quarter of Southeast Quarter of Northwest Quarter	10
SWSESE	Southwest Quarter of Southeast Quarter of Southeast Quarter	10
SWSESW	Southwest Quarter of Southeast Quarter of Southwest Quarter	10
SWSW	Southwest Quarter of Southwest Quarter-Section	40
SWSWNE	Southwest Quarter of Southwest Quarter of Northeast Quarter	10
SWSWNW	Southwest Quarter of Southwest Quarter of Northwest Quarter	10
SWSWSE	Southwest Quarter of Southwest Quarter of Southeast Quarter	10
SWSWSW	Southwest Quarter of Southwest Quarter of Southwest Quarter	10
W½	West Half-Section	320
W½E½	West Half of East Half-Section	160
W½N½	West Half of North Half-Section (same as NW)	160
W½NE	West Half of Northeast Quarter	80
W½NENE	West Half of Northeast Quarter of Northeast Quarter-Section	20
W½NENW	West Half of Northeast Quarter of Northwest Quarter-Section	20
W½NESE	West Half of Northeast Quarter of Southeast Quarter-Section	20
W½NESW	West Half of Northeast Quarter of Southwest Quarter-Section	20
W½NW	West Half of Northwest Quarter-Section	80
W½NWNE	West Half of Northwest Quarter of Northeast Quarter-Section	20
W½NWNW	West Half of Northwest Quarter of Northwest Quarter-Section	20
W½NWSE	West Half of Northwest Quarter of Southeast Quarter-Section	20
W½NWSW	West Half of Northwest Quarter of Southwest Quarter-Section	20
W½S½	West Half of South Half-Section	160
W½SE	West Half of Southeast Quarter-Section	80
W½SENE	West Half of Southeast Quarter of Northeast Quarter-Section	20
W½SENW	West Half of Southeast Quarter of Northwest Quarter-Section	20
W½SESE	West Half of Southeast Quarter of Southeast Quarter-Section	20
W½SESW	West Half of Southeast Quarter of Southwest Quarter-Section	20
W½SW	West Half of Southwest Quarter-Section	80
W½SWNE	West Half of Southwest Quarter of Northeast Quarter-Section	20
W½SWNW	West Half of Southwest Quarter of Northwest Quarter-Section	20
W½SWSE	West Half of Southwest Quarter of Southeast Quarter-Section	20
W½SWSW	West Half of Southwest Quarter of Southwest Quarter-Section	20
W½W½	West Half of West Half-Section	160

Appendix C - Multi-Patentee Groups

The following index presents groups of people who jointly received patents in Kemper County, Mississippi. The Group Numbers are used in the Patent Maps and their Indexes so that you may then turn to this Appendix in order to identify all the members of the each buying group.

Group Number 1
ABBOTT, Willis; JOHNSTON, Warren B

Group Number 2
ABELS, Mary; JACKSON, Harris

Group Number 3
ABERNATHY, John T; BEVILL, Thomas L

Group Number 4
ABERNATHY, John T; BURNETT, Boling C

Group Number 5
ABERNATHY, John T; CHEATHAM, Thomas M

Group Number 6
ABERNATHY, John T; DICKINS, Robert

Group Number 7
ABERNATHY, John T; ELLIOT, James

Group Number 8
ABERNATHY, John T; HENDERSON, John

Group Number 9
ABERNATHY, John T; HOLDERNESS, Mckinney

Group Number 10
ABERNATHY, John T; HOLDERNESS, Mckinney T

Group Number 11
ABERNATHY, John T; RUPERT, James C

Group Number 12
ABERNATHY, John T; TUTT, James B

Group Number 13
ABERNATHY, John T; WALKER, Lawrence W

Group Number 14
ABERNATHY, John T; YOUNG, Robert M

Group Number 15
ADAMS, Irvin; PEARL, Sylvester; WEIR, Andrew; WEIR, Robert

Group Number 16
ADAMS, Irvin; WEIR, Andrew

Group Number 17
ADAMS, Irvine; PEARL, Sylvester; WEIR, Robert

Group Number 18
ALLEN, Charles; MCRAE, James

Group Number 19
ALLEN, John; MARTIN, Joseph

Group Number 20
ALLEN, John; SANDERS, Jeremiah

Group Number 21
ANDERSON, Alexander; BARTON, John F

Group Number 22
ANDERSON, Alexander; CARTER, John

Group Number 23
ANDERSON, Alexander; PAGE, Willis

Group Number 24
ANDERSON, Joshua; BURFOOT, Mitchell

Group Number 25
ARCHER, Alexander; PAGE, Willis

Group Number 26
BACON, Christopher B; MILLS, Willard C

Group Number 27
BALDWIN, Frances; TURNER, Beloved L

Group Number 28
BARFOOT, John; BOSTIAN, Matthew

Group Number 29
BARNES, James; LEWIS, Moses

Group Number 30
BARTLETT, James; PIERCE, George

Group Number 31
BARTLETT, John; GRANT, Reuben H

Group Number 32
BELCHER, Branch; WELLS, Daniel

Group Number 33
BENNETT, Anthony; GREENE, Daniel

Group Number 34
BENNETT, Anthony; PICKETT, James

Group Number 35
BENNETT, Anthony; WINSTON, Joel W

Group Number 36
BENNETT, Louvenia; CONN, Louvenia

Group Number 37
BENTON, John; HARPER, George W

Group Number 38
BESTER, Daniel P; MCGEE, Thomas

Group Number 39
BEVILL, Thomas L; COOPWOOD, Thomas

Group Number 40
BEVILL, Thomas L; GREENE, Daniel

Group Number 41
BEVILL, Thomas L; HODGES, Armstrong J

Group Number 42
BIRDSONG, James P; BIRDSONG, Mary S

Group Number 43
BLAKELY, Robert; WARD, Ebon P

Group Number 44
BLANTON, James A; ROGERS, John

Group Number 45
BONNER, John; HANLEY, James

Group Number 46
BORDEN, Joseph; GREENE, Daniel

Group Number 47
BORDEN, Joseph; HARRISON, Simmons

Group Number 48
BOSTIAN, John; BOSTIAN, Matthew

Group Number 49
BOSTIAN, John; WARREN, Joseph M

Group Number 50
BOSTIAN, Matthew; WARREN, Joseph M

Group Number 51
BOWEN, Horatio; TAYLOR, Swepson

Group Number 52
BOZEMAN, Nancy C; BOZEMAN, Thomas C

Group Number 53
BRICKELL, Joseph J; MCMAHON, John J

Group Number 54
BROADWAY, William; VANDEVANDER, Jacob

Group Number 55
BROWN, Amanda V; BROWN, David W

Group Number 56
BROWNLEE, William R; RUPERT, John

Group Number 57
BROWNLEE, William R; WALTER, Henry

Group Number 58
BUCHANNAN, Henry; PEARL, Sylvester

Group Number 59
BUCHANNON, Henry; PEARL, Sylvester

Group Number 60
BURNETT, Boling C; DICKINS, Robert

Group Number 61
BURNETT, Boling C; HOLDERNESS, Mckinney

Group Number 62
BURNETT, Boling C; MAHON, Archimedes

Group Number 63
BURNETT, Boling C; MCCRANIE, Malcolm

Group Number 64
BURNETT, Boling C; MOODY, Washington

Group Number 65
BURNETT, Boling C; PAGE, Elijah

Group Number 66
BURNETT, Boling C; RICHEY, James; STEWART, Hugh C

Group Number 67
BURNETT, Boling C; RUPERT, James C

Group Number 68
BURNETT, Boling C; SANDERSON, Amos

Group Number 69
BURNETT, Boling C; WALTHALL, Madison

Group Number 70
BURNETT, Boling C; WATTERS, Stacy B

Group Number 71
BURNETT, Boling C; WEIR, Adolphus G

Group Number 72
BUTTERWORTH, Samuel F; COOPWOOD, Thomas

Group Number 73
BUTTERWORTH, Samuel F; FERGUSON, Elijah

Group Number 74
BYRN, John W; MARSHALL, Solomon

Group Number 75
BYRN, Samuel H; HOUSTON, Robert F

Group Number 76
CALLAHAN, Henry; CALLAHAN, Mary

Group Number 77
CANNON, George W; CANNON, William

Group Number 78
CANNON, William; CARTER, Clark

Group Number 79
CARLISLE, Edward K; DADE, Henry C

Group Number 80
CARLISLE, Edward K; EVANS, William

Group Number 81
CARLISLE, Edward K; JEMISON, John S

Group Number 82
CARTER, John; THOMAS, Page

Group Number 83
CARTER, John; YOUNG, Alexander F

Group Number 84
CARTER, John; YOUNG, Thomas T

Group Number 85
CAVANAH, James R; PEDEN, William T

Group Number 86
CHARLTON, Tapley; MOSELEY, William A

Group Number 87
CHILDS, Morgan; HATCH, Lemuel N

Group Number 88
CLARK, Gilbert; CLARK, John; CLARK, William

Group Number 89
CLARK, William W; PORTER, John C

Group Number 90
CLEMENT, Benjamin; HOLDERNESS, Mckinney

Group Number 91
COLBERT, William; GRAHAM, Christiana; GRAHAM, George J

Group Number 92
COLE, Lewis; JACK, Abner M

Group Number 93
COLE, Roscow; COOPWOOD, Thomas

Group Number 94
COLE, Roscow; HODGES, Armstrong J

Group Number 95
COLE, Roscow; HOLDERNESS, Mckinney

Group Number 96
COLE, Roscow; WINSTON, William B

Group Number 97
COLEMAN, Benjamin; JOHNSON, Warren B

Group Number 98
COLGLAZER, John; COOPWOOD, Thomas; OREILLY, Edmond; OREILLY, Nicholas

Group Number 99
CONELLY, John; JACKSON, Andrew

Group Number 100
COOLEDGE, Jonathan; JACKSON, Andrew

Group Number 101
COOLEDGE, Jonathan; LANG, William

Group Number 102
COOLEDGE, Jonathan; PHARMER, Calvin

Group Number 103
COOPER, Jesse; CORLEY, John

Group Number 104
COOPWOOD, Thomas; DENTON, Isaac

Group Number 105
COOPWOOD, Thomas; DICKINS, Robert

Group Number 106
COOPWOOD, Thomas; ELLIOT, James

Group Number 107
COOPWOOD, Thomas; ESTELL, John

Group Number 108
COOPWOOD, Thomas; FRANKLIN, Sidney S

Group Number 109
COOPWOOD, Thomas; GREENE, Daniel

Group Number 110
COOPWOOD, Thomas; HENDERSON, John

Group Number 111
COOPWOOD, Thomas; MOODY, Washington

Group Number 112
COOPWOOD, Thomas; OREILLY, Nicholas

Group Number 113
COOPWOOD, Thomas; PFISTER, Amandtus S

Group Number 114
COOPWOOD, Thomas; RICHEY, James; STEWART, Hugh C

Group Number 115
COOPWOOD, Thomas; RUPERT, James C

Group Number 116
COOPWOOD, Thomas; WATTERS, Stacey B

Group Number 117
COOPWOOD, Thomas; WATTERS, Stacy B

Group Number 118
COOPWOOD, Thomas; WEST, Anderson

Group Number 119
COOPWOOD, Thomas; WILSON, Joseph

Group Number 120
COOPWOOD, Thomas; YOUNG, Robert M

Group Number 121
CROSBY, Richard; HERRINGTON, John

Group Number 122
DAVIES, John; DYER, Otis

Group Number 123
DAVIS, Philip W; FARMER, Thomas

Group Number 124
DICKINS, Robert; HOLDERNESS, Mckinney

Group Number 125
DOBBS, Charles; WELSH, George

Group Number 126
DOZIER, Judy; DOZIER, Robert

Group Number 127
DUNLAP, James; DUNLAP, Robert

Group Number 128
DYER, Otis; MOODY, Washington

Group Number 129
EARLE, Joseph B; LAKE, James

Group Number 130
EARLE, Joseph B; MCGEE, Thomas

Group Number 131
EARLE, Joseph B; RUPERT, John

Group Number 132
EARLE, Joseph B; SPENCER, Hezekiah G

Group Number 133
EARLE, Joseph B; STEELE, Abner A

Group Number 134
EARLE, Joseph B; WHITFIELD, Boaz

Group Number 135
EARLE, Joseph B; WINSTON, Joel W

Group Number 136
EARLE, Joseph B; WINSTON, William

Group Number 137
EDWARDS, Rigdon; GRIFFIN, Archibald M

Group Number 138
EGGERTON, George; HUNDLEY, Cecilius J; HUNDLEY, Solomon M

Group Number 139
ELLIOT, James; GILCHRIST, Malcolm

Group Number 140
ELLIOT, James; HOLDERNESS, Mckinney

Group Number 141
ELLIOT, James; SHIPP, Ervel

Group Number 142
ELLIOT, James; SMITH, James L

Group Number 143
ELLIOTT, James; GILCHRIST, Malcolm

Group Number 144
ELLIOTT, James; HARRIS, Thompson

Group Number 145
ELLIOTT, Jonathan; JENKINS, William

Group Number 146
ESTELL, John; HOLDERNESS, Mckinney

Group Number 147
ESTES, Benjamin; MCGEE, Micajah

Group Number 148
FELTON, Mary; FELTON, Thomas M

Group Number 149
FELTS, Caswell; STEELE, Abner A

Group Number 150
FELTS, Samuel D; HARRIS, Buckner; WEIR, Adolphus G

Group Number 151
FELTS, Samuel D; JOHNSON, Warren B

Group Number 152
FERGUSON, Elijah; NASH, Orsamus L

Group Number 153
FLEMMING, William H; JUDSON, Charles

Group Number 154
FLOURNOY, Lucy A; FLOURNOY, Martha C

Group Number 155
FLOYD, Presley; WHITE, Rebecca

Group Number 156
FOOTE, Hezekiah W; HUNTINGTON, Elisha

Group Number 157
FOX, William; MCGEE, Thomas

Group Number 158
FOX, William; TART, Thomas E

Group Number 159
GAINES, George S; GLOVER, Allen; GREENE, Daniel

Group Number 160
GAY, Arthur; SHIRLEY, Nathaniel

Group Number 161
GENTRY, John M; NEWTON, Matthew A

Group Number 162
GERMANY, Samuel; MORRIS, Turner

Group Number 163
GIBBS, James; LEWIS, Thomas

Group Number 164
GIFFORD, Alden; GILCHRIST, Malcolm; ORNE, Edward

Group Number 165
GILCHRIST, Malcolm; GREENE, Daniel

Group Number 166
GILCHRIST, Malcolm; MCALLISTER, Collin

Group Number 167
GILCHRIST, Malcolm; SCOTT, Christopher C

Group Number 168
GOODE, Sidney M; SCUDDY, Joseph B

Group Number 169
GOYNES, Wiley W; PARKER, Isaac

Group Number 170
GRANT, Reuben H; HARRIS, Robert E

Group Number 171
GREEN, Daniel; LAKE, James

Group Number 172
GREEN, Daniel; PETTUS, Alice T

Group Number 173
GREEN, Daniel; PUCKETT, James

Group Number 174
GREEN, Daniel; ROGERS, John D; ROGERS, Lieuen

Group Number 175
GREEN, Daniel; SPENCER, Hezekiah G

Group Number 176
GREEN, Daniel; STEELE, Abner A

Group Number 177
GREEN, Daniel; STEELE, Richard G

Group Number 178
GREEN, Daniel; WINSTON, Joel W

Group Number 179
GREENE, Daniel; HUBBARD, Samuel; LEWIS, Rufus G; TAPPAN, John

Group Number 180
GREENE, Daniel; JENKINS, John H

Group Number 181
GREENE, Daniel; LAKE, James

Group Number 182
GREENE, Daniel; LEVENS, Joshua B

Group Number 183
GREENE, Daniel; LEWIS, Rufus G

Group Number 184
GREENE, Daniel; MALONE, John

Group Number 185
GREENE, Daniel; MCGEE, Thomas

Group Number 186
GREENE, Daniel; MOSELEY, John T

Group Number 187
GREENE, Daniel; PETTUS, Alice T

Group Number 188
GREENE, Daniel; ROGERS, John D; ROGERS, Lewin

Group Number 189
GREENE, Daniel; ROGERS, John D; ROGERS, Lieuen

Group Number 190
GREENE, Daniel; ROGERS, John D; ROGERS, Lieven

Group Number 191
GREENE, Daniel; RUPERT, James C

Group Number 192
GREENE, Daniel; RUPERT, John

Group Number 193
GREENE, Daniel; SCOTT, Christopher C

Group Number 194
GREENE, Daniel; SCOTT, Francis T

Group Number 195
GREENE, Daniel; STEELE, Richard G

Group Number 196
GREENE, Daniel; THURMOND, Powhatten B

Group Number 197
GREENE, Daniel; WINSTON, Joel W

Group Number 198
GREENE, Daniel; YOUNG, Samuel

Group Number 199
GREGORY, Henry; MARS, James

Group Number 200
GRIFFIN, Archibald M; HODGES, Philemon

Group Number 201
GRIFFIN, Archibald M; MULLINS, Burkley

Group Number 202
GRIFFIN, Archibald M; STEWART, Malcolm M

Group Number 203
GRIFFIN, Archibald M; UPCHURCH, Benjamin

Group Number 204
GRIFFIN, Richard; STEELE, Griffin

Group Number 205
GRIFFITH, Edward; GRIFFITH, Ralph

Group Number 206
GRIFFITH, Ralph; SCONYERS, William

Group Number 207
GRIGGS, Green B; RUPERT, James C

Group Number 208
GRIGGS, Green; JINCKS, William

Group Number 209
GRIGSBY, Joseph; HARRIS, Robert E

Group Number 210
GRIGSBY, Joseph; HARRIS, Robert E; HARRIS, Wiley P

Group Number 211
GRIGSBY, Joseph; HARRIS, Robert E; YOUNG, Samuel

Group Number 212
GRIGSBY, Joseph; HARRIS, Wiley P

Group Number 213
GRIGSBY, Joseph; YOUNG, Samuel

Group Number 214
HALE, Charles K; MILLS, Willard C

Group Number 215
HAMBRICK, John; SCITZS, Henry

Group Number 216
HARBOUR, John; SMITH, Reuben

Group Number 217
HARDY, Charles; PERSONS, Nicholas W

Group Number 218
HARRELL, Alfred G; ROSS, Michael

Group Number 219
HARRELL, John B; ROSS, Michael

Group Number 220
HARRIS, William H; SIMMONS, John

Group Number 221
HATCH, Lemuel N; LINCECUM, Grant

Group Number 222
HEARON, Ananias; SIGGARS, William

Group Number 223
HENDRICK, Bernard G; JACOWAY, Benjamin J

Group Number 224
HERRINGTON, John; SHUMATE, Daniel D

Group Number 225
HILLHOUSE, Jesse S; SCOTT, Francis T

Group Number 226
HODGES, Armstrong J; WALTHALL, Madison

Group Number 227
HODGES, Armstrong J; WINSTON, William B

Group Number 228
HOLDERNESS, Mckinney; RICHEY, James; STEWART, Hugh C

Group Number 229
HOLDERNESS, Mckinney; RUPERT, James C

Group Number 230
HOLDERNESS, Mckinney; WALTHALL, Madison

Group Number 231
HOLDERNESS, Mckinney; WINSTON, William B

Group Number 232
HUBBARD, Samuel; LEWIS, Moses; LEWIS, Rufus G; TAPPAN, John

Group Number 233
HUBBARD, Samuel; LEWIS, Rufus G; LEWIS, William M; TAPPAN, John

Group Number 234
HUBBARD, Samuel; LEWIS, Rufus G; TAPPAN, John

Group Number 235
HUBBARD, Samuel; LEWIS, Rufus G; TAPPAN, John; WHITSETT, John C

Group Number 236
HUGHES, Benjamin J; JORDEN, Henry A; WHITEHEAD, James

Group Number 237
HUMPHRIES, William W; ONEILL, Patrick

Group Number 238
HUNDLEY, Joel; WATSON, Edwin H

Group Number 239
HUNNICUTT, Leona P; WATSON, Leona P

Group Number 240
HUNTER, Ellen; JEMISON, Ellen

Group Number 241
HUTCHINS, James L; HUTCHINS, Washington P

Group Number 242
JACKSON, Andrew; VANDEAVENDER, Christopher

Group Number 243
JACKSON, Harris; WARE, John

Group Number 244
JACOWAY, Benjamin J; PIERCE, George

Group Number 245
JAGGERS, John; STEEL, Lemuel G

Group Number 246
JENKINS, William; MASSEY, David

Group Number 247
JOHNSON, David; WITHERS, Robert W

Group Number 248
JOHNSON, James; SANDERS, Jerrimiah

Group Number 249
JOHNSON, Thomas G; WHITE, Dorset

Group Number 250
JOHNSON, Warren B; SMITH, Ephraim

Group Number 251
JOHNSON, Warren B; WELSH, James

Group Number 252
JOHNSON, William H; MCCRORY, Allen

Group Number 253
JOHNSTON, Warren B; VAUGHAN, Malinda

Group Number 254
JONES, Alfred; YOUNG, Samuel

Group Number 255
JONES, Britain; PENNINGTON, Lawrence

Group Number 256
JONES, Ezekiel; PAGE, Willis

Group Number 257
JONES, Gabriel; OLIVE, Anthony

Group Number 258
KEENAN, Francis; PACE, Edwind

Group Number 259
KEMPER, County Of; LANKAM, Solomon

Group Number 260
KNAPP, Frederick; VAUGHAN, James

Group Number 261
KOONCE, Michael; WILLIAMS, Jeptha

Group Number 262
LAKE, James; MCGEE, Thomas

Group Number 263
LAKE, James; PAGE, Willis

Group Number 264
LEWIS, Moses; WHITSETT, John C

Group Number 265
LEWIS, Rufus G; MCGEE, Thomas

Group Number 266
LEWIS, Rufus G; SANDERS, Jesse P

Group Number 267
LEWIS, Rufus G; SAUNDERS, Jesse P

Group Number 268
LEWIS, Rufus G; WHITSETT, John C

Group Number 269
LEWIS, William M; SCOTT, Christopher C

Group Number 270
LILES, Samuel; RUPERT, John

Group Number 271
LLOYD, John E; SPINKS, Enoch

Group Number 272
LLOYD, John E; SPINKS, John

Group Number 273
LLOYD, John; MCGEE, Thomas

Group Number 274
LOWE, William; PEDEN, John S

Group Number 275
LYLE, David; MEYATTE, Peter

Group Number 276
LYLE, David; SMYTH, John B

Group Number 277
MADISON, James A; MADISON, Narcissa M

Group Number 278
MALONE, John; RUPERT, John

Group Number 279
MARSHALL, Solomon; MCCRORY, Allen

Group Number 280
MATTHEWS, Isaac; MCKELVIN, Benjamin A

Group Number 281
MAYNOR, Samuel H; RIGBY, Bryant; SCITZS, Henry

Group Number 282
MCCOWN, James; WALL, James

Group Number 283
MCDONALD, Daniel; WHITE, Isham

Group Number 284
MCGEE, Thomas; SPINKS, Enoch

Group Number 285
MCGEE, Thomas; STEELE, Abner A

Group Number 286
MCGEE, Thomas; STEELE, Richard G

Group Number 287
MCGEE, Thomas; TARTT, Thomas E

Group Number 288
MCGEE, Thomas; WELSH, George

Group Number 289
MCGEE, Thomas; WELSH, John V

Group Number 290
MCGEE, Thomas; WINSTON, Joel W

Group Number 291
MCGOWEN, James; MCGOWEN, Samuel

Group Number 292
MCINTYRE, Angus; MCKELVIN, Benjamin A

Group Number 293
MCLAMORE, Henry; MCLAMORE, Mary J

Group Number 294
MCLAUGHLIN, Charles; ROUNDTREE, Wright

Group Number 295
MINNIECE, Emma; RORY, Emma Minniece

Group Number 296
MOODY, Washington; ONEIL, Patric

Group Number 297
MOORE, John D; POPE, Tripp

Group Number 298
MORRIS, Lewis; TUTT, James B

Group Number 299
MOSELY, William A; ROSS, Michael

Group Number 300
MOSLEY, John T; MOSLEY, William A

Group Number 301
NASH, Ezekiel; NASH, Orsamus L

Group Number 302
NASH, Orsamus L; SMITH, James H

Group Number 303
NETTLES, Zachariah; WHITE, John S

Group Number 304
NICHOLSON, Isaac W; ROWE, Shadrack

Group Number 305
ODEN, Berline K; ODEN, George W

Group Number 306
OWEN, John; WEIR, Adolphus G

Group Number 307
PAGE, Thomas; PAGE, Willis

Group Number 308
PENNINGTON, Lawrence; YOUNG, Samuel

Group Number 309
PERKINS, Mary O; PERKINS, Silvester

Group Number 310
PHARMER, Calvin; PHARMER, Sydney

Group Number 311
POOL, Benjamin; RILEY, Peter

Group Number 312
POWELL, Martin; WHITSETT, John C

Group Number 313
PULLER, William P; STEPHENS, Moses

Group Number 314
RHODES, John P; WHITEHEAD, Gilford

Group Number 315
RIDDLE, Joseph N; WHITE, Robert W

Group Number 316
RIGBY, Bryant; WARREN, William H

Group Number 317
RILEY, Peter; RUPERT, James C

Group Number 318
RODES, Agnes; TURNER, Beloved L

Group Number 319
RUPERT, James C; RUPERT, John

Group Number 320
RUPERT, James C; SANDERS, Jeremiah

Group Number 321
SCOTT, Francis T; SCOTT, William T

Group Number 322
SHARP, Groves D; SHARP, Matilda A

Group Number 323
SITZS, Henry; WHITFIELD, Boaz

Group Number 324
SMITH, James H; WESTMORELAND, Mark

Group Number 325
SMITH, Tillotson P; SNEED, Peter

Group Number 326
STEELE, Samuel; WHITFIELD, Boaz

Group Number 327
STOVALL, Lewis; SWEARINGEN, Morgan

Group Number 328
STRAIT, John; WELLS, Samuel G

Group Number 329
TUCKER, John; WILSON, George

Group Number 330
ULMER, Mary; ULMER, Richard

Group Number 331
VANDEVANDER, Christopher; VANDEVANDER, Hiram

Group Number 332
WALTHALL, Madison; WINSTON, William B

Group Number 333
WARD, Ellen; WARD, William

Group Number 334
WARE, Nimrod W; WILLIAMS, Benjamin

Group Number 335
WATTS, Haden; WATTS, Sealy

Group Number 336
WHITE, Isaac; WHITE, Rebecca

Group Number 337
WHITFIELD, Archimedes M; WHITFIELD, Boaz

Group Number 338
WILKS, John W; WILSON, Henry R

Group Number 339
WINDHAM, Martha A; WINDHAM, S S

Group Number 340
YOUNG, George; YOUNG, Martha J

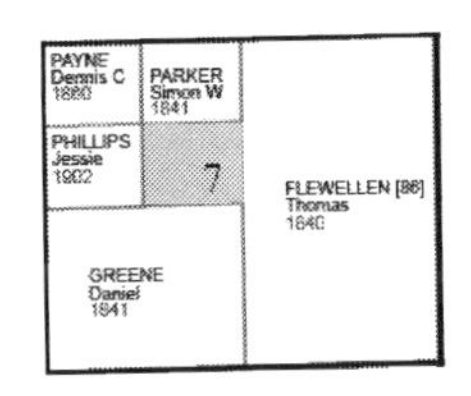

Extra! Extra! (about our Indexes)

We purposefully do not have an all-name index in the back of this volume so that our readers do not miss one of the best uses of this book: finding misspelled names among more specialized indexes.

Without repeating the text of our "How-to" chapter, we have nonetheless tried to assist our more anxious researchers by delivering a short-cut to the two county-wide Surname Indexes, the second of which will lead you to all-name indexes for each Congressional Township mapped in this volume :

For your convenience, the "How To Use this Book" Chart on page 2 is repeated on the reverse of this page.

We should be releasing new titles every week for the foreseeable future. We urge you to write, fax, call, or email us any time for a current list of titles. Of course, our web-page will always have the most current information about current and upcoming books.

Arphax Publishing Co.
2210 Research Park Blvd.
Norman, Oklahoma 73069
(800) 681-5298 toll-free
(405) 366-6181 local
(405) 366-8184 fax
info@arphax.com

www.arphax.com

How to Use This Book - A Graphical Summary

Part I

"The Big Picture"

Map A ▸ *Counties in the State*
Map B ▸ *Surrounding Counties*
Map C ▸ *Congressional Townships (Map Groups) in the County*
Map D ▸ *Cities & Towns in the County*
Map E ▸ *Cemeteries in the County*
Surnames in the County ▸ *Number of Land-Parcels for Each Surname*
Surname/Township Index ▸ Directs you to Township Map Groups in Part II

The Surname/Township Index can direct you to any number of **Township Map Groups**

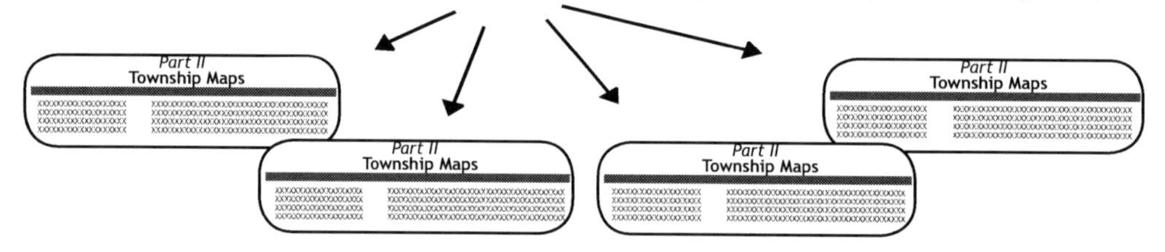

Part II

Township Map Groups

(1 for each Township in the County)

Each Township Map Group contains all four of of the following tools . . .

Land Patent Index ▸ *Every-name Index of Patents Mapped in this Township*
Land Patent Map ▸ *Map of Patents as listed in above Index*
Road Map ▸ *Map of Roads, City-centers, and Cemeteries in the Township*
Historical Map ▸ *Map of Railroads, Lakes, Rivers, Creeks, City-Centers, and Cemeteries*

Appendices

Appendix A ▸ *Congressional Authority enabling Patents within our Maps*
Appendix B ▸ *Section-Parts / Aliquot Parts (a comprehensive list)*
Appendix C ▸ *Multi-patentee Groups (Individuals within Buying Groups)*

Made in the USA
Middletown, DE
22 May 2021